MOUS *Essentials*

WORD 2000

KEITH MULBERY
UTAH VALLEY STATE COLLEGE

Prentice
Hall

Upper Saddle River, New Jersey

MOUS Essentials: Word 2000

Trademark Acknowledgments

Editor-in-Chief:
Mickey Cox

Acquisitions Editor:
Lucinda Gatch

Assistant Editor:
Jennifer Cappello

Managing Editor:
Monica Stipanov

Editorial Assistant:
Mary Toepfer

Director of Strategic Marketing:
Nancy Evans

Marketing Manager:
Kris King

AVP/Director of Production & Manufacturing:
Michael Weinstein

Manager, Production:
Gail Steier de Acevedo

Project Manager:
Tim Tate

Manufacturing Buyer:
Natacha St. Hill Moore

Associate Director, Manufacturing:
Vincent Scelta

Book Design:
Louisa Klucznik/Graphic World Inc.

Cover Design:
Pisaza Design Studio, Ltd.

Composition:
Gillian Hall, The Aardvark Group

About the Author

Keith Mulbery taught computer applications and business communication at Bowling Green State University and is currently teaching computer applications in the Business Systems Administration Department at Utah Valley State College. Specifically, he teaches Word, Excel, PowerPoint, Access, Windows, Internet Explorer, and WordPerfect. Keith received his B.S. and M.Ed. (majoring in Business Education) from Southwestern Oklahoma State University. Keith has written several word processing textbooks on Word and WordPerfect. In addition, he was the developmental editor for *Word 2000 Essentials Intermediate* and *Word 2000 Essentials Advanced*, which were published by Prentice Hall. Keith also conducts hands-on computer application workshops at the local, state, and national levels, including at the National Business Education Association Convention. He is a Microsoft Office User Specialist in Word, Excel, and PowerPoint 2000.

Dedication

This book is dedicated to my parents, Kenneth and Mary Lu, and to my grandparents. Through them, I learned the value of hard work, passion for my work, and the importance of education.

Acknowledgments

Several people contributed to the publication of this book. Sincere appreciation is expressed to the following key people at Prentice Hall: **Lucinda Gatch**, **Monica Stipanov**, **Tim Tate**, **Kris King**, and **Mary Toepfer**. In addition, I appreciate **Nancy Sixsmith's** careful copy edits. In addition, **Brent Wiscombe** and **SuAnn Butler** reviewed the manuscript from a student's perspective.

Furthermore, I would like to acknowledge the authors, especially **Cheryl Hanewicz**, of previous *Essentials* and *MOUS Essentials* books. Some of their ideas and exercises have been incorporated into this book. In addition, **Russell Norton**, **Kevin Staheli**, and **Mike Warren** (students at Utah Valley State College) let me use their business communication report as a data file for exercises in Project 6.

Contents at a Glance

Table of Contents

Introduction

Essentials courseware from Prentice Hall is anchored in the practical and professional needs of all types of students. Each title in the series reflects a "learning-by-doing" approach that encourages you to grasp application-related concepts as you expand your skills through hands-on tutorials.

The *MOUS Essentials* series has an added focus—preparing you for certification as a Microsoft Office User Specialist. The Specialist designation distinguishes you from your peers as knowledgeable in using Office products, which can also make you more competitive in the job market.

The Specialist program is available for many Office 2000 applications at both Core and Expert User levels. You can learn more about the Specialist program by reviewing Appendix B, "Preparing for MOUS Certification," and by visiting the www.mous.net Web site.

How To Use This Book

You have selected a book providing a comprehensive approach to learning Word, with emphasis on skill sets designated by Microsoft as *Core* or *Expert* for purposes of certification as a Microsoft Office User Specialist. Please take a few moments to familiarize yourself with the icons used in this book and its conventions. If you have questions or comments, visit the related Prentice Hall *MOUS Essentials* Web site at www.prenhall.com/mousessentials.

Each *MOUS Essentials* text consists of modular lessons built around a series of numbered step-by-step procedures that are clear, concise, and easy to review. Brief explanations are provided at the start of each lesson and, as needed, between steps. Many lessons contain additional notes and tips.

A *MOUS Essentials* book may contain anywhere from 15–21 projects, three appendixes, and a glossary. Each project covers one area (or a few closely related areas) of application functionality, and is divided into lessons related to that topic. For example, a project on inserting and formatting graphics includes lessons on inserting an image, moving and deleting an image, sizing an image, wrapping text around an image, inserting an image from the Web, creating a text box, selecting borders and fills, and using WordArt. Each lesson presents a specific task or closely related set of tasks in a manageable chunk that's easy to assimilate and retain.

Each element in a *MOUS Essentials* title is designed to maximize your learning experience. Here's a list of the *MOUS Essentials* project elements and a description of how each element can help you:

- **Required MOUS Objectives Table**   These tables are organized into three columns: Objective, Required Activity for MOUS, and Exam Level. The Objective column lists the general objectives of the project. The associated MOUS requirements for each objective are listed in the Required Activity for MOUS column. The particular exam levels of those activities—Core or Expert—are listed in the Exam Level column. Look over the objectives and MOUS requirements on the opening page of each project before you begin, and review them after completing the project to identify the main goals for each project.

- **Key Terms**   This book includes useful vocabulary words and definitions, specific to the application. Key terms introduced in each project are listed in alphabetic order on the opening page of the project. These key terms then appear in bold italic within the text and are defined during their first occurrence in the project. Definitions of key terms are also included in the glossary.

- **Why Would I Do This?**   You are studying Word to accomplish useful tasks in the real world. This brief section at the beginning of each project tells you why these tasks or procedures are important. What can you do with the knowledge? How can these application features be applied to everyday tasks?

- **MOUS Office Core Objective Icon**   This icon indicates that a lesson or exercise relates to a specific MOUS Core-level skill. MOUS skills may be covered by a whole lesson or perhaps just a single step within a lesson. They may also be covered in an end-of-project exercise.

- **MOUS Office Expert Objective Icon**   This icon indicates that a lesson or exercise relates to a MOUS Expert-level skill. There may be a mix of Core and Expert objectives within a project. Some objectives are both Core and Expert, as well.

- **Lessons**   Most lessons contain one or more tasks that correspond to an objective or MOUS requirement, which are listed on the opening page of the project. A lesson consists of step-by-step tutorials, associated screen captures, and the sidebar notes of the types described later. Although each lesson often builds on the preceding one, the lessons have been made as modular as possible. For example, you can skip tasks that you've already mastered and begin a later lesson, if you choose.

- **Step-by-Step Tutorials**   The lessons consist of numbered, bolded, step-by-step instructions that show you how to perform the procedures in a clear, concise, and direct manner. These hands-on tutorials, which are the "essentials" of each project, let you "learn by doing." A short paragraph may appear after a step to clarify the results of the step. Screen captures are provided after key steps so that you can compare the results on your monitor. To review the lesson, you can easily scan the bold, numbered steps.

- **Exam Notes**   These sidebars provide information and insights on topics covered on MOUS exams. You can easily recognize them by their distinctive icon. It's well worth the effort to review these crucial notes again after completing a project.

- **Inside Stuff**   Inside Stuff comments provide extra tips, shortcuts, and alternative ways to complete a process, as well as special hints. You may safely ignore these for the moment to focus on the main task at hand, or you may pause to learn and appreciate these tidbits.

- **If You Have Problems...**   These short troubleshooting notes help you anticipate or solve common problems quickly and effectively. Even if you don't encounter the problem at this time, do make a mental note of it so that you know where to look when you find yourself having difficulties.

- **Summary**   This section provides a brief recap of the activities learned in the project. The summary often includes suggestions for expanding your knowledge.

- **Checking Concepts and Terms**   This section offers optional true/false and multiple-choice questions designed to check your comprehension and to assess retention. If you need to refresh your memory, the relevant lesson number is provided after each question. For example, [L5] directs you to review Lesson 5 for the answer.

- **Skill Drill**   This section enables you to check your comprehension, evaluate your progress, and practice what you've learned. The exercises in this section build on and reinforce what you have learned in each project. Generally, the Skill Drill exercises include step-by-step instructions. A Core or Expert icon indicates whether a MOUS required activity is introduced in a Skill Drill exercise.

■ **Challenge**   This section provides exercises that expand on or relate to the skills practiced in the project. Each exercise provides a brief narrative introduction followed by instructions. Although the instructions are written in a step-by-step format, the steps are not as detailed as those in the Skill Drill section. Providing fewer specific steps, the Challenge section helps you learn to think on your own. A Core or Expert icon indicates whether a MOUS required activity is introduced in a Challenge exercise.

■ **Discovery Zone**   These exercises require advanced knowledge of project topics or application of skills from multiple lessons. Additionally, these exercises might require you to research topics in Help or on the Web to complete them. This self-directed method of learning new skills emulates real-world experience. A Core or Expert icon indicates whether a MOUS required activity is introduced in a Discovery Zone exercise.

■ **PinPoint Assessment**   Each project ends with a reminder to use MOUS PinPoint training and testing software to supplement the projects in the book. The software aids you in your preparation for taking and passing the MOUS exams. A thorough explanation of how to use the PinPoint software is provided in Appendix A, "Using the MOUS PinPoint 2000 Training and Testing Software."

Typeface Conventions Used in this Book

We have used the following conventions throughout this book so that certain items stand out from the rest of the text:

■ Key terms appear in **_bold italic_** the first time they are defined.

■ Monospace type appears frequently and looks `like this`. It is used to indicate 1) text that you are instructed to key in; 2) text that appears on screen as warnings, confirmations, or general information; 3) the name of a file to be used in a lesson or exercise; and 4) text from a dialog box that is referenced within a sentence, when that sentence might appear awkward if the dialog box text were not set off.

■ Hot keys are indicated by underline. Hotkeys are the underlined letters in menus, toolbars, and dialog boxes that activate commands and options, and are a quick way to choose frequently used commands and options. Hot keys look like this: File, Save.

How To Use Student Data Files on the CD-ROM

The CD-ROM accompanying this book contains PinPoint as well as all the data files for you to use as you work through the step-by-step tutorials within projects and the Skill Drill, Challenge, and Discovery Zone exercises provided at the end of each project. The CD contains separate parallel folders for each project.

The names of the student data files correspond to the filenames called for in the textbook. Each filename includes six characters[md]an initial letter indicating the application, a dash, two digits indicating the project number, and two digits indicating the file number within the project. For example, the first file used in Word Project 3 is named **W-0301**. The third file in Word Project 14 is named **W-1403**. The Word document named **W-Stufiles.doc** on the companion Web site (www.prenhall.com/mousessentials) provides a complete listing of data files by project, including the corresponding names used to save each file.

Please refer to the Readme file on the CD for instruction on how to use your CD-ROM.

Supplements

Instructors get extra support for this text in the following supplements:

- *Instructor's Resource CD-ROM* —The Instructor's Resource CD-ROM includes the entire Instructor's Manual for each application in Microsoft Word format and also contains screen shots that correspond to the solutions for the lessons in the book. A computerized testbank is included to create tests, maintain student records, and to provide online practice testing. Student data files and completed solutions files are also on the CD-ROM. PowerPoint slides, which elaborate on each project, are also included.

- *Companion Web Site (www.prenhall.com/mousessentials)* —For both students and instructors, the companion Web site includes all the ancillary material to accompany the *MOUS Essentials* series. Students can also access the Interactive Study Guide on-line, allowing them to evaluate their understanding of the key concepts of each application with instant feedback on their results. Instructors will find the data and solutions files, Instructor's Manual, and PowerPoint slides for each application.

Microsoft Word 2000 MOUS Core and Expert User Skills

Each MOUS exam includes a list of required tasks you may be asked to perform. This list of possible tasks is categorized by skill area. The following tables list the skill areas and where their required tasks can be found in this book. Table A contains the Core-level tasks; Table B contains the Expert-level tasks.

 **Table A   Microsoft Word 2000 Core MOUS Skills**

Skill Set	Required Activity for MOUS	Project	Lesson(s)	Page(s)
Working with text	Use the Undo, Redo, and Repeat commands	4	4	80
	Apply font formats (Bold, Italic and Underline)	3	1	52
	Use the SPELLING feature	4	6	83
	Use the THESAURUS feature	4	7	86
	Use the GRAMMAR feature	4	6	83
	Insert page breaks	6	1	120
	Highlight text in document	3	5	61
	Insert and move text	2	5	35
		4	2	75
	Apply Cut, Copy, Paste, and Paste Special by using the Office Clipboard	4	2	75
	Copy formats using the Format Painter	3	4	59
	Select and change font and font size	3	2	54
	Find and replace text	12	1	280
	Apply character effects (superscript, subscript, strikethrough, small caps and outline)	3	3	56
	Insert date and time	2	5	35
	Insert symbols	3	8	65
	Create and apply frequently used text with AutoCorrect	4	5	82
Working with paragraphs	Align text in paragraphs (Center, Left, Right and Justified)	5	3	100
	Add bullets and numbering	5	5	104
	Set character-, line-, and paragraph-spacing options	3	3	56
		5	2	98
	Apply borders and shading to paragraphs	5	6	107
	Use indentation options (Left, Right, First Line, and Hanging Indent)	5	4	102
	Use the TABS command (Center, Decimal, Left and Right)	8	4	182
		12	3	287
		12	4	290
	Create an outline-style numbered list	12	6	293
	Set tabs with leaders	12	4	290
Working with documents	Print a document	1	6	14
	Use Print Preview	1	5	13
	Use Web Page Preview	1	5	13
		21	1	498
	Navigate through a document	2	2	30
		6	8	139

Core Level MOUS Skills (continued)

Skill Set	Required Activity for MOUS	Project	Lesson(s)	Page(s)
	Insert page numbers	6	3	125
	Set page orientation	13	2	309
	Set margins	5	1	96
	Use GoTo to locate specific elements in a document	2	2	30
	Create and modify page numbers	6	3	125
	Create and modify headers and footers	6	6	135
	Align text vertically	6	2	123
	Create and use newspaper columns	13	1	308
	Revise column structure	13	3	311
	Prepare and print envelopes and labels	2	7	41
		2	8	42
	Apply styles	14	3	339
	Create sections with formatting that differs from other sections	6	2	123
		6	7	137
	Use click and type	1	3	9
Managing files	Use Save	1	4	11
	Locate and open an existing document	2	1	28
	Use Save As (different name, location, or format)	1	4	11
		14	8	349
	Create a folder	18	2	436
	Create a new document using a Wizard	14	2	337
		21	1	498
	Use Save as Web Page	1	4	11
		21	1	498
	Use templates to create a new document	14	1	334
	Create hyperlinks	17	2	412
		21	7	513
	Use the Office Assistant	1	7	16
	Send a Word document via email	11	7	268
Using tables	Create and format tables	7	1	152
		7	6	161
		8	6	185
		8	8	188
	Add borders and shading to tables	7	7	163
	Revise tables (insert and delete rows and columns, change cell formats)	7	3	155
		7	4	157
		8	2	178
	Modify table structure (merge cells, change height and width)	7	5	158
		8	1	176
	Rotate text in a table	8	7	187
Working with pictures and charts	Use the Drawing toolbar	10	1	222
		10	2	224
	Insert graphics into a document (WordArt, ClipArt, Images)	9	1	196
		9	5	203
		9	8	210
		21	5	509

Expert   Table B   Microsoft Word 2000 Expert MOUS Skills

Skill Set	Required Activity for MOUS	Project	Lesson(s)	Page(s)
Working with paragraphs	Apply paragraph and section shading	5	6	107
	Use text flow options (widows/orphans options and keeping lines together)	6	4	128
	Sort lists, paragraphs, and tables	5	4	102
		8	5	183
		12	5	292
Working with documents	Create and modify page borders	5	6	107
	Format first page differently from subsequent pages	6	3	125
		6	7	137
	Use bookmarks	17	1	410
	Create and edit styles	6	5	131
		14	4	341
		14	5	344
	Create watermarks	10	4	229
	Use find and replace with formats, special characters, and non-printing elements	12	2	283
	Balance column length (using column breaks appropriately)	13	5	317
	Create or revise footnotes and endnotes	6	5	131
	Work with master documents and subdocuments	17	6	422
	Create and modify a table of contents	17	5	420
	Create cross-references	17	3	414
	Create and modify an index	17	4	416
Using tables	Embed worksheets in a table	11	3	259
	Perform calculations in a table	8	3	179
	Link Excel data as a table	11	6	265
	Modify worksheets in a table	11	4	262
Working with pictures and charts	Add bitmapped graphics	9	6	206
	Delete and position graphics	9	2	198
	Create and modify charts	10	6	236
		10	7	240
	Import data into charts	10	8	243
Using mail merge	Create main document	16	3	390
	Create data source	16	1	384
	Sort records to be merged	16	2	387
	Merge main document and data source	16	4	292
	Generate labels	16	5	393
	Merge a document using alternate data sources	16	6	396
Using advanced features	Insert a field	20	2	478
		20	3	480
	Create, apply, and edit macros	15	5	368
		15	6	370
		15	7	372

Expert Level MOUS Skills (continued)

Skill Set	Required Activity for MOUS	Project	Lesson(s)	Page(s)
	Copy, rename, and delete macros	15	8	374
	Create and modify forms	20	1	476
	Create and modify a form control (add an item to a drop-down list)	20	4	481
		20	5	482
		21	6	510
	Use advanced text alignment features with graphics	9	4	201
	Customize toolbars	18	5	441
		18	6	443
Collaborating with workgroups	Insert comments	19	1	454
	Protect documents	19	6	465
	Create multiple versions of a document	19	5	463
	Track changes to a document	19	3	458
	Set default file location for workgroup templates	14	9	351
		20	1	476
	Round-trip documents from HTML	21	8	515

Getting Started with Word 2000

Key terms introduced in this project include

- adaptive menu
- buttons
- Click and Type feature
- close
- Control menu box
- default
- document window
- drop-down list
- end-of-document marker
- exit
- Formatting toolbar
- full menu
- grayed out

- Help
- Help Topic pane
- horizontal scrollbar
- hypertext link
- insertion point
- maximize
- menu
- menu bar
- minimize
- Navigation pane
- Office Assistant
- restore
- ruler

- save
- ScreenTip
- scroll buttons
- shortcut
- short menu
- Standard toolbar
- status bar
- submenu
- title bar
- vertical scrollbar
- view buttons
- word-wrap feature

Objectives	Required Activity for MOUS	Exam Level
➤ Start Word and Explore the Word Screen		
➤ Use Menus and Toolbars		
➤ Enter Text in a Document	Use Click and Type	Core
➤ Save a Document	Use Save	Core
	Use Save As (different name, location, or format)	Core
	Use Save As Web Page	Core
➤ Use Print Preview	Use Print Preview	Core
	Use Web Page Preview	Core
➤ Print a Document	Print a document	Core
➤ Get Help	Use the Office Assistant	Core
➤ Close a Document and Exit Word		

Why Would I Do This?

Word processing is possibly the most commonly used type of software. People around the world, from students to business professionals, use word processing programs such as Microsoft Word, also known as Word, for a variety of simple to complex tasks. You can create letters, research papers, newsletters, brochures, and other documents with Word. You can even create and send email and produce Web pages with Word.

And, after you create your documents, you need to edit and format them. These tasks are a snap with Word. But first, you need to learn your way around the Word window and understand how to create, save, and print your documents. In this project, you learn all of that, plus how to use the built-in Help feature. Let's get started!

Lesson 1: Starting Word and Exploring the Word Screen

Starting Word is the first step to learning and using the software. Your exciting experience with Word all begins with the Start button on the taskbar. After you start Word, you learn your way around the Word screen.

To Start Word and Explore the Word Screen

Start

1 **Click the Start button on the left side of the Windows taskbar.**
The Start menu appears. Use this menu to start programs, get help, choose computer settings, and shut down your computer.

2 **Move the mouse pointer to the Programs menu item.**
The Programs menu appears on the right of the Start menu, as shown in Figure 1.1.

Figure 1.1
Using the Start button makes it easy to open Word.

Word shortcut on the Desktop

Click to see Programs menu

Click to start Microsoft Word

Click Start button

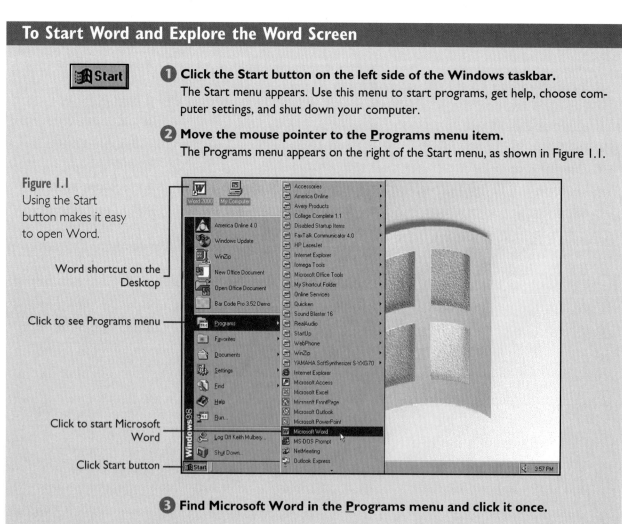

3 **Find Microsoft Word in the Programs menu and click it once.**

⊠ If You Have Problems...
If you don't see Microsoft Word on the Programs menu, ask your instructor for further assistance.

ⓘ Inside Stuff: Using the Word Shortcut Icon
If you see the Word shortcut icon on the Windows desktop, you can double-click it to immediately start Word, instead of using the Start menu.

Word opens and a blank document appears, as you can see in Figure 1.2. The Word window consists of a large area on which you place your text, graphics, and many different buttons, icons, and menus—all designed to help you create the perfect document for any occasion.

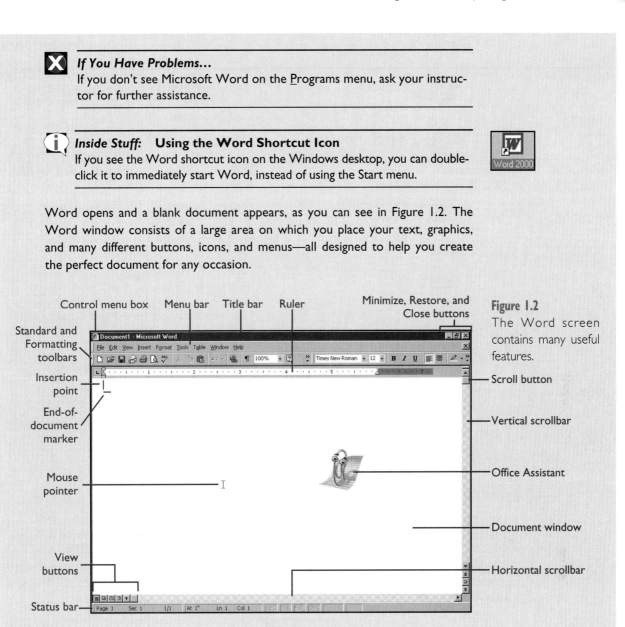

Figure 1.2
The Word screen contains many useful features.

Don't be intimidated by the number of items onscreen. You will continue to learn about these as you work through this book.

Table 1.1 lists the default screen elements and gives a brief description of each element. **Default** refers to standard settings, such as margins, which are determined by Microsoft Word. Word uses these settings unless you change them. Figure 1.2 shows the elements listed in Table 1.1 and Table 1.2.

Table 1.1   Icons and Buttons on the Microsoft Word Screen

Icon	Element	Description
	Control menu box	Displays menu that controls the application program. Double-click the box to exit (close) the application program.
	***Minimize* button**	Reduces the current document to an icon on the taskbar. If only one document is open, clicking the Minimize button reduces Word to an icon on the taskbar.
	***Restore* button**	Restores the window to its previous size.
	***Maximize* button**	Restores the window to the full-screen size.
	Close button	Closes the document window. If only one document is open, you see another Close button on the same row as the Menu Bar. Click the top Close button to close (exit) Word. Click the bottom Close button to close only the current document window.
	Insertion point	Shows your location in the document.
	End-of-document marker	Indicates the end of the document. Appears only in Normal View.

Table 1.2   Parts of the Microsoft Word Screen

Element	Description
Title bar	Shows the name of the file you are currently working on. If you haven't saved the document, Word displays a document number, such as Document2. Also shows the name of the program, such as Microsoft Word.
Menu bar	Lists categories of menus that contain options from which to choose.
Standard toolbar	Contains a row of buttons that perform routine tasks, such as opening, saving, and printing a file. Other toolbars are available for specific types of tasks.
Formatting toolbar	Contains a row of buttons that perform functions to enhance the appearance of your documents.
Ruler	Shows the location of tabs, indents, and left and right margins.
Document window	Displays text and formats for documents you create.
Vertical scrollbar	Moves up and down in a document.
Scroll buttons	Move quickly through a document. You can scroll up or down, one page at a time, or scroll to a particular object within the document.
View buttons	Switch between different view modes. These options are also available on the View pull-down menu.
Horizontal scrollbar	Adjusts horizontal view (left to right).
Status bar	Displays the current page number and location of the insertion point. Also displays active modes, such as Overtype.
Office Assistant	Provides help for questions you pose.

You can refer to Figure 1.2, Table 1.1, and Table 1.2 to learn the parts of the Word screen. With a little practice, it won't take long until you know each item on the Word screen and how to use it.

Lesson 2: Using Menu Bars and Toolbars

Menu bars and toolbars make it easy to find and use various features in Word. For example, if you need to insert page numbers or format a document, those commands are literally at your fingertips.

Word's commands are organized in menus. The **menu bar** lists nine menu categories, such as File. When you click a menu name, you see a **menu**, which is a list of commands.

Word's menus appear as short or full menus. The **short menus**, also called **adaptive menus**, display a list of commonly used commands (see Figure 1.3). As you work with Word, the short menus adapt to your use.

Figure 1.3
The short format menu displays the most recently used commands.

A moment after opening a short menu, or when you click the down-pointing arrows, you see the **full menu**, which includes all commands in that menu category (see Figure 1.4). When you select a command from the full menu, Word adapts the short menu by including that command the next time you display the menu.

Additional options appear ⎯

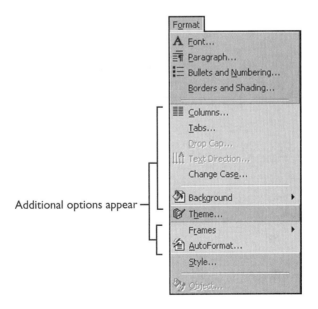

Figure 1.4
The full-format menu displays all format commands.

To Use the Menu Bar

1 Click File on the menu bar.
The File menu displays, listing the last four to nine documents used on your computer (see Figure 1.5). Your list might show different document names.

Figure 1.5
The File menu shows the most commonly used file commands.

Click to see File menu

List of last four to nine documents used

Position mouse pointer to see more options

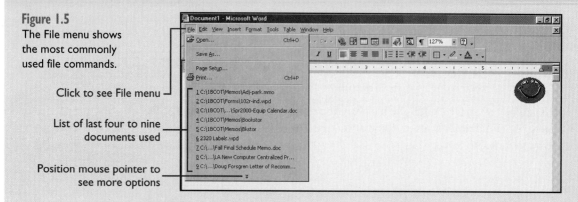

2 Move the mouse pointer to the bottom of the File menu, where you see the arrows.
You now see the full menu, which contains additional options, such as Send To and Properties. Table 1.3 describes the different types of menu options.

Table 1.3 Types of Menu Options

Characteristic	Description	Example
... (ellipsis)	Displays a dialog box with specific task-related options.	Print...
▶ (triangle)	Displays a *submenu*, a menu of more specific options, to the side of the current menu.	Send To ▶
No symbol	Performs the task immediately without providing additional options.	Exit
✓ (check mark)	Indicates that an option is turned on or active.	✓ Standard
Gray option name	Indicates that the option is currently unavailable (*grayed-out*).	Cut

3 If you decide not to select a menu option, click File again on the menu bar to close it.

 ***Inside Stuff:* Closing Menus**
You can also close a menu by pressing Esc twice or by pressing Alt once, or by clicking outside of the menu, such as in the document window.

Inside Stuff: **Selecting Menus from the Keyboard**

You can also use the keyboard to select from the menu bar. Notice that one letter (often the first) of each menu bar option is underlined. For example, F is underlined in File. To choose a particular menu, press Alt+the underlined letter. For example, pressing Alt+F displays the File menu.

When the menu displays, press ↓ or ↑ to highlight an option; then press ↵Enter to select that option. You can also press the underlined letter to immediately select the option of your choice. For example, press C for Close on the File menu.

The menus also display keyboard ***shortcuts***, such as Ctrl+S for Save (see Figure 1.5). By using keyboard shortcuts, you can keep your hands on the keyboard and maybe save a little time.

The Standard and ***Formatting toolbars*** contain ***buttons***, or little pictures that represent different tasks. When you click a button, Word performs the action or task associated with that button. Some buttons contain the same commands that you see in menus. For example, click the Save button to save a file. Clicking the Save button might be faster than opening the File menu and choosing the Save command.

Currently, the Standard and Formatting toolbars share one row. In the next exercise, you learn how to separate them to see all buttons on both toolbars at the same time. Plus, you learn about ScreenTips.

To Use Toolbars

❶ Move the mouse pointer to the New Blank Document button on the Standard toolbar.

When you position the mouse pointer on a button, Word displays the name of the button in a little yellow box, called a ***ScreenTip***. You should see the ScreenTip `New Blank Document (Ctrl+N)` now.

 If You Have Problems...

If the menus and ScreenTips do not show the shortcut keys, choose Tools, Customize, click the Options tab, click the Show ScreenTips in toolbars check box, make sure the Show shortcut keys in ScreenTips check box is selected, and then click Close.

❷ Click View on the menu bar to see the View menu.

❸ Choose Toolbars.

You see a list of different toolbars, plus the Customize option (see Figure 1.6). The check marks indicate the active toolbars.

continues ▶

To Use Toolbars   (continued)

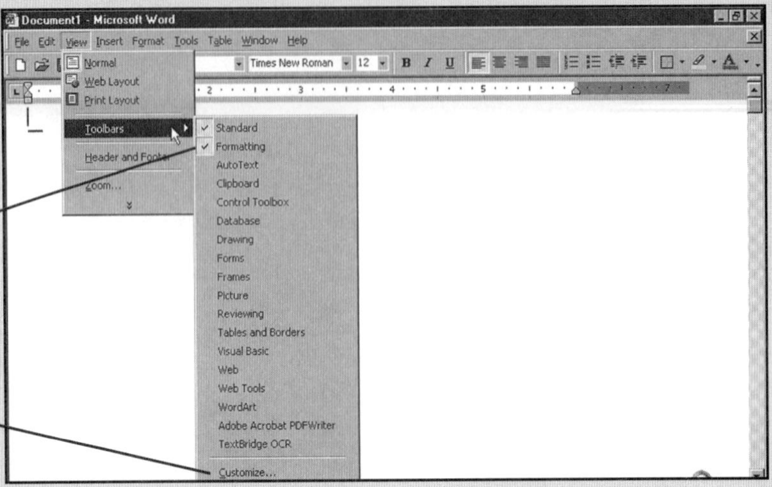

Figure 1.6
The Toolbars sub-menu lets you display, hide, and customize toolbars.

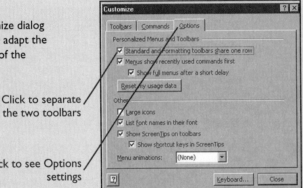

Active toolbars indicated by check marks

Choose Customize to adjust toolbar settings

4 Click Customize at the bottom of the menu.
The Customize dialog box appears, so you can adjust the way the toolbars appear on your screen (see Figure 1.7).

Figure 1.7
The Customize dialog box lets you adapt the appearance of the toolbars.

Click to separate the two toolbars

Click to see Options settings

5 Click the Options tab; then click the Standard and Formatting toolbars share one row check box to uncheck it.
This option is no longer selected.

6 Click Close.
The Standard and Formatting toolbars now appear on separate rows, as shown in Figure 1.8.

Figure 1.8
The Standard and Formatting toolbars appear on separate rows.

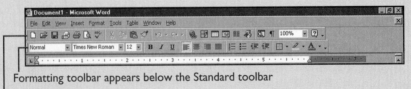

Formatting toolbar appears below the Standard toolbar

Standard toolbar appears first

Inside Stuff: **Customizing the Toolbar**
Instead of choosing View, Toolbars, Customize, you can right-click any button on the toolbar and choose Customize. You see the same Customize dialog box.

Lesson 3: Entering Text in a Document

You can begin entering text for your document as soon as you start Word. When you begin a new document, Word provides default settings, such as the margins, tabs, font, and font size. The **document window** is where you type and format your documents, and the insertion point should appear below the ruler.

In this lesson, you enter text using the default settings.

To Enter Text in a Document

1 Type the following text in the document window:

Your proposal contains some excellent ideas for the new advertising campaign. We are very impressed with your knowledge of the company and of our target market.

Don't press ⏎Enter when you reach the end of a line. When you enter more text than can fit on the current line, the **word-wrap feature** continues text to the next line when it runs out of room on the current line.

 If You Have Problems...
If the document area is gray instead of white, the Word document window isn't active and you need to start a new document. Click the New Blank Document button on the left side of the Standard toolbar.

2 Press ⏎Enter twice when you reach the end of a single-spaced paragraph.

Pressing ⏎Enter tells Word to go to the next line. Pressing ⏎Enter a second time leaves one blank line between paragraphs.

3 Continue by typing the following paragraph:

Brent Anderson, vice president of advertising, wants to set up a meeting for you to formally present your proposal to the board of directors. Please call me at 555-0201 to set up a meeting within the next two weeks.

Figure 1.9 shows what your document should look like.

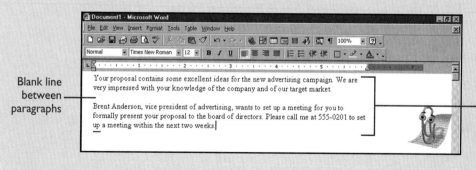

Blank line between paragraphs

Figure 1.9
Your document now contains two paragraphs.

Your line endings may differ

4 Leave your new Word document onscreen to continue with the next exercise.

Exam Note: Correcting Mistakes

When you take the MOUS tests, you are penalized for typographical errors. You should always proofread and correct errors before continuing to the next exam task.

If you make a mistake as you type the paragraphs, you can press ⎵Backspace to delete text to the *left* of the insertion point or you can press ⎵Del to delete text to the *right* of the insertion point. After deleting incorrect letters, type the correct letters.

If you see wavy red lines below a word, the word is not in Microsoft's main dictionary. You see these red lines below misspelled words and proper nouns. Simply right-click the word and choose the correct spelling from the menu that displays. You learn more about correcting spelling errors in Project 4, "Editing Documents."

  Inside Stuff: Seeing Dots and Symbols

You might see dots between words and a paragraph (¶) symbol at the end of the paragraphs. You learn about these marks in Project 2, "Working with a Document." For now, click the Show/Hide ¶ button on the Standard toolbar to turn off the symbols.

 Word 2000 introduces a new feature called **Click and Type** that lets you double-click in any area of the document and type new text in Print Layout View. Depending on where you double-click, you can type text at the left margin, tabbed in from the left margin, centered between the margins, or flush with the right margin.

To Use Click and Type

❶ Choose <u>V</u>iew and then choose <u>P</u>rint Layout from the <u>V</u>iew menu.
The end-of-document marker disappears in Print Layout view. However, you can use the Click and Type feature.

❷ Position the mouse pointer about one-half inch below your last paragraph and centered between the left and right edges of the screen.
Figure 1.10 shows the mouse pointer. The horizontal lines by the mouse pointer indicate that text will be centered when you double-click.

Figure 1.10
Double-click and type to enter text at a particular location.

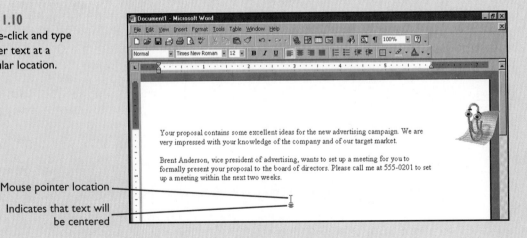

Mouse pointer location —

Indicates that text will be centered —

If You Have Problems...

If you don't see the horizontal lines by the mouse pointer, you might be in Normal view instead of Print Layout view. Click the Print Layout View button above the left side of the status bar.

If Click and Type is still not working, you need to activate it. To do this, choose <u>T</u>ools and choose <u>O</u>ptions from the <u>T</u>ools menu. Click the Edit tab, click the Enable <u>c</u>lick and type check box, and click <u>O</u>K.

3 Double-click in the center point and type your name.
Your name is centered between the left and right margins.

4 Leave the document onscreen to continue with the next lesson.

Lesson 4: Saving a Document

Your document is not saved or stored for you to use in the future. The document exists only in the computer's random-access memory (RAM) and will be lost if the computer crashes or unexpectedly shuts down. For this reason, you should save your documents frequently. **Save** refers to the process of storing a document for future use. When you save a document for the first time, you designate the location where you're storing the file (for example, on the hard drive or on a floppy disk) and you assign a name to the document.

To Save a Document

1 Insert a new, formatted floppy disk into the disk drive.

2 With your new Word document open, choose <u>F</u>ile, Save <u>A</u>s.
The Save As dialog box appears (see Figure 1.11). The first step in saving your file is to choose a location where you would like to keep it.

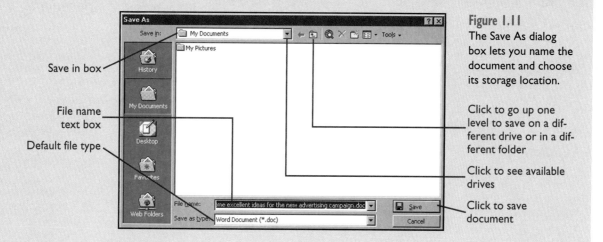

Save in box

File name text box

Default file type

Figure 1.11
The Save As dialog box lets you name the document and choose its storage location.

Click to go up one level to save on a different drive or in a different folder

Click to see available drives

Click to save document

By default, Word saves documents in the My Documents folder on the hard drive.

continues ▶

To Save a Document   (continued)

❸ Click the drop-down arrow on the right side of the Save in text box.

You see a list of available drives on your computer system (see Figure 1.12). This book assumes that you save and open documents on a floppy drive, typically designated as 3 1/2 Floppy (A:). Ask your instructor for the correct location for saving any files you create during this course.

Figure 1.12
The Save in **drop-down list** shows you the available drives where you can save your documents.

Save data files to this drive

Choose this option if saving to a Zip disk

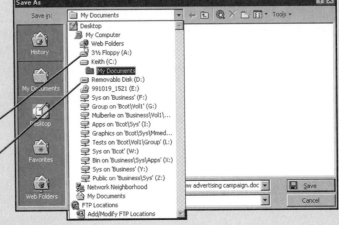

❹ Choose 3 1/2 Floppy (A:) from the Save in list.

 If You Have Problems...

If the Save in option displays Desktop and you don't see a list of drives, ask your instructor how to proceed.

❺ Press Alt+N to make the File name text box active. Now you can type over the suggested filename.

❻ Type Campaign Proposal in the File name text box. You have just named your file.

When you type a filename, it replaces the default name suggested by Word. You can assign filenames using up to 255 characters, including both upper- and lowercase letters, numbers, some symbols, and spaces.

❼ Click Save in the bottom-right corner of the dialog box.

Leave your Word document onscreen to continue with the next lesson.

 If You Have Problems...

If you try to save to a floppy disk and get an error message, there are several possible reasons. First, make sure you have correctly inserted a disk in the disk drive. Second, make sure you have selected the correct drive; many computers have more than one storage drive. Some network drives may prohibit users from storing files in these locations.

If you are saving to a floppy disk, the disk should be formatted and the write-protect tab should not cover the opening on the disk. Ask your instructor if you need help formatting a disk or determining whether the write-protect tab is on or off.

Exam Note: **Using Save versus Save As**

The first time you save a document, you can use either <u>S</u>ave or Save <u>A</u>s. Either way, you see the Save As dialog box. After you save a document, however, <u>S</u>ave and Save <u>A</u>s have two different effects.

If you modify a document and use <u>S</u>ave, Word saves the changes under the same filename without displaying the Save As dialog box. Use <u>S</u>ave to save a document under the same filename and then continue entering text and formatting it.

At other times, you might want to assign a different name to a modified document so that you have the original document as well as the modified document. Use Save <u>A</u>s to save the document with a different filename or to a different location. For example, you might want to save a document in two different locations: on a Zip disk and on your hard drive. To do this, click the Save <u>i</u>n drop-down arrow and choose the drive and folder in which to save the modified document. Furthermore, you might want to save a document in a non-Word format. To do this, click the Save as <u>t</u>ype drop-down arrow and choose the file type, such as `Text Only (*.txt)`.

 Inside Stuff: **Saving Methods**

You can also press Ctrl+S or click the Save button on the Standard toolbar to save a document. Note that the toolbar does *not* contain a button for Save As.

 Exam Note: **Saving a Document as a Web Page**

You might want to save a document in a format that is viewable on the World Wide Web (Web). You can save an existing document as a Web page without knowing HTML programming language. Choose <u>F</u>ile, Save as Web Page. Specify the Web page title, filename, and location. The Save as <u>t</u>ype option defaults to `Web Page (*.htm; *.html)` automatically.

Lesson 5: Using Print Preview

Before printing a document, you should preview it to make sure it looks the way you want it to look. If the document is formatted correctly, you can then print it. If not, you can correctly format the document before printing it.

To Use Print Preview

1 **Click the Print Preview button on the Standard toolbar.**

You see a preview of what the printed document will look like (see Figure 1.13).

continues ▶

To Use Print Preview   (continued)

Figure 1.13
The Print Preview window shows how the printed document will look.

Click to print
View percentage
Closes Print Preview window
Click mouse pointer to magnify the preview

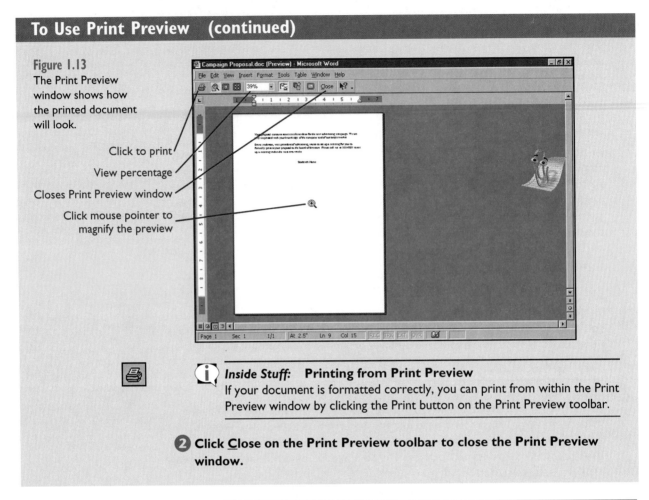

Inside Stuff: **Printing from Print Preview**
If your document is formatted correctly, you can print from within the Print Preview window by clicking the Print button on the Print Preview toolbar.

② **Click Close on the Print Preview toolbar to close the Print Preview window.**

Inside Stuff: **Print Preview Options**
You can press ⏎Enter to move text down or display the Ruler to change margins to balance text on a page if needed. The Print Preview toolbar contains buttons for magnifying the page onscreen, displaying one page, displaying multiple pages, or shrinking the document to fit.

Exam Note: **Web Page Preview**
If you want to see how a document will look on the Web, choose File, Web Page Preview.

Lesson 6: Printing a Document

After previewing a document and adjusting the format, if needed, you are ready to print it. You can quickly print the entire document by clicking the Print button on the Standard toolbar. If you need to specify print settings, such as the number of copies to print, you need to display the Print dialog box.

To Print a Document

 Make sure the printer is turned on, has paper, and is online.
Ask your instructor if you need further assistance in using the printer.

2 **Click <u>F</u>ile and then choose <u>P</u>rint from the <u>F</u>ile menu.**

** Inside Stuff: Print Keyboard Shortcut**
You can press Ctrl+P to display the Print dialog box.

The Print dialog box appears (see Figure 1.14).

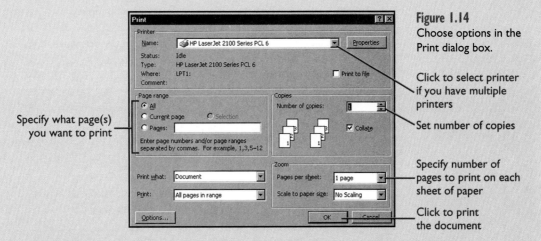

Specify what page(s) you want to print

Figure 1.14
Choose options in the Print dialog box.

Click to select printer if you have multiple printers

Set number of copies

Specify number of pages to print on each sheet of paper

Click to print the document

** Inside Stuff: Clicking the Print Button**
Clicking the Print button on the Standard toolbar sends the entire document to the printer without displaying the Print dialog box. Although this is a fast way to print a document, it doesn't give you the opportunity to select print options.

---

3 **Ask your instructor which printer name is correct for the system you're using. If needed, click the drop-down arrow to the right of the <u>N</u>ame option and choose the correct printer name from the list.**

4 **Click OK to print your document.**
Word sends a copy of the document to the printer. Leave your Word document onscreen to continue with the next lesson.

After you print a document, make sure the text looks good on paper. Check the format. You might need to adjust the formatting and print the document again.

Inside Stuff: Print Options
The Print dialog box contains many useful options. For example, you can print only the page that contains the insertion point (Curr<u>e</u>nt page) or a range of pages, such as pages 3–10 (Pa<u>g</u>es). Furthermore, you can print several copies of the document (Number of <u>c</u>opies), print miniature copies of pages on a single sheet of paper (Pages per s<u>h</u>eet), or adjust the document text size to fit on a particular type of paper (Scale to paper si<u>z</u>e).

Lesson 7: Getting Help

When you work with Word, you will probably need to know about a specific feature or how to perform a certain task. Although you are learning a lot about Word by completing this book, you might run across a situation in which you need assistance. Word contains an on-screen assistance feature called Help. **Help** provides information about Word features and step-by-step instructions for performing tasks. A quick way to get the help you need is to use the **Office Assistant**, Microsoft's animated Help feature, to find the answer to a specific question.

 Exam Note: **Using Help During a MOUS Exam**

While you can't use books, notes, or ask other people questions during a MOUS exam, you can use the Help feature built into the software. However, don't use Help as an alternative for knowing how to use the software; if you do, you probably won't have time to complete all tasks on the test.

To Get Help

① **If the Office Assistant does not appear on your screen, choose Help on the menu bar and then choose Show the Office Assistant.**

The Office Assistant appears as one of several different animated characters, such as Clippit the paper clip, Rocky the dog, Nibbles the cat, F1 the robot, and so on. Later, you will learn how to change these characters.

 Inside Stuff: **Displaying the Office Assistant**

To display the Office Assistant quickly, press F1 at any time or click the Microsoft Word Help button on the Standard toolbar.

② **Click the Office Assistant to display a balloon with the following message: What would you like to do?**

The Office Assistant is now ready for you to ask it a question (see Figure 1.15). Type a word, phrase, or full-length question. The more specific you are with your questions, the better the Office Assistant is able to direct you. After you type a question and click Search, the balloon displays a list of topics.

Figure 1.15
Use the Office Assistant to help you use Word.

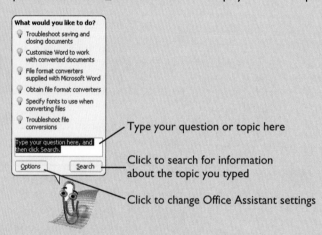

Type your question or topic here

Click to search for information about the topic you typed

Click to change Office Assistant settings

③ **Type menus and then click Search.**

The Office Assistant displays a listing of topics related to menus (see Figure 1.16).

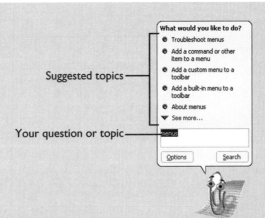

Suggested topics

Your question or topic

Figure 1.16
The Office Assistant provides topics to answer your question.

4 **Click the topic titled About menus.**

The Microsoft Word Help window appears, as shown in Figure 1.17. The left side, called the **Navigation pane**, contains tabs (Contents, Answer Wizard, and Index). The right side, called the **Help Topic pane**, contains information about the topic you selected. The Help window probably covers part of your document. Don't worry about this; the document window enlarges when you close the Help feature. Underlined keywords and phrases appearing in a different color are called **hypertext links**. When you click a hypertext link, you see additional information.

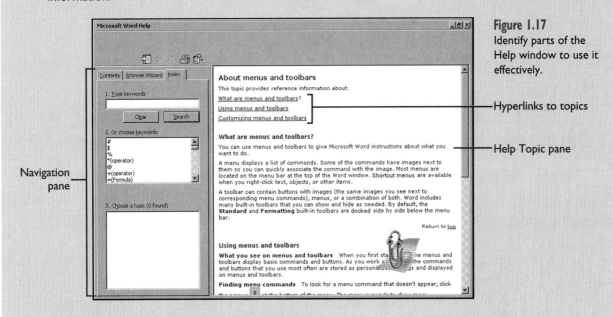

Navigation pane

Figure 1.17
Identify parts of the Help window to use it effectively.

Hyperlinks to topics

Help Topic pane

[X] ***If You Have Problems...***
If you don't see the Navigation pane, click the Show button on the Help toolbar.

5 **Click the Index tab in the Navigation pane, if necessary.**

The Index feature lets you type a topic and search through the alphabetical index of topics. The first step is to enter keywords (particular words that might be found in the Help topics) and then click the Search button. Alternatively, you can scroll through the list of keywords in the index to find what you're looking for.

continues ▶

To Get Help   (continued)

6 **Type toolbar in the Type keywords text box.**
You see a list of topics in the Choose a topic list box.

7 **Double-click toolbars in the Or choose keywords list box.**

8 **Click Rename toolbars in the Choose a topic list box.**
When you click a topic, you see topical information in the Help Topic pane (see Figure 1.18). Some topics are primarily descriptions, as you saw earlier. Other topics provide step-by-step instructions for completing a task.

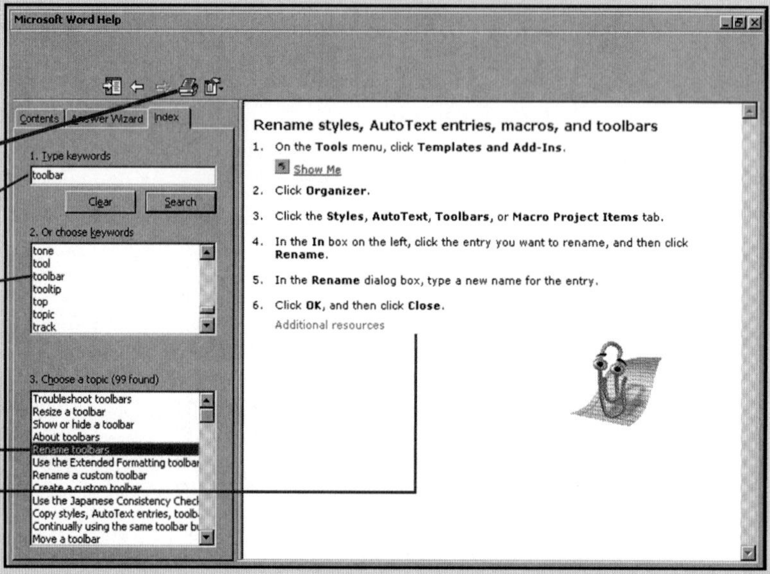

Figure 1.18
Use the Index to find specific information.

Click to print information in Help Topic pane

Type keywords here

Double-click word in alphabetical list

Click to choose topic

Step-by-step instructions

Microsoft Word Help

Contents | Answer Wizard | Index

1. Type keywords
toolbar

[Clear] [Search]

2. Or choose keywords
tone
tool
toolbar
tooltip
top
topic
track

3. Choose a topic (99 found)
Troubleshoot toolbars
Resize a toolbar
Show or hide a toolbar
About toolbars
Rename toolbars
Use the Extended Formatting toolbar
Rename a custom toolbar
Create a custom toolbar
Use the Japanese Consistency Check
Copy styles, AutoText entries, toolb
Continually using the same toolbar b
Move a toolbar

Rename styles, AutoText entries, macros, and toolbars

1. On the **Tools** menu, click **Templates and Add-Ins**.
   Show Me
2. Click **Organizer**.
3. Click the **Styles, AutoText, Toolbars,** or **Macro Project Items** tab.
4. In the **In** box on the left, click the entry you want to rename, and then click **Rename**.
5. In the **Rename** dialog box, type a new name for the entry.
6. Click **OK**, and then click **Close**.
   Additional resources

(i) ***Inside Stuff:*** **Printing Help Topics**
You might want to print the Help topic to have it handy. Printing the Help topic allows you to close the Microsoft Word Help window. You can read your printed copy as you perform the tasks on your document.

9 **Click the Close button in the top-right corner of the Microsoft Word Help window.**
This closes Help and displays your document on the whole screen again. Leave the document onscreen to continue with the next lesson.

  If You Have Problems...
If Office Assistant can't find topics related to the question you type, a balloon appears and tells you so. Make sure your question doesn't contain any misspelled words or type a more specific question and click Search again.

Inside Stuff: Changing the Office Assistant
To change the Office Assistant image, right-click the Office Assistant and select
Choose Assistant. When you see a gallery, scroll through the available images to select a different one. You can select other Office Assistant settings by right-clicking
the Office Assistant and choosing Options.

Some Office Assistant images might not be available. You might be prompted to insert the installation CD to use a particular assistant.

Another useful feature is What's This?, which displays a ScreenTip about a screen item. To
use this feature, choose Help, What's This, or press ⬆Shift+F1. When the pointer resembles a question mark with an arrow, click the mouse pointer on the screen item that you
don't understand. Word then provides a ScreenTip that describes that feature. Press
⬆Shift+F1 to turn off the What's This? feature.

If you can't find the information you need within Word, you can access resources available
on the World Wide Web. Assuming you have Internet access, you can choose Help, Office
on the Web to view information on Microsoft's Web site for Word.

Lesson 8: Closing a Document and Exiting Word

When you finish working on your documents, you should properly **close** the files (that is, remove them from the screen). When you finish using Word, you should **exit** (close down)
the Word software. If you simply turn off the computer, you might lose valuable work and
create problems within the computer itself. Because you saved the document in Lesson 4
and have not made any changes to it, you can close the document without having to save
again.

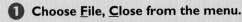
To Close a File and Exit Word

❶ Choose File, Close from the menu.

 Inside Stuff: Other Close Methods
You can also close a document by pressing Ctrl+F4 or by clicking the document close button on the far right side of the menu bar.

The file closes immediately. If you haven't saved the document after modifying it,
Word displays a dialog box that asks if you want to save the changes. Click Yes
to save the file before closing it or click No to close the document without saving the changes.

❷ Choose File, Exit from the menu to close Word.
If other Word files are open, they close immediately if you saved them. If other
files have been modified since you last saved them, Word prompts you to save
them before the program closes. After Word closes, you see the Windows
Desktop if no other programs are running.

 Inside Stuff: Exiting with the Control Menu Box
You can also exit Word by double-clicking the Control menu box or by
clicking the Close button in the top-right corner of the Word window.

This concludes Project 1. You can reinforce and expand your knowledge and skills by completing the end-of-project activities that follow the summary.

Summary

You are now familiar with some of the Word screen components. You can also use the menu bar and toolbars to access commands easily. You can enter text, save the document for future use, and print the document. Use the Office Assistant and the Help feature to learn more about the exciting things you can do with Word.

For more information about these and other features, ask the Office Assistant for help or choose Help, Office on the Web. These sources provide a vast array of information to help you become comfortable with and proficient at using Word.

Also, check out the MOUS Objective list in the book to find specific topics on the Word 2000 MOUS exam and where the topics are discussed. In addition, remember to use the index at the back of this book; it's an excellent way to find the *exact* pages that discuss particular topics.

Checking Concepts and Terms

True/False

For each of the following, check *T* or *F* to indicate whether the statement is true or false.

__T __F **1.** The Click and Type feature lets you single-click anywhere in the document and type text at that location. [L3]

__T __F **2.** If you want to assign a new name to a modified document that was previously saved, choose the Save option. [L4]

__T __F **3.** To see a preview of how a printed document will look, select Print Preview from the View menu. [L5]

__T __F **4.** Click the Print button to display the Print dialog box, in which you can set specific options, such as number of copies to print. [L6]

__T __F **5.** The Office Assistant provides access to a variety of topics to help you use Word. [L7]

Multiple Choice

Circle the letter of the correct answer for each of the following.

1. What feature displays an animated graphic that provides onscreen help? [L7]

  a. standard toolbar

  b. Office Assistant

  c. Help Index

  d. Navigation pane

2. What happens when you choose a menu option that displays a triangle? [L2]

  a. You see a submenu.

  b. A dialog box appears.

  c. Word immediately performs the command.

  d. The menu closes.

3. Which of the following does not happen when you use the Save command? [L4]

  a. Word saves an existing document with the same filename.

  b. The document closes.

  c. The Save As dialog box appears if you haven't saved the document before.

  d. You are able to use the document in the future.

4. If you want to scroll through an alphabetical list of Help topics, which Help feature do you use? [L7]

    a. Index

    b. Contents

    c. Office Assistant

    d. Answer Wizard

5. Which of the following can you do in the Print Preview window? [L5]

    a. see the amount of space for the margins

    b. type and edit text

    c. look at the overall format of the document

    d. all of the above

Screen ID

Label each element of the Word screen shown in Figure 1.19.

Figure 1.19

A. Formatting toolbar

B. insertion point

C. mouse pointer

D. Standard toolbar

E. status bar

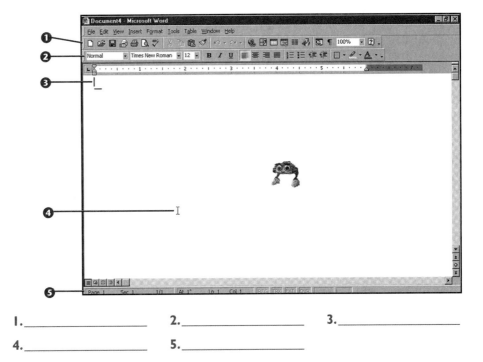

1._____ 2._____ 3._____

4._____ 5._____

Skill Drill

Skill Drill exercises reinforce project skills. Each skill reinforced is the same, or nearly the same, as a skill presented in the project. Each exercise includes a brief narrative introduction, followed by detailed instructions in a step-by-step format.

1. Exploring Menus and Using Toolbars

You want to review some menus and toolbars. The more you study the screen components, the more you understand the structure and logic of using Word.

1. Start Word.

2. Press (Alt)+(A) to display the Table menu. (You press (A) because **a** is underlined in Table.)

3. Click the arrows to display the full Table menu.

4. Try choosing Merge Cells. (Nothing happens because the option is grayed-out. It is available only when you perform a specific task first.)

5. Press (Alt) once to close the Table menu without choosing any options.

6. Choose View and then choose Toolbars to display the Toolbars submenu.

7. Click Drawing to display the Drawing toolbar. (It appears at the bottom of the Word screen.)

8. Position the mouse pointer over the blue A button on the Drawing toolbar. (You should see the ScreenTip, Insert WordArt.)

9. Repeat Steps 6 and 7 to hide the Drawing toolbar.

10. Click the right mouse button on any button on the Standard toolbar.

11. Choose Customize from the toolbar list.

12. Click the Options tab.

13. Look at the Show shortcut keys in ScreenTips option. If it is selected, click Close. Otherwise, click

Show shortcut keys in ScreenTips check box to select it and then click Close.

14. Position the mouse pointer on the second button on the Standard toolbar to see the ScreenTip, Open (Ctrl + O).

15. Choose File, Close to close the document. Click No if you are prompted to save the document. Choose File, Exit if you need to end your work session.

2. Creating, Saving, and Printing a Document

You need to compose a short note to your two primary supervisors, telling them that you need to come in later on Friday because you have a special test in the morning. You create and save the first note; then you change the supervisor's name and save the modified document with a new filename.

1. Type **Dear Ms. Turner:** and press ⏎Enter twice.

2. Type the following paragraph:

   This Friday I have a special test in my history class at the local community college. This test is scheduled during a specific time, which is controlled by the instructor. I would appreciate being able to come in to work at 11:30 instead of my usual 8:30 time. Thank you for working around my college class schedule.

3. Choose File, Save As.

4. Click the Save in drop-down arrow and choose the appropriate drive in which you have been instructed to save documents.

5. Type **Turner Note** in the File name text box.

6. Click Save to save the document.

7. Press ⏎Enter twice after the last paragraph, type **Sincerely yours,** press ⏎Enter four times, and then type your name.

8. Click the Save button on the Standard toolbar to save the modified document under the same filename, Turner Note.

9. Click the Print Preview button on the Standard toolbar.

10. Click the Close button to close the Print Preview window.

11. Choose File, Print, and then click OK to print the document.

12. Click to the left of Ms. Turner on the first line and press Del until you have deleted her name.

13. Type **Mr. Baxter** for your other supervisor's name. Make sure there is still a colon after the name.

14. Choose File, Save As to assign a new name to the modified document.

15. Make sure the correct drive is displayed in the Save in option. Change it if necessary.

16. Type **Baxter Note** in the File name text box and click Save.

17. Click the Print button on the Standard toolbar to print the document without displaying the Print dialog box.

18. Choose File, Close to close the document.

19. Choose File, Exit if you need to exit Word now. Leave Word open if you are continuing with the next exercise.

3. Using the Office Assistant and the Help Index

You want to continue topics in the Help Index and then print a Help topic.

1. Click the Office Assistant if it's displayed. If it's not displayed, choose Help, Show the Office Assistant and then click it.

2. Click the Options button to display the Office Assistant dialog box.

3. Click the Use the Office Assistant check box to deselect it. Then click OK.

4. Press F1 to display the Microsoft Word Help window.

5. Click the Index tab in the Navigation Pane.

6. Type **save** and click the Search button.

7. Read about the first topic.

8. Scroll through the topic to continue reading information about saving documents.

9. Click the Close button in the top-right corner of the Microsoft Word Help window to close it.

10. Continue working in Word if you wish to complete the Challenge exercises, or choose File, Exit to close Word.

Challenge

Challenge exercises expand on or are somewhat related to skills presented in the lessons. Each exercise provides a brief narrative introduction followed by instructions in a numbered-step or bullet-list format that are not as detailed as those in the Skill Drill exercises.

I. Creating, Modifying, Saving, and Printing a Letter

You want to write a short note to your word processing instructor to let him or her know your goals for learning Microsoft Word. Use Figure 1.20 as a guide for the format.

1. Type today's date and press ↵Enter four times.

2. Type your instructor's name and address on separate lines. Press ↵Enter twice after the address.

3. Type the greeting, press ↵Enter twice, and type a first paragraph about yourself.

4. Save the document on your data disk as **Introduction**.

5. Type a second paragraph that describes why you are learning Word. Then complete the rest of the letter with a complimentary closing and your name.

6. Save the modified document as **Introduction Letter for Instructor**.

7. Preview, print, and close the document.

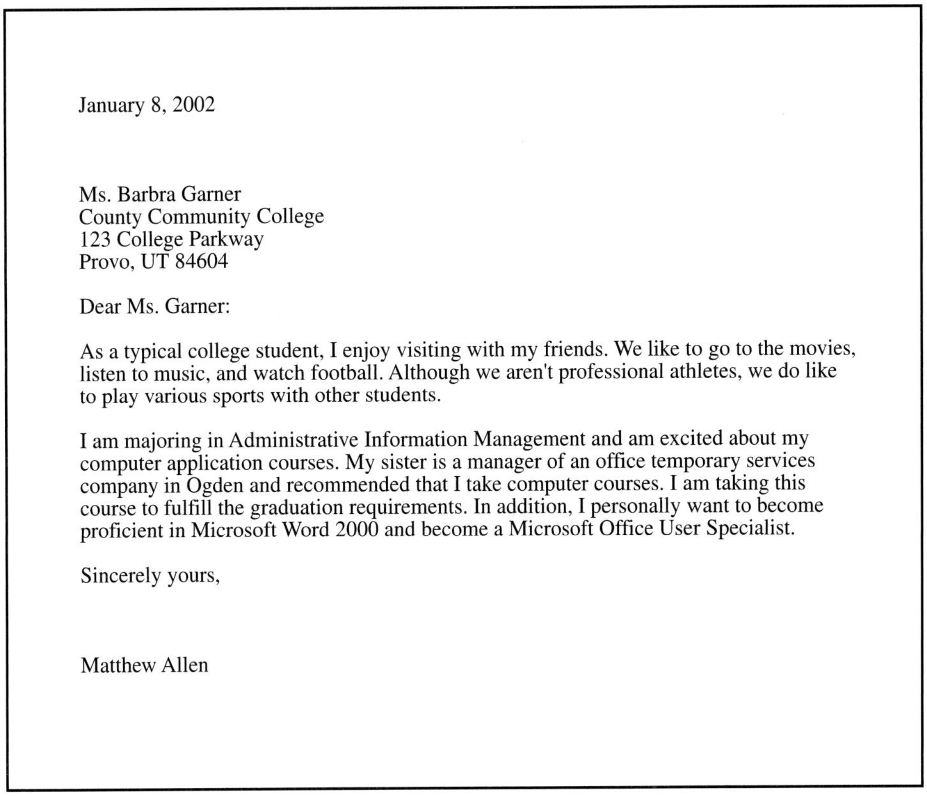

Figure 1.20
Use this sample letter to create and format your letter.

January 8, 2002

Ms. Barbra Garner
County Community College
123 College Parkway
Provo, UT 84604

Dear Ms. Garner:

As a typical college student, I enjoy visiting with my friends. We like to go to the movies, listen to music, and watch football. Although we aren't professional athletes, we do like to play various sports with other students.

I am majoring in Administrative Information Management and am excited about my computer application courses. My sister is a manager of an office temporary services company in Ogden and recommended that I take computer courses. I am taking this course to fulfill the graduation requirements. In addition, I personally want to become proficient in Microsoft Word 2000 and become a Microsoft Office User Specialist.

Sincerely yours,

Matthew Allen

2. Creating, Saving as a Different File Format, and Printing Two Copies of a Phone List

You want to create a phone list that contains numbers for 10 people. Use phone numbers of your friends and family. You want to save the file in ASCII text format so that you can give the document on disk to other people who don't have Microsoft Word.

1. Create a phone list by typing names at the left margin and pressing Tab⇄ to type the phone numbers. You might have to press Tab⇄ an extra time to align the phone numbers.

2. Save the phone list with these specifications:
   a. **Phone List** is the filename.
   b. It should be saved to a Zip disk or personal network drive.
   c. It is in a Text Only (*.txt) file format.

3. Preview the document and then print three copies of it.

3. Using the Office Assistant

The Help Contents section provides general topics to get users started with Word. You want to learn about scrolling.

1. Display the Office Assistant.

2. Ask the Office Assistant about **new features** and choose the first suggested topic.

3. When the Help window appears, select the option that will provide you with information about Office 2000's new look.

4. Read through the topical information and print the Help topic.

5. Click some hyperlinks for additional information.

Discovery Zone

Discovery Zone exercises help you gain advanced knowledge of project topics and/or application of skills. These exercises focus on enhancing your problem-solving skills. Numbered steps are not provided, but you are given hints, reminders, screen shots, and/or references to help you reach your goal for each exercise.

1. Saving a File with a Password

You need to create a highly confidential document. You want to save the document so that the user must enter a password to open the document. Use the Help Index or Office Assistant to find out how to save a document with a password. Print the specific step-by-step help instructions.

Compose a document that briefly discusses the difference between Save and Save As. Type two paragraphs. Save the document on your data disk as **Saving Documents** with the password **Secret**. Print the document.

2. Moving a Toolbar

Use the Office Assistant to help you find information about **moving toolbars**. Print the Help topic and then move the Formatting toolbar to the left side of the screen. Then move the toolbar back to its original location. If it combines with the Standard toolbar, separate them again by using the process you completed in Lesson 2.

PinPoint Assessment

You have completed this project and its associated lessons, and have had an opportunity to assess your skills through the end-of-project questions and exercises. Now use the PinPoint software Evaluation Mode to further assess your comprehension of the specific exam activities you have just learned. You can also use the PinPoint Trainer Mode and the Show Me tutorials to practice these exam activities.

Project 2

Working with a Document

Key terms introduced in this project include

- AutoComplete
- Full Screen view
- Insert mode
- inside address
- Normal view
- opening
- Overtype mode
- Print Layout view
- salutation
- scrolling
- selecting
- selection bar
- zoom

Objectives	Required Activity for MOUS	Exam Level
➤ Open an Existing Document	Locate and open an existing document	Core
➤ Scroll in a Document	Navigate through a document	Core
	Use Go To to locate specific elements in a document	Core
➤ Select Text		
➤ Delete and Change Text		
➤ Insert Text	Insert and move text	Core
	Insert date and time	Core
➤ Change View Modes		
➤ Create Envelopes	Prepare and print envelopes and labels	Core
➤ Create Labels	Prepare and print envelopes and labels	Core

Why Would I Do This?

In Project 1, "Getting Started with Word 2000," you learned how to create, save, print, and close a document. You often need to access a previously created document and modify it. This is one of the best features of a word processing program; you can start a document, save what you've created so far, and return to modify it at a later date. For example, you might be working on a business proposal for a client. Because the proposal evolves over time, you can add to and modify the existing document until you complete it.

In this project, you learn how to open a document that is identical to Campaign Letter, which you created in Project 1, "Getting Started with Word," and modify it to produce a letter. You also learn the different ways you can view your document with Word's viewing options and the advantages of each view.

 ## Lesson 1: Opening an Existing Document

One of the greatest benefits of using a computer is the capability to save documents and then use them again later. Using documents previously created saves valuable time in re-typing and reformatting the document.

Opening is the process of displaying a previously saved document. After you open a document, you can make changes, add new text, format text, save it, and print it.

To Open an Existing Document

① **If Word is not already running on your system, start the program, as described in Project 1. Insert the accompanying CD-ROM in the CD-ROM drive of your computer.**

② **Click the Open button on the Standard toolbar.**
The Open dialog box appears, as shown in Figure 2.1. Notice that it looks similar to the Save As dialog box you saw when you saved a document in Project 1.

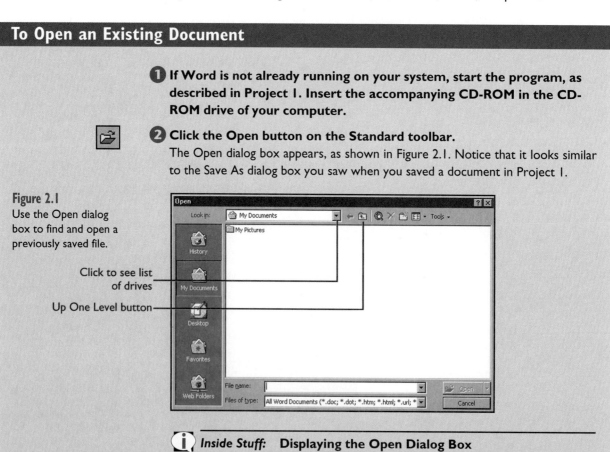

Figure 2.1
Use the Open dialog box to find and open a previously saved file.

Click to see list of drives

Up One Level button

Inside Stuff: **Displaying the Open Dialog Box**
You can also display the Open dialog box by choosing <u>F</u>ile, <u>O</u>pen, or by pressing Ctrl+O.

③ Click the arrow to the right of the Look in box.

The Look in list is identical to the Save in list you saw in Project 1. It lists the available storage drives, such as 3 1/2 Floppy (A:).

④ Choose the CD-ROM drive that contains the data files that accompany this book.

 If You Have Problems...

If you don't have the CD-ROM that accompanies this book, ask your instructor where the data files are stored (for example, the hard drive or school network). You might need to download the student data files from the Prentice Hall Web site. See the information at the beginning of this book for more information.

⑤ Double-click Project 02 folder on your CD-ROM.

The data files are stored in categories called ***folders***. Each folder name correlates to a project in this book. For example, all files you need to open for this project are stored in Project 02 on the CD-ROM.

⑥ Click W-0201 in the file list to select it.

⑦ Click Open.

Word accesses the document from your CD-ROM and displays it in a document window. The filename W-0201 appears on the title bar (see Figure 2.2).

Filename on
title bar

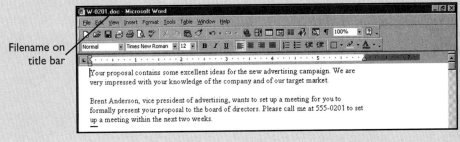

Figure 2.2
Your document is open and displayed onscreen.

⑧ Keep the document onscreen to continue with the next lesson.

From now on, you'll be instructed to simply open a file and save it with a different filename. Remember that you cannot save a file back to the CD-ROM; you need to save files to a data disk, Zip disk, or a network drive, if available.

 Inside Stuff: **Opening Recently Used Files**

The File menu lists the last four documents that have been used on your computer. If this menu lists the name of the document you want to work with, you can choose it from the menu to open that document. If the current disk does not contain the file, you see an error message.

You can customize the number of recently used files that are listed. Choose Tools, Options. Click the General tab. Specify how many filenames you want to list in the `Recently used file list` number box and then click OK.

Lesson 2: Scrolling in a Document

To make changes and corrections quickly and easily, you need to know the various ways of *scrolling*, or moving around in a document. For example, you can use either the mouse or the keyboard to move the insertion point in Word. Table 2.1 shows useful keyboard shortcuts for moving around in a document.

Table 2.1   Keyboard Shortcuts for Working in a Document

Key(s)	Moves the Insertion Point
←	one character to the left
→	one character to the right
↑	up one line
↓	down one line
Home	to the beginning of the line
End	to the end of the line
PgUp	up one window or page
PgDn	down one window or page
Ctrl+Home	to the beginning of the document
Ctrl+End	to the end of the document
Ctrl+←	one word to the left
Ctrl+→	one word to the right
Ctrl+↑	up one paragraph
Ctrl+↓	down one paragraph
Ctrl+PgUp	to the top of the previous page
Ctrl+PgDn	to the top of the next page

The **W-0201** file should be open on your screen. In the next exercise, you practice scrolling through the letter using both the mouse and the keyboard.

To Scroll Through the Document

❶ Press Ctrl+End **to move the insertion point to the end of the W-0201 document.**

❷ Position the mouse pointer to the immediate left of the word proposal **on the first line in the first paragraph; then click the left mouse button.**
When the mouse pointer is shaped like an I-beam, click within the document to place the insertion point at that location. This is a fast way of positioning the insertion point when you want to add new text within an existing paragraph.

❸ Press Ctrl+↓ **to position the insertion point on the blank line between paragraphs.**

❹ Press Ctrl+↓ **again to position the insertion point at the beginning of the next paragraph.**
Every time you press ↵Enter, you create a paragraph. Word treats blank lines as paragraphs as well as regular text paragraphs.

5 **On the vertical scrollbar, click the down scroll arrow two times.**

Clicking items on the vertical scrollbar, such as the down scroll arrow or the up scroll arrow, does not move the insertion point. Using the vertical scrollbar merely lets you see different parts of the document. The insertion point remains where you last positioned it (see Figure 2.3).

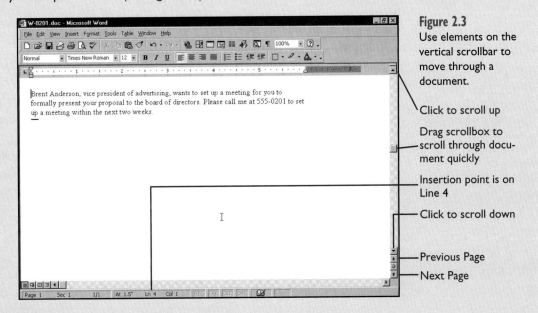

Figure 2.3
Use elements on the vertical scrollbar to move through a document.

Click to scroll up

Drag scrollbox to scroll through document quickly

Insertion point is on Line 4

Click to scroll down

Previous Page

Next Page

6 **Click and drag the scrollbox to the top of the vertical scrollbar. You can now see the top of your document again.**

If your document contains more than one page, you see a ScreenTip noting the page number, such as Page 3, as you click and drag the scrollbox.

7 **Press Ctrl+Home to move the insertion point to the top of the document.**

Take a minute now to practice some of the other keyboard shortcuts that were listed in Table 2.1.

In most cases, you save changes to your document before continuing to the next lesson. Because you just practiced scrolling in the document, you don't need to save the document because no changes were made.

8 **Keep the document onscreen to continue with the next lesson.**

ⓘ *Inside Stuff:* **Select Browse Object**

Clicking the Select Browse Object button displays a palette (see Figure 2.4), so you can choose the object to which you want to quickly move the insertion point.

Next button

Select Browse Object button

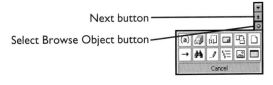

Figure 2.4
Choose how you want to move the insertion point by selecting an option on the Select Browse Object palette.

The default object is Page, which lets you move the insertion point to the top of the previous page or to the top of the next page. When you select a different browse object, such as Heading, the double arrows appear in blue. When you click the Next button, Word takes you to the next object, such as the next heading.

Click the Select Browse Object button and choose Page to change the browse mode back to page.

  Exam Note: **Using the Go To Option**

You can move the insertion point to a specific location by using the Go To option in the Find and Replace dialog box. Click <u>E</u>dit, <u>G</u>o To, or press Ctrl+G to display the Go To options. See Figure 2.5 for an example of the Go To options.

Figure 2.5
Use the Go To option to specify where you want to quickly position the insertion point.

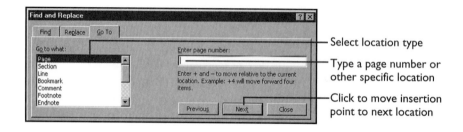

Select location type

Type a page number or other specific location

Click to move insertion point to next location

Lesson 3: Selecting Text

Making changes to a Word document is a simple process, especially when you can select text to change it. For example, you might want to delete an entire sentence or group of sentences. Instead of deleting characters one by one with +Backspace or Del, you can select and delete text.

Selecting is the action of defining an area of text so you can do something to it, such as delete or format it. When you select text, Word displays it in white with a black background. In this lesson, you learn how to select text.

To Select Text

❶ **Double-click the word proposal in the first paragraph to select it and the space after it.**

> *Inside Stuff:* **Selecting by Clicking the Selection Bar**
> You can also select text by clicking the *selection bar*, the space in the left margin area where you see a right-pointing arrow. Click once to select the current text line. Double-click to select the current paragraph, and triple-click to select the entire document.

❷ **Press and hold down Ctrl; then click anywhere in the first sentence of the first paragraph.**
This action selects the entire sentence, along with any additional blank spaces after the period.

❸ **Triple-click anywhere inside the first paragraph.**
This action selects the entire paragraph (see Figure 2.6).

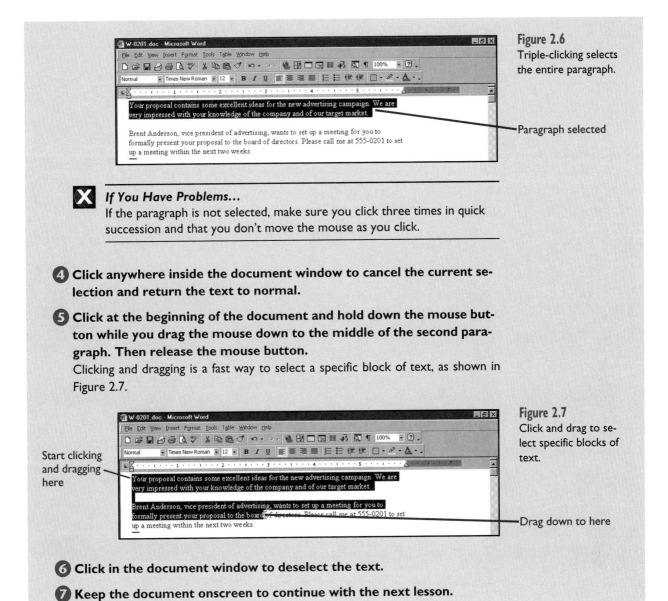

Figure 2.6
Triple-clicking selects the entire paragraph.

Paragraph selected

X *If You Have Problems...*

If the paragraph is not selected, make sure you click three times in quick succession and that you don't move the mouse as you click.

---

4 **Click anywhere inside the document window to cancel the current selection and return the text to normal.**

5 **Click at the beginning of the document and hold down the mouse button while you drag the mouse down to the middle of the second paragraph. Then release the mouse button.**

Clicking and dragging is a fast way to select a specific block of text, as shown in Figure 2.7.

Figure 2.7
Click and drag to select specific blocks of text.

Start clicking and dragging here

Drag down to here

6 **Click in the document window to deselect the text.**

7 **Keep the document onscreen to continue with the next lesson.**

X *If You Have Problems...*

If you click and drag too fast, you might end up selecting too much text. If this happens, try this method instead of clicking and dragging: Click at the point where you want to start selecting text, press and hold down ◆Shift, and click at the point where you want to end the selected text. This selects from the insertion point to the place where you ◆Shift+click.

(i) *Inside Stuff:* **Selecting Text with the Keyboard**

You can also use the arrow keys on the keyboard to select text. You might find this method more convenient when selecting a small section of text or if you prefer to keep your hands on the keyboard. First, you position the insertion point where you want to start selecting text. Press ◆Shift and then use the arrow keys to select text. Release ◆Shift to end the selection. Press any arrow key to turn off the selection.

If you want to select the entire document, press Ctrl+A.

Lesson 4: Deleting and Changing Text

As you read the first draft of your letter, you may decide that you don't like the way a particular sentence sounds or you may find that you have simply entered the wrong information. Word lets you delete text you don't want, enter new text, and correct existing text. In this lesson, you learn how to make basic corrections to text in a document.

To Delete and Change Text

1 **In W-0201, double-click the word new on the first line of the first paragraph.**
You want to replace the word new with summer.

2 **Type summer.**
When you select text and type new text, the new text replaces the selected text.

3 **Position the insertion point at the beginning of the word very in the second sentence of the first paragraph.**

4 **Press Ctrl+Del to delete the word to the right of the insertion point.**

> **ⓘ** **Inside Stuff:** **Deleting Text**
> You can delete the word to the left of the insertion point by pressing Ctrl+◆Backspace. To delete larger sections of text, select the text first, and then press Del.

5 **Position the insertion point before the first 0 in the phone number.**
This phone number is incorrect. You need to replace it with the correct phone number.

OVR

6 **Double-click the OVR indicator on the status bar.**
The OVR indicator appears darker. You are now in the **Overtype mode**, which overwrites (or replaces) existing text as you type new text.

7 **Type 2486 to insert the correct phone number and replace the old number, as shown in Figure 2.8.**

Figure 2.8
Your letter now reflects several corrections.

The word *very* is deleted

The word *new* is replaced with the word *summer*

Corrected phone number

Overtype mode indicator

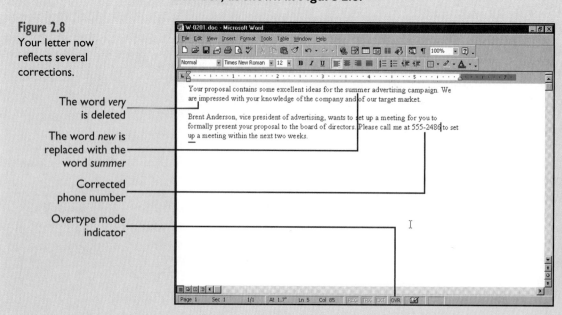

If You Have Problems...
If you forget to turn off the Overtype mode, you might accidentally delete text and replace it with other text instead of simply inserting new text. Double-click the OVR indicator on the status bar to turn off the Overtype mode.

8 **Double-click the OVR indicator to return to the Insert mode.**

9 **Choose File, Save As.**

10 **Click the Save in drop-down arrow and choose the drive containing the data or Zip disk you're saving to.**

11 **Type `Campaign Proposal Letter` in the File name text box and click Save.**
You have just saved the changes with a new name, Campaign Proposal Letter. Leave the document onscreen to continue with the next lesson.

 Inside Stuff: **Insert and Overtype Modes**
In addition to clicking OVR on the status bar, you can press Insert on the keyboard to toggle between the Insert and Overtype modes.

Lesson 5: Inserting Text

In the last lesson, you learned to turn on the Overtype mode and type over existing text. The default mode is the **Insert mode**, which lets you insert new text within existing text. Word inserts new text at the insertion point's location; the existing text then makes room for the new text as you type it.

Now that you have corrected the paragraphs, you need to insert other elements to complete the letter. You need to insert the date at the top of the letter, along with the **inside address** (the address of the person who will receive the letter). You also need to insert the **salutation** (otherwise known as the greeting) and the closing.

To Insert New Text

1 **In `Campaign Proposal Letter`, press Ctrl+Home to move the insertion point to the beginning of the first paragraph in the document.**

2 **Choose Insert, Date and Time.**
This option displays the Date and Time dialog box (see Figure 2.9). The dialog box shows sample dates and times. You can choose from a variety of date and time formats for practically any situation.

continues ▶

To Insert New Text (continued)

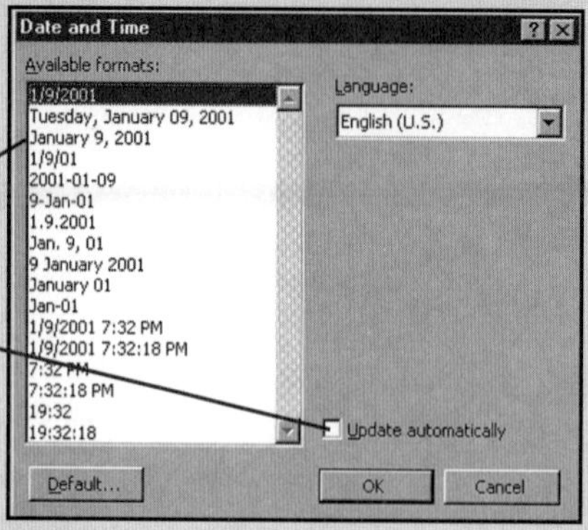

Figure 2.9
Select the date/time
format you want to
use in your document.

Click this date format

Click to automatically
update the date/time

For this letter, choose the format that spells out the name of the month, followed by the numeric day, and then followed by a four-digit year (for example, February 17, 2001).

③ **Double-click the date format to add the date to your letter.**

④ **Press ⏎Enter four times to add blank lines between the date and inside address.**

⑤ **Type the following text, pressing ⏎Enter once after each line:**
Ms. Rebecca Farnsworth
Farnsworth Advertising
5350 North Edgewood Drive
Provo, UT 84604
Word moves the existing paragraphs down to make room for the new lines of text you are inserting. Your letter should look like Figure 2.10.

Figure 2.10
Your letter now
includes the date and
inside address.

Date

Blank space created
by pressing ⏎Enter
four times

Inside address

Insertion point

Insertion point
on Line 9

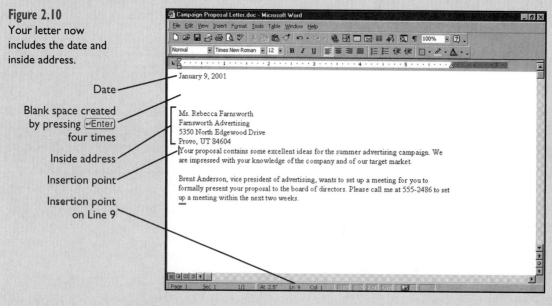

⑥ **Press ⏎Enter again to leave one blank line between the inside address and the salutation.**

⑦ **Type Dear Ms. Farnsworth: and press ⏎Enter twice.**
You should now have one blank line between the salutation and the first line of the first paragraph.

Inside Stuff: **Using the Letter Wizard**
The Office Assistant might appear, asking if you want help to create the letter. If you ask for help, the Office Assistant starts the Letter Wizard, which helps you create letters and gives you a variety of formats from which to choose. For example, you can choose letter formats, recipient information, and letter design by selecting from the Letter Wizard options. If you don't want the Office Assistant's help, click Cancel to finish the letter yourself.

8 **Press Ctrl+End and press ↵Enter twice to move the insertion point to the end of the letter.**

9 **Type Sincerely and then press ↵Enter four times to allow enough room to sign your printed letter.**

10 **Type your name.**
The letter is now complete. Compare your letter with the one in Figure 2.11.

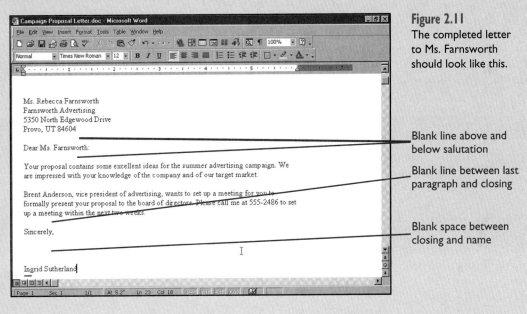

Figure 2.11
The completed letter to Ms. Farnsworth should look like this.

Blank line above and below salutation

Blank line between last paragraph and closing

Blank space between closing and name

11 **Click the Save button to save the changes. Keep the letter onscreen as you continue with the next lesson.**

 Inside Stuff: **Using the AutoComplete Feature**
If you start typing the current date, you see a ScreenTip that displays the full date, such as **March 15, 2001**. When you see this ScreenTip and press ↵Enter, Word automatically completes the date for you. This feature, known as *AutoComplete*, helps complete other text as well.

Use the Help feature to learn how to create your very own AutoComplete entries to save typing time. For example, you can create an AutoText entry that completes your name when you start typing it.

Exam Note: **Update Date and Time Automatically**

If you want the date to update automatically when you open or print the document, click the Update automatically check box at the bottom of the Date and Time dialog box. This process inserts the date (and time) as a field.

You can also insert a date or time field by choosing Insert, Field. Click the Date and Time category and insert Date and/or Time.

If you want to update the time while a document is open, click on the time field and press F9.

Lesson 6: Changing View Modes

When you work with a document, you might want to adjust how it appears on the screen. For example, you can adjust the document to display the layout with the margins or you can maximize the amount of screen space devoted to seeing text. In addition, you can adjust how the spacing or size of the characters appears on your screen without changing the size of the printed characters. This lesson teaches you how to use view options to focus on particular elements of your document, such as layout or text.

The default view option is ***Normal***, which shows text without displaying space for margins, page numbers, or other supplemental text. Normal view is appropriate when you are simply typing and editing text and you want to use the screen space for displaying text without seeing the margins.

To Change View Options

1 **Press Ctrl+Home to move your insertion point to the top of the document.**

2 **Click the Print Layout View button to the left of the horizontal scrollbar.**

Print Layout view shows you what the document will look like when it's printed. This view shows margin space, graphics locations, headers, footers, and page numbers. Although your document does not contain headers, footers, or page numbers, you can look at the margins (see Figure 2.12).

Figure 2.12
You see the document's layout in Print Layout view.

Top margin
Left margin
Vertical ruler
Right margin
View buttons

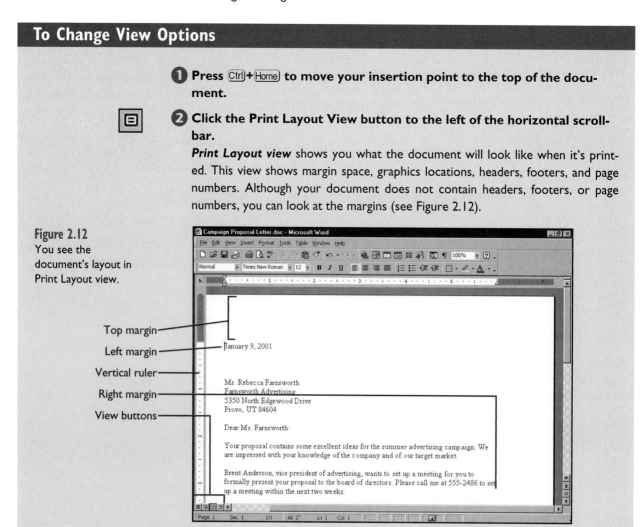

Notice that the end-of-document marker does *not* appear in Print Layout view.

③ Click the Normal View button to change back to the regular view.
The end-of-document marker appears again in Normal view. Although you can see more text in Normal view, you still want to see more text on your screen.

④ Choose View and click the down arrows at the bottom of the menu to display the full View menu.

⑤ Choose Full Screen.
Full Screen view uses the entire screen to display the document text, as shown in Figure 2.13. In this view, you do *not* see the title bar, menu bar, toolbars, or other Word elements. However, you do see the end-of-document marker.

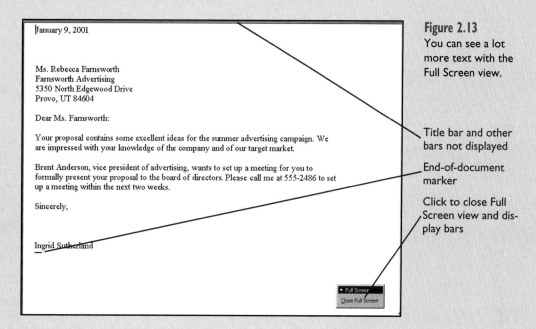

Figure 2.13
You can see a lot more text with the Full Screen view.

Title bar and other bars not displayed

End-of-document marker

Click to close Full Screen view and display bars

⑥ Click Close Full Screen or press Esc to close the Full Screen view.

ⓘ Inside Stuff: Working in the Full Screen View
Although you can't see the menu bar, you can still access the menus. Simply press Alt and the hotkey to display the desired menu. For example, press Alt + V to display the View menu.

The keyboard shortcut for closing the Full Screen view is Alt + C.

---

⑦ Click the Zoom drop-down arrow.
You see the Zoom menu (see Figure 2.14), which lets you change the *zoom*, or magnification percentage, of your document onscreen.

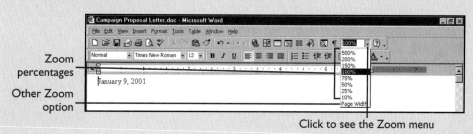

Zoom percentages

Other Zoom option

Click to see the Zoom menu

Figure 2.14
Select a zoom option for displaying the document on your screen.

continues ▶

To Change View Options   (continued)

8 Choose 150%.

The document is now displayed at 150% of its regular screen size, as shown in Figure 2.15. Changing the zoom does not, however, change the size of the text when it is printed.

Figure 2.15
Increase the zoom percentage to make text bigger onscreen.

Current zoom percentage

Larger text onscreen

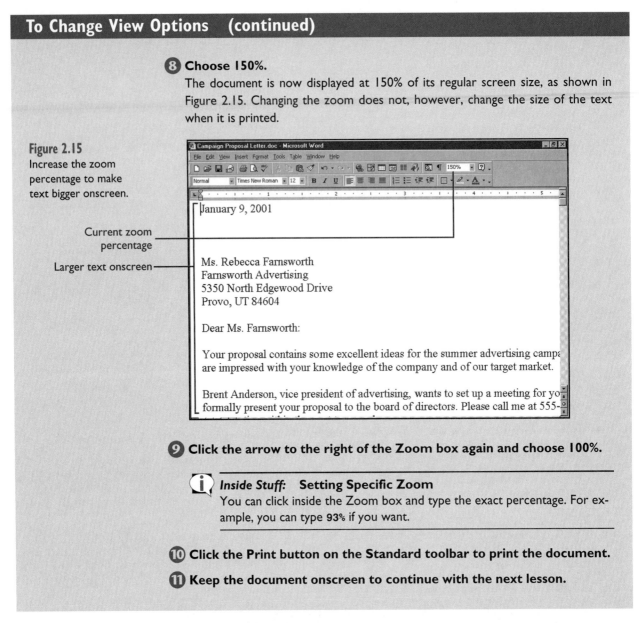

9 Click the arrow to the right of the Zoom box again and choose 100%.

ⓘ *Inside Stuff:*   **Setting Specific Zoom**
You can click inside the Zoom box and type the exact percentage. For example, you can type **93%** if you want.

10 Click the Print button on the Standard toolbar to print the document.

11 Keep the document onscreen to continue with the next lesson.

Although the Zoom menu gives you several percentages and options to choose from, you might want to magnify your document at a different percentage. To do this, choose <u>V</u>iew, <u>Z</u>oom. The Zoom dialog box provides preset options and a P<u>e</u>rcent option that allows you to specify the exact magnification (see Figure 2.16).

Figure 2.16
Use the Zoom dialog box to specify a particular percentage.

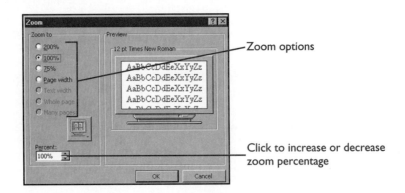

Zoom options

Click to increase or decrease zoom percentage

Inside Stuff: Using Zoom Options
When you select the Print Layout view, you can select Whole Page or Two Pages from the Zoom menu. Viewing the whole page or two pages is nice because it allows you to see the overall layout, such as spacing and margins. These options are not available when you use the Normal view.

Lesson 7: Creating Envelopes

You have a printed copy of your letter, but you need an envelope to mail it. Use Word's Envelope feature to quickly create and print an envelope for your letter. The Envelope feature creates the address from the existing letter and lets you select the envelope type and other options. In this lesson, you create and print an envelope for the `Campaign Proposal Letter` that is displayed on your screen.

To Create an Envelope

❶ Choose Tools, Envelopes and Labels.

❷ Click the Envelopes tab if it's not already selected.
The Envelopes and Labels dialog box appears, as shown in Figure 2.17. Word copies the inside address from your letter to the Delivery address section in the dialog box.

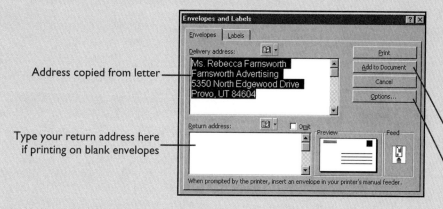

Figure 2.17
Select the options you want to create an envelope for your letter.

Address copied from letter

Type your return address here if printing on blank envelopes

Click to add envelope to document

Click to select envelope size and printing options

❸ Click Add to Document.
This inserts a new page at the beginning of the document, before the letter. The envelope is on page zero.

❹ Click the Print Layout View button to the left of the horizontal scrollbar.

❺ Click the Zoom drop-down arrow and choose 50%.
The envelope text now looks like it's placed on an envelope onscreen (see Figure 2.18).

continues ▶

To Create an Envelope (continued)

Figure 2.18
The envelope text looks like an envelope in Print Layout view.

Envelope at beginning of document

Letter after envelope

Envelope on page 0

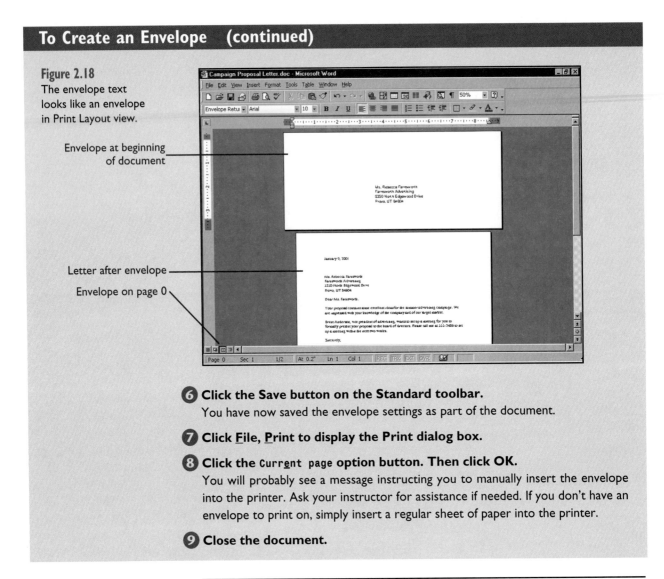

6 **Click the Save button on the Standard toolbar.**
You have now saved the envelope settings as part of the document.

7 **Click File, Print to display the Print dialog box.**

8 **Click the Current page option button. Then click OK.**
You will probably see a message instructing you to manually insert the envelope into the printer. Ask your instructor for assistance if needed. If you don't have an envelope to print on, simply insert a regular sheet of paper into the printer.

9 **Close the document.**

(i) *Inside Stuff:* **Creating Envelopes**
You can select a variety of envelope options by clicking Options in the Envelopes and Labels dialog box. For example, you can select a different envelope size, add a barcode, and specify how you want to insert the envelope into the printer.

 Lesson 8: Creating Labels

Instead of printing addresses on envelopes, you might want to print addresses on labels. Word's Label feature provides a variety of label formats, such as address, data disk, file folder, name badge, and video label. The label choices correspond to brand-name label product numbers, such as Avery 5160 Address labels. In this lesson, you select an address label format and enter data into some labels.

To Create Address Labels

 1 **Click the New Blank Document button on the Standard toolbar to start a new document.**

2 Choose **T**ools, **E**nvelopes and Labels to display the Envelopes and Labels dialog box.

3 Click the **L**abels tab.

You can type an address into the Address text box, start a new label document, and select different label formats (see Figure 2.19).

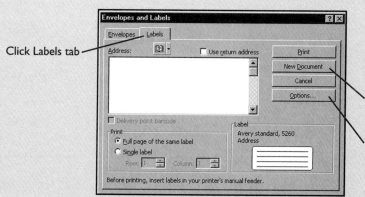

Click Labels tab

Figure 2.19
The Labels tab displays several options for customizing labels.

Click here to create a new label document

Click this button and choose specific label type

4 Click **O**ptions.

Before creating a label document, you should specify which label format and the printer settings you want (see Figure 2.20). Most Avery-brand label products are listed.

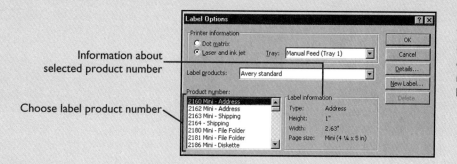

Information about selected product number

Choose label product number

Figure 2.20
The Label Options dialog box lets you choose a label product number and other label settings.

5 Scroll through the Product number list box and click 5160 – Address.

6 Click OK.

7 Click New **D**ocument.

You see boxes representing the labels. You type an address in the first label and press Tab↹ until the insertion point is in the next label. Depending on the label product number you choose, you might need to press Tab↹ one or two times to move to the next label.

8 Type the addresses shown in Figure 2.21. Remember to press Tab↹ twice to get from one label to the next.

continues ▶

To Create Address Labels (continued)

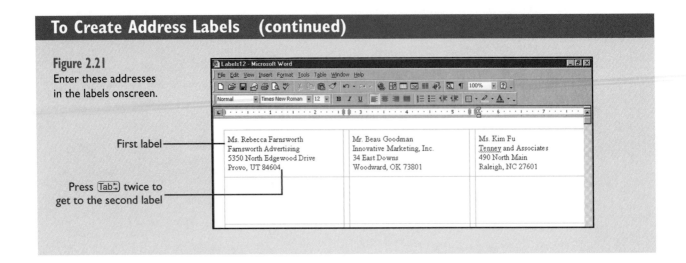

Figure 2.21
Enter these addresses in the labels onscreen.

First label ——

Press Tab twice to get to the second label

Inside Stuff: Creating Return Address Labels
You can create a sheet of personal address labels for yourself quickly and easily. Simply type your name and address in the <u>A</u>ddress box, choose the label format you want, and click the **Full page of the same label** option button. When you click New <u>D</u>ocument, Word creates an entire sheet of labels for you!

Summary

In this project, you learned some very important word processing tasks. You learned how to open a document that you previously saved and how to efficiently navigate through it. You also learned how to select, insert, and delete text. In addition, you learned how to change the view options to see your document from different perspectives. Finally, you created an envelope and mailing labels.

Now you're ready to reinforce your knowledge by completing the end-of-project exercises. In addition, experiment with features. For example, create labels for videos. Furthermore, you can expand your knowledge and skills by using Help to find out more about the topics covered in this project.

Checking Concepts and Terms

True/False

For each of the following, check *T* or *F* to indicate whether the statement is true or false.

__T __F **1.** When you display the Open dialog box, you typically need to choose the drive and folder containing the document you wish to open. [L1]

__T __F **2.** Triple-clicking the mouse selects the current sentence. [L3]

__T __F **3.** By default, when you type text within an existing document, the text types over the original text. [L4]

__T __F **4.** Normal view shows more of your document onscreen than Print Layout view does. [L7]

__T __F **5.** Even if you display the Envelopes and Labels dialog box when a letter is displayed onscreen, you must type in the delivery address yourself. [L7]

Multiple Choice

Circle the letter of the correct answer for each of the following.

1. What feature would you use to adjust the percentage a document that displays onscreen? [L6]

    a. Print Layout

    b. Zoom

    c. Full Screen

    d. Normal view

2. Which menu lists the most recently used documents? [L1]

    a. Edit

    b. Format

    c. Open

    d. File

3. Why would you use the Date and Time dialog box to insert the date or time? [L5]

    a. You can choose from a variety of formats.

    b. You can select an option to update the date the next time you open the file.

    c. Using the dialog box might be faster than typing

    a full date, such as Saturday, January 26, 2002.

    d. all of the above

4. What option is the most efficient for moving the insertion point from page 3 of your document to the top of page 12? [L3]

    a. Press Ctrl+PgDn nine times.

    b. Click the Next Page button nine times.

    c. Display the Go To dialog box, type **12**, and click the Go To button.

    d. Press ↓ repeatedly until you're on page 12.

5. When you create labels, which of the following steps should you perform first? [L8]

    a. Type names and addresses.

    b. Choose the label product number.

    c. Click the New Document button in the dialog box.

    d. Press Tab⇥ to separate addresses into separate labels.

Screen ID

Label each element of the Word screen shown in Figure 2.22.

Figure 2.22

A. end-of-document marker

B. Normal View button

C. Print Layout View button

D. Select Browse Object button

E. Zoom

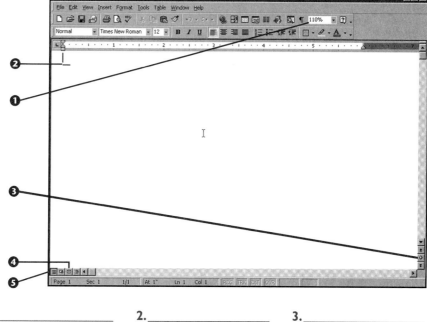

1._____   2._____   3._____

4._____   5._____

Skill Drill

Skill Drill exercises reinforce project skills. Each skill reinforced is the same, or nearly the same, as a skill presented in the project. Each exercise includes a brief narrative introduction, followed by detailed instructions in a step-by-step format.

1. Opening and Scrolling in a Document

You know you can perform the same tasks with different methods. Because you want to learn the different methods and see which you like best, you decide to practice some of the different ways to open a document and then scroll through it.

1. Press Ctrl+O to display the Open dialog box.

2. Click the Look in drop-down arrow and choose the drive that contains the CD-ROM that accompanies this book.

3. Double-click **Project 02** folder, click **W-0202**, and press ↵Enter to open the document.

4. Choose File, Save As.

5. Click the Save in drop-down arrow and choose the drive that contains your data disk or Zip disk.

6. Type **Chambers Letter** in the File name box and then click OK.

7. Choose File, Close to close the document.

8. Choose File and look at the bottom of the menu.

9. Choose D:\Project 02\Chambers Letter from the bottom of the menu.

10. Press Ctrl+Home to move the insertion point to the beginning of the document.

11. Click and drag the scrollbox until the ScreenTip shows **Page: 1**; then release the mouse button.

12. Click the Previous Page button.

13. Click the Next Page button.

14. Press Ctrl+End to move the insertion point to the end of the document.

15. Press Ctrl+G to display the Go To option.

16. Type **0** in the Enter page number box, click Go To, and then click Close.

17. Click at the beginning of the first paragraph in the letter.

18. Press Ctrl+↓ twice to move the insertion point to the beginning of the second paragraph.

19. Leave the document onscreen to continue to the next exercise.

2. Selecting, Changing, and Inserting Text

You want to use the same letter to send to someone else. Instead of typing a new letter, you decide to select and delete the original envelope, and select and replace the inside address and salutation. In addition, you need to insert new text using the Insert mode.

1. With **Chambers Letter** onscreen, select the entire inside address.

2. Type the following new address while the old address is selected:

   Mr. Aaron Chambers
   McClure and Associates
   305 West Main Street
   Toledo, OH 43615

3. Select Ms. Farnsworth in the salutation; then type **Mr. Chambers**.

4. Click the Normal View button to the left of the horizontal scrollbar.

5. Position the mouse pointer in the left margin. The mouse pointer is an arrow pointing to the right.

6. Click and drag to select the envelope, including the lines that mention the section break. Press Del to delete the entire envelope page.

7. Click to the right of the hyphen in the phone number.

8. Double-click OVR on the status bar, type **7356**, and double-click OVR again.

9. Click to the left of vice president in the second paragraph, type **senior**, and press Spacebar.

10. Click at the beginning of the second paragraph and type the following paragraph:

    As you are probably aware, we're expecting sales from the summer campaign to generate a 25 percent increase over last summer's campaign. The economy is very favorable, and we have a lot of new products to hit the market.

11. Press ⏎Enter twice after the paragraph to have a blank line between paragraphs.

12. Click to the left of economy and type **regional**. Make sure you have a space before and after the new word.

13. Click to the left of the date and press Ctrl+Del four times to delete the date. Don't delete any hard returns.

14. Choose Insert, Date and Time.

15. Click the third format in the **Available formats** list box and then click OK.

16. Click the Save button on the Standard toolbar and keep the document on the screen to continue to the next exercise.

3. Viewing the Document and Creating an Envelope

You want to review view options to look at the overall format and to adjust the magnification onscreen. Then, you need to create an envelope for your letter.

1. With **Chambers Letter** onscreen, click the Print Layout View button to the left of the horizontal scrollbar.

2. Choose View, Zoom to display the Zoom dialog box.

3. Click the Percent increment button to **125%** and click OK.

4. Click the Normal View button to the left of the horizontal scrollbar.

5. Click the Zoom drop-down arrow and choose 75%.

6. Choose Tools, Envelopes and Labels.

7. Click the Add to Document button.

8. Save the document with the envelope.

9. Print the envelope and letter.

10. Close the document.

Challenge

Challenge exercises expand on or are somewhat related to skills presented in the lessons. Each exercise provides a brief narrative introduction, followed by instructions in a numbered-step or bullet-list format that are not as detailed as those in the Skill Drill section.

1. Editing a Discount Message

You work for Mega Music, a regional retail store that sells CDs, cassettes, and movies. To promote your store to the college students, you are offering a special sale to them. You need to open the document a co-worker created and edit it.

1. Open **W-0203** and save it as **Mega Music**.

2. Change the case of the title to all capital letters.

3. Delete **or copy your official class schedule** from the second paragraph.

4. Change the street address number to **2286** and insert **North** between the street number and name.

5. Insert a line between the CD and video lines for **15% off on all cassette tapes**.

6. Select the four lines about the discount percentages and press Tab↹ once.

7. Change the case of the last two sentences in the last paragraph so that only the first letter of each sentence is capitalized.

8. Save the document and print it.

2. Editing a Memo

You composed a memo to inform employees about a new parking rule. You need to open it and make a few changes before sending it out.

1. Open **W-0204** and save it as **Parking Memo**.

2. Select Normal view and then change the zoom to Page Width.

3. Delete the asterisk on the Date line, and use the Date and Time dialog box to insert today's date. Use the format that provides the weekday (such as Monday) with the full date.

4. Delete the asterisk on the From line and type your name. Make sure that the date and your name line up with the word New on the Subject line.

5. Press Tab⇄ to line up All Employees with the other items in the memorandum heading.

6. Use the most efficient method for changing 8:30 to 8:45.

7. Select the last sentence in the memo and replace it with **We appreciate your cooperation during this construction period.**

8. Use the keyboard shortcut to change these words to all caps: Date, To, From, and Subject.

9. Save the document, print it, and close it.

3. Letter Requesting Donations from a Retail Store

You belong to a campus organization. Your organization is sponsoring a track meet for underprivileged children in your area. As president of the organization, you are responsible for writing letters to local retail stores to solicit donations for the event. You want to receive cash and food donations. The money will help defray the cost of sponsoring the event, and the food donations will help your members prepare a cookout after the event.

1. From a blank document window, insert the date and the following inside address:

```
Mr. John Davis
Fresher Groceries, Inc.
344 NW First
Racine, WI 53402
```

2. Insert and correctly format the salutation.

3. Type a three-paragraph letter that describes what your organization is sponsoring and the type of donations you seek. End with a statement showing appreciation for any donation the retailer might provide.

4. Include an appropriate closing with your name. Type your organization name on the line below your typed name.

5. Save the document as **Donation Letter**.

6. Create an envelope without a return address. Insert the envelope in the document.

7. Save the document and print both the envelope and the letter.

Discovery Zone

Discovery Zone exercises help you gain advanced knowledge of project topics and/or application of skills. These exercises focus on enhancing your problem-solving skills. Numbered steps are not provided, but you are given hints, reminders, screen shots, and/or references to help you reach your goal for each exercise.

1. Creating a Sheet of Disk Labels

As an assistant for a computer consulting company, you are responsible for preparing data disks that contain documents that the clients will use during the consultations.

From a new document window, create a sheet of labels using the Avery 6460 Remove 'Em laser diskette labels. Type the following text for the label and make sure the same text repeats on each label. Place the labels in a new document window; don't print from within the Envelopes and Labels dialog box.

> **Word 2000 Introduction**
>
> **Computer Essentials Training**
>
> **April 3, 2001**
>
> **Trainer: your name**

Save the sheet of labels as **Word Disk Labels** and print the labels on a regular sheet of paper.

2. Creating a Small Envelope with a Barcode

One of your college professors said he would mail your final grade to you if you provide a self-addressed stamped envelope. You only have 6 1/2 inch × 3 5/8 inch-sized envelopes.

Create the envelope in the Envelopes and Labels dialog box. Use your name and address in the Delivery address section and your professor's name and address in the Return address section. If needed, use Help to learn how to select an envelope size and how to insert a barcode on the envelope. Make these adjustments before adding the envelope to your document. Save the document as **College Instructor Envelope** and print the envelope.

PinPoint Assessment

You have completed this project and its associated lessons, and have had an opportunity to assess your skills through the end-of-project questions and exercises. Now use the PinPoint software Evaluation Mode to further assess your comprehension of the specific exam activities you have just learned. You can also use the PinPoint Trainer Mode and the Show Me tutorials to practice these exam activities.

Working with Text

Key terms introduced in this project include

- character effects
- character spacing
- designer font
- em dash
- en dash
- font
- font size
- Format Painter

- formatting marks
- hard return
- heading
- highlight
- kerning
- nonbreaking hyphen
- nonbreaking space

- position
- sans serif font
- scale
- serif font
- spacing
- text enhancements
- WYSIWYG

Objectives	Required Activity for MOUS	Exam Level
➤ Enhance Text	Apply font formats (Bold, Italic, and Underline)	Core
➤ Change the Font and Font Size	Select and change font and font size	Core
➤ Select Character Effects and Spacing	Apply character effects (superscript, subscript, strikethrough, small caps, and outline)	Core
	Set character, line, and paragraph spacing options	Core
➤ Copy Formats with Format Painter	Copy formats using the Format Painter	Core
➤ Highlight Text	Highlight text in document	Core
➤ Display Formatting Marks		
➤ Insert Nonbreaking Spaces and Hyphens		
➤ Insert Symbols	Insert symbols	Core

Why Would I Do This?

In the last project, you used basic editing techniques such as deleting and inserting text. You are now ready to learn how to make document text look better. In this project, you learn to change the appearance of your text by adding bold, italic, and underlining. You also learn how to change the font, font size, and font color of your text to add emphasis and draw the reader's eye to specific parts of your document. These features, and others you'll learn about, make your documents look more professional.

 ## Lesson 1: Enhancing Text

In the last project, you learned how easy it is to select and delete text. In addition to deleting selected text, you can enhance the appearance of text by applying bold, italic, underline, or color. These text formats, known as **text enhancements**, emphasize ideas as well as improve readability and clarity.

Table 3.1 shows the toolbar buttons and keyboard shortcuts that you use to apply these text enhancements.

Table 3.1   Text Enhancement Buttons

Button	Button Name	Keyboard Shortcut
B	Bold	Ctrl+B
I	Italic	Ctrl+I
U	Underline	Ctrl+U
A ▾	Font Color	

To Enhance Text

① Open W-0301 and save it as Office Software.
Currently, the document looks very plain. However, by the time you're done enhancing the text, it will look a lot better.

② Click and drag across Microsoft Word at the beginning of the second full paragraph.
You want the software name to stand out from the rest of the paragraph.

 ③ Click the Bold button on the Formatting toolbar.
The selected text, Microsoft Word, is now bold, so it stands out from the regular text. After bolding the title, you need to deselect it.

④ Click inside the selected text to deselect it.
Notice how boldface text differs from regular text (see Figure 3.1).

 Inside Stuff: Using Bold, Italic, and Underline
Although both bold and italic formatting emphasize text, use bold for stronger emphasis and italic for lesser emphasis.

Some reference manuals specify that you apply bold and underline to report **headings**—descriptive words or phrases placed between sections to help readers understand the organization of your document.

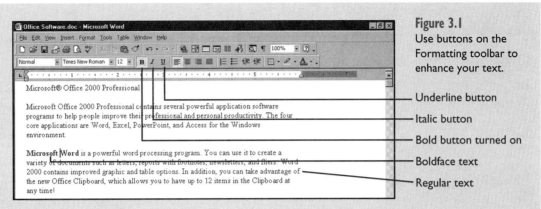

Figure 3.1
Use buttons on the Formatting toolbar to enhance your text.

— Underline button

— Italic button

— Bold button turned on

— Boldface text

— Regular text

5 Select Microsoft Word again.

6 Click the Font Color drop-down arrow on the Formatting toolbar.

The Font Color palette appears (see Figure 3.2), so you can choose a color for the selected text. As you move your mouse over each color, you see a ScreenTip that tells you the exact color name, such as Blue, Light Blue, and Sky Blue.

 If You Have Problems...
If you click the Font Color button (instead of the drop-down arrow), you immediately apply the default color, which is the last color someone selected. If this happens, select your text and make sure you click the Font Color drop-down arrow to see the palette. The new color you choose replaces the previous color.

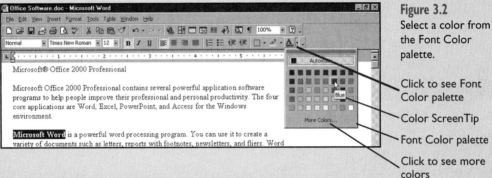

Figure 3.2
Select a color from the Font Color palette.

— Click to see Font Color palette

— Color ScreenTip

— Font Color palette

— Click to see more colors

7 Click Blue on the color palette to apply blue color to the selected text; then deselect the text.

Microsoft Word is now bold and blue (see Figure 3.3).

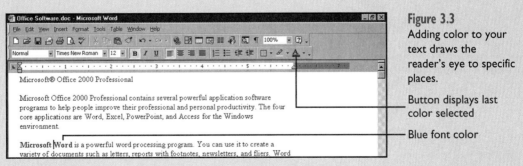

Figure 3.3
Adding color to your text draws the reader's eye to specific places.

— Button displays last color selected

— Blue font color

8 Click the Save button.

9 Keep the document onscreen to continue with the next lesson.

Lesson 2: Changing the Font and Font Size

Font refers to the overall appearance—style, weight, and typeface—of a set of characters. You can choose from literally thousands of fonts. Fonts are available from a variety of sources. For example, printers come with built-in fonts they can produce. You can also purchase font software from companies such as Adobe. Fonts range in appearance from very professional to informal, fun fonts. Figure 3.4 illustrates some examples of different fonts.

Figure 3.4
Different fonts are appropriate for different occasions.

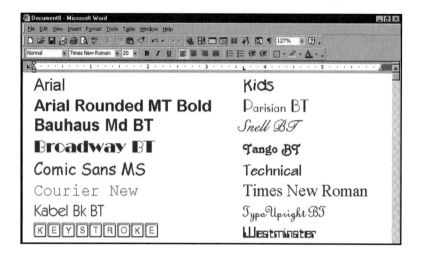

When choosing a font, consider the font's readability, its suitability to the document's purpose, and its appeal to the reader. Most fonts are classified as serif or sans serif. A **serif font**, such as Times New Roman, has tiny lines at the ends of the characters that help guide the reader's eyes across the line of text. Serif fonts should be used for text-intensive reading, such as paragraphs.

A **sans serif font**, such as Arial, does not have the tiny lines or extensions on the characters. Although a sans serif font has a crisp, clean look, it is difficult to read in large blocks of text, such as paragraphs. Use sans serif fonts for titles, headings, and other short blocks of text.

A **designer font** is a special font used in creative documents, such as wedding announcements, fliers, brochures, and other special-occasion documents. Examples of designer fonts include Broadway BT, Comic Sans MS, and Keystroke.

In addition to choosing the font, you should also consider the font size. **Font size** is the height of the characters, which is typically measured in points. One vertical inch contains about 72 points. You should use between 10-point and 12-point size for most correspondence and reports. Point sizes below 10 are difficult to read for detailed text and point sizes above 12 are too big for regular paragraphs.

Currently, your document is formatted in 12-point Times New Roman. You want to apply 24-point Arial to the title to make it stand out.

To Change the Font and Font Size

❶ In the open Office Software document, position the mouse pointer to the left side of the title Microsoft Office 2000 Professional.

❷ Click the mouse pointer in the selection bar area to select the title.
You must select text to apply a different font and font size to it.

❸ Click the Font drop-down arrow on the Formatting toolbar.
The Font menu displays the available fonts for the current printer (see Figure 3.5). You can scroll through the list to see all the available fonts.

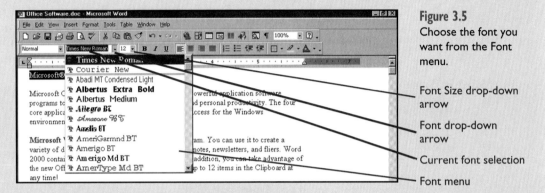

Times New Roman

Figure 3.5
Choose the font you want from the Font menu.

Font Size drop-down arrow

Font drop-down arrow

Current font selection

Font menu

❹ Scroll down through the menu and choose Arial.
The title appears in Arial font. Notice that the Font button displays the font, **Arial**, for the currently selected text.

❺ Click the Font Size drop-down arrow.
You see a list of different font sizes, ranging from 8 to 72.

12

❻ Choose 24 from the Font Size list and then click inside the text to deselect it.
The title is now bigger at 24-point size (see Figure 3.6). Notice that the Font Size button on the Formatting toolbar displays the font size, **24**, at the insertion point's location.

Current font selected

12-point Times New Roman for regular text

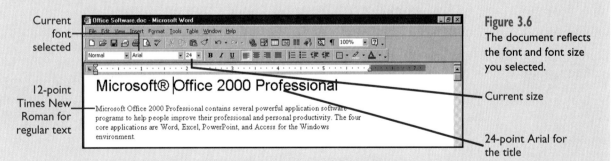

Figure 3.6
The document reflects the font and font size you selected.

Current size

24-point Arial for the title

Titles are typically printed in a larger point size, but be careful that the title isn't too overpowering compared to the regular document text.

continues ▶

To Change the Font and Font Size   (continued)

 Inside Stuff: **Keyboard Shortcuts for Changing Font Size**
Select text and press `Ctrl`+`[` to decrease the font size one point at a time, or press `Ctrl`+`]` to increase the font size one point at a time.

7 **Save the document and keep it onscreen to continue with the next lesson.**

 Inside Stuff: **Font and Font Size Keyboard Shortcuts**
If your mouse isn't working, you can still access Font and Font Size on the Formatting toolbar. Press `Ctrl`+`Shift`+`F` to activate the Font button. Press `Ctrl`+`Shift`+`P` to activate the Font (point) Size button. For either list, press `↑` or `↓` to scroll through the list. You see only the font name or font size on the respective button as you press the scrolling keys on your keyboard.

 ## Lesson 3: Selecting Character Effects and Spacing

In addition to changing the font face and font size, you might want to apply other font or character characteristics. ***Character effects*** are special formats that you apply to characters. Font effects include strikethrough, superscript, subscript, emboss, and other special effects. You can even apply onscreen text effects or specify character spacing.

In this lesson, you apply a character effect and set character spacing between letters in the title.

To Apply Character Effects

1 **In the Office Software document, select ® in the title.**
You want to apply the superscript font effect to the registered trademark symbol.

2 **Choose Format, Font to display the Font dialog box.**
The Font dialog box (see Figure 3.7) contains options for selecting the font, font style, size, font color, underline options, and character effects.

Figure 3.7
Use the Font dialog box for more specific font options.

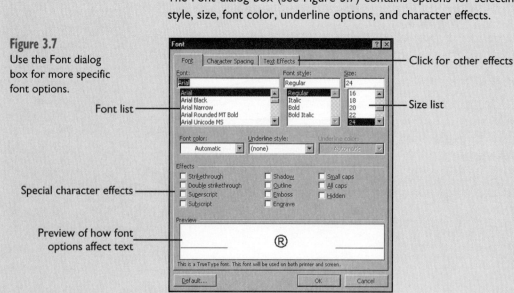

Font list

Special character effects

Preview of how font options affect text

Click for other effects

Size list

Inside Stuff: **Font Dialog Box Keyboard Shortcut**
The keyboard shortcut for accessing the Font dialog box is Ctrl+D.

❸ **Click the Superscript check box.**
A check mark appears in the check box to let you know the option is selected. The Preview window shows you that superscript text appears in smaller size and above the baseline.

❹ **Click OK and deselect the text.**
Figure 3.8 shows the superscript symbol.

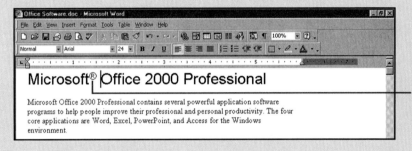

Figure 3.8
The superscript character effect is applied to the symbol.

Superscript symbol

 Inside Stuff: **Text Effects**
You can select onscreen text effects to draw attention to selected text. Click the Text Effects tab in the Font dialog box. You can choose effects such as Blinking Background, Las Vegas Lights, and Marching Red Ants. These effects are for onscreen reading only; they do not appear on print-outs.

❺ **Save the document and keep it onscreen to continue with the next exercise.**

 Inside Stuff: **Keyboard Shortcuts for Special Effects**
You can choose some character effects by using keyboard shortcuts. Table 3.2 shows the available keyboard shortcuts.

Table 3.2   Special Effects Keyboard Shortcuts

Keyboard Shortcut	Effect
Ctrl+⬆Shift+=	Superscript
Ctrl+=	Subscript
Ctrl+⬆Shift+D	Double Underline
Ctrl+⬆Shift+W	Underline Words Only
Ctrl+⬆Shift+K	Small Caps
Ctrl+⬆Shift+A	All Caps
Ctrl+⬆Shift+H	Hidden Text
Ctrl+Spacebar	Removes Character Effects

The Font dialog box contains a set of options to adjust the character spacing. **Character spacing** is the amount of space between printed characters. Although most character spacing is acceptable, some character combinations appear too far apart or too close together in large-sized text. In this lesson, you need to add a little character spacing between f and t in Microsoft and between ff in Office so that the characters are properly spaced apart.

To Adjust Character Spacing

1 Select ft in Microsoft in the title.
The characters are too close together and need to be separated.

2 Choose Format, Font to display the Font dialog box.

3 Click the Character Spacing tab.
You have four options for adjusting the character spacing (see Figure 3.9). **Scale** increases or decreases the text horizontally as a percentage of its size. **Spacing** controls the amount of space between two or more characters. **Position** raises or lowers text from the baseline without creating superscript or subscript size. **Kerning** automatically adjusts spacing between characters to achieve a more evenly spaced appearance.

Figure 3.9
Use character spacing options to properly space between characters.

Click to expand or condense space

Set exact spacing

Preview of character spacing

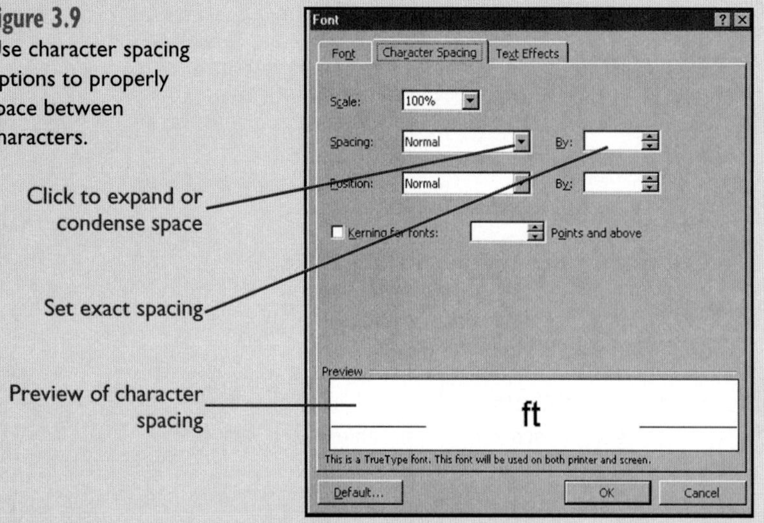

4 Click the Spacing drop-down arrow and choose Expanded.
The Spacing By option displays 1 pt, which increases the amount of space between characters by 1 point.

5 Click the Spacing By increment button five times to display 1.5 pt and click OK.
The selected letters have a little space between the characters now. Let's also adjust the character spacing between ff in Office.

6 Select ff in Office in the title.

7 Choose Format, Font.
The Font dialog box displays the Character Spacing options.

8 Click the Spacing drop-down arrow, choose Expanded, and click the Spacing By increment button to 1.5 pt, and click OK.

⑨ Deselect the text onscreen.
Figure 3.10 shows the better character spacing between the two sets of letters.

1.5 space between two characters

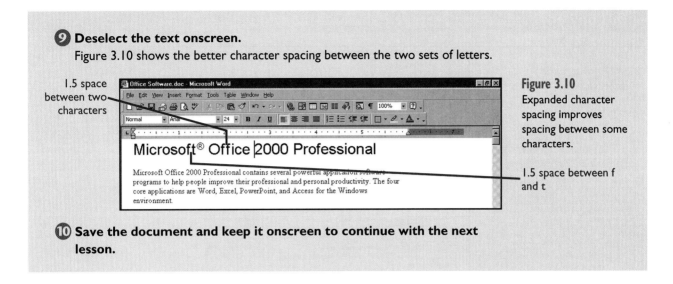

Figure 3.10
Expanded character spacing improves spacing between some characters.

1.5 space between f and t

⑩ Save the document and keep it onscreen to continue with the next lesson.

 Exam Note: **Using the Correct Character Spacing Option**
When taking the Word MOUS exam, make sure you read the task carefully so you know which option you should use. Often test takers get in a hurry and mistakenly set *line* spacing instead of *character* spacing.

Lesson 4: Copying Formats with Format Painter

Similar headings and text within a document should have the same formatting. However, selecting every heading individually and clicking the desired format buttons (such as bold, underline, and font color) can be time-consuming.

By using the **Format Painter**, you can copy existing text formats to ensure consistency. As an added bonus, using the Format Painter takes fewer mouse clicks to format text than formatting each instance individually. In this lesson, you use Format Painter to copy formats (bold and blue color) from the first software name to the other software names.

 Exam Note: **Single- and Double-Clicking the Format Painter Button**
If you single-click the Format Painter button, you can copy the formats only one time; then Word turns off Format Painter.

If you double-click the Format Painter button, you can continue formatting additional text. To turn off Format Painter when you're done, click the Format Painter button once.

To Copy Formats Using Format Painter

❶ In the Office Software document, click anywhere inside the bold, blue Microsoft Word.
This task lets Word know what formats you want to copy.

❷ Double-click the Format Painter button on the Standard toolbar.
When you double-click the Format Painter button, the mouse pointer turns into a paintbrush next to the I-beam (see Figure 3.11). Be careful where you click and drag with the Format Painter turned on; Word immediately formats any characters you select.

continues ▶

To Copy Formats Using Format Painter (continued)

Figure 3.11
The Format Painter
is turned on.

Double-click to turn on
Format Painter

Click inside formatted
text before turning on
Format Painter

Mouse pointer shape
when Format Painter
is on

Need to format text

Information on the
status bar

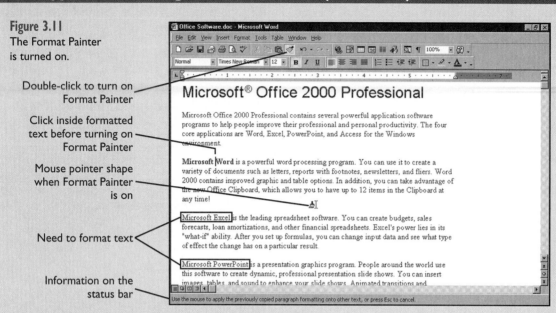

③ **Select** `Microsoft Excel` **at the beginning of the next paragraph.**
The second software name now has the same text enhancements as the first heading. Using Format Painter saves you from having to click two separate buttons (Bold and Font Color) to format the text.

④ **Click the scroll-down arrow on the vertical scrollbar until you see the last two paragraphs.**
You need to select the software names at the beginning of these two paragraphs.

⑤ **Select** `Microsoft PowerPoint` **and then select** `Microsoft Access` **to apply the text enhancements to these two software names.**
After formatting the last text, turn off the Format Painter.

⑥ **Click the Format Painter button to turn off this feature.**

⑦ **Click inside the text to deselect it.**
The software names at the beginning of each paragraph are now formatted consistently (see Figure 3.12).

Figure 3.12
The formatted
software names stand
out.

Format Painter
turned off

Formatted text

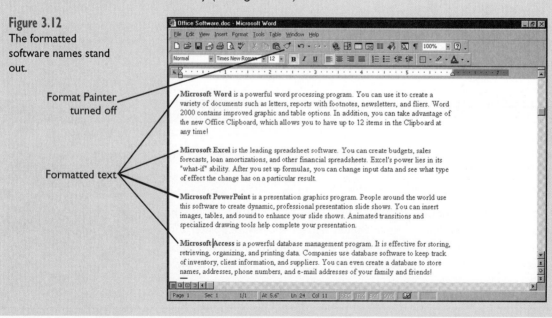

8 **Save the document and keep it onscreen to continue with the next lesson.**

 Exam Note: **Using Format Painter**

Completely format a section of text with the text enhancements that you want. Make sure the insertion point is inside the formatted text before turning on the Format Painter. If the insertion point is elsewhere when you turn on the Format Painter, you might apply the wrong formats to other text.

 Inside Stuff: **Formatting Headings**

Instead of using Format Painter, you can create a paragraph style and apply it to your document headings. The benefit of a style over using Format Painter is that you can quickly edit the style formats and all text formatted by that style is immediately updated. With Format Painter, you have to reapply the formats to the headings. Use the index at the back of this book to locate pages that discuss paragraph styles.

Lesson 5: Highlighting Text

People often use a highlighting marker to highlight important parts of textbooks, magazine articles, and other documents. You can use the **Highlight** feature to draw the reader's attention to important information within the documents you create.

After reviewing the Office Software document, you decide to highlight "improve their professional and personal productivity."

To Highlight Text

1 **In the Office Software document, press** `Ctrl`+`Home` **to position the insertion point at the beginning of the document.**

2 **Select the phrase "improve their professional and personal productivity" in the first paragraph.**
You want to highlight this phrase so it will stand out.

 If You Have Problems...
If you have trouble clicking and dragging to select text, you can use keyboard shortcuts. First, position the insertion point at the beginning of the word *improve*; press and hold down `Shift` while you click after the *y* in *productivity*.

3 **Click the Highlight button on the Formatting toolbar.**
Word uses the default highlight color to highlight the text you selected. After you click the Highlight button, the text is deselected (see Figure 3.13).

continues ▶

To Highlight Text (continued)

Figure 3.13
Use the Highlight feature to point out important information.

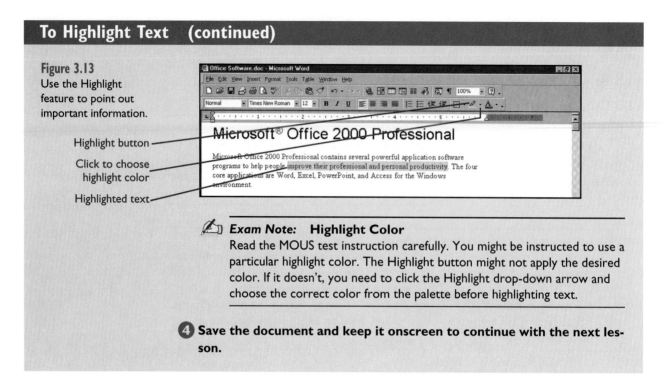

Highlight button ——

Click to choose highlight color

Highlighted text ——

  Exam Note: Highlight Color

Read the MOUS test instruction carefully. You might be instructed to use a particular highlight color. The Highlight button might not apply the desired color. If it doesn't, you need to click the Highlight drop-down arrow and choose the correct color from the palette before highlighting text.

4 **Save the document and keep it onscreen to continue with the next lesson.**

 Inside Stuff: **Using the Highlight Feature**

You can click the Highlight button before selecting text. When you do this, the mouse pointer resembles a highlighting pen. You can then click and drag across text you want to highlight. The Highlight feature stays on, so you can highlight additional text. When you finish, click the Highlight button to turn it off. To remove highlight, select the highlighted text, click the Highlight drop-down arrow and choose None.

Inside Stuff: **Printing Highlighted Text**

If you have a color printer, you see the highlight colors on your printout. If you're using a black-and-white printer, the highlight appears in shades of gray. Make sure you can easily read the text with the gray highlight. If not, select a lighter highlight color and print it again.

Lesson 6: Displaying Formatting Marks

The document on your screen looks basically like what its printout looks like. This is known as "What You See Is What You Get" (**WYSIWYG**). Usually, you see exactly what you've done to format your document. However, this is not always true. For example, you might not know at a glance whether you pressed Tab⇆ or Spacebar to indent text. Although in the short run either method might not be a problem, the spacing might look different if you print your document on a different system.

To help you see how your document is formatted, display formatting marks. **Formatting marks** are nonprinting symbols and characters that indicate spaces, tabs, and hard returns. A **hard return** is where you press ⏎Enter to start a new line instead of letting Word wrap text to the next line. Table 3.3 shows common formatting marks and what they indicate.

Table 3.3   Formatting Marks

Symbol	Description
.	space
o	nonbreaking space
-	hyphen
—	nonbreaking hyphen
→	tab
¶	end of paragraph

To Show and Hide Formatting Marks

1 **Click the Show/Hide ¶ button on the Standard toolbar.**

> *Inside Stuff:* **Keyboard Shortcut for Displaying Nonprinting Symbols**
>
> You can press Ctrl+◆Shift+8 to display or hide the nonprinting symbols.

You now see formatting marks within your document, as shown in Figure 3.14. Although these marks display onscreen, they do not appear in your printed document.

Indicates a space

Indicates the end of a paragraph

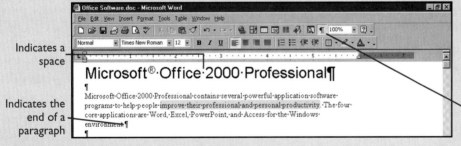

Figure 3.14
Display formatting marks to help you see how a document is formatted.

Click to display or hide the formatting marks

2 **Position the insertion point on the blank line after the title.**

3 **Press Tab‡. You now see a right arrow, or tab mark, between the title and the first paragraph, as shown in Figure 3.15.**

Tab formatting marker

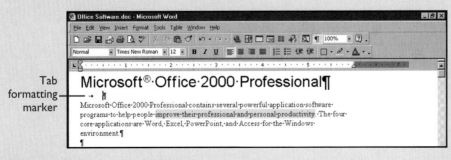

Figure 3.15
The formatting mark for a tab looks like an arrow.

4 **Press ◆Backspace to delete the tab marker.**

continues ▶

To Show and Hide Formatting Marks   (continued)

⑤ Keep the document onscreen to continue with the next lesson.
You don't need to save the document because you returned it to its original format after deleting the tab marker.

ⓘ *Inside Stuff:*   **Displaying Formatting Marks**
If you don't see all three types of formatting marks, you need to display the Options dialog box to change the default. To view all formatting marks, choose <u>T</u>ools on the menu bar and choose <u>O</u>ptions. When the Options dialog box appears, click the View tab and then click the <u>A</u>ll check box in the Formatting marks section. Click OK to close the dialog box.

Lesson 7: Inserting Nonbreaking Spaces and Hyphens

By now you know that the word-wrap feature wraps a word to the next line if it doesn't fit at the end of the current line. Occasionally, word-wrapping between certain types of words is undesirable; that is, some words should be kept together. For example, the date March 31 should stay together instead of separating between lines. Other items that should stay together include names, such as Ms. Stevenson, and page references, such as page 15.

To prevent words from separating due to the word-wrap feature, insert a ***nonbreaking space***. Some people might refer to a nonbreaking space as a hard space.

As you review your document, you notice that the words "Word" and "2000" word-wrap between the two words. You want to keep "Word 2000" together on the same line.

To Insert a Nonbreaking Space

❶ In the `Office Software` document, click the Show/Hide ¶ button on the Standard toolbar if the formatting marks are not already displayed.

❷ Position the insertion point after "Word" at the end of the second line in the second paragraph.
You need to delete the regular space after "Word" and replace it with a nonbreaking space to keep "Word 2000" together (see Figure 3.16).

Figure 3.16
You need to keep "Word 2000" together.

First word

Second word wrapped to next line

Regular space symbol

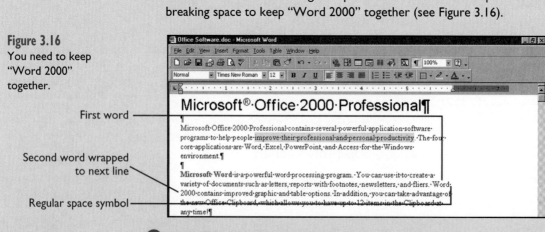

❸ Press `Del` to delete the regular space.
This brings "Word 2000" together without any space between the two words.

4 **Press** Ctrl + ⇧Shift + Spacebar.

Word now keeps "Word 2000" together (see Figure 3.17). Notice the difference in the nonbreaking space symbol and the regular space symbol.

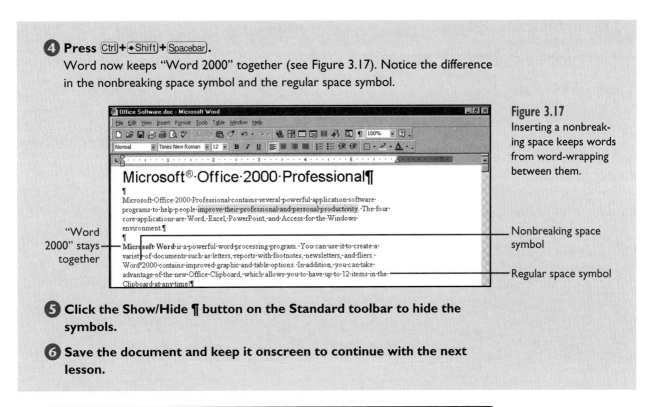

"Word 2000" stays together

Figure 3.17
Inserting a nonbreaking space keeps words from word-wrapping between them.

Nonbreaking space symbol

Regular space symbol

5 **Click the Show/Hide ¶ button on the Standard toolbar to hide the symbols.**

6 **Save the document and keep it onscreen to continue with the next lesson.**

 Inside Stuff: **Nonbreaking Hyphens**

Hyphens cause another word-wrap problem. Words containing hyphens can word-wrap at the hyphen location, causing undesirable results. Certain hyphenated text, such as phone numbers, should stay together.

To keep hyphenated words together, replace the regular hyphen with a nonbreaking hyphen. A *nonbreaking hyphen* keeps text on both sides of the hyphen together. To insert a nonbreaking hyphen, press Ctrl + ⇧Shift + - .

When you display the formatting symbols, a regular hyphen looks like a hyphen. A nonbreaking hyphen appears as a wider hyphen. However, the nonbreaking hyphen looks like a regular hyphen when printed.

Lesson 8: Inserting Symbols

Although the keyboard contains some keys that produce symbols, such as the plus sign (+), hundreds of other symbols are not on the standard keyboard. For example, you might want to insert an **em dash**, a dash the width of a lowercase m, to indicate a pause or change in thought. You might also need to insert an **en dash**, a dash the width of a lowercase n, to indicate a series, such as pages 9–15.

You can display the Symbol dialog box to insert these special dashes, a copyright symbol, or a trademark symbol. In addition, you can select from a variety of specialized symbols such as a plane, data disk, spider web, and book. In this lesson, you insert the Windows symbol in the first paragraph.

To Insert a Symbol

1 **In the `Office Software` document, position the insertion point to the left of environment at the end of the first paragraph.**
This is where you want to insert the symbol.

2 **Choose Insert, Symbol.**
The Symbol dialog box appears (see Figure 3.18). It has two tabs—Symbols and Special Characters. The Symbols tab provides access to hundreds of special symbols; the Special Characters tab provides access to standard characters, such as the em dash.

Figure 3.18
The Symbol dialog box displays a variety of special symbols.

Click to see other characters

Click to select a font

Click this symbol

3 **Click the Font drop-down arrow and choose Wingdings if it is not already selected.**

(i) ***Inside Stuff:*** **Unique Symbols**
Some of the most interesting and diverse symbols are located in Wingdings, Wingdings 2, Wingdings 3, Webdings, and WP IconicSymbolsA and WP IconicSymbolsB.

4 **Click the symbol in the bottom-right corner.**
This is the symbol that looks like the Windows emblem.

5 **Click Insert to place the symbol at the insertion point.**
The Cancel button changes to the Close button after you insert a symbol.

6 **Click Close to close the Symbol dialog box.**
Figure 3.19 shows the symbol in the paragraph. You probably need to insert a space after the symbol to separate it from the next word.

Figure 3.19
The symbol appears in the document.

Wingdings symbol inserted

Need a space here

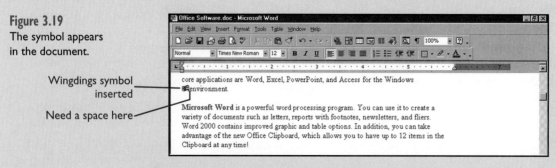

7 **Press Spacebar to separate the symbol and the word environment.**

8 **Save the document and close it.**

Exam Note: **Using Common Symbols**

If you're asked to insert a common symbol, such as an em dash, copyright symbol, or registered symbol, you can insert them from the Special Characters section of the Symbol dialog box (see Figure 3.20), or you can use the keyboard shortcuts, if available.

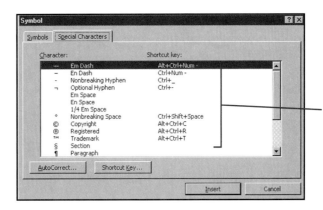

Figure 3.20
Insert special characters when needed in documents.

Keyboard shortcuts are available for some characters

Summary

In this project, you learned how to make text stand out by using text enhancements such as bold, underline, italic, and font color. You also know what types of fonts are appropriate for text and headings and how to increase font size. By using Format Painter, you can save time by copying text formats to other text in your document. Furthermore, you can highlight text to draw attention to important ideas.

You can make documents look more professional by using nonbreaking spaces and hyphens correctly and adjust character spacing when needed. Finally, display the nonprinting symbols to help you see spacing, tabs, and hard returns.

Checking Concepts and Terms

True/False

For each of the following, check *T* or *F* to indicate whether the statement is true or false.

__T __F   **I.** To italicize existing text, you must first select it. [L1]

__T __F   **2.** You should set line spacing to adjust the space between letters that touch each other horizontally. [L3]

__T __F   **3.** Before turning on the Format Painter to format other headings, place the insertion point inside the original formatted heading. [L4]

__T __F   **4.** When you display the nonprinting formatting symbols, you see a special code that indicates where you turned bold on and off. [L6]

__T __F   **5.** When you access the Symbols dialog box, click the Symbols tab to see a short list of common typing symbols, such as the em dash and registered symbol. [L8]

Multiple Choice

Circle the letter of the correct answer for each of the following.

1. All of the following have keyboard shortcuts except: [L1]

    a. underline

    b. font color

    c. bold

    d. italic

2. How many points are in a vertical inch? [L2]

    a. 10

    b. 12

    c. 24

    d. 72

3. Which effect only appears onscreen and not on a
printout? [L3]

    a. Blinking background

    b. Superscript

    c. Strikethrough

    d. Emboss

4. What nonprinting format symbol represents a nonbreaking space? [L7]

    a. •

    b. ¶

    c. →

    d. o

5. Look at Figure 3.4 and identify an example of a
serif font.

    a. Arial Rounded MT Bold

    b. Courier New

    c. Keystroke

    d. Westminster

Screen ID

Label each element of the Word screen shown in Figure 3.21.

Figure 3.21

    A. Format Painter button

    B. Highlight button

    C. Nonbreaking space symbol

    D. Paragraph symbol

    E. Tab symbol

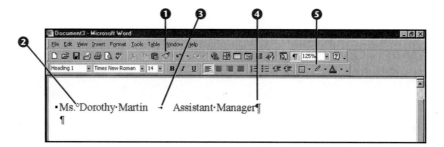

1._____ 2._____ 3._____

4._____ 5._____

Skill Drill

Skill Drill exercises reinforce project skills. Each skill reinforced is the same, or nearly the
same, as a skill presented in the project. Each exercise includes a brief narrative introduction,
followed by detailed instructions in a step-by-step format.

1. Using Text Enhancements, Font Options, and Format Painter to Enhance a Newsletter

You work for an apartment complex manager. She just finished typing the October newsletter and wants you to enhance its appearance.

1. Open **W-0302** and save it as **October Newsletter**.
2. Click and drag across the first two lines of text.
3. Click the Font drop-down arrow and choose Arial Rounded MT Bold or Kabel Dm BT.
4. Deselect both lines and select the first line only.
5. Click the Font Size drop-down arrow and choose 20.
6. Select the first heading, "Water Hoses".
7. Click the Bold button.
8. Click the Font Color drop-down arrow and choose Pink.
9. Click inside the "Water Hoses" heading to deselect it and then double-click the Format Painter button.
10. Scroll down to see "Thermostat Settings" at the top of the screen.
11. Click and drag across "Thermostat Settings" with the Format Painter mouse pointer.
12. Click and drag across "Sidewalk Salt" and then click and drag across "Laundry Room Hours."
13. Click the Format Painter button to turn off this feature.
14. Save the document and keep it onscreen to continue with the next exercise.

2. Applying Character Effects, Character Spacing, and Highlighting

You decide to apply the Small Caps character effect to the second line to add some contrast to the headings. In addition, you notice that some characters are too close together in the main title and need to be separated. Finally, you decide to highlight an important phrase for your readers.

1. In the **October Newsletter** document, select October 2001 Newsletter.
2. Choose Format, Font. If needed, click the Font tab.
3. Click the Small caps check box, and then click OK.
4. Click and drag across "rtm" in the main title.
5. Choose Format, Font.
6. Click the Character Spacing tab.
7. Click the Spacing drop-down arrow and choose Expanded.
8. Click the Spacing By increment button to 1.3 and then click OK.
9. Click inside the document to deselect the text.
10. Press and hold down Ctrl while you click the mouse button on the sentence **Please disconnect these hoses by October 15.** in the second paragraph.
11. Click the Highlight button.
12. Save the document and keep it onscreen to continue with the next exercise.

3. Inserting a Nonbreaking Space and Symbols

The newsletter is almost done. However, you need to insert a nonbreaking space to keep "7 a.m." together. In addition, you want to insert en dashes in the times to look professional.

1. In the **October Newsletter** document, press Ctrl+End to position the insertion point at the end of the document.
2. Click the Show/Hide ¶ button to see the nonprinting symbols if they are not already displayed.
3. Click to the immediate right of 7 and press Del to delete the regular space symbol.
4. Press Ctrl+⬆Shift+Spacebar to insert a nonbreaking space.
5. Click after Monday on the previous line and press Del to delete the regular space symbol.
6. Choose Insert, Symbol.
7. Click the Special Characters tab.
8. Click En Dash, click Insert, and then click Close to insert an en dash between Monday and Thursday.
9. Click after Friday on the next line and press Del to delete the regular space symbol.
10. Press Ctrl+- (minus key on the numeric keypad) to insert an en dash without having to access the Symbol dialog box.
11. Save the document, print it, and then close it.

Challenge

Challenge exercises expand on or are somewhat related to skills presented in the lessons. Each exercise provides a brief narrative introduction followed by instructions in a numbered-step or bullet-list format that are not as detailed as those in the Skill Drill section.

1. Enhancing a Letter to a Student Organization

You prepared a response to a student organization that is interested in holding a fundraiser for a charitable contribution. You work with the student organizations to inform them of the required sales tax forms for their vendors. You now want to enhance the letter to make certain points stand out.

1. Open **W-0303** and save it as **Gift and Craft Show Tax Letter**.

2. Emphasize the subject line by bolding it and applying Arial Narrow font to "Sales Tax Forms for the Gift and Craft Fair."

3. Use Bright Green highlight on the phrase "return the master forms to the tax commission's office by December 15."

4. Display the formatting marks. Insert nonbreaking spaces and hyphens in the appropriate locations. (*Hint*: You need at least one of each.)

5. Italicize the last sentence in the third paragraph and apply Red font color.

6. Save the document and print it.

2. Creating a Health Benefits Memo

You work in your company's Benefits Office. You need to prepare a memo to inform employees of a few changes and of upcoming seminars that further explain the changes.

1. From a new window, create the document shown in Figure 3.22.

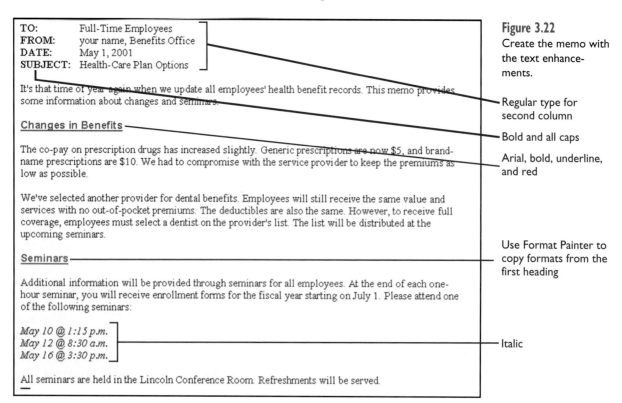

Figure 3.22
Create the memo with the text enhancements.

Regular type for second column

Bold and all caps

Arial, bold, underline, and red

Use Format Painter to copy formats from the first heading

Italic

2. Apply the text enhancements, as shown in the figure.

3. Display the formatting marks. Insert blank lines as needed to make sure you have two paragraph marks at the end of the TO, FROM, and DATE lines. Make sure you have three paragraph marks after the SUBJECT line.

4. Right-click words that have red wavy lines below them and correct these spelling errors.

5. Select the dates at the bottom of the memo, press ⌨Tab⇆ to indent them, and apply red font color to them.

6. Highlight the last sentence in Turquoise.

7. Insert nonbreaking spaces and hyphens, if needed.

8. Save the document as **Health Benefits Memo** and print it.

3. Enhancing an Advertisement Flier

In Project 2, you created an announcement to college students about your Mega Music store's special discount. Now you want to create and enhance a flier to go on bulletin boards around the campus.

1. Open **W-0304** and save it as **Mega Music Flier**.

2. Select the entire document and apply 20-point Comic Sans MS font.

3. Select the first two lines in the document and apply 28-point Arial Rounded MT Bold in Pink font color. (If you don't have Arial Rounded MT Bold, ask your instructor for an alternative font face.)

4. Apply an appropriate highlight color to the three lines that list the discount percentages.

5. Delete the asterisk and insert the Webdings symbol that looks like two masks, the symbol that you often see for theatrical events. The symbol is in the third column on the sixth row of symbols. Select the symbol and apply 72-point size with Pink font color.

6. Insert the telephone symbol from the Wingdings symbols at the beginning of the phone number on the last line of the document.

7. Save the document and print it.

Discovery Zone

Discovery Zone exercises help you gain advanced knowledge of project topics and/or application of skills. These exercises focus on enhancing your problem-solving skills. Numbered steps are not provided, but you are given hints, reminders, screen shots, and/or references to help you reach your goal for each exercise.

1. Enhancing a Restaurant Review Article

You are the newly appointed restaurant critic for your college newspaper. Your first article is to introduce your column and define your grading scale. Open **W-0305** and save it as **Restaurant Review Article 1**. Change * to your name and ** to your email address, such as **name@college.edu**.

Apply 12-point Bookman Old Style to the entire document. Apply 18-point Arial, Plum font color, and Blinking Background text effect to the title. Use your judgment in adjusting character spacing as needed within the title. Also, activate kerning for point sizes above 16. Insert any necessary nonbreaking spaces or hyphens in the correct locations.

Use Figure 3.23 to finish formatting the document. Pay close attention to detail. Use the Symbol dialog box to locate and insert é in the last sentence.

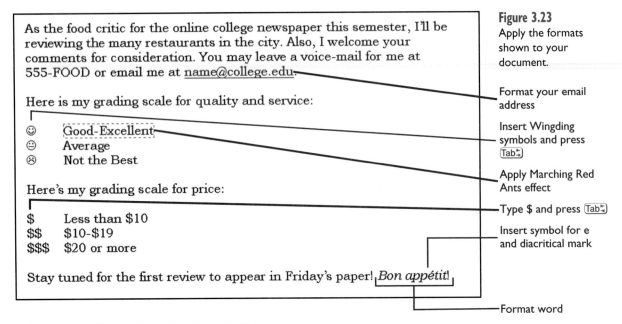

As the food critic for the online college newspaper this semester, I'll be reviewing the many restaurants in the city. Also, I welcome your comments for consideration. You may leave a voice-mail for me at 555-FOOD or email me at name@college.edu.

Here is my grading scale for quality and service:

☺   Good-Excellent
☺   Average
☹   Not the Best

Here's my grading scale for price:

$ Less than $10
$$ $10-$19
$$$ $20 or more

Stay tuned for the first review to appear in Friday's paper! *Bon appétit!*

Figure 3.23
Apply the formats shown to your document.

Format your email address

Insert Wingding symbols and press Tab

Apply Marching Red Ants effect

Type $ and press Tab

Insert symbol for e and diacritical mark

Format word

2. Creating a Notice for a Professor's Door

You are a student worker for a department on your college campus. You've been asked to create a notice to tape to a professor's door. Create the notice shown in Figure 3.24 by using the formats specified.

Apply a custom color to the title using these settings: Hue 238, Sat 128, Lum 133, Red 194, Green 72, and Blue 121. Use Help, if needed, to learn how to create a custom font color.

Save the document as **Van Buren Door Notice** and print it. Fold the note in half, just below the last text line.

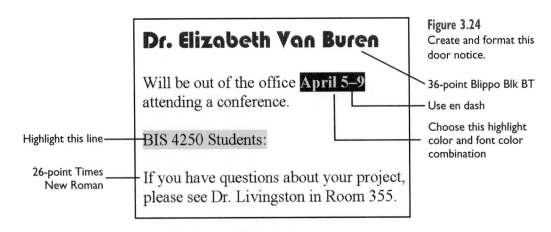

Dr. Elizabeth Van Buren

Will be out of the office April 5–9 attending a conference.

BIS 4250 Students:

If you have questions about your project, please see Dr. Livingston in Room 355.

Highlight this line

26-point Times New Roman

Figure 3.24
Create and format this door notice.

36-point Blippo Blk BT

Use en dash

Choose this highlight color and font color combination

PinPoint Assessment

You have completed this project and its associated lessons, and have had an opportunity to assess your skills through the end-of-project questions and exercises. Now use the PinPoint software Evaluation Mode to further assess your comprehension of the specific exam activities you have just learned. You can also use the PinPoint Trainer Mode and the Show Me tutorials to practice these exam activities.

Project 4

Editing Documents

Key terms introduced in this project include

- action
- active window
- AutoCorrect
- casing
- copy

- cut
- object
- Office Clipboard
- paste

- Redo feature
- Repeat command
- synonym
- Undo feature

Objectives	Required Activity for MOUS	Exam Level
➤ Change the Case of Text		
➤ Move and Copy Text	Insert and move text	Core
	Cut, Copy, Paste, and Paste Special using the Office Clipboard	Core
➤ Copy Between Document Windows		
➤ Use Undo, Redo, and Repeat Features	Use the Undo, Redo, and Repeat command	Core
➤ Use AutoCorrect	Create and apply frequently used text with AutoCorrect	Core
➤ Correct Spelling and Grammatical Errors	Use the SPELLING feature	Core
	Use the GRAMMAR feature	Core
➤ Use Thesaurus	Use the THESAURUS feature	Core

Why Would I Do This?

You can now create documents with text enhancements, such as bold, font, and color. You are now ready for some common editing tasks to affect the organization and accuracy of your documents.

In this project, you learn how to change capitalization style, rearrange text, and copy text from one document to another. In addition, you learn how to correct spelling and grammatical errors, as well as how to use Thesaurus to improve word choices.

Lesson 1: Changing the Case of Text

It's frustrating to discover you've typed an entire paragraph (or more) in all capital letters before realizing you've forgotten to turn off Caps Lock! Instead of deleting and retyping everything you've worked so hard to type, you can select the text and change its *casing*, which is how the text is capitalized.

In this lesson, you realize that a full paragraph is capitalized. You need to change the casing of the text to be consistent with the other paragraphs.

To Change the Case of Text

1 **Open W-0401 and save it as Benefits Status Report.**
The third paragraph is formatted in all capital letters. You want to select a different case style. Also note that spelling errors, such as "VIALBE" are not detected in all capital letters.

2 **Select the third paragraph, which is currently formatted in all capital letters.**
You must select the text that you want to change to a different case.

3 **Choose Format, Change Case.**

 If You Have Problems...
If you don't see the Change Case option, position the mouse pointer on the downward pointing arrows at the bottom of the Format menu to see the full menu.

The Change Case dialog box appears (see Figure 4.1). Sentence case capitalizes only the first letter of each sentence. lowercase changes all selected text to lowercase letters. UPPERCASE changes all selected text to all capital letters. Title Case capitalizes the first letter of each word. tOGGLE cASE reverses the capitalization of selected text. For example, it changes uppercase letters to lowercase and lowercase letters to uppercase.

Figure 4.1
The Change Case dialog box contains options for changing the capitalization of selected text.

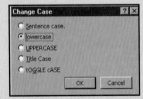

4 **Click Sentence case and click OK.**
Now only the first letter of each sentence is capitalized. After changing casing, you should read the text and individually capitalize the first letter of proper nouns.

⑤ Deselect the paragraph.
Figure 4.2 shows how your paragraph should look after changing the case.

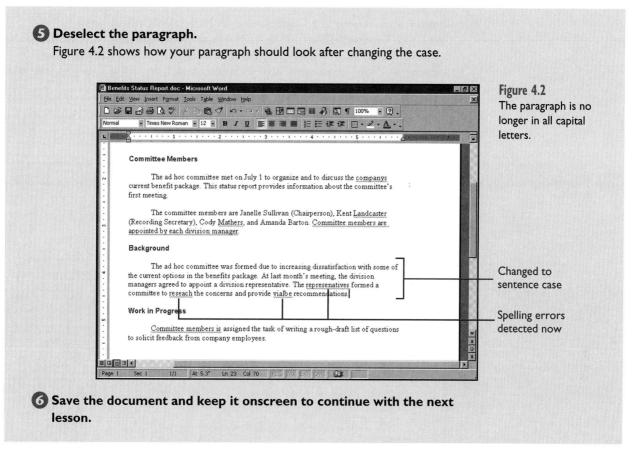

Figure 4.2
The paragraph is no longer in all capital letters.

Changed to sentence case

Spelling errors detected now

⑥ Save the document and keep it onscreen to continue with the next lesson.

  Inside Stuff: **Using Title Case**
After you use the <u>T</u>itle Case option from the Change Case dialog box on headings, you should lowercase small words, such as **in** and **the** in the middle of the heading.

  Inside Stuff: **Using Keyboard Shortcuts**
You can press ⇧Shift+F3 to change selected text to uppercase, lowercase, or sentence caps. Keep pressing this shortcut to cycle through the casing options until the text appears in the casing you want.

To quickly change selected text to all capitals, press Ctrl+⇧Shift+A.

Lesson 2: Moving and Copying Text

After you create a document, you might decide to rearrange sentences and paragraphs to improve the clarity and organization of the content. You might need to move a paragraph to a different location, rearrange the sentences within a paragraph, or move sentences from different paragraphs to form one paragraph.

The three main terms that describe moving and copying text are cut, copy, and paste. When you **cut** text, you remove it from its present location. When you **copy** text, you leave the original text in its current location and make a copy to put elsewhere. When you **paste** text, you insert the cut or copied text in the new location.

The **Office Clipboard** is an area in memory reserved for text and objects you cut and copy. An **object** is a non-text item such as clip art, bar charts, and so on. When you cut or copy text or an object, the text or object stays on the Clipboard. You can then paste it repeatedly to different locations.

Exam Note: **Using the Clipboard with Multiple Applications**
The Office Clipboard is particularly helpful for copying items from one application, such as Excel, to another application, such as Word. In Project 11, "Integrating Information," you learn how to copy Excel data into a Word document by using the Clipboard.

In this lesson, you move the Background section from its current location so that it's above the Committee Members section.

To Move and Copy Text

¶

1 In the `Benefits Status Report` document, click the Show/Hide ¶ button to display the nonprinting symbols.

2 Select the Background heading, the paragraph below it, and the paragraph symbol above "Work in Progress," as shown in Figure 4.3.

Figure 4.3
The Background section, including its blank lines, is selected.

Click to cut selected text

Start clicking and dragging here

Include paragraph symbol in selected area

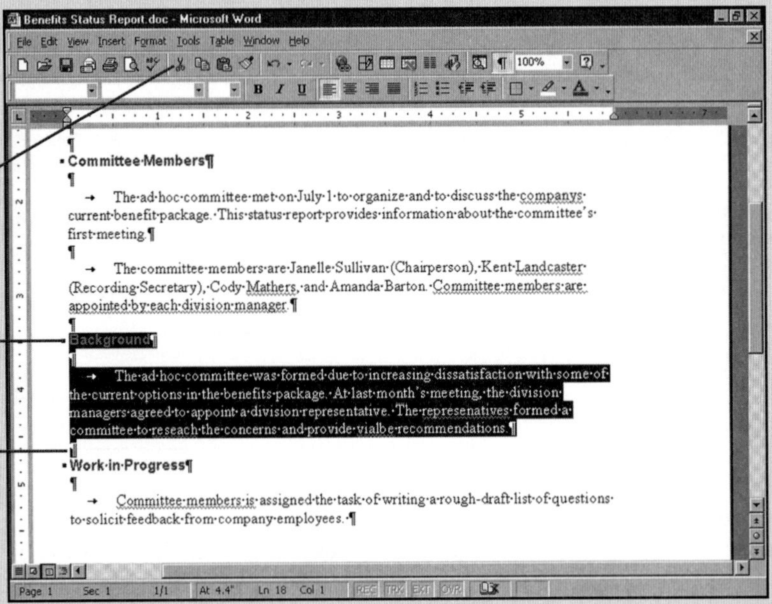

 If You Have Problems...
If you're having problems selecting this text, place the insertion point at the beginning of the word Background, and press Ctrl+↑Shift+↓ four times.

The Background section is selected, so you can move it. You must select text and any blank lines you want to cut or copy. Make sure the paragraph symbol between the paragraph and the next heading is selected.

 3 Click the Cut button on the Standard toolbar.
The Background section disappears from the document. It is stored in the Office Clipboard.

4 Position the insertion point to the left of the letter C in the heading Committee Members.
After cutting or copying text, you need to place the insertion point where you want the text to appear. In this document, you want to place the Background section before the Committee Members section.

⑤ Click the Paste button on the Standard toolbar.
When you paste the Background section in its new location, the Committee Members section moves down to accommodate it (see Figure 4.4).

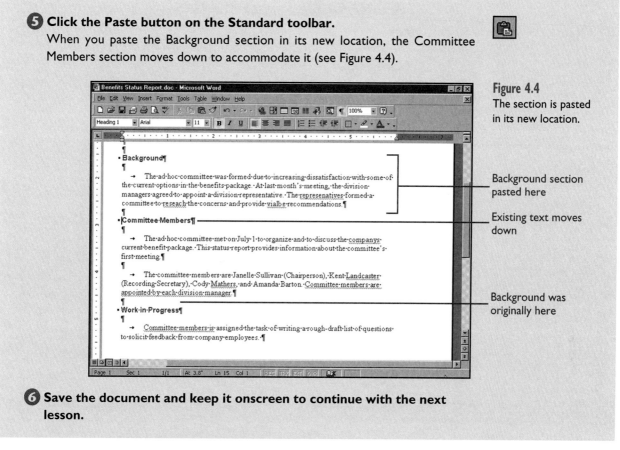

Figure 4.4
The section is pasted in its new location.

Background section pasted here

Existing text moves down

Background was originally here

⑥ Save the document and keep it onscreen to continue with the next lesson.

 Exam Note: **Copying and Pasting Text**
The steps for copying text are the same as those for cutting text. The only difference is that you click the Copy button instead of the Cut button. After copying text, position the insertion point where you want the copy to appear and then click the Paste button. The original text remains in place and a copy is created elsewhere.

In addition to using the Cut, Copy, and Paste buttons, you can use the following methods for moving and copying text:

- To move text, point inside the selected text and drag it to a new location. When you release the mouse button, the text is moved from its original location to the new location. If you hold down Ctrl while dragging, you copy the selected text rather than cut it.
- Press Ctrl+X to cut text, Ctrl+C to copy text, and Ctrl+V to paste text.
- Choose Cut, Copy, and Paste from the Edit menu.
- Right-click in the selected area to see a shortcut menu and then select Cut, Copy, or Paste.

You can cut or copy up to 12 items to the Office Clipboard. By default, when you click the Paste button, Word pastes the last item you cut or copied to the Office Clipboard. If you want to select a previous item in the Clipboard, you need to display the Clipboard toolbar by choosing View, Toolbars, Clipboard.

The Clipboard toolbar shows how many items are currently in the Office Clipboard. To see what an item is, position the mouse pointer on it to see the ScreenTip, as shown in Figure 4.5. (Your Clipboard might have different items than the one shown in the figure.) Click an item to paste it at the insertion point location.

Figure 4.5
The Clipboard toolbar displays the Clipboard contents and buttons for pasting items in your document.

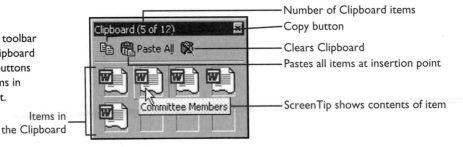

- Number of Clipboard items
- Copy button
- Clears Clipboard
- Pastes all items at insertion point
- ScreenTip shows contents of item

Items in the Clipboard

Committee Members

 Click the Paste All button to paste all of the Office Clipboard items at the insertion point location.

 Click the Clear Clipboard button to clear the items in the Office Clipboard.

Lesson 3: Copying Between Document Windows

In business, people often reuse information from previous reports and documents as they prepare new reports. In addition, people often work in teams, write their individual assignments, and send their documents to a team leader to collate. In these situations, you can open two or more documents and easily copy information from one document window to another. This process saves you from having to retype the information.

In this lesson, you copy some information from another document and paste it in your current document.

To Copy and Paste Between Document Windows

❶ **With `Benefits Status Report` onscreen, open `W-0402` and click the Show/Hide ¶ button to display the formatting marks.**
The document that contains the insertion point is in the *active window*.

❷ **Select the Employee Concerns heading, the paragraph below it, and the three indented lines. Make sure you include the paragraph mark that represents the blank line below "Tuition Reimbursement."**
Figure 4.6 shows the text that you should have selected.

Figure 4.6
Select the text in the document that you want to copy to the first document.

Selected text

Active window

Click to toggle back to this document

3 Click the Copy button.
This copies the selected text to the Office Clipboard.

4 Click the Benefits Status Report.doc button on the Windows taskbar.
You can go back and forth between open documents by clicking their respective buttons on the taskbar. Now Benefits Status Report is the active document.

5 Position the insertion point to the left of Work in Progress, and click the Paste button.
Figure 4.7 shows where the pasted text appears.

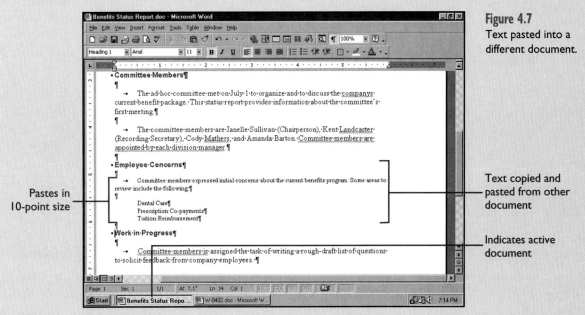

Pastes in 10-point size

Text copied and pasted from other document

Indicates active document

Figure 4.7
Text pasted into a different document.

6 Select the 10-point paragraph and three indented lines that were pasted.
You need to apply 12-point size to the regular text to make it consistent with the rest of your document. Note, however, that the heading "Employee Concerns" maintains its original format and font size.

7 Click the Font Size drop-down arrow, choose 12, and deselect the text.
Now the pasted text appears in 12-point (see Figure 4.8).

continues ▶

To Copy and Paste Between Document Windows (continued)

Figure 4.8
Pasted text is now correctly formatted.

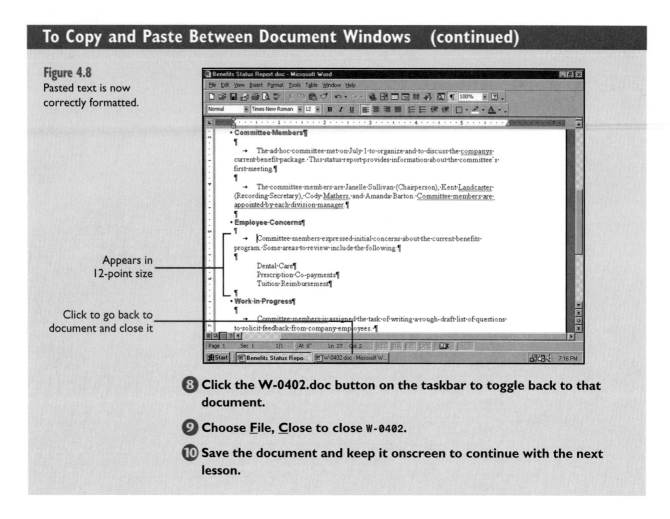

Appears in 12-point size

Click to go back to document and close it

⑧ **Click the W-0402.doc button on the taskbar to toggle back to that document.**

⑨ **Choose File, Close to close W-0402.**

⑩ **Save the document and keep it onscreen to continue with the next lesson.**

 ## Lesson 4: Using Undo, Redo, and Repeat Features

The **Undo feature** reverses actions you perform in a document. When you use Undo, Word reverses actions in sequential order—starting with the last action you performed. Clicking Undo again reverses the second-to-the-last action, and so on.

For example, assume that you paste a paragraph in the wrong location. Using the Undo feature removes the pasted text. If you accidentally click the Underline button, using the Undo feature removes the underline. Undo works for almost every action you perform within a document—formatting, deleting, sorting, placing graphics, and so on. Some actions cannot be reversed with Undo, though. For example, if you choose Save instead of Save As, you can't undo the saving process.

In this lesson, you "accidentally" delete a sentence in the first paragraph. You use Undo to restore the deleted text. In addition, you use Undo to remove underlining from a sentence.

To Undo Actions

① **In the Benefits Status Report document, position the insertion point in the first sentence in the first paragraph.**

② **Press and hold Ctrl while clicking the first sentence.**
This is the sentence you "accidentally" delete.

③ Press Del.

The sentence is not in the Clipboard because you deleted it instead of cutting it. Figure 4.9 shows the document after deleting the sentence.

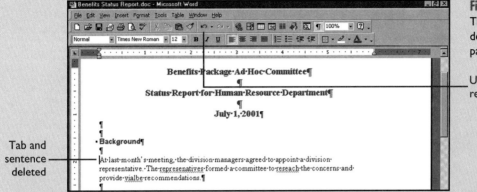

Figure 4.9
The sentence is deleted from the paragraph.

Undo button reverses actions

Tab and sentence deleted

④ Click the Undo button on the Standard toolbar.

> **ⓘ Inside Stuff: Undo Keyboard Shortcut**
> The keyboard shortcut for undo is Ctrl+Z.

The Undo feature reserves your last action. In this case, your last action deleted a sentence. Clicking Undo restores the deleted text.

⑤ Select the first sentence if it is not already selected, and click the Underline button to underline the sentence.

⑥ Deselect the sentence to see the underlined text.

You realize you accidentally clicked the Underline button.

⑦ Click the Undo button.

Undo reverses the last action by removing the underline from the selected text.

⑧ Save the document and keep the document onscreen to continue with the next lesson.

✗ If You Have Problems...

If Undo doesn't undelete the text or remove the underline, you probably performed another action on the document. Any change you make to the document, such as adding a space, is considered an **action**.

ⓘ Inside Stuff: Undo List

Clicking the Undo button reverses the last action. If you need to restore previous actions, click the Undo button again. Each time you click the Undo button, you work backward, reversing actions you have taken.

You can reverse a series of actions by clicking the Undo drop-down arrow. When you select an action from the list, Word reverses the most recent actions, including the one you select. Figure 4.10 shows that the last four actions will be undone.

Figure 4.10
The Undo list lets you reverse the last several actions at one time.

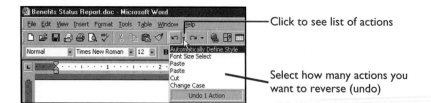

Click to see list of actions

Select how many actions you want to reverse (undo)

Exam Note: **Using the Redo Feature**

If you decide you don't want to reverse an action after clicking the Undo button, click the **Redo** button to reverse the Undo action. The Redo button is grayed-out if you have not used the Undo feature in a document.

Exam Note: **Using the Repeat Command**

The ***Repeat command*** duplicates or repeats the last action or command you executed. For example, if you applied Blue font color to selected text, you can use the Repeat command to repeat the application of Blue font color to other text. The Repeat command can also repeat something you typed or complex formatting.

To use the Repeat command, choose Edit, Repeat or press Ctrl+Y. If Word is unable to repeat your last action, the Edit menu will display Can't Repeat.

 Lesson 5: Using AutoCorrect

AutoCorrect corrects errors "on the fly," which means it corrects errors as you type them. For example, it changes "teh" to "the." It also corrects other types of errors, such as capitalization at the beginning of a sentence. It even helps you change manually typed symbols to unique symbols, such as changing :) to ☺. You can even insert AutoCorrect entries to change abbreviations to fully expanded text, such as changing "uvsc" to "Utah Valley State College."

In this lesson, you type a sentence at the end of the document. Although you type it with errors, AutoCorrect corrects the errors for you.

To Use AutoCorrect

① In the Benefits Status Report document, press Ctrl+End, and click the Show/Hide button to turn off the formatting marks.

② Type teh and press Spacebar.
When you press Spacebar, AutoCorrect changes teh to the and capitalizes the first letter of the sentence.

③ Type ad hoc comittee will reconvene next week to reveiw the questons and prepare a tenative questionaire.
Your sentence should look like the one shown in Figure 4.11.

Figure 4.11
AutoCorrect corrects some spelling errors as you type them.

Capitalized and corrected spelling

Correctly spelled words

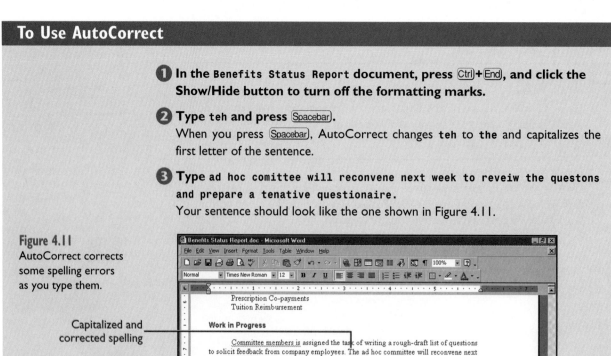

Now let's look at AutoCorrect to see what words are detected and corrected for you.

4 **Choose Tools, AutoCorrect to display the AutoCorrect dialog box.**

 If You Have Problems...
If you don't see AutoCorrect on the Tools menu, click the down-pointing arrows to display the full Tools menu.

5 **Click the scroll-down arrow on the right side of the dialog box to scroll through the list until you see the word committee in the second column.**
The first column shows misspelled words, and the second column shows the correct spellings, as shown in Figure 4.12.

Options to correct capitalization errors

When you type this...

...Word replaces it with this

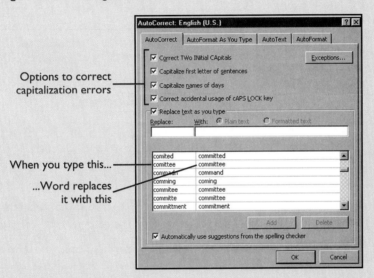

Figure 4.12
AutoCorrect corrects some spelling errors as you type them.

6 **Click Cancel to close the dialog box.**

7 **Save the document and keep it onscreen to continue with the next lesson.**

 Exam Note: **Adding Entries**
You can add words you typically misspell or abbreviations in AutoCorrect. Assume you typically misspell **business** as **busenes**. You can type **busenes** in the Replace text box and **business** in the With text box in the AutoCorrect dialog box. After entering the two words, click Add to add the entry.

Lesson 6: Correcting Spelling and Grammatical Errors

Even the best typists make mistakes. The Spelling and Grammar feature identifies potentially misspelled words, duplicate words, and irregular capitalization. In addition, it detects errors in grammar, style, punctuation, and word usage.

Recall from Project I that red wavy lines below words indicate misspelled words. The green wavy lines indicate possible grammar problems. You can right-click words with the red or green wavy underlines, and then choose the correct spelling or grammar.

However, you can keep typing and correct the errors later. In this lesson, you double-click the Spelling and Grammar Status button on the status bar to display the shortcut menus with suggested spellings. The button displays a red X when the document contains spelling or grammatical errors. It displays a red check mark when the document does *not* contain spelling and grammatical errors.

To Spell-Check a Document

1 In the Benefits Status Report **document, position the insertion point at the beginning of the document.**

2 **Double-click the Spelling and Grammar Status button on the status bar.**
Word displays the shortcut by the first spelling error, which is representatives (see Figure 4.13).

Figure 4.13
Choose the correct spelling from the menu.

Choose this word

Misspelled word

Double-click to detect next spelling or grammatical error

July 1, 2001

representatives

Ignore All
Add

AutoCorrect
Language
Spelling...

Background

The ad hoc committee was formed due to increasing dissatisfacti the current options in the benefits package. At last month's meeting, the managers agreed to appoint a division representative. The representatives committee to reseach the concerns and provide viable recommendations.

Committee Members

Page 1   Sec 1   1/1   At 1"   Ln 1   Col 1   REC TRK EXT OVR

3 **Choose** representatives **at the top of the shortcut menu.**
Word replaces the original word with the replacement word you choose.

4 **Double-click the Spelling and Grammar Status button on the status bar.**
The next misspelled word is reseach.

5 **Choose** research **from the shortcut menu.**

6 **Double-click the Spelling and Grammar Status button and choose** viable **for the next error.**
Instead of continuing to double-click the Spelling and Grammar Status button, you decide to start the Spelling and Grammar checking feature.

7 **Click the Spelling and Grammar button on the Standard toolbar.**
Figure 4.14 shows companys detected as an error. Word provides three suggestions.

Figure 4.14
Choose the correct suggestion from the dialog box.

Click correct suggestion

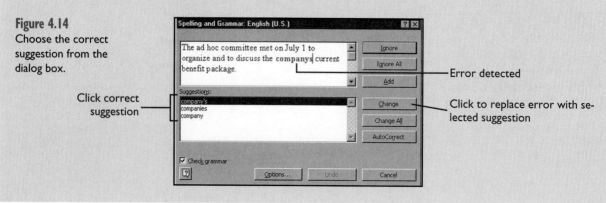

Error detected

Click to replace error with selected suggestion

8 **Click `company's` in the Suggestions box and then click Change.**

Word detects **Landcaster** because it's not in the dictionary. Because this word is spelled correctly, you can ignore it.

9 **Click Ignore.**

Word also detects **Mathers**. You can ignore this word also.

10 **Click Ignore.**

Word detects a grammatical error (see Figure 4.15). The selected sentence is written in passive voice. The suggestion restates the sentence in active voice.

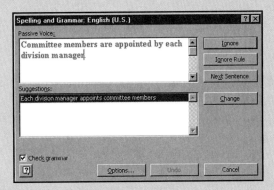

Figure 4.15
Word detects a grammatical error.

11 **Click Change to change the selected text to active voice.**

Word now detects a subject-verb agreement error (see Figure 4.16). You have two choices.

Error detected ———

Two suggestions ———

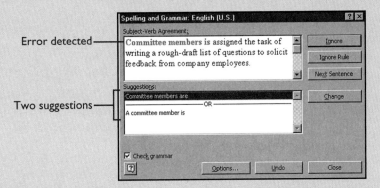

Figure 4.16
You need to correct the subject-verb agreement error.

12 **Make sure "Committee members are" is highlighted in the Suggestions box and then click Change.**

13 **Click OK when you see, `The spelling and grammar check is complete`.**

14 **Save the document and keep it onscreen to continue with the next lesson.**

 Inside Stuff: **Changing Spelling and Grammar Options**

If you want to select the way Word checks spelling and grammar, click Options in the Spelling and Grammar dialog box (see Figure 4.17). Click the Writing style drop-down arrow and choose a different grammar style, such as Formal or Technical, if desired.

Figure 4.17
Choose spelling and
grammar options.

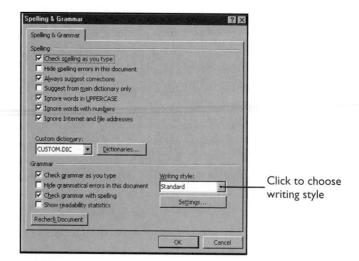

Click to choose
writing style

(i) *Inside Stuff:* **Proofreading Is Essential**
Although Word can help detect misspelled words for you and make it easy to correct them, you are still responsible for proofreading your documents. Word can't always determine whether you used words correctly, such as to, too, and two.

(i) *Inside Stuff:* **Learning About the Error**
If you don't understand why Word detected a grammatical error with the green wavy lines, right-click the error and choose About this Sentence from the shortcut menu. Word displays grammar information and rules, along with samples to help you better understand the error.

 ## Lesson 7: Using Thesaurus

Finding the perfect word to communicate your ideas clearly is sometimes difficult. You might type a word but then realize it doesn't quite describe what you're thinking. It might not have the impact for which you were searching. The Thesaurus tool helps you choose words to improve the clarity of your documents. You can select **synonyms**, words with similar meanings, from Word's Thesaurus feature and get your point across with greater ease.

To Use Thesaurus

❶ **In the Benefits Status Report document, click in the word "formed" in the first paragraph.**

❷ **Choose Tools, Language, Thesaurus.**

(i) *Inside Stuff:* **Thesaurus Keyboard Shortcut**
Press ⬆Shift+F7 to access Thesaurus from the keyboard.

Thesaurus appears with a list of possible replacement words (see Figure 4.18). If a word has multiple meanings, you can click a meaning and see different synonyms on the right side of the dialog box.

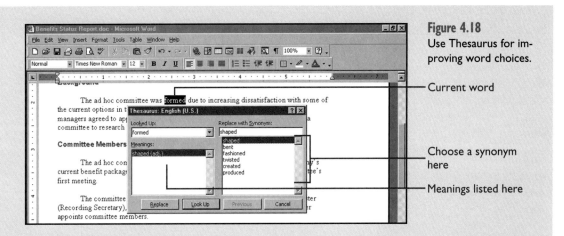

Figure 4.18
Use Thesaurus for improving word choices.

Current word

Choose a synonym here

Meanings listed here

X ***If You Have Problems...***
You see an error message if Thesaurus is not loaded on your computer. If you have the Microsoft Office 2000 installation CD, insert it and follow the prompts to install Thesaurus.

---

3 **Click `created` in the Replace with Synonym box, and then click Replace.**
Word replaces the current word with the synonym you select.

4 **Right-click `agreed` in the first paragraph.**
A shortcut menu appears with a Synonyms option. Choosing a synonym from this menu might be preferable to using the Thesaurus dialog box.

5 **Choose Synonyms.**
Figure 4.19 shows a list of synonyms for the current word.

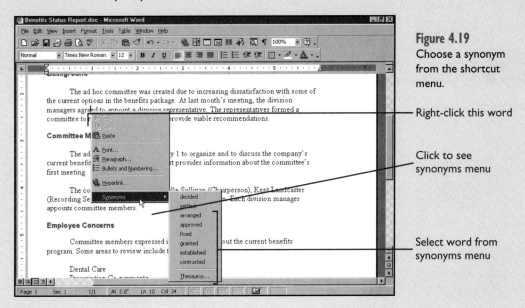

Figure 4.19
Choose a synonym from the shortcut menu.

Right-click this word

Click to see synonyms menu

Select word from synonyms menu

6 **Choose `decided`.**
Word replaces agreed with decided.

7 **Save the document and close it.**

Summary

You now know how to perform several essential tasks to enhance text and improve the clarity of your document. First, you learned how to quickly change the case of selected text instead of retyping it. In addition, you moved text to a different location and copied text from one document to another. You'll probably find the Undo and Redo features handy to reverse actions you've performed in a document. You also learned how to correct spelling and grammatical errors and to improve word choices by choosing synonyms. You also know that AutoCorrect works for you to correct errors as you type.

You can extend your learning by exploring some of the other options in AutoCorrect, Spelling and Grammar, and Thesaurus. In addition, practice using the Office Clipboard to store up to 12 items and then paste them at one time.

Checking Concepts and Terms

True/False

For each of the following, check *T* or *F* to indicate whether the statement is true or false.

__T __F   **1.** If you accidentally capitalized all words in a paragraph, the most appropriate Change Case option is Title Case. [L1]

__T __F   **2.** Before using the Cut command, you must first select text. [L2]

__T __F   **3.** You can use the Undo feature to reverse the second-to-the-last action without reversing the last action. [L4]

__T __F   **4.** The AutoCorrect feature corrects some misspelled words as you type. [L5]

__T __F   **5.** A green wavy line below a word indicates that the word is possibly misspelled. [L6]

Multiple Choice

Circle the letter of the correct answer for each of the following.

1. What Change Case option capitalizes the first letter after a punctuation mark, such as the period, question mark, or exclamation mark? [L1]

  a. Sentence Case

  b. Title Case

  c. tOGGLE cASE

  d. UPPERCASE

2. What is the keyboard shortcut for cutting text? [L2]

  a. Ctrl+C

  b. Ctrl+X

  c. Ctrl+Z

  d. Shift+F3

3. What feature reverses the last action you performed on the document? [L4]

  a. Redo

  b. Paste

  c. Undo

  d. Format Painter

4. AutoCorrect does all except for which one of the following? [L6]

  a. Corrects some misspelled words as you type

  b. Capitalizes the first letter of a sentence if you don't

  c. Changes some keyboard symbols to other symbols, such as a smiley face

  d. Places red wavy lines below grammatical errors

5. What is the purpose of using Word's Thesaurus? [L7]

   a. You can choose words that improve the clarity of your document.

   b. Word corrects misspelled words for you automatically.

   c. You can eliminate passive voice.

   d. It corrects mistakes as you type.

Screen ID

Label each element of the Word screen shown in Figure 4.20.

Figure 4.20

A. Clear Clipboard button

B. Copy button

C. Paste button

D. Spelling and Grammar button

E. Paste button

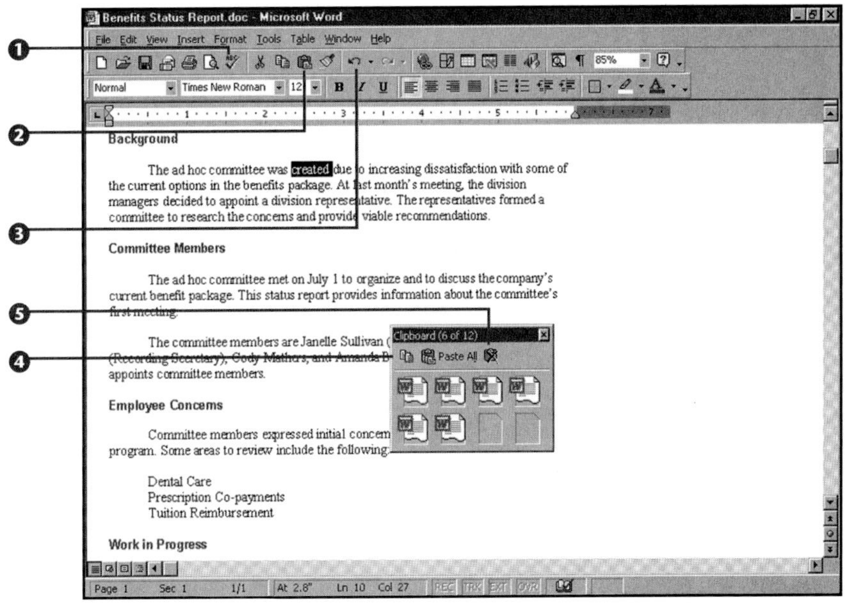

1._____   2._____   3._____

4._____   5._____

Skill Drill

Skill Drill exercises reinforce project skills. Each skill reinforced is the same, or nearly the same, as a skill presented in the project. Each exercise includes a brief narrative introduction, followed by detailed instructions in a step-by-step format.

1. Changing Casing and Reversing Actions

You just finished composing a status report memo to your manager. You need to make some changes in capitalization. You also might need to use Undo and Redo if you use the wrong casing style on text.

1. Open **W-0403**, change Andy Barton's name to your name, and save it as **Newsletter Memo**.

2. Double-click the word Subject.

3. Choose Format, Change Case.

4. Click the UPPERCASE option and then click OK.

5. Select the first heading, News articles.

6. Press (⬆Shift)+(F3) three times to choose the Title Case capitalization style.

7. Use the same process to apply the Title Case capitalization style to the other two headings.

8. Select and bold Winter Newsletter.

9. Click the Undo button twice—once to remove bold from Winter Newsletter and again to change the casing style of the last heading.

10. Click the Redo button to reverse the last Undo action. In other words, you are restoring the Title Case capitalization style to the last heading that you applied in Step 6.

11. Save the document and keep it onscreen to continue with the next exercise.

2. Moving and Copying Text

As you read through the memo, you decide to move the Art Work section below the News Articles section. You also need to copy a paragraph from another document and paste it in the current document.

1. In the **Newsletter Memo** document, click at the beginning of the heading Art Work.

2. Click the Show/Hide ¶ button to see the nonprinting symbols if they are not already displayed.

3. Select the **Art Work** heading and the paragraph below it. Make sure you include the ¶ symbol below the paragraph.

4. Click the Cut button to remove the selected text from its location.

5. Position the insertion point to the left of the Classified Advertisements heading.

6. Click the Paste button to paste the text between the News Articles and Classified Advertisement sections.

7. Select the sentence that begins with "The residents have expressed…," which is the last sentence in the Classified Advertisement section.

8. Press Ctrl+X to cut the sentence.

9. Position the insertion point at the beginning of the sentence that begins with "We are currently ac-

cepting…" in the same paragraph, and press Ctrl+V to paste it as the second sentence in the paragraph.

10. Press Spacebar, if necessary, to have a space between sentences.

11. Open **W-0404**, select the second paragraph and the blank line below it, and press Ctrl+C to copy it to the Clipboard.

12. Close **W-0404**.

13. Position the insertion point below the paragraph in the Classified Advertisement section, press ↵Enter, and click the Paste button to paste the text you had copied from the other document.

14. Make sure you have one blank line above the pasted paragraph. Make adjustments as needed.

15. Selected the pasted paragraph and choose 12-point size, if it does not appear in 12-point.

16. Save the document and keep it onscreen to continue with the next exercise.

3. Using AutoCorrect, Spelling and Grammar Checking, and Thesaurus

You need to add a sentence to the document. As you quickly type it, you make some mistakes. AutoCorrect will correct them for you. Furthermore, you need to spell-check the document, correct grammatical errors, and find an appropriate synonym for a word in the document.

1. In the **Newsletter Memo** document, position the insertion point at the end of the first paragraph in the News Articles section.

2. Type the following sentence exactly as shown with mistakes: **some topiks for artecles include informing residents ofthe new recycling program and trafic issues during home football games in september and october.**

3. Check to make sure AutoCorrect corrected the misspelled words as you typed them.

4. Position the insertion point at the beginning of the document and click the Spelling and Grammar button on the Standard toolbar.

5. Click **schedule** in the Suggestions box and click Change.

6. Click Change to change **dilegently** to **diligently**.

7. Click Change to correct the double comma error.

8. Click Ignore Rule when Word detects **art work** as a compound word.

9. Click Change to change **severel** to **several**.

10. Click Change to change **libary** to **library**.

11. Click Change to change **deal** with **deals** to correct the subject-verb agreement error.

12. Click Change to change **its** to **it's** to correct the commonly confused word error.

13. Click Ignore All when Word detects **Paramore** as not being in the dictionary.

14. Click <u>C</u>hange to change **busineses** to **businesses**.

15. Click OK when Word informs you that it is done checking the spelling and grammar.

16. Right-click currently in the first paragraph in the **Classified Advertisements** section, choose S<u>y</u>nonyms, and choose presently.

17. Save the document, print it, and close it.

Challenge

Challenge exercises expand on or are somewhat related to skills presented in the lessons. Each exercise provides a brief narrative introduction followed by instructions in a numbered-step or bullet-list format that are not as detailed as those in the Skill Drill section.

1. Correcting Errors in a Letter

You work as an assistant for a real estate company. One of the agents wrote a letter to condominium owners who have expressed interest in selling their condominiums. The agent asked you to make necessary corrections.

1. Open **W-0405** and save it as **Condominium Sales Letter**.

2. Start typing the date. When you see the ScreenTip of today's date, press `↵Enter` to complete it.

3. Double-click the Spelling and Grammar Status button on the status bar to display the first spelling or grammatical error, and correct it. Continue doing this until you correct all errors.

4. Choose an appropriate synonym for **maximum** in the last paragraph.

5. Select the appropriate casing for the third paragraph. Manually capitalize any letters that should remain capitalized.

6. Select the four items below the third paragraph, press `Tab↹`, and italicize them.

7. Apply bold to the first paragraph.

8. Select Sincerely and capitalize it.

9. Delete the first sentence in the first paragraph.

10. Click the drop-down arrow to the right of the Undo button. Select Undo actions starting with bolding text to the latest action.

11. Save the document and print it.

2. Enhancing and Editing a Welcome Letter

You live in a townhouse condominium complex in Amarillo, Texas. You are also on the welcome committee that greets new residents as they buy a townhouse. You have prepared a welcome letter and need to enhance and correct it.

1. Open **W-0406** and save it as **Welcome New Owners**.

2. Start typing today's date at the top and press `↵Enter` when AutoComplete displays the full date.

3. Open **W-0407** and copy the Swimming Pool paragraph and the blank line below it. Paste the text at the beginning of the lawn care paragraph in the Welcome New Owners document. (The paragraphs should remain separate with one blank line between them.) Close W-0407.

4. Apply Arial Narrow, bold, and Green font color to the first occurrence of Madison Village. Use Format Painter to apply these formats to the other Madison Village occurrences.

5. Select Title Case for each of these headings: lawn care, snow removal, and workout room.

6. Select Lawn Care and bold and underline it. Use Format Painter to copy these formats to the other two headings.

7. Move the Snow Removal paragraph below the Workout Room paragraph.

8. Check the spacing between paragraphs and make necessary adjustments.

9. Delete the Snow Removal paragraph; then undo the action.

10. Use the Spelling and Grammar feature to correct all spelling and grammatical errors. You might need to manually change a to an in the Snow Removal paragraph if the Spelling and Grammar feature does not catch the error.

11. Save the document and print it.

3. Correcting Errors and Enhancing Minutes from a Meeting

You are the secretary for a condominium association. You need to enhance the minutes and correct errors in them.

1. Open **W-0408** and save it as **Association Minutes**.

2. Type the following sentence *exactly* as shown at the end of the Minutes paragraph and let AutoCorrect correct errors for you: **teh minutes were aproved as corected.**

3. Enhance the title by applying boldface, Arial, and Violet font color to it.

4. Enhance the headings by applying 11-point Arial, bold, and Violet font color. Use Format Painter to help copy the formats from one heading to the other headings.

5. Use the appropriate Change Case option on the headings as you did in the lesson; make sure they are consistently formatted. You need to manually lowercase prepositions, such as "to."

6. Move the Condominium Dues section above the Parking Regulations section. You should have one blank line between paragraphs.

7. Use the Spelling and Grammar feature to help you correct the errors. Ignore people's names. You might need to manually edit a spelling error if the Spelling and Grammar feature does not suggest the correct spelling.

8. Choose an appropriate synonym for the word additional in the Condominium Dues paragraph.

9. Save the document and print it.

Discovery Zone

Discovery Zone exercises help you gain advanced knowledge of project topics and/or application of skills. These exercises focus on enhancing your problem-solving skills. Numbered steps are not provided, but you are given hints, reminders, screen shots, and/or references to help you reach your goal for each exercise.

1. Creating AutoCorrect Entries

You really like how AutoCorrect can correct some errors as you type. After reading the Exam Note at the end of Lesson 5, "Using AutoCorrect," you want to create a couple of AutoCorrect entries. You want to be able to type an abbreviation and have Word automatically change it to full text.

Read the Exam Note in Lesson 5 again and use onscreen Help to learn how to create and use AutoCorrect entries. Then, create the following two entries:

- ccc for College Computer Club
- your initials for your full name

Be careful when creating the entry for your name. Some names may expand state abbreviations or simple words, which you don't want to do. For example, a person named **Ingrid Smith** should not use **is** as an AutoCorrect entry.

Create the document shown in Figure 4.21. Use your initials for Vice President and Activities Director instead of xyz. Word should automatically expand the abbreviations as you type them. Select the title and use the keyboard shortcut for changing the case to uppercase.

Make two more copies of the list, so you have three copies of the list on one piece of paper. Save the document as **Computer Club Officers** and print it.

Figure 4.21
Create the list of computer club officers.

Ccc Officers

The ccc officers for the 2001-02 academic year are listed below:

President   Vicki Kamoreaux

Vice President   xyz

Secretary   Tyler Jorgenson

Treasurer   Gloria Rokovitz

Activities Director xyz

2. Compiling an Information Sheet by Using the Office Clipboard

You have a master file of workshop descriptions that your training company provides to business people in the area. You need to prepare a custom workshop program for one of your clients. In a new document window, type the title in 16-point Arial font, bold, Small Caps effect. Triple-space after the title, select 12-point Bookman Old Style font, and type the paragraph shown in Figure 4.22. Save the document as **Workshops for Bradshaw**.

COMPUTER WORKSHOPS FOR BRADSHAW AND ASSOCIATES

We are pleased to provide the workshops you requested for individuals in your organization. According to our agreement, you may send up to 15 individuals to each session listed below. The workshops are scheduled for May 18 in your conference room. If you have additional questions, please call <u>Taralyn VanBuren at 555-7843</u>.

Figure 4.22
Create the introductory information.

Open **W-0409**. Refer to Lesson 2, "Moving and Copying Text," and onscreen Help to learn about the Office Clipboard and how to use it to collect and paste several items at once.

Display the Clipboard toolbar. Clear any existing items in the Clipboard and copy the paragraphs to the Clipboard in this order: Upgrade to Word 2000, Automating Your Work, and Collaborating on Documents. Paste the entire Clipboard contents below the introductory paragraph in Workshops for Bradshaw. Make sure you have one blank line between paragraphs and that the pasted paragraphs have the same font and font size as the introductory paragraph. Save the document and print it.

Change Bradshaw and Associates to **The Rowley Group**. Save the modified document as **Workshops for Rowley**. Delete the paragraphs about the workshops. Clear the Clipboard. Click **W-0409** on the taskbar to go back to this document, and copy these paragraphs in this order to the Clipboard: Basic Formatting with Word, Graphics Jamboree, Integrating Excel Data into Word, and Organizing Items in Tables. Paste the entire Clipboard contents at the bottom of The Rowley Group document. Adjust the font and font size, if necessary, to be consistent with the first paragraph. Save the document and print it. Close all open documents.

PinPoint Assessment

You have completed this project and its associated lessons, and have had an opportunity to assess your skills through the end-of-project questions and exercises. Now use the PinPoint software Evaluation Mode to further assess your comprehension of the specific exam activities you have just learned. You can also use the PinPoint Trainer Mode and the Show Me tutorials to practice these exam activities.

Formatting Documents

Key terms introduced in this project include

- alignment
- border
- bullet
- bulleted list
- double indent
- double-space

- first line indent
- hanging indent
- left indent
- line spacing
- margins
- paragraph spacing

- reverse text effect
- shading
- single-space
- spinners
- What's This?

Objectives	Required Activity for MOUS	Exam Level
➤ Set Margins	Set margins	Core
➤ Set Line and Paragraph Spacing	Set character, line, and paragraph spacing options	Core
➤ Select Text Alignment	Align text in paragraphs (Center, Left, Right, and Justified)	Core
➤ Indent Text	Use indentation options (Left, Right, First Line, and Hanging Indent)	Core
	Sort lists, paragraphs, and tables	Expert
➤ Insert Bulleted and Numbered Lists	Add bullets and numbering	Core
➤ Add Borders and Shading to Text	Apply borders and shading to paragraphs	Core
	Apply paragraph and section shading	Expert
	Create and modify page borders	Expert
➤ View Paragraph Formats Using the What's This? Feature		

Why Would I Do This?

So far, you've created documents using the default settings. Those settings are acceptable for some basic documents. However, you probably want to have control over the format settings used for different types of documents. In this project, you learn a lot of common formatting techniques that can make your documents look professional.

 ## Lesson 1: Setting Margins

A document's **margins** determine the amount of white space around the text. When you start a new document, the default top and bottom margins are 1 inch from the top and bottom edges of the page, and the default left and right margins are 1.25 inches from the left and right edges of the page. These margin settings are acceptable for many documents. However, you should change margins when doing so improves the appearance of your document. General or company reference manuals specify certain margin settings for particular documents.

In this lesson, you learn how to set different margin widths in a document.

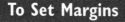
To Set Margins

1 **Open W-0501 and save it as Annual Report.**
The report is currently formatted by the default margins.

2 **Choose File, Page Setup.**
The Page Setup dialog box appears, as shown in Figure 5.1. This dialog box has four tabs. By default, the Margins tab is positioned in front of the other tabs. The Preview area displays a sample document so that you can preview changes before you apply them to the document.

Figure 5.1
The Page Setup dialog box contains the margin options.

Click the Margins tab

Margin settings

Preview area

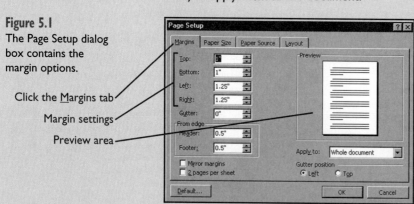

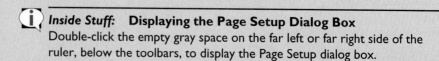

(i) *Inside Stuff:* **Displaying the Page Setup Dialog Box**
Double-click the empty gray space on the far left or far right side of the ruler, below the toolbars, to display the Page Setup dialog box.

3 **Click Margins if the margin options are not displayed.**

4 **Type 1.5 in the Top text box.**
Because the Top text box is selected when you first open the Page Setup dialog box, you simply type the margin setting you want; the number you type replaces the original setting.

Inside Stuff: **Setting Margins**
You don't have to type the inch mark (") when you set a margin. Word assumes you are setting margins in inches. You can press Tab to go from one margin text box to another.

Instead of typing a margin setting, you can click the up and down arrows, called *spinners*, at the right side of each margin text box to increase or decrease the margin setting.

5 **Press Tab.**
The **B**ottom text box is now active and ready for you to type a new setting for this margin.

6 **Type 1.25 and click OK.**
The 1.5-inch top and 1.25-inch bottom margins change the document, as shown in Figure 5.2. The margins are visible in Print Layout view.

Click and drag to set left margin

Gray indicates margin space

ScreenTip identifies margin

Print Layout View button

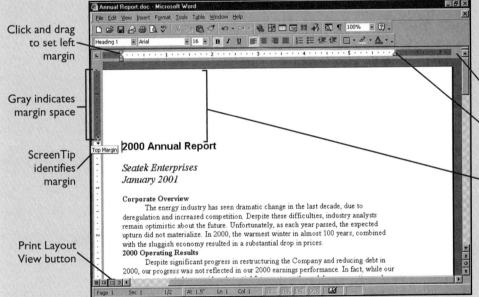

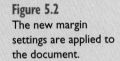
Figure 5.2
The new margin settings are applied to the document.

Double-click here to display Page Setup dialog box

Click and drag to set right margin

1.5-inch top margin

7 **Save the document and keep it onscreen to continue with the next lesson.**

 Inside Stuff: **Setting Margins on the Ruler**
When you display the document in Print Layout view, you can set the margins on the ruler. You can set the left and right margins on the horizontal ruler and the top and bottom margins on the vertical ruler.

As shown in Figure 5.2, the white area on the ruler displays the typing area between the margins and the dark gray area represents the margins. To change the margins, click and drag the margin markers on the ruler. You see a two-headed arrow as you click and drag the margin markers.

 Exam Note: **Setting Margins**
When you take the MOUS exam, read the instructions carefully. The test might require that you change the left and right margins. People who get in a hurry accidentally change the top and bottom margins instead, thus losing points on their test scores.

Lesson 2: Setting Line and Paragraph Spacing

Line spacing is the amount of vertical space from the bottom of one text line to the bottom of another. You use line spacing to control the amount of space between text lines in Word.

When you create a new document, Word **single-spaces** the document text, which means that text lines are close together with a small space to separate the lines. Although some documents, such as letters, should be single-spaced, other documents look better double-spaced. For example, a long report is typically easier to read if it is double-spaced.

Use the Line Spacing feature to change the amount of space between lines of text. If you click inside a paragraph and change the line spacing, only that paragraph is affected. To change line spacing for multiple paragraphs, you must select them first. In this lesson, you change the line spacing to double for most of the document.

To Change Line Spacing

1 **In the Annual Report document, position the insertion point at the beginning of the Corporate Overview heading.**
Before setting the line spacing, you must select the paragraphs that you want to format. In this document, you want to format all document text except the titles.

2 **Press** Ctrl+⇧Shift+End **to select text from the insertion point to the end of the document.**

3 **Choose Format, Paragraph.**
The Paragraph dialog box appears, as shown in Figure 5.3. Make sure the Indents and Spacing tab is displayed.

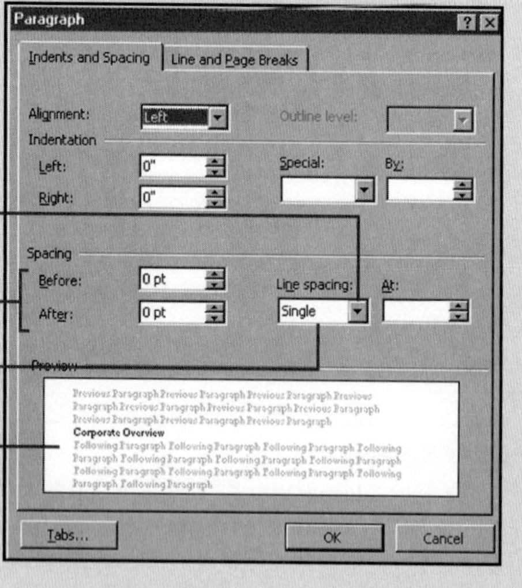

Figure 5.3
Set the line spacing in the Paragraph dialog box.

Click to display line spacing options

Paragraph spacing options

Current line spacing

Preview window shows paragraph formats

 Inside Stuff: **Displaying the Paragraph Dialog Box**
You can also display the Paragraph dialog box by right-clicking within a paragraph and choosing Paragraph from the shortcut menu.

4 **Click the Line spacing drop-down arrow.**
You see a list of line spacing options. Table 5.1 at the end of this lesson lists and describes the different line-spacing options.

5 **Choose Double from the list; then click OK.**

The Double option double-spaces the selected text. When you *double-space* text, Word leaves one blank line between lines within a paragraph. Each soft re-turn and each hard return in the selected area are doubled.

ⓘ *Inside Stuff:* **Line Spacing Keyboard Shortcuts**
Use the following keyboard shortcuts to change line spacing for selected text: Ctrl+①for single-spacing, Ctrl+②for double-spacing, and Ctrl+⑤for 1.5 spacing.

---

6 **Click in the document window to deselect the text.**

7 **Press Ctrl+Home to return the insertion point to the beginning of the document and deselect the text.**

8 **Click the Show/Hide ¶ button on the Standard toolbar.**

Your document should look like Figure 5.4.

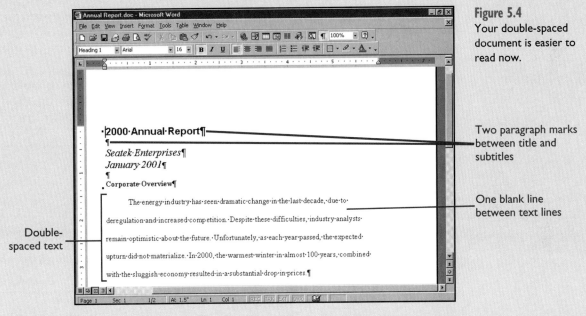

Figure 5.4
Your double-spaced document is easier to read now.

Two paragraph marks between title and subtitles

One blank line between text lines

Double-spaced text

9 **Save the document and keep it onscreen to continue with the next lesson.**

Table 5.1   Line-Spacing Options

Spacing Option	Description
Single	Places text line immediately beneath the previous line.
1.5 Lines	Leaves one and one-half the amount of space of single-spacing.
Double	Doubles the amount of space between lines.
At Least	Specifies the minimum amount of spacing between lines, based on what you type as the value. Word adjusts the spacing as needed to make room for larger fonts or graphics.
Exactly	Specifies an exact spacing measurement. Word cannot adjust the line spacing to make room for larger elements.
Multiple	Specifies how much Word can adjust the line spacing (up or down) by a particular percentage. For example, 1.25 increases the space by 25 percent; .75 decreases the space by 25 percent. You can also enter full values, such as **3** to triple-space text.

Exam Note: **Paragraph Spacing**

You might want to keep text single-spaced by adjusting the spacing between paragraphs (i.e., change the space created by paragraph marks when you press ⏎Enter). For example, you might want to have single-spaced paragraphs with the equivalent of double-spacing between paragraphs.

You can achieve this effect by setting the *paragraph spacing*, which controls the amount of space before or after the paragraph. Access the Paragraph dialog box and change the <u>B</u>efore or Aft<u>e</u>r spacing. For example, changing the After spacing to 12 points creates a double-space after the paragraph.

Lesson 3: Selecting Text Alignment

Alignment refers to the placement of text between the left and right margins. The default alignment is Align Left, which aligns text with the left margin. Table 5.2 lists and describes the four alignment options.

Table 5.2   Alignment Options

Button	Option	Keyboard Shortcut	Description
▤	Align Left	Ctrl+L	Aligns text on the left margin only. The left side appears smooth and the right side appears ragged.
▤	Center	Ctrl+E	Centers text between the left and right margins.
▤	Align Right	Ctrl+R	Aligns text at the right margin only. The right side appears smooth and the left side appears ragged.
▤	Justify	Ctrl+J	Aligns text along the left and right margins, so both sides appear smooth. Inserts extra space between words to justify the text.

In this lesson, you decide to justify the paragraphs to make them look more professional. The smooth edges on the left and right sides provide a cleaner look for the document. Also, you decide to center the title between the margins.

To Change the Alignment

1 **In the `Annual Report` document, choose Edit, Select All.**
Because you want to justify the text in the whole document, you must first select the entire document.

2 **Click the Justify button on the Formatting toolbar.**
When you justify text, Word inserts a small amount of space between the characters so that the text aligns at both the left and right margins. Notice, however, that you see one space symbol between words, even in justified text. Justified text creates a more formal appearance than left-aligned text.

3 **Click in the document window to deselect text.**
You now want to center the title between the margins.

4 **Position the insertion point within the 2000 Annual Report title.**

Exam Note: **Changing Alignment for a Paragraph**
When you want to change the alignment for a single paragraph, click within that paragraph (such as a title followed by a hard return) and click the alignment button. Only that paragraph's alignment changes.

---

5 **Click the Center button on the Formatting toolbar to center the title between the left and right margins.**

6 **Select the two-line italicized subtitles, and then click the Center button on the Formatting toolbar to center them.**

7 **Deselect the text.**
Figure 5.5 shows the centered titles and justified paragraphs.

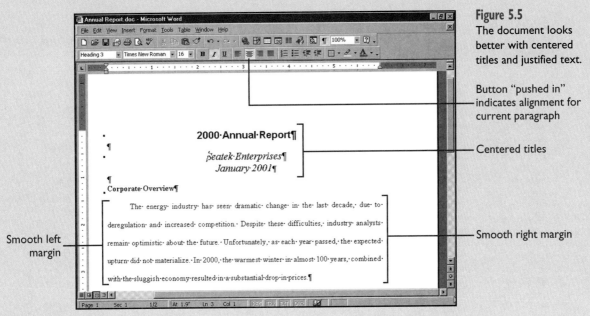

Figure 5.5
The document looks better with centered titles and justified text.

Button "pushed in" indicates alignment for current paragraph

Centered titles

Smooth right margin

Smooth left margin

8 **Save the document and keep it onscreen to continue with the next lesson.**

Inside Stuff: **Aligning New Text**
In the previous exercise, you changed the alignment for existing text by selecting it first. You can also select alignment before typing a document. For example, you can select Center alignment and then type a document title, press ⏎Enter two or three times, and then select Justify alignment. All new text from that point forward is automatically justified without selecting it first.

 ## Lesson 4: Indenting Text

By now, you know to press Tab⇄ to indent the first line of a paragraph. This format is typical in formal reports, letters, and legal documents. Sometimes, however, you might want to indent an entire paragraph from the left margin or indent a paragraph from both margins. To indent an entire paragraph, you set options in the Indentation section of the Paragraph dialog box.

As you review the annual report, you see a quotation from the Chief Financial Officer, Grant Keeper, at the top of the third page. Often, you see a paragraph of quoted text indented from both margins, which is called a **double indent**. In addition, the paragraph is single-spaced. You need to apply both formats to the quoted paragraph in your document.

To Indent Text

1 **In the** Annual Report **document, position the insertion point within the following quotation that is found on page 2.**
"2001 is the year we take the bull by the horns. Everyone at Seatek must pull together and work toward our mutual success. I'm counting on every employee to focus on our common goals to improve the financial status of the Company."

This quotation needs to be indented (see Figure 5.6). Because you are formatting a single paragraph, you don't need to select it first. Simply position the insertion point within the paragraph that you want to format.

Figure 5.6
Quotations that are full paragraphs should be double-indented and single-spaced.

Quotation

Quotation location

> 2001·is·the·year·we·take·the·bull·by·the·horns.·Everyone·at·Seatek·must·pull·
> together·and·work·toward·our·mutual·success.·I'm·counting·on·every·employee·to·focus·
> on·our·common·goals·to·improve·the·financial·status·of·the·Company.¶
>
> Goals·for·2001¶
>
> Fully·implementing·our·strategic·action·plan·will·take·several·years·to·complete·
> and·2001·will·be·no·less·critical·than·2000.·In·pursuing·the·second·year·of·our·plan,·we·

Page 2   Sec 1   2/2   At 6.4"   Ln 14   Col 1   REC TRK EXT OVR

2 **Choose F̲ormat, P̲aragraph to display the Paragraph dialog box.**
You need to change the settings in the Indentation section.

3 **In the Indentation section, click the L̲eft increment button until you see 0.5″ in the Left text box.**

4 **Click the R̲ight increment button until you see 0.5″ in the Right text box.**

 Exam Note: **Setting a Left Indent Only**
You might be required to set only a **left indent**, which indents a paragraph from the left margin only. If so, make sure you use the left indent only.

⑤ Click the Line spacing drop-down list arrow and choose Single to format the paragraph as single-spaced text.

⑥ Click the Spacing After increment button to 12 points.

⑦ Click OK.

The quotation paragraph is indented on both sides and is single-spaced. The document should now look like Figure 5.7.

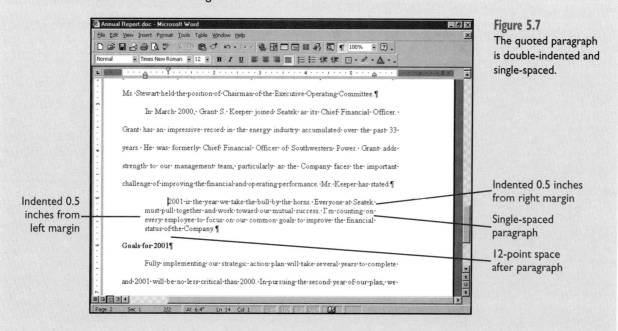

Figure 5.7
The quoted paragraph is double-indented and single-spaced.

You need only one hard return *before* the quoted text because double-spacing is in effect until the beginning of the quoted paragraph. You need either two hard returns or a 12-point spacing after the quoted paragraph because single-spacing is in effect until you reach the beginning of the following paragraph.

⑧ Click the Show/Hide ¶ button to turn off the formatting marks.

⑨ Save the document and keep it onscreen to continue with the next lesson.

You can indent or decrease indents from the Formatting toolbar. You can also set indents on the ruler. Figure 5.8 shows the toolbar and ruler indent items.

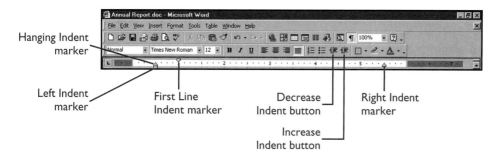

Figure 5.8
Use the toolbar or ruler to indent text

***Inside Stuff:* Indent and Decrease Indents**

Click the Decrease Indent button to decrease indented text a 1/2 inch (pull the text back to the left). The keyboard shortcut for decreasing indented text is Ctrl+⬆Shift+M.

Click the Increase Indent button to increase the indent by 1/2. The keyboard shortcut for indenting text from the left side is Ctrl+M.

You can also set indents on the ruler. Click and drag the Left Indent marker to set the amount of space to indent text from the left margin.

Click and drag the Right Indent marker to set the amount of space to indent from the right margin.

 ***Exam Note:* First Line Indent**

A *first line indent* automatically indents the first line of each paragraph. You can specify how much to indent the text. To set a first line indent, click the <u>S</u>pecial drop-down arrow in the Paragraph dialog box and choose First line. Set the amount of space for the indent, such as 0.5 inches, in the B<u>y</u> text box. Alternatively, you can click and drag the First Line Indent marker on the ruler.

 ***Exam Note:* Hanging Indent**

A **hanging indent** keeps the first line of a paragraph at the left margin and indents the rest of the lines of that paragraph from the left margin. Bibliographic entries are typically formatted with a hanging indent.

To create a hanging indent, display the Paragraph dialog box, click the <u>S</u>pecial drop-down arrow, and choose Hanging. In the B<u>y</u> text box, specify the amount of space you want to indent the second and subsequent lines within the paragraph.

 Alternatively, you can click and drag the Hanging Indent marker on the ruler to set a hanging indent for the current paragraph.

The keyboard shortcut for creating a hanging indent is Ctrl+T. If you accidentally indent a hanging indent too far, press Ctrl+⬆Shift+T to reduce the hanging indent.

  ***Exam Note:* Sorting Paragraphs**

You might need to sort paragraphs in a document. For example, if the bibliographic entries are not alphabetized by authors' last names, you need to sort them. Complete these steps:

1. Select the paragraphs you want to sort.

2. Choose T<u>a</u>ble, <u>S</u>ort.

3. Click OK.

 # Lesson 5: Inserting Bulleted and Numbered Lists

In word processing, a **bullet** is a special symbol used to attract attention to something on the page. People often use a **bulleted list** to itemize a series to make it stand out and be easy to read. For example, the objectives and terminology appear in bulleted lists on the first page of each project in this book. Use bulleted lists for listing items that can go in any order; use a numbered list for a list of items that must be in sequential order.

In this lesson, you create a bulleted list of goals for the coming year.

To Create a Bulleted List

1 **In the `Annual Report` document, click the Normal View button.**

2 **Press `Ctrl`+`End` to position the insertion point at the end of the document; then press `↑` once.**

This location is where you want to create a bulleted list that itemizes the company's goals for the upcoming year.

3 **Click the Bullets button on the Formatting toolbar.**

Word indents the bullet, which is a round dot, and then indents from the bullet for you to type text.

 If You Have Problems...

Word creates a bulleted list based on the last bullet type selected. If you see a different bullet shape, such as a check mark, choose Format, Bullets and Numbering. Click the sample bulleted list with round bullets and click OK.

---

4 **Type the following sentence and press `Enter` after it.**

`Pursue innovative marketing techniques.`

When you press `Enter`, Word inserts another bullet, followed by an indent (see Figure 5.9).

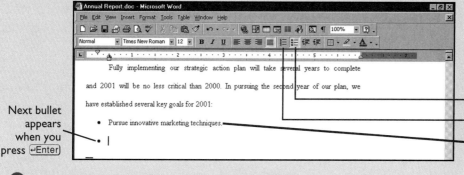

Next bullet appears when you press `Enter`

Figure 5.9
Using the Bullet feature helps you quickly create a bulleted list.

Creates bulleted list

Creates numbered list

First bullet and text

5 **Type the following paragraph and press `Enter`.**

`Increase usage of existing computer systems by hiring in-house training personnel and establishing a continuing schedule of training classes.`

6 **Type the following paragraph and press `Enter`.**

`Implement an electronic project management program in all business units and corporate headquarters.`

7 **Type the following paragraph and press `Enter`.**

`Reduce the travel and expenditures for the Company by closely evaluating each request for viability.`

Your document should look like Figure 5.10. You need to get rid of the bullet below the last item. Notice that the bulleted list might span two pages. Don't worry about this now; you'll learn how to keep text together in Project 6, "Formatting Documents with Multiple Sections."

continues ▶

To Create a Bulleted List (continued)

Figure 5.10
Your completed
bulleted list makes the
items stand out.

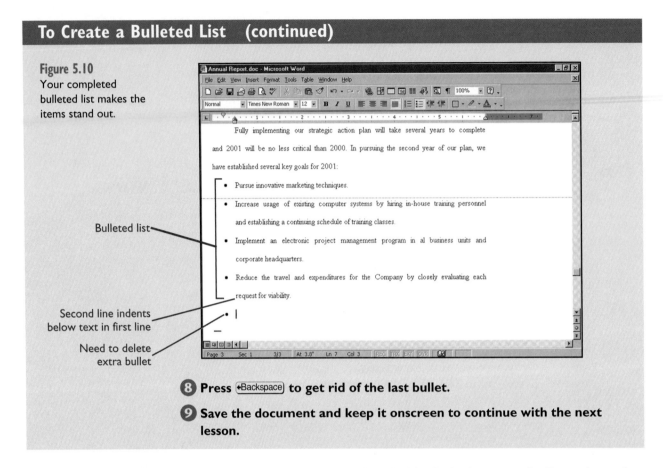

Bulleted list

Second line indents
below text in first line

Need to delete
extra bullet

8 Press +Backspace to get rid of the last bullet.

9 Save the document and keep it onscreen to continue with the next lesson.

You can create a numbered list by clicking the Numbering button on the Formatting toolbar. Word starts numbering the paragraphs as you type them. You can add or delete items within a bulleted or numbered list. When you do, the numbered list automatically renumbers itself.

You can also choose other bullet and number styles by choosing Format, Bullets and Numbering. When the Bullets and Numbering dialog box appears (see Figure 5.11), click the style you want and then click OK.

Figure 5.11
Select a different bullet
or numbering style
for your list.

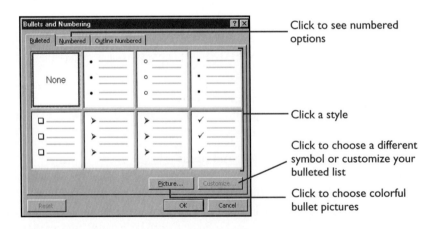

Click to see numbered options

Click a style

Click to choose a different symbol or customize your bulleted list

Click to choose colorful bullet pictures

You can customize your bulleted list or choose another symbol from hundreds of symbols in Word. To do this, click an existing bullet in the Bullets and Numbering dialog box and then click the Customize button. Figure 5.12 shows the Customize Bulleted List dialog box, in which you can set the indent for the bullet. By default, bullets are indented 0.25 inches from the left margin; however, you can place bullets at the left margin by changing the indent to 0 inches. You can also set the amount of space for indenting text after the bullet.

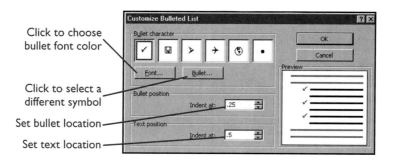

Figure 5.12
Customize your bulleted list.

Click to choose bullet font color

Click to select a different symbol

Set bullet location

Set text location

Click Font to select a font color for the bullets. If you want to choose a different symbol, click Bullet. When you click Bullet, you see the Symbols dialog box that you worked with in Lesson 8, "Inserting Symbols," of Project 3, "Working with Text." Choose a font, such as Wingdings, select the symbol you want, and click OK. Word uses that symbol to create your bulleted list.

Lesson 6: Adding Borders and Shading to Text

You can draw attention to an entire paragraph by putting a border around it. A **border** is a line that surrounds a paragraph or group of paragraphs. You can select the setting, line style, color, and width. To further enhance a border, you can also apply **shading**, a background color behind the text. Unlike a highlight color that places a color behind the text only, shading fills in the space between lines also.

You decide to add a border with shading for the double-indented paragraph.

To Add a Border and Shading

1 **In the `Annual Report` document, click inside the double-indented paragraph on page 2.**

2 **Choose F**o**rmat, B**o**rders and Shading.**
The Borders and Shading dialog box appears, as shown in Figure 5.13. This dialog box is where you select how you want the border to appear.

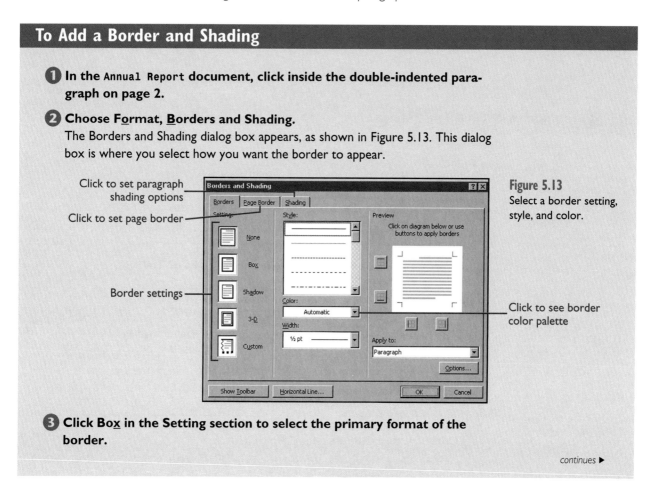

Click to set paragraph shading options

Click to set page border

Border settings

Figure 5.13
Select a border setting, style, and color.

Click to see border color palette

3 **Click Bo**x **in the Setting section to select the primary format of the border.**

continues ▶

To Add a Border and Shading   (continued)

4 **Click the <u>C</u>olor drop-down arrow.**
A color palette appears, so you can choose the color you want for the border (see Figure 5.14).

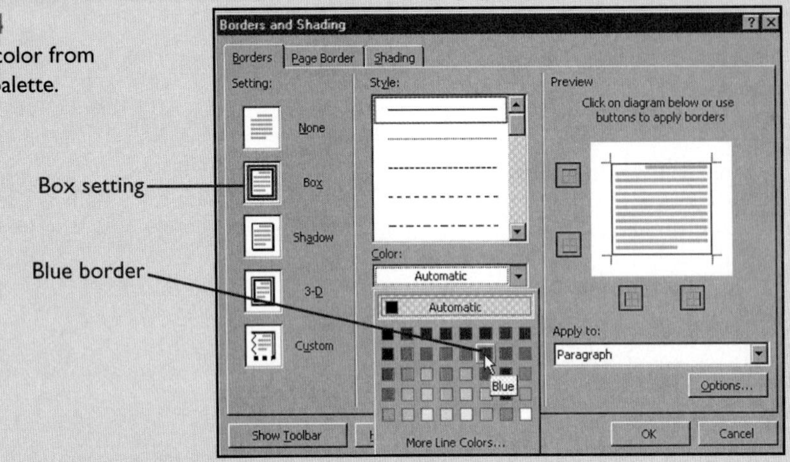

Figure 5.14
Choose a color from
the color palette.

Box setting

Blue border

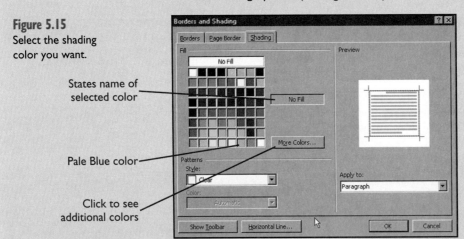

5 **Click Blue (the third color from the right on the second row).**
The color palette closes and you see the blue color displayed.

6 **Click the <u>S</u>hading tab at the top of the dialog box.**
You see shading options (see Figure 5.15).

Figure 5.15
Select the shading
color you want.

States name of
selected color

Pale Blue color

Click to see
additional colors

7 **Click Pale Blue, the third color from the right on the last row.**

ⓘ *Inside Stuff:*   **Choosing Border and Shading Colors**
Choose complementary colors for the border and shading. Typically, you should choose a darker border color and a lighter shading color. If the shading color is too dark, the text will be difficult to read.

You can create a *reverse text effect*, which is an appearance that uses a dark background with a lighter colored font. For example, choose Blue shading color and Yellow font color.

---

8 **Click OK and then deselect the text.**
Word applies a blue shadow border with Pale Blue shading around the selected paragraph, as shown in Figure 5.16.

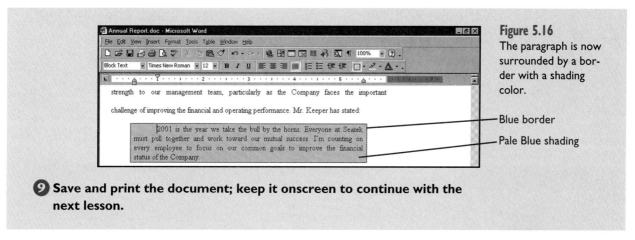

Figure 5.16
The paragraph is now surrounded by a border with a shading color.

Blue border

Pale Blue shading

 9 **Save and print the document; keep it onscreen to continue with the next lesson.**

Expert

Exam Note: **Choosing a Page Border**

You can also create a border for the entire page. Click the Page Border tab at the top of the Borders and Shading dialog box and choose the options you want (see Figure 5.17). Instead of using line page borders, you can select from a variety of creative page borders. Click the Art drop-down arrow to see fun image borders, such as hearts and stars.

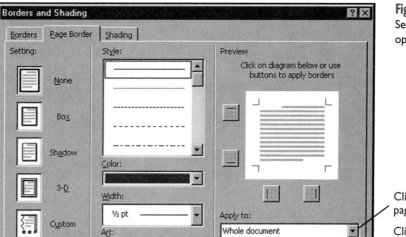

Figure 5.17
Select page border options.

Click to specify which pages will have border

Click to customize the page border

Click to select an art border

With page borders, you can choose the pages on which you want to place the border. Click the Apply to drop-down arrow and choose from Whole document, This section, This section—First page only, or This section—All except first page. If your document contains section breaks, which you'll learn about in Project 6, you can apply different page borders to each section.

In addition, click Options to customize the page border. For example, you can set the page border margins.

Lesson 7: Viewing Paragraph Formats Using the What's This? Feature

In Project 3, you clicked the Show/Hide ¶ button to see simple format codes, such as spaces, nonbreaking spaces, tabs, and paragraph marks. Although this feature is helpful, it doesn't inform you of other character or paragraph formatting. To display character and paragraph formatting information, use **What's This?**. When you activate What's This?, the mouse pointer displays a question mark by it. Click any text to see the character and paragraph formatting.

Using the What's This? Feature to See Formatting

1 **In the open Annual Report document, choose Help, What's This?**

> ⓘ **Inside Stuff: What's This? Keyboard Shortcut**
> Press ⇧Shift+F1 to activate or deactivate the What's This? feature.

The mouse pointer looks like an arrowhead with a question mark. You are ready to click the text to see its formatting.

2 **Click the paragraph that has the border.**

Figure 5.18 shows the formatting information about the text in which you clicked. The top part shows paragraph formatting, and the bottom half shows font formatting. In this text, the paragraph is formatted with a 0.5-inch left indent, first line, and right indent. The paragraph is justified with a 12-point spacing after. The font formatting is 12-point Times New Roman.

Figure 5.18
Use the What's This? feature to see paragraph formatting.

Information about options set in Paragraph dialog box

Other paragraph formats

Font settings

What's This? mouse pointer

Note on status bar

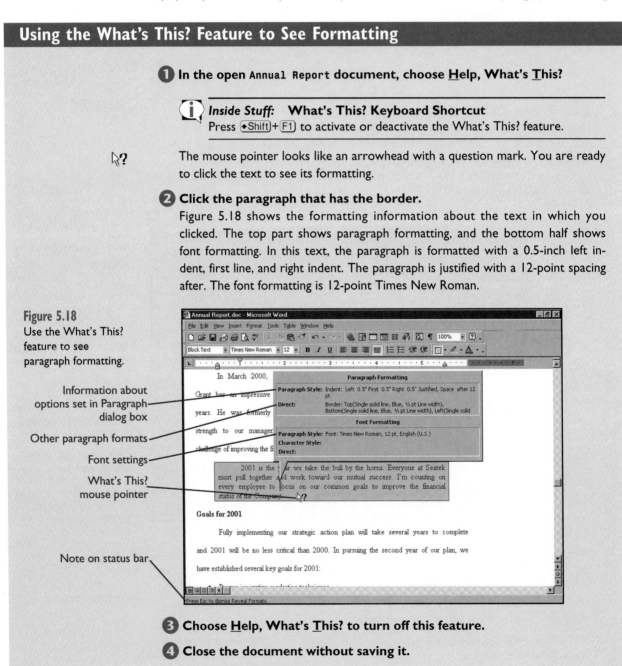

3 **Choose Help, What's This? to turn off this feature.**

4 **Close the document without saving it.**

Inside Stuff: Additional What's This? Uses
You can also use the What's This? feature to find out more information about a
toolbar button. After activating What's This?, click a toolbar button. Instead of activating the button's task, Word displays information about that button (see
Figure 5.19).

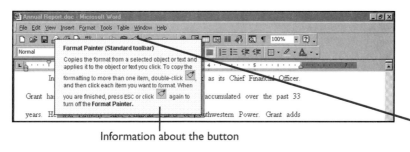

Information about the button

Figure 5.19
You can also use
What's This? to find
out information about
a toolbar button.

Click this button with
the What's This?
mouse pointer

Summary

In this project, you learned some exciting methods to enhance the appearance of your documents. You made the text easier to read by using double-spacing and paragraph spacing, inserting bulleted and numbered lists, and adding a border with shading. You also learned how
to set margins, change the alignment, and indent text. All of these formatting techniques dramatically improve the professionalism of the document you create.

Although these features are a great way to start improving your documents, Word offers a
lot more enhancements. Use the Help feature to learn more about formatting options, especially those found in the Page Setup, Paragraph, and Borders and Shading dialog boxes. There
are no limits to what you can do with these features!

Checking Concepts and Terms

True/False

For each of the following, check T or F to indicate whether the statement is true or false.

__T __F   1. The default left and right margins are 1
      inch each. [L1]

__T __F   2. To double-space existing text, you must
      first select the text. [L2]

__T __F   3. You see additional space symbols be-
      tween words when you select Justify
      alignment. [L3]

__T __F   4. To end a bulleted list, press Del to delete
      the extra bullet. [L5]

__T __F   5. When you create a border, it applies to
      the paragraph that contains the insertion
      point. [L6]

Multiple Choice

Circle the letter of the correct answer for each of the following.

1. What term refers to the way text lines up at the
left and right margins? [L3]

   a. line spacing

   b. margins

   c. justified text

   d. alignment

2. What feature keeps the first line of a paragraph at the left margin and indents the rest of the paragraph? [L4]

a. indent

b. double indent

c. hanging indent

d. double-spacing

3. What format is most appropriate for emphasizing a list of items in sequential order? [L5]

a. bulleted list

b. numbered list

c. border

d. highlight

4. All of the following are border options except _____. [L6]

a. style

b. color

c. setting

d. position

5. To see information about character and paragraph formatting, press which of the following and click in the text you want to know about? [L7]

a. ⬆Shift + F3

b. F1

c. ⬆Shift + F1

d. Ctrl + T

Screen ID

Label each element of the Word screen shown in Figure 5.20.

Figure 5.20

A. Bullets

B. Hanging Indent Marker

C. Increase Indent

D. Justify

E. What's This?

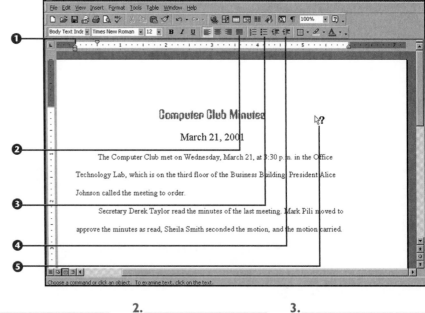

1._____   2._____   3._____

4._____   5._____

Skill Drill

Skill Drill exercises reinforce project skills. Each skill reinforced is the same, or nearly the same, as a skill presented in the project. Each exercise includes a brief narrative introduction, followed by detailed instructions in a step-by-step format.

1. Setting Margins and Text Alignment

You created a short report for a class and know that the report's appearance would be improved if the margins were changed. After checking a standard reference manual, you decide to set a 1.5-inch top margin and 1-inch left and right margins. In addition, you need to center the title and justify the rest of the document.

1. Open **W-0502** and save it as **Internet Report**.
2. Choose File, Page Setup.
3. Type **1.5** in the Top text box.
4. Press Tab twice, and type **1** in the Left text box.
5. Press Tab, and type **1** in the Right text box.
6. Click OK.
7. Choose Edit, Select All.
8. Click the Justify button on the Formatting toolbar.
9. Click in the document window to deselect text.
10. Position the insertion point within the title **Using the Internet** and click the Center button on the Standard toolbar.
11. Select the subtitle **Internet Protocol**; then click the Center button on the Formatting toolbar.
12. Repeat step 11 for these two subtitles: **Domain Names** and **Problems**.
13. Save the document and leave it onscreen to continue with the next exercise.

2. Changing Line Spacing and Double-Indenting Text

You decide to change the line spacing in your document to double-spacing to improve its readability. You decide to double-space all of the text except for the title. Then you need to double-indent and single-space a long quotation.

1. In the **Internet Report** document, position the insertion point at the beginning of the first paragraph.
2. Select the paragraphs you want to format by pressing Ctrl+Shift+End.
3. Press Ctrl+2 to double-space the selected text.
4. Position the insertion point before the text .edu on page 2.
5. Hold down Shift and click at the end of the .org paragraph to select the paragraphs about domain names.
6. Choose Format, Paragraph.
7. Click the drop-down arrow next to the Line spacing box.
8. Choose Single from the list.
9. Click the Spacing After increment button to 12 points and click OK.
10. Position the insertion point in the last paragraph of the document.
11. Choose Format, Paragraph to display the Paragraph dialog box.
12. In the Indentation section, click the Left increment button until you see 0.5" in the Left text box.
13. Click the Right increment button until you see 0.5" in the Right text box.
14. Click the Line spacing drop-down arrow and choose Single.
15. Click OK.
16. Save the document and keep it onscreen to continue with the next exercise.

3. Creating a Bulleted List, Applying Borders and Shading, and Using What's This?

The list of domain conventions is difficult to read. You determine that including a bullet before each convention will improve both the appearance and readability of the list.

1. With the **Internet Report** onscreen, position the insertion point before the text .edu on page 2.
2. Select the list of domains.
3. Click the Bullets button on the Formatting toolbar.
4. With the list of domains still selected, choose Format, Borders and Shading.
5. Click the Borders tab, if needed, and click the Shadow setting.
6. Click the Color drop-down arrow and click Orange.
7. Click the Shading tab.

8. Click Tan, the second color from the left on the last row.

9. Click OK.

10. Choose <u>H</u>elp, What's <u>T</u>his?

11. Click within the domain names you just formatted. Read the information to verify the paragraph formats.

12. Press ⎋Esc⎋ to turn off the What's This? feature.

13. Save the document, print it, and close it.

Challenge

Challenge exercises expand on or are somewhat related to skills presented in the lessons. Each exercise provides a brief narrative introduction followed by instructions in a numbered-step or bullet-list format that are not as detailed as those in the Skill Drill section.

1. Editing a Welcome Letter

You composed a letter to welcome new members to an organization for which you are president. You use several of the formatting techniques you learned in this project to improve the appearance of the letter.

1. Open **W-0503** and save it as **Welcome Letter**.

2. Change Ken's name to your name in the signature block.

3. Select the entire document, choose 12-point Bookman Old Style font, and Justify alignment.

4. Select the salutation through the last paragraph. Set a 12-point spacing after paragraph.

5. Select the Date, Time, and three Where lines. Set 1.5-inch left and right indents, 0 points spacing after, and a blue paragraph border. Click on the last Where line and set a 12-point spacing after paragraph.

6. Set 2-inch top and bottom margins. Use your judgment to set the left and right margins. Make sure the text looks balanced on the page.

7. Use the What's This? feature to check the formats of the indented text.

8. Save the document and print it.

2. Formatting an Invitation to a Halloween Party

You are having a Halloween party at your home and decide to create your own invitations. You create the text first and then want to improve it by changing fonts, changing text alignment, creating a fun bulleted list, and adding a page border.

1. Open **W-0504** and save it as **Halloween Party**.

2. Set a 2.5-inch top margin and 1.75-inch left and right margins.

3. Set the line spacing to double-spacing.

4. Make the first line of the invitation (**Hey! It's a Halloween Party!**) larger (at least 30-point) and bolder by using the Font dialog box. Because this is a fun invitation, try a different font, such as Chiller, Dauphin, Desdemona, or Cooperplate Gothic Bold. Apply your font choice to the last line of the invitation so both lines have the same appearance.

5. Pick another font for the body of the invitation. Select one that coordinates with the one you used for the title.

6. Select the When, Where, Why, and RSVP lines. Display the Bullets and Numbering dialog box. Customize the bulleted list by choosing a Halloween-type symbol, such as the spider or spider web, from the Webdings font. Select orange font for the bullets.

7. Center the first line of the invitation. Left-align the body of the invitation and the bulleted list. Center the last line of the invitation.

8. Select a Halloween theme page border from the Art drop-down list. Select an appropriate page border color.

9. Make adjustments in internal spacing (line or paragraph) and font sizes to spread the text out, so it's not all clustered together.

10. Save the document and print it.

3. Creating and Formatting a Reference Page (Bibliography)

You compiled a list of references about desktop publishing and proofreading. You need to type and format the reference list using the *Chicago Manual of Style*.

1. In a new document window, set a 2-inch top margin.

2. Type the title, **Reference List**, centered between the left and right margins. Triple-space after the title.

3. Create the following references using hanging indents and italicize the book titles. Keep the entire list single-spaced for now (no blank lines between reference entries).

    Studer, Linda I. and Marvin Jacobs. *Graphic Design for 21st Century Desktop Publishers*. North Olmsted: Words & Pictures Publishing, 1999.

    Beach, Mark, *Getting it Printed*, revised edition. Cincinnati: North Light Books, 1993.

    Smith, Debra A. and Helen R. Sutton. *Powerful Proofreading Skills: Tips, Techniques and Tactics*. Menlo Park: Crisp Publications, Inc., 1994.

    Anderson, Laura Killen. *Handbook for Proofreading*. Lincolnwood: NTC Business Books, 1996.

4. Insert nonbreaking spaces, if needed, to keep appropriate words together.

5. Select the reference four entries and set a 16-point spacing after paragraph.

6. Use the Sort command to sort the selected paragraphs in alphabetical order. (Refer to the Exam Note at the end of Lesson 4.)

7. Adjust spacing after the title, if needed to maintain the triple-space. (Check the paragraph spacing for the blank lines to make sure it is 0 points before the first reference entry.)

8. Select the title and apply Small Caps effect, and 14-point Arial Rounded MT Bold (or Arial with bold).

9. Save the document as **Reference List** and print it.

Discovery Zone

Discovery Zone exercises help you gain advanced knowledge of project topics and/or application of skills. These exercises focus on enhancing your problem-solving skills. Numbered steps are not provided, but you are given hints, reminders, screen shots, and/or references to help you reach your goal for each exercise.

1. Creating a Health Information Sheet

As part of an assignment in a health class, you create an information sheet on osteoarthritis to share with your classmates.

Open **W-0505** and save it as **Osteoarthritis**. Apply the formats as indicated in Figure 5.21. Use one of these sans serif fonts for the title and two headings: Arial Rounded MT Bold, AvantGarde with bold font style, or Kabel Dm BT. Use Bookman Old Style font for the paragraph and numbered items. When creating the page border, select the fourth style from the bottom of the Style list. Select other border options based on the figure.

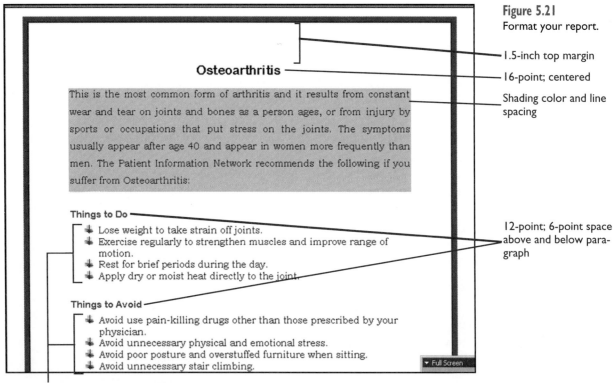

Figure 5.21
Format your report.

1.5-inch top margin

16-point; centered

Shading color and line spacing

12-point; 6-point space above and below paragraph

Picture bulleted list with adjusted special indent

2. Formatting a Course Description Document

Refer to Figure 5.22 to create a course description document. Create the customized bulleted list using the disk symbol found in the Wingdings font.

Specify two pages per sheet and then set 0.4-inch inside and outside margins, keeping the default left and right margins. Use Help and explore the Page Setup dialog box margin options. Duplicate (copy) the information from the top to the bottom half of the sheet of paper. Delete a blank third page if one appears. Save the document as **Course Descriptions** and print it.

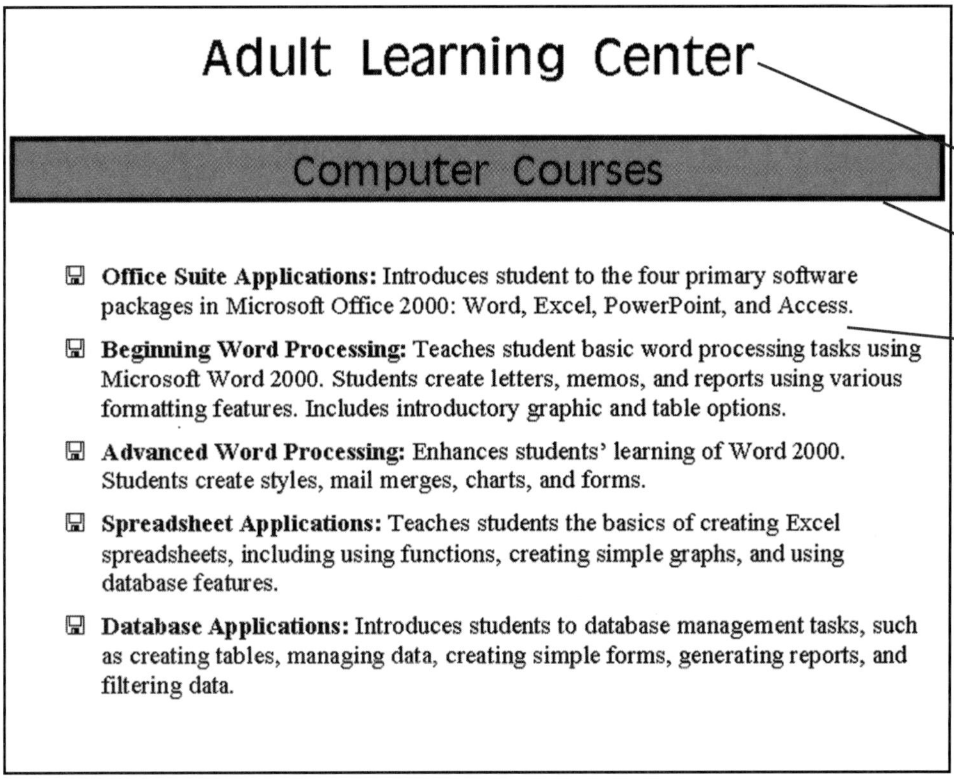

Figure 5.22
Create and format the course description sheet.

Adult Learning Center

Computer Courses

Sans serif font such as Kabel Md BT

Black, 3-pt. width border, shading, and sans serif font

6-point spacing after paragraph

- **Office Suite Applications:** Introduces student to the four primary software packages in Microsoft Office 2000: Word, Excel, PowerPoint, and Access.

- **Beginning Word Processing:** Teaches student basic word processing tasks using Microsoft Word 2000. Students create letters, memos, and reports using various formatting features. Includes introductory graphic and table options.

- **Advanced Word Processing:** Enhances students' learning of Word 2000. Students create styles, mail merges, charts, and forms.

- **Spreadsheet Applications:** Teaches students the basics of creating Excel spreadsheets, including using functions, creating simple graphs, and using database features.

- **Database Applications:** Introduces students to database management tasks, such as creating tables, managing data, creating simple forms, generating reports, and filtering data.

Edit your document by using course descriptions for computer courses at your school or training center. Look at course catalogs to create your descriptions. Save the revised document as **My College Course Descriptions**.

PinPoint Assessment

You have completed this project and its associated lessons, and have had an opportunity to assess your skills through the end-of-project questions and exercises. Now use the PinPoint software Evaluation Mode to further assess your comprehension of the specific exam activities you have just learned. You can also use the PinPoint Trainer Mode and the Show Me tutorials to practice these exam activities.

Project 6

Formatting Longer Documents

Key terms introduced in this project include

- Document Map
- endnote
- footer
- footnote
- footnote reference mark
- footnote text
- hard page break
- header
- orphan
- section break
- separator line
- soft page break
- suppress
- vertical alignment
- widow

Objectives	Required Activity for MOUS	Exam Level
➤ Insert Section and Page Breaks	Insert page breaks	Core
➤ Center Text Vertically on a Page	Align text vertically	Core
	Create sections with formatting that differs from other sections	Core
➤ Insert Page Numbers	Insert page numbers	Core
	Create and modify page numbers	Core
	Format first page differently than subsequent pages	Expert
➤ Prevent Text from Separating Across Page Breaks	Use text flow options (Widows/Orphans options and keeping lines together)	Expert
➤ Create Footnotes and Endnotes	Create or revise footnotes and endnotes	Expert
	Create and edit styles	Expert
➤ Create Headers and Footers	Create and modify headers and footers	Core
➤ Create Sectional Headers and Footers	Create sections with formatting that differs from other sections	Core
	Format first page differently than subsequent pages	Expert
➤ Navigate Through a Document	Navigate through a document	Core

Why Would I Do This?

In the last project, you learned some important formatting elements, such as margins, alignment, and line spacing. Word offers additional format features that improve the appearance of your documents.

In this project, you learn how to insert section and page breaks, center text vertically on a title page, and insert page numbers. In addition, you create footnotes, endnotes, headers, and footers. Finally, you keep bulleted text from spanning page breaks and use navigation features to get around a long document.

 ## Lesson 1: Inserting Section and Page Breaks

When you set some formats, such as margins, Word applies those formats to the *entire* document. However, you might need to apply different formats throughout the document. Therefore, you need to insert **section breaks**, which are markers that divide the document into sections that you can format separately.

In this lesson, you insert a section break so that you can format the title page differently from the rest of the document.

To Insert a Section Break

❶ Open W-0601 and save it as Desktop Publishing.
The first page contains information for a title page and regular document text. You need to start the document text on a new page. More importantly, you need to be able to format the title page differently from the document text.

❷ Position the insertion point to the left of Design Guidelines on Line 24.
You want the document title to start a new section.

❸ Choose Insert, Break.
The Break dialog box contains options for inserting page and section breaks (see Figure 6.1). Table 6.1 at the end of this exercise describes the options in the Break dialog box.

Figure 6.1
Use the Break dialog box to insert page and section breaks.

Page break option

Section break options

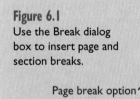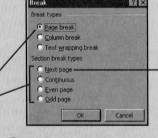

Inserts section break to start a new page

❹ Click the Next page option and click OK.
Figure 6.2 shows the section break in Normal view. You see a double dotted line and **Section Break (Next Page)**. The title page is Section 1, and the document text is Section 2. Now you can format each section separately.

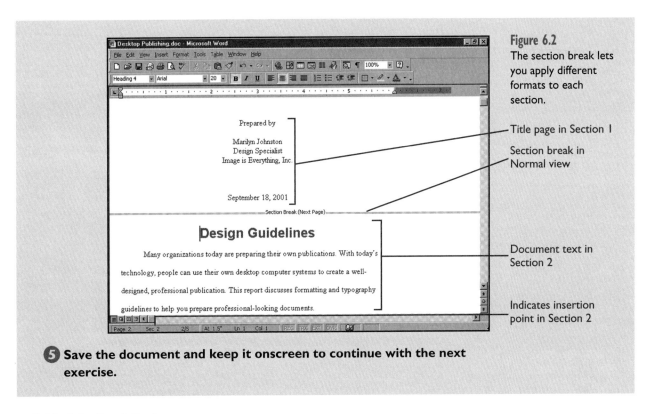

Figure 6.2
The section break lets you apply different formats to each section.

— Title page in Section 1

Section break in Normal view

Document text in Section 2

Indicates insertion point in Section 2

 Save the document and keep it onscreen to continue with the next exercise.

Table 6.1   Break Options

Option	Description
<u>P</u>age break	Inserts a hard page break (starts a new page) within the same section.
<u>C</u>olumn break	Starts a new column within columnar text.
Text <u>w</u>rapping break	Stops entering text on the current line and continues text on the next blank line. Useful for positioning text below a picture or table.
<u>N</u>ext page	Inserts a section break by starting a new page. Allows you to apply different formats to different sections.
Con<u>t</u>inuous	Starts a new section on the *same* page. Useful for creating different formats, such as margins, on the same page of a newsletter.
<u>E</u>ven page	Starts a new section by forcing text to appear on the next available even-numbered page. If the next page is an odd-numbered page, Word leaves that page blank.
<u>O</u>dd page	Starts a new section by forcing text to appear on the next available odd-numbered page. Useful for making sure all new sections or chapters start on the right-hand side of a double-sided document.

Exam Note: **Section Break Types**
When you take the MOUS exam, be sure you read the question carefully to see which type of section break is requested. You might be instructed to insert a *continuous* section break instead of starting a new page section break.

You might want to use the same formatting but start text on a new page instead of waiting for Word to start a new page for you. The page breaks inserted by Word are called **soft page breaks** because they change if you add or delete text. If you want to start a new page within the same section, insert a **hard page break**.

Your current document contains data for a bibliography page. Because you want it to have the same formatting as the regular document text, you need to insert a hard page break instead of a section break.

To Insert a Hard Page Break

1 **In the Desktop Publishing document, press Ctrl+End to position the insertion point at the end of the document; then position the insertion point at the beginning of the line that contains the heading Bibliography.**
You want to start a new page for the bibliography.

2 **Choose Insert, Break.**

3 **Make sure the Page break option is selected and then click OK.**
The bibliography starts on a new page (see Figure 6.3). Notice that it is still in Section 2 instead of starting a new section. In Normal view, you see a dotted line and Page Break to indicate a hard page break.

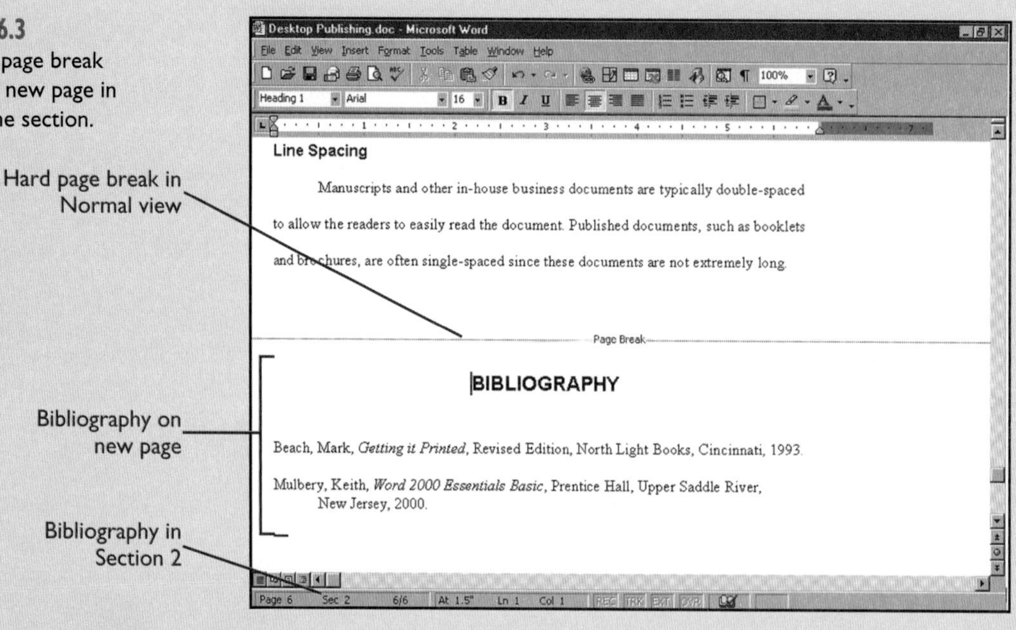

Figure 6.3
A hard page break starts a new page in the same section.

Hard page break in Normal view

Bibliography on new page

Bibliography in Section 2

4 **Click the Print Layout View button and scroll up to see the last paragraph on the previous page.**
In Print Layout view, you don't see any special notes that indicate a section break or a hard page break. However, if you click the Show/Hide ¶ button, you do see the note Section Break (Next Page).

5 **Save the document and keep it onscreen to continue with the next lesson.**

ⓘ *Inside Stuff:*   **Hard Page Break Keyboard Shortcut**
You can insert a hard page break quickly by pressing Ctrl+↵Enter.

Lesson 2: Centering Text Vertically on a Page

Typically, the first page in a document or research paper is the title page. The standard format is to center it horizontally and vertically. In Project 5, "Formatting Documents," you learned to use Center alignment to center text horizontally. In this lesson, you learn to center text vertically on a page. You use the **_vertical alignment_** option in the Page Setup dialog box to position text between the top and bottom edges of a page.

In this lesson, you choose center vertical alignment to center the title page text between the top and bottom margins.

To Center Text Vertically on a Page

1 **In the open** Desktop Publishing **document, press** Ctrl+Home **to position the insertion point at the beginning of the document.**

2 **Choose** **F**ile, Page Set**u**p.
The Page Setup dialog box appears with the margin options displayed. You need to display the layout options.

3 **Click the** **L**ayout tab.
The layout options appear, as shown in Figure 6.4. The default vertical alignment places text at the top of the page.

Click to choose the text affected by formats

Current vertical alignment

Click to see alignment options

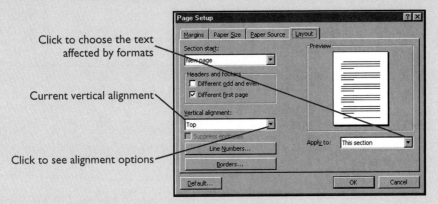

Figure 6.4
The Layout tab contains the vertical alignment option.

4 **Click the** **V**ertical alignment drop-down arrow.

5 **Choose Center.**
The **V**ertical alignment option now displays Center. The App**l**y to option displays This section.

 If You Have Problems...
If the App**l**y to options are only Whole document and This point forward, you need to make sure you have a _section break_—not a hard page break—after the title page. Using a hard page break does not let you vertically center the title page only; Word would vertically center the entire document.

6 **Click OK.**

continues ▶

To Center Text Vertically on a Page   (continued)

100% ▾

7 **Click the Zoom drop-down arrow on the Standard toolbar and choose Two Pages.**
The title page is now centered vertically on the page, as shown in Figure 6.5. In this document, the remaining pages use top vertical alignment because they are in a different section.

Figure 6.5
The title page is centered vertically.

Starts in Section 2

Text centered vertically on page

Insertion point on Page 1 in Section 1

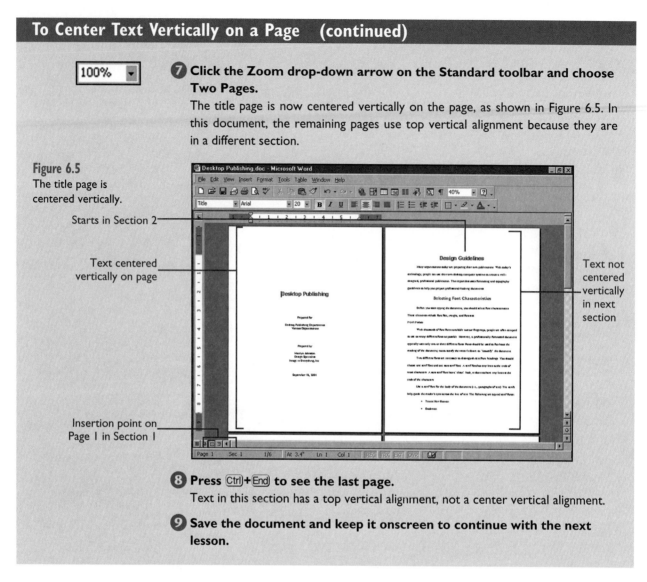

Text not centered vertically in next section

8 **Press** Ctrl+End **to see the last page.**
Text in this section has a top vertical alignment, not a center vertical alignment.

9 **Save the document and keep it onscreen to continue with the next lesson.**

When you select options in the Page Setup dialog box, you specify the amount of text to which you wish to apply the formats. Table 6.2 lists and describes the Apply to options.

Table 6.2   Page Setup Apply to Options

Option	Description
Whole Document	Applies formats to the entire document, regardless of where the insertion point is when you access the dialog box.
This Point Forward	Applies formats from the current page to the end of the document.
This Section	Applies formats to the current section only; other sections retain their formats.
Selected Text	Applies formats to only the text you selected prior to accessing the Page Setup dialog box.

✍ Exam Note: Page Setup Options for Different Sections
You might be instructed to specify different page setup options for different sections of a document. Make sure you click in the specified section before accessing the Page Setup dialog box. Then, ensure that the Apply to option is This section.

Lesson 3: Inserting Page Numbers

Page numbers are essential in long documents. They serve as a convenient reference point for the writer and the reader. Without page numbers in a long document, you would have difficulty trying to find text on a particular page or trying to tell someone else where to locate a particular passage in the document.

Use the Page Numbers feature to automatically insert page numbers throughout your document. You select the page-number position (top or bottom of the page) and the alignment (left, center, right, inside, or outside). Word not only inserts page numbers but also updates the numbers when you add or delete pages. In this lesson, you insert page numbers in your report.

To Insert Page Numbers

① In the `Desktop Publishing` document, position the insertion point at the top of the document and make sure you are displaying the document in Print Layout View with the Two Pages zoom option.

While selecting page-numbering options, you need to instruct Word not to number the title page.

 Inside Stuff: **Using Page Numbers in Sections**

Although your document is divided into two sections, Word applies page numbering to the entire document, continuing page numbers from one section to the next. To prevent a page number from appearing on the title page, you need to position the insertion point on that page before you access the Page Numbers feature.

② Choose Insert, Page Numbers.

The Page Numbers dialog box appears so you can choose the position and alignment of the page numbers (see Figure 6.6).

Click to change alignment

Deselect to suppress page number on first page

Click to set additional options

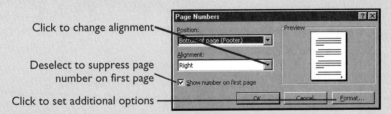

Figure 6.6
Choose the page number position and alignment.

③ Click the Alignment drop-down arrow and choose Center.

This option centers the page numbers between the left and right margins, similar to the Center alignment you used in Project 5.

④ Click the `Show number on first page` check box to deselect this option.

By deselecting `Show number on first page`, you *suppress*, or "hide," the page number. The page is still counted as Page 1, but the page number does not appear.

 Inside Stuff: **First Page In Each Section**

The page-numbering feature applies throughout the document. When you deselect `Show number on the first page`, Word suppresses the page number on the first page of *every* section.

continues ▶

To Insert Page Numbers   (continued)

⑤ Click OK.

Word does not show a page number on the title page or the next page because each page is the first page in its respective section (see Figure 6.7).

Figure 6.7
Page numbers don't appear on the first page in each section.

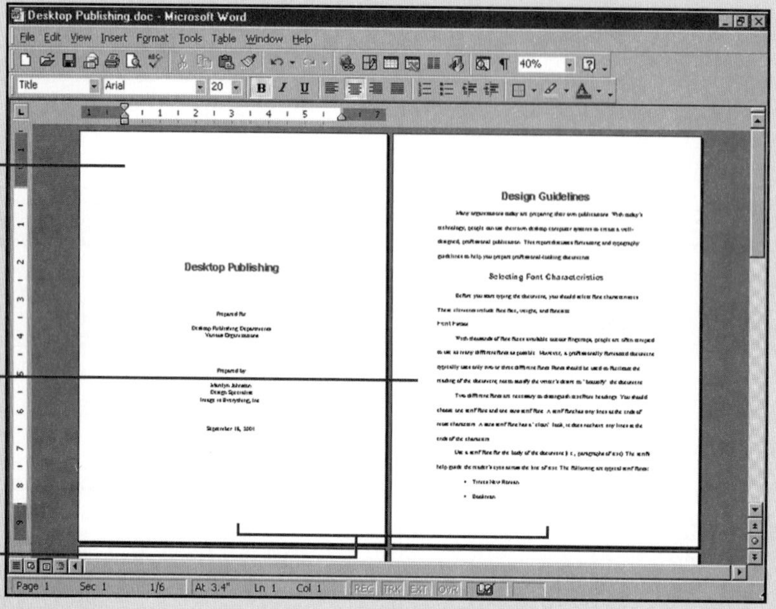

First page in Section 1 ——

First page in Section 2 ——

No page number displayed

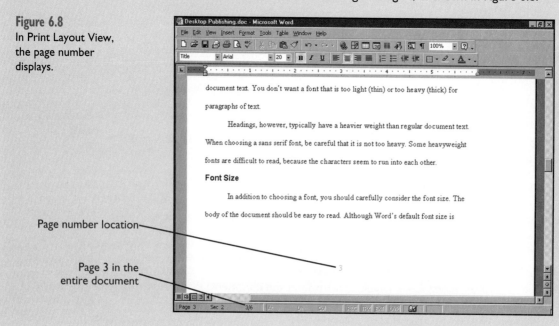

Word automatically switches to the Print Layout view, so you can see page numbers. Normal view does not display page numbers.

⑥ Click the Zoom drop-down arrow and choose 100%.

⑦ Scroll to the bottom of page 3.

In Print Layout view, you see the page number at the bottom of the third page. It is centered between the left and right margins, as shown in Figure 6.8.

Figure 6.8
In Print Layout View, the page number displays.

Page number location ——

Page 3 in the entire document ——

The page numbers actually appear, starting with the second page within Section 2. Word, however, counts the title page as page 1 and the first page of Section 2 as page 2. Typically, you should count the first page of the body of the report as page 1. Therefore, in the next exercise, you position the insertion point at the beginning of Section 2 and restart the section page numbers at 1 again.

To Restart Page Numbers in Section 2

1 **Position the insertion point at the top of page 2, the first page of the body of the document.**

The first page of the body of the report—not the title page—should count as Page 1. Therefore, you must change the page number value back to 1 on this page.

2 **Choose Insert, Page Numbers.**

3 **Make sure the Alignment is Center and that Show number on first page is deselected.**

4 **Click Format to display additional options.**

The Page Number Format dialog box appears (see Figure 6.9). You need to start the page numbering back to 1 for this section.

Continues numbering pages from previous section

Click to start page numbering with 1

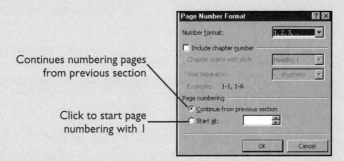

Figure 6.9
Change the page numbering back to 1 for Section 2.

5 **Click the Start at option button and type 1.**

6 **Click OK; then click OK in the Page Numbers dialog box.**

The first page in Section 2 is counted as page 1 within its section (see Figure 6.10).

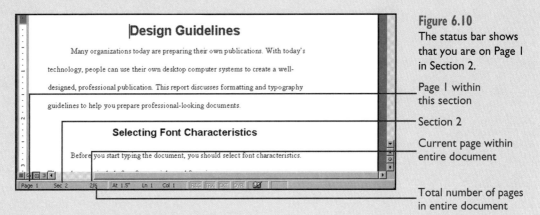

Figure 6.10
The status bar shows that you are on Page 1 in Section 2.

Page 1 within this section

Section 2

Current page within entire document

Total number of pages in entire document

7 **Scroll to the bottom of Page 2 within Section 2.**

The page number is page 2 in Section 2. It is the third page in the entire document (see Figure 6.11).

continues ▶

To Restart Page Numbers in Section 2 (continued)

Figure 6.11
The page number is now Page 2.

Page number

Page 3 in entire document

Section 2

Page 2

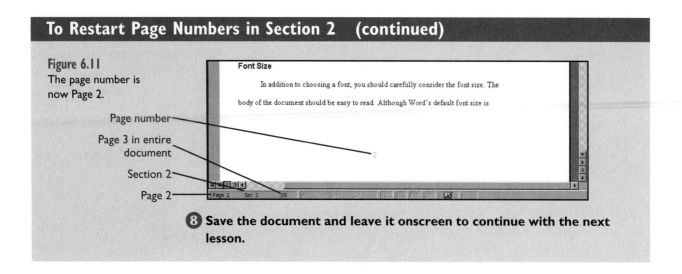

Font Size

In addition to choosing a font, you should carefully consider the font size. The body of the document should be easy to read. Although Word's default font size is

⑧ **Save the document and leave it onscreen to continue with the next lesson.**

Core ✍ *Exam Note:* **Modifying Page Numbering**

You might decide to change one or more page-numbering options. For example, you might want to choose a different page number alignment, start at a different page number, or use a different numbering format such as lowercase Roman numerals.

To change page numbering, position the insertion point at the beginning of the section you want to change and access the Page Numbers dialog box. Make the changes you want and click OK.

You can apply other formats, such as font and font color, to a page number by editing it within its header or footer. Lesson 6, "Creating Headers and Footers," and Lesson 7, "Creating Sectional Headers and Footers," discuss headers and footers.

Expert # Lesson 4: Preventing Text from Separating Across Page Breaks

To achieve a professional appearance, certain types of text should not separate between pages. For example, your document should not contain widows or orphans. A **widow** is the last line of a paragraph that appears by itself at the top of a page. An **orphan** is the first line of a paragraph that appears by itself at the bottom of a page. However, you don't have to worry about widows and orphans, because Word's Widow/Orphan Control feature is a default option. Word also typically keeps a heading from being the last line on a page with the following paragraph on the next page.

However, Word lets other text separate between pages. For example, it does not keep bulleted lists or tabulated text together on a page. Your document has a bulleted list on pages 1 and 2 in Section 2.

ⓘ *Inside Stuff:* **Widow and Orphan Control**

Word can identify widows and orphans because lines within a paragraph end in a soft return. The Widow/Orphan Control can't keep bulleted list items together, however, because each line ends with a hard return instead of a soft return.

In this lesson, you select the bulleted list and use the Keep with ne<u>x</u>t option in the Paragraph dialog box.

To Keep Text from Separating Across Page Breaks

1 In the `Desktop Publishing` document, make sure the document is displayed in **Normal** view.

2 Scroll through the document so you see the bottom of page 1 and the top of page 2 in Section 2.

You see two bulleted items at the bottom of page 1 and the remaining bulleted list on the next page.

3 Click and drag to select the entire bulleted list, which spans both pages.

You need to select the text that you want to keep from separating across pages (see Figure 6.12).

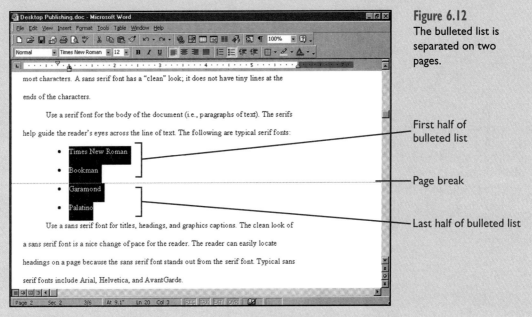

Figure 6.12
The bulleted list is separated on two pages.

First half of bulleted list

Page break

Last half of bulleted list

4 Choose F**o**rmat, **P**aragraph to display the Paragraph dialog box.

5 Click the Line and **P**age Breaks tab.

The Widow/Orphan Control option is selected. Although it keeps at least two lines of a paragraph together on each page, it does not keep lines together that end with a hard return. You need to select the Keep with ne**x**t option (see Figure 6.13).

continues ▶

To Keep Text from Separating Across Page Breaks   (continued)

Figure 6.13
Select options to keep
text together between
breaks.

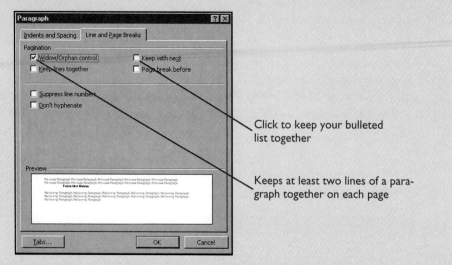

Click to keep your bulleted
list together

Keeps at least two lines of a paragraph together on each page

6 **Click the Keep with next check box and then click OK.**
Word now keeps the entire bulleted list together, as shown in Figure 6.14.
Because the bulleted list can't fit at the bottom of page 1, it appears at the top of
page 2.

Figure 6.14
The bulleted list stays
together on the same
page now.

Page break shifts up

Entire bulleted list on
same page

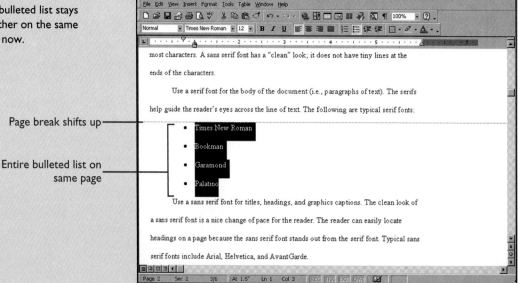

X **If You Have Problems...**
If the entire bulleted list does not appear at the top of page 2, switch to
the Print Layout view and then back to Normal view.

7 **Deselect the bulleted list.**

8 **Save the document and keep it onscreen to continue with the next
lesson.**

Inside Stuff: Keep Entire Paragraph Together
If you don't want a paragraph to span between pages, click inside the paragraph and display the Paragraph dialog box. Click the Keep lines together option and then click OK.

Lesson 5: Creating Footnotes and Endnotes

Footnotes are notes that appear at the bottom of a page and **endnotes** are notes that appear at the end of a document. You use footnotes or endnotes to give credit to the sources you used for information you quote or cite in your document. You can also use footnotes or endnotes to provide supplemental information about a topic that is too distracting in the body of the document.

Word numbers the footnotes and reserves space at the bottom of the same page for the footnote text. In addition, when you add or delete footnotes or endnotes, Word automatically renumbers the remaining notes for you. In this lesson, you create two footnotes and then edit one of them.

 Inside Stuff: Footnote Keyboard Shortcut
The keyboard shortcut for creating a footnote is Alt+Ctrl+F.

To Create Footnotes

1 In the Desktop Publishing **document, position the insertion point at the end of the first full paragraph on page 2 in Section 2.**
The insertion point should be after the period ending with Avant Garde.

2 Choose Insert, Footnote.
The Footnote and Endnote dialog box appears (see Figure 6.15).

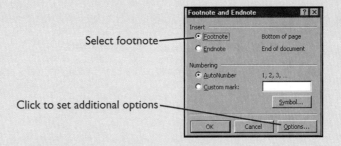

Figure 6.15
Specify whether you want to create footnotes or endnotes.

 Exam Note: Creating Endnotes
If you are instructed to create an endnote, click the Endnote option.

3 Make sure the Footnote option is selected and click OK.
Word inserts a superscript 1 in the document and displays the footnote window at the bottom of the screen.

 Inside Stuff: Customizing Footnotes or Endnotes
Creating notes in Normal view gives you a separate window for the notes. You can customize some options by clicking the drop-down arrow and choosing the item you want to customize.

continues ▶

To Create Footnotes (continued)

4 **Type the following footnote text, italicizing the book title and inserting a nonbreaking space in p. 101.**

Keith Mulbery, *Word 2000 Essentials Basic*, Prentice Hall, Upper Saddle River, New Jersey, 2000, p. 101.

To separate this footnote from the next one you create, you need to press ⏎Enter.

5 **Press ⏎Enter to leave one blank line between footnotes.**

Your footnote should look like the one shown in Figure 6.16.

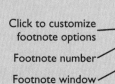

Figure 6.16
The footnote provides a reference to where you obtained the information.

Click to customize footnote options

Footnote number

Footnote window

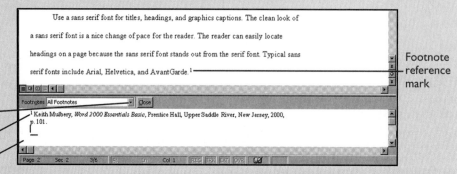

Use a sans serif font for titles, headings, and graphics captions. The clean look of a sans serif font is a nice change of pace for the reader. The reader can easily locate headings on a page because the sans serif font stands out from the serif font. Typical sans serif fonts include Arial, Helvetica, and AvantGarde.[1]

Footnote reference mark

Footnotes | All Footnotes | Close

[1] Keith Mulbery, *Word 2000 Essentials Basic*, Prentice Hall, Upper Saddle River, New Jersey, 2000, p. 101.

Page 2 Sec 2 3/6 At Ln Col 1 REC TRK EXT OVR

6 **Click Close above the footer to close the footer window.**

A footnote consists of two parts: the footnote reference mark and the corresponding footnote. The **footnote reference mark** is a superscript number that appears in the body of the text. The **footnote text**, which contains the actual footnote information, appears at the bottom of the page. You see a **separator line**—a horizontal line that separates the body of the document from the footnotes.

7 **Position the insertion point at the end of the paragraph immediately before the Weight heading on page 2.**

8 **Choose Insert, Footnote and click OK.**

9 **Type the following footnote text, making sure you italicize the book title.**

Mark Beach, *Getting it Printed*, Revised Edition, North Light Books, Cincinnati, 1993, p. 16.

You have one blank line between the footnotes because you pressed ⏎Enter in step 5 to separate the footnotes (see Figure 6.17).

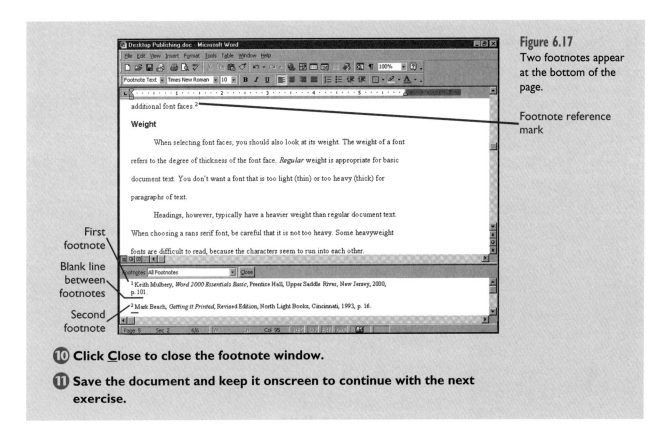

Figure 6.17
Two footnotes appear at the bottom of the page.

Footnote reference mark

First footnote

Blank line between footnotes

Second footnote

⑩ Click Close to close the footnote window.

⑪ Save the document and keep it onscreen to continue with the next exercise.

 Inside Stuff: **Editing Notes**
Although footnote reference marks appear in Normal view, the footnote text does not. However, you can edit footnote text by double-clicking the footnote reference mark.

 Inside Stuff: **Moving, Copying, and Deleting Notes**
You can cut and paste the footnote reference mark if you created the footnote in the wrong place. You can also copy and paste a footnote reference mark if you cite the same source later. Doing so saves you from re-creating the footnote text. Finally, you can delete the note reference marker to delete the note text itself. Remember to select the reference mark before using cut, copy, or delete.

The default font size for notes is 10-point. Also, the first line of the footnote is not indented as it should be, according to some reference manuals. Therefore, you need to change the font size and set a first-line indent for your footnotes to look better. In the next exercise, you change the footnote style.

Changing the Footnote Style

① In the Desktop Publishing document, choose Format, Style.
Figure 6.18 shows the Styles dialog box. You learn more about styles in Project 14, "Working with Styles and Templates." For now, you are modifying the format for your footnotes.

continues ▶

Changing the Footnote Style (continued)

Figure 6.18
Display the Styles
dialog box to change
the footnote style.

Displays list of styles ⎯

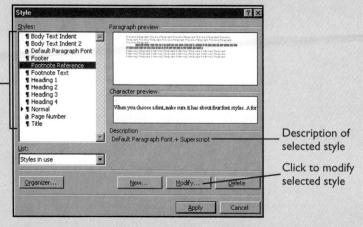

Description of
selected style

Click to modify
selected style

2 Click Footnote Text in the <u>S</u>tyles list.
This is the style you need to modify to change the font size and set a first-line indent for the footnote text.

3 Click <u>M</u>odify.
The Modify Style dialog box displays the style name and description of the footnote text style (see Figure 6.19).

Figure 6.19
The Modify Style
dialog box lets you
change the style
settings.

Click to change
style's formats

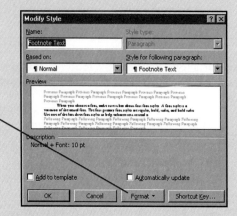

4 Click F<u>o</u>rmat and choose <u>F</u>ont.
The Font dialog box appears, so you can select the font attributes for the footnote text.

5 Click 12 in the <u>S</u>ize list box and click OK.

**6 Click F<u>o</u>rmat and choose <u>P</u>aragraph; then click the <u>I</u>ndents and
Spacing tab, if needed.**
The Paragraph dialog box appears, so you can set paragraph options, such as first
line indent.

7 Click the <u>S</u>pecial drop-down arrow, choose First line, and click OK.

8 Click OK in the Modify Style dialog box.

9 Click Close in the Style dialog box.

⑩ Double-click either the first or second footnote reference mark in the body of the document.

Figure 6.20 shows that the first line in each footnote is indented. Both footnotes appear in 12-point.

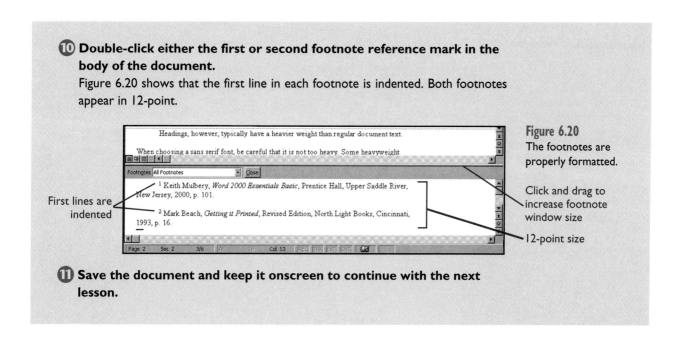

First lines are indented

Figure 6.20
The footnotes are properly formatted.

Click and drag to increase footnote window size

12-point size

⑪ Save the document and keep it onscreen to continue with the next lesson.

Lesson 6: Creating Headers and Footers

A **header** contains standard text at the top of most pages in a document. A **footer** contains standard text at the bottom of most pages in a document. You can insert text, page numbers, dates, and filenames in headers and footers. Headers and footers are typically used in long documents, such as reports, legal briefs, medical transcripts, and proposals.

Each section in a document can have different information in a header. For example, the header in your book changes to reflect the project discussed in that section.

In this lesson, you create a header containing the title of the report.

To Create Headers

① In the Desktop Publishing document, press Ctrl+Home to position the insertion point at the top of the document.

② Choose View, Header and Footer.

Word switches to the Print Layout view. The Header and Footer toolbar appears in the middle of the screen (see Figure 6.21). Table 6.3 at the end of this lesson describes the Header and Footer toolbar buttons. The header area is outlined at the top of the screen. Word displays information that the header will appear on the first page in Section 1.

continues ▶

To Create Headers (continued)

Figure 6.21
Type in the header area and use toolbar buttons to customize the header.

Indicates header for Section 1

Header area

Header and Footer toolbar

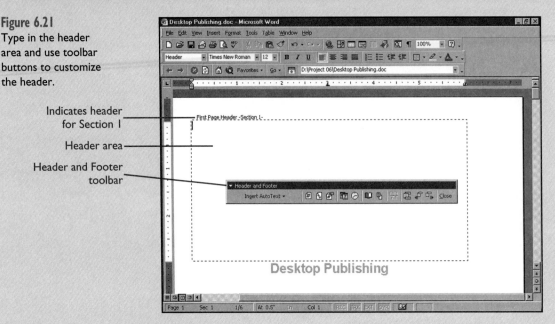

③ **Type Desktop Publishing.**
You want to insert the date at the right side of the header.

④ **Press Tab↹ twice—once to get to the center point and again to align text at the right side of the header.**

⑤ **Click the Insert Date button on the Header and Footer toolbar.**

⑥ **Click Close on the Header and Footer toolbar.**
When you click Close, the Header and Footer toolbar disappears, and the insertion point is inside regular document text.

⑦ **Click the Print Layout View button, click the Zoom drop-down arrow, and choose Two Pages.**
Figure 6.22 shows that the header appears at the top of every page of the document.

Figure 6.22
The header appears at the top of each page.

Header on Page 1 in Section 1

Header on Page 1 in Section 2

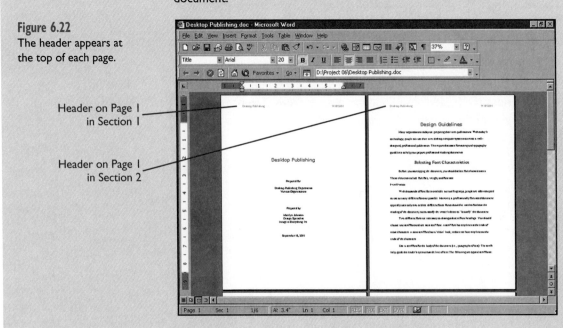

8 **Save the document and keep it onscreen to continue with the next lesson.**

Table 6.3   Header and Footer Toolbar Buttons

Button	Button Name	Description
Insert AutoText ▾	Insert AutoText	Inserts items such as the filename, filename and path, and creation data.
[#]	Insert Page Number	Inserts a code to display the page number.
[⊕]	Insert Number of Pages	Inserts a code to display the total number of pages in a document.
[✎]	Format Page Number	Lets you choose the page number format, such as the number format and whether you want continuous page numbers or new page numbers for a section.
[📅]	Insert Date	Inserts a code to display the current date.
[🕐]	Insert Time	Inserts a code to display the current time.
[📖]	Page Setup	Displays the Page Setup dialog box so that you can set different headers and footers for odd- and even-numbered pages and different headers and footers for the first page in a section.
[📄]	Show/Hide Document Text	Shows or hides the document text.
[📑]	Same as Previous	Links the header or footer to the same header or footer in the previous section when clicked. Click to set different headers and footers for the current section.
[🔁]	Switch Between Header and Footer	Switches between the header and footer window.
[⬅]	Show Previous	Shows the previous header or footer.
[➡]	Show Next	Shows the next header or footer.
Close	Close Header and Footer	Closes the header or footer window and hides the Header and Footer toolbar.

Lesson 7: Creating Sectional Headers and Footers

In the last lesson, you learned how to create a basic header or footer. By default, Word places the header on every page of the document. However, you probably don't want to have a header on the title page. Therefore, you must create a *blank* header on the first page of Section 1, which contains the title page, and create another header for Section 2, which contains the document text.

To Create Sectional Headers

1 In the `Desktop Publishing` document, click the Zoom drop-down arrow and choose 100%.

2 With the insertion point on the title page, choose **V**iew, **H**eader and Footer to display the header window.

3 Select the text and date; then press Del.
You need to delete the header text on the first page of Section 1. Now you're ready to go to Section 2 and create the header for that section.

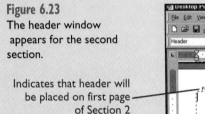

4 Click the **Show Next** button on the Header and Footer toolbar.
Word displays the header window for Section 2 (see Figure 6.23).

Figure 6.23
The header window appears for the second section.

Indicates that header will be placed on first page of Section 2

Indicates that header will be same as previous section's header

Page Setup button

Click to break link with previous header

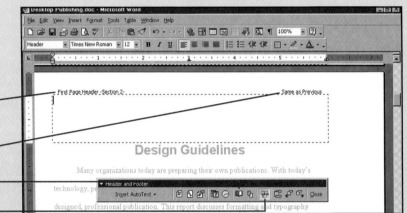

5 Click the **Page Setup** button on the Header and Footer toolbar.
You want the header to appear on all pages in section, not just the first page in Section 2.

6 Click the **Different first page** check box to deselect it, and then click **OK**.
The note about the header window changes to `Header - Section 2-`. The header you're about to type will appear on all pages of Section 2.

7 Click the **Same as Previous** button to deselect it.
The Same as Previous note disappears from above the header window. Deselecting Same as Previous breaks the link to the header in the previous section. Now, you can create a header for Section 2 without it also appearing in Section 1.

8 Type `Desktop Publishing`, press Tab↹ twice, and click the **Insert Date** button on the Header and Footer toolbar.
The header for Section 2 appears in the header window (see Figure 6.24).

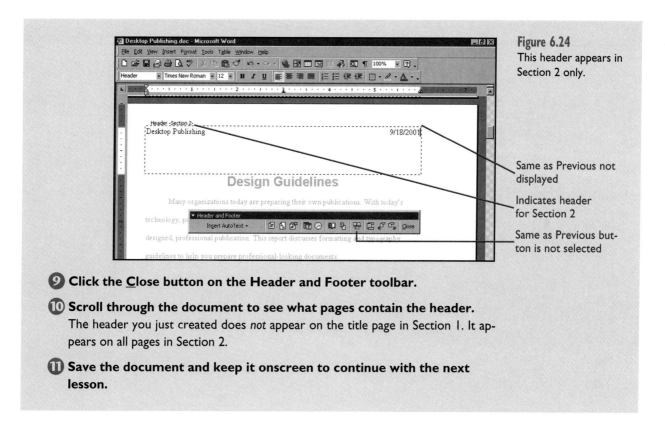

Figure 6.24
This header appears in Section 2 only.

Same as Previous not displayed

Indicates header for Section 2

Same as Previous button is not selected

9 **Click the Close button on the Header and Footer toolbar.**

10 **Scroll through the document to see what pages contain the header.**
The header you just created does *not* appear on the title page in Section 1. It appears on all pages in Section 2.

11 **Save the document and keep it onscreen to continue with the next lesson.**

 ***Exam Note:*   Multiple Headers and Footers**
You might need to create a different header on the first page of a section that is different from the rest of its section. If so, skip steps 5 and 6 in the previous exercise. After creating the header on the first page of a section, click Show Next to show the header for the second page of that section. The header you create there applies to the rest of that section.

You can also create one header for even-numbered pages and one for odd-numbered pages. Click the Page Setup button, click the **Different odd and even** check box, and click OK. You'll see a note that says **Odd Page Header** above the header window. The header text you create applies to odd-numbered pages only. Click the Show Next button to create a header for even-numbered pages. The note above the header window displays **Even Page Header**.

Lesson 8: Navigating Through a Document

You learned how to scroll and how to use the Go To feature in Project 2, "Working with a Document." Although those navigation features are helpful, you are now ready to learn additional navigation features for longer documents.

The **Document Map** feature displays a window that lists the structure of headings in your document. You can quickly display a particular section by clicking the heading in the Document Map. Furthermore, you use the Select Browse Object button to browse by footnotes or sections.

To Navigate Through Documents

❶ In the open `Desktop Publishing` **document, press** Ctrl+Home **and click the Normal View button.**

❷ Click the Document Map button on the Standard toolbar.
The Document Map appears on the left side of the document window (see Figure 6.25).

Figure 6.25
The Document Map shows the structure of your document.

Document Map button

Document Map window

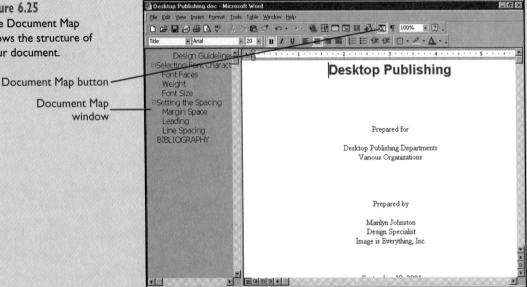

❸ Click `Setting the Spacing` **in the Document Map window.**
Word takes you to that section immediately (see Figure 6.26).

Figure 6.26
Clicking a heading in the Document Map takes you to that location.

Click this heading

Insertion point jumps to this heading

Select Browse Object button

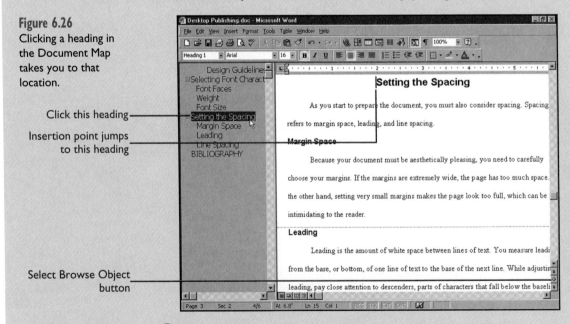

❹ Click the Document Map button to turn off this feature.
Now you want to scroll by jumping from heading to heading.

5 **Click the Select Browse Object button below the vertical scrollbar buttons.**

The Select Browse Object palette appears (see Figure 6.27). Table 6.4 at the end of this lesson lists the buttons on the palette.

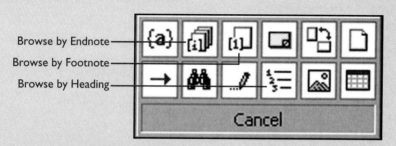

Browse by Endnote

Browse by Footnote

Browse by Heading

Figure 6.27
Choose a method for browsing through your document.

6 **Click the Browse by Heading button.**

Word moves the insertion point to the next heading: Margin Space. Notice that the Previous and Next buttons turn blue, indicating that you are browsing by any object *except* by page. When you position the mouse on top of these buttons, the ScreenTip displays Previous Heading and Next Heading, respectively.

7 **Click the Next Heading button.**

The insertion point jumps to the next heading: Leading.

8 **Click the Next Heading button again.**

The next heading is Line Spacing.

9 **Click the Select Browse Object button and click the Browse by Page button.**

This changes the browse back to the original default, which is browsing by page. The Previous and Next buttons are black again.

10 **Save the document and close it.**

Table 6.4   Select Browse Object Buttons Options

Option	Button Name
{a}	Browse by Field
	Browse by Endnote
	Browse by Footnote
	Browse by Comment
	Browse by Section
	Browse by Page
→	Go To
	Find
	Browse by Edits
	Browse by Heading
	Browse by Graphic
	Browse by Table

Summary

You learned a lot of valuable formatting features in this project. Now you can center text vertically on a page, insert page numbers, create headers, and insert page breaks. In addition, you learned how to create footnotes to document your sources in a research paper and how to navigate quickly through your documents using Document Map and the Select Browse Object options. Plus, your documents will look professional when you make sure bulleted lists are not separated across page breaks.

You can now expand your knowledge and skills of these and related features by using Help. For example, you might want to learn more about section breaks and the other buttons on the Header and Footer toolbar. In addition to using Help, complete the following exercises to reinforce and expand your skills.

Checking Concepts and Terms

True/False

For each of the following, check *T* or *F* to indicate whether the statement is true or false.

__T __F   **1.** If you have a document with regular page breaks instead of section breaks, selecting center vertical alignment only affects the current page. [L1–2]

__T __F   **2.** When you turn on page numbers, Word displays page numbers for all sections, not just the current section. [L3]

__T __F   **3.** If a bulleted list separates between two pages, you should insert a hard page break before the first bulleted item. [L4]

__T __F   **4.** By default, footnotes have the same point size that body text does. [L5]

__T __F   **5.** When the Same as Previous button is active on the Header and Footer toolbar, the header in the current section is identical to the header in the last section. [L7]

Multiple Choice

Circle the letter of the correct answer for each of the following.

1. What is the keyboard shortcut for inserting a hard page break? [L1]

a. ⏎Enter

b. Ctrl+⏎Enter

c. Ctrl+Break

d. Pause+Break

2. The Vertical alignment option is found in which tab of the Page Setup dialog box? [L2]

a. Margins

b. Paper Size

c. Paper Source

d. Layout

3. Which option should you use to keep a selected numbered list together? [L4]

a. Widow/Orphan control

b. Keep lines together

c. Keep with next

d. Page break before

4. Which of the following is an original default for footnotes? [L5]

   a. Footnotes appear in 12-point Times New Roman.

   b. The first line of each footnote is indented.

   c. Footnotes appear at the bottom of the page.

   d. Word automatically inserts one blank line between footnotes.

5. What types of items can you put into a header or footer? [L7]

   a. page numbers

   b. text

   c. date

   d. all of the above

Screen ID

Label each element of the Word screen shown in Figure 6.28.

Figure 6.28

A. Document Map

B. footnote

C. header text

D. total number of pages in document

E. third section

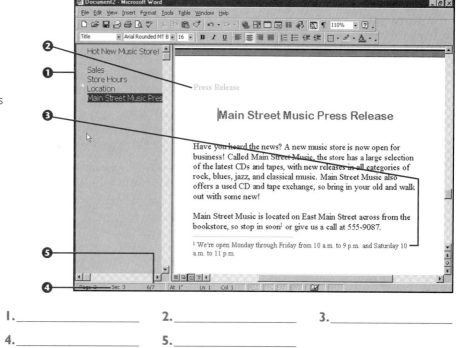

I._____ 2._____ 3._____

4._____ 5._____

Skill Drill

Skill Drill exercises reinforce project skills. Each skill reinforced is the same, or nearly the same, as a skill presented in the project. Each exercise includes a brief narrative introduction, followed by detailed instructions that are provided in a step-by-step format.

1. Inserting Breaks, Centering Text Vertically, and Using Document Map

You have created a research paper for your business communication class. You need to replace a hard page break with a section break so that you can vertically center the title page without centering the rest of the document. You also need to add two hard page breaks in Section 2.

1. Open **W-0602** and save it as **Interview Paper**.

2. Click the Normal View button.

3. Click on the page break line between the title page and the next page.

4. Press ⟨Del⟩ to remove the hard page break.

5. Choose Insert, Break. Click the Next page option and click OK to insert a section break.

6. Press ⟨Ctrl⟩+⟨Home⟩ to position the insertion point on the title page.

7. Choose File, Page Setup and click the Layout tab.

8. Click the Vertical alignment drop-down arrow and choose Center.

9. Check to see that the Apply to option displays **This Section**. Click OK.

10. Click the Document Map button on the Standard toolbar.

11. Click Pre-interview Impression Effects in the Document Map window to move the insertion point there.

12. Press ⟨Ctrl⟩+⟨↵Enter⟩ to insert a hard page break.

13. Click Perception in the Interview in the Document Map window and then press ⟨Ctrl⟩+⟨↵Enter⟩ to insert a hard page break.

14. Click the Document Map button to remove the Document Map from the screen.

15. Save the document and keep it onscreen to continue with the next exercise.

2. Inserting Page Numbers and Using Text Flow Options

You decide to insert page numbers in your document so that your readers can easily locate specific sections of the paper. You want page numbers to begin with the main document and not the title page. In addition, you need to keep a heading from being isolated at the bottom of a page.

1. In the **Interview Paper** document, position the insertion point at the top of the document (the title page).

2. Make sure you are displaying the document in Print Layout view with the Two Pages zoom option. (If the Document Map appears, turn it off.)

3. Choose Insert, Page Numbers.

4. Click the Alignment drop-down arrow and choose Center.

5. Click the **Show number on the first page** check box to deselect this option (if it is selected) and then click OK.

6. Click the Zoom drop-down arrow and choose 100%. Scroll to the bottom of page 3 to check the placement of the page number.

7. Position the insertion point at the top of page 2, the first page of the body of the document.

8. Choose Insert, Page Numbers and deselect the **Show number on the first page** check box.

9. Click Format to display additional options.

10. Click the Start at option and type **1**.

11. Click OK and then click OK in the Page Numbers dialog box.

12. Scroll to the bottom of the page and check to see that the page number has changed to 1.

13. Click the Normal View button.

14. Scroll through the document so you see the bottom of page 2 and the top of page 3 in Section 2.

15. Drag across the heading The Bias of Information Processing and the first two lines of the following paragraph. Choose Format, Paragraph to display the Paragraph dialog box.

16. Click the Line and Page Breaks tab.

17. Click the **Keep with next** check box and click OK. If the heading does not appear at the top of page 3, click the Print Layout View button and then click the Normal View button again.

18. Repeat this process with any other headings that have separated incorrectly.

19. Save the document and keep it onscreen to continue with the next exercise.

3. Inserting a Footnote and Creating Sectional Headers

You decide to create footnotes that supplement the text contained in paragraphs. In addition, you want to create a header for Section 2.

1. In the open **Interview Paper** document, click the Normal View button.

2. Display the first page in Section 2.

3. Position the insertion point after skill tests, in the second paragraph.

4. Choose Insert, Footnote and click OK.

5. Type the following footnote text:

   `Skill tests provide valuable information to see if an applicant possesses a certain skill. For example, word processing applicants typically take a skill test to see if they can correctly format documents in a timely manner.`

6. Click the Close button to close the footnote window.

7. Position the insertion point at the beginning of the document.

8. Choose View, Header and Footer.

9. Click the Show Next button on the Header and Footer toolbar.

10. Click the Page Setup button on the Header and Footer toolbar.

11. Click the Different first page check box to deselect it and then click OK.

12. Deselect the Same as Previous button on the Header and Footer toolbar.

13. Type **The Personal Interview**, press Tab↹ twice, and type your name.

14. Select the header text and choose 12-point Times New Roman.

15. Click the Close button on the Header and Footer toolbar.

16. Save the document, print it, and close it.

Challenge

Challenge exercises expand on or are somewhat related to skills presented in the lessons. Each exercise provides a brief narrative introduction followed by instructions in a numbered-step or bulleted-list format that are not as detailed as those in the Skill Drill section.

1. Formatting a Status Report

You composed a status report for division managers concerning an upcoming Information Technology Training Conference. You open it and make a few changes before sending it out.

1. Open **W-0603** and save it as **Status Report**.

2. On the blank line above the title, create the title page shown in Figure 6.29. Apply bold to the two-line title only; the rest of the title page should *not* be bold.

3. Apply Center alignment for the text you typed on the title page.

4. Insert a section break after the date. Then, vertically center text in the first section only (i.e., the title page).

5. Select text, starting with the first paragraph to the end of the document, and apply Justify alignment.

6. Select the bulleted list and use the feature that prevents a page break within this text.

7. Insert page numbers in the bottom center of the pages. Do not display a page number on the title page. Make sure the page number value starts at 1 on the first page of the body of the report.

8. Save the document, print it, and close it.

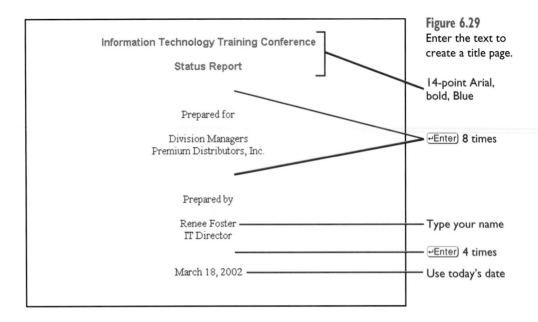

Figure 6.29
Enter the text to create a title page.

14-point Arial, bold, Blue

Enter 8 times

Type your name

Enter 4 times

Use today's date

2. Formatting a Report About the Internet

You created a document that discusses domain names and Internet protocol. Before printing and distributing copies to clients at a regional meeting, you need to format it with a header, page number, and footnotes.

1. Open **W-0604** and save it as **Domain Name**.

2. Set a 1.25-inch bottom margin.

3. Format the title in 14-point Avant Garde Md BT, bold, and Indigo font color. Format the heading Internet Protocol in 12-point Avant Garde Md BT, bold, Indigo. Use the Format Painter to copy the Internet Protocol formats to the remaining headings.

4. Create a blank header on the first page by selecting Different first page in the Page Setup dialog box.

5. Show the next header, which is for page 2 of the document. Type **Domain Names and the Internet** at the left side of the header, insert the date in the center, and type your name on the right side of the header.

6. Create a footer that contains a hard return and then centers the page number. (The page won't display on page 1.)

7. Create a footer after the second sentence in the first paragraph below the Domain Names heading on the first page. Use the following information:

   IP Addresses are also like Social Security Numbers. Each person has his or her own number for identification purposes.

8. Position your insertion point at the end of the document and insert the following footnote:

   Mikki Barry (Internet Policy Consultants), Internet article, http://www.mids.org/legal/dispute.html, 1996.

9. Modify the Footnote Text style by changing the font size to 12 and selecting the First line special indent.

10. Use the Document Map feature to go to **The trailing domain**.

11. Select the paragraphs that start with the domain names. The first domain name is .edu. Create a customized bulleted list with an appropriate symbol.

12. Save the document, print it, and close it.

3. Formatting a Document for Lab Assistants

You work for the College of Business Lab Center. Your supervisor typed a memo and job description list for the lab assistants. You need to finish formatting the document for your supervisor.

1. Open **W-0605** and save it as **Lab Assistant Rules**.
2. Insert a section break at the beginning of the title College of Business.
3. Vertically center text in the first section.
4. Create an empty footer in the first section.
5. Create a footer for the second section, making sure it is not linked to the first section. Type **Job Description** at the left side, insert a page number in the center, and insert the date on the right side. Format the page number to start at 1 for the first page in Section 2.
6. Save your document, print it, and close it.

Discovery Zone

Discovery Zone exercises help you gain advanced knowledge of project topics and/or application of skills. These exercises focus on enhancing your problem-solving skills. Numbered steps are not provided, but you are given hints, reminders, screen shots, and/or references to help you reach your goal for each exercise.

1. Formatting an Endnotes Page

You are asked to create an endnotes page for a report you have written for your Advanced Word Processing class. An endnotes page places the endnotes on a separate page at the end of the body of a report.

Open **W-0606** and save it as **Font Characteristics**. Insert your name and the current date on the title page.

Before creating the endnotes, you need to research endnote options to learn about the line that separates the notes from the text.

When you create the following endnotes, do *not* press ⏎Enter after each endnote.

Display the document in Normal view. Create the following endnote at the end of the third paragraph: **Mark Beach, *Getting It Printed*, Revised Edition, North Light Books, Cincinnati, 1993, p. 16.** Before closing the endnote window, display the endnote separator line and delete it.

Create the following endnote at the end of the fourth paragraph: **Marvin Jacobs, *Graphic Design for Desktop Dummies*, Ameritype & Art Inc., Cleveland, 1993, p. 26.**

Create the following endnote at the end of the last paragraph: **Dan Poynter, *The Self-Publishing Manual: How to Write, Print, and Sell Your Own Book*, Ninth edition, revised, Para Publishing, Santa Barbara, 1996, p. 106.**

Create a new section page at the end of your document. Set a 2-inch top margin for this section, and center **ENDNOTES** and set single-spacing. Triple-space after the title and select Left alignment. Select ENDNOTES and apply Arial bold. Edit the Endnote Text style by changing the font size to 12 and apply a First line indent, and set 12-point paragraph spacing after. View the document in Print Layout.

Create a header for Sections 2 and 3 that displays the page number at the right side. The page number should not appear on the title page or first page of the report. Make sure the page number appears on the Endnotes page and continues from Section 2.

Create a footer for Sections 2 and 3 that displays the filename and path field at the left margin and your name at the right margin. Make sure the footer appears on the Endnotes page.

Save the report again. Print the document using the 2 pages per sheet option.

2. Formatting a Research Paper

Your team conducted research and wrote a document about outsourcing. You are in charge of formatting the document before submitting it to the company president. The information is stored in two files to make it easier to format. The first document contains the title page, transmittal memo, and abstract. The second document contains the main report.

Open **W-0607** and save it as **Outsourcing Document 1**. Insert a section break to separate the title page from the memo. Insert a hard page break to separate the memo from the abstract. Vertically center text on the title page. Insert page numbers with the following specifications: no page number on the title page, page number in the bottom center location starting on the memo, lowercase Roman numerals for page numbers, and the memo counted as page ii. Make sure the page number appears on the memo and for the rest of the document. Set 1.5 inch left margins for the entire document because you plan to have the document spiral-bound. Save and print the document.

Open **W-0608** and save it as **Outsourcing Document 2**. One of your teammates inserted notes in parentheses, such as (1), indicating where you should create footnotes. You need to delete these parenthetical notes and insert the following footnotes:

First footnote: **J. Norman, 1997, "More Companies Outsourcing the Extras, Focusing on Core,"** *The Orange County Register*, **http://www.kentuckyconnect .com/heraldleader/news/110397/fb5core.html, November 11, 1998.**

Second footnote: **Ibid.**

Third footnote: **Jean Simpson, April 6, 1998, "Temp-to-Perm Hiring," http:// www.meansimpson.com/temptoperm.htm, February 5, 2000.**

Fourth footnote: **Dan Geslison, Director of Human Resources, Nature's Sunshine Products Inc., (Interviewed by Mike Warren), November 20, 1998.**

Fifth footnote: **Ibid.**

Sixth footnote: **J. Norman, 1997, "More Companies Outsourcing the Extras, Focusing on Core,"** *The Orange County Register*, **http://www.kentuckyconnect .com/heraldleader/news/110397/fb5core.html, November 11, 1998.**

Seventh footnote: **Clark, Thomas & Winters, 1998, http://www.ctw.com/labor.htm, December 1, 1998.**

Eighth footnote: **Lebau & Neuworth, 1998, "Did You Know?" http://www.lebau-neuworth.com/didyouknow/, December 4, 1998.**

Ninth footnote: **Dan Geslison, Director of Human Resources, Nature's Sunshine Products Inc., (Interviewed by Mike Warren), November 20, 1998.**

Tenth footnote: **S. Mayer, October 22, 1995, "U.S. Businesses Using More Temporary Workers, Agencies," Knight-Ridder/Tribune Business News, http://web1.searchbank.com/infotrac/session/996/574/341514w7/12!xrn_54, November 11, 1998.**

Eleventh footnote: **B. Czegel,** *Running an Effective Help Desk*, **Canada: John Wiley & Sons, 1994, p. 308.**

Twelfth footnote: **Dan Geslison, Director of Human Resources, Nature's Sunshine Products Inc., (Interviewed by Mike Warren), November 20, 1998.**

Thirteenth footnote: **A. Brockhoff, May 1, 1998, "Temps Spark Revolution: Companies Search Nationwide to Fill Jobs with Temporary Workers,"** *The Kansas City Business Journal*, **http://web3.searchbank.com/infotrac/session/ 472/112/329105w7/12!xrn_6, November 11, 1998.**

Fourteenth footnote: **R. D. Vrancken, September 1995, "Exploring Outsourcing as a Process,"** *Outsourcing, Insourcing or Resourcing?*, **http://www.isdesignet .com/IsdesigNET/Magazine/Sep'95/Outsourcing.html, November 11, 1998.**

Fifteenth footnote: **Dan Geslison, Director of Human Resources, Nature's Sunshine Products Inc., (Interviewed by Mike Warren), November 20, 1998.**

Modify the Footnote Text style by applying 12-point font size, first line indent, and 12-point paragraph spacing after.

Create a header that appears on odd-numbered pages only. Do not display the header on the first page, however. Type **Outsourcing: Will it Work for Us?** at the left margin, insert the page number at the right side, and insert a hard return. Create a header that appears on even-numbered pages with the page number on the left side, type **An In-depth Report** on the right side, and insert a hard return.

Insert a hard page break, if needed, before ECONOMIC CONSIDERATIONS OF OUTSOURCING, EFFECT ON OUTSOURCING ON GENERAL EFFICIENCY, GENERAL FINDINGS, and REFERENCES.

Save the document and print it. You might want to print it with the 2 pages per sheet option selected to save paper.

PinPoint Assessment

You have completed this project and its associated lessons, and have had an opportunity to assess your skills through the end-of-project questions and exercises. Now use the PinPoint software Evaluation Mode to further assess your comprehension of the specific exam activities you have just learned. You can also use the PinPoint Trainer Mode and the Show Me tutorials to practice these exam activities.

Project 7

Creating and Formatting Tables

Key terms introduced in this project include

- borders
- cell
- column
- column headings
- column width
- gridlines
- row
- row height
- shading
- table
- table alignment

Objectives	Required Activity for MOUS	Exam Level
➤ Create a Table	Create and format tables	Core
➤ Enter Text in a Table		
➤ Insert Rows and Columns	Revise tables (insert & delete rows and columns, change cell formats)	Core
➤ Delete Rows and Columns	Revise tables (insert & delete rows and columns, change cell formats)	Core
➤ Adjust Column Widths and Row Height	Modify table structure (merge cells, change height and width)	Core
➤ Format a Table	Create and format tables	Core
➤ Apply Shading and Borders	Add borders and shading to tables	Core
➤ Move and Position a Table		

Why Would I Do This?

Sometimes, you might want an easy way to organize a series of data in a columnar list format. Although you could align text with tabs, you have more format control when you create a table. A **table** is a series of rows and columns that neatly organize data. Each **row** presents data going across the table (left to right), and each **column** presents data vertically in the table. The intersection of a row and column is called a **cell**.

You can create tables to store customer names and addresses, phone lists, personal inventories, calendars, project forms, and so on. After you complete this project, you'll probably think of additional ways you can use tables in your own documents.

Lesson I: Creating a Table

You can create a table between paragraphs in a letter, memo, or report; or you can create a table as a separate document. Before you create a table, you should think about what data you want to include and how you want to organize it. Doing so helps you create an appropriate table structure from the beginning, but you can always change the table later.

In this lesson, you work for a local bookstore named Open Book Store. Your manager, Gabriel Thompson, asked you to insert a table that lists some books that are on sale this month. You decide to create a table to include book titles, authors' names, ISBN numbers, and sale prices. You also decide to list four books that are on sale. Your table will consist of four columns and four rows.

To Create a Table

1 **Open W-0701 and save it as** `Book Sales Letter`.

2 **Position the insertion point on the blank line above Sincerely.**
You need to position the insertion point where you want to create the table. Although you really want the table between the second and third paragraphs, you'll insert the table after the third paragraph and then learn how to move it in a later lesson.

3 **Click the Insert Table button on the Standard toolbar.**
Word displays a table grid. You click and drag through the grid to specify how many columns and rows you want in your table.

4 **Position the mouse pointer on the fourth cell down in the fourth column.**
The grid shows that you are creating a table with four rows and four columns (see Figure 7.1).

Figure 7.1
You have selected four rows and four columns on the grid.

First number indicates rows

Second number indicates columns

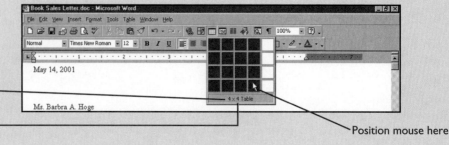

Position mouse here

5 **Click the mouse button in the cell.**

You now have a new table in your document (see Figure 7.2). By default, Word creates evenly spaced columns between the left and right margins. Your table contains *gridlines*, lines that separate cells within the table.

Table positioned after last paragraph

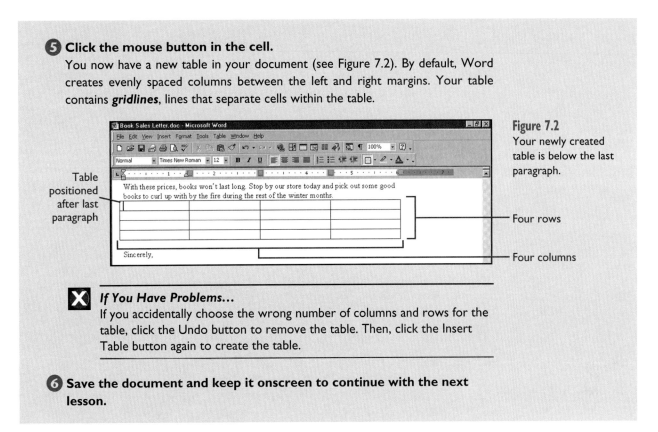

Figure 7.2
Your newly created table is below the last paragraph.

Four rows

Four columns

X ***If You Have Problems...***

If you accidentally choose the wrong number of columns and rows for the table, click the Undo button to remove the table. Then, click the Insert Table button again to create the table.

6 **Save the document and keep it onscreen to continue with the next lesson.**

(i) ***Inside Stuff:*** **Creating a Table**

You can also create a table from the Insert Table dialog box (see Figure 7.3). To do this, choose Table, Insert, Table. Specify the number of columns and rows you want and click OK.

Set number of columns

Set number of rows

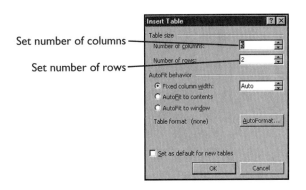

Figure 7.3
Use the Insert Table dialog box to create a table.

Lesson 2: Entering Text in a Table

After creating a table, you are ready to enter text into the cells. Type directly in the cell, letting text word-wrap within the cell. When you are ready to type in the next cell, press Tab.

You are now ready to type book titles, author names, ISBN numbers, and sale prices in your table. The insertion point is in the first cell, so you can start typing the first item now.

To Enter Text in a Table

1 **In the Book Sales Letter document, type the following book title in the first cell.**

Tuesdays with Morrie: An Old Man, A Young Man, and the Last Great Lesson

The book title wraps within the same cell, making the first row taller.

 Exam Note: **Pressing ⏎Enter in a Table**

Do not press ⏎Enter within the cell. Let Word word-wrap text within the cell. Inserting a hard return can cause problems when you adjust the column widths later.

---

2 **Press Tab⇄ to move the insertion point to the next cell to the right on the same row.**

3 **Type Mitch Albom in the cell.**

4 **Press Tab⇄ and type 0385484518.**

5 **Press Tab⇄ and type $13.97.**

You are ready to type text on the next row. Instead of pressing ⏎Enter to get to the next row, press Tab⇄. When you press Tab⇄ in the last cell on a row, Word moves the insertion point to the first cell on the next row.

6 **Type the rest of the table text shown in Figure 7.4. Do not press Tab⇄ after typing $12.00 in the last cell.**

Figure 7.4
Finish typing text in your table.

With these prices, books won't last long. Stop by our store today and pick out some good books to curl up with by the fire during the rest of the winter months.			
Tuesdays with Morrie: An Old Man, a Young Man, and the Last Great Lesson	Mitch Albom	0385484518	$13.97
Harry Potter and the Sorcerer's Stone	J. K. Rowling	0590353403	$12.57
The Testament	John Grisham	0385493800	$19.57
Storm of the Century	Stephen King	067103264X	$12.00

Type data in last three rows

☒ *If You Have Problems...*

If you accidentally press Tab⇄ in the last cell and create a new row at the end of the table, click the Undo button to remove the extra row.

---

7 **Save the document and keep it onscreen to continue with the next lesson.**

Table 7.1 lists different methods for moving around in a table.

Table 7.1   Moving the Insertion Point in a Table

To Move to the	Press
Next cell to the right	Tab
Cell to the left	Shift + Tab
First cell in column	Alt + PgUp
Last cell in column	Alt + PgDn
First cell in current row	Alt + Home

Lesson 3: Inserting Rows and Columns

After creating the table, you might decide to add another row or column. For example, you might realize that you left out information in the middle of the table or you might want to create a row for **column headings**—text that appears at the top of each column describing that column.

In this lesson, you decide to add a row at the top of the table to type in column headings. Before inserting a row, however, you need to position the insertion point on the row below or above where you want to insert the new row.

To Insert a Row

❶ In the Book Sales Letter document, position the insertion point within any cell on the first row.

Remember that rows go across, not down. You will insert a row in the wrong place if the insertion point is not on the first row.

❷ Choose Table, Insert to display the Table Insert menu options for inserting columns and rows (see Figure 7.5).

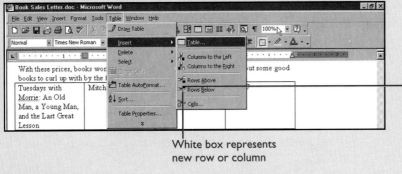

Figure 7.5
Use the Table, Insert menu to insert columns or rows.

Black box represents current cell

White box represents new row or column

❸ Choose Rows Above.

Word inserts a new row above the current one. The new row is currently selected.

❹ Click in the first cell.

continues ▶

To Insert a Row   (continued)

5 **Type the following data in cells on the first row:**

`Title of Book`

`Author`

`ISBN`

`Sale Price`

Your table now contains all the data you want to include (see Figure 7.6).

Figure 7.6
Your table now contains column headings.

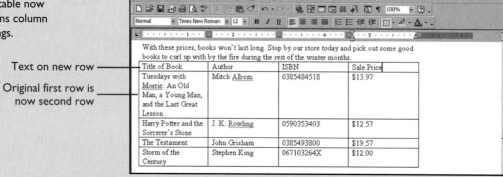

Text on new row ——

Original first row is now second row

6 **Click in the last cell on the last row—the cell containing $12.00.**

You want to add a row below the last row for another book that's on sale.

7 **Press** `Tab`.

Pressing `Tab` in the last cell on the last row creates a new row below the original last row.

8 **Type the following information on the last row:**

`Seize the Night`

`Dean R. Koontz`

`0783811640`

`$18.87`

Your table contains data on the new row at the bottom of the table (see Figure 7.7).

Figure 7.7
Your table now contains six rows.

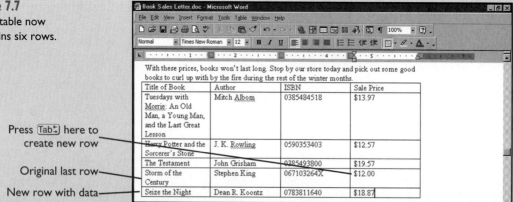

Press `Tab` here to create new row

Original last row

New row with data

9 **Save the document and keep it onscreen to continue with the next lesson.**

Exam Note: Inserting Columns

You can insert a new column to the left or right of the column containing the insertion point. For example, if the insertion point is in the second column and you insert a column to the left, the new column becomes the second column, and the original second column becomes the third column. When you insert a column, the existing columns decrease in width to make room for the new column.

Lesson 4: Deleting Rows and Columns

After creating a table, you might decide that you no longer need a particular row or column. You can delete a row or column just as easily as you insert rows and columns. In this lesson, you realize that your bookstore only has one copy of *Storm of the Century* and will not receive more for another month. Therefore, you decide to remove this book from your list of sale items.

To Delete a Row

1 **In the Book Sales Letter document, position the insertion point in the fifth row, the row that contains the *Storm of the Century* information.**

You must first position the insertion point in any cell on the row that you want to delete.

2 **Choose T**able, **Delete.**

The Delete options include Table, Columns, Rows, Cells.

3 **Choose Rows.**

Word deletes the row containing the insertion point (see Figure 7.8).

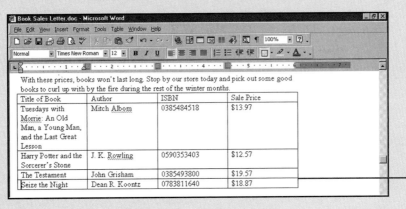

Figure 7.8
Your table contains five rows after deleting a row.

Row deleted between these two rows

4 **Save the document and keep it onscreen to continue with the next lesson.**

 Inside Stuff: Deleting Cell Contents

Instead of deleting a row or column, you might want to keep the table structure but delete the text in the cells. To delete just the text, select the cells containing text you want to delete and then press Del. This leaves empty cells in which you can type new text.

Lesson 5: Adjusting Column Width and Row Height

When you create a table, Word creates evenly spaced columns. **Column width** is the horizontal space or width of a column. You may, however, need to adjust the column widths based on the type of data you type in the column. For example, the book title column should be wider and the sale price column should be narrower in your current table.

Furthermore, you might want to adjust the row height. **Row height** is the vertical distance from the top of the row to the bottom of the row. By default, Word expands the row height when text word-wraps within a cell on that row. To make the column headings on the first row stand out, you want to make this row taller.

To Adjust Row Height and Column Widths

1 In the Book Sales Letter document, make sure you're displaying the document in **Print Layout** view at 100% zoom.

2 Position the mouse pointer on the gridline that separates the first and second rows.

As Figure 7.9 shows, a two-headed arrow appears, indicating that you can adjust the height by clicking and dragging the gridline.

Figure 7.9
Click and drag the gridline when you see a two-headed arrow.

Move Table Column markers

Mouse pointer on gridline

Adjust Table Row markers

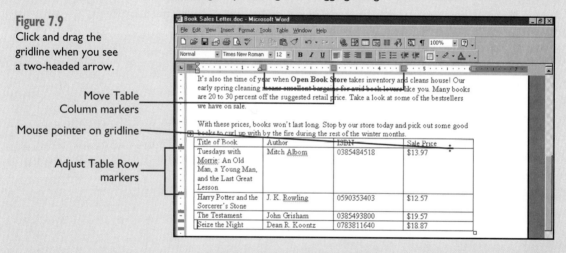

ⓘ **Inside Stuff: Using the Markers to Adjust Width and Height**
You can click and drag the Adjust Table Row marker to change the row height and the Move Table Column marker to change a column width.

3 Click and drag the gridline down to make the row about twice its original size, as shown in **Figure 7.10**.

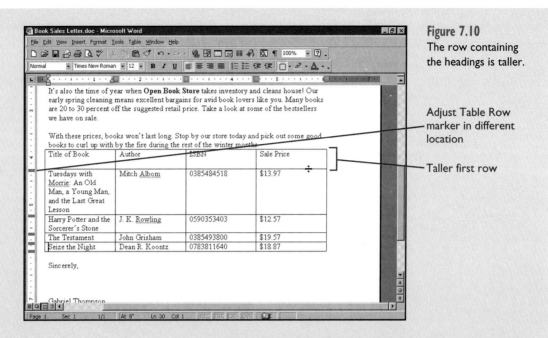

Figure 7.10
The row containing the headings is taller.

Adjust Table Row marker in different location

Taller first row

You now need to adjust the column widths. The first column needs to be wider, whereas the remaining columns need to be narrower.

> **Inside Stuff: Decreasing Widths Before Increasing Other Widths**
> Before making a column wider, you should adjust other columns that need to be narrower. If you make one wider and then decrease other column widths, you might have to go back and increase the first column width again.

4 **Position the mouse pointer on the vertical gridline on the right side of the sales price column.**
The mouse pointer is a two-headed arrow, indicating that you can change the column width (see Figure 7.11).

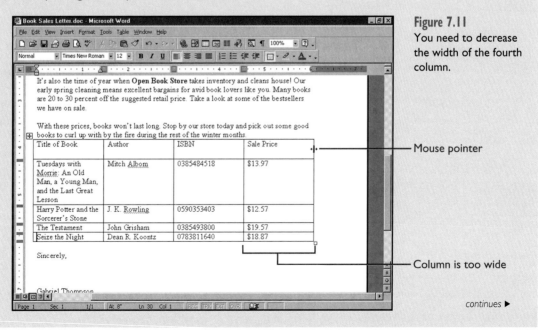

Figure 7.11
You need to decrease the width of the fourth column.

Mouse pointer

Column is too wide

continues ▶

To Adjust Row Height and Column Widths   (continued)

5 **Double-click the gridline.**
Double-clicking a vertical gridline adjusts the column width based on the text in that column. The fourth column is now narrower.

6 **Double-click the vertical gridline between the third and fourth columns to decrease the width of the third column.**

7 **Double-click the vertical gridline between the second and third columns.**
The last three columns look better than they did when they were wider. Now you can increase the width of the first column.

8 **Double-click the vertical gridline between the first and second columns.**
The first column is wider to accommodate the text in that column (see Figure 7.12).

Figure 7.12
The table looks better after adjusting column widths.

Column widths decreased

Wider first column

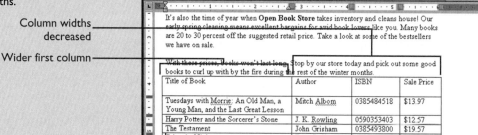

9 **Save the document and keep it onscreen to continue with the next lesson.**

  Exam Note: **Adjusting Exact Column Widths**
If instructed, you can specify an *exact* measurement for column widths. To do this, select the column for which you want to adjust its width. (If you don't select the column first, Word might not accept the column widths you set.) Choose Table, Table Properties. Then, click the Column tab, click the Preferred width check box, and set a specific setting (see Figure 7.13).

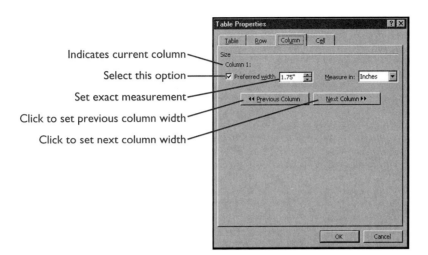

Figure 7.13
Set a specific column width.

Indicates current column
Select this option
Set exact measurement
Click to set previous column width
Click to set next column width

If you want to set the same width for all columns, click the Table tab in the Table Properties dialog box and set the Preferred width there.

 Exam Note: Setting Cell Formats
You might need to set cell formats. With the insertion point in the cell(s) you want to format, display the Table Properties dialog box and click the Cell tab. Choose the vertical alignment for text in the cell (Top, Center, or Bottom). You can also click Options to display the Cell Options dialog box (see Figure 7.14). This dialog box lets you set the margins within the cell.

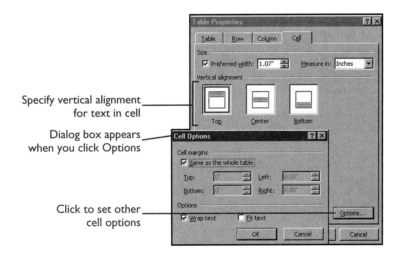

Figure 7.14
Set cell options to improve how text appears in the cell.

Specify vertical alignment for text in cell
Dialog box appears when you click Options
Click to set other cell options

Lesson 6: Formatting a Table

After creating a table, entering data, and adjusting the structure, you need to format the table. You can use many common formatting techniques you already know, such as bold, font color, font, font size, bullets, and more. In addition, you can select formats from the Tables and Borders toolbar.

You want the headings to stand out, so you decide to use center alignment, boldface, and center vertical alignment for the first row.

To Format the Table

1 In the Book Sales Letter document, choose <u>V</u>iew, <u>T</u>oolbars, Tables and Borders.
The Tables and Borders toolbar appears as a floating palette by the table.

2 Position the mouse pointer between the left gridline and the text in the first cell on the first row.

> (i) *Inside Stuff:*   **Moving the Toolbar**
> You might need to move the Tables and Borders toolbar so you can position the mouse pointer between the gridline and text. To do this, simply click and drag the toolbar to another location on your screen.

The mouse pointer looks like a solid black arrow (see Figure 7.15).

Figure 7.15
You want to format the first row of the table.

Mouse pointer

Tables and Borders toolbar

Click to set text alignment within cells

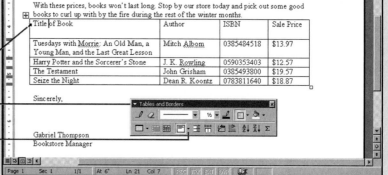

3 Double-click to select the entire row.
When you double-click the mouse when the mouse pointer appears as a solid black arrow, you select text on the current row. Single-clicking selects the current cell's text.

4 Click the Bold button on the Formatting toolbar.

5 Click the Font drop-down arrow and choose **Arial Narrow**.

6 Click the drop-down arrow to the right of the Alignment button on the Tables and Borders toolbar.
You see a palette of alignment styles (see Figure 7.16). The default is Align Top Left, which aligns text in the top left corner of the cell.

Figure 7.16
Select how you want text aligned in the selected cells.

Align Top Left, default

Align Center (horizontally and vertically)

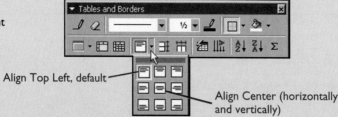

7 Click the Align Center button; then, click in the first cell to deselect the text.
The text on the first row is boldface, centered horizontally, and centered vertically, as shown in Figure 7.17. When you point on the Align button, the ScreenTip displays Align Center.

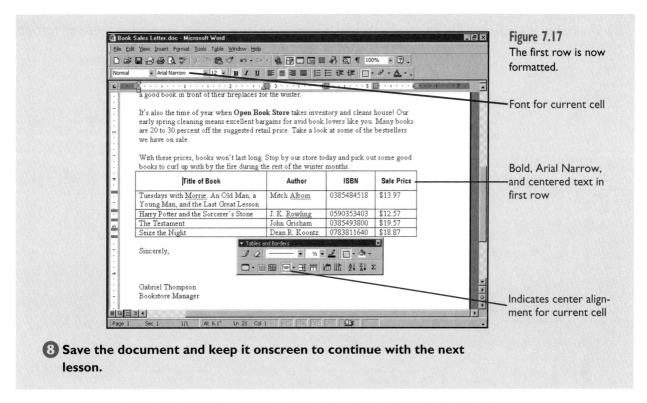

Figure 7.17
The first row is now formatted.

Font for current cell

Bold, Arial Narrow, and centered text in first row

Indicates center alignment for current cell

8 **Save the document and keep it onscreen to continue with the next lesson.**

 Exam Note: Formatting Tables
You can also change text color, font, and font size to enhance the appearance of your table. To apply these attributes, select the cell or cells you want to format; then choose options in the Font dialog box or from the Formatting toolbar.

Lesson 7: Applying Shading and Borders

You can also enhance the appearance of a table by selecting shading and border options. *Shading* refers to the background color within a cell or group of cells. Table shading is similar to the Highlight feature that places a color behind text. *Border* refers to the line style around each cell in the table. The default line style is a single line.

You decide to further enhance your table by shading the first row, so it will stand out.

To Select Table Shading

1 **In the Book Sales Letter document, make sure the Tables and Borders toolbar is displayed.**

2 **Select the text on the first row of the table.**

3 **Click the drop-down arrow to the right of the Shading Color button on the Tables and Borders toolbar.**
You see the Shading Color palette, as shown in Figure 7.18.

continues ▶

To Select Table Shading   (continued)

Figure 7.18
Select a color from
the palette to shade
cells.

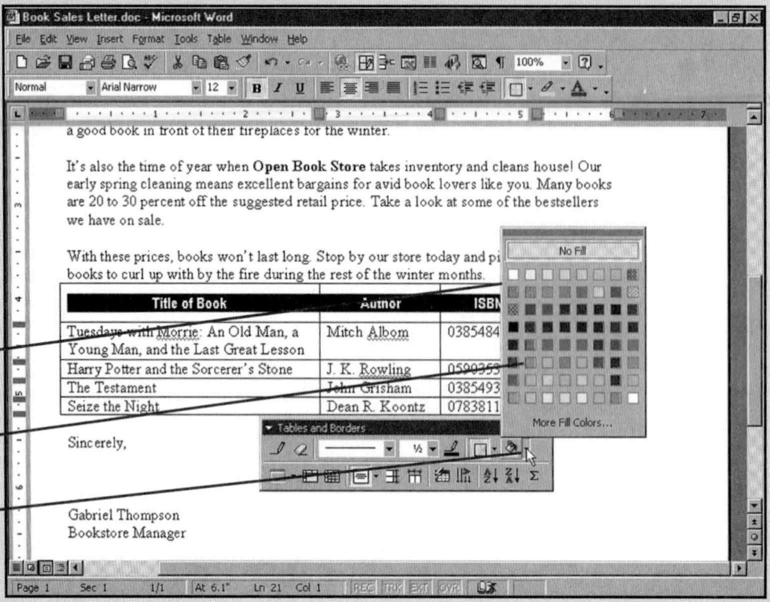

Shading Color palette

Light Orange

Click to see Shading
Color palette

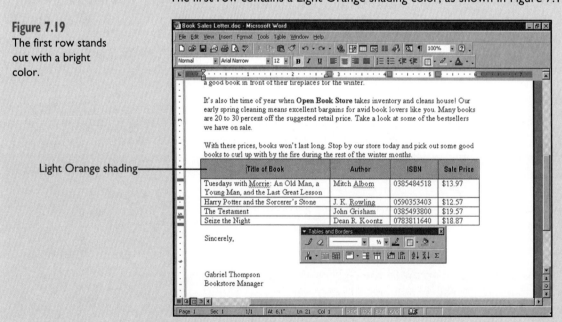

> **ⓘ** *Inside Stuff:*   **Selecting a Color**
> When you position the mouse pointer on a color, Word displays a
> ScreenTip that tells you the exact name of the color, such as Sky Blue.

④ Click the Light Orange color.

⑤ Deselect the row to see the color.
The first row contains a Light Orange shading color, as shown in Figure 7.19.

Figure 7.19
The first row stands
out with a bright
color.

Light Orange shading

⑥ Close the Tables and Borders toolbar to remove it from the screen.

**⑦ Save the document and keep it onscreen to continue with the next
lesson.**

> **✍ Exam Note: Table Borders**
>
> In Project 5, "Formatting Documents," you learned how to insert a border around a paragraph. Although you see borders for your table, you can customize the borders. To do this, choose Table, Table Properties. Then, click the Borders and Shading button. You'll see options similar to those you used for paragraph borders.
>
> Remember that some colors do not print well or might cause text to be difficult to read on a black-and-white printout.

Lesson 8: Moving and Positioning a Table

After creating a table, you might decide to move it to a different location. In your current letter, you want the table above, not below, the last paragraph. In this lesson, you position the table and make sure you have a blank line before and after the table. Doing so helps separate the table from the preceding and following text, which makes the printout look more professional.

To Move the Table

① **In the Book Sales Letter document, adjust the view to see the table and the first two paragraphs.**

② **Make sure the insertion point is inside the table; then position the mouse pointer on the table marker.**

You should see a four-headed arrow, indicating that you can move the entire table.

③ **Click and drag the table marker to the blank line above the last paragraph.**

As you drag the table marker, you see a dotted line indicating where you're moving the table. When you release the mouse, Word moves the table to that location (see Figure 7.20). The top left corner of the table is positioned where you see the four-headed mouse pointer.

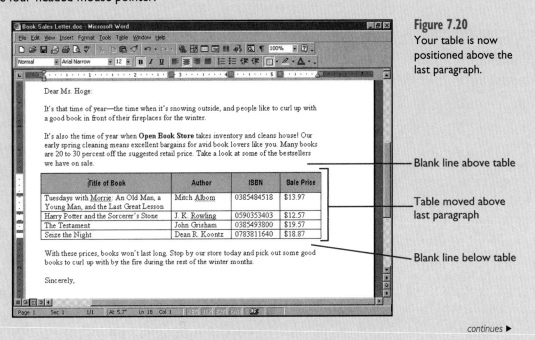

Figure 7.20
Your table is now positioned above the last paragraph.

— Blank line above table

— Table moved above last paragraph

— Blank line below table

continues ▶

To Move the Table (continued)

④ **Make sure you have one blank line above and below the table.**

⑤ **Save the document and print it.**

ⓘ *Inside Stuff:* **Positioning a Table**

Table alignment refers to the location of a table between the margins. If the table does not fill the space between the left and right margins, Word positions the table at the left margin. You can center the table between the margins or allow text to wrap around the table. To adjust the table alignment, choose Table, Table Properties, and click the Table tab (see Figure 7.21). Click the desired Alignment option and Text Wrapping option. You can also click Positioning to see additional options.

Figure 7.21
Select where you want to position the table.

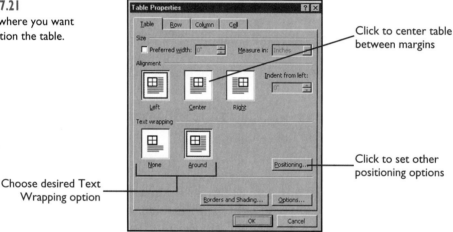

Click to center table between margins

Click to set other positioning options

Choose desired Text Wrapping option

Summary

After completing these lessons, you know how to create a table, adjust the structure, and format the data. You can create exciting tables that look professional by centering text, shading cells, and positioning the table. In addition, you know how to move a table to a new location.

You probably noticed a lot of different buttons on the Tables and Borders toolbar. To learn more about these buttons, point to the button to see the ScreenTip displaying the button's name. Then access onscreen Help to learn about these additional table buttons.

Checking Concepts and Terms

True/False

For each of the following, check *T* or *F* to indicate whether the statement is true or false.

__T __F   **1.** After you type text within a cell, you should press ⏎Enter to be able to type in the next cell in that column. [L2]

__T __F   **2.** When you insert a column to the left of the first column, the original first column becomes the second column. [L3]

__T __F   **3.** Double-clicking a vertical gridline adjusts the column width, based on the largest item in that column. [L5]

__T __F   **4.** Shading refers to changing the color of the text within a table. [L7]

__T __F   **5.** By default, Word centers a table between the left and right margins if it does not span the space between the margins. [L8]

Multiple Choice

Circle the letter of the correct answer for each of the following.

1. If the insertion point is in the last cell on the first row, what key(s) should you press to go to the first cell on the next row? [L2]

   a. Ctrl + G

   b. ⬆Shift + Tab⇄

   c. Alt + Home

   d. Tab⇄

2. Assume that you created a table with the names of the months in the first column. Each row lists data for that particular month. The insertion point is in the first cell on the third row. This row list goals for April. You realize that you left out the goals for March. What should you do? [L3]

   a. Choose Table, Insert, Columns to the Left.

   b. Choose Table, Insert, Columns to the Right.

   c. Choose Table, Insert, Rows Above.

   d. Choose Table, Insert, Rows Below.

3. What happens when you press Tab⇄ when the insertion point is in the last cell in the last row? [L3]

   a. Word inserts a new row above the current row.

   b. Word inserts a new row below the current row.

   c. The insertion point appears in the paragraph below the table.

   d. The insertion point stays in the cell because it's already in the last cell of the table.

4. Refer to Figure 7.20 in Lesson 8. If the insertion point is in the cell that contains $13.97 and you choose Table, Delete, Rows, what happens? [L4]

   a. You delete just the text $13.97.

   b. You delete the Sale Price column.

   c. You delete the entire second row.

   d. You delete the entire fourth row.

5. All of the following help make the first row stand out except: [L6, 7]

   a. shading

   b. boldface

   c. taller height

   d. smaller font size

Screen ID

Label each element of the Word screen shown in Figure 7.22.

Figure 7.22

A. Adjust Table Row marker

B. Center Alignment button

C. column

D. row

E. Shading Color button

F. Table marker

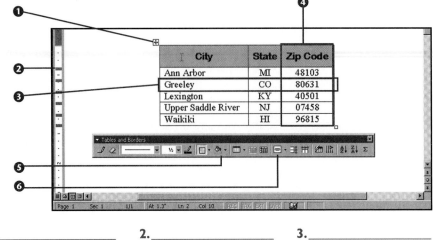

I._____ 2._____ 3._____

4._____ 5._____ 6._____

Skill Drill

Skill Drill exercises reinforce project skills. Each skill reinforced is the same, or nearly the same, as a skill presented in the project. Each exercise includes a brief narrative introduction, followed by detailed instructions in a step-by-step format.

I. Creating a Table of Seminars

As the assistant to David Zaugg, you need to create a table that lists upcoming seminars for employees in the Dallas area.

1. Open **W-0702** and save it as **Dallas Seminars**.

2. Position the insertion point between the first and second paragraphs.

3. Choose Ta̲ble, I̲nsert, T̲able.

4. Type **4** in the **Number of c̲olumns** box, press (Tab⁺̣), and type **5** in the **Number of r̲ows** box. Then, click OK.

5. Type the data shown in Figure 7.23.

6. Save the table and continue with the next exercise.

Figure 7.23
Create this table in the memo.

October 17	8:00-10:00 a.m.	Working with Difficult Customers	Baker Room
October 17	1:30-3:30 p.m.	Communicating with Subordinates	Texas Ballroom
October 18	8:00-10:00 a.m.	Resolving Customer Complaints	Suite 495
October 18	9:30-11:30 a.m.	Climbing the Corporate Ladder	Texas Ballroom
October 18	3:30-5:30 p.m.	Analyzing Data	Suite 495

2. Adjusting the Table Structure

You need to add a row at the top of the table to enter column headings to identify the data. You also need to add a row at the bottom of the table. David Zaugg, your supervisor, just informed you that one seminar was canceled; therefore, you need to delete that row. You also decide to adjust column widths and row height.

1. With **Dallas Seminars** onscreen, position the insertion point in any cell on the first row.

2. Choose Table, Insert.

3. Choose Rows Above.

4. Click in the first cell.

5. Type the following data in cells on the first row:

   Date

   Time

   Topic

   Room

6. Click in the last cell on the last row, the cell containing Suite 495, and press Tab.

7. Type the following data in the cells on the new row:

   October 19

   9:30-11:30 a.m.

   Working with Managers

   Suite 495

8. Click in the cell containing Climbing the Corporate Ladder.

9. Choose Table, Delete, Rows to delete the row.

10. Position the mouse pointer on the vertical gridline on the right side of the last column and double-click to decrease its width.

11. Double-click the vertical gridline between the Date and Time columns.

12. Double-click the vertical gridline between the Time and Topic columns.

13. Double-click the vertical gridline between the Topic and Room columns.

14. Click and drag the horizontal gridline between the first and second rows down to double the height of the first row.

15. Save the document and keep it onscreen with continue to the next exercise.

3. Formatting a Table

You want the column headings to stand out, so you plan to add bold, centering, and shading to the first row. In addition, you want to right-align text in the second column. Finally, you realize the table is in the wrong location and needs to be moved.

1. In the **Dallas Seminars** document, choose View, Toolbars, Tables and Borders.

2. Select the first row by positioning the mouse pointer between the left gridline and the text in the first cell and double-clicking.

3. Click the Alignment drop-down arrow on the Tables and Borders toolbar.

4. Click the Align Center button.

5. Click the Bold button on the Formatting toolbar.

6. Click the Shading Color drop-down arrow and choose Light Green.

7. Deselect the first row.

8. Click and drag to select times (but not the column heading) in the second column.

9. Click the Justify Right button on the Formatting toolbar.

10. Position the mouse pointer on the table marker.

11. When you see the four-headed arrow, click and drag the table marker straight down and position the table between the second and third paragraphs.

12. Make sure you have one blank line above and below the table.

13. Save, print, and close the document.

Challenge

Challenge exercises expand on or are somewhat related to skills presented in the lessons. Each exercise provides a brief narrative introduction followed by instructions in a numbered- or bulleted-list step format that are not as detailed as those in the Skill Drill section.

1. Creating a Table in a Flier

The Life and Learning Center at a college is sponsoring two series of workshops: one series to improve student success and one series on effective writing. You've been asked to create and format a table in the flier that will be distributed on campus.

1. Open **W-0703** and save it as **Workshops**.

2. Create a table with two columns and six rows. Place the table between the Free Workshops and Sponsored By text lines. Use the following information to create the table:

Student Success Series	**Effective Writing Series**
Taking Notes	**Using Proper Punctuation**
Using Textbooks Effectively	**Writing Creatively**
Improving Concentration	**Correcting Common Mistakes**
Managing Time	**Streamlining Prose**
Taking Tests	**Proofreading Carefully**

3. Select the table and apply 16-point Times New Roman.

4. Emphasize the *first row* by applying these formats: Arial Narrow, bold, 0.5 inch row height, centered vertically and horizontally.

5. Apply Yellow font color and Blue shading for the first row.

6. Double-click the vertical gridlines to adjust the column widths.

7. Display the Table Properties dialog box and select **Center** table alignment to center the table between the left and right margins.

8. Add some blank lines between Workshops and the table and between the table and Sponsored By.

9. Center the document vertically.

10. Insert a row after the fourth row. Type the following information in the new row:

Overcoming Text Anxiety	**Revising Globally**

11. Apply the Pencil art border to the document.

12. Save the document and print it.

2. Creating a Table of People Involved in a Book Project

You are an assistant for a book publisher. Your supervisor wants you to create a table that lists the key people involved with an Office 2000 book.

1. In a new document window, type the title **Office 2000 Book Project** and triple-space after the title.

2. Apply these formats to the title: center-align, bold, 16-point Antique Olive or Arial Rounded MT Bold, Blue font color.

3. Create a table after the hard returns. Use the information shown in Figure 7.24.

Name	Job Title	Phone Number
Monica Stewart	Author	(801) 555-8237
Susan Layne	Developmental Editor	(580) 555-7033
Justin Fields	Project Editor	(201) 555-4387
Melody Linsky	Proofreader	(419) 555-2031
Louisa Kindel	Indexer	(734) 555-2499
Andy Walsh	Layout Technician	(201) 555-8108
Nate Stone	Usability Tester	(801) 555-1634

Figure 7.24
Create the table of key project people.

4. Insert a row above the developmental editor and enter the following data:

   Greg Simon   **Acquisitions Editor**   **(201) 555-8642**

5. Insert a row below the project editor and enter the following data:

   Tim Cromwell   **Copy Editor**   **(201) 555-8265**

6. Apply Pale Blue shading to the entire table.

7. Set a 0.25 inch row height for the entire table.

8. Choose Align Center Left from the Tables and Borders toolbar to align text at the left side of the cell, but center text vertically in the cell.

9. Select the third column and choose Align Center.

10. Adjust the column widths and cell margins as needed.

11. Apply these formats to the first row (the column headings row): Align Center, bold, Blue font color.

12. Center the table between the left and right margins. (Make sure you center the *table*, not the text.)

13. Save the document as **Book Project** and print it.

3. Creating Tables for Candle Scents and Prices

You work for Heavenly Scents Candles, a company that makes and distributes a variety of candle fragrances. You just wrote a letter to a customer who is interested in your candles. Now, you need to create two tables: one to list candle fragrances and one for sizes and pricing.

1. Open **W-0704** and save it as **Candle Letter**.

2. Create the first table below the first paragraph. Use the information shown in Figure 7.25.

Standard Scents	Exotic Scents
Cinnamon	Pina Colada
Peach	Raspberry Delight
Mulberry	Mango
Vanilla	Passion Fruit

Figure 7.25
Create the table of fragrances.

3. Add a row at the bottom of the table for **Apple Spice** and **Tropical Mist**, two popular standard and exotic scents.

4. Delete the row containing **Peach** and **Raspberry Delight** because you ran out of those scents and won't have any more for another month.

5. Apply these formats to the first row: centered vertically and horizontally, bold, 11-point Arial, Violet font color, Yellow shading color, and 0.35 inch row height.

6. Apply a Light Yellow shading color to the rest of the table.

7. Adjust the column widths.

8. Create another table after the second paragraph using the information shown in Figure 7.26. Make sure you have one blank line above and below the table.

Size	Price
8 ounce	$9.95
16 ounce	$17.95
26 ounce	$19.95
28 ounce	$22.95

Figure 7.26
Create the table for pricing.

9. Insert a column between the two existing columns in the second table. Enter this data:

   Description

   Round Jar

   Round Jar

   Octagon Jar; 2 Wicks

   Square Jar; 2 Wicks

10. Apply these formats to the first row of the second table: centered vertically and horizontally, bold, 11-point Arial, Yellow font color, Violet shading color, and 0.35-inch row height.

11. Apply Lavender shading color to the rest of the second table.

12. Adjust column widths as needed for the second table.

13. Center-align the data in the first and third columns of the second table.

14. Center both tables between the left and right margins.

15. Make sure you have one blank line above and below each table.

16. Select the second table and apply a 1.5-point border to the outside of the table. (This applies a thicker outside border and removes the cell borders inside the table.)

17. Replace the regular hyphens with nonbreaking hyphens in the phone number.

18. Save the document and print it.

Discovery Zone

Discovery Zone exercises help you gain advanced knowledge of project topics and/or application of skills. These exercises focus on enhancing your problem-solving skills. Numbered steps are not provided, but you are given hints, reminders, screen shots, and/or references to help you reach your goal for each exercise.

1. Enhancing the Candle Letter Tables

You want to further enhance the tables you created in Challenge 3. Open **Candle Letter** and save it as **Candle Letter Update**.

Use Help to learn how to create captions for tables. Create a caption for each table that reflects the table content. Keep the caption brief. Use the option to place the caption above the tables. After creating the captions, center them above their respective tables.

Select the first table and apply these border options: Grid setting, ninth line style, Pink line color, applied to the table. Also choose a Rose shading color for the table. Italicize the fragrance names, but not the column headings. Apply the same border style to the bottom of the first row. *Hint:* Look at the buttons in the Preview section of the dialog box to apply a border to a certain part of the cell.

Select the second table and apply these border options: Box setting, Yellow line color, 3-point width, applied to table. Also add a Yellow bottom border to the first row only.

Save the document and print it.

2. Creating a Table of Potential Computer Systems

Your supervisor asked you to research six different computer systems and provide the following details in a table: brand name and model number, hard-drive capacity, RAM, megahertz, other features (such as CD-ROM or DVD; Jazz or Zip drive), and price. Choose one major computer retailer to complete your research. You might want to conduct Internet research by looking at the retailer's Web site. Choose models with similar features so the comparison will be appropriate.

Write a memo to your supervisor that explains where you got the research and create a table that compares the computer systems. Apply appropriate formatting that you learned in this project. For example, select shading and borders; set column widths and row height; choose fonts, font sizes, and font color to make the table look good. Use Help to learn how to select landscape page orientation. Explore the Tables and Borders toolbar.

Save your document as **Computer Systems Memo** and print it.

PinPoint Assessment

You have completed this project and its associated lessons, and have had an opportunity to assess your skills through the end-of-project questions and exercises. Now, use the PinPoint software Evaluation Mode to further assess your comprehension of the specific exam activities you have just learned. You can also use the PinPoint Trainer Mode and the Show Me tutorials to practice these exam activities.

Using Additional Table Options

Key terms introduced in this project include

- AutoFormat
- AutoSum
- cell margins
- cell references
- decimal tab
- functions
- mathematical operators
- merge cells
- Sort Ascending
- Sort Descending
- sorting
- split cells

Objectives	Required Activity for MOUS	Exam Level
➤ Merge and Split Cells	Modify table structure (merge cells, change height and width)	Core
➤ Adjust Cell Formats	Revise tables (insert and delete rows and columns, change cell formats)	Core
➤ Perform Calculations in a Table	Perform calculations in a table	Expert
➤ Align Numerical Values	Use TABS command (Center, Decimal, Left and Right)	Core
➤ Sort Data in a Table	Sort lists, paragraphs, tables	Expert
➤ Draw a Table	Create and format tables	Core
➤ Rotate Text in a Table	Rotate text in a table	Core
➤ Use AutoFormat	Create and format tables	Core

Why Would I Do This?

I n the last project, you learned how to create and format tables. Although you have strong skills in tables now, you might need to apply other table formats. For example, you might need to perform calculations in a table, sort data within a table, or adjust cell margins.

 ## Lesson 1: Merging and Splitting Cells

Many tables contain a title on the first row, followed by the column headings. To make a title span across all columns, you must **merge cells** by combining them into one wide cell. In this project, you are sending a letter with a table invoice to a customer who ordered books from your company, Open Book Store. You need to merge cells for a title and also at the bottom of the table.

To Merge Cells

1 Open W-0801 and save it as Book Invoice Letter.

2 Choose **View, Toolbars, Tables and Borders** to display this toolbar.
The Tables and Borders toolbar contains a button to merge cells together.

3 Scroll down in the document to see the table. Click and drag across the cells on the first row, which are currently empty.
In order to merge cells into one cell, you must first select them.

 4 Click the **Merge Cells** button on the Tables and Borders toolbar.

> **Inside Stuff: Merging Cells**
> Another way of merging cells is to choose Table, Merge Cells.

5 Click in the cell to deselect it.
Word combines all four cells on the first row into one wide cell that spans all four columns (see Figure 8.1).

Figure 8.1
The first row contains one cell.

Merge Cells button

Merged cell on first row

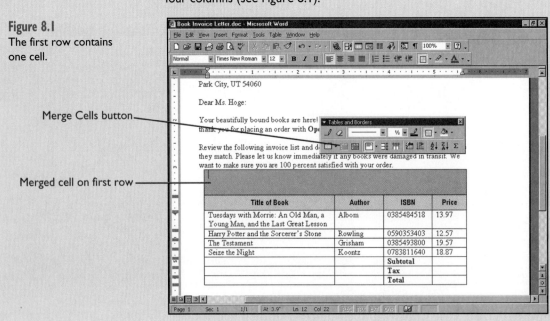

6 Click the Alignment button on the Tables and Borders toolbar and then click Align Center.

You want to center the title vertically and horizontally in the first cell.

7 Type `Your Book Order Invoice` in the first cell.

8 Select the title, click the Font drop-down arrow and choose Arial, and click the Font Size drop-down arrow and choose 18, and click the Bold button. Then deselect the text.

Your table now has a title that spans over the four columns (see Figure 8.2).

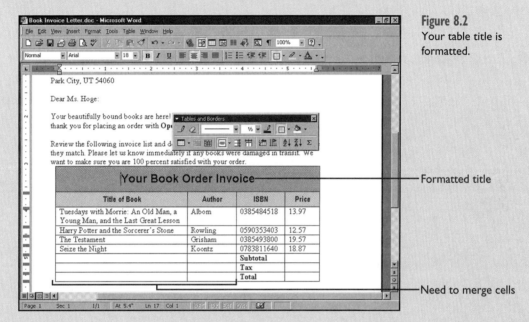

Figure 8.2
Your table title is formatted.

Formatted title

Need to merge cells

9 Click and drag to select the six empty cells at the bottom of the first two columns.

You want to combine these cells because you won't be typing any data in them.

10 Click the Merge Cells button on the Tables and Borders toolbar.

11 Click in the cell to deselect it.

Your table looks better after merging those cells (see Figure 8.3).

Figure 8.3
Empty cells are merged together.

Merged into one cell

12 Save the document and keep it onscreen to continue with the next lesson.

Inside Stuff: Splitting Cells
The opposite of merging cells is called splitting cells. **Splitting cells** divides one or more cells into multiple cells. When you click the Split Cells button, you select how many columns or rows you want from the original cell (see Figure 8.4).

Figure 8.4
Use the Split Cells dialog box to divide a cell.

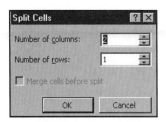

 Lesson 2: Adjusting Cell Formats

You have already applied some formatting to cells. For example, you have bolded, centered, and selected fonts and font sizes for cells. In addition to using these formats, you might want to set other formats. In this lesson, you learn how to set **cell margins**, the amount of space from the cell borders to the text. This is similar to setting margins for a document.

To Set Cell Margins

❶ In the Book Invoice Letter document, select the authors' names but not the column heading.
You want to maintain the current column width, but you want to adjust the cell margins to better position the text within the cells.

 Exam Note: Setting Cell Formats
Before accessing the Table Properties dialog box, make sure you have selected the appropriate cell or cells. Otherwise, you might accidentally format the wrong cells and lose points on the MOUS exam.

❷ Choose Table, Table Properties to display the Table Properties dialog box.

❸ Click the Cell tab.

 Inside Stuff: Setting Vertical Alignment
Although you can select vertical alignment in this dialog box, you've been using the Align button on the Tables and Borders toolbar. The Align button lets you set both the horizontal and vertical alignment at the same time.

❹ Click Options in the bottom-right corner of the dialog box.
The Cell Options dialog box appears (see Figure 8.5). The default margin settings are 0 inches at the top and bottom and 0.08 inches at the left and right for all cells in a table.

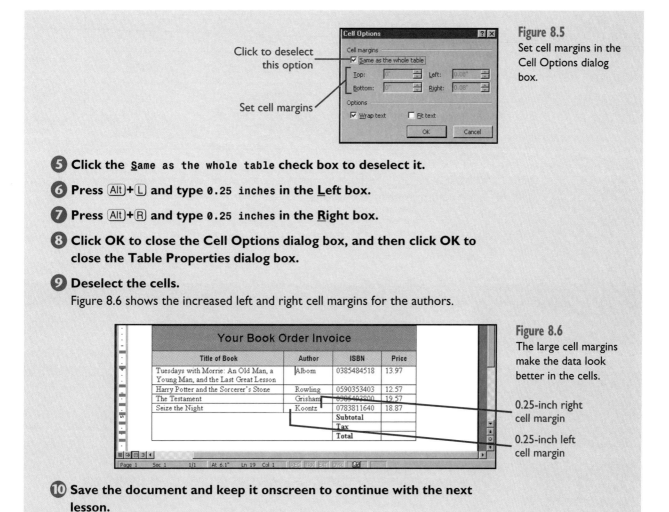

Figure 8.5
Set cell margins in the Cell Options dialog box.

Click to deselect this option

Set cell margins

5 Click the <u>S</u>ame as the whole table check box to deselect it.

6 Press Alt+L and type 0.25 inches in the <u>L</u>eft box.

7 Press Alt+R and type 0.25 inches in the <u>R</u>ight box.

8 Click OK to close the Cell Options dialog box, and then click OK to close the Table Properties dialog box.

9 Deselect the cells.
Figure 8.6 shows the increased left and right cell margins for the authors.

Figure 8.6
The large cell margins make the data look better in the cells.

0.25-inch right cell margin

0.25-inch left cell margin

10 Save the document and keep it onscreen to continue with the next lesson.

Lesson 3: Performing Calculations in a Table

Tables often contain numerical data that need to be calculated. For example, your table might contain salary data. You can add the salaries together to find the total salary budget or you might want to find the average salary.

Word provides various formulas that you can use to perform calculations within a table. You can use predefined formulas, known as **functions**, to perform tasks, such as adding a group of values. You can also create basic formulas with **mathematical operators**, such as add, subtract, multiply, and divide.

To save you from entering values again within a formula, insert **cell references**, such as A3, that refer to the particular cells that contain the values you want to calculate. Figure 8.7 illustrates cell references.

Figure 8.7
Use cell references in formulas.

Cell A1	Cell B1	Cell C1
Cell A2	Cell B2	Cell C2
Cell A3	Cell B3	Cell C3
Cell A4		Cell B4

The first column is A, the second column is B, and so on. The first row is 1, the second row is 2, and so on. On the fourth line, two cells are merged into one wide cell, which is Cell A4. The next cell over is B4, even though the cells above it are in Column C.

In this lesson, you insert a function that calculates the subtotal, a formula that calculates the tax, and a formula that adds the subtotal and tax for the grand total.

To Perform Calculations

1 In the `Book Invoice Letter` document, make sure the **Tables and Borders toolbar is visible.**

2 **Position the insertion point in the cell to the right of Subtotal.**
This is the cell that needs to display the subtotal of the books ordered.

Σ

3 **Click the AutoSum button on the Tables and Borders toolbar.**
AutoSum calculates the sum or total of values stored in cells either immediately above or to the left of the current cell (see Figure 8.8).

Figure 8.8
AutoSum calculates the total amount of books purchased.

AutoSum button

Cell C7 contains sum of books

Calculate tax in Cell C8

Calculate total in Cell C9

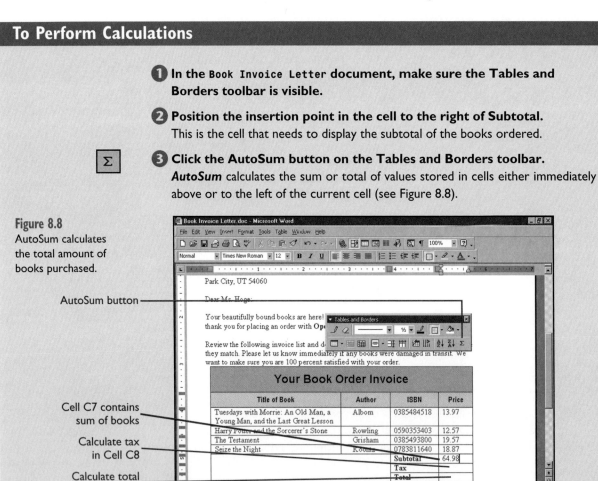

4 **Position the insertion point in the cell to the right of Tax.**
You need to create a formula that multiplies the total book price by the tax rate, which is seven percent.

Exam Note: **Cell References**

Keep in mind that the table has four columns (A–D) for the first six rows. After that, the table has only three columns (A–C). Using cell references, the formula to calculate taxes is =C7*.07, because C7 is where the total book price is stored.

5 Choose Table, Formula.

Word displays the Formula dialog box, so you can create the formula you need (see Figure 8.9).

Formula
Formula:
=SUM(ABOVE)
Number format:
Paste function:
Paste bookmark:
OK
Cancel
Type formula here
Choose a number format
Click to see list of functions

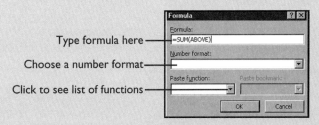

Figure 8.9
Create your formulas in the Formula dialog box.

6 Press Backspace until you completely delete the existing formula in the Formula text box.

7 Type `=C7*.07` in the Formula text box.

You must start formulas with the equals sign. C7 refers to the value stored in Cell C7, which is $64.98. The seven percent tax rate, converted to a decimal value, is .07.

Inside Stuff: **Number Formats**

When you create a formula, you can also choose a number format. For example, you can click the Number format drop-down arrow and choose $#,##0.00;($#,##0.00) to display dollar signs by the result.

8 Click OK.

The tax is 4.55. Now, you need to add the total cost of the books and the tax together to determine the total amount the customer owes.

9 Click in the cell to the right of Total.

10 Choose Table, Formula.

11 Delete the existing formula, type `=C7+C8`, and then click OK.

The total amount of the books and tax is 69.53 (see Figure 8.10).

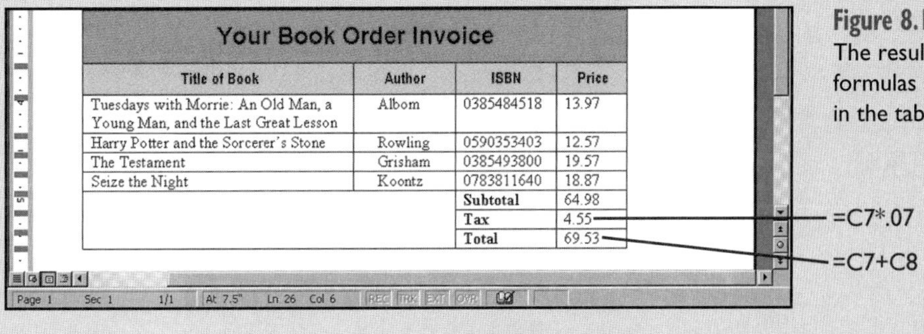

Your Book Order Invoice
Title of Book | Author | ISBN | Price
Tuesdays with Morrie: An Old Man, a Young Man, and the Last Great Lesson | Albom | 0385484518 | 13.97
Harry Potter and the Sorcerer's Stone | Rowling | 0590353403 | 12.57
The Testament | Grisham | 0385493800 | 19.57
Seize the Night | Koontz | 0783811640 | 18.87
Subtotal | 64.98
Tax | 4.55
Total | 69.53
=C7*.07
=C7+C8
Page 1 Sec 1 1/1 At 7.5" Ln 26 Col 6

Figure 8.10
The results of your formulas are displayed in the table.

12 Save the document and keep it onscreen to continue with the next lesson.

Exam Note: **Updating Formula Fields**

If you change a value in the table, Word does *not* automatically update the formula results. You must click in the result cells, such as the subtotal cell, and press F9.

 # Lesson 4: Aligning Numerical Values

When a table contains numerical values, the values might not align on the decimal point. You can select the numerical values and set a ***decimal tab*** to align values on their decimal points at a particular setting. In this lesson, you need to align the dollar values in the last column.

To Align Numerical Values

1 **In the Book Invoice Letter document, select the first four values in the last column.**

You should select values to set a decimal tab. If you don't select values, only the current cell contains the decimal tab.

 Inside Stuff: **Setting Decimal Tabs for Values and Formula Results**

Word won't let you select all values, including the formula results, and then set a decimal tab. You must format the values first and then format the formula results separately.

2 **Click the Left Tab button on the left side of the ruler three times to see the Decimal Tab button.**

The tab button changes to reflect the type of tab you can set. The Decimal Tab button looks like an upside-down T with a decimal point.

3 **On the ruler, click in the middle of the fourth column to set a decimal tab.**

Figure 8.11 shows the values aligned on the decimal point. Notice the exact location you should click to set the decimal tab on the ruler.

Figure 8.11
The decimal tab aligns the values on the decimal points.

Decimal Tab button

Click here to set decimal tab

Values aligned

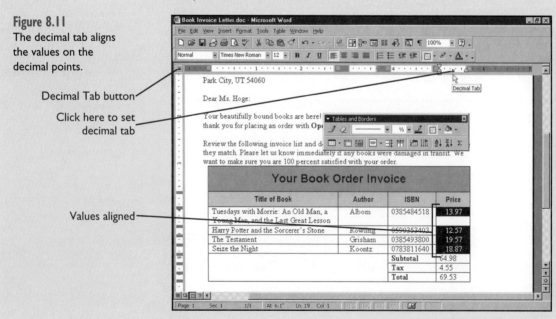

4 **Select the last three values in the fourth column.**

You need to set a decimal tab at the same location to align these formula results. You don't have to click the Decimal Tab button on the left side of the ruler because it is already selected.

5 **Click the ruler to set a decimal tab in the same location that you set a decimal tab for the other values.**

6 **Deselect the formula results.**

Figure 8.12 shows that the formula results are aligned on the decimal point.

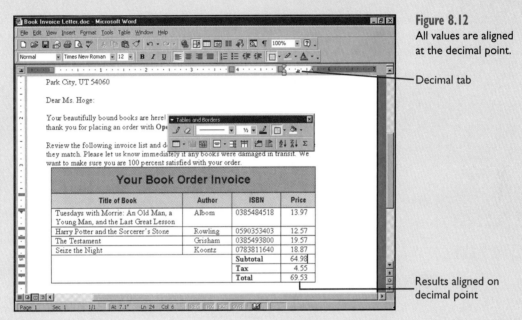

Figure 8.12
All values are aligned at the decimal point.

—Decimal tab

Results aligned on decimal point

7 **Save the document and keep it onscreen to continue with the next lesson.**

 Inside Stuff: Setting Other Tabs

When you set decimal tabs within a table, the selected values immediately align at the decimal point. However, if you set other tabs, you must press `Ctrl`+`Tab⇆` to align regular text within a cell.

Lesson 5: Sorting Data in a Table

After entering data in a table, you might want to rearrange the order of the data. The process of rearranging data in a table is called *sorting*.

Word provides two ways of sorting data in tables—Sort Ascending and Sort Descending. *Sort Ascending* arranges data in ascending or increasing order. Word arranges text in alphabetical order and numerical data in sequential order. *Sort Descending* arranges data in descending or reverse order. Word arranges text in reverse alphabetical order and numerical data from high to low.

 Expert

✍️ ***Exam Note:*** **Sorting Data in a Table**
You don't have to select the column or table to sort by a column. Simply click in a cell in the column you wish to sort and click either the Sort Ascending or Sort Descending button.

If your table contains merged cells, you must select the data to sort and use the Sort Text dialog box.

In this lesson, you want to sort the table in alphabetical (ascending) order by authors' names. Because you merged cells in a previous lesson, you must select the data to sort.

To Sort Data in a Table

1 **In the `Book Sales Letter` document, select all data columns for the four books, but don't select the first two rows or the rows containing formulas.**
Figure 8.13 shows the cells you should select.

Figure 8.13
Select these rows in your table.

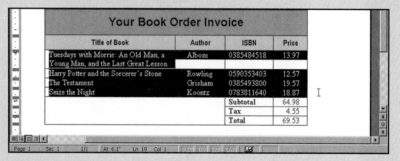

2 **Choose T̲able, S̲ort.**
The Sort dialog box lets you choose which column to sort and how to sort it (see Figure 8.14).

Figure 8.14
Use the Sort Text dialog box to sort table data.

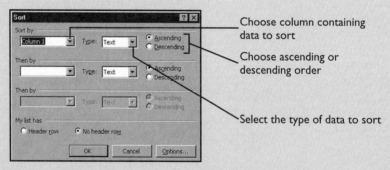

Choose column containing data to sort

Choose ascending or descending order

Select the type of data to sort

3 **Click the `Sort` by drop-down arrow and choose Column 2.**
Column 2 contains the authors' names.

4 **Leave Text as the Type and Ascending selected.**
You can choose Text, Number, or Date as the Type option.

 Inside Stuff: **Multiple Sorts**
You can choose up to three sort levels. For example, you can sort a table first by city, second by last name, and third by first name. Choose the sort order starting with the most common element, such as city.

5 **Click OK and deselect the table cells.**
The authors' names are now alphabetized (see Figure 8.15).

Your Book Order Invoice			
Title of Book	**Author**	**ISBN**	**Price**
Tuesdays with Morrie: An Old Man, a Young Man, and the Last Great Lesson	Albom	0385484518	13.97
The Testament	Grisham	0385493800	19.57
Seize the Night	Koontz	0783811640	18.87
Harry Potter and the Sorcerer's Stone	Rowling	0590353403	12.57
		Subtotal	64.98
		Tax	4.55
		Total	69.53

Figure 8.15
The names are sorted in ascending order.

Alphabetized names

6 **Save the document and close it.**

 Exam Note: Sorting Other Text
You can use the Sort Text dialog box to sort paragraphs and lines. To select other types of text, select the text you want to sort, and choose T**a**ble, **S**ort.

Lesson 6: Drawing a Table

So far, you have created tables by using the Insert Table button on the Standard toolbar or by choosing T**a**ble, **I**nsert, **T**able. You can also create tables by drawing them. Drawing a table might be an easier method of creating complex tables with varying number of columns, rows, widths, and heights.

To start drawing a table, you click the Draw Table button on the Tables and Borders toolbar. You click and drag to define the table area. Then you can click and drag within the table to draw lines to form columns and rows. In this lesson, you create a partial schedule for conference sessions.

To Draw a Table

1 **In a new document window, click the Tables and Borders button on the Standard toolbar.**
You need to display the Tables and Borders toolbar that contains the Draw Table button.

2 **Click the Draw Table button on the Tables and Borders toolbar.**
The mouse pointer looks like a pencil. You are ready to click and drag the outside border of the table.

3 **Click in the top left side of the document window, where the insertion point is blinking.**

4 **Click and drag diagonally, down to the 2-inch mark on the vertical ruler and right to the 5-inch mark on the horizontal ruler.**
You've created the outside area of the table (see Figure 8.16).

continues ▶

To Draw a Table   (continued)

Figure 8.16
The outside area of
the table is drawn.

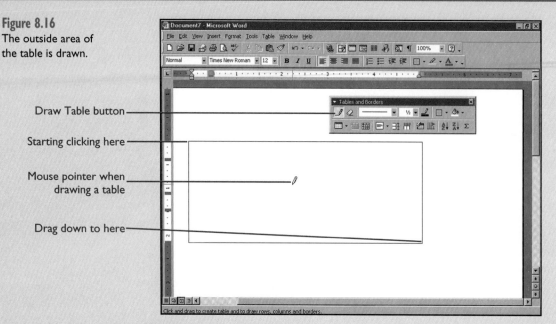

Draw Table button

Starting clicking here

Mouse pointer when
drawing a table

Drag down to here

⑤ **Use Figure 8.17 as a guide to click and drag to draw the lines within
the table.**

Figure 8.17
Draw the lines in the
table.

Check ruler to draw
column lines

Check ruler to draw
row lines

Eraser button

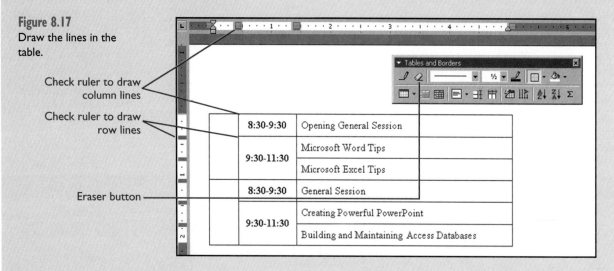

8:30-9:30	Opening General Session
9:30-11:30	Microsoft Word Tips
	Microsoft Excel Tips
8:30-9:30	General Session
9:30-11:30	Creating Powerful PowerPoint
	Building and Maintaining Access Databases

As you start clicking within the table, you see dotted lines. Word quickly inserts
a line there, thus forming columns and rows.

 ⓘ *Inside Stuff:*   **Erasing Mistakes**
If you accidentally draw a line in the wrong place, click the Eraser button
on the Tables and Borders toolbar. The mouse pointer looks like an eraser; click on the line you want to erase. To continue drawing lines, click the
Draw Table button again.

⑥ **Click the Draw Table button to turn off this feature.**

⑦ **Use Figure 8.17 to enter and format text.**

8 **Click and drag border lines if you need to adjust the column widths or row heights.**

9 **Save the document as** Sessions **and keep it onscreen to continue with the next lesson.**

Lesson 7: Rotating Text in a Table

In order to have enough space for all table columns, you might need to rotate text in a narrow column. The Change Direction button lets you rotate text to face upright, left, or right. In this lesson, you rotate the names of two weekdays to fit in the narrow column in your table.

To Rotate Text

1 **In the** Sessions **document, click in the first narrow cell in the first column.**
Before typing text in this cell, let's change the text direction.

2 **Click the Change Text Direction button** *twice* **on the Tables and Borders toolbar.**

3 **Type** Thursday **in the cell.**
The top of the text is on the left side of the cell.

4 **Click in the next narrow cell.**
You need to change the direction of text in this cell also.

5 **Click the Change Text Direction button** *twice* **on the Tables and Borders toolbar.**

6 **Type** Friday **in the cell.**

7 **Select the two narrow cells, click the Align button, and choose Align Center.**
Figure 8.18 shows the rotated text that is centered vertically and horizontally in the cells.

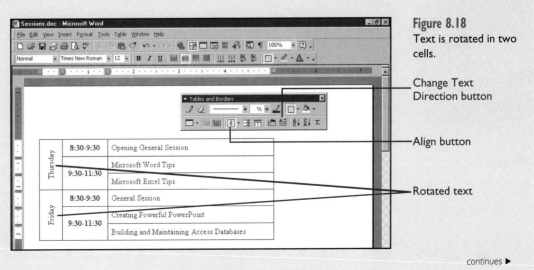

Figure 8.18
Text is rotated in two cells.

Change Text Direction button

Align button

Rotated text

continues ▶

To Rotate Text   (continued)

8 **Save the document and keep it onscreen to continue with the next lesson.**

 ## Lesson 8: Using AutoFormat

Although you can apply various formats to a table, you might want to see special table formats provided by AutoFormat. **AutoFormat** is a feature that applies predefined styles, such as borders and shading, to tables. In this lesson, you want to apply an AutoFormat style to your table to see what it will look like.

To Use AutoFormat

1 **In the** Sessions **document, make sure the Tables and Borders toolbar is displayed.**

 2 **Click the Table AutoFormat button on the toolbar.**
The Table AutoFormat dialog box contains various formats you can apply to your table (see Figure 8.19). You can also choose or avoid applying certain formats.

Figure 8.19
Use Table AutoFormat
to apply formats to
your table.

3 **Click Colorful 1 in the Forma_ts list box.**
You see a sample table formatted by the Colorful 1. You like the format but don't want to apply the format to the first row because it doesn't contain headings.

4 **Click the Heading _rows check box to deselect it, and click OK.**
Word applies the Colorful 1 settings to your table (see Figure 8.20).

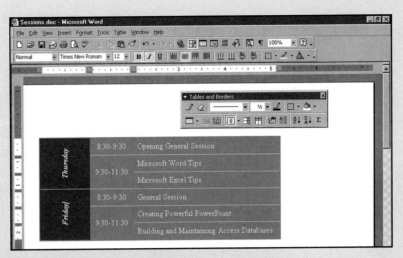

Figure 8.20
The table is formatted by the Colorful 1 AutoFormat.

 Save the document, print it, and close it.

Inside Stuff: **Undo a Table AutoFormat**

If you don't like how Table AutoFormat applies formats to your table, click the Undo button. You can select a different Table AutoFormat, select other check boxes, or deselect check boxes to change how formats are applied.

Summary

Throughout this project, you learned some exciting ways to adjust tables. You can merge and split cells to create a more effective table, adjust cell margins to make text look better, and align values in cells by setting a decimal tab. In addition, you can perform calculations, such as adding and multiplying values. You also learned how to sort table rows, rotate text in cells, draw a table with the mouse, and use AutoFormat.

To expand your knowledge, explore other options in the dialog boxes you encountered in this project. Also, experiment with the other buttons on the Tables and Borders toolbar. Finally, complete the following exercises to reinforce the skills you developed in this project.

Checking Concepts and Terms

True/False

For each of the following, check *T* or *F* to indicate whether the statement is true or false.

__T __F **1.** You must select cells before merging them together. [L1]

__T __F **2.** Changing margins for text in a table is a column option. [L2]

__T __F **3.** Word automatically updates the results of formulas when you change a value. [L3]

__T __F **4.** If your table does not contain merged cells, you can sort table data without selecting it first. [L5]

__T __F **5.** You can specify the exact degree, such as 175, for rotating text in a table. [L7]

Multiple Choice

Circle the letter of the correct answer for each of the following.

1. Which toolbar contains the AutoSum button? [L3]

a. Standard

b. Formatting

c. Tables and Borders

d. Formula

2. What term refers to the processing of combining cells into one cell? [L1]

a. Split

b. Merge

c. Join

d. Connect

3. After changing values in a table, you should click in a formula cell and press what button to update the formula results? [L3]

a. ⬆Shift + F1

b. ↵Enter

c. Ctrl + Tab⇆

d. F9

4. If you want to sort values to display them from high to low, what button should you click? [L5]

a. Sort Descending

b. Sort Ascending

c. AutoSum

d. AutoFormat

5. What button lets you rotate text in a cell? [L7]

a. Align Center

b. Sort Ascending

c. AutoSum

d. Change Text Direction

Screen ID

Label each element of the Word screen shown in Figure 8.21.

Figure 8.21

A AutoSum

B Merge Cells

C Sort Ascending

D Sort Descending

E Split Cells

1._____   2._____   3._____

4._____   5._____

Skill Drill

Skill Drill exercises reinforce project skills. Each skill reinforced is the same, or nearly the same, as a skill presented in the project. Each exercise includes a brief narrative introduction, followed by detailed instructions in a step-by-step format.

1. Merging Cells and Adjusting Cell Margins

You created a table to compare the budgeted and actual expenses for February. The office manager is concerned that the company is going over budget in several categories. You need to insert a row and merge cells to create a title row. In addition, you want to set cell margins to balance text.

1. Open **W-0802** and save it as **February Expense Memo**.

2. Click the Tables and Borders button on the Standard toolbar to display the Tables and Borders toolbar.

3. Click in the first row of the table and choose Table, Insert, Rows Above.

4. With the entire first row selected, click the Merge Cells button on the Tables and Borders toolbar.

5. Type **February Expenses**. *Note:* The title should be bold because the row takes on the bold from the previous row.

6. Click the Align Top Left button on the Tables and Borders toolbar and choose Align Center.

7. Select the cells containing values, as well as the two empty cells at the bottom of those columns.

8. Choose Table, Table Properties.

9. Click the Cell tab and then click Options.

10. Click the **Same as the whole table** check box to deselect it.

11. Press Alt+L and type **0.35** in the Left box.

12. Press Alt+R and type **0.35** in the Right box.

13. Click OK to close the Cell Options dialog box and then click OK to close the Table Properties dialog box.

14. Deselect the cells, save the document, and keep it onscreen to continue with the next exercise.

2. Performing Calculations and Aligning Values

You need to calculate the total budgeted and actual expenses. In addition, you want to align the values on the right side. Because the values do not contain decimal points, you do not have to set a decimal tab; you can simply choose the Align Top Right option.

1. With **February Expense Memo** onscreen, click in the empty cell at the bottom of the Budgeted column.

2. Click the AutoSum button on the Tables and Borders toolbar.

3. Click in the empty cell at the bottom of the Actual column.

4. Click the AutoSum button to insert the actual expense total.

5. Click the Align button on the Tables and Borders toolbar and choose Align Top Right.

6. Save the document and keep it onscreen to continue with the next exercise.

3. Sorting Table Data

You want to arrange the expenses in order from the highest to the lowest actual expense. In addition, you want to apply a Table AutoFormat style to the table.

1. In the **February Expense Memo** document, select the four expense rows by clicking and dragging from Supplies to 435. Do not include the row headings or total row.

2. Choose Table, Sort.

3. Click the **Sort by** drop-down arrow and choose Column 3.

4. Make sure the Type option shows Number.

5. Click the Descending option button.

6. Click OK.

7. Click the Table AutoFormat button on the Tables and Borders toolbar.

8. Scroll through the Formats list and choose Grid 8.

9. Click the First column check box to deselect it.

10. Click the Last row check box to select it.

11. Click OK.

12. Click and drag across Expense, Budgeted, and Actual to select these cells.

13. Click the Bold button.

14. With the three cells still selected, click the Font Color button and choose Indigo.

15. Deselect the cells.

16. Save, print, and close the document.

Challenge

Challenge exercises expand on or are somewhat related to skills presented in the lessons. Each exercise provides a brief narrative introduction followed by instructions in a numbered-step or bullet-list format that are not as detailed as those in the Skill Drill section.

1. Creating a Flight Table Within a Memo

You work for a travel company in Chicago. Although you provided a customer with information about her upcoming flights via a fax, you want to send her a letter containing a table of her itinerary.

1. Open **W-0803** and save it as **Flight Memo to Schuster**.

2. Select the Departs column and split it into two columns. Deselect **Merge cells before split**. Type the following information into the column created by the split:

   Arrives

   11:07 a.m.

   3:34 p.m.

   12:00 p.m.

   4:05 p.m.

   12:05 p.m.

   8:00 p.m.

3. Select the cells containing time and apply the Align Top Right alignment option. Also set 0.13-inch cell margins for these cells. *Note:* You might need to decrease the margins a fraction if 0.13 inches makes the text word-wrap in the cells.

4. Apply the Align Center alignment to the first row. Increase the row height to 0.3 inches.

5. Merge the first cell containing a value with the empty cell below it. Repeat this process for the other two values and their empty cells. Then apply Align Center Left to the three cells containing values.

6. With the three costs selected, set an appropriate decimal tab.

7. Center the text in the Flight Number column.

8. Keep the same widths for the Date and Destination columns. Adjust the cell margins to make the data look better within the cells.

9. Insert a row at the bottom of the table and merge the first five cells.

10. Type **Total Cost** in the newly merged cell and apply bold and Align Top Right formats.

11. Use AutoSum to calculate a total at the bottom of the Cost column. Set the same decimal tab for this cell as you did for the other costs.

12. Change 362.00 to **362.75**, and change 374.50 to **374.32**.

13. Click in the total and use the function key that updates the total. *Hint:* Refer to the exam note at the end of Lesson 3 to find out how to update the total.

14. Save and print the document.

2. Preparing a Distributor Table

Your company, Heavenly Scents Candles, has increased sales throughout several states. Your supervisor prepared a table that lists the cities and sales for this year and last year. You need to sort the table by state and then by city. In addition, you need to calculate the amount of increase, insert totals, and improve the table's appearance.

1. Open **W-0804** and save it as **Candle Distributor Sales**.

2. Without selecting the table, display the Sort Text dialog box. Choose State for the primary sort in ascending order and City for the secondary sort in ascending order. Make sure you choose the option that lets Word know your table has a header row.

3. Create a formula that finds the difference between this year's amount and last year's amount for the first city. Remember to use cell references. The increase for Colorado Springs is 15,000. Because you can't copy the formula for the other cities, you must create formulas for each city. Be careful when typing cell formulas and spot-check the answers for accuracy.

4. Select the cells containing values and set 0.28-inch left and right cell margins.

5. Align the values on the right side.

6. Insert a row at the bottom of the table. Type **Totals** in bold italic below the last city. Calculate the totals for the three value columns.

7. Save and print the document.

8. Keep the first listing of Colorado. Delete Colorado in the next two cells. *Note:* You're deleting the text, not the entire rows. Then merge the empty cells with the cell containing Colorado.

9. Repeat the basic process in Step 8 for the remaining states.

10. Select the cells containing the four state names and change the text direction so that the top is on the left side of the cell. Decrease the column width for the first column.

11. Select the entire table and choose 0.3-inch row height.

12. Apply Pale Blue shading and Align Center to the state names.

13. Apply Align Center Left alignment to the cities.

14. Apply Align Center Right alignment to the values.

15. Save the document as **Final Candle Sales Memo** and print the document.

3. Sorting and Formatting a Phone List

You prepared a list of some important business contacts. To make the list easier to use, you need to sort it by city, last name, and first name. In addition, you need to apply other formatting techniques.

1. Open **W-0805** and save it as **Business Contacts**.

2. Center the data on the first row.

3. Sort the table in this order of priority: (1) city, (2) last name, and (3) first name. Don't let the header row sort. Sort all three columns in ascending order.

4. Insert a row at the top of the table and merge the cells. Type the title **Important Business Contacts** in boldface, 14-point Arial.

5. Set a 0.4-inch row height and Align Center for the first row.

6. Apply Blue font color and Pale Blue shading for the first row.

7. Center the Phone Number column.

8. Keep the first three column widths and the same alignment. Set appropriate cell margins to make the text look good.

9. Center the table structure itself between the left and right margins.

10. Save the document and print it.

11. Apply a List 8 Table AutoFormat without formatting the first column. You need to bold the second row again.

12. Save the document as **Business Contacts List** and print it.

Discovery Zone

Discovery Zone exercises help you gain advanced knowledge of project topics and/or application of skills. These exercises focus on enhancing your problem-solving skills. Numbered steps are not provided, but you are given hints, reminders, screen shots, and/or references to help you reach your goal for each exercise.

1. Completing a Fourth-Quarter Sales Table

You've been asked to compile the weekly sales for the fourth quarter for 2001. You want to show the average weekly sales per month. Open **W-0806** and save it as **Fourth-Quarter Sales**.

Insert a row below each month's fourth week. In the new cells in the second column, type **Weekly Average**. Use the Formula dialog box to insert the Average function. Use Help and explore the function options. Remember to use cell references in the formulas. *Hint:* Use a colon to separate the beginning and ending cells in the range to average. Apply bold and Blue font color to the average values.

Merge each month's name with the empty cells below it. Then rotate the names of the months, so the top of the text is on the left side. Adjust the column width as needed. Center-align, bold, and apply Light Yellow shading to the month names.

Apply Yellow shading, 0.4-inch row height, bold, and Align Center to the first row. Center text in the second column and decrease its column width.

Set a 1.4-inch width for the cells in the last column. Then, adjust the cell margins for these cells or set a decimal tab to make the values look good in their cells. Center the table itself between the left and right margins.

2. Preparing a Personal Budget

You want to prepare a table that lists your typical expenses for each month in this semester (or quarter). The first column should list the expense categories and the other columns should list the expenses per month.

Include categories such as rent or mortgage, tuition, books, utilities, groceries, and so forth. Include a total row that shows the total for each month.

Apply formatting techniques you learned in this project and the last project. Use appropriate column widths, cell margins, alignment, shading, etc. to enhance the table.

Save the table as **Personal College Expenses** and print it.

Pinpoint Assessment

You have completed this project and its associated lessons, and have had an opportunity to assess your skills through the end-of-project questions and exercises. Now use the PinPoint software Evaluation Mode to further assess your comprehension of the specific exam activities you have just learned. You can also use the PinPoint Trainer Mode and the Show Me tutorials to practice these exam activities.

Inserting and Formatting Graphics

Key terms introduced in this project include

- associated keywords
- border
- clip art
- Clip Gallery

- fill
- gradient
- hypertext link
- sizing handles

- text box
- tight wrap
- WordArt
- wrapping style

Objectives	Required Activity for MOUS	Exam Level
➤ Insert an Image	Insert graphics into a document (WordArt, Clip Art, Images)	Core
➤ Move and Delete an Image	Delete and position graphics	Expert
➤ Size an Image		
➤ Wrap Text Around an Image	Use advanced text alignment features with graphics	Expert
➤ Insert an Image Saved from the Web	Insert graphics into a document (WordArt, Clip Art, Images)	Core
	Add bitmapped graphics	Expert
➤ Create a Text Box		
➤ Select Borders and Fills		
➤ Use WordArt	Insert graphics into a document (WordArt, Clip Art, Images)	Core

Why Would I Do This?

Some of the most exciting features of Word are its graphics capabilities. You can insert *clip art*, graphic images, or drawings, in any document. Use clip art to enhance fliers, brochures, newsletters, and announcements. You can also create other graphics elements to enhance documents.

Lesson I: Inserting an Image

Office 2000 comes with an enormous number of clip art images. You can find images representing people, animals, special occasions, and more! Depending on how Office 2000 was installed on your computer, you may have just a few or all of these images. In addition to using these images, you can obtain clip art from Microsoft's Web page at **www.microsoft.com** or purchase clip art packages at a computer supply store.

In this lesson, you insert clip art in a company newsletter. You search through the Clip Gallery to locate a particular image that corresponds with text in the document. The **Clip Gallery** is a collection of images, sound clips, and motion clips.

 Inside Stuff: Appropriate Uses of Images
Be sure to read about the legal uses of clip art images, whether you're using Microsoft's clip art or other clip art you've purchased. Although some clip art is acceptable for use in an educational environment, it may not be legal to use in some advertising situations.

To Insert an Image

1 Open W-0901 **and save it as** June Newsletter**.**

2 Position the insertion point at the end of the document by pressing Ctrl+End**.**

3 Choose **I**nsert, **P**icture, **C**lip Art.
The Insert ClipArt dialog box appears, as shown in Figure 9.1. The dialog box displays the Clip Gallery, so you can select pictures, sound, or motion clips. The Pictures tab organizes images into categories, such as Animals, Entertainment, and Seasons.

Figure 9.1
Select an image
category.

Click to get clips
from Web site

Image categories

Click to see
other
categories

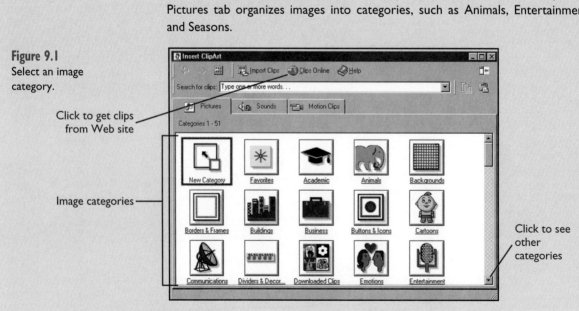

You want to select a dental image, which can be found in the Healthcare and Medicine category.

4 **Scroll through the picture categories and click Healthcare & Medicine to see a gallery of healthcare images (see Figure 9.2).**

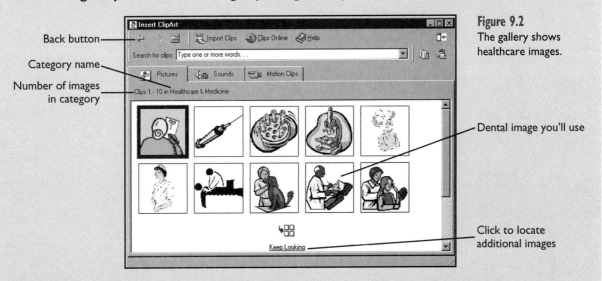

Back button

Category name

Number of images in category

Dental image you'll use

Click to locate additional images

Figure 9.2
The gallery shows healthcare images.

5 **Right-click the dental image and choose Insert.**
Word inserts the image at the insertion point location. You need to close the dialog box to see the image in your document.

 Inside Stuff: **Other Ways to Insert Images**
You can use the Copy and Paste commands to insert an image. Simply click an image and click the Copy button within the dialog box. Then, click in your document and click the Paste button on the Standard toolbar.

You can also click the image to see a palette of four buttons. Click the Insert Clip button to insert the image.

---

6 **Click the Close button in the upper-right corner of the dialog box.**
The image appears at the end of the document, causing the last text line to move down (see Figure 9.3).

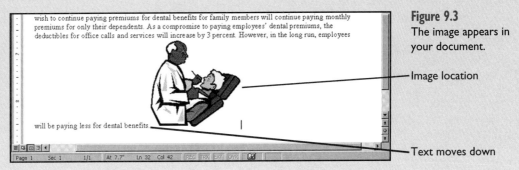

Figure 9.3
The image appears in your document.

Image location

Text moves down

7 **Save the document and keep it onscreen to continue with the next lesson.**

***Exam Note:* Using Other Images**

You can insert almost any type of image by choosing Insert, Picture, From File. Some image file types you can use include Joint Photographic Experts Group (.jpg), Windows Bitmap (.bmp), Graphics Interchange Format (.gif), and Windows Metafile (.wmf). Word can insert these types of files without any special conversion.

If you want to insert other types of graphics files, such as a WordPerfect (.wpg) graphics image, you must install the graphics filters from the installation CD first.

 ***Inside Stuff:* Scanning a Picture**

If you have a scanner attached to your computer, you can scan a picture to use as an image within Word. Choose Insert, Picture, From Scanner or Camera. Refer to the Help topic `Scan a picture and insert it in a document` for more information about inserting an image into your document by using a scanner.

 ## Lesson 2: Moving and Deleting an Image

After inserting an image, you might want to move it around on the page until you are satisfied with its location. If you want to move an image to another area that you currently see onscreen, you can click and drag the image there.

In this lesson, you move the image below the heading and position it in the left margin.

 ***Exam Note:* Moving an Image to an Unseen Area**

If you can't see the part of the document to which you want to move the image, do *not* click and drag. Doing so might cause your screen to scroll so quickly through the document that you won't be able to stop at the place you want to drop the image.

Instead, click the image and then click the Cut button. Position the insertion point where you want the image to appear and click the Paste button. This is easier than clicking and dragging the image from page to page.

To Move an Image

❶ In the June Newsletter document, click the image to select it.
Word displays *sizing handles*—little black boxes that appear around the image so that you can adjust the image's size and move it elsewhere (see Figure 9.4).

 If You Have Problems...
If you don't see the Picture toolbar, choose View, Toolbars, Picture to display the Picture toolbar.

❷ Position the mouse pointer on the image and hold down the mouse button.
You see a gray box below the mouse pointer arrowhead. This means that you are about to move the image.

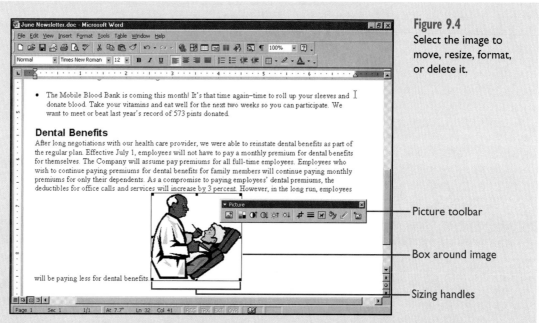

Figure 9.4
Select the image to move, resize, format, or delete it.

Picture toolbar

Box around image

Sizing handles

3 **Click and drag the image to the beginning of the following paragraph—the paragraph immediately below Dental Benefits.**

The shadow cursor that follows your mouse pointer lets you know where the image will appear when you release the mouse button.

4 **Release the mouse button at the beginning of the paragraph.**

The image appears at the beginning of the paragraph, as shown in Figure 9.5. The image and last paragraph might appear at the top of the second page or it might still appear at the bottom of the first page.

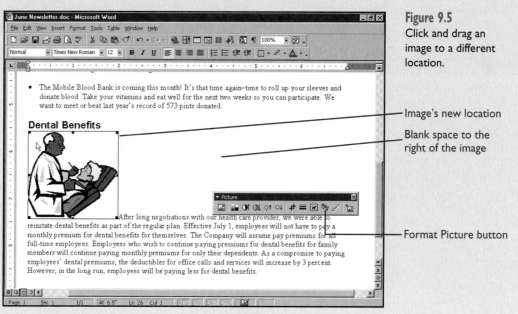

Figure 9.5
Click and drag an image to a different location.

Image's new location

Blank space to the right of the image

Format Picture button

5 **Click outside the image.**

Clicking outside the image deselects it so you can work elsewhere in your document.

6 **Save the document and keep it onscreen to continue with the next lesson.**

✍ *Exam Note:* **Deleting an Image**
If you want to delete an image, click it to select it. Then, press Del.

Lesson 3: Sizing an Image

When you insert an image in a document, it comes in at a predetermined size. Most of the time, you need to adjust the image's size so that it fits better within the document.

In this lesson, you decide on a specific size for the image. You want it to be 1.6 inches tall and 1.69 inches wide. To set a specific size, you need to access the Format Picture dialog box.

To Change the Image's Size

① **In the June Newsletter document, click the dental image to select it.**
The Picture toolbar should appear. If it doesn't, right-click the Standard toolbar and choose Picture.

② **Click the Format Picture button on the Picture toolbar.**
The Format Picture dialog box appears. You use this dialog box to select the format settings for your images.

③ **Click the Size tab.**
You see the options for setting the size of your image, as shown in Figure 9.6.

Figure 9.6
Use the Format Picture dialog box to specify an exact size for your image.

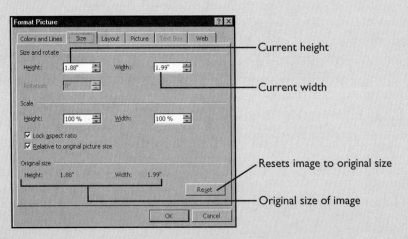

Current height
Current width
Resets image to original size
Original size of image

④ **Click and drag across 1.88 inches in the Height box.**

⑤ **Type 1.6.**
When you select the current setting and type, the new setting replaces the old setting. Also, you don't have to type the inch mark.

⑥ **Press Tab⇆ to make the Width box active.**
The width should automatically change to 1.69 inches.

⑦ **Click OK.**

⑧ **Scroll to the bottom of page 1.**
The picture and part of the last paragraph now fit at the bottom of page 1. The image is slightly smaller, as shown in Figure 9.7.

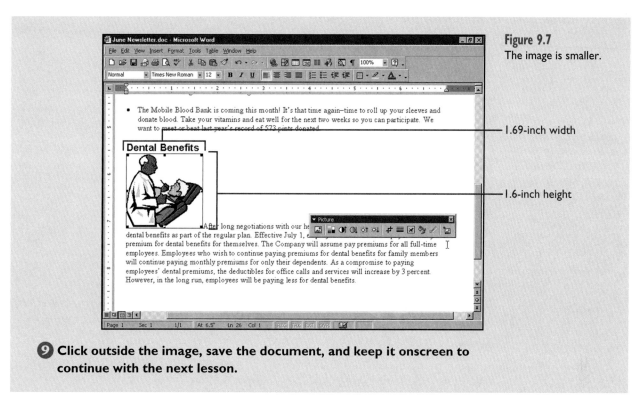

Figure 9.7
The image is smaller.

— 1.69-inch width

— 1.6-inch height

9 **Click outside the image, save the document, and keep it onscreen to continue with the next lesson.**

 Inside Stuff: **Using the Sizing Handles**
If you don't need an exact size, you can click and drag the sizing handles to adjust the image's size. Table 9.1 describes how to use the sizing handles.

Table 9.1   Adjusting the Image's Size with the Sizing Handles

Desired Result	Do This:
Increase the width	Click and drag either the middle-left or middle-right sizing handle away from the image.
Decrease the width	Click and drag either the middle-left or middle-right sizing handle toward the image.
Increase the height	Click and drag the upper-middle or bottom-middle sizing handle away from the image.
Decrease the height	Click and drag the upper-middle or bottom-middle sizing handle toward the image.
Adjust the height and the width at the same time	Click and drag a corner sizing handle at an angle to adjust height and width.

Lesson 4: Wrapping Text Around an Image

Word places text above and below an image when you first insert it. Although some images look better with no text to the left or right sides, you might want to wrap text around the image. ***Wrapping style*** refers to the way text wraps around an image. You can have text appear on top of or behind an image, wrap tightly around the outer edges of the image itself, or wrap above or below the image.

In this lesson, you choose ***tight wrap*** to wrap text around the edge of the image itself instead of the square boundary of the image.

To Wrap Text Around an Image

1 In the `June Newsletter` document, click the image to select it.

2 Click the Text Wrapping button on the Picture toolbar to see a list of text-wrapping options, as shown in Figure 9.8.

Figure 9.8
The text-wrapping options specify the way text wraps around the image.

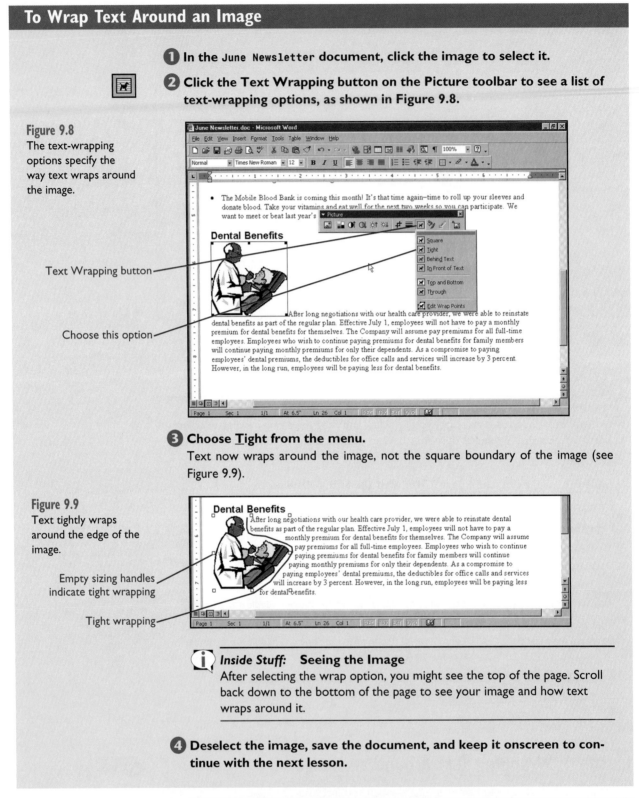

Text Wrapping button

Choose this option

3 Choose **T**ight from the menu.
Text now wraps around the image, not the square boundary of the image (see Figure 9.9).

Figure 9.9
Text tightly wraps around the edge of the image.

Empty sizing handles indicate tight wrapping

Tight wrapping

ⓘ *Inside Stuff:* **Seeing the Image**
After selecting the wrap option, you might see the top of the page. Scroll back down to the bottom of the page to see your image and how text wraps around it.

4 Deselect the image, save the document, and keep it onscreen to continue with the next lesson.

✎ *Exam Note:* **Selecting Wrap Style and Alignment**
You can display the Format Picture dialog box and then click the Layout tab to select a wrapping style (see Figure 9.10). In addition, you can choose the horizontal alignment of the image, such as centering it between the left and right margins. The Horizontal alignment options are available for any wrapping style *except* `In line with text`.

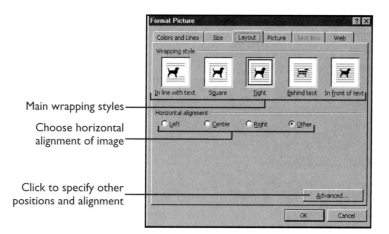

Figure 9.10
You can select a wrapping style and horizontal alignment.

Main wrapping styles

Choose horizontal alignment of image

Click to specify other positions and alignment

 Inside Stuff: **Top and Bottom Wrap**
If you want to place an image between paragraphs without text wrapping on either the left or right sides, you need to choose Top and Bottom as the wrap option. You can choose this option by clicking the Text Wrapping button on the Picture toolbar or by clicking Advanced within the Layout tab of the Format Picture dialog box.

Lesson 5: Inserting an Image Saved from the Web

The Internet contains a vast number of clip art images. You can use a search engine, such as Excite, to search for Web sites that contain clip art images that you can purchase or download free. For example, registered users of Microsoft Word can download additional clip art free.

 Inside Stuff: **Using Downloaded Clip Art**
When you find clip art on the Internet, you need to review that particular Web site's policy on acceptable use of its images. Many sites allow you to download a copy for your personal use only. Others might allow you to include their images in limited advertising, brochures, and company newsletters. You are typically restricted from making unlimited copies of the clip art for other people or selling the clip art for personal gain.

In this lesson, you explore downloadable images on Microsoft's Web site and insert a photo into your document.

To Download an Image from a Web Site

1 **In the June Newsletter document, click at the beginning of the first paragraph and choose Insert, Picture, Clip Art.**
The Insert ClipArt dialog box appears. Instead of choosing an image on your computer, you want to download a picture from Microsoft's Web site.

2 **Click Clips Online at the top of the dialog box.**

3 **Click OK when you see a dialog box telling you that the clips you select will be added to your Clip Gallery.**
Internet Explorer starts and displays the End-User License Agreement. Read through the agreement to learn about acceptable uses of the clips.

continues ▶

To Download an Image from a Web Site   (continued)

4 **Click Accept when you read and agree to accept the terms.**
The Microsoft Clip Gallery Live Web page appears (see Figure 9.11).

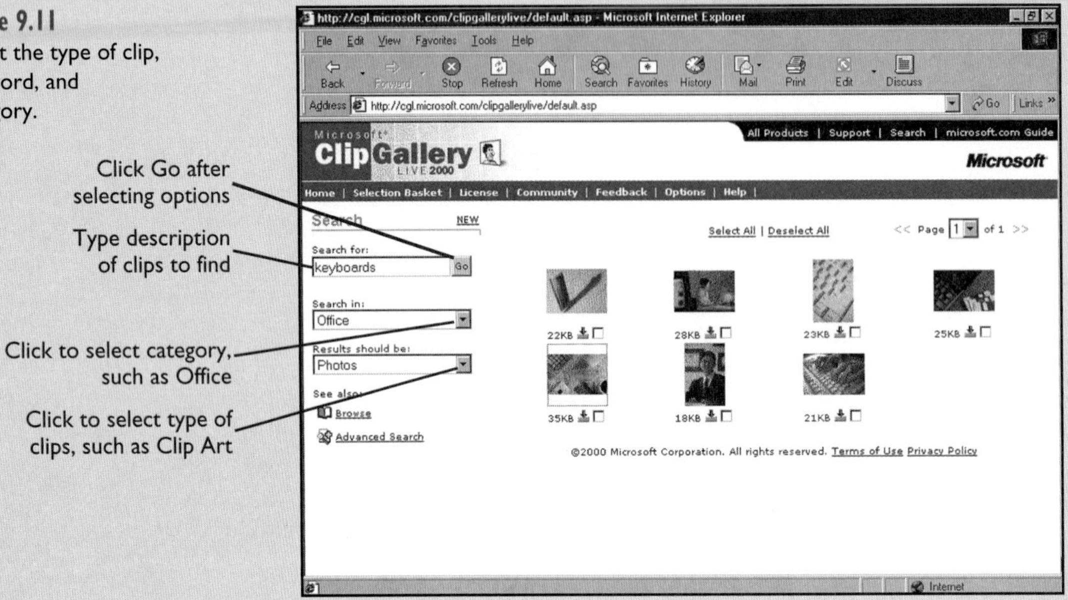

Figure 9.11
Select the type of clip,
keyword, and
category.

Click Go after
selecting options

Type description
of clips to find

Click to select category,
such as Office

Click to select type of
clips, such as Clip Art

(i) *Inside Stuff:*   **Different Web Options**
Web pages constantly change; therefore, you might see different objects and images in the Web page on your screen than those shown in this book. You should be able to use the category and search options to locate the images specified in the steps.

---

5 **Type keyboards in the Search for text box.**
You want to find images of keyboards.

6 **Click the Search in drop-down arrow, scroll through the list and choose Office.**
The Office category should contain images of keyboards.

7 **Click the Results should be drop-down arrow and choose Photos; then click the Go button.**
You should see photos that include keyboards.

8 **Click the photo that contains a keyboard, mouse, and cup of coffee.**
The image appears in a separate preview window (see Figure 9.12). You also see a list of associated keywords to the right of the image. *Associated keywords* are words that describe the clip. Microsoft uses keywords to help organize clips and help you find clips that contain the same keywords. The keywords are formatted as hypertext links. When you click a *hypertext link*, you connect to another Web page.

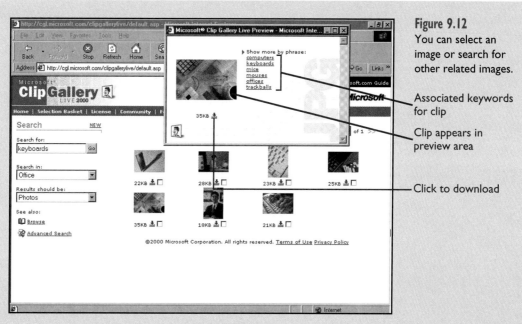

Figure 9.12
You can select an image or search for other related images.

Associated keywords for clip

Clip appears in preview area

Click to download

9 **Click the download icon to download the image.**
The picture is downloaded into the Clip Gallery.

 If You Have Problems...
If you are using Netscape, the image is not automatically downloaded. You must choose to save the image to your network drive, hard drive, or data disk. The saved image is not included in the Clip Gallery. You must select it by choosing Insert, Picture, From File.

10 **Right-click the image and choose Insert to insert the picture in your document.**

 If You Have Problems...
If you don't see the image you just downloaded, click the Downloaded Clips category, right-click the image, and choose Insert.

11 **Close the Insert Clip Art dialog box; close the Internet Explorer window; and sign off from your online service if necessary.**

 Inside Stuff: **Using the Downloaded Clip Again**
When you initially download a clip, it automatically appears in the Insert Clip Art dialog box window. You can use the downloaded clip again at any time. The next time you display the Insert Clip Art dialog box, click the category that contains the clip you downloaded from Internet Explorer. The clip is typically downloaded into the same category in which you selected it from the Web site.

After you insert the image, you need to decrease the size of the picture and place it in the right margin.

To Adjust the Picture

❶ Click the Format Picture button on the Picture toolbar.

❷ Click the Size tab and type 1 in the H̲eight box.

❸ Click the Layout tab and click the Sq̲uare wrapping style.

❹ Click the R̲ight horizontal alignment, and then click OK.

The picture is now positioned on the right side of the paragraph, as shown in Figure 9.13.

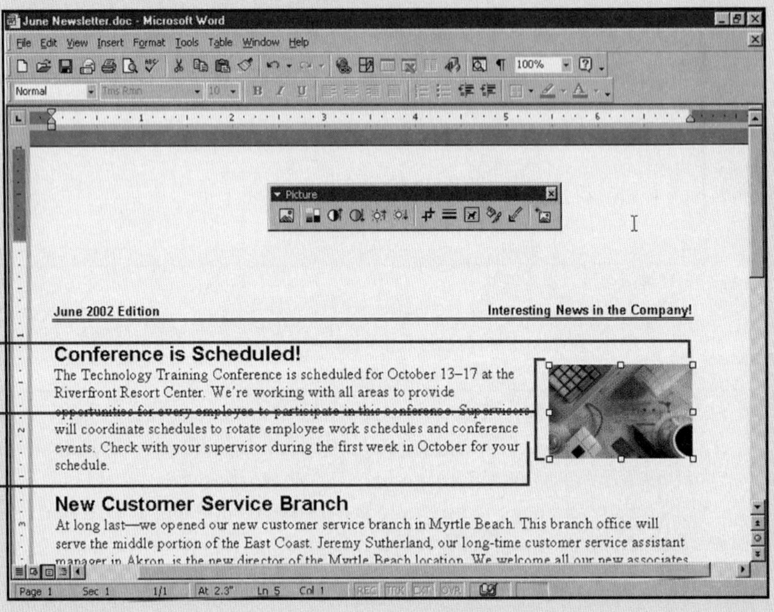

Figure 9.13
The image down-loaded from the Internet is now formatted in your document.

Photo at right margin ——

1-inch height ——

Square wrapping style ——

❺ Deselect the image, save the document, and keep it onscreen to continue with the next lesson.

Exam Note: **Saving Other Images from the Internet**
When you want to save a graphic image from another Web site, right-click the image and choose Save Picture As. You can typically save images in jpeg, bmp, or gif format. Then choose I̲nsert, P̲icture, F̲rom File to insert the image you downloaded from the Internet.

Lesson 6: Creating a Text Box

In addition to inserting clip art, you might want to create a text box. A **text box** is a graphics object containing text; it is useful for grabbing the reader's attention. You can place the text box within a paragraph, add a border, and use other graphics options to customize the way the text appears.

Text boxes are used to draw attention to text on the page. Magazines typically use text boxes to highlight a quote, special information, or exciting news. To make a text box stand out, you should select a different font and font size. In this lesson, you create a text box to make people more inclined to read information on the page.

To Create a Text Box

1 In the June Newsletter document, position the insertion point at the beginning of the Just a Reminder heading.

2 Choose Insert, Text Box.

You must draw the box area where you want to place the text box.

3 Click and drag to form a small box that looks like the one in Figure 9.14.

To do this, start clicking on the first line of the following paragraph at about the 5-inch mark. Then, drag down and to the right until the mouse pointer is at the end of the last line of the same paragraph at the right margin.

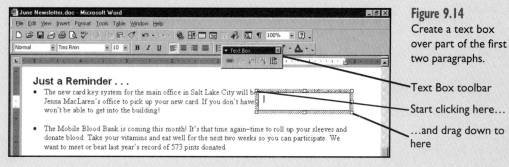

Figure 9.14
Create a text box over part of the first two paragraphs.

Text Box toolbar

Start clicking here...

...and drag down to here

4 Click the Font drop-down arrow on the Formatting toolbar and choose Arial Rounded MT Bold or Arial Black.

You want to choose a sans serif font to stand out from the serif font used in the paragraphs.

5 Click the Font Size drop-down arrow and choose 12.

You want to make the text bigger to draw the reader's eyes to the text box.

6 Type Get Your New Key Card! in the text box.

7 Click and drag the bottom middle sizing handle down to the left to increase the height of the text box a little if you can't read the text you just typed. Decrease the width a little to balance the text on two lines.

Your text box now contains text in a different font and font size. Now you need to adjust the wrap option so that the text box does not cover up regular text in the paragraphs.

8 Position the mouse pointer along the outer border of the text box.

9 When you see a four-headed arrow, right-click the border of the text box and choose Format Text Box from the shortcut menu.

You see the Format Text Box dialog box. It looks similar to the Format Picture dialog box you used in previous lessons.

10 Click the Layout tab.

11 Click the Square wrapping option and click the Right horizontal alignment option; then click OK.

The text box does not cover the paragraph text any more, as shown in Figure 9.15.

continues ▶

To Create a Text Box   (continued)

Figure 9.15
The text in your text
box stands out.

Text box font

Text box font size

Square wrapping option

Click and drag to right to
decrease width

Click and drag down to
increase height

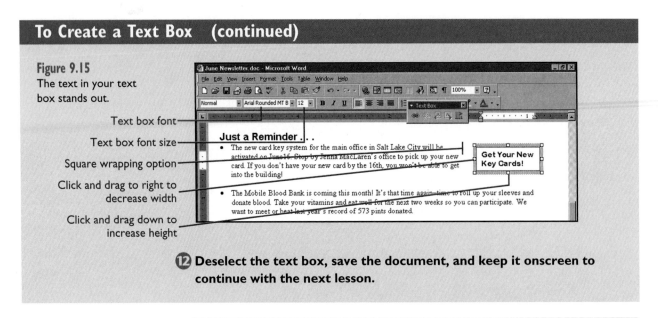

🔟 **Deselect the text box, save the document, and keep it onscreen to
continue with the next lesson.**

ⓘ *Inside Stuff:*   **Formatting a Text Box**
Instead of right-clicking the border of the text box and choosing Format Text B<u>o</u>x,
you can choose F<u>o</u>rmat, Text B<u>o</u>x from the menu bar.

Lesson 7: Selecting Borders and Fills

You can enhance text boxes and images by selecting fills and borders. **Fill** refers to a shading
color that appears in the background of a text box or around the image within its square
boundaries. A **border** is a line style that creates a frame around an object.

The text box currently has a single black line border. In this lesson, you choose a pale blue fill
and a dark blue border.

To Select Borders and Fills

❶ **In the June Newsletter document, position the mouse pointer on the
text box border and click the right mouse button.**
You see the shortcut menu of options to adjust the text box settings.

❷ **Choose Format Text B<u>o</u>x and click the Colors and Lines tab.**
You see the options to specify a fill color and line color and style.

❸ **Click the <u>C</u>olor drop-down arrow in the Fill section of the dialog box.**
You see a color palette from which to choose a fill color (see Figure 9.16).

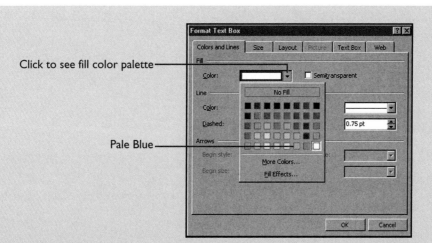

Click to see fill color palette ⎯

Pale Blue ⎯

Figure 9.16
Select the color you want to fill in the text box background.

④ **Click the Pale Blue color.**

⑤ **Click the Line Color drop-down arrow option. You see the same colors for the line color.**

> ⓘ ***Inside Stuff:*** **Choosing Fill and Border Colors**
> Choose complementary fill and border colors. For example, choose Light Blue fill and Dark Blue border color.

⑥ **Click the Blue color.**

⑦ **Click the Style drop-down arrow and choose 3 pt.**

⑧ **Click OK.**
Your text box looks much better with a touch of color (see Figure 9.17).

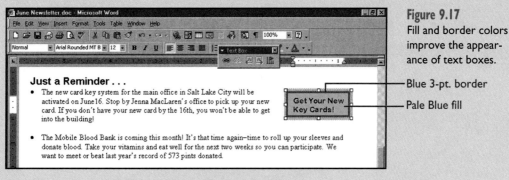

Figure 9.17
Fill and border colors improve the appearance of text boxes.

⎯ Blue 3-pt. border
⎯ Pale Blue fill

⑨ **Deselect the text box, save the document, and keep it onscreen to continue with the next lesson.**

ⓘ ***Inside Stuff:*** **Customizing the Fill Color**
You can choose additional colors besides those shown on the Fill color palette. Click More Colors on the palette and click the Custom tab in the Colors dialog box. You can click any part of the color pad to choose any color you see on the color palette.

In addition, you can select special fill effects by choosing Fill Effects from the Fill color palette. For example, you can blend two colors (such as Light Blue and Dark Blue) to form a ***gradient*** appearance. In addition, you can choose from a variety of texture backgrounds, such as marble.

Lesson 8: Using WordArt

Another exciting graphic feature is WordArt. **WordArt** shapes text into designs for you. You can use WordArt to create unique banners and titles for fliers, brochures, and other advertising documents. Because WordArt is a graphic object, you can use similar options to those you used to customize your clip art.

In this lesson, you create a WordArt object for the title of your newsletter.

To Create WordArt

1 In the June Newsletter document, position the insertion point at the top of the document.

2 Choose Insert, Picture, WordArt.
The WordArt Gallery dialog box appears (see Figure 9.18). The first step is to select a style or shape for your text.

Figure 9.18
Select a style or shape for your text.

Click this style

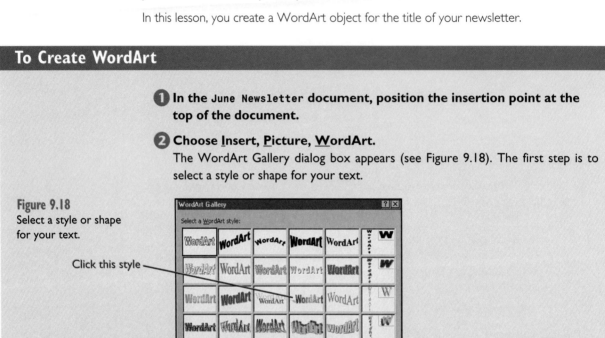

3 Click the fourth style on the third row.

4 Click OK.
The Edit WordArt Text dialog box appears, as shown in Figure 9.19. This is where you type the text and select the font and font size you want.

Figure 9.19
Type and format your WordArt text.

Click to select a font
Click to select a font size
Type text here

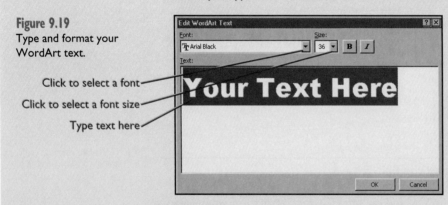

5 Type The Millennium Group in the text area.
You need to choose a smaller font for your title.

6 Click the Size drop-down arrow and choose 28; then click OK.
Although the insertion point was at the beginning of the document, the WordArt object appears in a different position (see Figure 9.20).

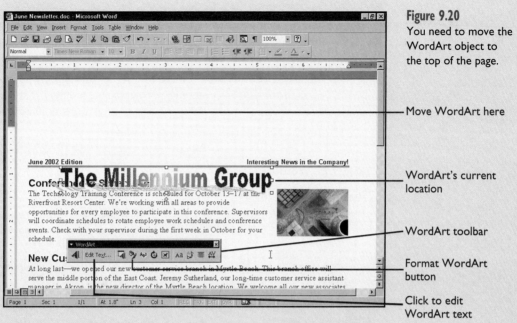

Figure 9.20
You need to move the WordArt object to the top of the page.

—Move WordArt here

—WordArt's current location

—WordArt toolbar

—Format WordArt button

—Click to edit WordArt text

7 Position the mouse pointer inside the WordArt area. Click and drag the WordArt to the top of the page.

8 Click the Format WordArt button on the WordArt toolbar.
You see the Format WordArt dialog box, which is similar to the Format Picture dialog box.

9 Click the Layout tab, click the Square wrapping style, click Center alignment, and click OK.
Your WordArt object is now positioned at the top of the page and is centered between the left and right margins (see Figure 9.21).

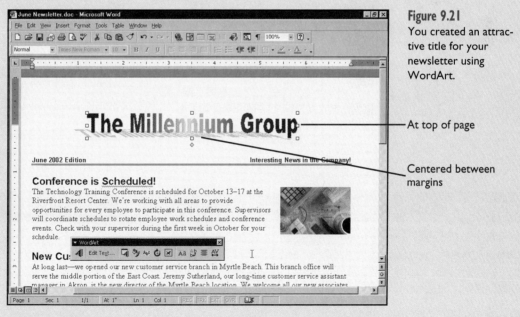

Figure 9.21
You created an attractive title for your newsletter using WordArt.

—At top of page

—Centered between margins

10 Deselect the WordArt object, save the document, print it, and then close the document.

***Exam Note:*   Customizing WordArt**

If you need to edit your WordArt object later, double-click the WordArt object to change the text, font, or font size.

If you want to customize the WordArt object, click it to see the WordArt toolbar. Then you can select options from the toolbar to enhance the appearance of the object. For example, you can rotate the object, select a different style from the gallery, or choose a different shape. Table 9.2 lists the functions of different WordArt toolbar buttons.

Table 9.2   WordArt Buttons

Button	Button Name	Description
	Insert WordArt	Displays the WordArt Gallery dialog box so that you can choose a style and then type WordArt text.
Edit Text...	Edit Text	Displays dialog box to edit text, font, and font size.
	WordArt Gallery	Displays Gallery to choose a different style.
	Format WordArt	Displays the Format WordArt dialog box to change size, layout, etc.
	WordArt Shape	Displays palette of various shapes for the WordArt.
	Free Rotate	Displays rotation handles (green circles) to click and drag to rotate the WordArt.
	Text Wrapping	Displays list of text wrapping options, such as Top and Bottom.
	WordArt Same Letter Height	Adjusts WordArt letters so that they are the size height.
	WordArt Vertical Text	Changes WordArt to a vertical object.
	WordArt Alignment	Displays palette of alignment options, such as Stretch Justify.
	WordArt Character Spacing	Lets you adjust spacing between characters.

Summary

You should be able to create exciting graphics in your documents now. You can insert clip art, photos, change the clip's size and location, and adjust the text wrap style. In addition, you can create attention-getting text boxes with pleasing fill and border colors. Finally, you learned how to design exciting WordArt objects to make headings and banners.

Although much information about graphics is included here, Word provides many more choices for customizing pictures, text boxes, and WordArt. You can learn a lot by simply exploring the different options on the toolbars and by using onscreen Help. Plus, you'll learn more graphic options in the next project.

Checking Concepts and Terms

True/False

For each of the following, check *T* or *F* to indicate whether the statement is true or false.

__T __F   **1.** If you want to move an object to a location you can't see onscreen, you should click and drag the image there. [L2]

__T __F   **2.** If you click and drag the middle-right sizing handle to the left, you decrease the width of an image. [L3]

__T __F   **3.** Square wrap enables text to wrap on both sides of the image but maintains a box around the image. [L4]

__T __F   **4.** When you first create a text box, its wrapping style is Square. [L6]

__T __F   **5.** A fast way to edit the text in WordArt is to double-click the object. [L8]

Multiple Choice

Circle the letter of the correct answer for each of the following.

1. All of the following are graphic image types *except* _____. [L1]

a. .jpg

b. .gif

c. .doc

d. .bmp

2. You can do all of the following to an image that has sizing handles around it except _____. [L2–4]

a. adjust the image's width

b. move the image to a different location

c. increase the height of the image

d. adjust the text wrapping around the image

3. Which wrap option allows text to wrap around the specific image itself, not the graphics area? [L4]

a. Square

b. Tight

c. Top to Bottom

d. Through

4. Which of the following format techniques does not highlight the information in a text box? [L6]

a. 8-point size

b. light fill color

c. using a different font, such as Arial

d. interesting text

5. What option lets you select a color background within a text box? [L7]

a. highlight

b. border

c. fill

d. wrapping

Screen ID

Label each element of the Word screen shown in Figure 9.22.

Figure 9.22

A. Clip art image

B. Format Picture (Object) button

C. Text box

D. Text Wrapping button

E. WordArt

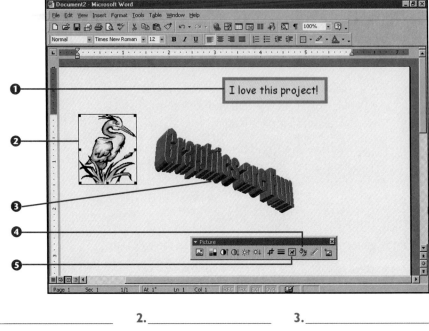

1._____ 2._____ 3._____

4._____ 5._____

Skill Drill

Skill Drill exercises reinforce project skills. Each skill reinforced is the same, or nearly the same, as a skill presented in the project. Each exercise includes a brief narrative introduction, followed by detailed instructions in a step-by-step format.

1. Inserting, Sizing, and Formatting a Bitmap Image

The local Parent Educator Association (PEA) has asked you to create this month's newsletter for parents about school activities. You have been given the basic text, but you decide that images, clip art, and quotes will enhance the newsletter's appearance and encourage parents to read it.

1. Open **W-0902** and save it as **PEA Newsletter**.

2. With the insertion point at the beginning of the document, choose Insert, Picture, From File.

3. Choose the drive that contains the CD-ROM that accompanies this book. Double-click the appropriate folders, double-click the **Project 09** folder, click PEA.bmp, and click Insert.

4. Click the image to display the sizing handles.

5. Click the Format Picture button on the Picture toolbar.

6. Click the Size tab.

7. Click and drag across the current Height setting, type **1.5"**, and click OK.

8. Save the document and keep it onscreen to continue with the next exercise.

2. Inserting, Sizing, and Formatting a Clip Art Image

You want to insert a fun clip art image from the Insert ClipArt dialog box. The Academic category might contain an appropriate image. After inserting the image, you need to adjust its size, layout, and wrap options.

1. In the open **PEA Newsletter** document, position the insertion point at the end of the first sentence after the heading Book Fair.

2. Choose Insert, Picture, Clip Art.

3. Click the Academic category, right-click the image of the three books, and choose Insert.

4. Click the Close button in the upper-right corner of the dialog box.

5. Click the Format Picture button on the Picture toolbar.

6. Click the Size tab, click and drag across the value in the Width box, and type **1.5**.

7. Click the Layout tab in the Format Picture dialog box.

8. Click the Square wrapping style, click the Right alignment option, and click OK.

9. Drag the image up a little, so the top of the image is aligned with the top of the Happenings heading.

10. Deselect the image, save the document, and keep it onscreen to continue with the next exercise.

3. Inserting a Text Box, Using Borders and Fills, and Creating WordArt

You decide to create a text box to emphasize information about the upcoming PEA Halloween Party for the children of the school. After creating the text box, you want to apply a light orange fill. Finally, you need to create a banner using WordArt.

1. In the open **PEA Newsletter** document, choose Insert, Text Box.

2. Click and drag to form a small box approximately 2 inches wide and 0.75 inches high below the last paragraph.

3. Click the Font Size drop-down arrow and choose 14. Click the Font drop-down arrow and choose Comic Sans MS.

4. Type the following lines in the text box:

   Friday, October 29

   6:30-8:00 p.m.

   Halloween Party

5. Click and drag the sizing handles to increase the text box a little if you can't read the text you just typed.

6. Right-click the text box and choose Format Text Box from the shortcut menu.

7. Click the Layout tab.

8. Click the Square wrapping option, click the Center alignment option, and click OK.

9. Click the Colors and Lines tab in the Format Text Box dialog box.

10. Click the Color drop-down arrow in the Fill section, and click Tan.

11. Click the Color drop-down arrow in the Lines section, and click Orange.

12. Click the Style drop-down arrow option and select the 2 point option.

13. Click OK and deselect the text box.

14. Position the insertion point at the top of the document and choose Insert, Picture, WordArt.

15. Click the third style on the third row and click OK.

16. Type **Maple Elementary** in the Text area.

17. Click the Size drop-down arrow, choose 40, and click OK.

18. Position the mouse pointer inside the WordArt area; click and drag the WordArt to the top of the page and right of the PEA Logo. Make sure the base of the dark green WordArt text aligns with the bottom of the triangle in the logo.

19. Deselect the WordArt object, save the document, and print it.

Challenge

Challenge exercises expand on or are somewhat related to skills presented in the lessons. Each exercise provides a brief narrative introduction followed by instructions in a numbered-step or bulleted-list format that are not as detailed as those in the Skill Drill section.

1. Editing a Fourth of July Invitation

You are in charge of the annual Family Fourth of July celebration. You decide to create an eye-catching invitation for your extended family members using WordArt, clip art, and a text box.

1. Open **W-0903** and save it as **Family Invitation**.

2. Apply the Fireworks Art border to the page. It is the 28th border option in the A<u>r</u>t border drop-down list.

3. Position your insertion point immediately before the Special Guests line. From the Home and Family clip art category, locate and insert the image of a grandpa and grandma having a picnic.

4. Use the Format Picture dialog box to set a 2.5-inch height.

5. Apply the Top and Bottom wrapping style with a Center alignment for the image.

6. Position your insertion point at the bottom of the document. From the Special Occasions clip art category, locate and insert the Fourth of July fireworks clip art image.

7. Apply these formats to the image you just inserted: 0.75 inches high, Center alignment, Top and Bottom wrapping style.

8. Position your insertion point between the lines **Grandpa is bringing his fiddle** and **Don't miss the fiddling and fireworks!** Create a text box approximately 2 inches wide and enter the following information in 14-point Times New Roman:

    Where: Anderson Memorial Park

    When: July 4, 3 p.m.

    RSVP: your name @ 555-8242

9. Adjust the width and height of the text box, as needed.

10. Apply a Red, 3-point border with a Light Yellow fill color.

11. Apply a Top and Bottom wrapping style, and center the text box between the left and right margins. Adjust the space above and below the text box.

12. Create a WordArt heading at the top of your invitation. The heading should read **Family 4th of July Picnic**. Use the WordArt style of your choice and adjust the position as needed.

13. Save the document and print it.

2. Enhancing a Halloween Invitation

You created a Halloween invitation. You want to search the Microsoft Clip Gallery Live to find an appropriate image. In addition, you want to create a title using WordArt.

1. Open **W-0904** and save it as **Halloween Party**.

2. Using the WordArt feature, insert **Halloween Party!** at the top of the invitation. Use the third style on the fourth row of the WordArt Gallery. Use 44-point Comic Sans MS. Set horizontal alignment to <u>C</u>enter.

3. Create a text box at the bottom of the invitation text. Type **Don't forget your costume!** in 24-point Comic Sans MS, bold, Orange font color. Set horizontal align-

ment to <u>C</u>enter. Select the Tan fill for the text box and set an Orange 3-point line border. Adjust the size of the text box as needed.

4. In the blank space below Let the Good Times Roll, insert a clip art image from Microsoft's Web site. Access Microsoft's Web site from the <u>C</u>lips Online option of the Insert ClipArt dialog box. Search for clips by using the keyword Halloween. Select an appropriate image and insert it into your invitation. Adjust the size, wrap style, and alignment of the image.

5. Apply a page border using an appropriate Halloween art border. Change the color of the art border to orange.

6. Choose the option to vertically center the page.

7. Save the document and print it.

3. Creating an Airline Information Sheet

You work for a small airline service that provides transportation from Oklahoma City to special-attraction vacation spots, such as Las Vegas, Denver, and Salt Lake City. You want to design an attractive information sheet about safety instructions for the passengers.

1. Open **W-0905** and save it as **Airline Information**.

2. Select the list of rules at the bottom of the document. Use the Bullets and Numbering dialog box to create a customized bulleted list using the Wingdings symbol of an airplane. *Note:* The airplane symbol is on the second row of symbols. Change the symbol font color to Blue, but make sure the text remains in Black.

3. Apply a paragraph border around the selected bulleted list. Select Light Yellow shading.

4. Position the insertion point at the beginning of the document and access the Microsoft Clip Gallery Live Web site.

5. Select the Transportation category in the Photos type.

6. Preview the clip of the plane with the sun in the background; then download it.

7. Insert the clip in your document. Move it to the right side of the paragraph. Set a 2-inch height, <u>B</u>ehind Text wrapping style in the Layout section, and a 58% picture Brightness.

8. Create a WordArt banner using the third style in the first column of the Gallery. Type **Sunset Airlines** for the text. Move the WordArt above the first paragraph, apply a S<u>q</u>uare wrap, and center it between the left and right margins.

9. Select Center vertical alignment in the Page Setup dialog box.

10. Save and print the document.

Discovery Zone

Discovery Zone exercises help you gain advanced knowledge of project topics and/or application of skills. These exercises focus on enhancing your problem-solving skills. Numbered steps are not provided, but you are given hints, reminders, screen shots, and/or references to help you reach your goal for each exercise.

1. Saving an Image from the Internet

A friend told you about a very interesting site containing beautiful computer-generated designs. The URL is **www.digitalblasphemy.com**. Ryan Bliss is the creator and copyright owner of the digital images. Access the Internet and connect to this Web site. Explore the different images. When you see an image you really like, click it to see it full-screen. Although you can download the image as wallpaper for your Windows desktop, you want to save the image to use in Word. Right-click the image and choose Save Picture As. Save the image as a bitmap or jpg file.

In Word, use the option that inserts a graphics file. Adjust the format to size the image and place it on the page. Write a brief paragraph about the **www.digitalblasphemy.com** Web site. Create a footnote that cites the Web site. Refer to a reference manual for the correct format for creating this type of footnote entry.

Save the document as **Digital Image** and print it. Compare your printouts and descriptions with your classmates.

2. Inserting Scanned Images in a Flier

You have been assigned to create a flier for a Hawaiian Touring Agency. The company has sent you three scanned photographs from the island of Kauai for you to include in the flier.

Open **W-0906** and save it as **Hawaiian Paradise**. Use Figure 9.23 on the next page to create the flier. Apply the formats as indicated. Set a 0.8-inch height and center the WordArt.

Insert Hawaii1.jpg, Hawaii2.jpg, and Hawaii3.jpg from the CD-ROM that accompanies this book. Apply a Square wrap for the three images. Use Help to learn how to overlap the images with the Order option. Use text boxes to create the captions for the photos. Save the document and print it.

PinPoint Assessment

You have completed this project and its associated lessons, and have had an opportunity to assess your skills through the end-of-project questions and exercises. Now use the PinPoint software Evaluation Mode to further assess your comprehension of the specific exam activities you have just learned. You can also the use the PinPoint Trainer Mode and the Show Me tutorials to practice these exam activities.

Escape to Paradise: Island of Kauai

With its unspoiled white sand beaches, dramatic emerald cliffs, and stunning waterfalls, Kauai is considered by many to be the gem of all the Hawaiian Islands.

Breathtaking Waterfalls

Tropical Settings

Ocean Views

For your most pleasurable visit to the paradise of Kauai, call Garden Island Tours. Our team of experts will guide you to the very best tours for you and your family, premier activities and restaurants at incredible discounts, and the location of secret island "hot spots." We'll help you make your visit both affordable and memorable.

800-555-8877

Garden Island Tours

Figure 9.23
Create the Hawaii flyer.

Fifth row, fifth style in WordArt

20-point Arial Black

14-point Arial, centered

12-point Arial, bold, italic

14-point Arial

WordArt, 18-point

WordArt, 18-point, Inflate shape

Using Additional Graphics Options

Key terms introduced in this project include

- anchor
- arrow
- chart
- chart area
- data labels
- data series
- datasheet
- grouped objects
- import
- layering

- legend
- organization chart
- placeholder
- plot area
- regrouping
- scribble line
- shape
- ungrouping
- value (z) axis title
- watermark

- workbook
- worksheet
- x-axis
- x-axis labels
- y-axis
- y-axis labels
- z-axis
- z-axis labels

Objectives	Required Activity for MOUS	Exam Level
➤ Draw and Format Shapes	Use the drawing toolbar	Core
➤ Draw and Format Lines	Use the drawing toolbar	Core
➤ Layer and Group Objects		
➤ Create Watermarks	Create watermarks	Expert
➤ Create Organization Charts		
➤ Create Charts	Create and modify charts	Expert
➤ Format Chart Elements	Create and modify charts	Expert
➤ Import Data into Charts	Import data into charts	Expert

Why Would I Do This?

Word 2000 contains a vast number of drawing tools to help you develop exciting, creative documents. You can draw a variety of shapes and lines, format these objects, and group them together. In addition, you can lighten images and place them behind text for a special visual effect.

Other valuable tools help you create and format organization charts and business charts. You can even import data from an Excel worksheet to create a chart within Word. In this project you learn how to accomplish these specialized graphics tasks.

Lesson 1: Drawing and Formatting Shapes

You can enhance the appearance of fliers and brochures by including shapes. A **shape** is a graphics object such as a circle or lightning bolt. Designers use shapes to draw attention to a particular section on a page, enhance a document, and create pictures.

In this lesson, you use the Drawing toolbar to draw and format a shape on top of an existing text box.

> **Inside Stuff: Changing the Zoom**
> As you draw objects in a document, you might want to decrease the zoom magnification to 75%. Doing so lets you see more document elements onscreen, which helps you position objects easier.

To Use an Object

1 Open W-1001 and save it as Safe Driving Tips; then scroll down to see the text box below the clip art image.
You want to draw a shape that covers the text box. Later, you bring the text box to the font and format it.

2 Click the Drawing button on the Standard toolbar.
The Drawing toolbar appears above the status bar. It contains buttons to help you draw and format various objects.

3 Click the AutoShapes button on the Drawing toolbar; then choose Basic Shapes.
Figure 10.1 shows a palette of basic shapes. Some of the shapes include a rectangle, a cube, a heart, and a moon.

Figure 10.1
Select a shape from the palette.

Regular Pentagon

AutoShapes button

> **Inside Stuff: Knowing the Shape Name**
> To find out the name of a shape on the palette, position the mouse pointer on top of a shape. You'll see a ScreenTip that tells you the shape's name, such as Regular Pentagon.

4 **Click the Regular Pentagon shape from the palette.**
The mouse pointer looks like a crosshair, which indicates that you need to click and drag to draw the shape.

5 **Using Figure 10.2 as a guide, position the mouse pointer at 1.5 inches from the left margin and 5 inches from the top margin; click and drag down and to the right to completely cover the text box.**

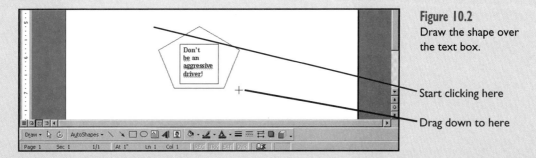

Figure 10.2
Draw the shape over the text box.

Start clicking here

Drag down to here

 Inside Stuff: **Viewing the Ruler**
If you do not see the horizontal ruler, choose View, Ruler to display it. If the vertical ruler does not appear, choose Tools, Options; click the View tab and choose Vertical ruler (Print view only).

The place you start clicking and dragging is the object's *anchor*—the location that the object is attached to.

6 **Click the Fill Color drop-down arrow on the Drawing toolbar.**
You see a color palette, similar to the paragraph shading color palette. When you choose a color, Word applies the fill color to the currently selected object.

7 **Click Dark Blue on the palette.**
The shape now has a Dark Blue fill color.

8 **Save the document and keep it onscreen to continue with the next lesson.**

 Exam Note: **Drawing Circles**
If you want to create a perfect one-inch circle, press and hold Ctrl while you click the Oval button. Word automatically draws a perfect circle in your document.

 Inside Stuff: **Sizing the Shape**
If the text box corners extend outside the shape area, you need to adjust the size of the shape. To make the shape bigger, click and drag one of its corner sizing handles. You might need to click and drag the shape to move it so it completely covers the text box.

The Drawing toolbar contains buttons to create a variety of objects, shapes, and lines. Table 10.1 shows and describes the buttons.

Table 10.1   Drawing Toolbar Buttons

Button	Name	Description
	Draw	Displays menu of drawing options, such as Order.
	Select Objects	Selects objects.
	Free Rotate	Displays rotation handles, so you can rotate an object.
AutoShapes ▾	AutoShapes	Displays a menu of predefined shapes, such as shapes and arrows.
	Line	Draws a straight line.
	Arrow	Draws a line with an arrow at the end.
	Rectangle	Draws rectangles and squares.
	Oval	Draws ovals and circles.
	Text Box	Creates a box in which you type and format text.
	Insert WordArt	Creates a WordArt object.
	Insert Clip Art	Inserts a clip art image.
	Fill Color	Changes the fill color of an object.
	Line Color	Changes the color of a line.
	Font Color	Changes the color of selected text.
	Line Style	Applies a line thickness or style to a selected line.
	Dash Style	Applies a dashed-line style to a selected line.
	Arrow Style	Applies an arrow style or direction to a selected line.
	Shadow	Applies a shadow to the selected object.
	3D	Applies a three-dimensional setting to the selected object.

Lesson 2: Drawing and Formatting Lines

You can also draw various lines in a document. When you choose Lines from the AutoShapes menu, you can select from Line, Arrow, Double Arrow, Curve, Freeform, or Scribble. A **scribble line** is like using a pencil to scribble on a piece of paper. You also have drawing tools to help you format your line by choosing a line color, arrow style, and so on. In this lesson, you draw a line with an **arrow**: a line with an arrowhead, circle, or diamond at the end.

To Draw an Arrow Line

1 **In the open** Safe Driving Tips **document, click the Arrow button on the Drawing toolbar.**

The mouse pointer looks like a crosshair, indicating that you are ready to click and drag to draw the line.

2 **Click to the right of the clip art of the driver, starting at 4.25 inches, and dragging toward the driver's face. Then, release the mouse button.**

The line begins at 4.25 inches and ends with an arrow pointing toward the driver's face (see Figure 10.3).

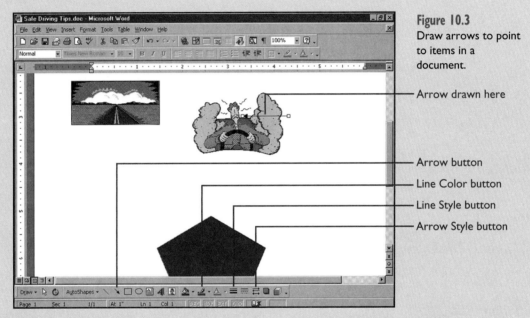

Figure 10.3
Draw arrows to point to items in a document.

Arrow drawn here

Arrow button
Line Color button
Line Style button
Arrow Style button

3 **Click the Line Color drop-down arrow on the Drawing toolbar and choose Blue.**

The selected line is blue.

4 **Click the Line Style button and choose 3 pt.**

The line is now thicker (see Figure 10.4).

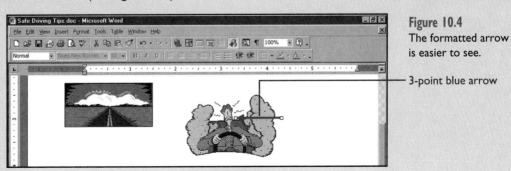

Figure 10.4
The formatted arrow is easier to see.

3-point blue arrow

5 **Save the document and keep it onscreen to continue with the next lesson.**

Inside Stuff: **Changing Line Attributes**
If you decide to change a line's attributes, click it to select it. You can then change the line style, color, and other characteristics.

 Exam Note: **Drawing Lines and Shapes On the MOUS Exam**
Be sure you read the instructions carefully when taking the MOUS exam. Make sure you are creating the exact type of line or shape specified. If you create the wrong line or shape, you lose points.

Lesson 3: Layering and Grouping Objects

When you create objects that overlap existing objects, Word places one object on top of an existing object. This process is called **layering** the objects. Object layering is similar to working on a project on a desk: you pick up a piece of paper and place it on top of another piece of paper as you sort through your research notes. At any time, you can dig through a pile of papers and put another paper on top of the current stack, or you can take the top piece of paper and put it at the bottom of the stack.

As you work with objects in Word, you can bring an object to the front one layer, push an object back one layer, move an object to the front of all layers, or push an object to the back of all layers.

In this lesson, you want to push the Regular Pentagon shape back behind the text box, so you can see the text in the text box.

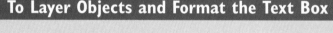
To Layer Objects and Format the Text Box

❶ In the open Safe Driving Tips document, click the Regular Pentagon shape to select it.
Because you can't see the text box to bring it forward, the easiest method is to push the shape behind the text box.

Draw ▾ **❷ Click the D̲raw button on the Drawing toolbar and then choose O̲rder.**
Figure 10.5 shows the O̲rder menu, which lists the methods for layering the current object. In your document, you only have two objects that overlap, so Send to Bac̲k and Send B̲ackward accomplish the same thing.

Figure 10.5
The Order menu lets you choose the object's layer.

Sends object to back of other objects

Sends object back one layer only

Click the Draw button

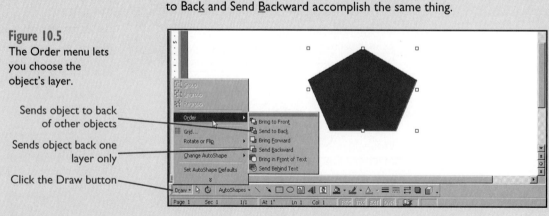

③ Choose Send to Back.

The shape is sent to the back of the overlapped objects, which brings the text box to the front (see Figure 10.6).

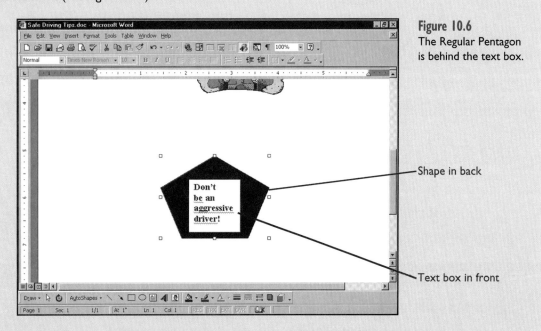

Figure 10.6
The Regular Pentagon is behind the text box.

Shape in back

Text box in front

 Inside Stuff: **Formatting the Text Box**
You can change the text box fill to match the shape's fill color. Doing so makes the text look like it's inside the shape, not a separate box.

---

④ Click the top left edge of the text box to select it.

⑤ Click the Fill Color drop-down arrow on the Drawing toolbar and choose Dark Blue.

The text box fill is identical to the shape's fill—Dark Blue. However, the black font color makes reading the text difficult. Therefore, you need to change the font color.

⑥ With the text box still selected, click the Font Color drop-down arrow and choose Yellow.

The Yellow font color of the text stands out from the Dark Blue fill color (see Figure 10.7).

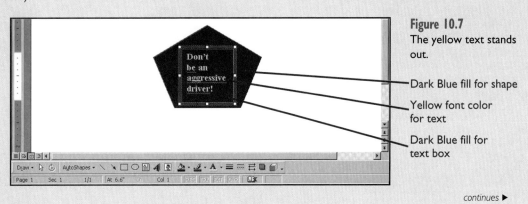

Figure 10.7
The yellow text stands out.

Dark Blue fill for shape

Yellow font color for text

Dark Blue fill for text box

continues ▶

To Layer Objects and Format the Text Box (continued)

7 **Right-click the black border for the text box and choose Format Text Box.**

8 **Click the Colors and Lines tab, click the Line Color drop-down arrow, click No Line, and then click OK.**
The black border around the text box is gone, which blends the text box and shape together.

9 **Save the document and keep it onscreen to continue with the next exercise.**

When you have several objects on a page, you might need to group them. **Grouped objects** are selected objects that act as a single object, which means you can move and format the objects as a group. In the next exercise, you group the text box and shape, and move them collectively to a different location.

To Group Objects

1 **In the Safe Driving Tips document, select the text box if it is not already selected.**
After selecting the text box, you need to add the Regular Pentagon shape to the selected object.

> **Inside Stuff: Selecting Objects**
> When you want to select multiple objects, you should select the interior objects first. Then, you can press ⬆Shift to select the outer object. If you select the outer object first, you might find selecting the interior object to be impossible.

2 **Press ⬆Shift while you click the outside border of the Regular Pentagon shape to select it.**
You should see sizing handles around both the text box and the shape (see Figure 10.8).

Figure 10.8
Both objects are selected.

Sizing handles around shape —

Sizing handles around text box —

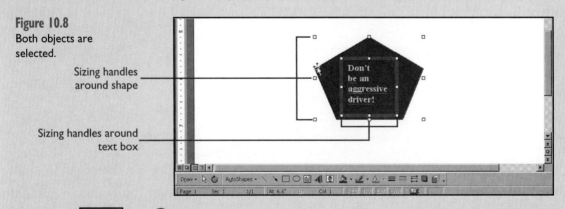

 3 **Click the Draw button on the Drawing toolbar and choose Group.**
You see only one set of sizing handles around the grouped objects.

④ Decrease the zoom magnification to 75%.

Decreasing the zoom magnification lets you see more of your document when you want to move objects.

⑤ Click and drag the grouped object to the right of the blue arrow.

Word moves both objects—the text box and the Regular Pentagon shape—to the right of the arrow (see Figure 10.9).

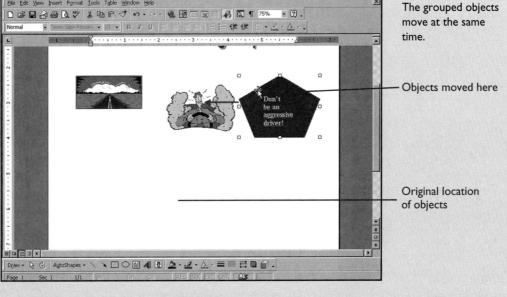

Figure 10.9
The grouped objects move at the same time.

Objects moved here

Original location of objects

⑥ Save the document and keep it onscreen to continue with the next lesson.

ⓘ **Inside Stuff: Ungrouping and Regrouping Objects**

You can separate grouped objects by **ungrouping** them. If you need to ungroup objects to format one object, click the grouped objects, click the D**r**aw button, and choose **U**ngroup. *Hint:* You might need to click the down-pointing arrows to see the full D**r**aw menu.

Word remembers how you grouped the objects. To group the objects back again, select one of the objects that was originally grouped, click the D**r**aw button and choose Regr**o**up. **Regrouping** is the process of grouping objects back together again.

Lesson 4: Creating Watermarks

A **watermark** is a "washed-out" graphic object or text that typically appears behind text. People use watermarks as an imprint for a logo that helps people remember and identify a company's image. You can also use watermarks as visual effects for creative documents, such as fliers, brochures, and newsletters.

In this lesson, you convert the road clip art into a watermark.

To Create a Watermark

1 In the Safe Driving Tips document, choose <u>V</u>iew, <u>T</u>oolbars, Picture to display the **Picture toolbar**.

2 Click the clip art image of the road to select it.

 3 Click the **Image Control** button on the **Picture toolbar** and then choose **W**atermark.

  Inside Stuff: **Adjusting the Brightness**

The Image Control button might not display options for other types of images or photos. If this happens, click the More Brightness button about seven or eight times to lighten the image into a watermark.

Figure 10.10 shows that the image is now a watermark.

Figure 10.10
The image is formatted as a watermark.

Watermark image

Image Control button

More Brightness button

Format Picture button

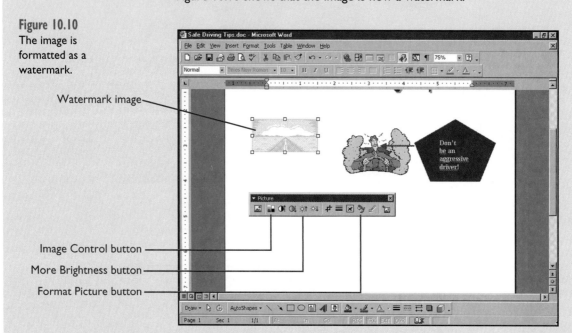

You need to enlarge the image and center it horizontally.

 4 Click the **Format Picture** button.

5 Click the **Size** tab, drag across the current value in the **Wi**<u>d</u>th box, and type 7.5".

A 7.5 inch width enlarges the image dramatically to fill a good portion of the page.

6 Click the **Layout** tab, make sure the **Square** wrapping style is selected, click the **C**enter horizontal alignment option, and then click **OK**.

The watermark is now larger and centered horizontally (see Figure 10.11). The watermark covers the other objects, so you need to send it to the back.

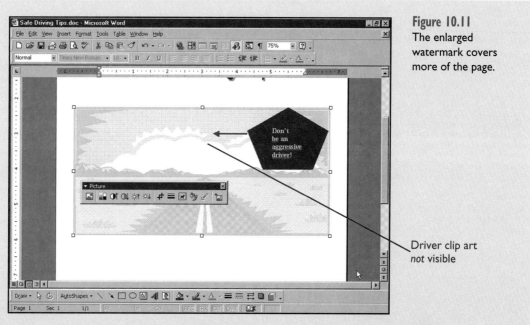

Figure 10.11
The enlarged watermark covers more of the page.

Driver clip art
not visible

7 **Click the Text Wrapping button on the Picture toolbar and choose Behind Text.**
Figure 10.12 shows that the other objects are visible and the watermark is behind everything.

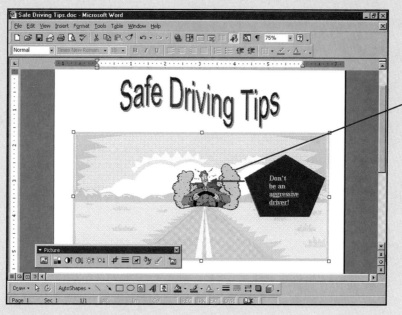

Figure 10.12
The watermark appears behind text now.

Driver clip art
visible now

8 **Save the document and close it.**

9 **Close the Picture toolbar.**

Exam Note: **Creating Watermarks in Headers**

You can create a watermark within a header. After displaying the header window, you insert a clip art image or photo. You then change the image to a watermark by displaying the Format Picture dialog box, clicking the Picture tab, clicking the <u>C</u>olor drop-down arrow in the Image control section, and choosing Watermark. If needed, you can adjust the Brightness and Contrast settings. You also need to select the Behin<u>d</u> Text wrap option.

When you create a watermark in a header, the watermark can appear on every page in the document or section.

You can also use a text box or WordArt object inside a header and convert it to a watermark.

Lesson 5: Creating Organization Charts

An **organization chart** shows the hierarchy of positions within an organization. The chart shows who reports to whom and the different positions within a department or division. In this lesson, you create an organization chart with a company president and three vice presidents. Then, you add two subordinate positions.

To Create an Organization Chart

1 Open W-1002 and save it as February 2002 Newsletter.

2 Position the insertion point on the blank line above the Three Growth Areas heading.
This is where you want the organization chart to appear.

2 Choose <u>I</u>nsert, <u>O</u>bject to open the Object dialog box.

3 Scroll through the list until you see MS Organization Chart 2.0 (see Figure 10.13).

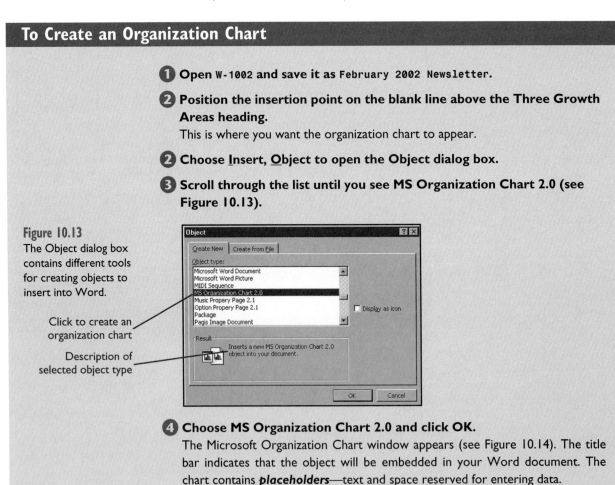

Figure 10.13
The Object dialog box contains different tools for creating objects to insert into Word.

Click to create an organization chart

Description of selected object type

4 Choose MS Organization Chart 2.0 and click OK.
The Microsoft Organization Chart window appears (see Figure 10.14). The title bar indicates that the object will be embedded in your Word document. The chart contains **placeholders**—text and space reserved for entering data.

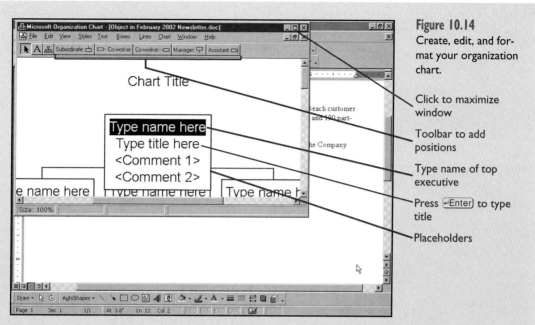

Figure 10.14
Create, edit, and format your organization chart.

Click to maximize window

Toolbar to add positions

Type name of top executive

Press ↵Enter to type title

Placeholders

5 **Click the Maximize button to maximize the Microsoft Organization Chart window and see more of the organization chart as you create and edit it.**

6 **Type** Jared Farnsworth **over the Type name here placeholder.**

7 **Press** ↵Enter **and type** President & CEO **over the Type title here placeholder.**

You don't have to replace the Comment placeholders. If you don't type text over them, they disappear when you go to another position.

8 **Press** Ctrl+↓ **to move to the first position on the next level.**

9 **Type the following data in the three remaining positions, pressing** ↵Enter **to move to the next placeholder for the current position. Press** Ctrl+→ **to go across the chart.**

Andrew Schultz	Marie Patterson	Amanda Gold
Vice President	Vice President	Vice President
International Affairs	Sales & Services	Finance

Your organization chart now contains names and titles, as shown in Figure 10.15. After typing **Finance**, the insertion point is in that field. You still see the <Comment 2> field. The comment placeholder, however, will not print.

continues ▶

To Create an Organization Chart (continued)

Figure 10.15
Your chart contains people's names and titles.

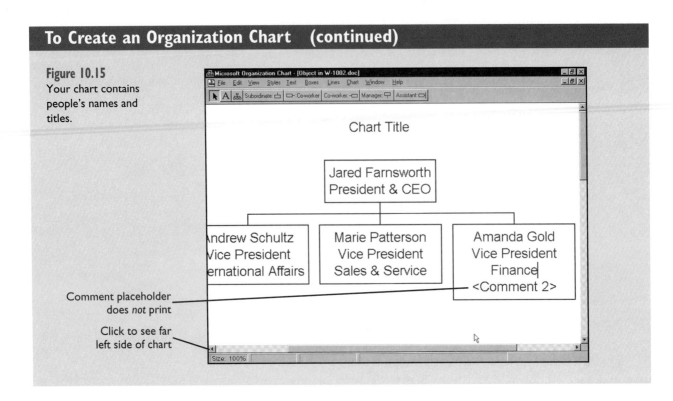

Comment placeholder does *not* print

Click to see far left side of chart

The default organization chart provides the main position and three subordinate positions. You, however, can add subordinates, co-workers, managers, and assistants. Let's add two subordinates for Marie Patterson.

To Add Positions

Subordinate:

1 **Click the Subordinate button on the toolbar.**
The mouse pointer displays as the icon you see on the Subordinate button.

2 **Click inside Marie Patterson's box.**
A subordinate position appears below Marie's box (see Figure 10.16).

Figure 10.16
A subordinate position is created under Marie Patterson.

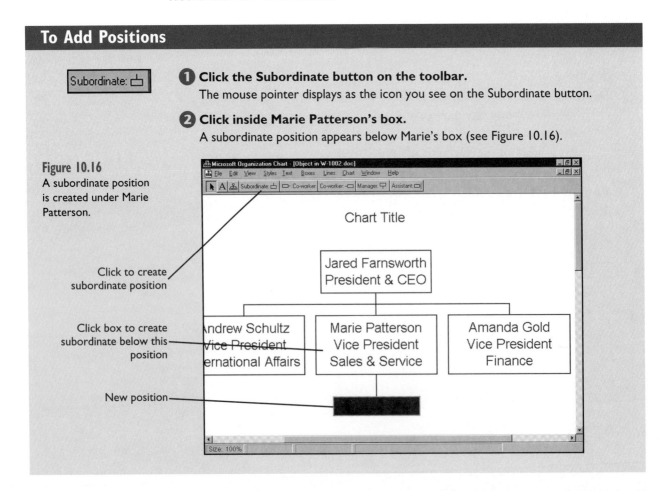

Click to create subordinate position

Click box to create subordinate below this position

New position

③ Click in the new position box.

Clicking in the new box displays the placeholders, so you can type text. You might need to scroll down to see the entire box.

④ Type the following data, pressing ⏎Enter to go from one placeholder to the next.

```
Janice Bronson
Regional Director
East Coast
```

You need to add a co-worker position for Janice. You want to place the co-worker's data to the right of Janice's box. Notice you have two Co-worker buttons on the toolbar. The second Co-worker button is the one that places a box to the right of the current one.

⑤ Click the Right Co-worker Button on the toolbar.

⑥ Click Janice's box to create a co-worker box to the right of that box.

 If You Have Problems...
If you accidentally create the wrong position, press Del while the box is selected. That will delete the box and you can try again.

⑦ Click in the new box and type the following data, pressing ⏎Enter to go from one placeholder to the next.

```
Daniel Neilson
Regional Director
West Coast
```

You are now ready to insert the organization chart into your document.

⑧ Click the Close button in the top right corner of the window and click Yes when you see the prompt The object has been changed. Do you want to Update Object in A:\Project 10\February 2002 Newsletter.doc before proceeding?

The organization chart appears in your document (see Figure 10.17).

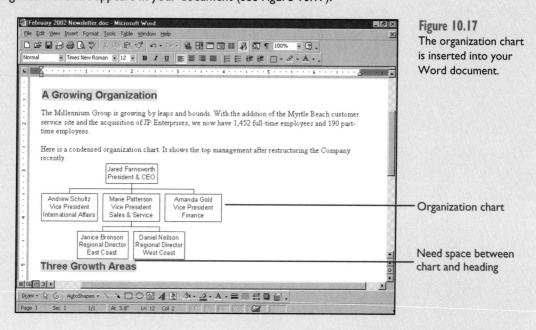

Figure 10.17
The organization chart is inserted into your Word document.

Organization chart

Need space between chart and heading

The chart will look better if you center it. Furthermore, you need to insert a hard return to separate the chart and the Three Growth Areas heading.

To Adjust the Chart

① **Press ⏎Enter to insert a blank line below the chart.**

② **Right-click the organization chart and choose Show Picture Toolbar.**

③ **Click the Text Wrapping button on the Picture toolbar and choose Top and Bottom.**

④ **Right-click the organization chart and choose Format Object.**

⑤ **Click the Layout tab, choose Center horizontal alignment, and click OK.**

The organization chart is better positioned on the page (see Figure 10.18).

Figure 10.18
The organization chart is now properly positioned.

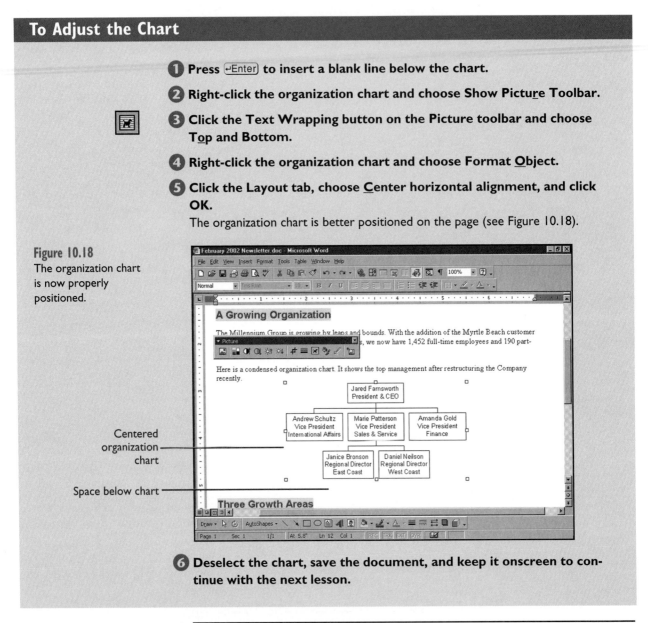

Centered organization chart

Space below chart

⑥ **Deselect the chart, save the document, and keep it onscreen to continue with the next lesson.**

ⓘ *Inside Stuff:*   **Editing Organization Charts**
After inserting an organization chart into Word, double-click it to display MS Organization Chart 2.0; then modify the chart.

If you do not want a position box, select it and press Del.

Furthermore, you can customize an organization chart by changing the lines, colors, and fill colors. Refer to Help within MS Organization Chart 2.0 for more information.

 Lesson 6: Creating Charts

Numerical data arranged in a table or in tabular columns is helpful for conveying values. However, numbers alone do not provide a great visual image. A ***chart***, on the other hand, is a visual representation of numerical data that enhances the reader's understanding and comprehension of the values. A chart helps you compare **data series**—values arranged in columns and rows. For example, a data series could be a set of values showing your phone bill for each of the past four months.

In this lesson, you create a chart using the Microsoft Graph feature. Figure 10.19 illustrates some components of a chart that you'll be working with in this lesson and the next lesson.

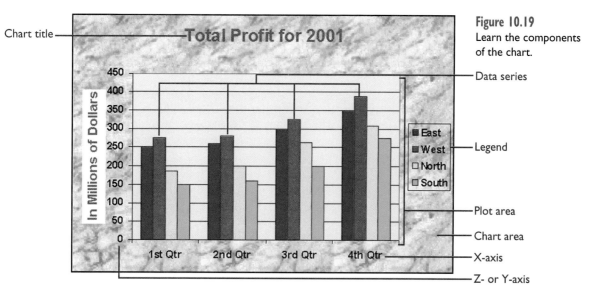

Figure 10.19
Learn the components of the chart.

To Create a Chart

1 **In the February 2002 Newsletter document, position the insertion point on the blank line below the last paragraph.**

2 **Choose Insert, Picture, Chart.**
Word inserts a chart and displays the **datasheet**, a table containing data used to create the chart (see Figure 10.20).

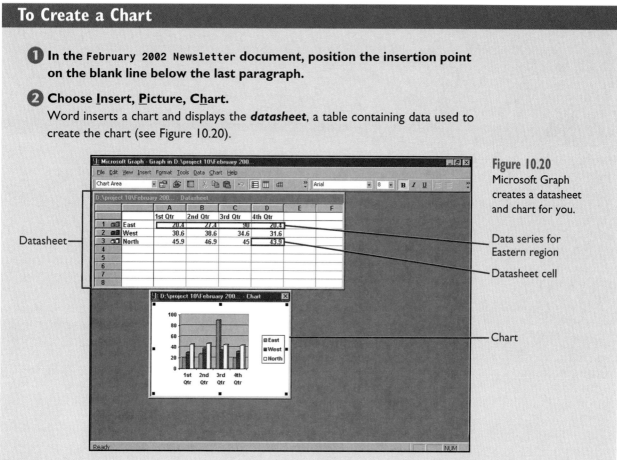

Figure 10.20
Microsoft Graph creates a datasheet and chart for you.

To Create a Chart   (continued)

The numbers in the first column represent a data series. The text in the second column, such as East, represents the name of a data series. Notice that the second column's text creates the **legend**—a color-coded key that indicates what color represents what region or data series. The **x-axis** indicates the time period (in quarters) for the categories. The first row below the alphabetic letters indicates a time period, such as 1st Quarter. This text appears as the **x-axis labels**, descriptions of each set of bars. The **z-axis** (or **y-axis**) displays bars representing quantities. The **z-axis** (or **y-axis**) **labels** show consistent increments to help you determine the value of each bar.

 Inside Stuff: Maximize the Chart Widow
You can create and format a chart better if you maximize the Microsoft Graph window. You might also need to click and drag the actual chart window below the datasheet.

❸ Click in the datasheet cell below North; type South and press ⏎Enter.
Entering data in the first column creates a new data series.

❹ Click and drag across the existing 12 values in the datasheet and press Del.
Before you start to enter your own values, you should clear the existing values. This way, you don't forget which values are yours and which values were sample values.

❺ Click in Cell A1, the first cell for the 1st Quarter sales for the East.

❻ Type 250, press ⏎Enter, type 275, press ⏎Enter, type 185, press ⏎Enter, and then type 150.
Figure 10.21 shows the data entered for the first-quarter for each region.

Figure 10.21
Data is entered for
the first quarter.

South entered——

Data for first quarter——

Other data deleted——

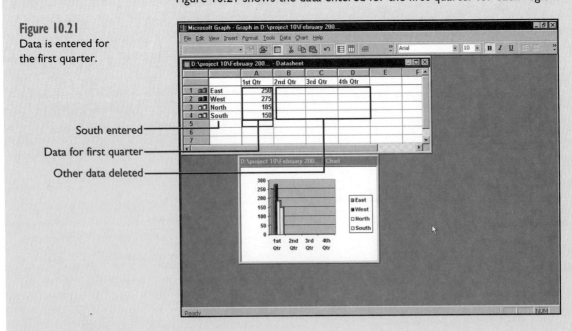

7 **Enter the following values for their respective quarters:**

2nd Qtr	3rd Qtr	4th Qtr
260	300	350
280	325	390
200	265	310
160	200	275

 Inside Stuff: **Scrolling in a Datasheet**

Press ⏎Enter to enter text in a cell and go down to the next cell. You can press Tab↹ to move to the next cell on the right, or you can press ⬆Shift+Tab↹ to move to the next cell on the left.

---

8 **Click the Close button in the top right corner of the window to close Microsoft Graph and insert the chart in your document.**

The chart appears on page 2 of your document. The chart is a little small.

9 **Right-click the chart and choose Format Object.**

10 **Click the Size tab, delete the existing width, and type 5".**

Now you want to adjust the layout and center the object.

11 **Click the Layout tab, click the Square wrapping option, click the Center horizontal alignment option, and then click OK.**

Figure 10.22 shows the bigger chart that is centered between the left and right margins.

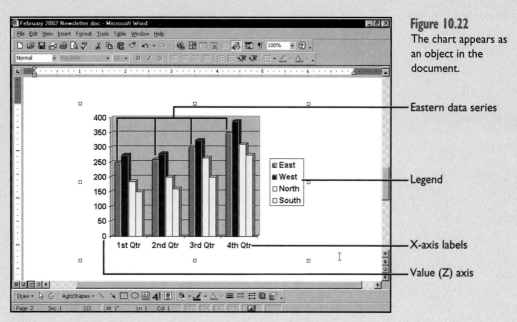

Figure 10.22
The chart appears as an object in the document.

— Eastern data series

— Legend

— X-axis labels

— Value (Z) axis

12 **Save the document and keep it onscreen to continue with the next lesson.**

 Exam Note: **Editing Data in the Datasheet**

If you need to edit chart data after inserting the chart into your Word document, double-click the chart. The datasheet appears, so you can edit values that are charted.

Lesson 7: Formatting Chart Elements

After creating a chart, you probably want to modify it. Microsoft Graph treats each part of the chart as a separate element that you can format. For example, you might want to add a chart title, change the font size for the legend, or change a color for a data series. In this lesson, you insert and format the chart title and adjust the font size of the legend.

To Format Chart Elements

1 In the February 2002 Newsletter document, double-click the chart to display the chart, datasheet, and chart options.

2 Click the View Datasheet button to hide the datasheet.
By hiding the datasheet, you can see the entire chart. If you need to see the datasheet again, click the View Datasheet button.

3 Choose <u>C</u>hart, Chart <u>O</u>ptions.
The Chart Options dialog box appears (see Figure 10.23). This dialog box contains several options for enhancing your chart.

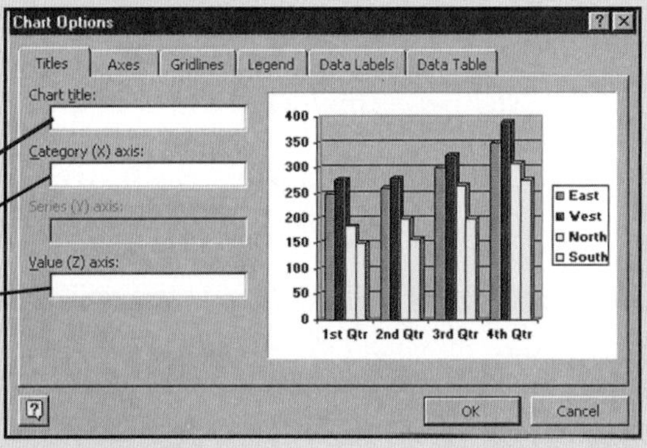

Figure 10.23
Use the Chart Options dialog box to enhance your chart.

Type title of chart here
Type title for X-axis here
Type title for Z-axis here

  Exam Note: **Creating a Value (Z) Axis Title**
The **value (z) axis title** is a heading that describes the values on the left side of the chart. You can create a title, such as **In Millions of U.S. Dollars**, to help clarify the values.

---

4 Type Total Profit for 2001 in the Chart <u>t</u>itle text box, and then click OK.
The chart title appears above the chart. By default, it is in 16-point Arial black.

5 Right-click the chart title and chose <u>F</u>ormat Chart Title.

  Inside Stuff: **Using the Format Object Button**
After clicking an object, such as the chart title, to select it, you can click the Format Object button to display a dialog box to format that particular object.

You see the Format Chart Title dialog box. The Font tab contains options that are similar to the regular Font dialog box.

6 Click the <u>C</u>olor drop-down arrow, choose Red, and click OK.
The chart title stands out in red. Now, let's decrease the font size for the text in the legend.

7 **Right-click the edge of the legend, and choose F̲ormat Legend.**

The Format Legend dialog box looks similar to the Format Chart Title dialog box. You can change font, font size, and color, among other things.

8 **Click 9 in the S̲ize list box and then click OK.**

Figure 10.24 shows the chart after changing the chart title color and decreasing the legend's font size.

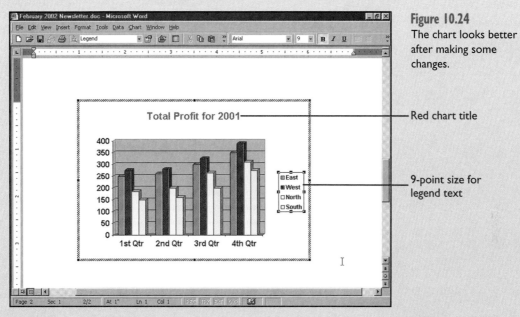

Figure 10.24
The chart looks better after making some changes.

Red chart title

9-point size for legend text

9 **Click the Chart Type button; if the Chart Type button is not visible, choose C̲hart, Chart T̲ype.**

Figure 10.25 shows the Chart Type dialog box. It displays a list of the major chart types and the subtypes. The current chart is a `Clustered column with a 3-D visual effect`. Because you are charting only quantities and time (quarters), there is no third-dimension. Using a 3-D chart distorts the data, making it more difficult to read.

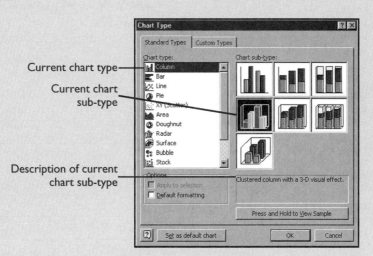

Figure 10.25
Choose the chart and chart sub-type.

Current chart type

Current chart sub-type

Description of current chart sub-type

10 **Click the first example in the Chart sub-t̲ype palette.**

The description says, `Clustered Column. Compares values across categories`.

continues ▶

To Format Chart Elements   (continued)

⑪ Click OK.

The chart is now a clustered column chart without the 3-D effect (see Figure 10.26).

Figure 10.26
The chart is easier to read without the 3-D effect.

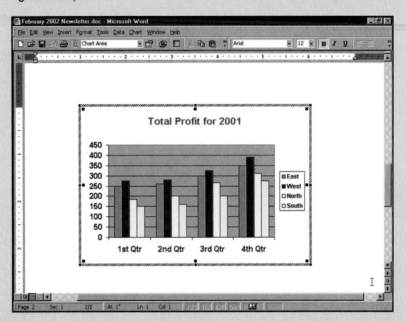

⑫ Click outside the chart area to close the Microsoft Graph application and return to the document window.

⑬ Save the document and keep it onscreen to continue with the next lesson.

Exam Note: **Changing Background Color**

The *plot area*, the area that displays the charted data series, is gray by default. You can change the chart area's background color by right-clicking the chart area and choosing Format Plot Area. Then, click the Patterns tab and choose the desired color; or click Fill Effects to select gradients, textures, or patterns.

The *chart area* is the white area containing all chart elements. By default, it is white. However, you can also choose its background color. Right-click in the chart area and choose Format Chart Area. Then, choose a pattern color, or click Fill Effects for more advanced background colors.

Exam Note: **Formatting the Data Series**

You can format a data series by right-clicking one of its bars and choosing Format Data Series. You can change the color for the data series, add *data labels* (values above the data series), or change other data series options.

Inside Stuff: **Displaying More Buttons On the Chart Toolbar**

You can see more Chart toolbar buttons if you click and drag the vertical line before the Font button below the current toolbar. Figure 10.27 shows the separated toolbars. Notice that you have buttons for formatting values, such as the Currency Style, Percent Style, and Comma Style buttons.

In addition, you can control the number of decimal points by clicking the Increase Decimal or Decrease Decimal button.

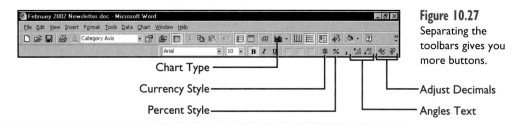

Chart Type ——————
Currency Style ——————
Percent Style ——————
—— Adjust Decimals
—— Angles Text

Figure 10.27
Separating the toolbars gives you more buttons.

Lesson 8: Importing Data into Charts

 Expert

If you have an Excel worksheet that contains data you want to chart, you can create the chart either in Excel or Word. If you decide to create the chart in Word, you can import the Excel data. **Import** refers to the process of bringing in data from another source application, such as bringing Excel data into Word.

An Excel file is called a **workbook**. Each workbook can contain several **worksheets**, or pages of data. In this lesson, you import a part of an Excel worksheet into the datasheet of Microsoft Graph.

To Import Data into Charts

1 **In the open February 2002 Newsletter document, position the insertion point on the blank line immediately above the 2001 Sales heading.**

2 **Choose Insert, Picture, Chart; then maximize the Microsoft Graph window.**
You need to import the Excel worksheet data into the datasheet.

3 **Click in the datasheet cell above East.**

4 **Click the Import File button on the toolbar.**

5 **Click the Look in drop-down arrow and choose the drive that contains your CD-ROM that accompanies this book. Double-click the Project 10 folder, and then double-click W-1003.xls.**
Excel workbook filenames end with the xls extension. The Import Data Options dialog box appears (see Figure 10.28). This is where you choose the worksheet number and range. You can also choose to overwrite or keep existing data in the datasheet.

Choose worksheet
in Excel workbook ——————

Choose what to import ——————

Default overwrites
existing data ——————

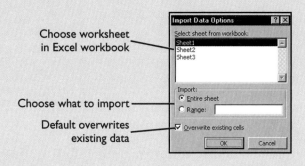

Figure 10.28
Choose how you want to import the data.

continues ▶

To Import Data into Charts   (continued)

6 **Click the Range option and type A3:D6.**

You don't want the entire worksheet page; you want a specific range or area within that sheet. The range address is A3 through D6. The colon separates the beginning and ending points of the range.

7 **Click OK.**

Figure 10.29 shows the imported data. Microsoft Graph inserts the column headings as a data series instead on the first row of the datasheet. You need to move the data to create the legend.

Figure 10.29
The data imports into the datasheet.

Move column headings to this row

Column headings treated as data series

Years treated as Area data series

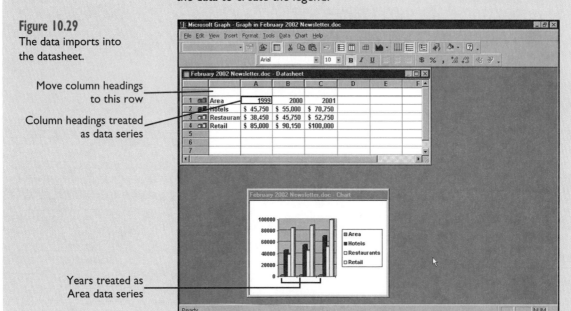

8 **Click and drag across Area, 1999, 2000, and 2001 to select these cells.**

9 **Click the Cut button, click in the first cell in the first row of the datasheet, and click the Paste button.**

The data is pasted on the first row; however, the datasheet now has an empty data series row, which you need to delete.

10 **Click in cell that displays 3-D Column in gray.**

11 **Choose Edit, Delete.**

The Delete dialog box appears (see Figure 10.30).

Figure 10.30
Use the Delete dialog box to delete parts of the datasheet.

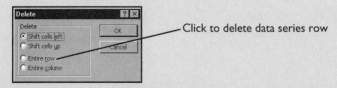

Click to delete data series row

12 **Click Entire row, and then click OK.**

The extra data series row is deleted.

13 **Click the Close button to close Microsoft Graph.**

The chart you created by importing Excel data appears in your document window (see Figure 10.31).

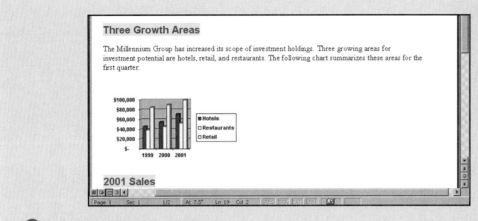

Figure 10.31
The chart contains imported Excel data.

 Save the document and close it.

 Inside Stuff: **Creating a Chart from a Word Table**
You can create a chart from a Word table. To do this, select the rows you want to chart; or choose Table, Select, Table to select the entire table. Then, access the Microsoft Graph feature. Microsoft Graph automatically uses the selected table data to create the chart.

Summary

You learned how to draw objects and lines. You can easily format these drawings by selecting their fill color and choosing other settings. By grouping and layering objects, you can create interesting visual effects.

You also know how to create an organization chart and business charts. In addition, you can import Excel worksheets into the datasheet to create a chart. To expand your knowledge and charting abilities, experiment with the Microsoft Graph menus, options, and toolbars.

Checking Concepts and Terms

True/False

For each of the following, check *T* or *F* to indicate whether the statement is true or false.

__T __F **1.** When you choose a shape from the shape palette, Word automatically inserts that shape for you. [L1]

__T __F **2.** To select multiple objects, hold down (⬆Shift) while you click each object. [L3]

__T __F **3.** You can convert an image to a watermark by changing the Image Control. [L4]

__T __F **4.** If you want a watermark to appear on all pages, you must create it in a header. [L4]

__T __F **5.** The only way to create a chart is from a Word table. [L6]

Multiple Choice

Circle the letter of the correct answer for each of the following.

1. What AutoShapes option do you click to see a palette that contains shapes such as a rectangle, pentagon, diamond, and heart? [L1]

   a. Lines

   b. Basic Shapes

   c. Stars and Banners

   d. Callouts

2. All of the following are buttons that help you format a line, *except*: [L2]

   a.

   b.

   c.

   d.

3. What term refers to placing objects in a certain order on top of each other? [L3]

   a. layering

   b. grouping

   c. ungrouping

   d. rotating

4. Which button contains an option to convert an image to a watermark? [L4]

   a.

   b.

   c.

   d.

5. What term refers to a set of the same colored bars in a chart? [L6]

   a. chart area

   b. data series

   c. plot area

   d. x-axis

Screen ID

Label each element of the Word screen shown in Figure 10.32.

Figure 10.32

A. data series

B. legend

C. plot area

D. value (z) axis title

E. x-axis

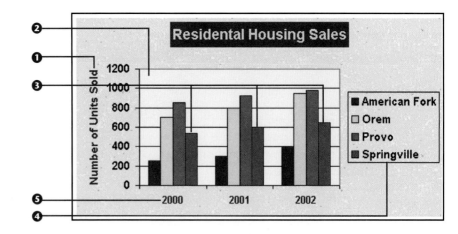

1._____   2._____   3._____

4._____   5._____

Skill Drill

Skill Drill exercises reinforce project skills. Each skill reinforced is the same, or nearly the same, as a skill presented in the project. Each exercise includes a brief narrative introduction, followed by detailed instructions in a step-by-step format.

1. Drawing and Formatting a Shape

You want to create a back-to-school flier for a public school. You plan to draw a banner shape and format it with fill color and wrap it behind text. In addition, you want to include a watermark.

1. Open **W-1004** and save it as **School Flier**.

2. Click the Drawing button on the Standard toolbar if the Drawing toolbar is not visible at the bottom of your screen.

3. Click the AutoShapes button and choose Stars and Banners.

4. Choose Horizontal Scroll.

5. Click and drag across the flier title, **Back to School**. Make sure the shape fits over the entire title.

6. Right-click inside the shape and choose Format AutoShape.

7. Click the Layout tab, click Behind text, click the Center option, and then click OK.

8. Click the Fill Color drop-down arrow on the Drawing toolbar and then choose Rose.

9. Choose File, Page Setup; click the Layout tab, click the Vertical alignment drop-down arrow, choose Center, and click OK.

10. Press Ctrl + Home to position the insertion point above the title.

11. Choose Insert, Picture, Clip Art.

12. Click the scroll down arrow several times and click the Seasons category.

13. Right-click the image of the schoolhouse and choose Insert. Click the Close button to close the Insert ClipArt dialog box.

14. Click the schoolhouse image to see the Picture toolbar.

15. Click the Image Control button on the Picture toolbar, and then choose Watermark.

16. Click the Format Picture button.

17. Click the Size tab, drag across the current value in the Width box, and type **6.5"**.

18. Click the Layout tab, click Behind text, and click OK.

19. With the watermark selected, click the Draw button on the Drawing toolbar, choose Order, and choose Send to Back.

20. Save the document, print it, and close it.

2. Creating a School Organization Chart with Objects

You want to create a simple organization chart showing the superintendent, three principals, and the teacher-of-the-year. In addition, you want to draw a shape with a text box and draw an arrow pointing to the teacher's box in the organization chart.

1. In a new document window, choose Insert, Object.

2. Scroll down, click MS Organization Chart 2.0, click OK, and click the Maximize button to maximize the chart window.

3. Type **Denise Kennison** over the **Type name here** placeholder, press Enter, and type **Superintendent** over the **Type title here** placeholder.

4. Press Ctrl + ↓, type **Cory Peters**, press Enter, and type **High School Principal**.

5. Press Ctrl + →, type **Darin Sabey**, press Enter, and type **Jr. High Principal**.

6. Press Ctrl + →, type **Luella Jayroe**, press Enter, and type **Grade School Principal**.

7. Click the Subordinate button, click Darin's box, type **Kevin Partee**, press Enter, and type **History Teacher**.

8. Scroll up to see **Chart Title** above the organization chart, click and drag across **Chart Title**, and type **City Public Schools**.

9. Click the Close button to close the Microsoft Organization Chart window. Click Yes if prompted to update the changes.

10. Click the A**u**toShapes button and choose **S**tars and Banners.

11. Choose Explosion 2 and click and drag about a 2.5-inch square object.

12. With the object selected, click the Fill Color drop-down arrow, and choose Yellow.

13. Click the Text Box button, and click and drag a box within the Explosion 2 object.

14. Click the Bold button, type **Teacher**, press ⏎Enter), type **Of The**, press ⏎Enter), and type **Year**.

15. If needed, click and drag the text box to fit better in the Explosion 2 shape.

16. With the text box selected, click the Fill Color button to apply Yellow fill.

17. Right-click the edge of the text box, choose Format Text B**o**x, click the Colors and Lines tab, click the Line C**o**lor drop-down arrow, choose No Line, and click OK to remove the text box border.

18. Click the Arrow button; click and drag an arrow from one of the Explosion 2 points to the box containing Kevin's name in the organization chart.

19. With the arrow selected, click the Line Color drop-down arrow, and choose Red.

20. With the arrow selected, click the Line Style button, and choose 1-1/2 pt.

21. Deselect the object.

22. Save the document as **School Organization Chart**, and print the document.

3. Creating and Formatting a Chart

As an assistant at a local high school, you've been asked to create a chart depicting the number of students in each grade for the past three years.

1. In a new document window, choose **I**nsert, **P**icture, **C**hart.

2. Click and drag across all the data in the datasheet and then press Del).

3. Type the following data in the datasheet, leaving the top left cell empty:

	2000	2001	2002
Freshmen	245	308	284
Sophomore	320	255	321
Junior	312	325	261
Senior	289	315	322

4. Click the Column D heading.

5. Choose **E**dit, Delete to clear the column.

6. Choose **C**hart, Chart **T**ype.

7. Click the Clustered Column chart sub-type and then click OK.

8. Choose **C**hart, Chart **O**ptions.

9. Click in the Chart **t**itle box and type **Ocean View High School**.

10. Click in the **V**alue (Y) axis box and type **Final Enrollment**; then click OK.

11. Right-click the chart title and choose **F**o**rmat Chart Title**.

12. Click the Font tab, click the **C**olor drop-down arrow, choose Orange, and click OK.

13. Right-click the legend and choose F**o**rmat Legend.

14. Click Regular in the Font style list, and click OK.

15. Click outside the chart area to close the chart feature.

16. Right-click the chart and choose Format **O**bject.

17. Click the Size tab, drag across the current value in the Wi**d**th box, and type **5"**.

18. Click the Layout tab, click the **S**quare wrap option, click the **C**enter horizontal alignment option, and click OK.

19. Save the document as **School Enrollment Chart**, print the document, and close it.

Challenge

Challenge exercises expand on or are somewhat related to skills presented in the lessons. Each exercise provides a brief narrative introduction followed by instructions in a numbered-step or bulleted-list format that are not as detailed as those in the Skill Drill section.

I. Creating a Valentine's Day Dance Flier

Your college is sponsoring a Valentine's Day dance. You've been asked to create the flier because of your excellent Word skills.

1. In a new document window, create a WordArt object using the third style on the first row of the WordArt Gallery. Type **Valentine's Day Dance**.

2. Format the WordArt by making these changes:

   a. Choose the Rainbow present gradient fill effect.

   b. Choose the Wave I WordArt shape.

   c. Select Square wrap with a <u>C</u>enter align.

   d. Set a 1.5-inch height.

3. Apply the 16th art page border.

4. Create a header with these specifications:

   a. Insert the clip art of the heart with the white cupid.

   b. Change the image to a watermark.

   c. Choose the appropriate text wrapping option for a watermark.

   d. Set a 6-inch height for the watermark.

   e. Select a Center horizontal alignment. Use the advanced layout option to center the image vertically.

5. Use the Click and Type feature to center text at the top of the watermark of the cupid. Select 24-point Comic Sans MS font with Red font color. Type the following text on three separate lines, with space between the lines:

        February 14

        8:30 p.m.-Midnight

        Student Center Ballroom

6. Draw a Heart AutoShape in the bottom left corner of the flier. Choose Red fill color. Copy the object to the right side of the flier.

7. Create a text box inside the left heart with these settings:

   a. **$5/Couple with Student ID** in bold

   b. White font color

   c. No fill color

   d. No line border

8. Create a text box inside the right heart with these settings:

   a. **Sponsored by the Student Government Association** in bold

   b. White font color

   c. No fill color

   d. No line border

9. Adjust the text boxes within their respective hearts. Group each text box with its heart.

10. Save the document as **Valentine's Day Dance** and print it.

2. Creating Organization Charts

You need to create two organization charts showing the hierarchy of your school. The first chart should reflect the structure of your administration and the second should reflect your business department.

1. Research the structure of your school hierarchy. Use the school's course catalog or browse the school's Web page, if it has one. Refer to Figure 10.33 for sample organizational charts. Sketch out the structure of your school before beginning this exercise. Refer to this sketch as you create your organization chart using MS Organization Chart 2.0.

2. Set 1-inch top, bottom, left, and right margins.

3. Create a heading using the title of your top administration. Center the heading and format it with 20-point Arial Black.

4. Create the organization chart and insert it into your document. Format it for Square wrapping and Center horizontal alignment.

5. Create a heading using the title of your department. Center-align the heading and format it as 20-point Arial Black.

6. Create the organization chart and insert it into your document. Format it for Square wrapping and Center horizontal alignment.

7. Adjust spacing as needed.

8. Save the document as **Organization** and print it.

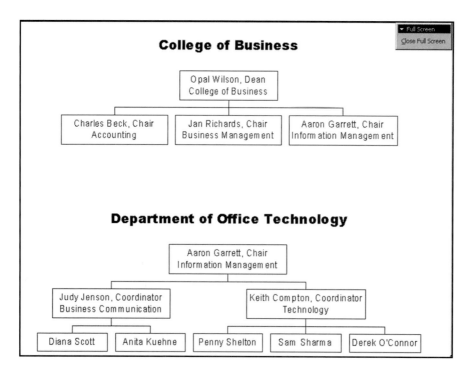

Figure 10.33
Use these sample charts to create your charts.

3. Creating a Chart from a Table

You are preparing a memo for the manager of a local music store. The memo contains a table that you want to chart.

1. Open **W-1005** and save it as **Music Sales Memo**.
2. Select the entire table, display Microsoft Graph, and then choose the Pie Chart sub-type.
3. Select a regular Pie chart.
4. From the Data menu, choose Series in Columns to create the chart correctly.
5. Create a title called **April Sales**.
6. Choose the Chart Options option that displays percent data labels.
7. Click outside the chart, set a 4.5-inch width, Square wrap, and Center horizontal alignment.
8. Select 8-point font size for the legend and 10-point font size for the data labels.
9. Choose None for the plot area fill and None for the plot area border.
10. Click and drag the plot area within the chart area to increase its size.
11. Format the data labels by choosing Inside End as the Label Position option for the alignment.
12. Close the chart, save the document, and print it.

Discovery Zone

Discovery Zone exercises help you gain advanced knowledge of project topics and/or application of skills. These exercises focus on enhancing your problem-solving skills. Numbered steps are not provided, but you are given hints, reminders, screen shots, and/or references to help you reach your goal for each exercise.

1. Importing Data to Create a Chart

A college friend is applying for a short-term loan to help cover college expenses. He created a simple worksheet listing his major expenses. He asked you to create a stacked bar chart depicting his expenses and insert it into a letter you helped him compose.

Open **W-1006** and save it as **Loan Letter**. Create a chart between the last two paragraphs, importing **W-1007.xls** into the datasheet. Use the stacked column chart sub-type. Include an appropriate title in Blue font color. Format the values on the y-axis for Currency with zero decimal places.

Change the colors for each data series to be brighter colors. Format the chart area to have a Marble textured-fill.

Set a 4.5 inch width and center the chart between the margins. Use a Top and Bottom wrap option. Decrease the font sizes for the legend, x-axis labels, and y-axis labels. Save the print the letter.

2. Creating a Workshop Flier

You need to create a flier advertising a workshop on conflict management. The flier will contain Word Art, AutoShapes, clip art, customized bulleted list, a text box, and a paragraph border.

Create the flier as shown in Figure 10.34. Use the Rounded Rectangular Callout AutoShape for the text, **Play nice, boys!** Group the callout and the clip art together. Use paragraph shading and font color to format the question. Save the document as **Conflict Resolution** and print it.

Play nice, boys!

Having trouble dealing with on-the-job conflict?

Sign up for a Conflict Management Workshop!

※ Reasoning with the unreasonable person

※ Keeping an open mind

※ Appearing *objective* not *emotional*

※ Establishing goodwill

※ Solving problems together

Conflict Management Workshop
September 23
8:30 a.m. – 12:00 p.m.
Cornerstone Hotel Ballroom
Call 555-HELP to register.

Figure 10.34
Create the flier with the graphics elements.

PinPoint Assessment

You have completed this project and its associated lessons, and have had an opportunity to assess your skills through the end-of-project questions and exercises. Now use the PinPoint software Evaluation Mode to further assess your comprehension of the specific exam activities you have just learned. You can also use the PinPoint Trainer Mode and the Show Me tutorials to practice these exam activities.

Integrating Information

Key terms introduced in this project include

- attachment
- blind courtesy copy
- cell
- destination program
- embedding
- importing
- linking
- Object Linking and Embedding (OLE)
- range
- source program
- Tile Windows Vertically option
- workbook
- worksheet

Objectives	Required Activity for MOUS	Exam Level
➤ Insert a File within the Current Document		
➤ Import Excel Data into Word		
➤ Embed Excel Data into Word	Embed worksheets in a table	Expert
➤ Modify Embedded Data	Modify worksheets in a table	Expert
➤ Embed an Excel Chart		
➤ Link Excel Data into Word	Link Excel data as a table	Expert
➤ Send a Word Document via Email	Send a Word document via email	Core

Why Would I Do This?

As you work on a document in Word, you might need to include additional information or objects that you saved in another Word document. You might also want to share Word documents by sending them as email messages or email attachments to other people.

In addition, you might want to use data that was created in another program. For example, you can insert spreadsheet data into a word processing document. The program used to create the original data is called the **source program**. The program that you bring the data into is called the **destination program**.

Lesson 1: Inserting a File Within the Current Document

You might need text that you saved as another file or you might want to insert text that someone sends to you as an email attachment. You can use the Insert File dialog box to insert an *entire* document within the current document. Inserting an existing document saves you time, so you don't have to type the same information again.

In this lesson, you are preparing an annual report. A colleague prepared a document that you need to insert within your document.

To Insert a File Within the Current Document

1 **Open W-1101 and save it as 2001 Annual Report.**
So far, your document contains three paragraphs. You need to insert another document between the second paragraph and the heading 2002 Capital Expenditures.

2 **Click at the beginning of the 2002 Capital Expenditures heading.**

3 **Choose Insert, File to display the Insert File dialog box.**
The Insert File dialog box looks similar to the Open dialog box. However, it inserts the document into the current document window (unlike Open, which opens the document into a different document window).

4 **Choose W-1102 and click Insert.**
Word inserts the W-1102 file at the insertion point location, as shown in Figure 11.1. Although the paragraphs are 12-point in W-1102, the paragraphs are inserted at 10-point. Notice that the headings maintain the same font and font size.

5 **Select the first imported paragraph, which begins with For the past several years.**

6 **Choose Times New Roman and 12-point from the Formatting toolbar; then deselect the text.**
You need to format the second imported paragraph.

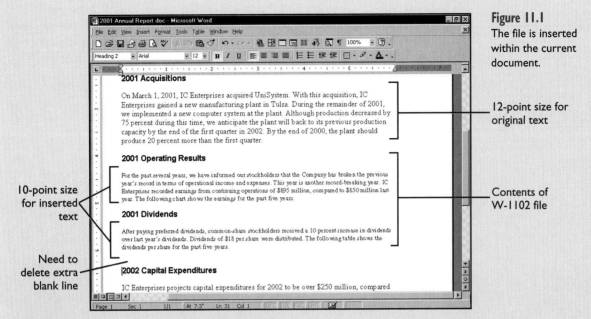

Figure 11.1
The file is inserted within the current document.

10-point size for inserted text

Need to delete extra blank line

12-point size for original text

Contents of W-1102 file

⑦ **Select the paragraph that begins with** `After paying preferred dividends`**; choose Times New Roman and 12-point size; then deselect the text.**

The paragraphs are now formatted to match the existing paragraphs in your document.

⑧ **Position the insertion point on the blank line above 2002 Capital Expenditures and press** `Del`**.**

Figure 11.2 shows the formatted imported paragraphs.

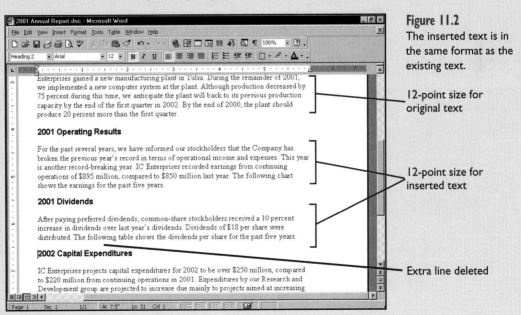

Figure 11.2
The inserted text is in the same format as the existing text.

12-point size for original text

12-point size for inserted text

Extra line deleted

⑨ **Save the document and keep it onscreen to continue with the next lesson.**

Lesson 2: Importing Excel Data into Word

Each Office 2000 program is designed to create documents for specific purposes. For example, use Word to create and format letters, memos, and reports; use Excel for creating spreadsheets to store, format, and calculate values. Although you should use the appropriate program for what you're doing, you might need the same data in another program. For example, you might need to include some Excel data in a proposal that you're creating in Word.

Importing is the process of inserting data created in the source program into the destination program. For example, when you insert Excel data into a Word document, you are importing that Excel data. In this lesson, you use the Copy and Paste commands to import part of an Excel worksheet into your Word document.

 Exam Note: Excel Terminology
You need to know some basic Excel terms to import data. **Workbook** refers to an Excel file. Each workbook can contain "pages" of data known as worksheets. A **worksheet** is a set of columns and rows that contains numerical data, descriptions, and formulas.

 Inside Stuff: Application Windows
While completing this lesson, make sure you are not running other applications, such as Internet Explorer or PowerPoint. The more applications you open, the greater the chance that your computer will lock up.

To Import Excel Data into Word

1 **In the 2001 Annual Report document, position the insertion point on the blank line above the 2002 Capital Expenditures heading.**
You should position the insertion point where you want to insert the worksheet data. Now, you need to start Excel and open the workbook that contains the data you want.

 2 **Click Start on the taskbar, choose Programs, and choose Microsoft Excel.**
Excel appears and covers the Word window. If you can still see part of the Word window, click Excel's Maximize button.

 3 **Click the Open button on the Excel Standard toolbar, open W-1103.xls, and save it as IC Data. Note: Excel adds the .xls extension when you save the workbook.**
You see the workbook in the Excel window, as shown in Figure 11.3. Each worksheet contains columns and rows, similar to a Word table—but noticeably bigger. The intersection of a column and row is called a **cell**.

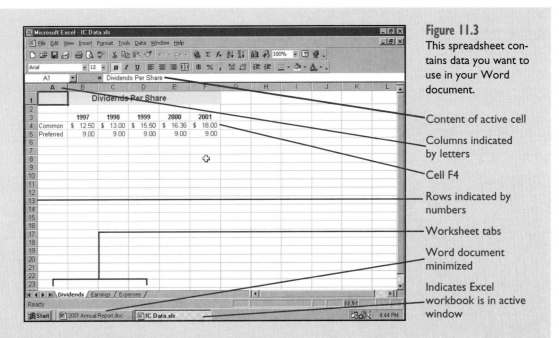

Figure 11.3

This spreadsheet contains data you want to use in your Word document.

Content of active cell

Columns indicated by letters

Cell F4

Rows indicated by numbers

Worksheet tabs

Word document minimized

Indicates Excel workbook is in active window

You see alphabetic labels at the top of the spreadsheet and numbered labels on the left side. These labels help you identify columns and rows, respectively, within the spreadsheet. For example, the cell containing $18.00 is cell F4.

 Exam Note: **Ranges**

A *range* is a rectangle block of cells in a worksheet. You typically identify the exact range that contains the data you want to import into your Word document.

---

4 **Position the mouse pointer in cell A3. When the mouse pointer resembles a big plus sign, drag down and over to cell F5, which contains 9.00, as shown in Figure 11.4.**

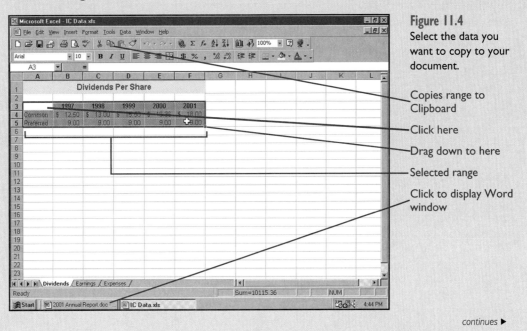

Figure 11.4

Select the data you want to copy to your document.

Copies range to Clipboard

Click here

Drag down to here

Selected range

Click to display Word window

continues ▶

To Import Excel Data into Word   (continued)

5 **Click the Copy button on Excel's Standard toolbar.**
The selected spreadsheet data is copied to the Clipboard. Once data is on the Clipboard, you can paste it in most Windows-based programs.

6 **Click the Word button on the taskbar to maximize Word.**
You know Excel is still open because you see the Excel button on the taskbar.

7 **Click the Paste button on the Standard toolbar.**
The spreadsheet data is pasted into the Word document as a table, as shown in Figure 11.5.

Figure 11.5
The Excel data is pasted into your Word document as a table.

Excel data pasted at the left margin

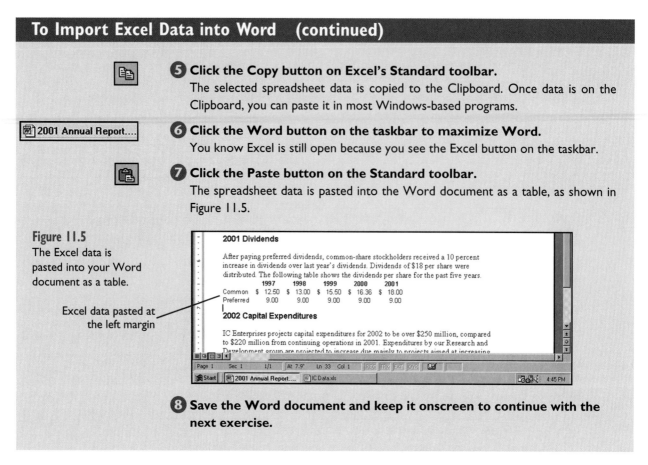

8 **Save the Word document and keep it onscreen to continue with the next exercise.**

When you paste worksheet data into Word, the formulas convert to numbers. Therefore, the results do not recalculate if you change numbers.

You need to format the table after importing the worksheet data. For this, you'll use some of the format techniques you learned in Project 7, "Creating and Formatting Tables."

To Format the Imported Table

1 **Right-click the imported table within Word and choose Table Properties.**
You want to apply a border around the outside edges of the table.

2 **Click the Borders and Shading button, click the Box setting, and click OK to close the Borders and Shading dialog box.**
You want to center the table between the left and right margins, so it looks balanced on the page.

3 **Choose Center alignment.**

4 **Click OK to close the Table Properties dialog box.**
The table is centered between the left and right margins. It looks better with a border around it. However, you notice that the decimal points don't line up. Because data formats do not import perfectly, you need to manually insert spaces to make the last row look better.

5 **Click before the first 9.00 and press** Spacebar.
The decimal point should align with the decimal in the second row.

6 **Repeat step 5 for the rest of the values on the last row.**
Figure 11.6 shows the formatted table of imported Excel data.

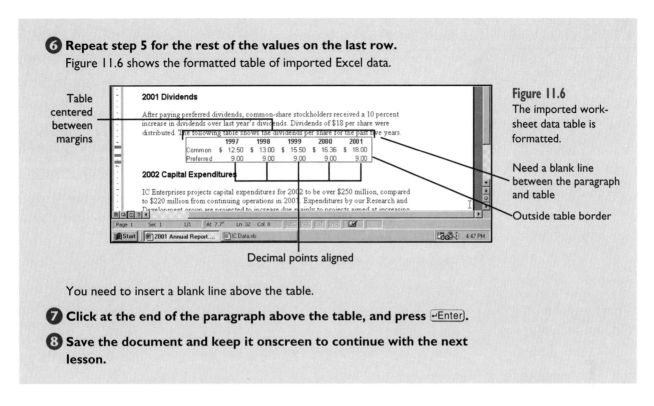

Table centered between margins

Figure 11.6
The imported worksheet data table is formatted.

Need a blank line between the paragraph and table

Outside table border

Decimal points aligned

You need to insert a blank line above the table.

7 **Click at the end of the paragraph above the table, and press ⏎Enter.**

8 **Save the document and keep it onscreen to continue with the next lesson.**

Lesson 3: Embedding Excel Data into Word

Although using Copy and Paste commands is helpful for inserting Excel data into Word, imported data has its limitations. For example, formulas convert to text, so you can't edit a value in Word and expect the results to recalculate.

Thanks to **Object Linking and Embedding (OLE)**, technology that lets you use objects between programs, you can edit embedded data and objects. **Embedding** is the process of importing data that can be edited within the destination program. You typically double-click an embedded object to edit it.

In this lesson, you embed Excel data into the annual report.

To Embed Excel Data into Word

1 **In the 2001 Annual Report document, position the insertion point at the end of the document.**

2 **Click the Excel button on the taskbar to display the Excel window; then press Esc to clear the Clipboard and turn off the moving dashed lines surrounding the selected range.**
A moving dashed line appears around a range when you click the Copy button. It remains onscreen, so you can paste the range several times, if needed. You must press Esc to clear the Clipboard and turn off the moving dashed lines; otherwise, you might accidentally enter or paste data over the original data.
You need to select the data you want to embed into Word.

3 **Click the Expenses worksheet tab at the bottom of the Excel window, select the range A1:C8, and click the Copy button.**

continues ▶

To Embed Excel Data into Word   (continued)

> **(i)** *Inside Stuff:*   **Range Identification**
> Ranges are typically identified by the starting and ending cells with a colon in between, such as A1:C8.

The first few steps of embedding are identical to the first few steps of importing: you select and copy the data you want in the source program.

4 **Click the Word button on the taskbar.**

5 **Choose Edit, Paste Special.**
The Paste Special dialog box appears (see Figure 11.7). You need to choose the type of data you're embedding.

Figure 11.7
The Paste Special dialog box embeds data into the destination program.

Click this option
Description of selected source

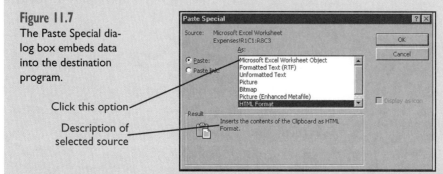

6 **Click Microsoft Excel Worksheet Object, and click OK.**
Figure 11.8 shows the embedded data. Unlike a regular Copy and Paste import that imports the data as a table, the embedded data contains sizing handles, indicating it is treated as an object.

Figure 11.8
Word treats embedded data as an object.

Sizing handles

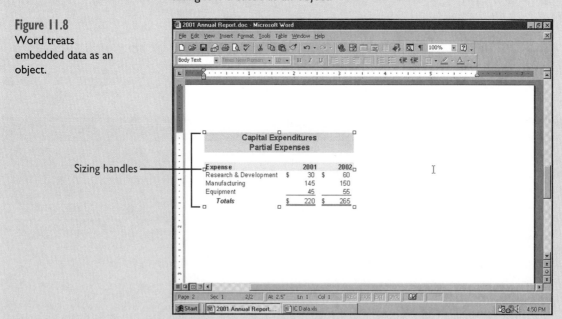

7 **Right-click the embedded data and choose Format Object.**
You see the Format Object dialog box, so you can set the object's formats, similar to setting clip art formats.

8 **Click the Layout tab, click the Square wrapping style, choose Center horizontal alignment, and then click OK.**

The embedded object is centered between the margins (see Figure 11.9).

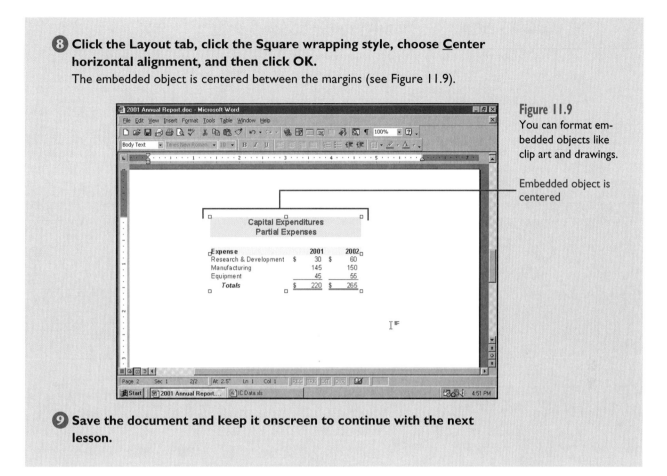

Figure 11.9
You can format embedded objects like clip art and drawings.

Embedded object is centered

9 **Save the document and keep it onscreen to continue with the next lesson.**

---

 *Exam Note: **Embedding a New Worksheet***

If you don't have existing data created in Excel, you can insert a new Excel worksheet within Word by clicking the Insert Microsoft Excel Worksheet button on the Standard toolbar. Choose the number of columns and rows from a palette, as you do when you click the Insert Table button.

You see an empty embedded worksheet that looks like a portion of an Excel worksheet. You can click and drag the bottom right corner of the embedded Excel object window to enlarge it. The Word menus and toolbars temporarily change to include Excel capabilities (see Figure 11.10).

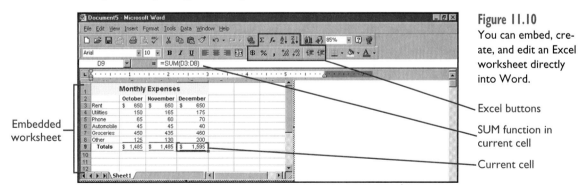

Figure 11.10
You can embed, create, and edit an Excel worksheet directly into Word.

Excel buttons

SUM function in current cell

Current cell

Embedded worksheet

Inserting a new Excel worksheet as an embedded object has advantages over a Word table. For example, you have more formatting options. Most importantly, you can easily create formulas, use Excel functions, and copy formulas. When you change a value, the results automatically recalculate, unlike formula results in a Word table.

Lesson 4: Modifying Embedded Data

You can edit embedded text by double-clicking the object. You see the column and row indicators inside the object window. Plus, you see Excel buttons and options within the Word window. These options allow you to format the embedded data without exiting the Word program.

When you edit embedded data, you change the data in the destination program (i.e., Word) only. These changes do not affect the original data in the source program (i.e., Excel).

In this lesson, you change a value in the embedded object.

To Modify Embedded Data

❶ **In the open** 2001 Annual Report **document, double-click the Capital Expenditures embedded object.**
Figure 11.11 shows the Excel tools for modifying the embedded object within Word.

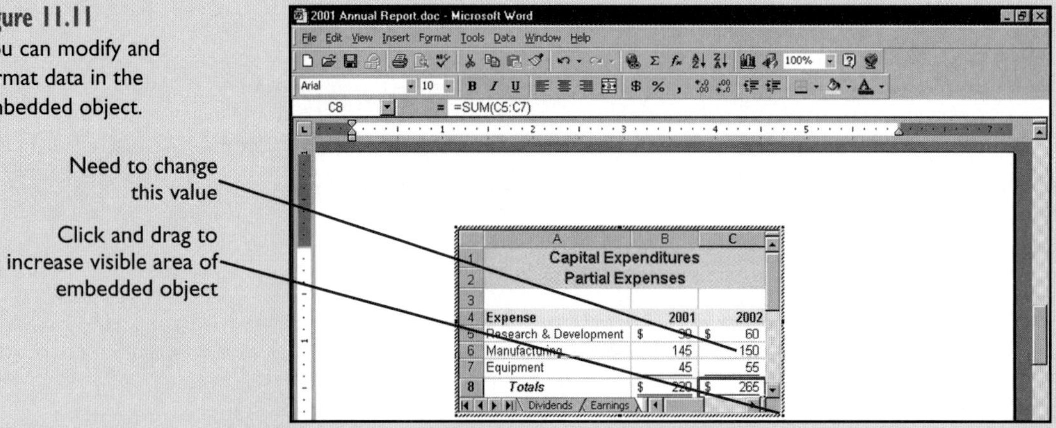

Figure 11.11
You can modify and format data in the embedded object.

Need to change this value

Click and drag to increase visible area of embedded object

	A	B	C
1	Capital Expenditures		
2	Partial Expenses		
3			
4	Expense	2001	2002
5	Research & Development	$ 50	$ 60
6	Manufacturing	145	150
7	Equipment	45	55
8	*Totals*	$ 250	$ 265

❷ **Click and drag the bottom right corner to enlarge the size of the worksheet window to see all of the embedded data.**

❸ **Click in cell C8.**
The formula bar displays the formula to calculate the total. The formula is =SUM(C5:C7).

❹ **Click in cell C6, the cell that contains 150.**

❺ **Type** 160 **and press** ↵Enter.
The total changes to reflect the new value. The new total is 275 (see Figure 11.12).

❻ **Click outside the embedded object.**
The menu bar and toolbars reflect Word capabilities again.

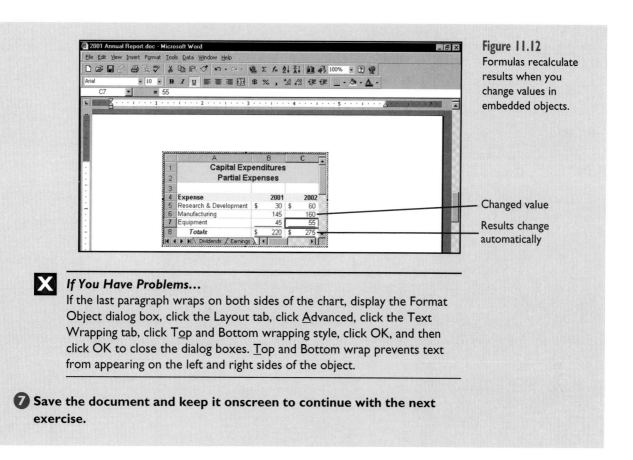

Figure 11.12
Formulas recalculate results when you change values in embedded objects.

Changed value

Results change automatically

 If You Have Problems...
If the last paragraph wraps on both sides of the chart, display the Format Object dialog box, click the Layout tab, click <u>A</u>dvanced, click the Text Wrapping tab, click T<u>o</u>p and Bottom wrapping style, click OK, and then click OK to close the dialog boxes. <u>T</u>op and Bottom wrap prevents text from appearing on the left and right sides of the object.

7 **Save the document and keep it onscreen to continue with the next exercise.**

(i) *Inside Stuff:*   **Formatting Embedded Data**
The F<u>o</u>rmat menu contains Excel options when you create and edit an embedded worksheet. Choose F<u>o</u>rmat, <u>C</u>ells to form worksheet cells. You can choose alignment, underline, and numerical formats for embedded cells.

The Formatting toolbar changes to reflect Excel capabilities. For example, you can format data for currency, indent text inside a cell, and so on.

Lesson 5: Embedding an Excel Chart

You can embed an Excel chart into a Word document. Embedding an Excel chart is helpful when the chart is already created. You don't have to re-create the chart in Word. Some people prefer creating charts in Excel because Excel contains more options than Word.

In this lesson, you embed an Excel chart at the end of the 2001 Operating Results section. When you embed a chart, you can either click the Paste button in Word; or choose <u>E</u>dit, Paste <u>S</u>pecial, click Microsoft Excel Chart Object, and click OK. Unlike Excel data, in which there is a difference between importing and embedding, both Paste and Paste Special embed a chart.

To Embed an Excel Chart

1 **In the open `2001 Annual Report` document, position the insertion point above the 2001 Dividends heading.**

2 **Click the Excel button on the taskbar to display the Excel program and worksheet.**

3 **Press `Esc`.**
Remember to press `Esc` to clear the Clipboard and turn off the moving dashed line.

4 **Click the Earnings worksheet tab at the bottom of the Excel window.**
This worksheet contains the chart that you want to embed into your Word document (see Figure 11.13).

Figure 11.13
You want to embed this chart into Word.

Click to select chart

Chart in Earnings worksheet

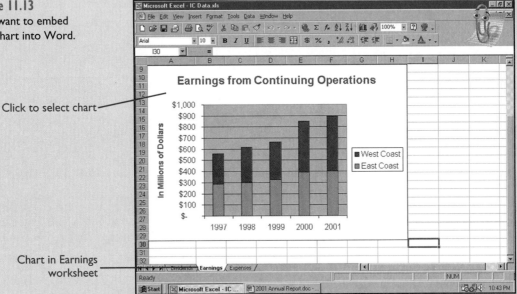

5 **Click the chart to select it.**

6 **Click the Copy button on the Standard toolbar in Excel.**
After copying the object to the Clipboard, you need to display Word and embed the chart.

7 **Click the Word button on the taskbar and then click the Paste button to embed the chart.**
The chart is embedded into Word. You should decrease its size.

8 **Right-click the chart object, and choose Format Object.**

9 **Click the Size tab, drag across the value in the Width box, type 4", and click OK.**
Figure 11.14 shows the embedded chart in Word.

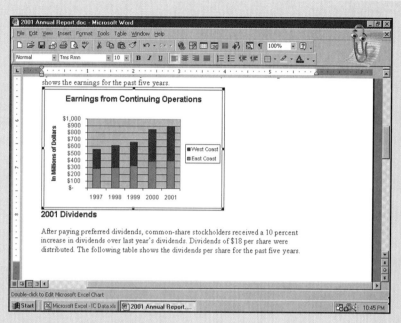

Figure 11.14
Word contains an
embedded Excel chart.

10 **Click outside the object to deselect it.**

11 **Save the document and keep it onscreen to continue with the next lesson.**

 Inside Stuff: **Modifying an Embedded Chart**

Double-click the chart to change the values that create the chart. Within the embedded chart window, click the worksheet tab containing the values that create the chart. When you change a value, the chart automatically changes. The original chart in the Excel workbook maintains the original settings, however.

 Inside Stuff: **Dragging and Dropping a Chart**

There's another easy way of copying and pasting a chart from Excel to Word. You can display both the Word and Excel windows side by side by using the **Tile Windows Vertically option**. To do this, right-click the gray space on the taskbar and choose Tile Windows V̲ertically.

After you select the chart, hold down Ctrl and drag the chart to where you want to copy it in the Word window. Release the mouse and Ctrl. A copy of the chart appears in Word. If you don't press and hold Ctrl during the entire drag-and-drop process, you move the chart instead of copying it.

Lesson 6: Linking Excel Data into Word

Linking is the process of inserting an object from another program in which the object is dynamically linked to the original data. If you change data in the original source program, the data updates in the destination program. In this lesson, you want to delete the embedded data and insert it again, but as a linked object.

To Link Excel Data

1 **With the 2001 Annual Report document onscreen, save the document as 2001 Annual Report with Link.**
You want to keep the original version with the embedded data, so you can compare the differences in embedded and linked objects.

2 **Click the Capital Expenditures embedded object at the end of the document; then press Del.**
Now you are ready to insert the object again to link to the original worksheet.

3 **Click the Excel button on the taskbar.**

4 **Click the Expenses tab.**

5 **Select the range A1:C8 and then click the Copy button.**
Like all previous methods, you must select and copy the data in the source program.

6 **Click the Word button on the taskbar.**
You are ready to paste the object as a link.

7 **Choose Edit, Paste Special.**

8 **Click the Paste link option on the left side of the dialog box.**
The Paste link option tells Word to insert the incoming object as a link instead of embedding the object with no connection to the source data.

9 **Click Microsoft Excel Worksheet Object and click OK.**
The Excel data comes in as an object, similar to embedded data. However, this time the data is linked to the original Excel worksheet data. If you change the original data, the linked data changes in Word.

10 **Right-click the object.**
Notice the shortcut menu displays the Linked Worksheet Object option (see Figure 11.15). You can edit or open the link if you want.

Figure 11.15
The shortcut menu contains an option for the linked object.

Choose option to edit or open the link

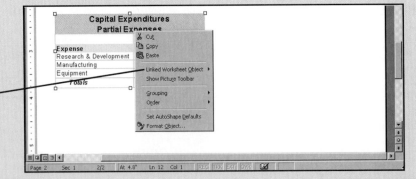

11 **Click outside the object, save the document, and keep it onscreen to continue with the next exercise.**

Now, let's change data in the Excel worksheet and see how those changes affect your linked object.

To Change the Source Data

1 **Click the Excel button on the taskbar and press Esc to clear the Clipboard and turn off the moving dashed lines around the selected range.**

2 **Click in cell C5, type 65, and press Enter.**
The 2002 total is now 270.

3 **Type 165 in cell C6 and press Enter.**

4 **Type 60 in cell C7 and press Enter.**
The 2002 total is 290.

5 **Save the Excel workbook and exit Excel.**
Word appears again. Notice the linked object reflects the changes you made in the Excel workbook (see Figure 11.16).

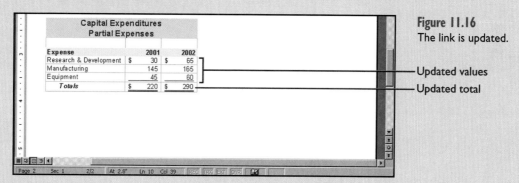

Figure 11.16
The link is updated.

—Updated values
—Updated total

6 **Save the document.**
Because you saved the linked object with a different filename, you can open the 2001 Annual Report to compare the difference in the linked and embedded object.

7 **Open 2001 Annual Report and scroll to the bottom of the document to see the embedded object.**

8 **Right-click a gray spot on the taskbar and choose Tile Windows Vertically.**
Figure 11.17 shows both documents onscreen. You might need to click the horizontal scrollbars to see the full objects. The linked object in 2001 Annual Report with Link shows the updated values in the workbook. The embedded object in 2001 Annual Report contains the original values.

continues ▶

To Change the Source Data (continued)

Figure 11.17
Compare the differences in linked and embedded objects.

Linked object contains new values and total

Embedded object contains old values and total

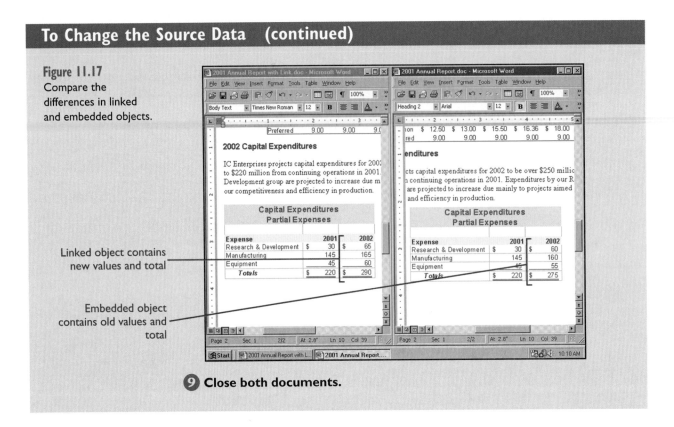

9 **Close both documents.**

Inside Stuff: **Importing, Embedding, and Linking**

You used three methods for inserting worksheet data into Word. Use the following guidelines to determine which method is appropriate for the situation:

■ **Import** when you want a permanent copy of the source data but do not need the data updated within Word.

■ **Embed** when you want to insert worksheet data or a chart and be able to modify it *within* Word. Also click the Insert Microsoft Excel Worksheet button to create a blank embedded worksheet within Word.

■ **Link** when you want to insert worksheet data that might change in the source worksheet and you want the updates to be reflected in your Word document.

Inside Stuff: **Displaying a Link as an Icon**

You can save disk space by inserting the link as an icon instead of displaying the actual linked data. When you are selecting options in the Paste Special dialog box, click the <u>D</u>isplay as icon check box.

Microsoft Excel Worksheet

You see an icon representing the linked data. You can access the source file by double-clicking the icon.

Lesson 7: Sending a Word Document Via Email

Often, you need to send documents in an electronic form to supervisors, clients, suppliers, and colleagues. You can email a document as the main part of the email message, or you can create an email message within Word and ***attach*** the document (that is, include a document as a separate file that is attached to the main email message).

Depending on the setup of your computer and the type of email program you and the recipient have, a Word document used as the main email message might lose its formats during transmission. However, a document file used as an attachment keeps its formats. The recipient simply saves the attached document on his or her computer and opens it in Word with the formats intact.

In this lesson, you create an email message for your supervisor and attach the 2001 Annual Report document.

 If You Have Problems...
Word tries to use Outlook to complete the email process. If you don't have Outlook installed on your computer, or if you aren't setup with an email account, you might not be able to complete all steps in this lesson.

To Email a Word Document as an Attachment

1 **Click the New Blank Document button to start a new document window.**

2 **Click the E-mail button on the Standard toolbar.**
The email header appears so you can enter the recipient's email address and subject line (see Figure 11.18). In addition, the toolbar provides options for sending the email. Table 11.1 at the end of this lesson describes the email buttons.

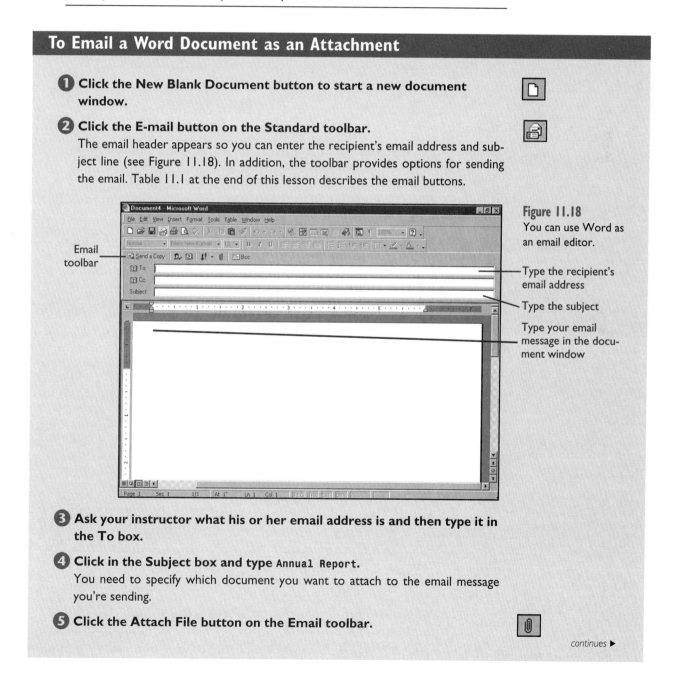

Figure 11.18
You can use Word as an email editor.

Email toolbar

Type the recipient's email address

Type the subject

Type your email message in the document window

3 **Ask your instructor what his or her email address is and then type it in the To box.**

4 **Click in the Subject box and type** `Annual Report`.
You need to specify which document you want to attach to the email message you're sending.

5 **Click the Attach File button on the Email toolbar.**

continues ▶

To Email a Word Document as an Attachment (continued)

6 **Choose the drive, folder(s), and 2001 Annual Report, and then click Attach.**

The Attach text box appears below the Subject text box. It shows you the file you attached to the email.

You need to type a short "cover letter" for the attached document.

7 **Click in the document window area and type the following paragraph:**

I'm attaching a copy of the 2001 Annual Report for you to review. Please let me know if you have additional information to include before I send the report to the stockholders.

8 **Press ⏎Enter twice and type your name.**

Figure 11.19 shows the completed email message.

Figure 11.19
You can use Word to create your email message.

Attached document ⟶

Email message ⟶

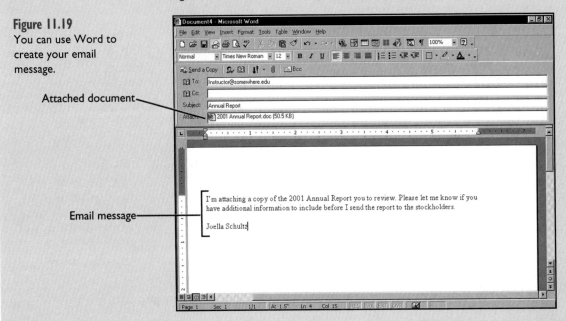

After completing the email message, you should spell-check it before sending it.

9 **Click the Spelling and Grammar button on the Standard toolbar, correct any errors, and close the dialog box.**

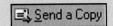

10 **Click the Send a Copy button on the Email toolbar to send the email to your supervisor.**

After the email is sent, the email text might remain onscreen. You can either save it or close the document.

11 **Save the document as Email Note and then close it.**

 Exam Note: Sending a Word Document as Email

To send an open Word document as the main email message, click the E-mail button. Word displays the email header to enter the recipient's email address.

Depending on how email is set up on your computer, you might be able to choose File, Send To. Choose Mail Recipient to send the current document as the email message or choose Mail Recipient (as Attachment) to send the document as an attachment to the email message.

Table 11.1   Buttons on the Email Toolbar

Icon	Element	Description
🖹 <u>S</u>end a Copy	<u>S</u>end a Copy	Sends the email and attachments to the recipient.
🖎	Check Names	Checks the recipient's email address in Outlook to make sure it is a legitimate email address.
📖	Address Book	Displays the Address Book, so you can select email addresses you've stored.
⬇ ▾	Set Priority	Specifies the priority of the email. The default is Normal Priority, but you can also choose <u>H</u>igh Priority or <u>L</u>ow Priority.
📎	Attach File	Lets you select a document to include as an attachment for the email. The recipient can save and open the attachment in the source program, such as Word.
📧 Bcc	Toggle Bcc	Displays or hides the Bcc text box. Use this option when you want to send a **blind courtesy copy**—a copy of the email message sent to another person, but the primary recipient does not know someone else is receiving the email.

Summary

When preparing reports in which text is entered into different documents, you can use the Insert File dialog box to insert a document within the current document. In addition, you can insert worksheet data by importing, embedding, and linking data from the source file in Excel to the destination file in Word. Finally, you can create an email message in Word and attach a Word document to an email message.

Use the built-in Help feature to learn more about embedding, linking, and emailing data. You should spend some time experimenting with different options and observing the results. To continue your learning, complete the following exercises.

Checking Concepts and Terms

True/False

For each of the following, check *T* or *F* to indicate whether the statement is true or false.

__T __F   **1.** When you copy Excel worksheet data and paste it into Word, the imported date is an embedded object. [L2]

__T __F   **2.** You can format an embedded object similar to formatting a picture in Word. [L3]

__T __F   **3.** When you double-click an embedded object, you see the original data in the source program. [L4]

__T __F   **4.** Editing values in an embedded object also changes the values in the source file. [L4]

__T __F   **5.** When you click the E-mail button on the toolbar, Word uses the open document as the main email message. [L7]

Multiple Choice

Circle the letter of the correct answer for each of the following.

1. When you use the Insert File dialog box, what happens to the file you select? [L1]

   a. The file's contents are inserted at the insertion point location within the current document.

   b. The document opens into a separate document window.

   c. The document is inserted at the beginning of the current document.

   d. The document is inserted at the end of the current document.

2. When you copy an Excel worksheet and paste it into Word, all of the following happen *except:* [L2]

   a. Formulas are converted to values.

   b. The imported data can be formatted as a table.

   c. Values with decimal points might not align in Word.

   d. You can display the Picture toolbar and format the data as an object.

3. Which option inserts Excel data in a way that lets you edit the values in Word and updates the formula results? [L3, 6]

   a. Copying and Pasting

   b. Embedding

   c. Linking

   d. Emailing

4. What option lets you embed or link Excel worksheet data into Word? [L3, 6]

   a. Paste

   b. Copy

   c. Paste Special

   d. Show as Icon

5. Which option inserts Excel data in a way that lets you modify the original Excel worksheet and the changes are automatically made in the Word data? [L6]

   a. Copying and Pasting

   b. Embedding

   c. Linking

   d. Emailing

Screen ID

Label each element of the Word screen shown in Figure 11.20.

Figure 11.20

A. Attach File button

B. E-mail button

C. embedded chart

D. source chart

E. worksheet tab

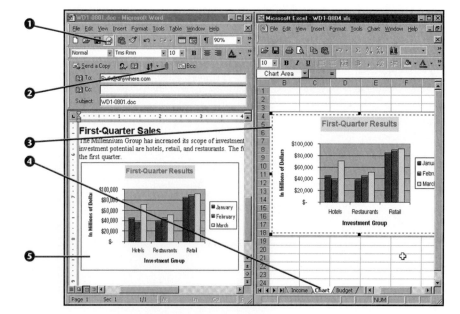

I. _____   2. _____   3. _____

4. _____   5. _____

Skill Drill

Skill Drill exercises reinforce project skills. Each skill reinforced is the same, or nearly the same, as a skill presented in the project. Each exercise includes a brief narrative introduction, followed by detailed instructions in a step-by-step format.

1. Inserting a Document Within the Current Document

You are writing an update to tell your family about your semester. You just finished the letter, but you want to include a document you always insert into your letters: a plea to get your family to help pay for your spring-break ski trip!

1. Open **W-1104** and save it as **Personal Letter**.
2. Position the insertion point at the beginning of the last paragraph.
3. Choose Insert, File.
4. Choose **W-1105** and click Insert.
5. Select the heading Spring Break is Around the Corner and the paragraph below it.
6. Choose 11-point Comic Sans MS font from the Formatting toolbar.
7. Deselect the text.
8. Select the heading Spring Break is Around the Corner and click the Bold button.
9. Save the document and leave the document onscreen to continue with the next exercise.

2. Embedding Excel Worksheet Data

You created a simple budget in Excel and want to copy it into your Word document.

1. With **Personal Letter** onscreen, position the insertion point between the two paragraphs in the Update on Expenses section.
2. Choose Start, Programs, Microsoft Excel.
3. Open **W-1106.xls** from within Excel.
4. Click in Cell A1 and drag down to Cell B10 to select the range that contains the budget data.
5. Click the Copy button in Excel.
6. Click the Word button on the taskbar.
7. Choose Edit, Paste Special.
8. Click Microsoft Excel Worksheet Object and click OK.
9. Right-click the embedded object and choose Format Object.
10. Click the Layout tab and click Center.
11. Click the Colors and Lines tab, click the Line Color drop-down arrow, and click Sea Green.
12. Click the Style drop-down arrow, choose 3 points, and click OK.
13. If part of the paragraph goes below the object, click and drag the object down just enough for the entire **In fact** paragraph to be above the object.
14. Save the document and keep it onscreen to continue to the next exercise. Keep Excel and the workbook open also.

3. Linking an Excel Chart and Emailing an Attached Word Document

Your Excel workbook also contains a pie chart that shows each expense's proportion of your total budget. You want to include it in your personal letter. Then, you plan to create an email message and attach the document.

1. With **Personal Letter** onscreen, position the insertion point on the blank line above Spring Break is Around the Corner.
2. Click the Excel button on the taskbar; press Esc to stop selecting the range.
3. Click the chart to select it and click the Copy button in Excel.
4. Click the Word button on the taskbar.
5. Choose Edit, Paste Special; click the Paste link option, and click OK.
6. Right-click the linked chart and choose Format Object.
7. Click the Size tab, delete the current value in the Width box, type **2.75"**, and click OK.

8. If the chart appears at the top of the document, change the zoom magnification to 50% and then click and drag the chart to the bottom of page 1, before the heading Spring Break is Around the Corner.

9. Click at the beginning of the heading Spring Break is Around the Corner and press `Ctrl`+`↵Enter` to insert a hard page break.

10. Save the document and close it; exit Excel.

11. Click the New Blank Document button on the Standard toolbar.

12. Click the E-mail button on the Standard toolbar.

13. Enter an email address in the To box and type **Personal Update** in the Subject box.

14. Click the Attach File button on the Email toolbar, select **Personal Letter.doc**, and click <u>A</u>ttach.

15. Click in the document window and type the following paragraph:

> **Hi everyone! I thought I'd drop you a note to let you know how things are going here at the College on Daytona Beach! Although you are still skeptical about why I chose this college, I assure you that I do more than surf the waves on weekends and maintain my tan!**

16. Click the <u>S</u>end a Copy button to send the email.

17. Save the document as **Personal Email Message** and close it.

Challenge

Challenge exercises expand on or are somewhat related to skills presented in the lessons. Each exercise provides a brief narrative introduction followed by instructions in a numbered-step or bulleted-list format that are not as detailed as those in the Skill Drill section.

1. Compiling a List of Workshops

You are in charge of the monthly status to division managers. This month's report concerns the upcoming Information Technology Training Conference. You want to add a sampling of the scheduled computer workshops.

1. Open **W-1107** and save it as **Conference Workshops**.

2. Position the insertion point at the end of the document. Insert the file **W-1108**. Check the spacing between paragraphs and correct it, if needed.

3. Format the inserted text to match the font used in the original document.

4. Each workshop has been assigned a number. Use the Cut and Paste commands to organize the workshops by number. Check the spacing between workshops and correct it, if needed.

5. Use the **Keep with ne<u>x</u>t** option, if needed, to make sure a heading isn't isolated from its paragraph between page breaks.

6. Save the document and print it.

2. Embedding a Mortgage Worksheet and Emailing it as an Attachment

A customer calls the loan officer at your mortgage company. The loan officer asks you to prepare a short letter that includes some calculations for the loan.

1. Open **W-1109** and save it as **Loan Letter** in Word; open **W-1110.xls** in Excel.

2. Select and copy the worksheet data (cells A1 through B8).

3. Embed the data as a Microsoft Excel Worksheet Object between the first and second paragraphs in your Word document.

4. Center the object between the margins.

5. Make sure you have only one blank line before and after the object.

6. Edit the embedded object within Word by changing the home price to **190000**. *Note:* You don't have to type the dollar sign and comma because the cell is already formatted.

7. Edit the sentence above the object to reflect the new monthly payment amount shown in the object.

8. Save the document, print it, and close it.

9. Create an email message by entering your instructor's email address, typing an appropriate subject line, and attaching the Loan Letter document.

10. Type a short paragraph that describes the document you're attaching.

11. Send the email and close the document.

3. Linking an Excel Chart and Updating the Link

You are preparing a report that announces the implementation of new technology for your company. You need to include a chart that was created in Excel. Because you want the chart in Word to reflect changes in the original Excel workbook, you need to link the chart.

1. Open **W-1111** in Word and save it as **CTA Implementation Report**.

2. Open **W-1112** in Excel and save it as **Phases**.

3. Select the chart and copy it to the Clipboard.

4. Link the chart at the bottom of the Word document.

5. Save the Word document and print it.

6. In the Excel workbook, make these changes:

   Phase 1 Hardware value: **1.4**

   Phase 2 Software value: **1.0**

   Phase 3 Software value: **0.75**

   Phase 4 Software value: **0.5**

   Phase 3 Training value: **0.5**

   Phase 4 Training value: **1.0**

7. Change the chart to a Clustered Bar Chart, similar to the way you changed chart types in Word.

8. Change the legend to 10-point size.

9. Select the chart and drag the bottom-middle sizing handle down about three rows to make the chart taller.

10. Save the Excel workbook and print it.

11. Save the Word document and print it.

Discovery Zone

Discovery Zone exercises help you gain advanced knowledge of project topics and/or application of skills. These exercises focus on enhancing your problem-solving skills. Numbered steps are not provided, but you are given hints, reminders, screen shots, and/or references to help you reach your goal for each exercise.

1. Preparing an Email Attachment with an Embedded Object

You need to prepare a flier to be used as an email attachment. The flier is designed to promote membership in your fitness center. Open **W-1113** and save it as **HealthFirst Fitness Club**. Insert **W-1114** between the first and second paragraphs. Make sure the inserted text's font size is consistent with the current document. Select the list and create a customized bulleted list with the symbol of a person lifting weights. *Note:* This symbol is found in the Webdings font.

Within Word, insert a new Excel worksheet with six rows and four columns. *Note:* Do not use the Excel program; create the worksheet within Word. Refer to the end of Lesson 3 for more information. Use Figure 11.21 to create the embedded worksheet. Adjust column widths as you adjust column widths in a Word table. For B1:D1, format the cells with the Wrap text alignment option. *Hint:* Look at the Format menu while creating the embedded object.

Do not type the dollar signs. Apply Currency Style numeric format to the first row and Comma Style numeric format to the rest of the values. Apply other formats as shown, such as Light Green fill color, Sea Green font color, bold, and centering.

	A	B Monthly Rate	C 1 Year Membership	D 2 Year Membership
1	Club			
2	Energetic	$ 45.00	$ 420.00	$ 774.00
3	HealthFirst	32.00	290.95	456.00
4	NewAge	38.50	325.50	525.50
5	Workout Rage	42.95	375.95	549.95

Figure 11.21
Create the embedded object within Word.

Center the object between the left and right margins. Use the Top and Bottom text wrap option. Apply a Sea Green 2 1/4-point border for the object. Save, print, and close the document.

Create an email message to your instructor using Word as the email editor. Type an appropriate subject line and attach the HealthFirst Fitness Club document. Type the following information for the email message:

> **We're excited that you are interested in information about HealthFirst Fitness Club, one of the largest fitness centers in the city. Please refer to the attached document for more information about our fitness center.**

Send the email message.

2. Linking a Chart for a Handout for Potential Investors

You need to create an information sheet for potential investors. The information sheet will have a link to the original chart in Excel, so you can change the Excel data at any time and the linked object in Word updates itself. Open **W-1115** in Word and save it as **Sales History**. Open **W-1116** in Excel and save it as **CTC Sales**.

Link the chart from Excel to Word. Center the chart between the left and right margins in Word. Save the document and print it.

In Excel, change the 2000 Courses to **90000**, and change the 2000 Tests to **95000**. Change the chart to a Clustered Column type. Change the chart tile font color to Blue and the fill color to Pale Blue. Select Light Yellow fill for the plot area. Change the Tests data series color to Red. Change the Miscellaneous data series color to Bright Green. Save the changes and print the workbook. Save the Word document and print it.

PinPoint Assessment

You have completed this project and its associated lessons, and have had an opportunity to assess your skills through the end-of-project questions and exercises. Now use the PinPoint software Evaluation Mode to further assess your comprehension of the specific exam activities you have just learned. You can also use the PinPoint Trainer Mode and the Show Me tutorials to practice these exam activities.

Project 12

Working with Documents

Key terms introduced in this project include

- bar tab
- demote
- leaders
- outline numbered list
- promote
- tabs

Objectives	Required Activity for MOUS	Exam Level
➤ Find and Replace Text	Find and replace text	Core
➤ Find and Replace Formatting	Use find and replace with formats, special characters and non-printing elements	Expert
➤ Set Tabs on the Ruler	Use TABS command (Center, Decimal, Left and Right)	Core
➤ Set Tabs in the Tabs Dialog Box	Use TABS command (Center, Decimal, Left and Right)	Core
	Set tabs with leaders	Core
➤ Sort Lists and Paragraphs	Sort lists, paragraphs, tables	Expert
➤ Create an Outline Style Numbered List	Create an outline-style numbered list	Core

Why Would I Do This?

As you work with long documents, you might need to change text or formats throughout the document. Furthermore, you might want to include a list based on tabs instead of creating a table. Finally, you might need to prepare a formal outline of a document that includes several levels instead of a simple numbered list.

In this project, you are sending a letter to a potential client who is interested in your company's training program. You need to find and replace text, find and replace formats, create and sort tabulated lists, and create an outline numbered list.

 ## Lesson 1: Finding and Replacing Text

After you create a document, you might decide to replace a certain phrase with a different phrase. For example, you might want to change "in my opinion" to "I believe" to make the text more concise. At other times, you might need to edit a status report about a project your team is working on. Because people frequently change jobs, your team members periodically change. Therefore, you need to find the original person's name and change it to reflect the replacement person's name.

The Find and Replace feature locates specific text (such as words or phrases) and replaces it with different text. Using Find and Replace saves you a lot of time because you don't have to read your entire document and identify the text to change. It ensures that you don't overlook an occurrence of the text you want to replace.

In this lesson, you decide to change the abbreviation **MS** to **Microsoft** in a letter to a potential customer who is interested in your training workshops.

To Find and Replace Text

❶ Open W-1201 and save it as Software Letter.
You see **MS** throughout the document.

❷ Choose Edit, Replace.

 Inside Stuff: **Keyboard Shortcuts**
Press Ctrl+F to find text, or press Ctrl+H to find and replace text.

The Find and Replace dialog box appears with the **Replace** tab options displayed (see Figure 12.1).

Figure 12.1
Type the text you want to find and replace.

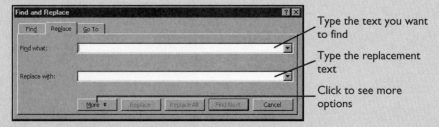

Type the text you want to find

Type the replacement text

Click to see more options

❸ Type MS in the Find what box.
MS is the text that you want to find.

❹ Press Tab↹ and type Microsoft in the Replace with box.
Microsoft is the replacement word for MS.

⑤ Click Replace All.

Word searches the entire document. It replaces all occurrences of MS with Microsoft. You should see a message: `Word has completed its search of the document and has made 10 replacements.`

⑥ Click OK to acknowledge the message and click Close to close the Find and Replace dialog box.

Word replaces the courtesy title `Ms` with `Microsoft` (see Figure 12.2). Capitalized occurrences of `MS` are also replaced with capitalized `MICROSOFT`. On Page 2, the word `programs` is replaced with `prograMicrosoft`. By default, Word does not look for `MS` as an individual word or for capitalized occurrences only. Therefore, any occurrence of `MS` or `ms` is replaced with `Microsoft`.

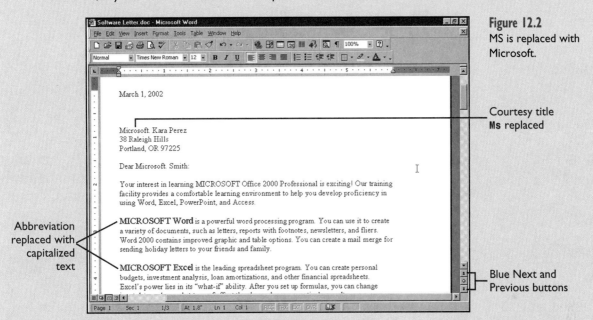

Figure 12.2
MS is replaced with Microsoft.

Courtesy title Ms replaced

Abbreviation replaced with capitalized text

Blue Next and Previous buttons

Notice that the Previous and Next buttons are blue, indicating that clicking them goes to something besides the previous and next pages. You can click the Select Browse Object button and choose Browse by Page to change the browse back to page.

ⓘ *Inside Stuff:*   **Selectively Finding and Replacing Text**

You can select which occurrences to find and replace by clicking Find Next instead of Replace All. When you click Find Next, Word finds the next occurrence of the text you entered. If you want to replace that occurrence, click Replace. If you don't want to replace that text, click Find Next to continue searching.

Because you don't want to change the courtesy title `Ms` to `Microsoft` and you don't want `programs` changed to `prograMicrosoft`, you need to undo the changes and set additional options in the Find and Replace dialog box.

⑦ Click the Undo button on the Standard toolbar.

⑧ Choose Edit, Replace.

The Find and Replace dialog box should display the text you entered into the Find what and Replace with boxes.

continues ▶

To Find and Replace Text   (continued)

9 Click **More** at the bottom of the dialog box.

The dialog box expands to show you more options (see Figure 12.3).

Figure 12.3
Select search options
to specify conditions
for finding and
replacing text.

Search options ——

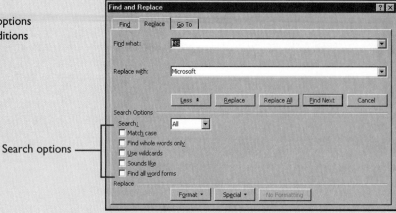

10 Click the **Match Case** check box.

Match Case makes sure that only occurrences with the same casing (capitalization) as MS are found.

11 Click the `Find whole words only` check box.

`Find whole words only` ensures that only occurrences of MS are found when they are individual words, not letters within other words—such as `programs`.

12 Click **Replace All**.

13 Click **OK** when you see the message `Word has completed its search of the document and has made 6 replacements.`

14 Click **Close** to close the **Find and Replace** dialog box.

This time only capitalized, whole-word occurrences of MS are found and replaced (see Figure 12.4).

Figure 12.4
Word replaces fewer
text items when you
select search options.

Ms not replaced ——

Regular capitalization ——

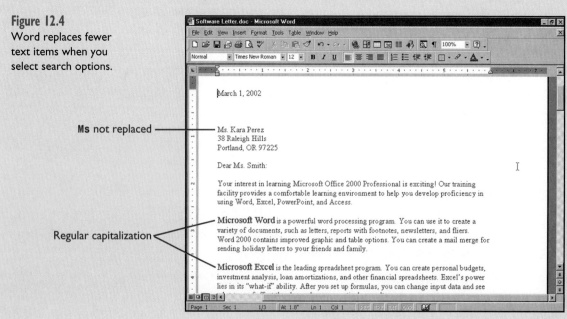

Save the document and keep it onscreen to continue with the next lesson.

 ***Exam Note:*   Restricting Find and Replace with Search Options**
To find exactly what you are looking for, use the appropriate options in the Search Options category of the Find and Replace dialog box. Table 12.1 describes these options.

Table 12.1   Search Options

Option	Description
Search:	Specifies the direction in which Word searches through your document. By default, Word searches the entire document (All). Choose Up to search from the insertion point toward the top of your document. Choose Down to search from the insertion point to the end of the document.
Match case	Select this check box to tell Word to search for only occurrences that appear in the same casing of the text you entered in the Find what box. Otherwise, Word finds text occurrences, regardless of capitalization. For example, Word finds **ms**, **MS**, and **Ms** if you don't select this option.
Find whole words only	Select this check box to ignore text when it is part of another word. If you want to find **man**, this option ignores words such as **manuscript** and **manipulate**.
Use wildcards	Selecting this option enables you to find words, even when you're not sure of their spelling, by using operators—such as ***** for any number of characters or **?** for one character—rather than letters. For example, searching for **w?n** finds **win** and **won**. If you select this option, click Special to see a list of search operators.
Sounds like	Select this check box to tell Word to stop on words that sound like or are spelled similar to the search text.
Find all word forms	Select this check box to find all forms or tenses of a word. For example, searching for **swim** finds **swam** and **swimming**.
Format	Click this button to find or replace formatting styles.
Special	Click this button to search for special non-text characters such as paragraph marks or nonbreaking spaces.
No Formatting	Click this button to turn off any formatting options that you selected, so you can search for text regardless of formatting.

Lesson 2: Finding and Replacing Formatting

In addition to finding and replacing text, you can find and replace certain types of formatting. For example, you might want to replace text formatted in Arial with Century Gothic. Furthermore, you might want to replace regular spaces with nonbreaking spaces between courtesy titles such as **Ms.** and people's last names. Figures 12.5 and 12.6, respectively, show you the menus that appear when you click Format and Special.

Figure 12.5
The Format menu lets
you choose formats to
find and replace.

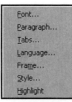

Font...
Paragraph...
Tabs...
Language...
Frame...
Style...
Highlight

Figure 12.6
The Special menu lets
you choose special
non-text items, such
as a nonbreaking
space.

Paragraph Mark
Tab Character
Comment Mark
Any Character
Any Digit
Any Letter
Caret Character
Column Break
Em Dash
En Dash
Endnote Mark
Field
Footnote Mark
Graphic
Manual Line Break
Manual Page Break
Nonbreaking Hyphen
Nonbreaking Space
Optional Hyphen
Section Break
White Space

In this lesson, you find text formatted in Blue font color and replace it with Red font color,
Arial, and bold.

To Find and Replace Formatting

① **In the open Software Letter document, choose Edit, Replace.**
You need to delete the text that you found and replaced in the last lesson.

② **Press Del to delete MS in the Find what box; press Tab⇆, and then press Del to delete the text in the Replace with box.**
You also need to remove the current search options.

③ **Click Match case to deselect this option; click Find whole words only to deselect this option.**
You are ready to specify the formatting characteristics you want to find and replace.

④ **Click in the Find what box to make it active.**

⑤ **Click Format and choose Font.**
You see the Find Font dialog box, which is similar to the Font dialog box you've used before (see Figure 12.7).

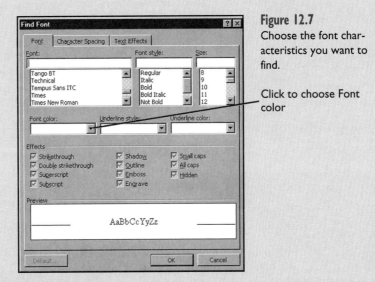

Figure 12.7
Choose the font char-
acteristics you want to
find.

Click to choose Font
color

6 **Click the Font color drop-down arrow, click Blue on the palette, and then click OK.**

X **If You Have Problems...**
You will have problems if you don't choose Blue as the font color. Make
sure the ScreenTip displays Blue on the color you pick; other shades of
blue, such as Dark Blue, won't work.

You see **Format: Font color: Blue** below the **Find what** box. Now you need
to specify the replacement formatting.

7 **Click in the Replace with box, click Format, and choose Font.**
The Replace Font dialog box appears with the same options.

8 **Scroll through the Font list and choose Arial.**

9 **Click Bold in the Font style list.**

10 **Click the Font color drop-down arrow, choose Red, and click OK.**
Figure 12.8 shows the Find and Replace dialog box with the formatting specifications.

Formatting to find ———

Replacement
formatting

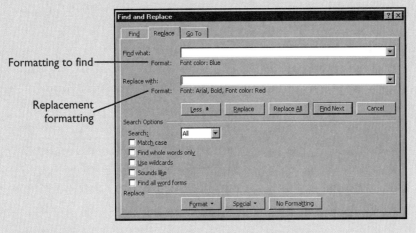

Figure 12.8
The dialog box shows
the formats you're
finding and replacing.

11 **Click Replace All.**

continues ▶

To Find and Replace Formatting (continued)

12 Click **OK** when you see the message `Word has completed its search of the document has made 4 replacements`; then click **Close** to close the **Find and Replace dialog box.**

13 **Scroll down to see some of the replacement formatting.**
Figure 12.9 shows the four formatting replacements.

Figure 12.9
Blue was replaced with Red, boldface, Arial.

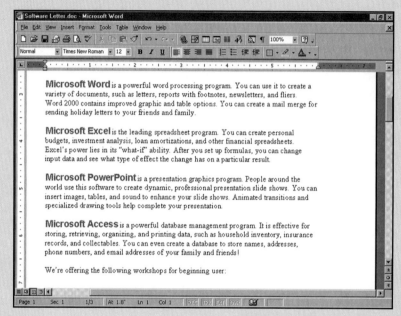

14 **Save the document and keep it onscreen to continue with the next lesson.**

 Inside Stuff: **Undoing Replacements**
If you don't get the results you expect from using Find and Replace, click the Undo button. Study the options and formatting selections in the Find and Replace dialog box and try again.

 Exam Note: **Removing Formatting Options**
Word maintains the options you set in the Find and Replace dialog box until you exit Word. If you need to find and replace other text, you might need to remove the formatting options you selected. To do this, click No Formatting at the bottom of the dialog box.

 Exam Note: **Finding and Replacing Paragraph Formats**
If you want to find and replace paragraph formats, click Special and choose Paragraph Mark. Word inserts ^p in the Find what box. You can then click Format and choose Paragraph to specify the type of formatting you want to find and replace.

Lesson 3: Setting Tabs on the Ruler

In Project 7, you learned how to create tables to organize data into columns and rows. You can set **tabs**—markers that specify the position for aligning text—to create organized lists. You can set left, center, right, and decimal tabs. In addition, you can set a **bar tab**, a marker that produces a vertical bar between two columns when you press (Tab⇄).

When you start a new document, Word uses the default tab settings. Every time you press (Tab⇄), the insertion point moves over one-half inch. You can use the Ruler to set tabs at any location.

In this lesson, you create a tabulated list that shows software prices on the second page of your letter.

To Set Tabs on the Ruler

1 **In the open Software Letter document, make sure you are in Print Layout view and 100% zoom magnification.**

> **X** **If You Have Problems...**
> If you don't see the Ruler below the Formatting toolbar, choose <u>V</u>iew, <u>R</u>uler.

2 **Position the insertion point on the blank line above the last paragraph on page 2.**
This is where you want to create the tabulated list.

3 **Click below the 1" marker on the Ruler.**
You should see a symbol that looks like an L, indicating a left tab setting (see Figure 12.10).

Click to change the tab alignment

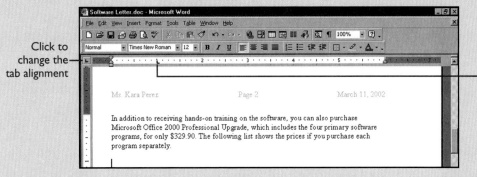

Figure 12.10
You have a 1" left tab setting on the Ruler.

Click to set left tab

> **ⓘ** **Inside Stuff: Setting Tabs Deletes Default Tabs**
> When you set a tab on the Ruler, Word deletes all default tab settings to the left of the one you set. For example, when you set a 1" left tab, Word deletes the original 0.5" tab setting. The tab settings on the right side of the 1" tab setting still exist until you set additional tabs. With each additional tab you set, the other default tab settings to the left of the new one are deleted.

4 **Click the Left Tab button on the left side of the Ruler.**
The button changes to reflect a different tab setting, which is a center tab. Table 12.2 at the end of this lesson shows the different tab alignment buttons that appear.

continues ▶

To Set Tabs on the Ruler   (continued)

 Inside Stuff: **Cycling through Tab Alignments**
If you click the tab button too many times, keep clicking it until it shows you the tab alignment you want. The button cycles through all tab alignments before displaying the Center Tab again.

⑤ Click below the 3" mark on the Ruler.
This sets a center tab at this location.

⑥ Click the Center Tab button on the left side of the Ruler to change to a Right tab.
You need to set a decimal tab, so you need to click the Right Tab button to change to a decimal tab.

⑦ Click the Right Tab button to change to a Decimal tab.
Now that the tab alignment is Decimal Tab, you are ready to set a decimal tab on the Ruler.

⑧ Click below the 4 7/8" mark on the Ruler.
Each tick mark represents one-eighth of an inch. The 4 7/8" mark is the last tick mark before 5". Figure 12.11 shows the tab settings on the Ruler.

Figure 12.11
The Ruler contains the new tab settings.

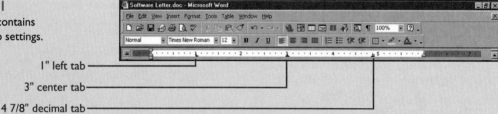

1" left tab ———————
3" center tab ———————
4 7/8" decimal tab ———————

⑨ Press (Tab↹) **and type** PowerPoint.

⑩ Press (Tab↹) **and type** Presentations.

⑪ Press (Tab↹), **type** $94.95, **and press** (↵Enter).

⑫ Type the rest of the tabulated list. Press (↵Enter) **after typing the last line.**

```
Excel     Spreadsheets          $102.95
Word      Word Processing        $79.95
Access    Database Management   $102.95
```

Figure 12.12 shows how the tabulated text appears.

Figure 12.12
The text is aligned by the tab types.

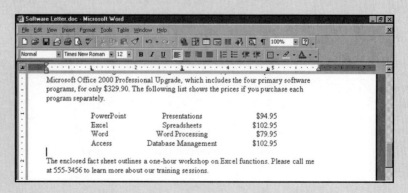

⒔ Save the document and keep it onscreen to continue with the next exercise.

After typing tabulated text, you should make sure it looks balanced on the page. You should ensure that you have the same amount of space before the first column and after the last column. Furthermore, you should balance the space between the columns.

In this lesson, you move the tab markers to balance the tabulated text.

Moving Tab Settings

❶ In the open Software Letter document, select the tabulated text you typed in the last exercise.
After typing the tabulated text, you must select it in order to add, delete, or move tab settings.

❷ Click the 1" tab marker and drag it to the left to the 6/8" position.
When you release the mouse, the entire first column moves to the left.

❸ Click the 4 7/8" tab marker to 5" position.

❹ Deselect the tabulated text.
The third column is decimal-aligned at 5". Moving these two tab settings provides the same amount of space between before the first column that you have after the last column (see Figure 12.13). The internal space between columns is balanced.

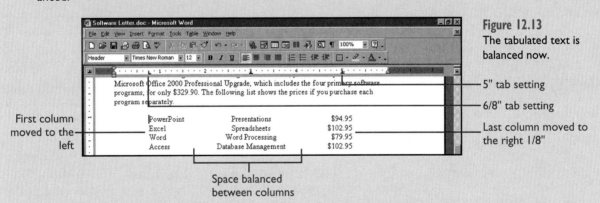

First column moved to the left

Space balanced between columns

Figure 12.13
The tabulated text is balanced now.

5" tab setting

6/8" tab setting

Last column moved to the right 1/8"

❺ Save the document and keep it onscreen to continue with the next lesson.

 Inside Stuff: **Setting Exact Measurements**
You can set a more precise measurement by holding onto Alt as you click and drag the tab marker along the Ruler. When you do this, Word displays the amount of space between the left margin and the tab setting and the amount of space between the tab setting and the right margin (see Figure 12.14).

Figure 12.14
Hold onto (Alt) to set
more precise tabs.

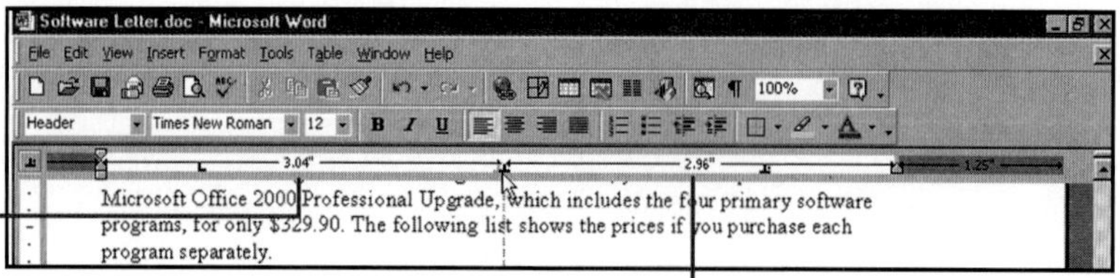

Amount of space between
left margin and tab setting

Amount of space between
tab setting and right margin

Microsoft Office 2000 Professional Upgrade, which includes the four primary software programs, for only $329.90. The following list shows the prices if you purchase each program separately.

Table 12.2   Tab Alignment Buttons

Symbol	Type	Description
L	Left Tab	Aligns text at the left side of the tab setting and continues to the right—similar to Left alignment.
⊥	Center Tab	Centers text on the tab setting; half of the characters appear on the left side and half of the characters appear on the right side of the tab setting.
⌐	Right Tab	Aligns text at the right side of the tab setting—similar to Right alignment.
⊥·	Decimal Tab	Aligns text at the decimal point.
I	Bar Tab	Inserts a vertical line at the tab setting; useful for separating tabular columns.
▽	First Line Indent	Sets the amount of space for indenting the first line of a paragraph.
△	Hanging Indent	Sets the indent for all lines of a paragraph except the first line.

Lesson 4: Setting Tabs in the Tabs Dialog Box

Instead of setting tabs on the Ruler, you can set tabs in the Tabs dialog box. The Tabs dialog box is helpful if you want an exact measurement that you can't set on the Ruler. Furthermore, you can set **leader** options that produce dots, a dashed line, or a solid line between the current column and the next column. Leaders help guide the reader's eyes across from one column to the next.

In this lesson, you want to create a two-column list that shows workshop topics and dates on the first page. You want to use the Tabs dialog box to produce the leader effect between the two columns.

To Set Tabs in the Tabs Dialog Box

❶ In the open Software Letter **document, position the insertion point the second blank line below the last paragraph on the first page.**

❷ Choose For̲mat, T̲abs.
The Tabs dialog box appears (see Figure 12.15).

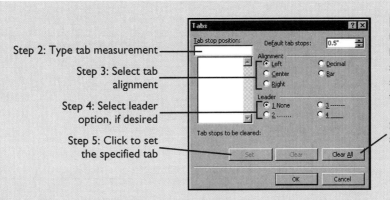

Figure 12.15
Use the Tabs dialog box to clear all tabs, select tab alignments, set tab locations, and tab leaders.

Step 2: Type tab measurement

Step 3: Select tab alignment

Step 4: Select leader option, if desired

Step 5: Click to set the specified tab

Step 1: Click to clear all tabs

❸ Click Clear All to clear all existing tabs.

❹ Click in the Tab stop position box, type 1, and click Set.
Word sets a 1" left tab.

❺ Type 5 in the Tab stop position box, click the Right alignment option, click the 2 option in the Leader section, and then click Set.
Word sets a 5" right tab with dot leaders (see Figure 12.16).

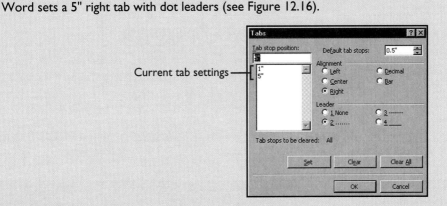

Current tab settings

Figure 12.16
The Tabs dialog box shows the current tab settings.

❻ Click OK.

❼ Type the following tabulated text, pressing Tab⇄ to start each line. Do not press ↵Enter after the last line.

```
Word Basics                     March 22
Excel Formulas and Functions    March 29
PowerPoint Drawings             April 11
Access Tables                   April 18
```

Figure 12.17 shows the tabulated text with the dot leaders between the first and second columns.

continues ▶

To Set Tabs in the Tabs Dialog Box (continued)

Figure 12.17
The tabulated text contains dot leaders between the columns.

1" left tab

5" right tab

Dot leaders between columns

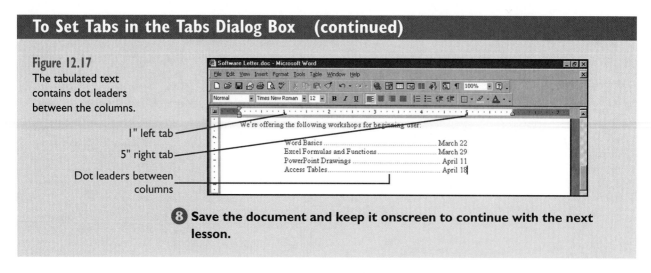

8 **Save the document and keep it onscreen to continue with the next lesson.**

(i) *Inside Stuff:* **Clearing One Tab Setting**
You can clear only one tab setting. Click the tab setting in the list box and click Clear.

Expert

Lesson 5: Sorting Lists and Paragraphs

After you type a tabulated list, you might decide to rearrange it. For example, you might want to organize the list by software name or by price. You can use the Sort Text dialog box to rearrange the tabulated text. Because each line ends with a paragraph mark, each tabulated line is treated as a separate text. Therefore, you must select all tabulated text to sort it.

In this lesson, you decide to sort the second tabulated text to arrange the data in alphabetical order by software name.

To Sort a Tabulated List

1 **In the open Software Letter document, select the four lines of the tabulated text on page 2.**

2 **Choose Table, Sort.**
The Sort Text dialog box appears (see Figure 12.18). You can specify up to three levels for sorting text.

Figure 12.18
Use the Sort Text dialog box to sort tabulated text.

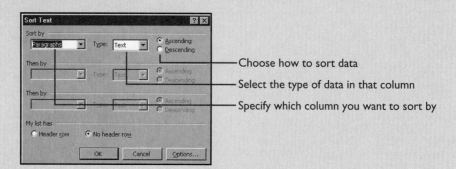

Choose how to sort data

Select the type of data in that column

Specify which column you want to sort by

3 **Click the Sort by drop-down arrow and choose Field 2.**
Field 1 is text at the left margin. Because your first column is tabbed over, that text is in Field 2.

4 **Click OK to sort the selected text; then deselect the text.**

The tabulated text is arranged in alphabetical (ascending) order by the software names in Field 2 (see Figure 12.19).

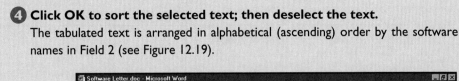
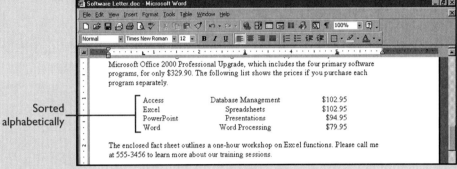

Sorted alphabetically

Figure 12.19
The text is sorted by software name.

5 **Save the document and keep it onscreen to continue with the next lesson.**

 Inside Stuff: **Sort Type**
The Type option changes based on the data you select. The different options are Text, Number, and Date.

Lesson 6: Creating an Outline Style Numbered List

In Project 5, "Formatting Documents," you created bulleted and numbered lists. The numbered lists were simple lists. However, if you need more detail, you should create an outline numbered list. An ***outline numbered list*** is a list that contains several levels of numbering in an outline format. You can choose from seven predefined outline numbered lists in Word or you can create your own customized outline numbered list.

In this lesson, you want to create an outline numbered list that shows topics covered in a particular computer workshop.

To Create an Outline Numbered List

1 **With the `Software Letter` document onscreen, press Ctrl+End to position the insertion point at the end of the document.**
The third page contains a heading for your outline numbered list.

2 **Choose Fo̲rmat, Bullets and N̲umbering.**
The Bullets and Numbering dialog box appears.

3 **Click the Ou̲tline Numbered tab.**
You see predefined outline numbering styles (see Figure 12.20). The first style to the right of None is similar to a formal outline. The second style is often used to create numbered paragraphs for policy and procedures manuals.

continues ▶

To Create an Outline Numbered List   (continued)

Figure 12.20
Select an outline
numbering style.

Click to create
formal outline

Heading outline styles

Click to customize
an outline

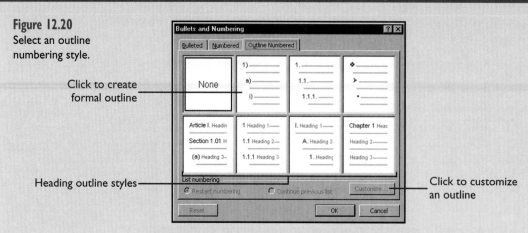

④ Click the first style to the right of None.
The Customize button is available after selecting a style.

⑤ Click OK.
Word inserts the first-level number, **1)** and indents the text you are about to type.

⑥ Type Formulas and press ⏎Enter.
Word inserts **2)** for the next outline number. However, you want to create a second-level entry instead of another first-level entry.

⑦ Press Tab↹, type Operators, and press ⏎Enter.
When you press Tab↹, Word changes **2)** to **a)**. When you press ⏎Enter, Word inserts **b)** automatically.

⑧ Type Order of Precedence and press ⏎Enter.
Word inserts **c)**, but you want to create a third-level entry.

⑨ Press Tab↹ to change c) to i).

⑩ Type Exponentiation and press ⏎Enter.

⑪ Type Multiplication and Division and press ⏎Enter.

⑫ Type Addition and Subtraction and press ⏎Enter.
You now want to create another second-level entry.

⑬ Press ⇧Shift+Tab↹ to change iv) to c).

⑭ Type Functions.
Figure 12.21 shows the outline numbered list so far.

Figure 12.21
Your outline contains
three levels.

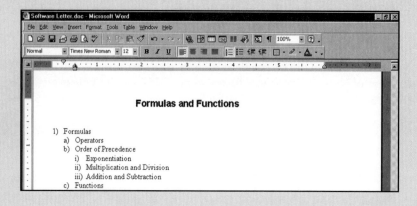

Now that you know how to use ⎡Tab⥺⎤ to create a sub-level entry and ⎡⬆Shift⎤+⎡Tab⥺⎤ to create a higher-level entry, you are ready to complete the outline numbered list.

⑮ Use Figure 12.22 to complete the outline.

1) Formulas
   a) Operators
   b) Order of Precedence
      i) Exponentiation
      ii) Multiplication and Division
      iii) Addition and Subtraction
   c) Functions
   d) Basics
      i) Syntax
         (1) Equals Sign
         (2) Function Name
         (3) Parameters
      ii) Examples
         (1) SUM
         (2) AVERAGE
   e) Specialized
      i) IF
      ii) VLOOKUP

Figure 12.22
Complete the outline numbered list.

⑯ Save the document and keep it onscreen to continue with the next exercise.

After reviewing your outline, you might decide to promote or demote entries. ***Promote*** means to change an outline entry to a higher-level entry. ***Demote*** means to change an outline entry to a lower-level entry.

You can display the document in Outline view to see the Outline toolbar. It contains buttons to help you promote and demote entries. In addition, you can move entries up or down.

In this lesson, you promote **Functions** to a first-level entry. You also want to move **IF** down below **VLOOKUP**.

Adjusting the Outline

❶ In the open Software Letter document, click the Outline View button above the status bar. 
Word displays outline icons by each paragraph in the document (see Figure 12.23). The outline appears to have lost its indents, but the indents will reappear when you change back to Print Layout view. The Outline toolbar appears below the Formatting toolbar.

continues ▶

Adjusting the Outline (continued)

Figure 12.23
The document is displayed in Outline view.

Outline toolbar
Promote button
Demote button
Move Up button
Move Down button
Outline View button

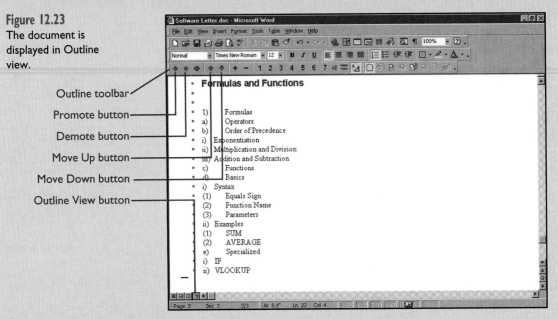

2 **Click on the line that contains c) Functions.**
You must click on the outline entry that you want to change.

3 **Click the Promote button on the Outline toolbar.**
Word changes it from **c)** to **2)**. All entries below this one are automatically renumbered.

4 **Click on the i) IF entry.**
You want to move this entry below the **VLOOKUP** entry.

5 **Click the Move Down button on the Outline toolbar.**
Figure 12.24 shows that the **IF** and **VLOOKUP** entries are reversed.

Figure 12.24
Your outline numbers change after modifying the outline.

Changed to first-level entry

Changed to first entry under Basics entry

IF entry moved below VLOOKUP entry

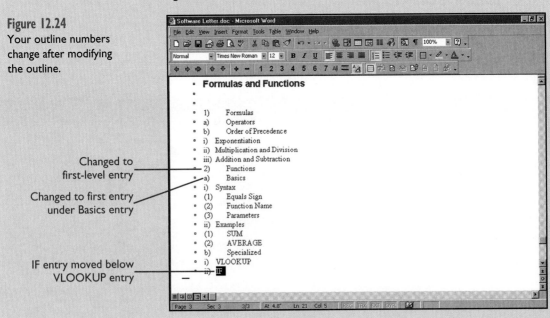

Inside Stuff: **Using the Outline Toolbar**
To learn about other buttons on the Outline toolbar, press ⬆Shift+F1.
When the What's This? mouse pointer appears, click a button to learn
more about it.

6 **Click the Print Layout button.**

7 **Save the document and close it.**

 Exam Note: **Creating a Customized Outline Numbered List**
You can create a customized outline numbered list. First, click an existing outline
numbered style in the Bullets and Numbering dialog box. Then, click Customize.
Figure 12.25 shows the Customize Outline Numbered List dialog box.

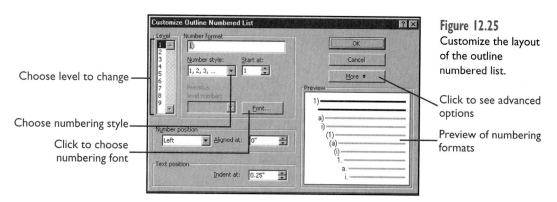

Choose level to change

Choose numbering style

Click to choose
numbering font

Figure 12.25
Customize the layout
of the outline
numbered list.

Click to see advanced
options

Preview of numbering
formats

You can choose the numbering style, such as **1, 2, 3** or **a, b, c**. You can also select a font for the numbers and specify other options.

Summary

You can improve your productivity by using the Find and Replace feature to search for text
with particular conditions and replacing it with other text. You can also find and replace
some formatting and create professional-looking lists by setting tabs on the Ruler or within
the Tabs dialog box. You also know how to sort tabulated text to arrange the data in a different order. Finally, you can create an outline numbered list to organize ideas in a hierarchy.

The features you learned help you maximize the ability to work with longer documents. To
further enhance your skills, use the built-in Help feature to learn more about format replacements, bar tabs, and customized outline numbered lists. Complete the following exercises to
broaden your knowledge and skills.

Checking Concepts and Terms ✓

True/False

For each of the following, check *T* or *F* to indicate whether the statement is true or false.

__T __F **1.** You probably don't need to set search options to find **IS** and replace it with **Information Systems**. [L1]

__T __F **2.** You can find paragraph formats, such as left alignment, and replace it with other paragraph formats, such as justified. [L2]

__T __F **3.** The default tabs are set at one-half inch increments. [L3]

__T __F **4.** To change tab settings for existing text, you can click inside any item in the list; you don't have to select text first. [L3]

__T __F **5.** When you sort tabulated text, text at the left margin is considered Field 1. [L5]

Multiple Choice

Circle the letter of the correct answer for each of the following.

1. What search option prevents **CTC** from finding **ctc** or **Ctc**? [L1]

a. Match case

b. Find whole words only

c. Use wildcards

d. Special

2. Assume you want to replace a regular space with a nonbreaking space. Which button do you click to be able to choose the Nonbreaking Space option? [L2]

a. Use wildcards

b. Format

c. Special

d. No Formatting

3. Which of the following is the Bar Tab button? [L3]

a.

b.

c.

d.

4. You can create all of the following types of tab leaders *except* _____. [L4]

a. continuous periods

b. continuous dashes or hyphens

c. alternating periods and spaces

d. solid underline

5. Which button demotes an outline entry? [L6]

a.

b.

c.

d.

Screen ID

Label each element of the Word screen shown in Figure 12.26.

Figure 12.26

A. Center tab

B. Demote button

C. Left tab

D. Promote button

E. Right tab

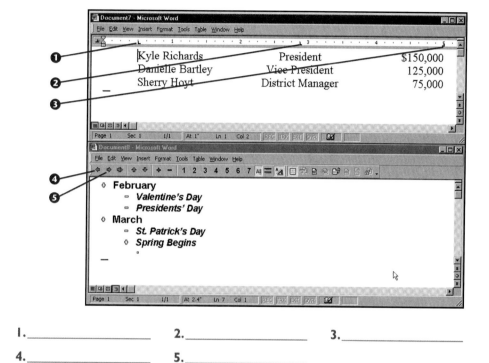

1. _____   2. _____   3. _____

4. _____   5. _____

Skill Drill

Skill Drill exercises reinforce project skills. Each skill reinforced is the same, or nearly the same, as a skill presented in the project. Each exercise includes a brief narrative introduction, followed by detailed instructions in a step-by-step format.

1. Using the Find and Replace Feature

You work for Computer Training Concepts, Inc., a company that provides training to small and large businesses in the country. After creating a proposal for a potential new client, you decide to find and replace most occurrences of **Computer Training Concepts** with **CTC** with formatting. In addition, you want to replace 14-point with 16-point and replace additional formatting.

1. Open **W-1202** and save it as **CTC Proposal**.

2. Choose Edit, Replace.

3. Type **Computer Training Concepts** in the Find what box.

4. Press Tab↹ and type **CTC** in the Replace with box.

5. Click More, if needed, to display additional options.

6. Click the No Formatting button, if it is available, to clear the formats for the Find what and Replace with criteria.

7. Make sure the insertion point is inside the Replace with box.

8. Click Format and choose Font.

   a. Click the Font color drop-down arrow and choose Indigo.

   b. Click Bold in the Font style list.

   c. Click OK.

9. Selectively find and replace text by completing the following steps:

   a. Click Find Next to start searching for text.

   b. Click Find Next to skip the main title and keep searching.

   c. Click Find Next to skip the first occurrence of **Computer Training Concepts** at the beginning of the first paragraph.

   d. Click Replace to replace the second occurrence in the first paragraph.

   e. Click Replace to replace the next occurrence.

   f. Click Find Next to skip the next occurrence.

   g. Click Replace to replace the next occurrence.

   h. Click Find Next to skip the next occurrence.

   i. Click Replace to replace the next occurrence.

   j. Click Find Next to skip the next occurrence, which is in the footer.

   k. Click OK when Word informs you that it has searched the document; keep the dialog box open.

10. You now need to find headings in 14-point and replace the formatting with 16-point, Indigo color, and paragraph spacing before and after. Complete these steps:

    a. Delete the text in the Find what box.

    b. Click Format and choose Font.

    c. Click 14 in the Size box and click OK.

    d. Delete the text in the Replace with box and then click No Formatting to remove the previous replacement formatting.

    e. Click Format and choose Font.

    f. Click 16 in the Size box, click the Font color drop-down arrow and choose Indigo, and click OK.

    g. Click Format and choose Paragraph.

    h. Click in the Before box and type 12 pt; click in the After box and type 12 pt; click OK.

    i. Click Replace All; click OK when Word informs you that it made eight replacements.

    j. Click Close to close the Find and Replace dialog box.

11. Save the document and keep it onscreen to continue with the next exercise.

2. Setting Tabs and Sorting Data

You need to type a short list in the **Budget** section of your proposal. To do this, you want to set tabs. After setting the tabs, you need to move a tab marker for better balance. Finally, you plan to sort the list in ascending order by cost.

1. In the open **CTC Proposal** document, position the insertion point at the end of the paragraph in the **Budget** section, and press **Enter** twice.

2. Choose Format, Tabs.

3. Click Clear All.

4. Type **1** in the Tab stop position box and click Set.

5. Type **5** in the Tab stop position box, click Right, click 3 in the Leader section, click Set, and then click OK.

6. Type the following tabulated text, pressing **Tab** for each column and pressing **Enter** after each line *except* the last line.

   ```
   Materials $95,000
   Personnel $200,000
   Travel    $150,000
   ```

7. Select the three-line tabulated text you just typed.

8. Click the 5" tab marker on the Ruler and drag it to 4.5".

9. With the tabulated text still selected, choose Table, Sort.

10. Click the Sort by drop-down arrow and choose Field 3 to sort by the column that contains the costs.

11. Click OK and then deselect the text.

12. Save the document and keep it onscreen to continue with the next exercise.

3. Creating an Outline Style Numbered List

To complete your proposal, you want to create an outline style numbered list in the **Proposal** section.

1. In the open **CTC Proposal** document, position the insertion point on the blank line below the paragraph in the **Proposal** section and then press ⏎Enter.

2. Choose Format, Bullets and Numbering.

3. Click the Outline Numbered tab.

4. Click the first style to the right of the None style, and then click OK.

5. Type **On-Site Delivery** and press ⏎Enter.

6. Press Tab⇄ and type the following, pressing ⏎Enter after each line:

   Small, hands-on classes held at your corporate locations

   One-on-one instruction for specific individuals

   CTC trainers available in person to answer questions

7. Press ⬆Shift+Tab⇄ to make the next item a first-level entry with **2)**.

8. Type **Off-Site Delivery** and press ⏎Enter.

9. Press Tab⇄ and then type the following, pressing ⏎Enter after each line *except* the last line:

   Retreats held with the specific intent to provide training

   Small, hands-on classes held at our state-of-the-art training facilities

   Toll-free telephone support

10. Save the document, print it, and close it.

Challenge

Challenge exercises expand on or are somewhat related to skills presented in the lessons. Each exercise provides a brief narrative introduction followed by instructions in a numbered-step or bulleted list format that are not as detailed as those in the *Skill Drill* section.

1. Creating a Memo with Tabulated Text

You want to send a memo to your company's employees about upcoming Word workshops. You want to align the colons in the heading, so you plan to set appropriate tabs. In addition, you create a tabulated list of workshops, dates, and times.

1. In a new document window, set a 1.5" top margin, and save the document as **Word Workshops**.

2. In the Tabs dialog box, clear existing tabs and set a 0.81" right tab and a 0.95" left tab.

3. Type the following heading with these specifications:

   a. Press Tab⇄ before typing the first column for each line.

   b. Type the bold, capitalized words. Turn off bold after typing the colon, press Tab⇄, and type the second column.

   c. Press ⏎Enter twice after typing each of the first three lines of the heading; press ⏎Enter three times after typing the subject line.

   TO: All Employees
   FROM: your name
   DATE: February 1, 2002
   SUBJECT: Word 2000 Workshops

4. Type the following paragraph:

   The Computer Services Department has completed the installation of the new computer systems and Microsoft Office 2000 software. We are offering the following training sessions to help you become more proficient in

> **Word 2000. All sessions will be held in Room 415. Please call Extension 5840 to register for workshops you'd like to attend.**

5. Double-space, clear existing tabs, and set the following tabs: 1" left, 3.38" center, and 5" right.

6. Type the following tabulated text:

New Features	**February 8**	**3:30 p.m.**
Section Formats	**February 22**	**9:00 a.m.**
Table Formats	**March 1**	**12:00 p.m.**
Excel Integration	**March 5**	**10:00 a.m.**
Styles & Templates	**March 29**	**3:30 p.m.**
Advanced Formats	**April 5**	**10:30 a.m.**

7. Select the tabulated text and move the second tab to the left about 1/8".

8. Save the document and print it.

2. Finding and Replacing Text and Formats in an Internet Report

The Internet report you prepared needs a few adjustments. You want to replace some text and formats before duplicating it for clients.

1. Open **W-1203** and save it as **Internet Information**.

2. Find all occurrences of **e-mail** and replace them with **email**.

3. Find the lowercase word **inform** and replace it with **notify**.

4. Find headings in underline, Green font, and Centered align; replace with these formats: Arial, Bold font style, Blue font color, Left align, 12 pt spacing before and 12 pt spacing after.

5. Select the bulleted list on page 2. Clear the existing Find and Replace settings. Find occurrences of Bold font style and replace them with these formats: Arial, Bold font style, 10-point size, and Blue font color.

6. Apply Blue font color and Yellow highlight color to the main title.

7. Save the document and print it.

3. Preparing an Outline Style Numbered List for Teachers

As a student assistant in your college's administration office, you have been asked to type an outline numbered list of teaching responsibilities.

1. In a new document window, set a 2" top margin, a 1" left margin, and a 1" right margin; save the document as **Teaching Responsibilities**.

2. Type **TEACHING RESPONSIBILITIES** centered in all caps, boldface. Turn off bold and Caps Lock before pressing ↵Enter. Press ↵Enter three times after the title and select Left alignment.

3. Create the outline numbered list using the style and format shown in Figure 12.27. After you select the appropriate outline style, click Customize to adjust the formats. Make the following adjustments to each level:

Level 1:	Aligned at 0"	Indent at 0.25"
Level 2:	Aligned at 0.25"	Indent at 0.65"
Level 3:	Aligned at 0.65"	Indent at 1.15"
Level 4:	Aligned at 1.15"	Indent at 1.75"

4. Type the outline numbered list shown in Figure 12.27.

Figure 12.27
Create the outline
numbered list.

1. RESPONSIBILITY TO SELF AND PROFESSION
   1.1. Seek the truth of subject matter.
   1.2. Stay informed by reading journals in respective field
2. RESPONSIBILITY TO STUDENTS
   2.1. Demonstrate minimum competencies for teaching.
      2.1.1. Develop a lesson plan.
      2.1.2. Select student instructional materials (e.g., textbooks, supplemental reading, etc.)
      2.1.3. Provide appropriate student laboratory experience.
      2.1.4. Introduce each lesson.
      2.1.5. Provide opportunities for student participation and feedback.
      2.1.6. Summarize the lesson at the conclusion of the each lecture.
      2.1.7. Assess student performance.
   2.2. Prepare each course.
      2.2.1. Determine course content based on official objectives.
      2.2.2. Prepare and distribute a detailed course syllabus.
         2.2.2.1. List major course objectives.
         2.2.2.2. Include instructor's name, office, phone, and email address.
         2.2.2.3. Describe attendance policy.
         2.2.2.4. Outline assignments and deadlines.
         2.2.2.5. Discuss testing procedures.
         2.2.2.6. Inform students of grading scale and weighted categories.
      2.2.3. Create appropriate testing materials.
   2.3. Determine teaching methods.

5. Click the Outline View button and do the following:

   a. Demote the last entry, **Determine teaching methods.**

   b. Move down **List major course objectives.**

6. Click the Print Layout View button.

7. For the first first-level entry, set a 12-pt paragraph spacing after.

8. For the second first-level entry, set a 12-pt paragraph spacing before and a 12-pt paragraph spacing after.

9. Select the title and apply Arial Rounded MT Bold font and Red font color.

10. Save the document and print it.

Discovery Zone

Discovery Zone exercises help you gain advanced knowledge of project topics and/or application of skills. These exercises focus on enhancing your problem-solving skills. Numbered steps are not provided, but you are given hints, reminders, screen shots, and/or references to help you reach your goal for each exercise.

1. Improving a Loan Document with Find and Replace and Tabs

Your small café is planning to expand, and you need to borrow money from a bank. Your business partner drafted the loan proposal and wants you to enhance its appearance. Open **W-1204** and save it as **IFC Proposal**.

Find and replace **IFC** with **International Food Cafe** with these formats: Bold Italic style,

Blue font color, 11-point Arial Narrow, and Highlight. Make sure that the replacement is in title case, not all caps.

Find occurrences of two paragraph marks and replace them with the following: one paragraph mark and a 0.5" first-line indent. Be sure to remove all previous find and replace settings first.

Find occurrences of **)** followed by a space; replace them with **)** followed by a nonbreaking space. Find occurrences of a hyphen; replace them with occurrences of a nonbreaking hyphen.

In the blank space after the second paragraph, set a 1.5" left tab and an appropriately spaced right tab with dot leaders. Type the following information:

```
Construction       $10,750.50
Decoration          $2,500.95
Demolition         $10,900.95
```

Select the tabulated list, change to single-spacing, and sort it in descending order by cost. If needed, adjust the location of the decimal tab. After deselecting the text, make sure you have one *blank* line between the last item and the next paragraph. Change the amount in the preceding paragraph to equal the total of the three expenses.

Click at the end of the second-to-the-last paragraph, press ⏎Enter), and change to single-spacing. Create the following list by setting appropriate tabs:

```
Quarter          Last Year         Next Year
   1             $20,000           $25,000
   2             $22,000           $26,000
   3             $23,000           $27,000
   4             $24,000           $28,000
```

The headings should be bold and underline. Make sure the space before **Quarter** is identical the space after **Next Year**. Select the four lines about quarterly sales, delete the left tabs and set center tabs, so the items are centered perfectly below their column headings. Now, select all lines in the tabulated list, insert bar tabs between the columns, and choose the **Keep with next** paragraph option to ensure the entire list stays on the same page.

Save the document and print it.

2. Outlining the Interview Speech

You want to prepare an outline of the interview speech you'll be giving at the local Chamber of Commerce next month. Open **W-1205** and save it as **Interview Speech Outline**. Edit the header by changing **Student's Name** to your name.

Apply Heading 1 style to the first line on page 1. *Hint:* The style button is the drop-down arrow to the left of Normal on the Formatting toolbar. It changes to Heading 1 after you select it. Apply Heading 2 to the second line on page 1 and to the first line on Page 2.

Display the document in Outline View and study the purpose of each button on the Outline toolbar. Display the first three heading levels. Expand the **Self-Fulfilling Prophecy** section. Move **Stereotypes** up twice and then expand that section. Save the document and print it.

In a new document window, create a corresponding table of contents using Figure 12.28. Set a 1.5" top margin, and set appropriate tabs. Save the document as **Interview TOC** and print it.

TABLE OF CONTENTS

The Personal Interview 1

Introduction 1

Pre-interview Impression Effects 1
Pre-interview Impressions 1
Self-Fulfilling Prophecy 2
The Bias of Information Processing 2

Perception of the Interview 3
The Unfavorable Information Effect.. 3
Interviewer Decision Styles 3
The Attribution Theory and Attribution Bias 3
Stereotypes 4
Non-Verbal Communications 4
Physical Characteristics 5

Figure 12.28
Create the table of contents for the interview document.

PinPoint Assessment

You have completed this project and its associated lessons, and have had an opportunity to assess your skills through the end-of-project questions and exercises. Now use the PinPoint software Evaluation Mode to further assess your comprehension of the specific exam activities you have just learned. You can also use the PinPoint Trainer Mode and the Show Me tutorials to practice these exam activities.

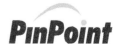

Working with Columns

Key terms introduced in this project include

- continuous section break
- drop cap
- gutter

- hyphenation zone
- landscape
- masthead

- nameplate
- page orientation
- portrait

Objectives	Required Activity for MOUS	Exam Level
➤ Create and Use Newspaper Columns	Create and use newspaper columns	Core
➤ Set the Page Orientation	Set page orientation	Core
➤ Revise Column Structure	Revise column structure	Core
➤ Insert Section and Column Breaks		
➤ Balance Column Length	Balance column length (using column breaks appropriately)	Expert
➤ Create Drop Caps		
➤ Hyphenate Text		

Why Would I Do This?

Dividing text into columns helps you create visually appealing, easy-to-read documents. Columns are frequently used to design newsletters, brochures, and advertising material. Many organizations prepare periodic newsletters for their employees, customers, or members.

Because newsletters contain several short articles, the text is easier to read in two or more columns than text that spans from the left to the right margin. The length of the line of text is shorter, which helps people read through each article faster.

 ## Lesson 1: Creating and Using Columns

You can designate columns before or after you compose the text for the document. However, you might find it's easier to create your text first and then apply columnar format to it.

You can create columns by using the Columns button on the Standard toolbar or by choosing <u>C</u>olumns from the F<u>o</u>rmat menu. Clicking the Columns button is a fast way of creating columns of equal width; if you need specific settings, however, you'll want to access the Columns dialog box. The dialog box lets you set different widths for columns and specify the space between columns.

In this lesson, you apply columns to a school newsletter you're working on.

To Create Newspaper Columns

1 Open **W-1301** and save it as **School Newsletter**.

2 **Click the Columns button on the Standard toolbar.**
Figure 13.1 shows the Columns grid, so you can choose how many columns you want.

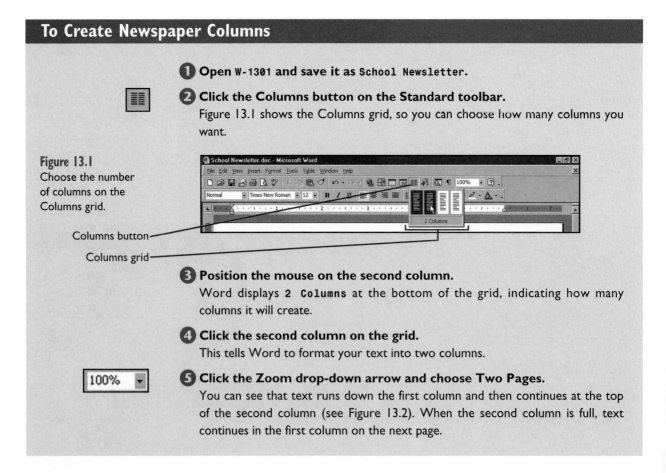

Figure 13.1
Choose the number of columns on the Columns grid.

Columns button
Columns grid

3 **Position the mouse on the second column.**
Word displays **2 Columns** at the bottom of the grid, indicating how many columns it will create.

4 **Click the second column on the grid.**
This tells Word to format your text into two columns.

5 **Click the Zoom drop-down arrow and choose Two Pages.**
You can see that text runs down the first column and then continues at the top of the second column (see Figure 13.2). When the second column is full, text continues in the first column on the next page.

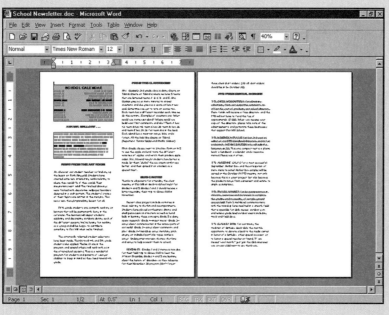

Figure 13.2
The document is formatted into newspaper columns.

6 **Click the Zoom drop-down arrow and choose 100%.**

7 **Save the document and keep it onscreen to continue with the next lesson.**

 Inside Stuff: **Removing Columns**
If you decide that you don't want multiple columns, click the Columns button and choose the first column. This formats the document back as one column, which is how regular text appears.

Lesson 2: Setting the Page Orientation

Page orientation refers to the way printed text appears on a sheet of paper. The two page orientations are portrait and landscape. *Portrait*, the default orientation, positions text parallel with the short side of the page, which is the top side. It derives its name because it is similar to a regular large-framed photograph. *Landscape* positions text parallel with the long side of the paper, which is the top side. The name is derived from the idea of looking at a wide picture of the landscape. Figure 13.3 illustrates portrait and landscape orientations.

Figure 13.3
Compare the difference in portrait and landscape orientation.

Typically, most correspondence and business reports are formatted in portrait orientation. Newsletters, brochures, and advertisements, however, are often formatted in landscape orientation.

In this lesson, you change the orientation to landscape to have a wider amount of space from the left to the right margin.

To Select Landscape Orientation

1 In the open `School Newsletter` document, choose <u>F</u>ile, Page Set<u>u</u>p.
You used the Page Setup dialog box to set margins, set header and footer options, and choose vertical alignment.

2 Click the Paper <u>S</u>ize tab.
The default paper size is Letter (8 1/2 x 11 inches). You can choose other paper sizes, such as Legal (8 1/2 x 14 inches). Notice that the default orientation is Portra<u>i</u>t (see Figure 13.4).

Figure 13.4
Choose the paper size and orientation in the Paper Size tab options.

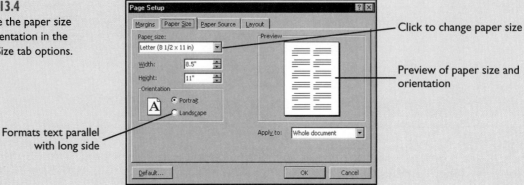

Click to change paper size

Preview of paper size and orientation

Formats text parallel with long side

3 Click the Land<u>s</u>cape option and then click OK.
Word formats the document in landscape orientation, which displays more text between the left and right margins. However, the length of the paper is shorter.

4 Click the Zoom drop-down arrow and choose Whole Page.

 If You Have Problems...
If the two columns do not widen to fill the extra space on the right side of the paper, click the Columns button and choose `2 Columns` again to reapply the column formatting.

Figure 13.5 shows the whole page in landscape orientation. The columns are wider because landscape provides a bigger width.

Figure 13.5
Landscape lets you have wider newspaper columns.

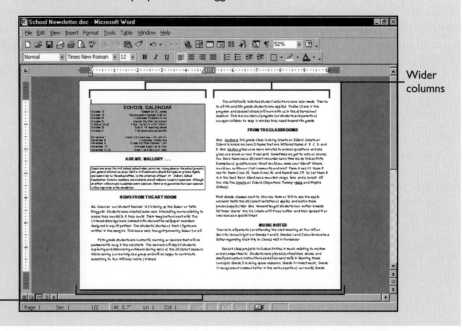

Wider columns

Landscape orientation

Save the document and keep it onscreen to continue with the next lesson.

 Inside Stuff: **Different Orientations in a Document**
You can have multiple page orientations in a document if your document is divided into sections.

Lesson 3: Revising Column Structure

After you apply column formatting to text, you might want to change it. For example, you might want to format the text into three columns instead of two columns. You can always change your mind and change the structure of your newspaper columns.

When you access the Columns dialog box, you can specify different widths for each column instead of using equal column width. If you don't like the default one-half inch space between columns, you can increase or decrease this space. Finally, you can insert a vertical line between columns to separate them.

 Inside Stuff: **Gutter**
Gutter is a desktop publishing term that refers to the space between columns.

In this lesson, you apply three columns to the newsletter. In addition, you want to set a 0.75-inch space and insert a vertical line between the columns.

To Revise Column Structure

1 **In the open** `School Newsletter` **document, choose F_ormat, _Columns.**
The Columns dialog box appears (see Figure 13.6). You can choose one of five preset column formats, or you can specify more columns in the _Number of columns box.

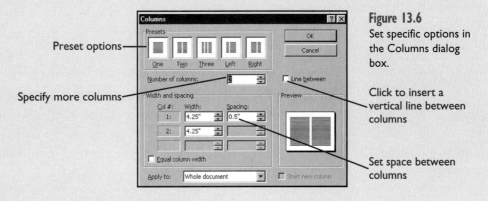

Preset options
Specify more columns

Figure 13.6
Set specific options in the Columns dialog box.

Click to insert a vertical line between columns

Set space between columns

 Inside Stuff: **Uneven Column Widths**
Choosing the _Left preset option creates a *smaller* left column with a bigger right column. Choosing the _Right preset option creates a *smaller* right column with a bigger left column.

---

continues ▶

To Revise Column Structure   (continued)

2 Click Three in the Presets section.
This formats your document text into three even columns.

3 Click the Line between check box.
This option creates a vertical line between the columns.

4 Drag across the setting in the Spacing box and type 0.75".
You just increased the space between the columns, which results in slightly smaller column widths.

5 Click OK.
Figure 13.7 shows the three-column text with a vertical line between columns. Notice that the space between columns is a little bigger.

Figure 13.7
Your document reflects the revised column structure.

Three columns

Vertical lines between columns

0.75 inch width between columns

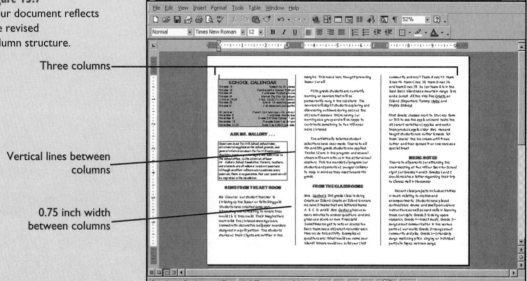

The right tab in the first column is off now that you've decreased the column width. You need to move the tab marker to the left, so the tabulated text fits within the border.

6 Click the Zoom drop-down arrow and choose 100%.

7 Select the list of tabulated dates in the first column.
Figure 13.8 shows that the second column of tabulated text extends past the border.

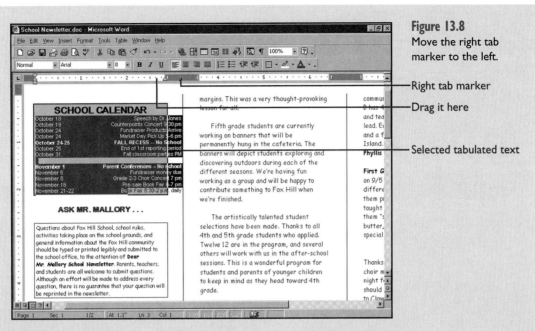

Figure 13.8
Move the right tab marker to the left.

Right tab marker

Drag it here

Selected tabulated text

8 **Click and drag the right tab marker to 2 5/8 inches on the Ruler; then deselect the text.**

The tabulated text now fits within the border after you move the tab to the left (see Figure 13.9).

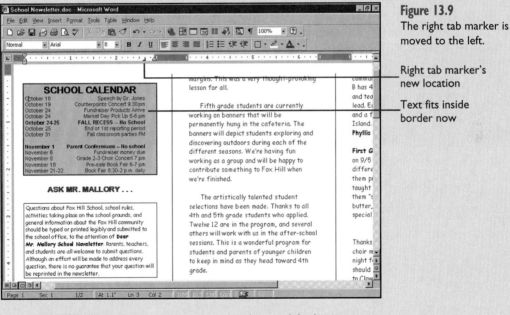

Figure 13.9
The right tab marker is moved to the left.

Right tab marker's new location

Text fits inside border now

9 **Save the document and keep it onscreen to continue with the next lesson.**

  Exam Note: Setting Different Widths

If you want specific different sizes for columns, access the Columns dialog box. When you deselect Equal column width, you see Width and Spacing text boxes for all columns, so you can set the exact width of each column and the space after that particular column.

Exam Note: **Setting Column Widths and Spacing on the Ruler**

You can use the Ruler to adjust column widths and spacing between columns. To change the size of two adjacent columns, click and drag the white dotted grid in the gray space between the columns. Word maintains the space between the columns while increasing a column and decreasing the other column. Figure 13.10 illustrates decreasing the first column's width while increasing the second column's width.

To change the gutter and one adjacent column, click and drag the outer gray edge. Dragging toward the column decreases its width and increases the gutter; dragging away from that column increases its width and decreases the gutter.

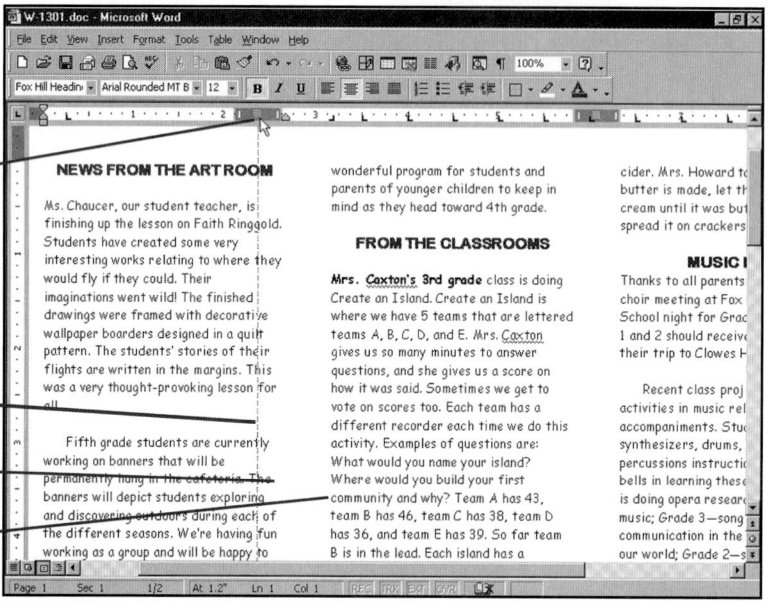

Figure 13.10
Adjust column widths by clicking and dragging the column grid in the gutter.

Click and drag

Indicates new right side of first column

Current right side of first column

Current left side of second column

Lesson 4: Inserting Section and Column Breaks

When you create a newsletter, you probably want a **masthead** (also known as a **name-plate**), which is the area on the first page that contains the title and date of the newsletter. The masthead usually spans all columns.

Unfortunately, Word doesn't let you simply create a masthead and then start columns after it. You must insert a **continuous section break**, a break that divides the document into sections but continues the next section on the same page instead of starting a new page. After you insert a continuous section break, you can format each section differently. You can format the masthead section with one column while keeping the multiple columns for the body of the newsletter, which is in a different section.

In this lesson, you insert a continuous section break at the beginning of the document, format the new section, and then insert a file that contains the masthead.

To Insert a Continuous Section Break and Format that Section

❶ In the open `School Newsletter` document, press `Ctrl`+`Home` **to position the insertion point at the beginning of the document.**

You need to insert a continuous section break before the first heading.

2 **Choose Insert, Break.**

The Break dialog box appears (see Figure 13.11).

Click to create a column break

Inserts section break on same page

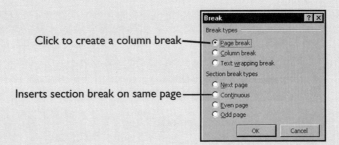

Figure 13.11
Click Continuous to create a section break on the same page.

3 **Click Continuous and click OK.**

Word inserts a section break but continues the section on the same page.

4 **Click the Show/Hide ¶ button on the Standard toolbar.**

You see two dotted lines with `Section Break (Continuous)` to indicate the section break.

5 **Press Ctrl+Home to position the insertion point at the beginning of the document—within the new section.**

The new section takes on the formats from the original section, which is set up for three columns. You need to remove column formatting in the first section.

6 **Click the Columns button on the Standard toolbar and choose 1 Column.**

Now you are ready to insert the file that contains the masthead.

7 **Choose Insert, File.**

8 **Choose W-1302 in the Project 13 folder and click Insert.**

Word inserts W-1302 in the first section, which is formatted for only one column (see Figure 13.12).

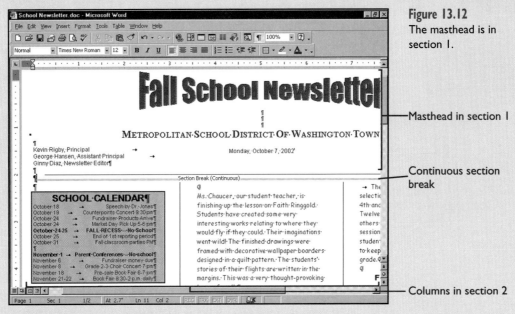

Figure 13.12
The masthead is in section 1.

Masthead in section 1

Continuous section break

Columns in section 2

9 **Save the document and keep it onscreen to continue with the next exercise.**

As you review your newsletter, you might want to start a new column to balance text better. In the next exercise, you notice a heading at the bottom of the first column and insert a column break to start the heading at the top of the second column.

To Insert a Column Break

1 In the open `School Newsletter` document, position the insertion point at the bottom of the first column, to the left of the heading **NEWS FROM THE ART ROOM**.

2 Choose <u>I</u>nsert, <u>B</u>reak.

3 Click the <u>C</u>olumn break option and click OK.
Word inserts a column break and places the heading at the top of a column.

4 Click and drag across the Zoom percentage on the Standard toolbar, type **90%**, and press ⏎Enter.
Figure 13.13 shows the heading at the top of the second column. You can see the `Column Break` note at the bottom of the first column.

Figure 13.13
Insert a column break to start a new column within the section.

Heading at top of column

Column break inserted here

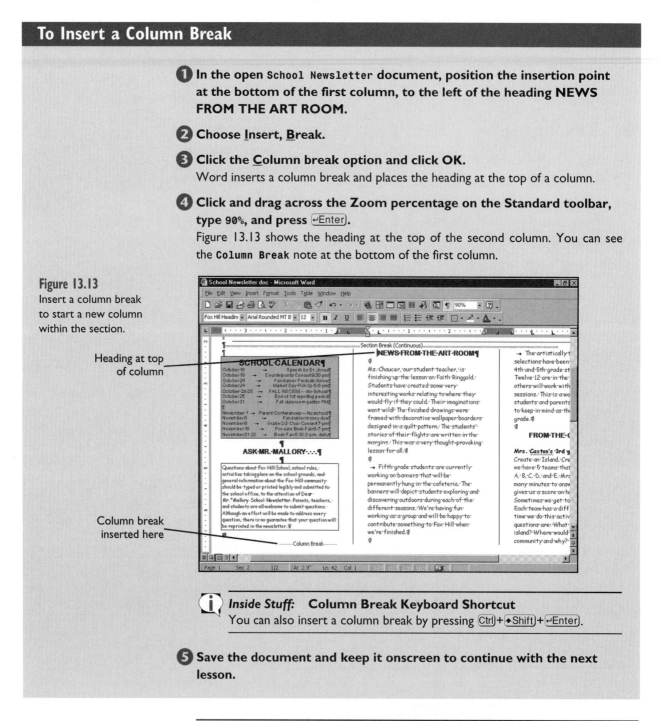

ℹ **Inside Stuff:** **Column Break Keyboard Shortcut**
You can also insert a column break by pressing Ctrl+⇧Shift+⏎Enter.

5 Save the document and keep it onscreen to continue with the next lesson.

ℹ **Inside Stuff:** **Deleting Section and Column Breaks**
If you decide to delete a section or column break, click the Normal View button. Position the insertion point to the left of the single or double dotted line and then press Del.

When you delete a section break, you delete the formats associated with that section. The section takes on the formats of the next section. For example, if you delete the section break after the masthead, the masthead takes on the two-column format that is stored in the second section.

Lesson 5: Balancing Column Length

If your newspaper columns take up more than one page, the columns on the first page are balanced. That means that the bottom of all columns end at about the same place. However, the last page that contains columns might not be full. If this is the case, the column lengths are not balanced. The last column might be shorter than the other columns. You can balance the column lengths on the last page by inserting a section break at the end of the last column.

In this lesson, you balance the columns on the last page of the newsletter.

To Balance Column Length

① **In the open** **School Newsletter** **document, press** Ctrl+End.
The insertion point is at the end of the document. Notice that the last column is shorter than the other two columns on the last page (see Figure 13.14).

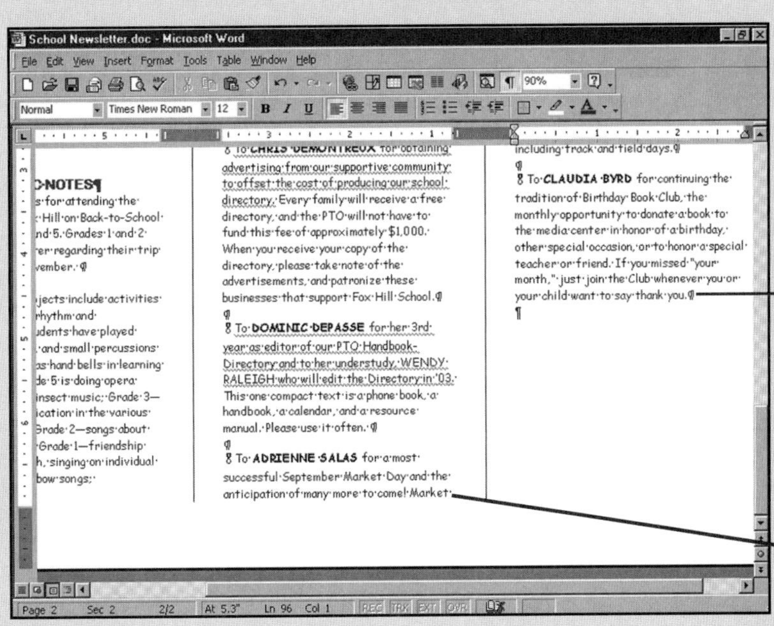

Figure 13.14
The last column on the last page is shorter than the other columns.

Short last column

Other column length

② **Choose** **Insert, Break.**

③ **Click Con̲tinuous and click OK.**
Figure 13.15 shows that the last column is *almost* as long as the other two columns. Word tries to balance the column lengths the best it can, based on the type of text in the columns.

continues ▶

To Balance Column Length (continued)

Figure 13.15
The last column is "balanced" with the other columns.

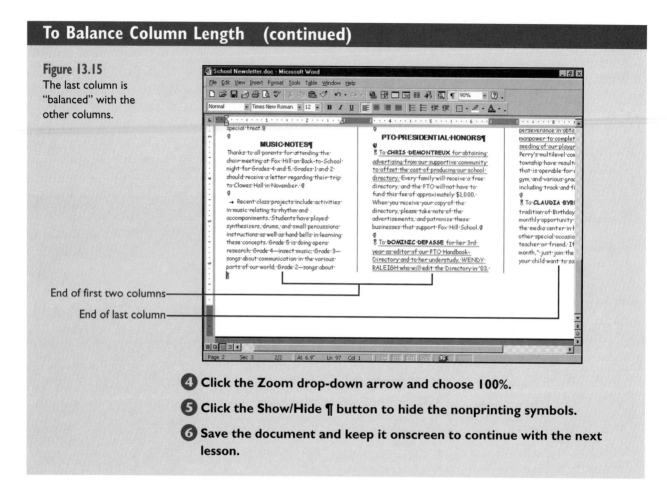

End of first two columns—

End of last column—

④ **Click the Zoom drop-down arrow and choose 100%.**

⑤ **Click the Show/Hide ¶ button to hide the nonprinting symbols.**

⑥ **Save the document and keep it onscreen to continue with the next lesson.**

Lesson 6: Creating Drop Caps

You can enhance the appearance of a newsletter by adding color, graphics, and drop caps. A **drop cap** is a big character that drops below the current line. Publishers often use drop caps for the first letter of the first paragraph in a chapter or section. For example, the first paragraph below each Why Would I Do This? section that starts each project begins with a drop cap.

In this lesson, you add a drop cap to the first paragraph in the second column. After creating the drop cap, you change its font color and shading color.

To Create a Drop Cap

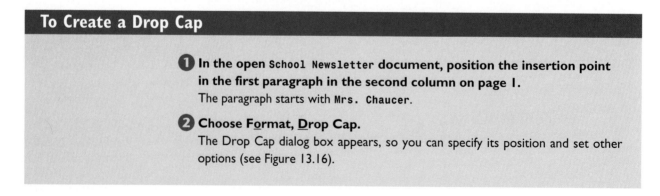

① **In the open School Newsletter document, position the insertion point in the first paragraph in the second column on page 1.**
The paragraph starts with Mrs. Chaucer.

② **Choose Format, Drop Cap.**
The Drop Cap dialog box appears, so you can specify its position and set other options (see Figure 13.16).

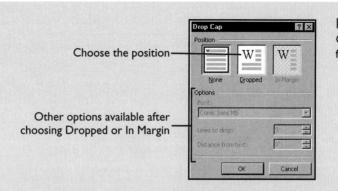

Choose the position

Other options available after
choosing Dropped or In Margin

Figure 13.16
Choose options to
format the drop cap.

❸ Click Dropped.
You can now choose other options, such as the drop cap's font.

❹ Click the Font drop-down arrow and choose Arial Rounded MT Bold.

❺ Click OK.
Figure 13.17 shows the drop cap created from the first letter of that paragraph.

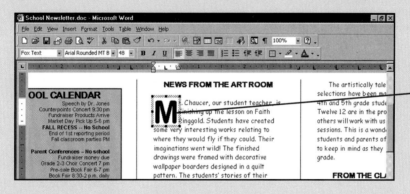

Figure 13.17
The drop cap is created from the first letter in the paragraph.

Drop cap

 Inside Stuff: **Creating a Drop Cap for a Word**
By default, Word creates a drop cap from the first letter in the paragraph.
You can create a drop for the first word in the paragraph by selecting it
before displaying the Drop Cap dialog box.

**❻ With the drop cap selected like a text box, click the Font Color button
and choose Blue.**
The drop cap is now blue.

❼ With the drop cap selected, choose Format, Borders and Shading.
You want to add a Pale Blue shading color behind the drop cap letter.

❽ Click the Shading tab in the dialog box.

**❾ Click Pale Blue, the third color from the right on the last row, and
then click OK.**
The drop cap is visually appealing with its font color and shading (see Figure 13.18).

continues ▶

To Create a Drop Cap (continued)

Figure 13.18
Font color and shading
enhance the drop cap.

Blue text color

Pale Blue shading color

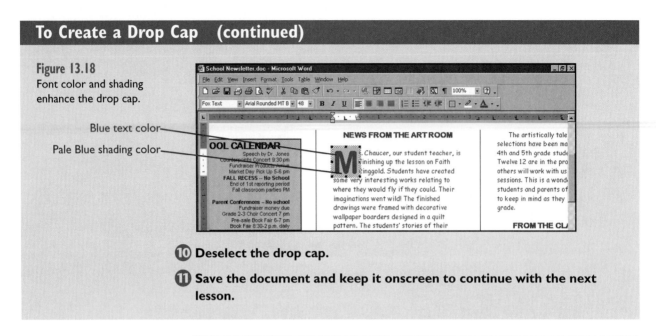

10 **Deselect the drop cap.**

11 **Save the document and keep it onscreen to continue with the next lesson.**

 Inside Stuff: **Reformatting the Drop Cap**
If you want to change drop cap options, right-click the edge of the drop cap and choose <u>D</u>rop Cap from the menu. You'll see the Drop Cap dialog box again.

 Inside Stuff: **Removing the Drop Cap Feature**
If you decide to remove a drop cap, click it to select it like a graphics box and choose <u>D</u>rop Cap to display the Drop Cap dialog box. Choose <u>N</u>one to remove the drop cap features and return the drop cap text back to regular text.

If you press Del when a drop cap is selected, you delete the drop cap and the text that created it.

Lesson 7: Hyphenating Text

By now, you know that the word-wrap feature wraps a word to the next line if it can't fit at the end of the existing line. However, word-wrap sometimes causes huge gaps at the right margin when it wraps a long word to the next line. You can smooth out the right margin by hyphenating words.

The Hyphenation feature identifies words that can partially fit at the end of the line; it fits as much of the word at the end of the line as it can, inserts a hyphen, and continues the rest of the word on the next line.

In this lesson, you hyphenate words to make the newsletter look more professional.

To Hyphenate Words

1 **In the open School Newsletter document, position the insertion point at the beginning of the document.**

2 **Choose <u>T</u>ools, <u>L</u>anguage, <u>H</u>yphenation.**
The Hyphenation dialog box appears (see Figure 13.19).

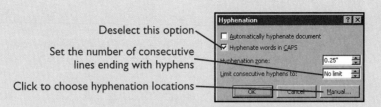

Deselect this option

Set the number of consecutive lines ending with hyphens

Click to choose hyphenation locations

Figure 13.19
Choose how you want to hyphenate the document.

③ If the Hyphenate words in <u>C</u>APS option is selected, deselect it.

④ Click the <u>L</u>imit consecutive hyphens to increment button to 2.
Avoid letting Word hyphenate the document automatically. It might hyphenate words in poor locations. You want to choose <u>M</u>anual because it gives you control over the hyphenation locations. You can choose to hyphenate words as Word suggests, or you can choose other hyphenation locations, or you can prevent a word from being hyphenated.

 Inside Stuff: **Hyphenating Words**
Do not hyphenate capitalized words, proper nouns such as a person's name, or words with fewer than six letters.

⑤ Click <u>M</u>anual.
The Manual Hyphenation dialog box appears with the first word that can be hyphenated (see Figure 13.20).

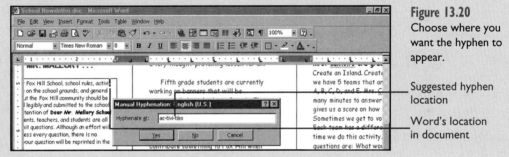

Figure 13.20
Choose where you want the hyphen to appear.

Suggested hyphen location

Word's location in document

⑥ Click <u>Y</u>es to hyphenate the word as suggested.
The Manual Hyphenation dialog box appears again, prompting you to hyphenate another word.

⑦ Click <u>Y</u>es to hyphenate most words. Do *not* hyphenate words that start with a capital letter, such as November, or that have only two letters before the hyphen, such as to-ward. Click <u>N</u>o to avoid hyphenating these types of words.
You should always make sure you have three letters before and after the hyphen. Having three letters on each side of the hyphen makes it easier for the reader to mentally complete the hyphenated word.

⑧ Click OK when you see the message Hyphenation is complete.

⑨ Scroll to the bottom of the second page.
Figure 13.21 shows the hyphenated document. When you click the Show/Hide ¶ button to view the nonprinting symbols, the hyphens inserted by the Hyphenation feature have a little vertical line on the right side; this helps you identify a hyphenation hyphen from a typed hyphen or nonbreaking hyphen. However, all hyphens print the same.

continues ▶

To Hyphenate Words (continued)

Figure 13.21
The document is hyphenated.

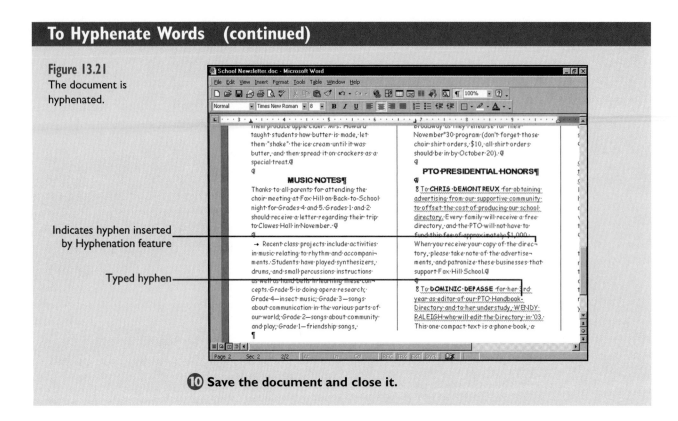

Indicates hyphen inserted by Hyphenation feature

Typed hyphen

 Save the document and close it.

ⓘ *Inside Stuff:* **Changing the Hyphenation Zone**

The *hyphenation zone* is an area at the end of a line that determines whether a word can potentially be hyphenated. If a word starts on or before the zone and extends past it, Word prompts you to hyphenate that word. If a word starts after the zone, Word wraps it to the next line.

The default zone is 0.25 inches. If you increase the zone, Word prompts you with *fewer* words to hyphenate. If you decrease the zone, Word prompts you with *more* words to hyphenate.

Summary

You can now create and format professional-looking newsletters. You learned how to create columns, insert a vertical line between columns, and adjust the column width and space between columns. In addition, you learned how to insert continuous section breaks to have a masthead centered over all newspaper columns. Adding a drop cap with a font color and shading adds a splash of color to make your newsletter more exciting! Finally, you learned how to hyphenate words to smooth-out the right margin.

Continue your knowledge and skills by experimenting with different options and column widths in the Columns dialog box. You might want to change column widths and gutters on the Ruler. In addition to experimenting, explore Help topics on columns, drop caps, and hyphenation. Then, complete the following exercises.

Checking Concepts and Terms

True/False

For each of the following, check *T* or *F* to indicate whether the statement is true or false.

__T __F   **1.** Creating columns from the Columns button creates evenly spaced columns. [L1]

__T __F   **2.** The default page orientation is landscape. [L2]

__T __F   **3.** To insert a vertical line between columns, you need to display the Drawing toolbar and click the Line button to draw a line yourself. [L3]

__T __F   **4.** Insert a column break to start text at the top of the next column. [L4]

__T __F   **5.** You can balance the last column on the last page by inserting a hard page break after it. [L5]

Multiple Choice

Circle the letter of the correct answer for each of the following.

1. What term refers to text that runs parallel with the long side of the paper? [L2]

   a. portrait

   b. newspaper columns

   c. section break

   d. landscape

2. What is the default space between columns? [L3]

   a. 0.25 inches

   b. 0.5 inches

   c. 0.75 inches

   d. 1 inch

3. What type of break must you insert to be able to have two types of column settings on the same page? [L4]

   a. Continuous section break

   b. Page break

   c. Column break

   d. Next page section break

4. You can set all of the following in the Drop Cap dialog box *except* _____. [L6]

   a. position

   b. font

   c. distance from text

   d. font color

5. Which of the following words is the most appropriate for being hyphenated? [L7]

   a. pro-grams

   b. No-vember

   c. re-source

   d. John-son

Screen ID

Label each element of the Word screen shown in Figure 13.22.

Figure 13.22

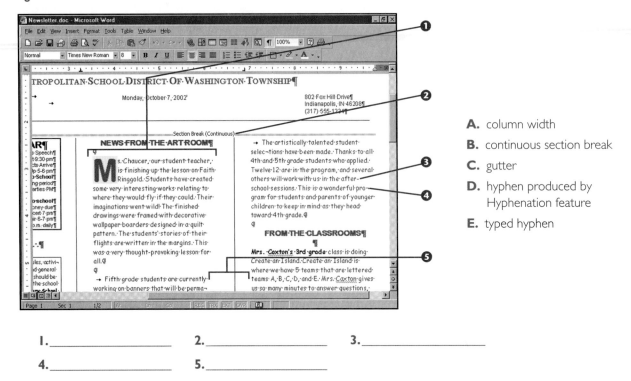

A. column width

B. continuous section break

C. gutter

D. hyphen produced by Hyphenation feature

E. typed hyphen

1._____ 2._____ 3._____

4._____ 5._____

Skill Drill

Skill Drill exercises reinforce project skills. Each skill reinforced is the same, or nearly the same, as a skill presented in the project. Each exercise includes a brief narrative introduction, followed by detailed instructions in a step-by-step format.

1. Inserting a Continuous Section Break and Changing the Page Orientation

In Project 9, you inserted WordArt, clip art, and a text box for the June newsletter for The Millennium Group. Now, you want to format the newsletter into columns. Before you do that, however, you need to insert a continuous section break between the masthead and the body of the newsletter. Plus, you want to print the document in landscape orientation.

1. Open **W-1303** and save it as **Revised June Newsletter**.

2. Position the insertion point on the left side of the heading Conference is Scheduled!

3. Choose Insert, Break.

4. Click the Continuous option, and then click OK.

5. Press Ctrl+Home.

6. Choose File, Page Setup.

7. Click the Paper Size tab.

8. Click the Landscape option.

9. Click the Apply to drop-down arrow, choose Whole Document, and click OK.

10. Save the document and keep it onscreen to continue with the next exercise.

2. Applying Columns and Inserting a Column Break

Now, you need to format the main part of the document into columns.

1. In the open **Revised June Newsletter** document, position the insertion point at the beginning of the heading Conference is Scheduled!

2. Choose Format, Columns.

3. Click the Right option to set two columns with a smaller right column.

4. Click the Line between check box, and then click OK.

5. Position the insertion point to the left of the heading Dental Benefits.

6. Choose Insert, Break.

7. Click the Column break option, and then click OK.

8. Click the Zoom drop-down arrow and choose Whole Page.

9. Click and drag the WordArt The Millennium Group to be centered between the left and right margins.

10. Click in the text that reads **Interesting Views**, located below the WordArt.

11. Click and drag the right tab from 7 inches to 8 7/8 inches. *Hint:* Don't worry if you can't see the full text after dragging the right tab marker—the text still prints.

12. Save the document and keep it onscreen to continue with the next exercise.

3. Creating a Drop Cap and Hyphenating the Newsletter

You want to enhance the newsletter by adding a drop-cap character and by hyphenating text.

1. In the open **Revised June Newsletter** document, position the insertion point at the beginning of the first paragraph, which begins with The Technology Training Conference.

2. Choose Format, Drop Cap.

3. Click the Dropped option, and then click OK.

4. With the drop cap selected, click the Font Color drop-down arrow and choose Yellow.

5. With the drop cap selected, choose Format, Borders and Shading.

6. Click the Shading tab, click Blue, and then click OK.

7. Deselect the drop cap.

8. Click after October, located at the end of the line, press Del to delete the soft space, and then press Ctrl + ⬆Shift + Spacebar to insert a nonbreaking space.

9. If needed, click and drag the photograph back to the left if it overlaps the vertical line and the second column.

10. Position the insertion point at the top of the document and choose Tools, Language, Hyphenation.

11. Make sure that Hyphenate words in CAPS is *not* selected.

12. Click the **Limit consecutive hyphens to** increment button to 2, and then click Manual.

13. Click Yes to hyphenate words when desired; click No to avoid hyphenating proper nouns and words with only two letters before the hyphen.

14. Click OK when the hyphenation process is complete.

15. Save the document, print it, and then close it.

Challenge

Challenge exercises expand on or are somewhat related to skills presented in the lessons. Each exercise provides a brief narrative introduction followed by instructions in a numbered-step or bulleted-list format that are not as detailed as those in the Skill Drill section.

1. Formatting the PEA Newsletter Into Columns

In Project 9, "Inserting and Formatting Graphics," you enhanced a PEA newsletter by adding WordArt, a text box, and clip art. Now, you want to format the newsletter into columns. In addition, you want to enhance its appearance by creating a drop cap and by hyphenating words.

1. Open **W-1304** and save it as **Revised PEA Newsletter**.
2. Format the entire document with landscape orientation.
3. Insert the appropriate type of section break by the heading Letter from the Principal.
4. Create three columns starting with the Letter from the Principal heading.
5. Revise the column structure by inserting vertical lines between the columns.
6. Move the text box to an appropriate empty space. This should make the document fit on one page.
7. Create a drop cap at the beginning of the first paragraph. Use the <u>D</u>ropped effect with only two lines to drop. Choose Arial as the drop cap font. Select Green font color for the drop cap.
8. Activate the Hyphenation feature. Deselect the option that hyphenates capitalized words.
9. Hyphenate words in appropriate locations. Do *not* hyphenate proper nouns or words with only two letters before the hyphen.
10. Save the document and print it.

2. Creating a Job Announcement Flier

You work as an assistant in the Human Resources Department at your university. Because of your knowledge and skills in Word 2000, you've been asked to create a job-announcement flier.

1. Open **W-1305** and save it as **Job Announcement**.
2. Position the insertion point at the end of the document and insert a continuous section break.
3. After the section break, insert the file **W-1306**.
4. Insert another continuous section break to the left of the heading Opening Date.
5. Format this section with two columns with a 1-inch space between columns.
6. Insert a column break after (5:00 p.m.).
7. Type the following information, inserting an en-dash symbol in the salary range:

   Department: Information Systems Management

   Salary: $50,000-$60,000, plus benefits
8. At the beginning of the heading APPLICATION INFORMATION, insert a continuous section break and format the following section with two columns with a 0.5-inch space between columns.
9. Select the text for the rest of the document, starting with APPLICATION INFORMA-TION, and choose 11-point size.
10. Apply bold and Times New Roman to the APPLICATION INFORMATION heading.
11. Bold and italicize **Submit application materials to:** in the first column.
12. Insert a column break at the beginning of the heading Knowledge, Skills, & Abilities.
13. Insert a continuous column break at the end of the document and set the format for one column only.
14. Press ↵Enter once and display the Drawing toolbar.
15. Draw a straight line from the left to the right margin at the bottom of the document. Choose Dark Blue line color and choose 4 1/2-pt line style.
16. Turn on hyphenation with a limit of two consecutive hyphens; hyphenate words in appropriate locations. Do *not* hyphenate compound words such as **post-secondary** that

are already hyphenated. Do *not* hyphenate proper nouns, capitalized words, words with only two letters before the hyphen, and the last word of a paragraph.

17. Insert a nonbreaking space in the appropriate location in the first column.

18. Save the document and print it.

3. Creating a List of Job Descriptions

You work for a major publisher. Your supervisor asked you to prepare a document that lists key personnel and their job descriptions. This information sheet will be sent to each author on the Office 2000 team, so they'll know who is responsible for different aspects of the publication process.

1. In a new document window, set a 2-inch top margin.

2. Center and type the title shown in Figure 13.23. Triple-space after the title. Select the title and apply 16-point Arial Rounded MT Bold font.

3. At the end of the document, insert a continuous section break and create two columns using the Left preset option.

4. Type the column heading **Publisher Contact** in boldface in the first column, set 12-point spacing after the paragraph, and then insert a column break. (The 12-point spacing after paragraph should continue for the rest of the document.)

5. Type the column heading **Job Description** in boldface in the second column. Then insert a continuous section break.

6. Finish typing the rest of the columnar text, inserting a column break after each person's name and inserting a continuous section break after each job description. You should have the equivalent of one blank line between rows with the 12-point spacing after paragraph.

7. Save the document as **Office 2000 Series** and print it.

Office 2000 Series

Publisher Contact	Job Description
Monica Anderson	<u>Executive Editor</u>: Coordinate all books in the Office 2000 series. Contact potential authors and issue contracts to final authors. Work with all publishing personnel. Determine budgets, sales forecasts, etc.
Michael Keyes	<u>Developmental Editor</u>: Work with author to organize topics for a final TOC. Review incoming chapters and provide suggestions for organization, content, and structure. Ensure that author is formatting the manuscript correctly.
Robyn Perkins	<u>Technical Editor</u>: Review first-draft of manuscript to ensure technical accuracy of the step-by-step lessons. Make notes of any missing or extra steps. Point out inconsistencies with menu names, options, etc., including capitalization. Make other notes from a student's perspective.
Dennis Stewart	<u>Copy Editor</u>: Proofread manuscript and correct errors in spelling, grammar, punctuation, wording, etc. Use the tracking feature in Word to make the online edits.

Figure 13.23
Create the job description information sheet.

Discovery Zone

Discovery Zone exercises help you gain advanced knowledge of project topics and/or application of skills. These exercises focus on enhancing your problem-solving skills. Numbered steps are not provided, but you are given hints, reminders, screen shots, and/or references to help you reach your goal for each exercise.

1. Creating a Flier to Sell a Condominium

You are trying to sell your condominium, so you can buy a house. You need to create an attractive flier using columns, column breaks, and section breaks to advertise your condo.

In a new document window, type and center the title shown in Figure 13.24. Apply 28-point Berlin Sans FB font fact or a similar sans-serif font. Apply Blue font color to the title.

In the Insert ClipArt dialog box, use the link that jumps to Microsoft's Clip Gallery Web site. Once you're at the site, search for photographs of apartment buildings. (Unfortunately, there aren't photos of townhouses.) Select the picture, as shown in Figure 13.24. Insert and format the picture in the document.

Create the address line using the same sans serif font you used for the title. Apply appropriate font color and highlight color. Enter and format the Special Features line. Create the columnar text with appropriate bullets. Enter the information at the bottom of the flier.

Adjust spacing between major sections to balance the space on the page. Save the document as **Condominium for Sale Flier** and print it.

2. Creating a Program for an Awards Banquet

You are the secretary for your college's Theatre Club. You are holding your spring awards banquet to honor those receiving awards for theatrical performances. You are responsible for preparing the program for the event.

In a new document window, set up the document for landscape orientation with 0.5-inch margins (all sides). Set up two columns with 0.5-inch spacing between columns. Save the document as **Awards Banquet Program**.

Because the program will be folded like a greeting card, you need to plan this document carefully. Pages 1 and 4 print on the same side of the sheet of paper, and pages 2 and 3 print on the other side of the sheet of paper. Page 1 is the cover; page 4 is the back cover. Pages 2 and 3 contain the program content. Because you're using column formatting, page 4 prints in the first column, and page 1 prints in the second column. On the second sheet of paper, page 2 prints in the first column, and page 3 prints in the second column.

Refer to Figure 13.25 on page 330 to create the back and front covers. Select the appropriate page orientation and choose Center vertical alignment. Type the text and apply the fonts as shown. Use Figure 13.26 on page 331 to create the inside pages of the program. Look at Microsoft's Clipart Gallery on the Web to find, download, and insert the clip art image shown. Type and format the text as shown in the figure. Use balanced spacing between sections.

Print the first page, which prints the back and front covers. Re-insert the paper into the printer and print the second page, which prints the inside columns. Ask your instructor if you need assistance in printing on both sides of the paper.

Spacious Condominium for Sale

1018 East Village Parkway, #214

Special Features:

- ➢ Over 1,600 Square Feet
- ➢ Fully **Finished** Basement
- ➢ Top-of-the-Line Gas Range/Oven
- ➢ Family Room
- ➢ Vaulted Ceilings in Upstairs Bedrooms
- ➢ Remote-controlled Ceiling Fans
- ➢ Fenced-in Private Back Yard
- ➢ One Covered & One Uncovered Parking Stalls

- ➢ 3 Bedrooms
- ➢ Full Bath Upstairs w/ 2 Sinks
- ➢ ¾ Bath/Laundry Room in Basement
- ➢ ½ Guest Bathroom on Main Floor
- ➢ Central Heating/Air Conditioning
- ➢ 5 Phone Outlets & 4 Cable Outlets
- ➢ Class to Shopping Mall
- ➢ Low Condo Fee Covers: Cable TV, Water, Sewer, Trash, and Lawn Care

All of these features and more for ONLY $120,900!!!

Call Kyle @ 555-SELL for more information

Figure 13.24
Create the condominium-for-sale flier.

Center and adjust size

Use appropriate break here

12-point Times New Roman for columns

Figure 13.25
Create the back and font cover.

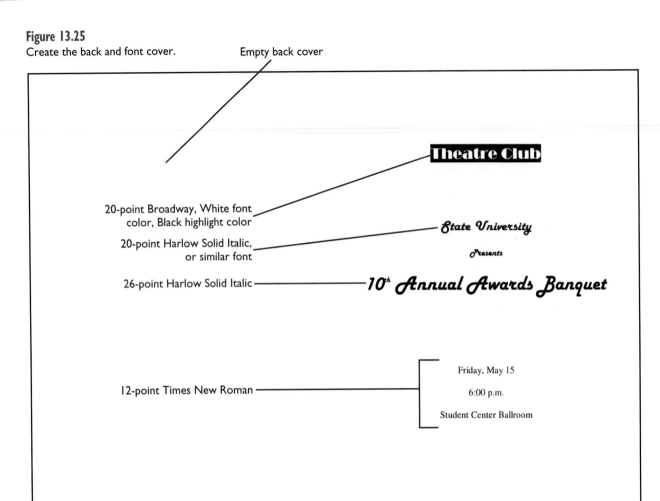

Empty back cover

Theatre Club

20-point Broadway, White font
color, Black highlight color

20-point Harlow Solid Italic,
or similar font

26-point Harlow Solid Italic

State University

Presents

10ᵗʰ Annual Awards Banquet

12-point Times New Roman

Friday, May 15

6:00 p.m.

Student Center Ballroom

Figure 13.26
Create the inside columns.

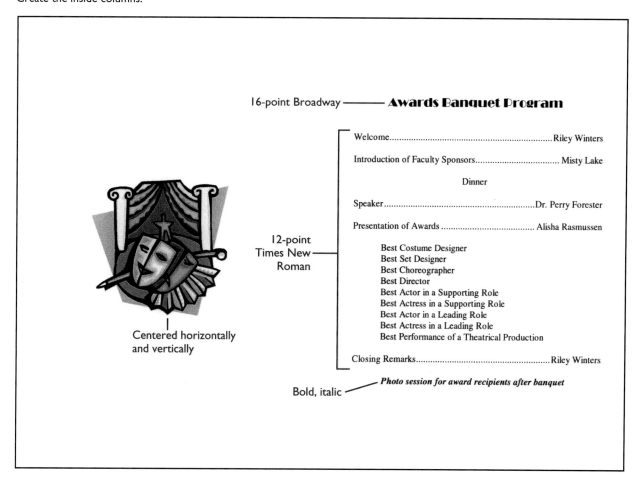

16-point Broadway ———— **Awards Banquet Program**

Welcome..Riley Winters

Introduction of Faculty Sponsors................................. Misty Lake

Dinner

Speaker...Dr. Perry Forester

Presentation of Awards .... Alisha Rasmussen

Best Costume Designer
Best Set Designer
Best Choreographer
Best Director
Best Actor in a Supporting Role
Best Actress in a Supporting Role
Best Actor in a Leading Role
Best Actress in a Leading Role
Best Performance of a Theatrical Production

Closing Remarks..Riley Winters

12-point Times New Roman

Centered horizontally and vertically

Bold, italic ——— *Photo session for award recipients after banquet*

PinPoint Assessment

You have completed this project and its associated lessons, and have had an opportunity to assess your skills through the end-of-project questions and exercises. Now use the PinPoint software Evaluation Mode to further assess your comprehension of the specific exam activities you have just learned. You can also use the PinPoint Trainer Mode and the Show Me tutorials to practice these exam activities.

Working with Styles and Templates

Key terms introduced in this project include

- boilerplate text
- character style
- Organizer
- paragraph style
- style
- template
- Word Wizard

Objectives	Required Activity for MOUS	Exam Level
➤ Use a Template to Create a New Document	Use templates to create a new document	Core
➤ Use a Word Wizard to Create a Document	Create a new document using a wizard	Core
➤ Use Word Styles	Apply styles	Core
➤ Create a Paragraph Style	Create and edit styles	Expert
➤ Create a Character Style	Create and edit styles	Expert
➤ Copy Styles to the Normal Template		
➤ Attach a Word Template to a Document		
➤ Create a New Template	Use Save As (different name, location, or format)	Core
➤ Set the Default Location for Workgroup Templates	Set default file location for workgroup templates	Expert

Why Would I Do This?

When you use a computer, you want to be as efficient as possible. You want to be able to create and format documents with minimal effort, yet give them a professional appearance. To become more efficient, you can use special Word features to create and format your documents.

As you create more and more documents, you'll notice a trend in the types of formats you use often. After you complete this project, you'll be able to create the formats once and use them over and over again without manually setting the formats each time you need them.

 ## Lesson 1: Using a Template to Create a New Document

If you're not sure how to format a certain type of document or if you want to save time by using existing document formats, you can use a Word template. A **template** is a framework of specifications for creating a document; it specifies a document's formats and might include some text and graphics. Each time you create a new document, you use the Normal template. It defines the 1.25 inch left and right margins, 1 inch top and bottom margins, Left alignment, 12 point Times New Roman, and other settings.

Word provides other templates for specific types of documents. You can use Word templates to create letters, memos, reports, resumes, agendas, calendars, and brochures. Each template contains the framework of formats and text to decrease the time it takes you to create a document.

In this lesson, you use the Professional Fax template, so you can send a fax to a customer at your mortgage company.

To Use the Professional Fax Template

① **Choose File, New.**
Figure 14.1 shows the New dialog box, which contains a variety of templates to choose from.

Figure 14.1
Choose the template for creating a new document.

Template categories

Templates

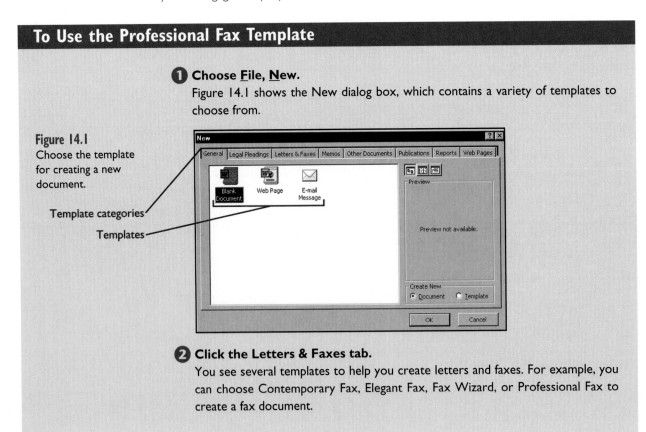

② **Click the Letters & Faxes tab.**
You see several templates to help you create letters and faxes. For example, you can choose Contemporary Fax, Elegant Fax, Fax Wizard, or Professional Fax to create a fax document.

3 **Click Professional Fax.**

The Preview window shows the overall formats and text created by the template you select.

4 **Click OK.**

Word uses the template's specifications to create the document's framework for you, thus saving you valuable time (see Figure 14.2).

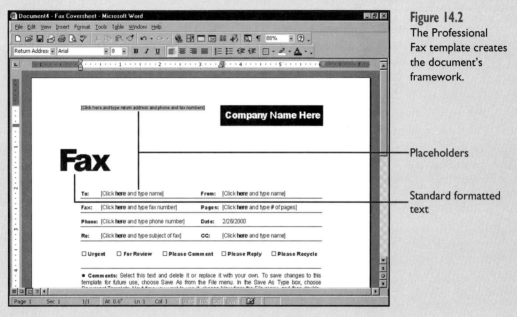

Figure 14.2
The Professional Fax template creates the document's framework.

5 **Save the document as Fax to Anita and keep it onscreen to continue with the next exercise.**

The document contains standard text, which is often referred to as **boilerplate text**. The text within brackets is simply a placeholder, indicating where you need to enter specific information. For example, **[Click here and type name]** is a placeholder for you to type the fax recipient's name. When you click a placeholder, that text is replaced with the text you type. In the next exercise, you replace the placeholders with text.

To Replace Placeholders

1 **In the open Fax to Anita document, click in the first placeholder, [Click here to type return address and phone and fax numbers], type 840 North Main, and press Spacebar.**

2 **Press and hold down Alt while you type 0149 from the number keypad.**
When you release Alt, Word inserts a circular bullet. This keyboard shortcut saves you from having to find the bullet in the Symbols dialog box.

3 **Press Spacebar, type Bolivar, MO 65613, and press ↵Enter.**

4 **Type Phone:, press Ctrl+Tab↹, type (417) 555-8000, and press ↵Enter.**

continues ▶

To Replace Placeholders   (continued)

5 Type `Fax:`, press Ctrl+Tab, and type `(417) 555-8500`.
Now you need to insert the name of your company.

6 Select `Company Name Here` and type `City Mortgage Corp.`

> **ⓘ** *Inside Stuff:*   **Enlarging the Company Name Space**
> If you type a long company name, the name word-wraps with the second column. The company name is actually in a table column cell. Therefore, you can increase the width of that column to avoid word-wrapping the company name.

7 **Replace the rest of the placeholders by entering the data shown in Figure 14.3.**

Figure 14.3
Finish entering data for the placeholders.

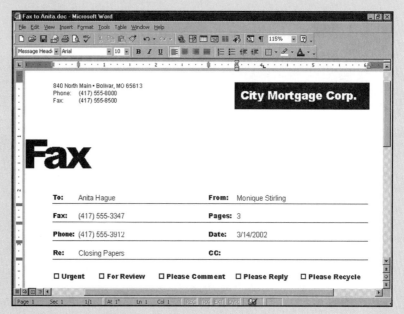

8 **Select the text after the word Comments.**
The sample paragraph tells you how you can save this document as a new template that will contain the text you entered. You'll create a template in Lesson 7.

9 **Type the following paragraph to replace the selected text:**

`Anita, the following pages contain the preliminary closing papers for your loan. Please bring a cashier's check in the amount of $30,000 with you when you come to the closing on Friday. Please call me if you have any questions.`

10 **Save the document and close it.**

 Exam Note: **Choosing a Template**
When you take the MOUS exam, read the template question carefully. Make sure you choose the *exact* template that it specifies. Don't get in a hurry and choose the wrong template. For example, don't choose Professional Letter if the test asks you to use Professional Fax.

Inside Stuff: **Downloading Additional Templates**

Microsoft's Web site (www.microsoft.com) contains additional templates you can download and use. You can use its search engine to search for Word 2000 templates. You can download a file that contains several templates. The Web site contains instructions for downloading and using the templates.

Some templates that were available when this project was being written include a contemporary press release, an invoice, a purchase order, a weekly timesheet, and a newsletter.

Lesson 2: Using a Word Wizard to Create a Document

When you were selecting a template in the previous lesson, you probably noticed templates that include the word wizard. A *Word Wizard* guides you through creating a document by asking questions and having you select from various options. The wizard uses your responses to customize the document based on the template.

In this lesson, you use the Calendar Wizard to create a monthly calendar.

To Use the Calendar Wizard

1 **Choose File, New.**

2 **Click the Other Documents tab.**
The Other Documents tab contains miscellaneous templates, such as the Calendar Wizard and resumes.

3 **Click Calendar Wizard and click OK.**
The Calendar Wizard starts by informing you of what it will create (see Figure 14.4). You see a task-completion process on the left side.

Figure 14.4
The Calendar Wizard leads you through the steps of creating a calendar.

4 **Click Next to continue using the Wizard.**
The Calendar Wizard's first screen asks you to select one of three different styles: Boxes & Borders, Banner, and Jazzy.

5 **Make sure the Boxes & Borders option is selected, and then click Next to go to the next step.**
You have two questions to answer in the next step. The first question asks you to choose between Portrait and Landscape direction. The second question asks if you want a picture.

continues ▶

To Use the Calendar Wizard (continued)

 Inside Stuff: **Creating a Balanced Calendar**
Because a monthly calendar has more columns than rows, you are recommended to leave the direction as <u>L</u>andscape.

Although you might want a picture in your calendar, don't click <u>Y</u>es. If you click <u>Y</u>es, the Wizard reserves a large amount of space on the left side for an image, which decreases the amount of space for the actual calendar. Instead of doing this, you can insert special images by special days of the month.

6 **Click <u>N</u>ext to go to the next step.**
The Wizard asks you to select the starting and ending dates (see Figure 14.5).

Figure 14.5
Choose the starting and ending months and years.

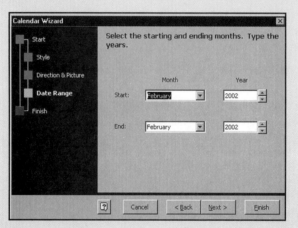

7 **Click the starting month drop-down arrow and choose February; click the increment button to change the year to 2002.**

8 **Click the ending month drop-down arrow and choose May; click the increment button to change the year to 2002.**

9 **Click <u>N</u>ext and then click <u>F</u>inish.**
Figure 14.6 shows the first month of the calendar generated by the Calendar Wizard.

Figure 14.6
The calendar is accurately created.

Office Assistant provides help

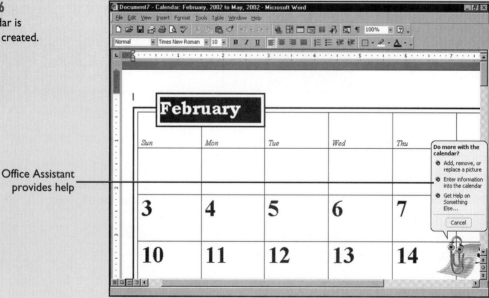

Save the document as `Monthly Calendar` **and close it.**

 Inside Stuff: **Enhancing the Calendar**
The calendar is created as a table. You can click inside any cell in the calendar and insert clip art and other images. In addition, you can select the days of the months and decrease the font size to allow more room to type important occasions, such as birthdays, holidays, etc.

Lesson 3: Using Word Styles

One of Word's most convenient and efficient attributes is the styles feature. A *style* is a group of formatting settings that you can apply to characters or paragraphs. Because a style contains several formats, you exert less effort in formatting text, such as headings. A single style might apply 16 point Arial, Blue font color, Center alignment, with a 12 point spacing after the paragraph. Instead of applying each of these formats individually, you apply your style that contains these formats.

The Normal.dot template contains about 104 different styles. Unless you specify a style, Word uses the Normal style. The Normal style contains these settings: 12 point Times New Roman, English, single-spacing, Left alignment, and widow/orphan control.

In this lesson, you apply the default Heading styles to an existing document.

To Use Existing Word Styles

1 **Open** W-1401 **and save it as** `Committee Status Report`.

2 **With the insertion point on the first line, click the Style drop-down arrow on the Formatting toolbar.**
The Style list appears, showing the most commonly used styles (see Figure 14.7).

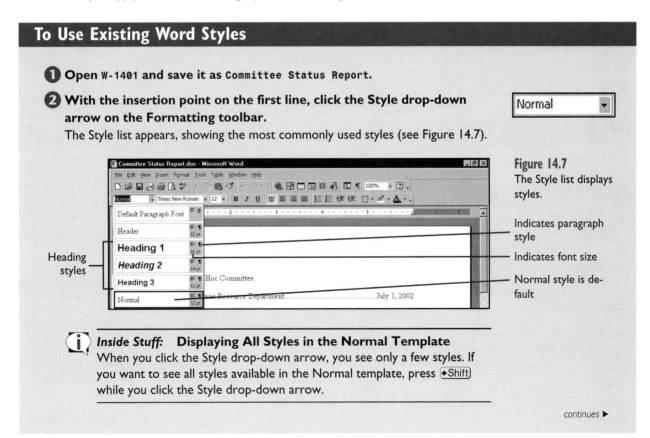

Figure 14.7
The Style list displays styles.

Indicates paragraph style

Indicates font size

Normal style is default

 Inside Stuff: **Displaying All Styles in the Normal Template**
When you click the Style drop-down arrow, you see only a few styles. If you want to see all styles available in the Normal template, press ◆Shift) while you click the Style drop-down arrow.

---

continues ▶

To Use Existing Word Styles (continued)

③ Choose Heading 1.
When you select a style, Word applies its formatting to the paragraph that contains the insertion point. The title is formatted in 16 point Arial. Notice that the Style button on the toolbar displays Heading 1, the name of the style used for that paragraph.

④ Click in the Committee Members heading.

⑤ Click the Style drop-down arrow and choose Heading 2.
The Heading 2 style formats the text in 14 point Arial italic.

⑥ Scroll down and apply the Heading 2 style to Background and Work in Progress.
Figure 14.8 shows the document after you apply the Heading 1 and Heading 2 styles.

Figure 14.8
The document is formatted with heading styles.

Style button indicates style for current paragraph

Heading 1 style

Heading 2 style

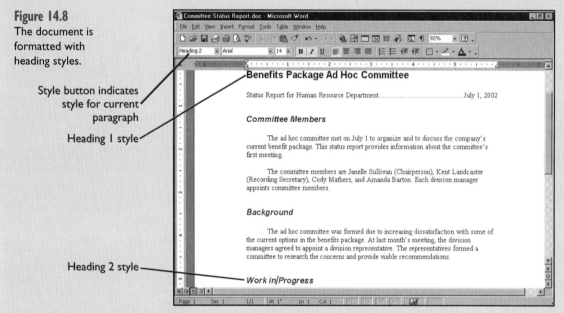

⑦ Save the document and keep it onscreen to continue with the next lesson.

 Inside Stuff: **Heading Styles**
The Heading styles also include space above and below the paragraph to separate the headings from the regular text. For example, Heading 2 includes 12 point spacing before and 3 point spacing after the paragraph. Heading styles also contain the Keep with ne<u>x</u>t option to make sure the heading isn't isolated at the bottom of a page.

Remember that you can view a paragraph's formats by using the What's This? feature. Press ◆Shift+F1 and click in the paragraph to see the formats. Figure 14.9 shows the formats for the Heading 2 style. Press ◆Shift+F1 again to turn off What's This?

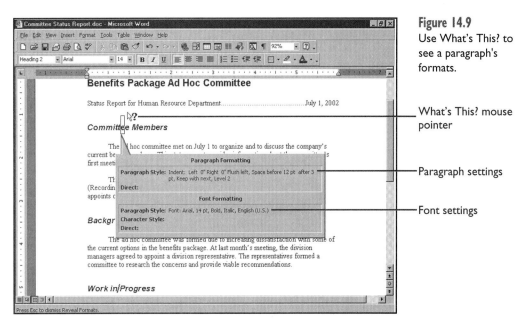

Figure 14.9
Use What's This? to see a paragraph's formats.

What's This? mouse pointer

Paragraph settings

Font settings

You can apply some styles by using keyboard shortcuts. Table 14.1 lists the keyboard shortcuts for some of Word's default styles.

Table 14.1   Keyboard Shortcuts for Styles

Keyboard Shortcut	Style
Alt + Ctrl + 1	Heading 1
Alt + Ctrl + 2	Heading 2
Alt + Ctrl + 3	Heading 3
Ctrl + ⇧Shift + L	List (for bullets)
Ctrl + ⇧Shift + N	Normal
Ctrl + ⇧Shift + S	Activates Style box on toolbar; press ↑ or ↓ to scroll through list.

Lesson 4: Creating a Paragraph Style

Although Word contains a great number of styles, you might want to create your own. You can create two different types of styles: paragraph and character. A ***paragraph style*** is a style that applies formats to an entire paragraph, or text separated by hard returns. Paragraph styles can include font formats and paragraph formats such as line spacing, indents, alignment, and spacing before and after the paragraph. The Heading 1 and Heading 2 styles you applied in the previous lesson are paragraph styles.

In this lesson, you create a paragraph style for the main heading in the status report.

To Create a Paragraph Style

1 In the open `Committee Status Report` document, position the insertion point on the first line and apply the Normal style again.

continues ▶

To Create a Paragraph Style   (continued)

2 **Choose Format, Style.**
The Style dialog box appears (see Figure 14.10). It contains a list of available styles, a preview of the currently highlighted style, and buttons to create, edit, and delete styles.

Figure 14.10
Use the Styles dialog box to create, modify, and delete styles.

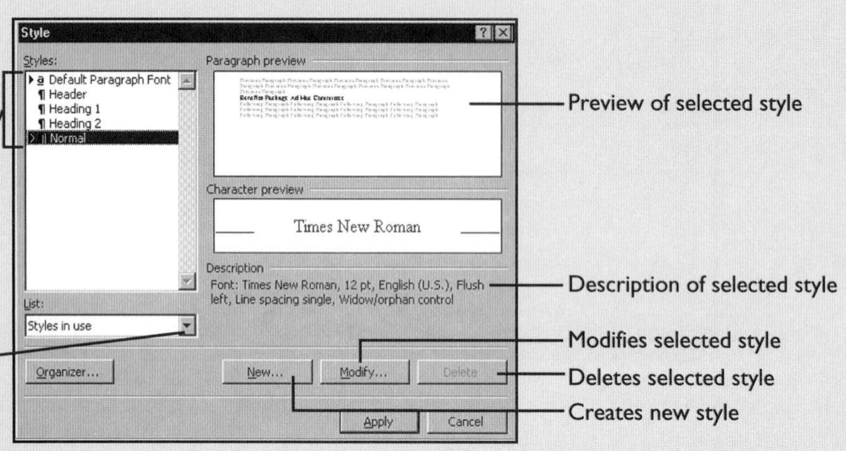

List of styles

Click to see all styles

Preview of selected style

Description of selected style

Modifies selected style

Deletes selected style

Creates new style

3 **Click New to create a new style.**
The New Style dialog box appears. You need to specify the style's name, type, and style that this style is based on.

4 **Type** Document Title **in the Name box.**

5 **Make sure the Style type is Paragraph, and make sure the Based on option is Normal.**

✎ **Exam Note:** **Basing the Style on Another Style**
If you want to include formats from an existing style, choose it from the Based on drop-down list. If you want to create a style from scratch without using existing styles, make sure the Based on option is Normal.

6 **Click Format.**
Figure 14.11 shows the different types of formats available. You can select formats such as fonts, tabs, and borders for your paragraph style.

Figure 14.11
Choose the formats you want to include in your style.

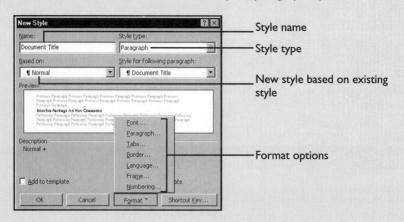

Style name

Style type

New style based on existing style

Format options

7 **Click Font.**
The Font dialog box appears, so you can choose font attributes.

8 **Choose Univers in the Font list; choose Bold in the Font style list; choose 16 in the Size list; click the Font color drop-down arrow and choose Blue; and then click OK.**

9 **Click Format and choose Paragraph.**
The Paragraph dialog box appears, so you can choose paragraph formats.

10 **Make sure the Indents and Spacing tab is selected; click the Alignment drop-down arrow and choose Centered; click the After increment button to 12 points; and click OK.**
Figure 14.12 shows the style's description after selecting the font and paragraph formats.

Preview of style —
Style formats —

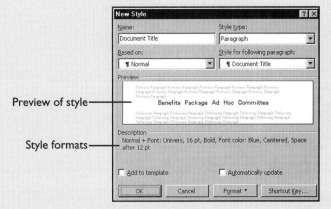

Figure 14.12
The description lists the formats you selected.

11 **Click OK to accept the style formats.**

12 **Click Apply to apply the style to the current paragraph, which is the title.**
Figure 14.13 shows the Document Title style applied to the heading.

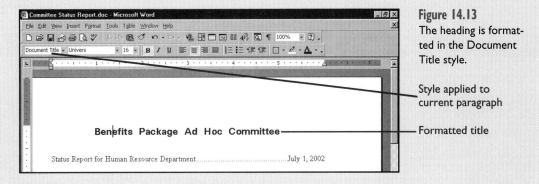

Figure 14.13
The heading is formatted in the Document Title style.

Style applied to current paragraph

Formatted title

13 **Save the document and keep it onscreen to continue with the next lesson.**

Exam Note: **Modifying a Style**

If you want to edit a style to change its formats, you need to select it in the Style dialog box and click **M**odify. The Modify Style dialog box appears, which looks similar to the New Style dialog box. Click F**o**rmat and change the formats, similar to choosing formats when you first create the style.

You can also modify a style without opening the Style dialog box. First, make the formatting changes to text affected by the style; second, select that text; third, click the Style drop-down arrow and select the current style. The Modify Style dialog box appears (see Figure 14.14), asking if you want to update the style with the new format or reapply the original style. Select **Update the style to reflect recent changes?** and click OK.

Figure 14.14
Modify a style
reflecting changes to
the document text.

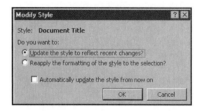

When you modify a style, Word automatically reformats text that is affected by that style. Using styles saves you valuable time in reformatting text throughout the document.

 # Lesson 5: Creating a Character Style

So far, you have applied paragraph styles using Word's Heading styles and your own Document Title style. However, you might want to create and apply a **character style**—a style that formats a portion of the text *within* a paragraph. Unlike a paragraph style that can format font, border, language, line spacing, alignment, and indents, a character style can format only fonts, borders, and languages.

In this lesson, you create a character style named ADC that applies font attributes to **ad hoc committee**.

To Create a Character Style

1 **In the open `Committee Status Report` document, click on the blank line below the title (to be in nonformatted area), and choose F**o**rmat, **S**tyle.**

2 **Click **N**ew.**
The New Style dialog box appears, so you can enter its name and specify its formats.

3 **Type `AHC` in the **N**ame box.**
You need to change the style type to Character.

4 **Click the Style t**y**pe drop-down arrow and choose Character.**

5 **Make sure the **B**ased on option is Default Paragraph Font.**
Now you're ready to select the formats for the character style.

6 **Click F_o_rmat and choose _F_ont.**
The Font dialog box appears, so you can choose the font attributes for the character style.

7 **Choose Arial Narrow in the _F_ont list, choose Bold Italic in the Font style list, and click OK.**
The New Style dialog box displays.

8 **Click OK and then click Close to return to the document.**
You are ready to apply the character style to the phrase ad hoc committee throughout the document.

9 **Select `ad hoc committee` in the first paragraph in the Committee Members section.**
Unlike applying a paragraph style where you simply choose the style without selecting text, you must select text before applying a character style.

10 **Click the Style drop-down arrow on the Formatting toolbar and choose AHC.**
Word applies the AHC style formats to the selected text.

11 **Deselect this occurrence.**

12 **Select `ad hoc committee` in the first paragraph in the Background section, apply the AHC style, and deselect the text.**
Figure 14.15 shows the AHC style applied to text.

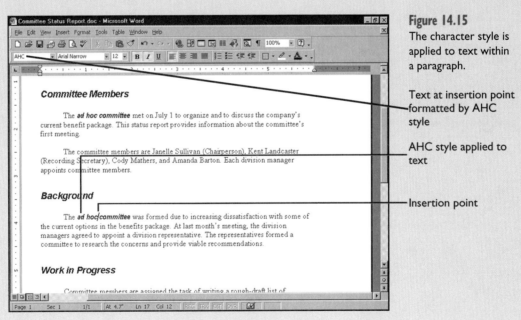

Figure 14.15
The character style is applied to text within a paragraph.

Text at insertion point formatted by AHC style

AHC style applied to text

Insertion point

13 **Save the document and keep it onscreen to continue with the next lesson.**

Lesson 6: Copying Styles to the Normal Template

You might use some styles you create for a particular document only, although you might want to use other styles in other documents. For example, you might want to use the Document Title paragraph style in other documents you create. Instead of re-creating this style in new documents, you can copy the style to the Normal.dot template, which is used when you create new documents.

In this lesson, you copy the two styles you created to the Normal.dot template to use in new documents you create based on that template.

To Copy Styles to the Normal Template

1 **Click the New Blank Document button on the Standard toolbar.**
A new blank document appears based on the Normal.dot template. You want to check the available styles.

2 **Click the Styles drop-down arrow.**
The two styles you created—Document Title and AHC—are not listed; only Word's default styles are listed.

3 **Close the document without saving it, and make sure `Committee Status Report` is open.**
Now you're ready to copy the styles to the Normal.dot template.

4 **Choose F̲ormat, S̲tyle.**

5 **Click O̲rganizer.**
The Organizer dialog box appears (see Figure 14.16). The **Organizer** is a tool that enables you to copy styles, AutoText entries, and other shareable items between two documents or between a document and a template.

Figure 14.16
Use the Organizer to copy styles to the Normal.dot template.

Styles in current document

Click to copy styles to Normal.dot

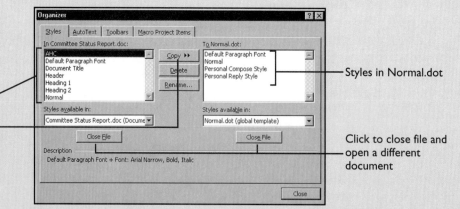

Styles in Normal.dot

Click to close file and open a different document

6 **Click AHC to select it and press** Ctrl **while you click `Document Title` in the I̲n Committee Status Report.doc list.**
You must select the styles you want to copy or delete.

7 **Click C̲opy to copy the styles to the Normal.dot template.**
The two styles are now listed in the T̲o Normal.dot list.

8 **Click Close to close the Organizer.**
Now, you want to create a new document to make sure the styles copied to Normal.dot.

9 Click the New Blank Document button and then click the Style drop-down arrow.

The AHC and Document Title styles are now available for every new document you create (see Figure 14.17).

AHC style

Document
Title style

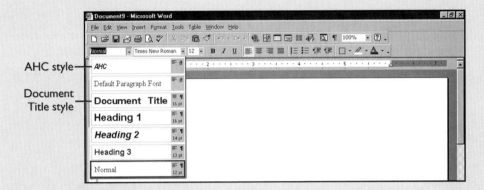

Figure 14.17
The styles you created are available for new documents.

 Inside Stuff: Changes Don't Affect Previously Saved Documents
Although you copied styles from a document to the Normal.dot template, these styles are available for *new* documents only. The styles are not available in previously saved documents—even though those documents might have been based on the Normal.dot template.

Let's now delete the styles you copied to the Normal.dot template.

10 Choose Format, Style and then click Organizer.

11 Click AHC and then Ctrl-click Document Title in the In Normal.dot list box to select these styles.

12 Click Delete, click Yes to All to confirm the deletion, and then click Close.

The AHC and Document Title styles are no longer available when you create documents based on the Normal.dot template.

13 Close the new file without saving it and keep the `Committee Status Report` onscreen to continue with the next lesson.

 Inside Stuff: Saving Changes to the Normal.dot Template
When you exit Word, you might be prompted to save changes to Normal.dot. This message appears because you copied styles and then deleted styles in the Normal.dot template. You can click No if you see this prompt.

Lesson 7: Attaching a Word Template to a Document

Word contains a variety of templates, in addition to the Normal template. Although the Normal template is a good general template with general formatting styles, you might need a template with different styles. Even after you create a document, you can attach a different template to the document.

In this lesson, you attach the Professional Report template to your status report.

To Attach a Different Template to a Document

1 **In the open `Committee Status Report` document, click in the title and apply the Heading 1 style again.**

2 **Choose F̲ormat, T̲heme.**
The Theme dialog box appears. You need to access the Style Gallery from here to choose a different template.

3 **Click S̲tyle Gallery at the bottom of the dialog box.**
The Style Gallery displays a list of Word templates (see Figure 14.18). When you select a template from the list, the P̲review window displays how that template affects your document.

Figure 14.18
Choose a template to attach to your document.

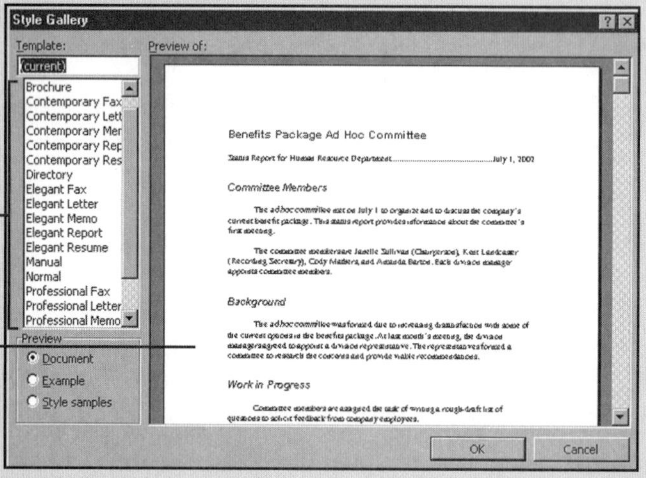

Choose from the template list

Preview of the way template affects document

4 **Scroll to the bottom of the T̲emplate list box, click Professional Report, and click OK.**
Figure 14.19 shows the document reformatted after you attach the Professional Report template. The styles within that template have different formats.

Figure 14.19
The Professional Template is attached to the document.

Different format for Heading 1

Heading 2 formats

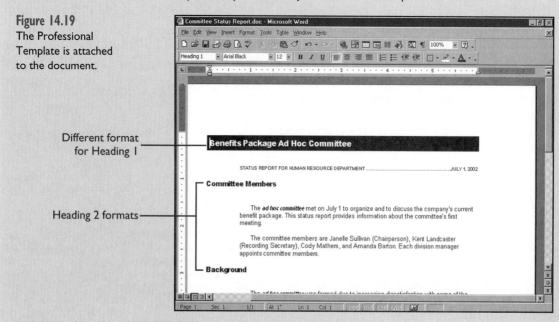

5 **Save the document and close it.**

Lesson 8: Creating a New Template

You will probably create many similar documents on the job or in your college classes. To ensure consistency of formatting, you should use a template. However, you might not want to use any of Word's templates. You can create your own template of formatting and text as a framework for creating new documents.

In this lesson, you want to use an existing document to create a form for coworkers to complete when they request the use of the conference room at your company. To save time creating the document in the future, you want to save the document as a template.

To Create a New Template

1 **Open** W-1402 **and save it as** Request for Conference Room.
You need to delete the existing variable data, so the form will be ready to fill in when you open it again.

2 **Click and drag to select** Myrna Rogan **and** Marketing; **press** Del.

3 **Select the dates and time and press** Del.

4 **Select the text in the Purpose of Room box and press** Del.
The document contains styles for the title and categories. Let's see what they are.

5 **Click the Style drop-down arrow.**
The two styles created specifically for this document are Form Title and Items (see Figure 14.20). The styles are saved with the document when you save it as a regular document or as a template.

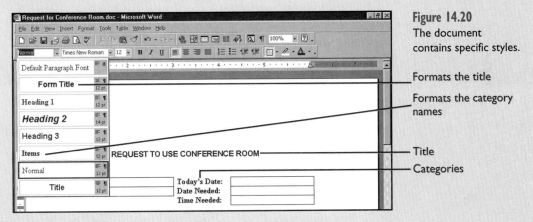

Figure 14.20
The document contains specific styles.

Formats the title

Formats the category names

Title

Categories

6 **Choose File, Save As.**

7 **Click the** Save as type **drop-down arrow and choose Document Template (*.dot).**
Word changes the Save in folder to Templates. This saves the template in the General tab of the New dialog box, so you can access it quickly when you need to use it as a template.

8 **Click Save.**
The form is now saved as a template.

9 **Close the document.**

Now, let's display the New dialog box and select the template you just saved. The template is listed in the General tab.

To Use the Template You Created

1 Choose File, New.
You should see Request for Conference, the template you created (see Figure 14.21).

Figure 14.21
Your template appears in the General category.

Your template

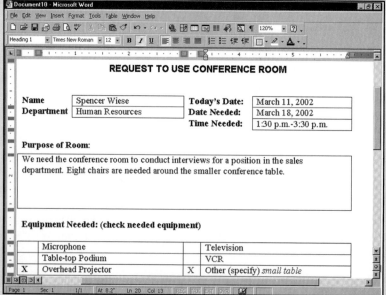

Inside Stuff: Your Template Name
The last few letters might not appear in the template name. Word truncates part of the template name in the New dialog box.

2 Click Request for Conference Room and click OK.
You are now ready to enter data into the form.

3 Use Figure 14.22 to enter data into the form.

Figure 14.22
Enter the data into the form.

REQUEST TO USE CONFERENCE ROOM

Name	Spencer Wiese	Today's Date:	March 11, 2002
Department	Human Resources	Date Needed:	March 18, 2002
		Time Needed:	1:30 p.m.-3:30 p.m.

Purpose of Room:

We need the conference room to conduct interviews for a position in the sales department. Eight chairs are needed around the smaller conference table.

Equipment Needed: (check needed equipment)

	Microphone		Television
	Table-top Podium		VCR
X	Overhead Projector	X	Other (specify) *small table*

4 Save the document as Request from Wiese and close it.

Inside Stuff: **Creating a Template from an Existing Template**
You can use an existing template to create a new template. Choose the template you want in the New dialog box. Before clicking OK, however, click the Template option. After clicking OK, make any formatting or text changes you want. When you save the document, Word automatically displays the Template folder in which to save the revised template. Enter a new name for the template and click Save.

 Inside Stuff: **Editing a Template**
You might decide to change formats, enter text, add a graphic, or modify styles within a template. Editing a template you created is similar to creating a new template from a Word template: Select the template in the New dialog box, click the Template option in the Create New category, and click OK. Make the modifications you need and save the template under the same template name.

 Inside Stuff: **Deleting a Template**
Your instructor might want you to delete the template you just created. If so, display the New dialog box. Right-click the template you created and choose Delete, and then click Yes to confirm the deletion.

Lesson 9: Setting the Default Location for Workgroup Templates

When you saved the template you created in the last lesson, Word saved it to the Templates folder by default. Although you can manually change the location as you're saving the template, you might want to designate a different default location for saving all new templates. For example, if several of your colleagues need access to the same template, you can set the default to save templates in a common location on your organization's network.

In this lesson, you set the default location for workgroup templates. Because you probably don't have access to save templates to your educational institution's network, let's set the default for your floppy disk drive.

To Set the Default Location for Workgroup Templates

❶ Choose Tools, Options.
The Options dialog box appears. This dialog box controls many facets of the Word environment.

❷ Click the File Locations tab.
Figure 14.23 shows the File Locations options. The Workgroup templates file type probably does not have a default location specified in the second column.

continues ▶

To Set the Default Location for Workgroup Templates   (continued)

Figure 14.23
Set the default file
locations.

Select this file type

Click to modify the
default location

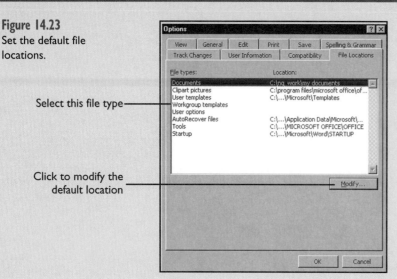

3 **Click Workgroup templates and then click <u>M</u>odify.**
The Modify Location dialog box lets you specify where you want to save templates by default. You can choose the drive letter and folder(s) where you want
to save templates.

4 **Click the Look <u>i</u>n drop-down arrow, choose 3 1/2 Floppy (A:), click
OK. Then click OK to close the Options dialog box.**
This sets the floppy drive as the workgroup location and closes the Modify
Location dialog box. Now let's open a file and save it as a template with the new
default location.

5 **Open** Request for Conference Room **and delete the variable data as you
previously did.**

6 **Choose <u>F</u>ile, Save <u>A</u>s.**

7 **Type** Conference Room **in the File <u>n</u>ame box.**

8 **Click the** Save as **type drop-down arrow and choose Document
Template (*.dot).**
Word displays the Template folder on the computer.

9 **Click the Save <u>i</u>n drop-down arrow and choose 3 1/2 Floppy (A:), and
then click <u>S</u>ave.**

10 **Close the document and choose <u>F</u>ile, <u>N</u>ew.**
Figure 14.24 shows both templates that you created.

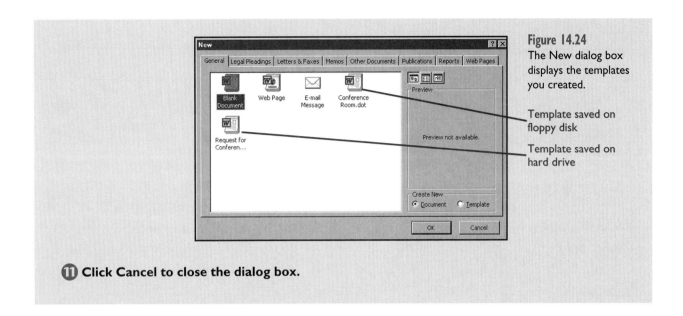

Figure 14.24
The New dialog box displays the templates you created.

Template saved on floppy disk

Template saved on hard drive

11 **Click Cancel to close the dialog box.**

Summary

You learned some excellent time-saving features in this project. You learned how to use existing Word templates, wizards, and styles to create and format new documents. In addition, you learned how to create and apply paragraph and character styles to improve efficiency and consistency throughout a document. You also learned how to save a regular document as a template to use in the future.

By attaching a different template to a document, your document can have a different appearance based on the new template's styles. Finally, you learned how to set a default location for workgroup templates that you can share with others at work. You can now explore Help menus about these topics, complete the following activities, and use the PinPoint software for reinforcement.

Checking Concepts and Terms

True/False

For each of the following, check *T* or *F* to indicate whether the statement is true or false.

__T __F **1.** The default template that is applied to each new document you create is the Normal.dot template. [L1]

__T __F **2.** A Wizard is a set of questions that you answer to set up a document based on a template. [L2]

__T __F **3.** Word provides three types of styles: document, paragraph, and symbol. [L4]

__T __F **4.** You must select text before applying a paragraph style. [L4]

__T __F **5.** You can use the Organizer to copy styles to the Normal template. [L6]

Multiple Choice

Circle the letter of the correct answer for each of the following.

1. Which template is used when you create a new blank document? [L1]

a. Normal

b. General

c. Professional Document

d. Report Wizard

2. Which dialog box lists template categories and specific templates? [L1]

a. Template

b. New

c. Open

d. Save As

3. Which format is *not* available when creating a character style? [L5]

a. Arial font

b. Red font color

c. Bold

d. Alignment

4. Which dialog box lets you attach a different template to the current document? [L7]

a. Style

b. New

c. Style Gallery

d. Options

5. When you save a document as a template, what is the filename extension? [L8]

a. .tmp

b. .doc

c. .tem

d. .dot

Screen ID

Label each element of the Word screen shown in Figure 14.25.

Figure 14.25

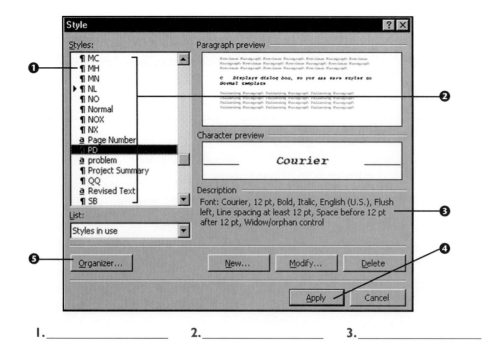

A. Indicates paragraph style

B. Formats current text with selected style

C. Displays dialog box, so you can save styles to Normal template

D. Style for current text

E. Style list

1._____ 2._____ 3._____

4._____ 5._____

Skill Drill

Skill Drill exercises reinforce project skills. Each skill reinforced is the same, or nearly the same, as a skill presented in the project. Each exercise includes a brief narrative introduction, followed by detailed instructions in a step-by-step format.

1. Using the Memo Wizard

You want to create a memo without spending a lot of time formatting it. Therefore, you decide to use the Memo Wizard to help you create a memo.

1. Choose File, New to display the New dialog box.
2. Click the Memos tab, click Memo Wizard, and click OK.
3. Click Next when the Memo Wizard dialog box appears.
4. Click the Contemporary option to select the style and click Next.
5. Click Next to accept the suggested title.
6. Make sure the Date, From, and Subject check boxes are checked.
7. Type your name in the From text box.
8. Type **Staff Meeting** in the Subject text box and then click Next.
9. Type **Denver Sales Staff** in the To text box.
10. Type **Jonathon Rivera** in the Cc text box and then click Next.
11. Click the Attachment check box and then click Next.
12. Click Next and then click Finish.
13. Click in the placeholder **[Click here and type your memo text]** and then type the following paragraph:

    Please plan on meeting next Friday at 2:30 p.m. in Room 505 for a staff meeting. We have several situations that must be addressed and resolved as soon as possible. The attached agenda provides details of the meeting.
14. Select the dateline through the end of the paragraph, click the Font Size drop-down arrow, and choose 11.
15. Save the document as **Staff Meeting Memo**, print it, and close it.

2. Applying Word Styles and Attaching a Different Template

You need to quickly format a report with Word's heading styles. After printing a copy, you decide to attach a different template to the document.

1. Open **W-1403** and save it as **Memo Newsletter**.
2. Click the Style drop-down arrow and choose Heading 1 for the title.
3. Click in News Articles between the first and second paragraphs.
4. Click the Style drop-down arrow and choose Heading 3.
5. Apply the Heading 3 style to Classified Advertisements and Art Work.
6. Save and print the document.
7. Choose Format, Theme.
8. Click Style Gallery.
9. Choose Contemporary Report and click OK.
10. Save the document as **Updated Memo Newsletter** and print it.

3. Creating and Applying Styles and Creating a Template

You want to open the original memo and create your own styles. After creating and applying styles, you decide to save the memo as a template to use in the future.

1. Open **W-1403** and save it as **Winter Newsletter Memo**.
2. Choose Format, Style, and click New.
3. Type **Side Heading** in the Name box, make sure the Style type is Paragraph, and click the Based on drop-down arrow and choose Normal.
4. Click Format, Font.

5. Choose Bauhaus Md BT in the Font list. If you don't have this font, use Kabel Md or another sans serif font.

6. Click Bold in the Font style list.

7. Click the Font color drop-down arrow and choose Red; then click OK.

8. Click Format, Paragraph; click the Alignment drop-down arrow; and choose Centered.

9. Click OK, click OK, and then click Close.

10. Apply the Side Heading style to the headings News Articles, Classified Advertisements, and Art Work.

11. Save the document and keep it onscreen.

12. Delete the date; choose Insert, Date and Time; click the third format; click the Update automatically check box, and click OK.

13. Delete the heading Winter Newsletter and type **Start here** at the beginning of the first paragraph.

14. Press Ctrl + ⬆Shift + End to select the rest of the document and then press Del.

15. Choose File, Save As.

16. Click the Save as type drop-down arrow and choose Document Template (*.dot).

17. Click the Save in arrow, choose the 3 1/2 Floppy (A:), and then click Save. Then, print the document.

Challenge

Challenge exercises expand on or are somewhat related to skills presented in the lessons. Each exercise provides a brief narrative introduction followed by instructions in a numbered-step or bulleted-list format that are not as detailed as those in the Skill Drill section.

I. Using the Letter Wizard

You want to use the Letter Wizard to create a letter. The Wizard asks you questions about how you want the letter formatted and provides boxes for you to enter data.

1. Display the New dialog box and select the Letter Wizard.

2. In the Letter Formats section, choose Contemporary Letter and Modified Block style.

3. In the Recipient Information section, enter **Ms. Isabel Kahn** as the recipient. Enter her address:

   342 Maple Drive

   Laurel, MD 20708

4. Use the Business salutation.

5. Enter your name as the sender and select one enclosure.

6. When the Wizard is finished, select the paragraph and delete it. Do *not* delete the paragraph mark, though.

7. Insert the file **W-1403**.

8. Vertically center the document.

9. Apply 12 point Bookman Old Style font to the letter.

10. Save the document as **Kahn Letter** and print it.

2. Creating and Applying Styles for Minutes of a Meeting

You want to create and apply styles to format the minutes for a condominium association meeting.

1. Open **W-1404** and save it as **September 2001 Minutes**.

2. Create a paragraph style with these specifications:

   a. Minutes Title (name)

   b. Normal (style basis)

    c. 16 point Tahoma font

    d. Teal font color

    e. Bold font style

    f. 12 point spacing after paragraph

    g. Centered alignment

3. Create a paragraph style with these specifications:

    a. Major Headings (name)

    b. Minutes Title (basis)

    c. 14 point Tahoma font

    d. Left alignment

    e. 18 point spacing before paragraph

    f. keep other formats carried over from the Minutes Title style

4. Apply the Minutes Title style to the first two lines of text in the document.

5. Apply the Major Headings style to the three major headings in the document.

6. Save and print the document.

7. Edit the Normal style by setting a 0.5 inch first line indent and double-spacing.

8. Edit the Major Headings style by changing the font size to 12 point, and setting a (none) special indent.

9. Set 1 inch left and right margins.

10. Delete extra blank lines caused by hard returns.

11. Create a character style named **Names** that adds bold and Teal font color. Apply this style to people's names throughout the document *except* those listed in the Call to Order section.

12. Save the document as **Revised September 2001 Minutes** and print it.

3. Creating a Table Template for a Publisher

You work as an editorial assistant at a publishing company. To help authors know with whom they are working, you frequently send out a contact sheet with the names, titles, and responsibilities. Because you use this format regularly, you want to create a template from a table.

1. In a new document window, set 1 inch left and right margins and a 2 inch top margin.

2. Create the table shown in Figure 14.26.

3. Set a 1.5 inch column width for the first column and 1.75 inch width for the second column.

4. Bold the first two rows. Use appropriate alignment.

[book title]		
Key Individual	**Title**	**Responsibilities**
	Executive Editor	Coordinate all books in the series. Contact potential authors and issue contracts to final authors. Work with all publishing personnel. Determine budgets, sales forecasts, etc.
	Developmental Editor	Work with author to organize topics for a final TOC. Review incoming chapters and provide suggestions for organization, content, and structure. Ensure that author is formatting the manuscript correctly.
	Technical Editor	Review first-draft of manuscript to ensure technical accuracy of the step-by-step lessons. Make notes of any missing or extra steps. Point out inconsistencies with menu names, options, etc., including casing. Make other notes from student perspective.
	Copy Editor	Proofread manuscript and correct errors in spelling, grammar, punctuation, wording, etc. Use the tracking feature in Word to make the online edits.

Figure 14.26
Create this table.

5. Set a 0.45 inch row height, 14 point Arial, vertical and horizontal centering. Use the font and shading colors as indicated in the figure.

6. Save the document as a template. Name the template **Editor Table**. Print the template and then close it.

7. Select the Editor Table from the New dialog box.

8. Delete the placeholder and type **Outlook 2000 Basics**.

9. Enter the following data in the first column: **Guy Demke**, **Esita Johnson**, **Tyler Kinikini**, and **Robert Loughlin**.

10. Save the document as **Outlook Editors** and print it.

Discovery Zone

Discovery Zone exercises help you gain advanced knowledge of project topics and/or application of skills. These exercises focus on enhancing your problem-solving skills. Numbered steps are not provided, but you are given hints, reminders, screen shots, and/or references to help you reach your goal for each exercise.

1. Using and Editing Styles from Another Document

You want to use the styles you created in the **Revised September 2001 Minutes** (Challenge 2) to format minutes from a special meeting. However, you know that copying the styles to the Normal.dot template won't work because the secretary already typed the new minutes.

Open **W-1405** and save it as **January 2002 Minutes**. Access the Organizer and close the existing files listed. Select Revised September 2001 Minutes on one side, and select January

2002 Minutes on the other side. Change the file type to All Word Documents to make sure you can find the doc files. Copy all styles from the Revised September Minutes document to the January 2002 Minutes document.

Apply the styles to the document you're currently working on. Modify the Minutes Title style by changing the font color to yellow and adding blue shading with no border lines. Modify the Major Headings style by changing the font color to blue and choosing no shading color. Modify the Normal style by adding Justified alignment.

Save and print the January minutes.

2. Creating a Newspaper Columns Template

You need to create a template for a monthly newsletter that you distribute to your company. The newsletter contains tips and tricks of software applications. The newsletter should have a standard masthead, continuous section break, newspaper columns, and a paragraph style for the article titles.

In a new document window, set 1 inch left and right margins and create the masthead shown in Figure 14.27.

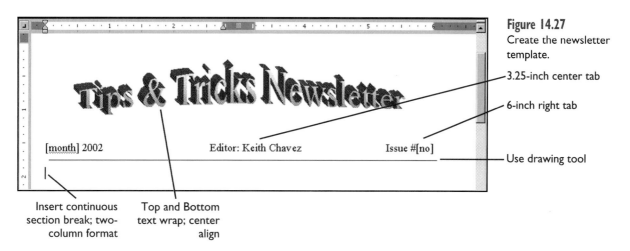

Figure 14.27
Create the newsletter template.

— 3.25-inch center tab

— 6-inch right tab

— Use drawing tool

Insert continuous section break; two-column format

Top and Bottom text wrap; center align

Create a paragraph style called **Article Title** with these formats: 12 point Arial Rounded Mt Bold, Orange font color, Center align, 8 point spacing after paragraph. Save the document as a template named **Tips Newsletter**, print it, and then close it.

Choose the Tips Newsletter in the New dialog box. Change the placeholder [month] to **April** and change [no] to **4**. Insert **W-1406** after the continuous section break. The file should be formatted into two columns. Apply the paragraph style to the headings. Make sure the document is formatted by 1 inch left and right margins. Insert a column break for the **Other Ctrl Keyboard Shortcuts** heading. Save the document as **April Tips Newsletter** and print it.

PinPoint Assessment

You have completed this project and its associated lessons, and have had an opportunity to assess your skills through the end-of-project questions and exercises. Now use the PinPoint software Evaluation Mode to further assess your comprehension of the specific exam activities you have just learned. You can also use the PinPoint Trainer Mode and the Show Me tutorials to practice these exam activities.

Project 15

Automating Your Work

Key terms introduced in this project include

- AutoComplete
- AutoText
- macro
- Microsoft Visual Basic
- record macro
- run macro

Objectives	Required Activity for MOUS	Exam Level
➤ Use AutoComplete to Insert AutoText Entries		
➤ Create AutoText Entries		
➤ Insert AutoText Entries		
➤ Edit and Delete AutoText Entries		
➤ Record Macros	Create, apply, and edit macros	Expert
➤ Run Macros	Create, apply, and edit macros	Expert
➤ Edit Macros	Create, apply, and edit macros	Expert
➤ Copy, Rename, and Delete Macros	Copy, rename, and delete macros	Expert

Why Would I Do This?

You probably find yourself typing the same text over and over. Some examples include typing your name, your department, your company name, a return address, a signature block, or an entire paragraph. Although typing these pieces of text doesn't take a lot of time in the short run, you spend extra time typing them over and over.

Word includes several features to help you automate tasks such as reusing text and formatting text. In this project, you use AutoText and macros to automate your work, thus improving your productivity.

Lesson 1: Using AutoComplete to Insert AutoText Entries

The ***AutoText*** feature lets you store many different pieces of text or graphics and retrieve them instantly into a document. The default AutoText entries include salutations such as Ladies and Gentlemen and To Whom it May Concern. Word includes other AutoText entries to insert other types of text, such as complimentary closings.

When you type a few key letters of an AutoText entry, ***AutoComplete*** displays a ScreenTip that shows you the entire AutoText entry. You can then press ⏎Enter to accept, let AutoComplete complete the rest of the AutoText entry, or keep typing. For example, when you start typing **Augu**, AutoComplete displays a ScreenTip **August**. Pressing ⏎Enter automatically completes the rest of the word for you.

In this lesson, you use AutoComplete to insert several AutoText entries.

To Use AutoComplete

1 **Open W-1501 and save it as Scholarship Application.**
You need to insert the date at the top of the letter. When you start typing the current month, Word typically displays the ScreenTip of the full month name. You can press ⏎Enter or F3 to complete the month's name. When you press Spacebar after the current month's name, AutoComplete displays the current date.

 Inside Stuff: **Typing Months**
Some months, such as May, might not appear as a ScreenTip when you starting typing them. Also, AutoComplete won't display a full date, such as October 12, 2002, if the current month is not October.

---

2 **Delete + at the top of the document and start typing the current month.**
Figure 15.1 shows a typical ScreenTip displaying a month after typing a few key letters of the month name.

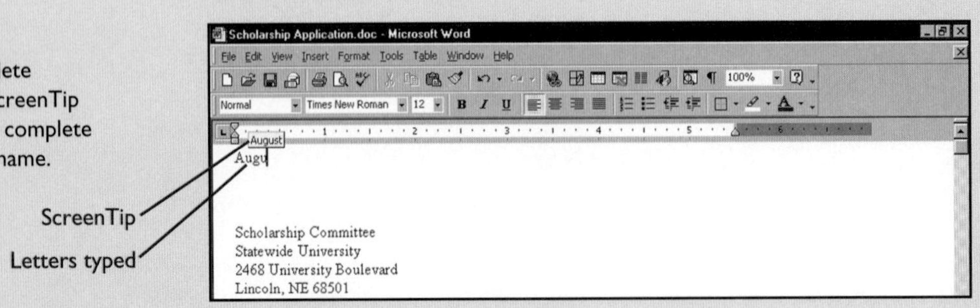

Figure 15.1
AutoComplete displays a ScreenTip to help you complete the month name.

ScreenTip
Letters typed

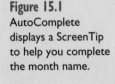

If You Have Problems...
If you do not see the date ScreenTip, this feature might be turned off. To turn on the feature, choose **T**ools, **A**utoCorrect; click the AutoText tab; click the **Show AutoComplete tip for AutoText and dates** check box; and then click OK.

3 **Press** ⏎Enter **or** F3 **when you see the AutoComplete ScreenTip.**
AutoComplete completes the rest of the month name for you. Now you're ready to have it help you insert the rest of the current date.

4 **Press** Spacebar.
AutoComplete displays the current date, such as **August 15, 2002** in the ScreenTip (see Figure 15.2).

Current month

Space

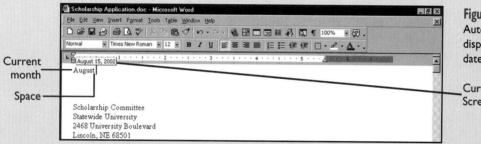

Figure 15.2
AutoComplete displays the current date in a ScreenTip.

Current date ScreenTip

5 **Press** ⏎Enter **or** F3 **to complete the rest of today's date.**
If you press ⏎Enter again, Word will insert a hard return. It only completes text instead of inserting a hard return if the AutoComplete ScreenTip appears.

6 **Delete ++ below the inside address and type** Ladi.
You should see the ScreenTip **Ladies and Gentlemen:**.

7 **Press** ⏎Enter **or** F3 **to complete the rest of the salutation.**
Now you're ready to insert a complimentary closing. By default, AutoText contains complimentary closings such as Sincerely, Sincerely yours, and Cordially. However, not all complimentary closings appear in ScreenTips.

8 **Scroll to the bottom of the letter, delete +++, and type** Cord.
You see the ScreenTip **Cordially** to complete the complimentary closing.

9 **Press** ⏎Enter **or** F3 **to complete the complimentary closing.**
Figure 15.3 shows the letter after inserting three AutoComplete entries.

continues ▶

To Use AutoComplete (continued)

Figure 15.3
The letter is complete with AutoComplete entries.

AutoComplete date

Decrease zoom to see all AutoText entries

Salutation AutoText

Complimentary closing AutoText

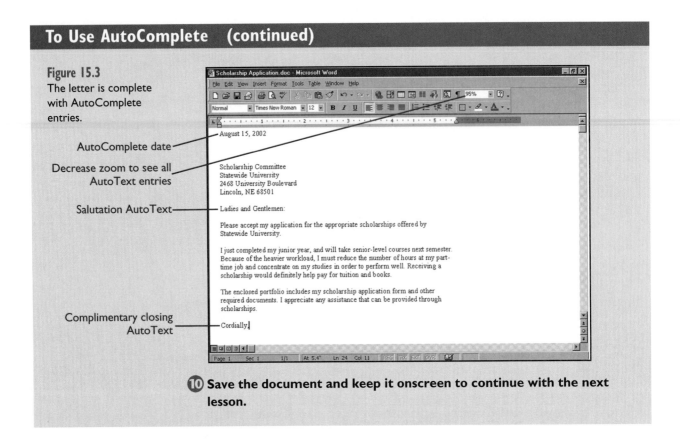

10 **Save the document and keep it onscreen to continue with the next lesson.**

Lesson 2: Creating AutoText Entries

In addition to the default AutoText entries, you might want to create AutoText entries for text you use on a regular basis. For example, you might want to create an AutoText entry for your return address, a signature block for a letter, or a standard paragraph you plan to use in several documents.

In this lesson, you create an AutoText entry for your complimentary closing, name, and return address.

To Create an AutoText Entry

1 **In the open** Scholarship Application **document, choose** **V**iew, **T**oolbars, AutoText.
Displaying the AutoText toolbar helps you create an insert AutoText entries. You want to replace Cordially with Sincerely yours.

2 **Select Cordially and type** Sincerely yours **to replace the selected text. Make sure you don't delete the comma or paragraph mark.**
The first step to create an AutoText entry is selecting the text or graphic that you want to be the AutoText entry.

3 **Select the signature block, which includes the complimentary closing, typed name, and address.**
Figure 15.4 shows the text you should select.

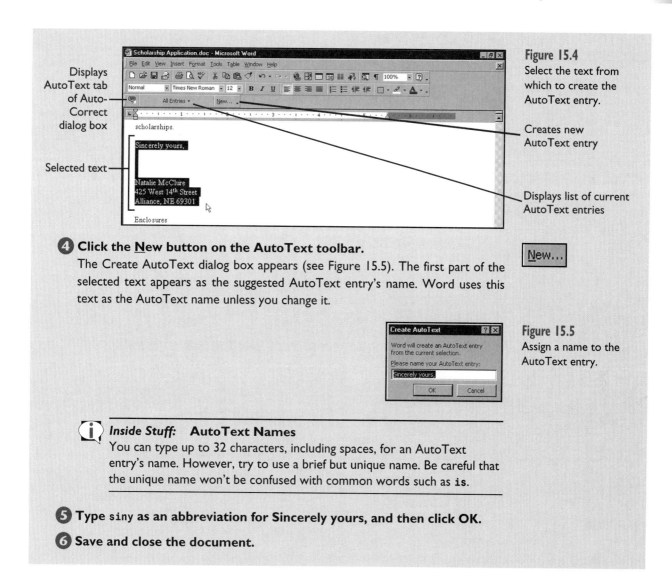

Displays AutoText tab of Auto-Correct dialog box

Selected text

Figure 15.4
Select the text from which to create the AutoText entry.

Creates new AutoText entry

Displays list of current AutoText entries

4 **Click the <u>N</u>ew button on the AutoText toolbar.**
The Create AutoText dialog box appears (see Figure 15.5). The first part of the selected text appears as the suggested AutoText entry's name. Word uses this text as the AutoText name unless you change it.

New...

Figure 15.5
Assign a name to the AutoText entry.

ⓘ *Inside Stuff:* **AutoText Names**
You can type up to 32 characters, including spaces, for an AutoText entry's name. However, try to use a brief but unique name. Be careful that the unique name won't be confused with common words such as **is**.

5 **Type siny as an abbreviation for Sincerely yours, and then click OK.**

6 **Save and close the document.**

 Exam Note: **Creating New Entries**
You can also create a new AutoText entry by choosing <u>I</u>nsert, <u>A</u>utoText, <u>N</u>ew or by pressing (Alt)+(F3) after selecting text.

Lesson 3: Inserting AutoText Entries

You can insert the AutoText entries into any new or existing document. In some cases, you see an AutoComplete ScreenTip to complete the entry, similar to the ScreenTips you saw in Lesson 1, for default AutoText entries. If the ScreenTip does not appear, you can press (F3) after typing the abbreviation.

You can also insert AutoText entries by clicking the All Entries button on the AutoText toolbar and then choosing the AutoText entry you want to insert.

All Entries ▾

In this lesson, you insert the AutoText entry you created in Lesson 2.

To Insert an AutoText Entry

1. **Click the New Blank Document button, if necessary, to start a new document.**

2. **Type siny.**
   You should see the AutoComplete ScreenTip that shows part of the AutoText entry.

3. **Press F3 to insert the AutoText entry.**
   Now let's try another way to insert an AutoText entry.

 All Entries ▾

4. **Press ↵Enter three times, and then click the All Entries button on the AutoText toolbar.**
   The AutoText entry you created is saved under the Normal category.

5. **Choose Normal from the list.**
   Figure 15.6 shows the All Entries menu with the **siny** entry stored in the Normal category.

Figure 15.6
Select an AutoText entry to insert.

Your entries stored in this category

AutoText entry created in Lesson 2

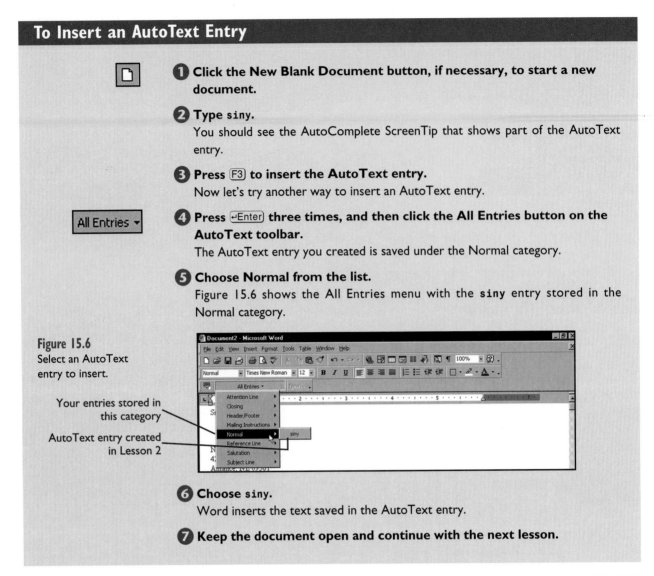

6. **Choose siny.**
   Word inserts the text saved in the AutoText entry.

7. **Keep the document open and continue with the next lesson.**

 Exam Note: **When You Don't Know AutoText Name**
You can display the AutoText section of the AutoCorrect dialog box and insert an AutoText entry from there. Simply click the AutoText button on the AutoText toolbar or choose Insert, AutoText, AutoText. Displaying the dialog box is necessary if you don't remember an AutoText entry name.

Lesson 4: Editing and Deleting AutoText Entries

After creating an AutoText entry, you might need to change its results. For example, you might need to correct an error, change the text, or format the text. In addition, you might decide to delete an AutoText entry that you no longer use.

In this lesson, you modify the **siny** AutoText entry. Later, you delete the entry.

To Edit an AutoText Entry

1 **In the open document, select the street address in the first signature block.**
Do not select the paragraph mark. To make sure you don't select the paragraph mark, click the Show/Hide ¶ button.

2 **Type 360 Pine Street to replace the original address.**

3 **Select the complimentary closing through the end of the ZIP Code for the first signature block.**
You need to have inserted the AutoText entry in a document and edit that text in order to change the AutoText entry.

4 **Click the AutoText button on the AutoText toolbar.**
The AutoCorrect dialog box appears with the AutoText options (see Figure 15.7).

Check this option for
AutoComplete feature

Select AutoText entry to edit

Click to add changes
to selected entry

Preview of selected
AutoText entry

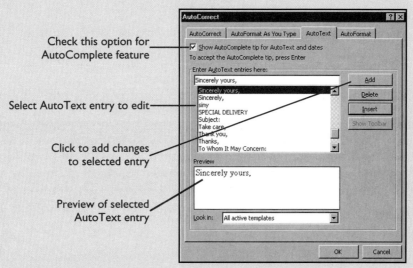

Figure 15.7
The AutoText tab
controls AutoText
entries.

5 **Scroll through the list of AutoText entries and click siny.**

6 **Click Add.**
You see a dialog box that asks `Do you want to redefine the AutoText entry?`

7 **Click Yes to redefine the entry and return to the document.**
The document text is still selected.

8 **Deselect the text and press ⏎Enter twice after the current text.**

9 **Type siny and press F3.**
Word inserts the AutoText entry with the new address.

10 **Close the document without saving it.**

Exam Note: **Deleting an AutoText Entry**

You can delete AutoText entries that you no longer use. Display the AutoText section of the AutoCorrect dialog box. Select the entry you want to delete, click <u>D</u>elete, and click OK to close the dialog box. You don't see a confirmation message to delete the entry; Word deletes it immediately when you click <u>D</u>elete.

If you type a deleted AutoText entry and press F3, you see the following message on the status bar: `The specified text is not a valid AutoText name. Use Insert AutoText to create AutoText entries.`

Ask your instructor if you should delete the AutoText entry **siny** on your computer system.

 # Lesson 5: Recording Macros

A *macro* is a small computer program you create to speed up repetitive tasks. Using a macro in Word is like tape-recording your favorite television show: you turn on the recorder, tape the show, and then play the show over and over.

The process of creating a macro is called *record macro*. When you record a macro, Word records a series of keystrokes and command selections. For example, you can record a macro that sets margins, vertical alignment, and horizontal alignment.

In this lesson, you record a macro that sets basic formats for a short business letter.

To Record a Macro

❶ In a new document window, choose <u>T</u>ools, <u>M</u>acro, <u>R</u>ecord New Macro.
The Record Macro dialog box appears (see Figure 15.8). You need to name the macro you're about to record. The macro name can consist of up to 80 characters, but no spaces.

Figure 15.8
Name the macro and set location in the Record Macro dialog box.

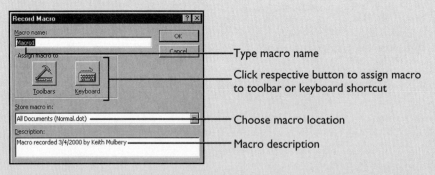

Type macro name

Click respective button to assign macro to toolbar or keyboard shortcut

Choose macro location

Macro description

 Inside Stuff: **Recording a Macro**

You can start recording a macro by double-clicking the gray REC indicator on the taskbar. When you double-click it, the Record Macro dialog box appears.

By default, the macro is saved to the Normal.dot template so that you can use it in all new documents. If you want, you can specify that the macro be stored with the current document only by clicking the <u>S</u>tore macro in drop-down arrow and choosing the name of your open document.

2 **Type** ShortLetter **in the Macro name box.**
You want to provide a short description in addition to your name and date.

3 **Click at the beginning of the Description box, type** Formats Short
Letters, **and then click OK.**
Word assigns the macro name you entered. You see a small Macro Record toolbar with two buttons. The REC indicator is bold on the status bar, indicating that
you are recording a macro (see Figure 15.9).

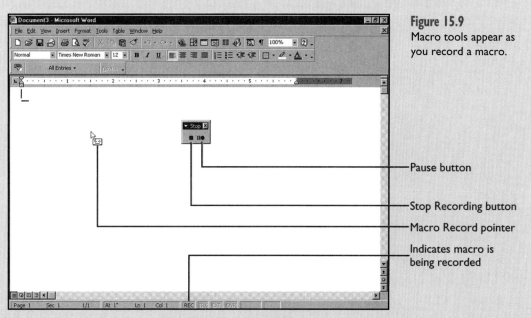

Figure 15.9
Macro tools appear as
you record a macro.

Pause button

Stop Recording button

Macro Record pointer

Indicates macro is
being recorded

4 **Choose File, Page Setup.**
You want to set bigger margins and vertically center the text.

5 **Click the Margins tab and set 2-inch left and right margins.**

6 **Click the Layout tab, click the Vertical alignment drop-down arrow,
choose Center, and click OK.**
Now, you want to be able to apply Justify horizontal alignment to an existing
document. To format existing text, you need to have the macro select the text
first.

7 **Press** Ctrl+A **to select everything in a document.**

8 **Click the Justify button on the Formatting toolbar.**
You are now ready to stop recording the macro.

9 **Click the Stop Recording button on the Macro toolbar.**
Clicking the Stop Recording button immediately stops recording your macro and
stores it for future use in whichever templates were indicated in the Record
Macro dialog box.

10 **Close the document without saving it.**

Exam Note: **Recording Unnecessary Actions**

Don't include unnecessary actions. Remember that Word records *everything* you do when you record a macro. For example, if you press `Ctrl`+`Home` to correct a mistake while recording the macro, Word records the command to move the insertion point to the beginning of the document. This can prove to be problematic if you run the macro in an existing document and the macro inserts or formats text in the wrong location.

 Inside Stuff: **Recording Formatted Text**

You can type text to include in a macro. If you want the macro text to contain character attributes such as bold or font color, you should turn on the attribute *before* typing that particular text, type the text, and then turn off that attribute. Word does not let you click and drag to select text in order to apply formatting.

If you already typed text and want to add an attribute, you can select the text by pressing `Shift` and an arrow key. Then, you can apply the attribute you want to the selected text.

 Exam Note: **Assigning a Macro to a Toolbar or Keyboard Shortcut**

You can have a macro appear as a toolbar button or you can assign a keyboard shortcut to run the macro. Click the appropriate button in the Record Macro dialog box.

When you click the <u>T</u>oolbar button, you see the Customize dialog box. At that point, you can click and drag your macro name to a toolbar.

When you click the <u>K</u>eyboard button, you see a dialog box to assign a keyboard shortcut. Be careful when assigning keyboard shortcuts. Most `Ctrl`-plus-letter and most `Ctrl`+`Shift`-plus-letter combinations are already reserved by Word.

 ## Lesson 6: Running Macros

The process of playing back or using a macro is called ***run macro***. When you run a macro, Word processes the series of commands and keystrokes saved in the macro. Running a macro is faster than manually choosing each command when you need to use a series of commands.

In this lesson, you open an existing letter and run the **ShortLetter** macro to format the letter.

 Inside Stuff: **Before Running Macros**

You should save a document before running a macro in it. If the macro produces undesirable results, you can close the document and open the saved version again.

To Run a Macro

 Open W-1502 and save it as Farnsworth Letter.

The letter contains the default 1.25-inch left and right margins, Top vertical alignment, and Left horizontal alignment. You want to run the macro to set margins and apply alignment settings.

Choose Tools, Macro, Macros.

(i) *Inside Stuff:* **Macros Keyboard Shortcut**
The keyboard shortcut for running macros is (Alt)+(F8).

The Macros dialog box appears (see Figure 15.10). You can select the macro file in the list or you can type the macro's name in the Macro name text box.

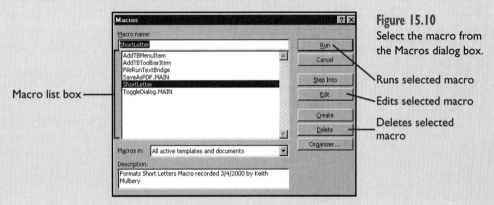

Figure 15.10
Select the macro from the Macros dialog box.

Runs selected macro

Edits selected macro

Deletes selected macro

Macro list box

2 **Choose** ShortLetter **and click** Run; **scroll down to see the letter, if needed.**
Word runs the macro and sets 2-inch left and right margins, selects Center vertical alignment, and selects Justify horizontal alignment (see Figure 15.11).

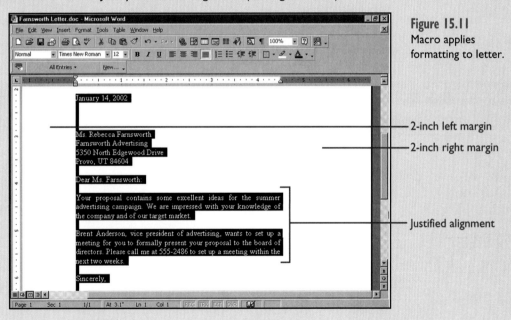

Figure 15.11
Macro applies formatting to letter.

2-inch left margin

2-inch right margin

Justified alignment

You can see that the text is vertically centered if you change the zoom to Whole Page or when you print the document.

continues ▶

To Run a Macro (continued)

 If You Have Problems...
The macro security level is too high if you receive a message stating that macros are disabled. A high security level protects you from running a macro that contains a virus. To disable this security so the macro can run, choose <u>T</u>ools, <u>M</u>acro, <u>S</u>ecurity. When the Security dialog box appears, select <u>L</u>ow and run the macro again. Be sure to reset the security to Medium or <u>H</u>igh after completing this project.

4 **Save and close the document.**

 Inside Stuff: **Formatting Text**
If your macro includes text, that text takes on the current document's formats when you run the macro. If you specially formatted the text while recording a macro, that special format is retained when you run the macro, regardless of the other document's formats.

 ## Lesson 7: Editing Macros

When you record a macro, the commands and text are recorded in a program called ***Microsoft Visual Basic***, an extremely powerful programming language for creating your own mini-applications within Word. If you need to edit a macro, you must open the Microsoft Visual Basic Editor. The macro contents appear as a series of comments.

In this lesson, you edit the **ShortLetter** macro you created in the last lesson.

To Edit a Macro

1 **Choose <u>T</u>ools, <u>M</u>acro, <u>M</u>acros.**

2 **Choose ShortLetter and click <u>E</u>dit.**
The Microsoft Visual Basic editor appears (see Figure 15.12).

Figure 15.12
Use Microsoft Visual Basic to edit the macro.

Macro name
Macro description
Programming language

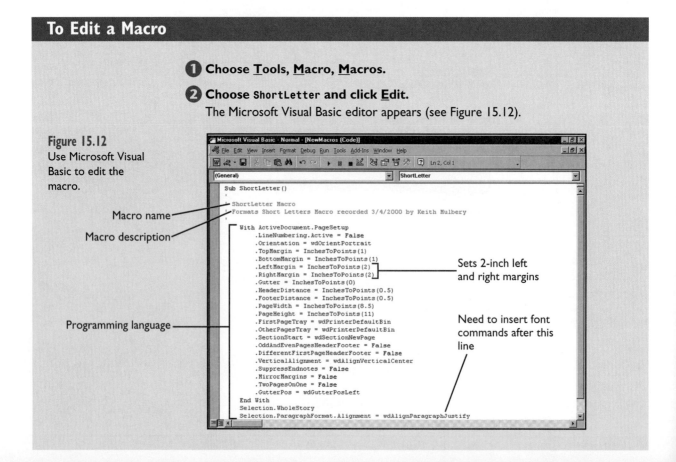

③ Click at the end of the second line from the bottom, after
`wdAlignParagraphJustify.`

You want to add command lines to apply Bookman Old Style font to selected text. The first command line indicates that you're working with font attributes.

④ Press ⏎Enter and type `With Selection.Font.`

The next line indicates the actual font name. If you don't have the font specified in the next step, ask your instructor what font name you should use.

⑤ Press ⏎Enter, press Tab⇆, and type `.Name = "Bookman Old Style".`

Make sure you have a space before and after =. Do *not* type the period after the closing quotation mark.

⑥ Press ⏎Enter.

⑦ Press ⬆Shift+Tab⇆ and type `End With.`

Pressing ⬆Shift+Tab⇆ outdents the next line. End With is the command that ends the set of commands such as changing font attributes. Figure 15.13 shows the edited macro.

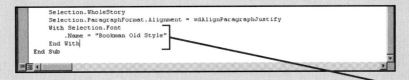

```
        Selection.WholeStory
        Selection.ParagraphFormat.Alignment = wdAlignParagraphJustify
        With Selection.Font
            .Name = "Bookman Old Style"
        End With
    End Sub
```

Figure 15.13
The macro contains new command lines.

Command lines to change font for selected text

⑧ Click the Save button; and then choose File, Close and Return to Microsoft Word.

 Exam Note: **Text Command Lines**

If you had typed text while recording a macro, you'd see text command lines such as the following:

`Selection.TypeText Text:="425 West Main Street"`

When you press ⏎Enter while recording a macro, the following command line is recorded:

`Selection.TypeParagraph`

You can insert these command lines within Microsoft Visual Basic if you need to. Be sure the text is surrounded in quotation marks.

Now, let's run the macro to make sure it applies Bookman Old Style font to a document.

To Run an Edited Macro

① Open `W-1502` **and save it as** `Farnsworth Letter 2.`

② Choose Tools, Macro, Macros.

③ Choose `ShortLetter` **and click Run.**

Figure 15.14 shows that the document is also formatted with Bookman Old Style after running the macro.

continues ▶

To Run an Edited Macro   (continued)

Figure 15.14
The document is
formatted with the
edited macro.

Selected text font

Bookman Old Style
applied to selected text

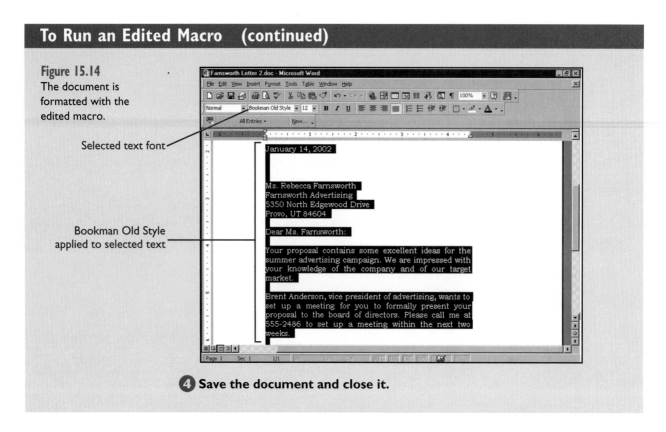

4 Save the document and close it.

It's helpful to have some knowledge of the Visual Basic programming language and how it works. When possible, you can make minor adjustments to improve the speed and efficiency of the macro. For example, you can remove unnecessary properties. Every time you choose a dialog box option for a macro, the macro recorder records all dialog box settings, even those you don't change. Figure 15.15 shows the **ShortLetter** macro after removing unnecessary command lines.

Figure 5.15
The macro is more
efficient after
removing unnecessary
lines.

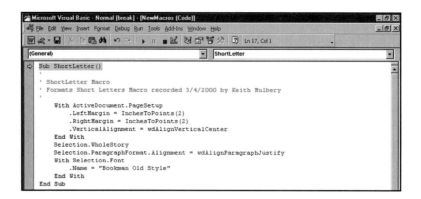

Expert Lesson 8: Copying, Renaming, and Deleting Macros

When you record macros, they are saved in the Normal.dot template, so you can use them with other documents. Within the template, macros are stored in a macro project called **NewMacros**, which is a collection of macros you've created. You can copy a macro project to another template or document. In addition, you can rename or delete macros.

In this lesson, you use the Organizer to copy a macro to a document.

To Copy a Macro

1 **Open W-1503 and save it as Green Tree.**

2 **Choose Tools, Macro, Macros.**
You need to display the Organizer to organize your macros.

3 **Click Organizer.**
The Organizer dialog box appears with the Macro Project Items tab selected (see Figure 15.16).

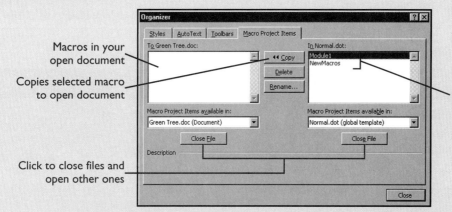

Macros in your open document

Copies selected macro to open document

Click to close files and open other ones

Figure 15.16
Use the Organizer to copy, delete, or re-name macros.

Macros in the Normal template

(i) *Inside Stuff:* **Closing and Opening Files**
Click Close to close the current file. The button changes to Open, so you can open a different file to use to copy macros.

---

4 **Make sure NewMacros is selected in the In Normal.dot list box.**

5 **Click Copy.**
The macro project is copied to the current document, which is **Green Tree.doc**. Let's now rename the macro.

6 **Click NewMacros in the Green Tree.doc list on the left side of the dialog box.**

7 **Click Rename.**
The Rename dialog box appears, so you can type in a new name for the macro.

8 **Type LetterMacro.**
Figure 15.17 shows the Rename dialog box with the new macro name.

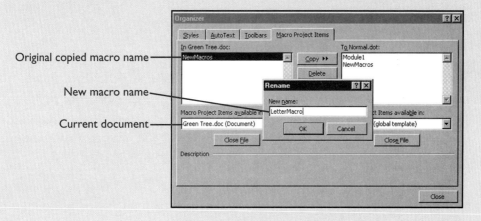

Original copied macro name

New macro name

Current document

Figure 15.17
Rename a macro through Organizer.

continues ▶

To Copy a Macro   (continued)

 Click OK to accept the new macro name; then click Close to close the dialog box.

 Save the document and close it.

✏️ *Exam Note:*   **Deleting a Macro**
You can delete a macro by choosing it and clicking <u>D</u>elete in the Macros dialog box. You can also select a macro within the Organizer and click <u>D</u>elete to delete it.

Summary

The AutoComplete feature helps you save typing time by displaying ScreenTips of AutoText entries; simply press ⏎**Enter** to insert the full text. You can also create your own AutoText entries and insert them into documents. In addition, you can edit an AutoText entry in a document window and save it again with the changes.

You learned how to create a simple formatting macro. You can perform simple edits in a macro. In addition, you can use Organizer to copy, rename, or delete a macro. By exploring the Help menus in Microsoft Visual Basic, you can learn more about its programming language.

Checking Concepts and Terms

True/False

For each of the following, check *T* or *F* to indicate whether the statement is true or false.

__T __F   **1.** AutoComplete displays ScreenTips for many AutoText entries. [L1]

__T __F   **2.** The first step to creating a new Auto-Text entry is displaying the AutoText tab of the AutoCorrect dialog box. [L2]

__T __F   **3.** When you type an AutoText entry, you can have it expand by pressing **F3**. [L3]

__T __F   **4.** When you record a new macro, it is stored in the Normal.dot template. [L5]

__T __F   **5.** When you edit a macro, the macro commands appear within a new Word document. [L7]

Multiple Choice

Circle the letter of the correct answer for each of the following.

1. What feature displays a ScreenTip to help you finish entering something? [L1]

  a. AutoComplete

  b. AutoText

  c. Template

  d. Macro

2. How do you edit an AutoText entry? [L4]

  a. Select the AutoText entry in the dialog box, click <u>E</u>dit, make your changes in the Preview window, and click OK.

  b. Delete the AutoText entry and start all over.

c. Insert the AutoText entry into a document window, edit the text in the document window, select it, and add it as an AutoText entry to replace the original one.

d. None of the above.

3. What term refers to the processing of playing back a macro? [L6]

a. record

b. run

c. apply

d. select

4. Which macro command inserts a hard return? [L7]

a. Selection.Enter

b. HardReturn.Enter

c. Selection.TypeParagraph

d. Selection.HardReturn

5. Which task is *not* available in the Organizer? [L8]

a. copy a macro

b. delete a macro

c. rename a macro

d. record a macro

Screen ID

Label each element of the Word screen shown in Figure 15.18.

Figure 15.18

A. AutoText button

B. Create AutoText button

C. Macro Record pointer

D. Record Macro Toggle

E. Stop Recording button

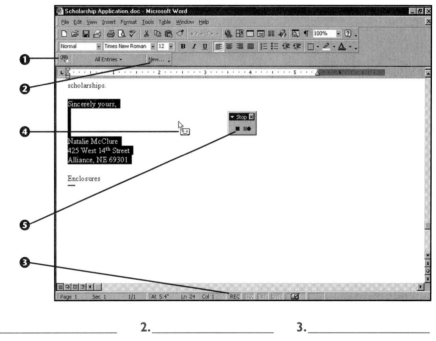

1._____   2._____   3._____

4._____   5._____

Skill Drill

Skill Drill exercises reinforce project skills. Each skill reinforced is the same, or nearly the same, as a skill presented in the project. Each exercise includes a brief narrative introduction, followed by detailed instructions in a step-by-step format.

1. Creating, Inserting, and Editing an AutoText Entry

One of your co-workers created a logo with the company name and address. You want to create an AutoText entry from it to use over and over. After inserting the AutoText entry, you decide to edit it to include some color.

1. Open **W-1504**; if the AutoText toolbar is not visible, choose <u>V</u>iew, <u>T</u>oolbars, AutoText.

2. Press Ctrl+A to select the entire document, which includes an image, the company name, address, phone number, and paragraph mark.

3. Click the <u>N</u>ew button on the AutoText toolbar, type **cta**, and click OK.

4. Close the document without saving it.

5. Open **W-1505** and save it as **Jordan Letter**.

6. With the insertion point at the top of the document, type **cta** and press F3 to insert the AutoText entry.

7. Save, print, and close the document.

8. In a new document, type **cta** and press F3 to insert the AutoText entry.

9. Press Ctrl+A to select the entire document.

10. Click the Font Color drop-down arrow and choose Dark Blue.

11. Click the AutoText button on the AutoText toolbar.

12. Select **cta** in the list of AutoText entries, click <u>A</u>dd, and click <u>Y</u>es to replace the entry.

13. Close the document without saving it.

14. Open **W-1506** and save it as **Rheta Letter**.

15. Click the All Entries button on the AutoText toolbar.

16. Choose Normal and then choose **cta**.

17. Save, print, and close the document.

2. Recording and Running a Macro

You frequently have identically structured tables that contain names and other data. Because the tables have the same construction, you want to create a macro that sorts the table in alphabetical order by last name.

1. Open **W-1507** and save it as **Table 1**.

2. Position the insertion point in the first column.

3. Choose <u>T</u>ools, <u>M</u>acro, <u>R</u>ecord New Macro.

4. Type **SortTable** in the <u>M</u>acro name box and click OK.

5. Choose T<u>a</u>ble, <u>S</u>ort.

6. Click the Sort by drop-down arrow and choose LastName.

7. Click the Then by drop-down arrow and choose FirstName; then click OK.

8. Click the Stop Recording button on the Macro toolbar.

9. Save, print, and close the document.

10. Open **W-1508** and save it as **Table 2**.

11. Choose <u>T</u>ools, <u>M</u>acro, <u>M</u>acros.

12. Choose SortTable and click <u>R</u>un.

13. Save, print, and close the document.

3. Editing and Running a Macro

You want to edit the **SortTable** macro by having it sort by company, then by last name, and finally by first name. After editing the macro, you'll run it again.

1. Choose <u>T</u>ools, <u>M</u>acro, <u>M</u>acros.

2. Choose **SortTable** and click <u>E</u>dit.

3. Delete 2 and type **3** in **FieldNumber:="Column 2"**.

4. Select and delete Column 1 in the command line **FieldNumber2 _ :="Column 1"**. There should be no space between the opening and closing quotation marks.

5. Click the Save button.

6. Choose <u>F</u>ile, <u>C</u>lose and Return to Microsoft Word.

7. Open **W-1508** and save it as **Table 3**.

8. Choose <u>T</u>ools, <u>M</u>acro, <u>M</u>acros.

9. Choose **SortTable** and click <u>R</u>un.

10. Save, print, and close the document.

Challenge

Challenge exercises expand on or are somewhat related to skills presented in the lessons. Each exercise provides a brief narrative introduction followed by instructions in a numbered-step or bulleted-list format that are not as detailed as those in the Skill Drill section.

1. Creating a Letterhead AutoText Entry

You want to create a letterhead AutoText entry that you can use for letters, memos, and advertisements.

1. In a new document window, select the Justify horizontal alignment and type **Computer Training Concepts, Inc.** in 28-point Times New Roman.

2. Select 12-point Times New Roman and type **6262 Technology Boulevard**.

3. Insert the computer symbol 🖥 from the Wingdings font in the Symbols dialog box. It is the second symbol from the right on the first row.

4. Type **Nashua, NH 03063**, insert the computer symbol, and then type **(603) 555-6262**.

5. Insert a space before and after each computer symbol.

6. Insert a hard return after the second line and choose Left horizontal alignment.

7. Select the two centered lines of text; set a box border setting with the eleventh border style. Apply a 10% style pattern.

8. Select the entire document and create an AutoText entry called **ctci**. Then, close the document without saving it.

9. In a new document window, type **Please call me if you have any questions, or if I can be of further assistance.** Then, create an AutoText entry from it. Select only the sentence and period; do *not* select the paragraph mark. Name the entry **plezcall**. Then, close the document without saving it.

10. Open **W-1509** and save it as **Response to Request**.

11. Insert the **ctci** AutoText entry at the top of the document.

12. Insert the **plezcall** AutoText entry at the end of the last paragraph.

13. Change **Your Name** to your name; save, print, and close the document.

14. Edit the **ctci** AutoText entry by adding Blue font color to the text and a Light Blue shading with a Clear style pattern.

15. Open **W-1510** and save it as **Letter to Terry**.

16. Insert the **ctci** AutoText at the top of the document.

17. Delete + and start typing today's date. Use AutoComplete to help you finish the date.

18. Delete ++ in the signature block, type **Your**, and accept the AutoComplete ScreenTip.

19. Save, print, and close the document.

2. Recording and Running a Macro that Creates a Table

Your company recently changed its name to sound more exciting. You are responsible for creating a macro that finds the old company name and replaces it with the new company name.

1. In a new window, create a macro named **ReplaceName**. Give it an appropriate description based on the situation.

2. Activate the Replace command.

3. Find occurrences of **Computer Training Concepts, Inc.** (with no special format-ting) and replace them with **Millennium Training**. Choose the options to format the replacements in Blue font color.

4. Use the Replace <u>A</u>ll command, click OK, and click Close.

5. Stop recording the macro.

6. Open **W-1511** and save it as **Company Proposal**.

7. Run the **ReplaceName** macro.

8. Save, print, and close the document.

3. Editing a Macro

You want to edit the macro to specify **Millennium Training Group** as the replacement text in Arial Rounded MT Bold.

1. Edit the macro **ReplaceName**.

2. Add **Group** to the command line that inserts the text **Millennium Training**. The new name should be **Millennium Training Group**. Watch the location of the text in relation to the quotation marks.

3. Add a command line to set a font replacement. Use these specifications:

   a. The new command should be *above* the replacement font color command.

   b. The first part of the command should be the same.

   c. The syntax for font face is **Name**.

   d. Use the same format for the equals sign and space before and after the equals sign.

   e. Type the font name **Arial Rounded MT Bold** in quotation marks.

4. Save and close the macro.

5. Open **W-1512** and save it as **Letter to Kara**.

6. At the beginning of the document, run the edited macro.

7. Save the document and print it.

Discovery Zone

Discovery Zone exercises help you gain advanced knowledge of project topics and/or appli-cation of skills. These exercises focus on enhancing your problem-solving skills. Numbered steps are not provided, but you are given hints, reminders, screen shots, and/or references to help you reach your goal for each exercise.

1. Creating a Table AutoText Entry

You work for a local bookstore named Open Book Store. You send semi-personal letters out to special customers to let them know about books on sale that are of particular interest to each of them. You want to create an AutoText entry that creates a table that creates the table structure and sets table formats, so you can insert the table without creating it from scratch each time.

Create the table shown in Figure 15.19. Apply the formats and shading shown in the figure. Look at the figure carefully; not all formats are spelled-out in the callouts. Center the table it-self between the margins and choose <u>N</u>one text wrapping. Apply Lavender shading color and Violet text color for the first row. Select the second and third columns and choose Center horizontal alignment. Save the AutoText entry as **tob**.

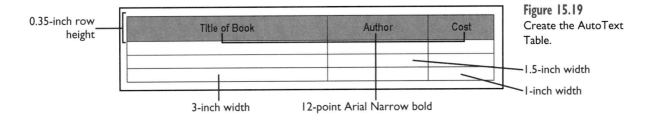

0.35-inch row height

	Title of Book	Author	Cost

Figure 15.19
Create the AutoText Table.

1.5-inch width
1-inch width

3-inch width   12-point Arial Narrow bold

Open **W-1513** and save it as **Hoge Letter**. Insert the AutoText table between the second and third paragraphs, and then enter the following data:

Exquisite Gardens	McDougal	$15.99
I'll Promise You a Rose Garden	Vanderbelt	$24.99
Know Your Flowers and Their Needs	Patterson	$19.95

Save, print, and close the document.

2. Editing the Sort Macro and Using the Organizer

You want to create a macro to sort a table, similar to the one you recorded in the Skill Drill section. Open **W-1507** and save it as **Table 4**. Record a macro named **SortClientTables** that sorts the table by last name and then by first name. Also record steps to save the document after sorting the table. Then, stop recording the macro. Save **Table 4** again and print it.

Open **W-1508** and save it as **Table 5**. Run the macro and print the document. The macro should save the document under the same filename. Then, close the document.

You want to edit the macro to first sort by company, then by last name, and finally by first name. You also want the macro to print the document after saving it and then close it. *Hint:* To know the Visual Basic command for printing a document, you might want to create a practice macro that prints a document and then edit it to view the command line, so you know what to insert in your SortClientTables macro. Edit your macro to reflect these additions. Then, close the Visual Basic editor. Be prepared to show your macro commands to your instructor.

Open **W-1514** and save it as **Table 6**. Run the macro, which should sort the table and save the document under the same filename and then print it.

Use the Organizer to copy the macro from the Normal.dot template to Table 6.doc. You'll need to open that file within the Organizer. After copying the macro to Table 6.doc, rename it as **EssentialsMacros** and save the document when prompted.

Completion Activities

After completing this project, ask your instructor if you should delete all AutoText entries and macros from the Normal.dot template. If you completed the activities on your home computer, you might want to delete them as well.

PinPoint Assessment

You have completed this project and its associated lessons, and have had an opportunity to assess your skills through the end-of-project questions and exercises. Now use the PinPoint software Evaluation Mode to further assess your comprehension of the specific exam activities you have just learned. You can also use the PinPoint Trainer Mode and the Show Me tutorials to practice these exam activities.

Using Mail Merge

Key terms introduced in this project include

- catalog main document
- data source
- fields
- filter
- form file
- main document
- mail merge
- merge field
- query
- record

Objectives	Required Activity for MOUS	Exam Level
➤ Create a Data Source	Create data source	Expert
➤ Sort Records in a Data Source	Sort records to be merged	Expert
➤ Create a Main Document	Create main document	Expert
➤ Merge the Main Document and Data Source	Merge main document and data source	Expert
➤ Create Mailing Labels to Merge with the Data Source	Generate labels	Expert
➤ Merge a Document Using an Access Database Table	Merge a document using alternate data sources	Expert
➤ Filter Records for a Merge		
➤ Create a Catalog Main Document		

Why Would I Do This?

 hen you want to send the same message to a number of people, you can use Word's Mail Merge feature. You need to create two types of files in order to use Mail Merge: a main document and a data source. A **main document** (also known as a **form file**) contains the information that stays the same for all recipients. A **data source** contains a record of information for each recipient. The process of bringing the main document and data source together is called a **mail merge**. Using Mail Merge saves you from having to retype the same document for each recipient.

In this project, you create a mail merge to send letters to people who registered for your Technology Training Conference.

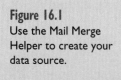 ## Lesson 1: Creating a Data Source

A data source contains **fields** or individual components of data. Common fields in a data source include first name, last name, address, city, state, and ZIP Code. You can also include fields for phone numbers and email addresses. A group of fields for a particular person or thing is called a **record**.

In this lesson, you first identify an existing letter you want to use as a main document and then you create the data source containing the records for the registered participants at the conference.

To Create a Data Source

1 **Open W-1601 and save it as Conference Form Letter.**
This is the letter that you want to send to all people who registered for the conference.

2 **Choose Tools, Mail Merge.**
The Mail Merge Helper dialog box appears (see Figure 16.1). It provides the three major steps for performing a mail merge.

Figure 16.1
Use the Mail Merge Helper to create your data source.

Click to start main document

Grayed-out until you choose a main document

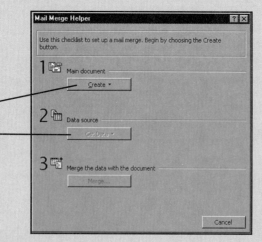

You must click Create and choose the type of main document you want to create from the list. Form Letters is the option used to create a main document so that Word creates a new page for every record in the data source during the merge. Although you won't complete the form letter at this time, you must select a main document in order for the Get Data option to be available.

3 Click Create and then choose Form Letters.

You see the following message: `To create the form letters, you can use the active document window Conference Form Letter.DOC or a new document window.`

4 Click Active Window to use the letter you opened.

The Mail Merge Helper dialog box now contains Edit to edit the main document. It also displays the merge type and main document file you selected. Notice that Get Data is now available.

5 Click Get Data and choose Create Data Source from the drop-down menu.

Figure 16.2 shows the Create Data Source dialog box, which contains a list of predefined field names. You can add additional field names, such as `Birthdate`, or remove fields you don't plan to use.

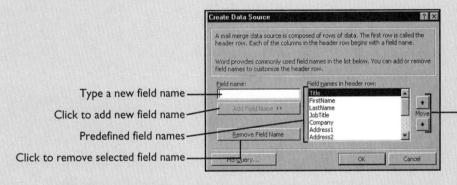

Type a new field name

Click to add new field name

Predefined field names

Click to remove selected field name

Figure 16.2
Specify the field names in the Create Data Source dialog box.

Click to move field names within list

✍ *Exam Note:*   **Adding a New Field**

To add a new field name, type it in the Field name box. Field names cannot contain spaces; however, you can make the field name look like two words by pressing ⟨Shift⟩+⟨-⟩ to create an underline between words. After typing the field name, click Add Field Name.

Let's remove the field names that you won't use.

6 Click Address2 and click Remove Field Name.

You also need to remove the Country, HomePhone, and WorkPhone fields. All of your participants work in the United States and you don't have their phone numbers at this time.

7 Scroll through the list, click Country, and click Remove Field Name.

8 Remove both the HomePhone and WorkPhone fields.

9 Click OK.

The Save As dialog box appears, so you can save the field names in a data source document.

10 Type `Conference Participants` in the File name box and then click Save.

Word saves the data source file and displays a message, indicating that you can add records to the data source or insert *merge fields* into the main document (see Figure 16.3).

continues ▶

To Create a Data Source (continued)

Figure 16.3
Indicate whether you want to work the data source or main document now.

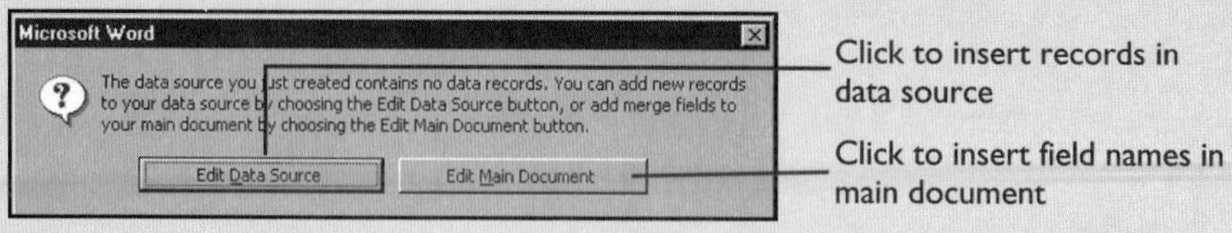

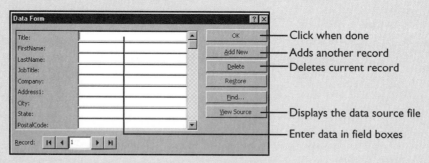

Click to insert records in data source

Click to insert field names in main document

11 **Keep the dialog box onscreen to continue with the next exercise.**

After selecting the field names and saving the data source, you are ready to enter records into the data source. In the next exercise, you enter data for five conference participants.

To Enter Data in a Data Source

1 **Click Edit Data Source.**
The Data Form dialog box appears, so you can enter the name and address for the first person (see Figure 16.4).

Figure 16.4
Enter the data in the Data Form dialog box.

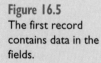

Click when done
Adds another record
Deletes current record

Displays the data source file

Enter data in field boxes

2 **Type Ms. in the Title box and press Tab.**
You can quickly enter data by pressing Tab to get from one field to the next.

3 **Enter the rest of the fields for the first record:**

Jeana
MacLaren
Benefits Coordinator
EcoSystems, Inc.
1603 South State
Orem
UT
84057

Figure 16.5 shows the Data Form dialog box after you enter Jeana's information.

Figure 16.5
The first record contains data in the fields.

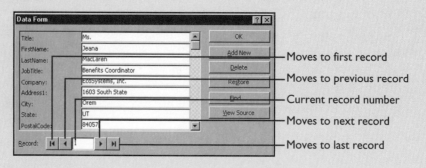

Moves to first record
Moves to previous record
Current record number
Moves to next record
Moves to last record

If You Have Problems...
If you need to correct mistakes, click in the text box that contains the mistake. You can also press ⟨⬆Shift⟩+⟨Tab⬌⟩ to move up a field within the record.

4 **Press ⟨⏎Enter⟩.**
Pressing ⟨⏎Enter⟩ in the last field starts a new record.

5 **Using the preceding steps, enter the following records in the Data Form dialog box, making sure you enter the correct data into each field. Do *not* type the comma after the city.**

```
Ms. Virginia Brewer
Office Manager
Downing and Associates
4400 Central Avenue N
Chicago, IL 60625
```

```
Ms. Marilyn Goldstein
Corporate Trainer
The Millennium Group
708 West Gibson
Indianapolis, IN 46230
```

```
Mr. Drew Pryzbyla
Executive Assistant
Matheson Group
12700 Michigan Avenue
Dearborn, MI 48126
```

```
Mr. Antonio Caldera
Customer Service Director
Metropolitan Products
700 Main Street
Evansville, IN 47708
```

 If You Have Problems...
You will have spacing problems if you press ⟨Spacebar⟩ after the last word in each field. Also, do *not* type the commas after the city names.

6 **Leave the Data Form dialog box onscreen to continue with the next lesson.**

Lesson 2: Sorting Records in a Data Source

Before merging the data source with the main document, you might want to rearrange the records in the data source. For example, you might want to sort the data source in alphabetical order by last name or in descending order by sales, if included. If you have a large number of form letters to mail, you can receive a special discount at the Post Office if you follow certain procedures. One procedure is to sort the letters by ZIP Code. You can save a lot of work hours if you sort the data source *before* merging instead of after merging and printing.

In this lesson, you view the data source and sort it by ZIP Code.

To Sort the Data Source Records

❶ In the open Data Form dialog box, click <u>V</u>iew Source.
The data source document appears in the form of a table (see Figure 16.6). The first row contains the field names. Each row is a record of data for a particular person and each column contains the fields of data.

Figure 16.6
The data source is arranged in a table.

Database toolbar —
Field names —
City field —
Drew's record —

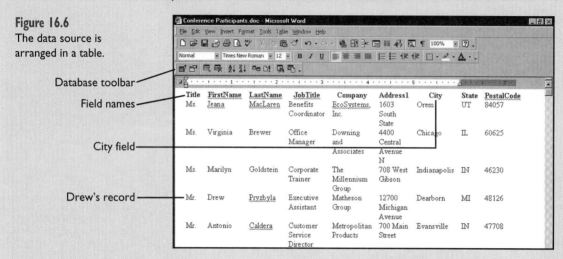

Don't worry about how text wraps inside the table cells; the word-wrapping does not affect how the data appears when you perform the merge.

❷ Click in PostalCode in the last column.
To sort a data source, you need to position the insertion point within the field by which you want to sort.

❸ Click the Ascending button on the Database toolbar.
Figure 16.7 shows the records are now sorted by ZIP Code. The lowest ZIP Code, which is **46230**, appears first.

Figure 16.7
The records are sorted by ZIP Code.

Sort Ascending button —
Sort Descending button —
Lowest ZIP Code —
Highest ZIP Code —

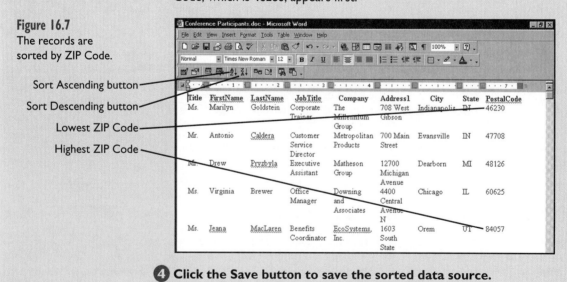

❹ Click the Save button to save the sorted data source.

Inside Stuff: Adding New Records
If you want to add new records, you can click the Data Form button or the Add New Record button, depending on whether you want to enter the data into the dialog box or as a row at the bottom of the table. After adding new records, you need to sort the data source again.

⑤ Keep Conference Participants onscreen to continue with the next lesson.

 Exam Note: Multiple Sort Levels
If you need to sort a data source into three levels (such as by city, then by last name, and then by first name), choose T̲able, S̲ort. The Sort dialog box lets you specify up to three levels for sorting a document. Choose the hierarchy of the sort by selecting the field names in the order that you want to sort the records.

The Database toolbar contains several useful buttons for working with the data source. For example, you can go back to the Data Source dialog box, add a new record, or sort the records. Table 16.1 describes these buttons. If you don't see the Database toolbar, choose View, T̲oolbar, Database.

Table 16.1   Icons and Buttons on the Microsoft Word Screen

Icon	Element	Description
	Data Form	Displays the Data Form dialog box again.
	Manage Fields	Displays the Manage Fields dialog box so you can add, delete, or rename field names.
	Add New Record	Adds a row at the bottom of the table, so you can enter data for a new record.
	Delete Record	Deletes the record that contains the insertion point.
	Sort Ascending	Sorts records in ascending order by the field that contains the insertion point.
	Sort Descending	Sorts records in descending order by the field that contains the insertion point.
	Insert Database	Inserts data from a database or other source into the table structure.
	Update Field	Updates the data in the current field.
	Find Record	Displays the Find in Field dialog box so you can search through a particular field to find records containing certain data.
	Mail Merge Main Document	Displays the mail merge main document that is associated with the data source.

Inside Stuff: **Opening the Data Source**

If you elect not to view the data source from the Data Form dialog box, you can display the data source at any time by opening it as a regular file.

  # Lesson 3: Creating a Main Document

You are now ready to insert the fields within your main document. When inserting fields, you need to press Spacebar and ↵Enter as needed to place the fields exactly where you want the data to be inserted during the merge.

In this lesson, you insert a date field and then create the inside address and salutation using the fields from your data source.

To Create the Main Document

1 **In the open Conference Participants document, click the Mail Merge Main Document button.**

This action switches to the main document file. The Mail Merge toolbar appears, so you can insert field names and perform the merge.

Inside Stuff: **Displaying the Main Document**

If you had *not* clicked View Source in the Data Form dialog box, you would have clicked OK. At that point, you see the main document.

---

2 **Type August 15, 2002 and press ↵Enter four times.**

You are ready to insert the fields to form the inside address. As you insert fields, you press Spacebar and ↵Enter as you would if you were typing regular text in an inside address.

3 **Click the Insert Merge Field button.**

Figure 16.8 shows a list of fields used in the data source.

Figure 16.8
Insert the fields in your main document.

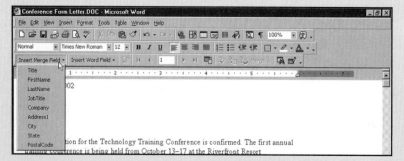

4 **Click Title and press Spacebar.**

Word inserts the Title field, and you pressed Spacebar to leave a space between it and the next field.

5 **Click the Insert Merge Field button, choose FirstName, and press Spacebar.**

6 **Click the Insert Merge Field button, choose LastName, and press ↵Enter.**

The next three fields need to be inserted on separate lines, so you'll press ↵Enter after inserting each field.

7 **Insert the JobTitle, Company, and Address fields on the next three lines.**

8 **Insert City, type a comma, press** Spacebar**, insert State, press** Spacebar**, and insert PostalCode.**

The inside address is complete; now you need to create the salutation.

9 **Press** ↵Enter **twice, type** Dear **and then press** Spacebar**.**

10 **Insert the Title field, press** Spacebar**, insert the LastName field, and then type a colon.**

Figure 16.9 shows what your main document looks like after inserting the fields. Double-check that the inside address and salutation match the figure.

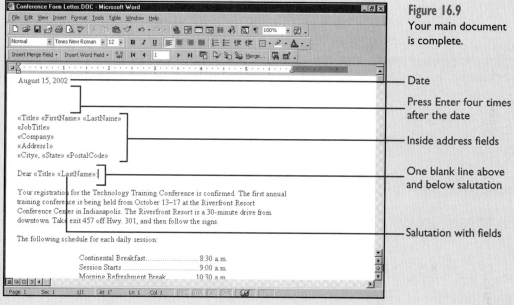

Figure 16.9
Your main document is complete.

— Date

Press Enter four times after the date

— Inside address fields

One blank line above and below salutation

— Salutation with fields

11 **Save the document and keep it onscreen to continue with the next lesson.**

 Inside Stuff: **Viewing the Merged Data Without Actually Merging**
You can see how the merged data looks when integrated into the main document. Click the View Merged Data button on the Mail Merge toolbar. The field codes are replaced with the merged data. You can then click the First Record, Previous Record, Next Record, and Last Record buttons to quickly view the other records. When you are done viewing the merged data, click the View Merged Data button again to display the field codes.

 Exam Note: **Displaying the Data Source**
You can quickly display the data source by clicking the Edit Data Source button on the Mail Merge toolbar. The Data Form dialog box appears, so you can edit the records or view the data source itself.

 Inside Stuff: **Inserting Data During a Merge**
You can click the Insert Word Field button and choose Fill-in to insert a fill-in field. This type of field is appropriate when you want to input text while the merge is being performed. Refer to Help for more information on this field and other Word fields.

 # Lesson 4: Merging the Main Document and the Data Source

After you create the data source and main document, you are ready to merge them together. When you merge these documents, Word matches the merge field codes in the main document with those in the data source. When a match is found, Word pulls the information from the data source and inserts it into the main document, replacing the merge fields. Word creates a new copy of the main document for each record in the data source.

In this lesson, you merge your data source with the main document.

To Merge the Documents

Merge...

1 **In the open** `Conference Form Letter` **document, click the Merge button.**
Word displays the Merge dialog box (see Figure 16.10). The default settings merge the data into a new document window. All data in the data source is used to perform the merge.

Figure 16.10
The Merge dialog box lets you specify how to perform the merge.

Click to perform the merge

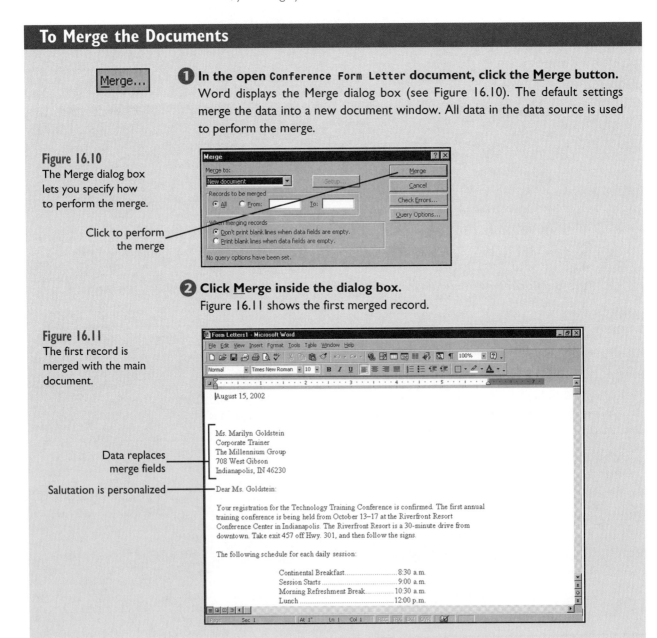

2 **Click Merge inside the dialog box.**
Figure 16.11 shows the first merged record.

Figure 16.11
The first record is merged with the main document.

Data replaces merge fields

Salutation is personalized

3 Save the merged document as `Conference Confirmation Letters`.

 If You Have Problems...

If you notice spacing errors, look for a trend. If you notice no space after the comma between the city and state in every merged letter, you need to insert a space in that location in the main document and merge again. If you notice irregular spacing errors on some but not all merged letters, then you have spacing problems in your data source. You should correct errors in either document and perform the merge again.

4 Print the merged letters and then close that document.

The main document and data source should still be open.

5 Close both documents.

The Mail Merge toolbar contains several buttons for merging documents. Table 16.2 describes these buttons.

Table 16.2 Icons and Buttons on the Microsoft Word Screen

Icon	Element	Description
	Mail Merge Helper	Displays the Mail Merge Helper dialog box, so you can choose the main document or data source, or perform the merge.
	Merge to New Document	Merges the main document and data source immediately into a new document.
	Merge to Printer	Merges and prints the documents without displaying the merged documents on screen.
	Start Mail Merge	Displays the Merge dialog box, so you can specify how the documents merge.

Lesson 5: Creating Mailing Labels to Merge with the Data Source

When you create merged letters, you obviously need to insert them into envelopes. You can either create an envelope or label main document to merge with the data source. Doing so helps you prepare the envelopes.

(i) *Inside Stuff:*   **Merging to Envelopes or Labels**

If you merge to envelopes, you will probably have to individually feed the envelopes into the printer if your printer does not have an envelope tray. This can be time-consuming!

However, merging to labels saves you time because fewer label sheets are printed. You can quickly remove the labels from the label sheet and attach them to envelopes.

In this lesson, you create a label main document to correspond with the letters you just merged and printed.

To Create a Label Main Document

1 In a new document window, choose Tools, Mail Merge.
The Mail Merge Helper dialog box appears.

2 Click Create and choose Mailing Labels.

3 Click Active Window when prompted.
Now, you need to get the data source. The major advantage of having a data source is that you can use it as many times as you want. It is not restricted to a single main document.

4 Click Get Data and choose Open Data Source.
You need to select the data source you created in Lesson 1.

5 Choose Conference Participants and click Open.
Figure 16.12 shows a message that you are ready to set up the main document.

Figure 16.12
Acknowledge the message about setting up your main document.

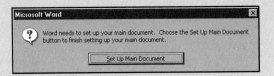

6 Click Set Up Main Document.
The Label Options dialog box appears, so you can select the label type to use as your main document (see Figure 16.13).

Figure 16.13
Choose the label you want for your main document.

Avery is the most common product

Choose the label product number

7 Make sure Avery standard is the selected Label products option.

8 Scroll through the Products number list box, choose 5160 – Address, and then click OK.
The Create Labels dialog box appears (see Figure 16.14). This is where you insert the field names to create the format for the way the addresses will appear on the labels.

Figure 16.14
Insert the field names to create the labels.

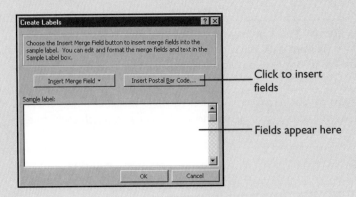

Click to insert fields

Fields appear here

9 **Click the Insert Merge Field drop-down arrow and insert the fields, spaces, and comma as shown in Figure 16.15.**

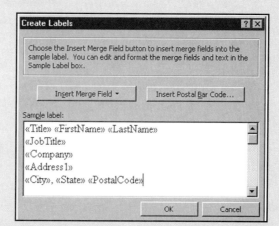

Figure 16.15
Create the label format.

10 **Click OK and keep the Mail Merge Helper dialog box onscreen to continue with the next exercise.**

After creating the format for the label main document, you are ready to perform the merge. When you merge the label with the data source, Word creates two documents: a sheet of labels with the field codes and a sheet of labels with the records inserted.

To Merge the Labels

1 **Click Merge in the Mail Merge Helper dialog box.**

2 **Click Merge in the Merge dialog box.**
Word merges the two documents and displays the resulting merged labels onscreen (see Figure 16.16).

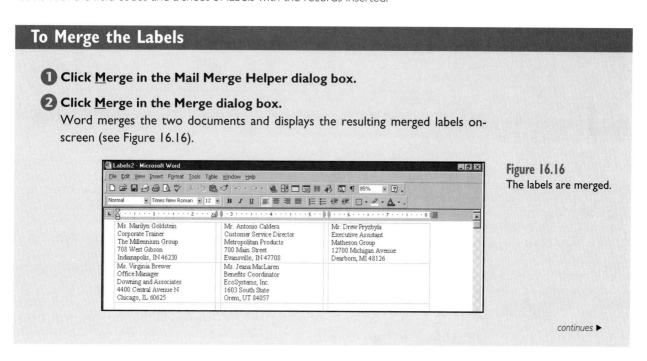

Figure 16.16
The labels are merged.

continues ▶

To Merge the Labels (continued)

 Inside Stuff: Showing Gridlines
If the gridlines don't appear showing you each label, you can display them by choosing Table, Show Gridlines. The gridlines are for visual purposes only to identify each label; the gridlines don't print.

❸ Save the document as Conference Mailing Labels, print it, and close it.
Figure 16.17 shows the label main document. Notice that it appears as a full sheet of labels with the merge fields.

Figure 16.17
The label main document contains merge fields.

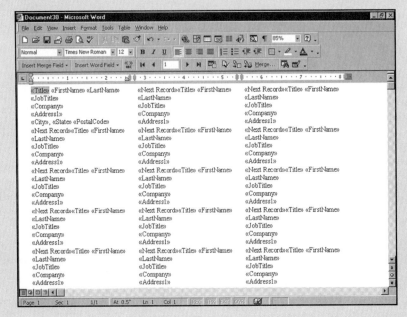

❹ Save the document as Conference Label Form File, print it, and close it.

 Inside Stuff: Generating Envelopes
You can generate envelopes to merge if you prefer envelopes more than labels. To generate envelopes, choose Envelopes instead of Mailing Labels when you click Create in the Mail Merge Helper dialog box. Similar to choosing a label format, you choose an envelope format and then insert the merge fields into the envelope window.

 ## Lesson 6: Merging a Document Using an Access Database Table

Often, employees must rely on data provided by others in their organization. You might have an occasion where you need to prepare a mail merge, but you don't have the data saved in a Word data source. Another employee has the data, but it was created in another program.

Word lets you use other document types, such as Access, Excel, and Outlook, as your data source. Without this ability, you'd have to retype all that data into Word.

In this lesson, you use an Access database table as your data source.

To Select an Access Table as a Data Source

1 **Open** W-1601 **and save it as** Additional Form Letter.
You need to set up this document again as a main document.

2 **Choose Tools, Mail Merge.**

3 **Click Create and choose Form Letters; then click Active Window when prompted.**
Now, you're ready to find the Access database and use it as your data source.

4 **Click Get Data and choose Open Data Source.**
Access database files contain an mdb extension; therefore, you need to change the file type to locate that file.

5 **Click the Files of type drop-down arrow and choose MS Access Databases (*.mdb;*.mde).**
All Access databases should appear in the dialog box.

6 **Select** W-1602.mdb **and click Open.**
The Microsoft Access dialog box appears (see Figure 16.18). This dialog box appears in case the database contains multiple tables of data. You need to choose the table you want as the data source.

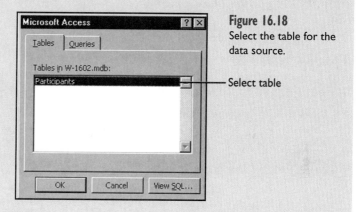

Figure 16.18
Select the table for the data source.

Select table

7 **Click OK, and then click Edit Main Document.**

8 **Type** August 15, 2002 **and press** ↵Enter **four times.**
You are ready to insert the merge fields to create the inside address and salutation.

continues ▶

To Select an Access Table as a Data Source   (continued)

Figure 16.19
Create the main
document based on
the Access table's field
names.

⑨

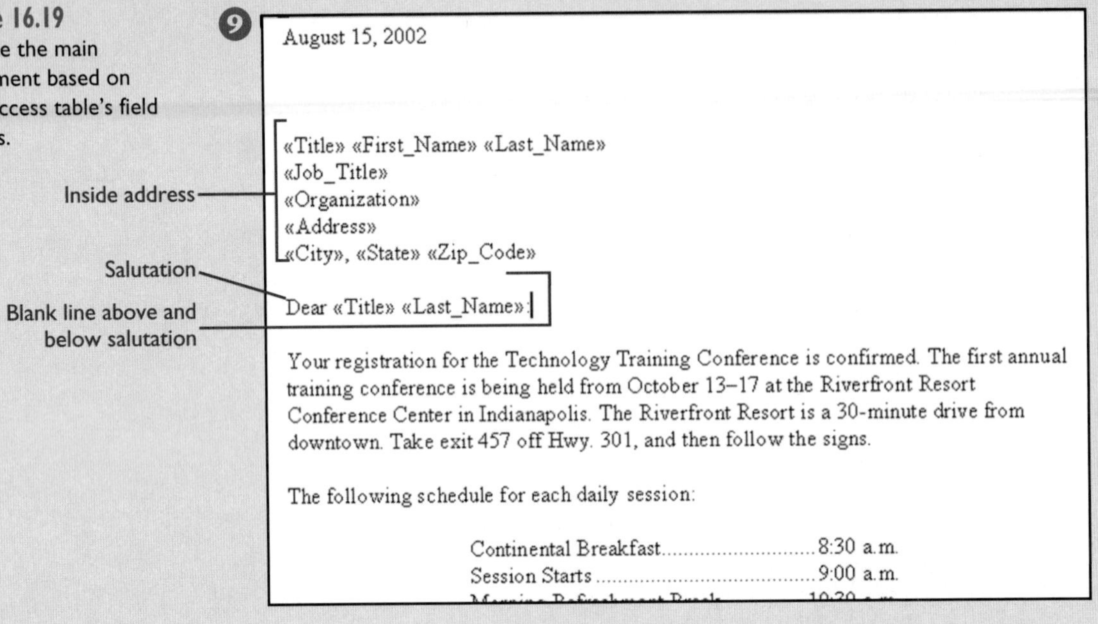

August 15, 2002

«Title» «First_Name» «Last_Name»
«Job_Title»
Inside address —— «Organization»
«Address»
«City», «State» «Zip_Code»

Salutation ——
Blank line above and
below salutation —— Dear «Title» «Last_Name»:

Your registration for the Technology Training Conference is confirmed. The first annual
training conference is being held from October 13–17 at the Riverfront Resort
Conference Center in Indianapolis. The Riverfront Resort is a 30-minute drive from
downtown. Take exit 457 off Hwy. 301, and then follow the signs.

The following schedule for each daily session:

Continental Breakfast............................8:30 a.m.
Session Starts ....9:00 a.m.
Morning Refreshment Break 10:30 a.m.

⑩ **Save the document.**
You are ready to merge the main document with the Access database table.

⑪ **Click the Merge button on the Mail Merge toolbar and then click
Merge in the Merge dialog box.**
Word retrieves the data from the Access table and merges it with the main
document.

⑫ **Save the merged document as** Additional Letters **and close it; keep**
Additional Form Letter **onscreen to continue with the next lesson.**

   Exam Note: Merging with an Excel Workbook
You can use an Excel workbook file as the data source. Typically, for an Excel workbook to work, you need to enter and format field names in the first row of the
worksheet. You can also range-name a part of the worksheet to use as a data
source.

To use an Excel workbook as a data source, click <u>G</u>et Data and choose <u>O</u>pen Data
Source, as you did for other data sources. In the Open dialog box, click the Files of
type drop-down arrow and choose MS Excel Worksheets (*.xls) to display all Excel
files. When you choose the file you want, you see the Microsoft Excel window. You
can use the entire spreadsheet or a range name. The rest of the process is the same
as you've done before for inserting merge fields into the main document.

Lesson 7: Filtering Records for a Merge

If you are working with a large data source, you might not want to include all records in the
merge. Therefore, you need to filter the records. A **filter** is a set of criteria that each record
must meet to be included in the merge process.

In this lesson, you set a filter to include records for participants who live in either Utah or
California.

To Filter Records to Merge

1 In the open `Additional Form Letter` document, click the **M**erge button on the Mail Merge toolbar.

2 Click **Q**uery Options on the right side of the Merge dialog box.

The Query Options dialog box appears (see Figure 16.20). The **F**ilter Records tab is where you define the criteria that states what records will merge. The term *query* is a database term that refers to a filtering tool to select records that meet particular criteria.

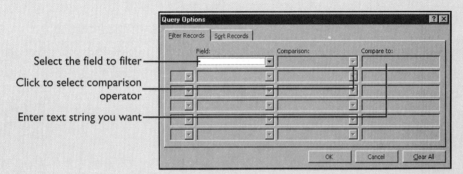

Figure 16.20
Specify the filter options.

 Inside Stuff: **Removing Filters**
Click **C**lear All to remove all filters in the dialog box.

---

3 Click the **Field** drop-down arrow and choose **State**.

The Comparison and Compare to options are available for specifying these options. Leave the Comparison operator as Equal to because you want to find states equal to UT.

4 Type `UT` in the **Compare to** box.

You want to also include participants from California. However, you must change And to Or because the participants can't live in Utah *and* California at the same time. When the And option is specified, the records must meet *both* conditions to be merged. When the Or option is specified, the records must meet *either* condition to be merged.

5 Click the drop-down arrow to the right of And and then choose **Or**.

6 Click the **Field** drop-down arrow for the second row and choose **State**.

7 Type `CA` in the **Compare to** box for the second row.

Figure 16.21 shows the conditions you specified.

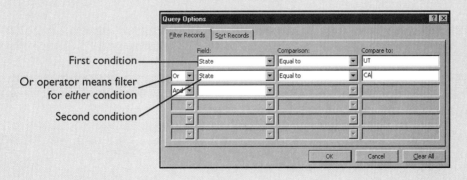

Figure 16.21
The conditions are set to filter the records.

continues ▶

To Filter Records to Merge (continued)

> **X** **If You Have Problems...**
> If you type the full state names **Utah** and **California**, no records will merge. This happens because the State field does *not* contain full state names; it contains the two-letter state abbreviation.

8 **Click OK and then click Merge in the Merge dialog box.**

Only six of the 10 records are merged (see Figure 16.22). The other records do not contain UT or CA in the State field.

Figure 16.22
Only records that meet the conditions are merged with the main document.

First merged record from California

Indicates six total letters merged

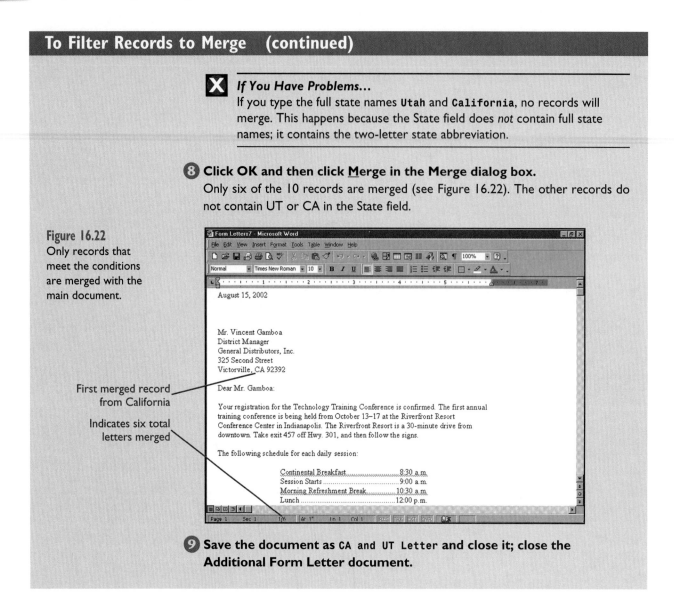

9 **Save the document as CA and UT Letter and close it; close the Additional Form Letter document.**

Lesson 8: Creating a Catalog Main Document

You might want to prepare a list of data source records, but you don't want to include all fields. For example, you might want to create a simple phone list with names and phone numbers only. Instead of merging into form letters, you can create a catalog. A **catalog main document** is a form document that creates a list during the merge instead of separately merged pages.

In this lesson, you create a catalog main document with the LastName, FirstName, and Company fields, so you'll have a check-off list when people show up during the conference.

To Create a Catalog

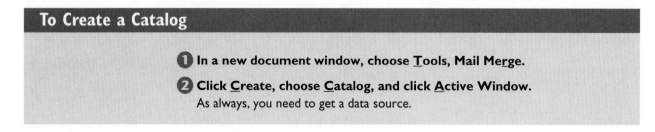

1 **In a new document window, choose Tools, Mail Merge.**

2 **Click Create, choose Catalog, and click Active Window.**

As always, you need to get a data source.

3 Click **Get Data** and choose `Conference Participants`, **the data source you created in Lesson 1.**

4 Click **Edit Main Document.**
You need to set left tabs on the Ruler to space the data apart.

5 Set these **left tabs: 0.5 inches, 2 inches, and 4 inches.**
You need to insert the three fields with tabs separating them.

6 Press (⏎Enter), press (Tab↹), **insert the LastName field; press** (Tab↹), **insert the FirstName field, press** (Tab↹); **insert the Company field and then press** (⏎Enter).

 If You Have Problems…
If you don't press (⏎Enter) after entering the field names, the merged document won't work correctly. Word won't know that you want to start the next record on the next line; it will try to continue inserting data at the end of the line.

You want to have a title and column headings in the merged list; however, you can't type those in the document window. If you do, the title and column headings will repeat for each record. Instead, you need to create a header with this information.

7 Choose **View, Header and Footer to display the Header window.**

8 Center and type `Conference Attendees` **in boldface, 14-point Arial; change back to 12-point Times New Roman and then press** (⏎Enter) **three times.**

9 Click the **Left alignment button; set 0.5-inch, 2-inch, and 4-inch left tabs; delete the 3-inch center tab; and type this text at the respective tabs:** `Last Name, First Name,` **and** `Company`.

10 Click the **Close button on the Header and Footer toolbar.**
Your document should look similar to the one in Figure 16.23.

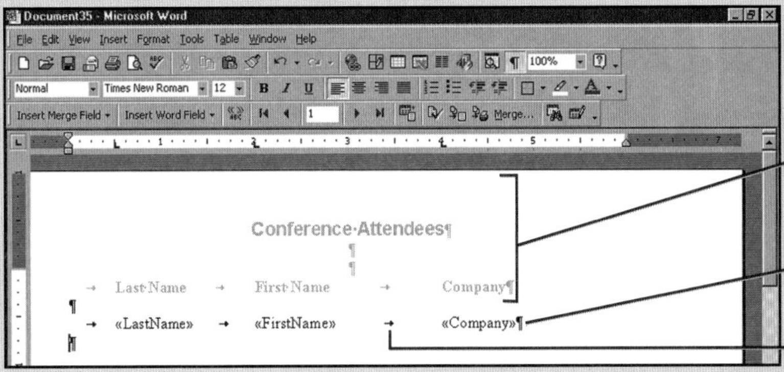

Figure 16.23
Your catalog main document is set up.

Header for title and column headings

Hard return to separate records

Merge fields separated by tabs

11 Save the document as `Conference Catalog` **and keep it onscreen to continue with the next exercise.**

You are ready to merge the catalog main document with the data source. Because you want an alphabetized list, you need to sort the data source while it merges with the main document.

To Merge the Catalog with the Data Source

① **With the** `Conference Catalog` **document onscreen, click the Mail Merge Helper button.**

② **Click** **M**erge **in the Mail Merge Helper dialog box.**
Before merging the documents, you want to sort the records.

③ **Click** **Q**uery Options **and then click the** **S**ort Records **tab.**
This section of the Query Options dialog box lets you specify up to three levels for sorting the records during the merge (see Figure 16.24).

Figure 16.24
Sort the records during the merge.

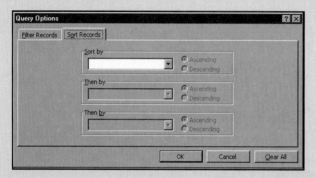

④ **Click the** **S**ort by **drop-down arrow and choose LastName.**
If you have several records with the same last name, you need to set a second sort level to further sort records by first name.

⑤ **Click OK and then click** **M**erge.
Figure 16.25 shows the results of merging the catalog main document with the data source.

Figure 16.25
The catalog produces a list.

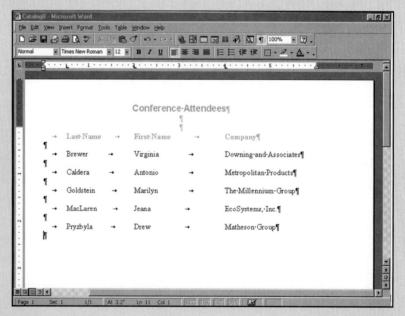

⑥ **Save the catalog list as** `Conference Participants List` **and close it; close** `Conference Catalog`.

Summary

In this project, you completed several merge processes. You first learned how to create a data source by identifying fields you want and removing fields you don't want. You then input data into the data source and sorted it. You learned how to insert merge fields into the main document and merge it with the data source.

You expanded your knowledge by creating a label main document, using alternate data sources such as Access tables, filtering records to include in a merge, and creating a catalog to make a list. You can expand your knowledge and develop advanced skills by exploring the dialog boxes, exploring Help, and completing the following activities.

Checking Concepts and Terms

True/False

For each of the following, check *T* or *F* to indicate whether the statement is true or false.

__T __F **1.** A main document contains records for different people. [L1]

__T __F **2.** If you want records to merge in a particular order, you should sort the data source prior to performing the merge. [L2]

__T __F **3.** To create merged labels, you must specify the label format as a main document. [L5]

__T __F **4.** If you want to filter records to merge records for people in Arizona and Nevada, you use the And operator. [L7]

__T __F **5.** A catalog main document creates a list of merged records. [L8]

Multiple Choice

Circle the letter of the correct answer for each of the following.

1. What term refers to a group of data for one person? [L1]

a. field

b. record

c. main document

d. data source

2. Which of the following is *not* a main document? [L1, 3, 5–6, 8]

a. Access database table

b. catalog

c. labels

d. form file

3. You can use all of the following as data sources *except* _____. [L2, 6]

a. Word data source

b. Excel worksheet

c. Access database table

d. PowerPoint slide show

4. What filter operator requires the records to match the comparison text? [L7]

a. Equal to

b. Match

c. Identical

d. Greater than or equal to

5. Which step comes first in the merge process? [L1]

   a. Creating a data source

   b. Inserting fields into a main document

   c. Filtering records

   d. Identifying the main document

Screen ID

Label each element of the Word screen shown in Figure 16.26.

Figure 16.26

A. Data Form button

B. Field

C. Field names

D. Mail Merge Main Document button

E. Record

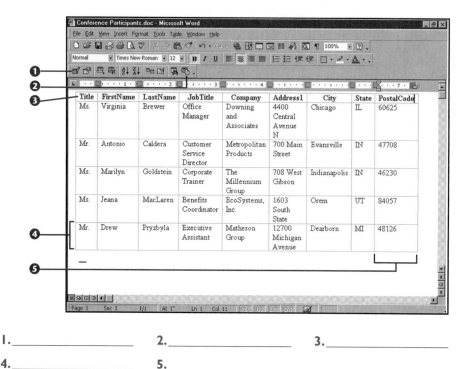

1._____ 2._____ 3._____

4._____ 5._____

Skill Drill

Skill Drill exercises reinforce project skills. Each skill reinforced is the same, or nearly the same, as a skill presented in the project. Each exercise includes a brief narrative introduction, followed by detailed instructions in a step-by-step format.

1. Creating and Sorting a Data Source

You are writing a holiday letter to send to your close friends from college. Although you're sending a form letter, you want it to appear somewhat personalized. You need to create a data source with your friends' names, addresses, and phone numbers.

1. Open **W-1603** and save it as **Holiday Form Letter**.

2. Choose Tools, Mail Merge; click Create, choose Form Letters, and click Active Window.

3. Click Get Data and choose Create Data Source.

4. Click Remove Field Name to remove the Title field.

5. Repeat the process you used in Step 4 to remove these fields: JobTitle, Company, Address2, Country, and WorkPhone; click OK to display the Save As dialog box.

6. Type **Friends Data File** in the File _name box and click _S_ave.

7. Click _E_dit Data Source when prompted.

8. Type **Ryan** in the FirstName field and press ↵Enter.

9. Type **Stewart** in the LastName field and press ↵Enter.

10. Type **358 Arbor Drive** in the Address1 field and press ↵Enter.

11. Type **Carmel** in the City field and press ↵Enter.

12. Type **IN** in the State field and press ↵Enter.

13. Type **46032** in the PostalCode field and press ↵Enter.

14. Type **(317) 555-6249** in the HomePhone field and press ↵Enter.

15. Using the preceding steps, enter the following records in the Data Form dialog box:

```
Alice Lorenzana
1571 Locust Street
Elkhart IN 46514
(219) 555-7947

Carol Montgomery
1159 Thickett Court
Columbus IN 47201
(812) 555-4163

Seth Higton
230 Sycamore
Silver Lake IN 46982
(219) 555-5026
```

16. Click _V_iew Source after entering the last record.

17. Click in the PostalCode field and click the Sort Ascending button.

18. Save the document, print it, and keep it onscreen to continue with the next exercise.

2. Creating a Main Document and Merging Documents

You are ready to insert the merge fields into your main document and then merge the documents.

1. In the open Friends Data File data source, click the Mail Merge Main Document button.

2. Delete *****, click the Insert Merge Field button, and choose FirstName.

3. Press Spacebar, click the Insert Merge Field button, choose LastName, and press ↵Enter.

4. Click the Insert Merge Field button, choose Address1, and press ↵Enter.

5. Click the Insert Merge Field button, choose City, type a comma, and then press Spacebar.

6. Click the Insert Merge Field button, choose State, and press Spacebar.

7. Click the Insert Merge Field button, choose PostalCode, and press ↵Enter twice.

8. Type **Dear**, press Spacebar, click Insert Merge Field, choose FirstName, and type a comma.

9. Save the main document and print it.

10. Click the _M_erge button on the Mail Merge toolbar.

11. Click _M_erge to merge the documents.

12. Save the merged documents as **Holiday Letters**, print them, and close the document; close the main document and the data source document.

3. Creating a Catalog Main Document

You want to create a list of your friends' names and phone numbers. You'll do this by creating a catalog main document and performing a merge.

1. In a new document window, choose _T_ools, Mail Me_r_ge.

2. Click _C_reate, choose _C_atalog, and click _A_ctive Window.

3. Click _G_et Data, choose _O_pen Data Source, choose **Friends Data File**, and click _O_pen.

4. Click Edit _M_ain Document.

5. Set 1-inch and 4-inch left tabs.

6. Press Tab⇄, click the Insert Merge Field button, and choose LastName.

7. Type a comma, press Spacebar, click the Insert Merge Field button, and insert FirstName.

8. Press Tab⇄, click the Insert Merge Field button, choose HomePhone, and press ↵Enter.

9. Choose _V_iew, _H_eader and Footer.

10. Click the Center button, click the Bold button, type **Phone Numbers**, and press ↵Enter twice.

11. Click the Close button on the Header and Footer toolbar.

12. Save the main document as **Friends Catalog**.

13. Click the Mail Merge Helper button and then click Merge.

14. Click Query Options and then click the Sort Records tab.

15. Click the Sort by drop-down arrow, choose LastName, and click OK.

16. Click Merge to perform the merge.

17. Save the catalog list as **Friends Phone List**, print it, and close it. Close other open documents.

Challenge

Challenge exercises expand on or are somewhat related to skills presented in the lessons. Each exercise provides a brief narrative introduction followed by instructions in a numbered-step or bulleted-list format that are not as detailed as those in the Skill Drill section.

1. Creating Cover Letters to Apply for Jobs

You are applying for jobs that were announced in a recent newspaper. You have created part of the form letter and need to create the data source, sort the data source by city, create the main document, merge the documents, and generate mailing labels.

1. Open **W-1604** and save it as **Cover Letter**; create it as the main document.

2. Create a data source with all fields *except* JobTitle, Address2, Country, HomePhone, and WorkPhone. Save the data source as **Job Contacts**. Enter the data shown in Figure 16.27. Make up your own company names.

Title	FirstName	LastName	Address1	City	State	PostalCode
Ms.	Heather	Landward	31 Imperial Place	Lafayette	IN	47905
Mr.	Craig	Hogue	2010 E 2nd Street	Bloomington	IN	47401
Mr.	Roger	Kirkland	1200 Shiloh Square	Evansville	IN	47714
Ms.	Rona	Dunn	5399 New Haven Ave.	Fort Wayne	IN	46803

Figure 16.27
Create the data source.

3. Sort the data source in alphabetical order by last name, save the document, and print it.

4. Insert fields into the main document to create a formal complete inside address and salutation. Use correct spacing and vertically center the document. Save the main document and print it.

5. Merge the documents, save the merged letters as **Cover Letters for Jobs**, and print the letters. Close all open documents.

6. Create a mailing labels main document using the **Job Contacts** data source. Create the same format as the inside address in the form letter. Merge the label main document with the data source. Save the merged labels as **Job Labels** and print the sheet of labels. Save the main document as **Job Form Labels**. Close all open documents.

2. Filtering an Access Table to Merge

Your company will unveil a new product in two weeks. As part of the marketing plan, you are sending out "teaser" literature to buyers in a specific area.

1. Open **W-1605** and save it as **Product Form Letter**.

2. Create a main document from the active window.

3. Select **W-1606.mdb**, an Access database, as the data source. The data source contains 20 records.

4. Insert the appropriate number of hard returns after the date, insert the merge fields to form an inside address, and create a salutation using people's first names.

5. Set up a filter that selects records of people living in the state of Wisconsin (WI). Also, set a sort criteria to sort the filtered records by city.

6. Merge to a new document. You should have three merged records.

7. Save the merged document as **Wisconsin Customers** and print it.

3. Creating a Bonus Memo Form Letter with Envelopes

You need to send out memos to individuals who are receiving a bonus this month. First, you'll prepare a short memo and designate it as the main document. You'll then create a data source, enter records, and filter the records during the merge.

1. In a new document window, create the memo shown in Figure 16.28, save it as **Bonus Form Memo**, and then designate it as the main document.

TO: «FirstName» «LastName»

FROM: District Manager

DATE: July 1, 2002

SUBJECT: Special Bonus

Congratulations! Your high evaluation score has earned you a special summer bonus. Because of your rating, I'm enclosing a check for $«Bonus».

This is our way of saying "thanks for doing a good job."

Enclosure

Figure 16.28
Create the main document.

2. Create the data source shown in Figure 16.29; name it **Employee Data File**. Use the fields as indicated and create any fields you need. Save and print the data source.

FirstName	LastName	Department	Extension	Bonus
Kim	Nettles	Human Resources	560	350
Jon	Zaugg	Marketing	605	400
Mike	Chadworth	Administration	610	350
Monica	Farnsworth	Human Resources	501	450
Patty	Stinson	Marketing	688	300
Mark	Sabey	Manufacturing	101	275
Amanda	Peterson	Manufacturing	103	425
Belinda	Wilson	Sales	716	415
Kalen	Nelson	Sales	900	360
Tim	Foster	Public Relations	783	415

Figure 16.29
Create the data source.

3. Insert fields in the appropriate locations in the main document, save it, and print the main document.

4. Set a filter to merge only records in which employees earn 400 or more. Sort the filtered records by last name.

5. Perform the merge.

6. Save the merged memos as **Bonus Memo $400** and print the memos.

7. Create an envelope main document for the memos. It should contain the first and last names with the department name on the second line. Merge the envelopes using the same filter conditions you used to merge the memos, save them as **Bonus Envelopes**, and print them. Close the envelope main document without saving it.

Discovery Zone

Discovery Zone exercises help you gain advanced knowledge of project topics and/or application of skills. These exercises focus on enhancing your problem-solving skills. Numbered steps are not provided, but you are given hints, reminders, screen shots, and/or references to help you reach your goal for each exercise.

1. Sorting, Filtering, and Merging an Excel Worksheet

Your company is hosting a special luncheon for employees hired during 1999. Someone in the Personnel Department has an Excel worksheet that contains employee information (names, addresses, year hired, emergency information, etc.).

Open **W-1607** to use the main document, and save it as **Invitation Form File**. Designate **W-1608.xls** as your data source. Insert the merge fields in the main document, using the first names in the salutation. Save the main document and print it.

Set a filter to include records between 1/1/999 and 1/31/1999 (including the beginning and ending dates). Set the specifications to sort the last names in alphabetical order before performing the sort. Save the merged letters as **1999 Employees** and print the letters.

2. Creating a Catalog of Employee Information

You want to create a reference list of each employee's emergency contact and phone number. Create a catalog main document in a new document window. Use the Excel worksheet **W-1608.xls** as the data source. Insert these fields, starting at the left margin: **Last Name**, **First Name** Tab⁺⃗ **Contact Name** Tab⁺⃗ **Contact Phone** Tab⁺⃗ **Relation**. Set 0.75-inch left and right margins and appropriate tabs.

Create a header in the catalog main document with **EMERGENCY CONTACT INFORMATION** centered, boldface, 14-point Arial. Set the same tabs you have in the document window. Type the following column headings in 12-point Times New Roman boldface: **Employee**, **Contact**, **Phone**, **Relation**. Insert one hard return after the column headings and close the header.

Set query options to sort the records by last name in ascending order. Merge the document. Save the merged document as **Emergency List** and print it. Save the catalog main document as **Emergency Catalog** and print it.

PinPoint Assessment

You have completed this project and its associated lessons, and have had an opportunity to assess your skills through the end-of-project questions and exercises. Now use the PinPoint software Evaluation Mode to further assess your comprehension of the specific exam activities you have just learned. You can also use the PinPoint Trainer Mode and the Show Me tutorials to practice these exam activities.

Creating Supplemental Document Components

Key terms introduced in this project include

- bookmark
- concordance file
- cross-reference

- hyperlink
- index
- marking

- master document
- subdocument
- table of contents

Objectives	Required Activity for MOUS	Exam Level
➤ Insert Bookmarks	Use bookmarks	Expert
➤ Insert a Hyperlink	Create hyperlinks	Core
➤ Create a Cross-Reference	Create cross-references	Expert
➤ Create an Index	Create and modify an index	Expert
➤ Create a Table of Contents	Create and modify a table of contents	Expert
➤ Create a Master Document and Subdocuments	Work with master documents and subdocuments	Expert

Why Would I Do This?

Well-prepared, long documents include special features to help readers locate information easily. For example, people often refer to a table of contents or an index to locate particular topics within a long document. Bookmarks and hyperlinks also help people jump to a particular location within a document onscreen. You can also break a long document into several documents to work with a smaller part of the document at a time.

In this project, you create and use various supplemental document components to assist readers.

 ## Lesson 1: Inserting Bookmarks

You already know how to use the Go To command to move to a particular page. In addition, you used the Document Map to jump to major sections within a document. In addition to these tools, you might want to insert bookmarks in a document. A **bookmark** is like a physical bookmark you use to mark the location in a document; however, it is an *electronic* bookmark as opposed to a physical piece of paper. Bookmarks are helpful to mark a location you're working on. You can scroll to other parts of a document and quickly go back to the bookmarked location.

In this lesson, you insert bookmark in a document.

To Insert a Bookmark

1 Open W-1701 and save it as Personal Interview.
You want to insert a bookmark for a sentence that introduces a bulleted list.

2 Position the insertion point to the left of the phrase The following factors affect validity in the last full paragraph at the bottom of page 1 in section 2.

3 Choose Insert, Bookmark.
The Bookmark dialog box appears (see Figure 17.1).

Figure 17.1
Use the Bookmark dialog box to add, delete, or go to a bookmark.

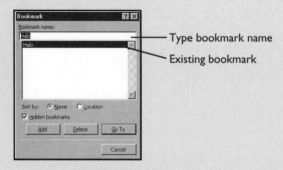

— Type bookmark name
— Existing bookmark

 ___Exam Note: Bookmark Names__
You cannot use a space or most symbols within a bookmark name. However, you can type an underscore between words. Although you can enter numbers within the bookmark name, you can't start a bookmark with a number.

4 **Type** `Validity_Factors` **in the Bookmark name box and then click Add.**
Word inserts a bookmark with the name you entered. You might see a big
I-beam that indicates the bookmark (see Figure 17.2).

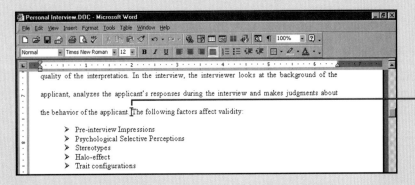

Figure 17.2
The bookmark
appears onscreen.

Bookmark indicator

 Inside Stuff: **Bookmark I-Beam**
If you don't see the big I-beam, choose Tools, Options; click the View tab;
click the Bookmarks check box; click OK.

Let's go back to the top of the document and use the Go To command to find
the bookmark.

5 **Press** Ctrl+Home**, and then press** Ctrl+G **to display the Go To dialog box.**

6 **Choose Bookmark in the Go to what list box.**
Word displays the first bookmark name, which is `Halo`, in the Enter bookmark
name text box.

7 **Click the Enter bookmark name drop-down arrow and choose
Validity_Factors.**
Figure 17.3 shows the bookmark you're about to go to.

Bookmark name

Click to see list of
bookmarks

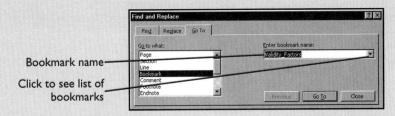

Figure 17.3
Choose the bookmark
name you want to go
to.

8 **Click Go To.**
The insertion point moves to the bookmark's location. The Find and Replace dialog box remains onscreen in case you want to go to another bookmark.

9 **Click Close to close the dialog box.**

10 **Save the document and keep it onscreen to continue with the next
exercise.**

 Inside Stuff: **Going to a Bookmark**
You can also choose Insert, Bookmark to see a list of bookmarks in the current document. Click a bookmark and then click Go To.

 ***Exam Note:* Deleting a Bookmark**
If you no longer need a bookmark, you can delete it. Display the Bookmark dialog box, click the bookmark, click <u>D</u>elete, and then click Close.

 # Lesson 2: Inserting a Hyperlink

If you send documents electronically via attachments to email, you might want to include hyperlinks. A Word ***hyperlink*** is an electronic code that jumps the insertion point to a different location or document when clicked. You can create hyperlinks that jump to a different location within the same document, to a specific location in another document, or to a Web page. You can create a hyperlink from text or a graphics image.

In this lesson, you create a hyperlink from an item on the bulleted list to the section that discusses that topic.

To Insert a Hyperlink

 ①In the open `Personal Interview` document, select Halo-effect at the bottom of page 1 in section 2.
You must select existing text to create a hyperlink from it.

 ②Click the Insert Hyperlink button on the Standard toolbar.

 ***Inside Stuff:* Insert Hyperlink Keyboard Shortcut**
Press Ctrl+K to display the Insert Hyperlink dialog box.

The Insert Hyperlink dialog box appears (see Figure 17.4). You can specify a file or Web page that you want the hyperlink to jump by or you can specify a bookmark within the current document.

Figure 17.4
Choose where you want the link to jump to.

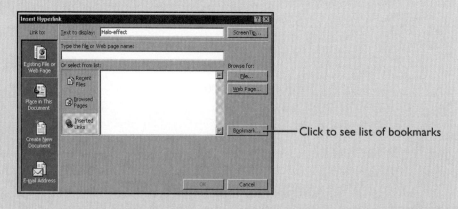

Click to see list of bookmarks

 ***Exam Note:* Hyperlinks to Files and Web Pages**
If you want to create a hyperlink to another document, enter its full path and filename (including the three-letter extension) in the `Type the file or Web page name` box. If you don't know the exact path, click <u>F</u>ile to browse your computer or your organization's intranet to locate the file.

Enter a uniform resource locator (URL), such as http://www.prenhall.com, to have the hyperlink jump to a Web page.

---

③ Click Bookmark.

When the Select Place in Document dialog box appears, you can choose either a heading or bookmark (see Figure 17.5).

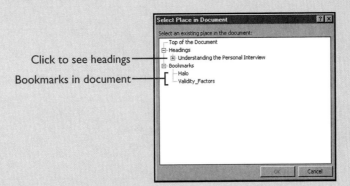

Click to see headings

Bookmarks in document

Figure 17.5
Choose a heading or bookmark.

④ Click Halo in the Bookmarks section, click OK, and then click OK to close the Insert Hyperlink dialog box.

Word converts the text to a hyperlink, which you can tell because the text is underlined and appears in blue.

⑤ Position the mouse pointer on top of the hyperlink text.

Figure 17.6 shows the formatted hyperlink text. The mouse pointer looks like a hand, which indicates that the text is a hyperlink.

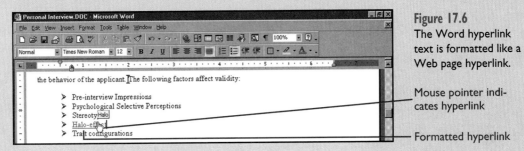

Figure 17.6
The Word hyperlink text is formatted like a Web page hyperlink.

Mouse pointer indicates hyperlink

Formatted hyperlink

⑥ Click the hyperlink text.

Word jumps you to the Stereotypes heading on page 7. The Web toolbar appears. You can click the Back button to go back to the previous location (see Figure 17.7).

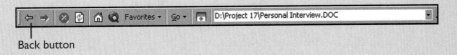

Back button

Figure 17.7
The Web toolbar appears when you click a hyperlink.

⑦ Save the document and keep it onscreen to continue with the next lesson.

 Inside Stuff: **Creating a Graphic Hyperlink**

You can create a hyperlink from a graphic image, such as a photo or clip art image. To do this, click the image to select it and then click the Insert Hyperlink button on the Standard toolbar. Choose a different file, a Web page, or a location in the current document to link to. The picture looks the same. When the mouse pointer is positioned on the image, it looks like the hand. Clicking the picture links to the location you specified.

Exam Note: Editing or Removing a Hyperlink
If you need to edit or remove a hyperlink, you must *right-click* it to display a short-cut menu instead of jumping to that link. Choose Hyperlink. You can then choose Edit Hyperlink or Remove Hyperlink (see Figure 17.8).

Figure 17.8
Choose from the
Hyperlink menu.

Displays dialog box to
edit hyperlink

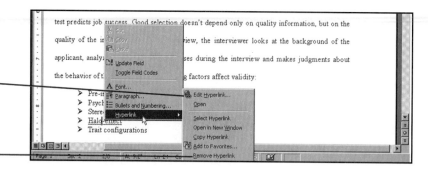

Removes link

Lesson 3: Creating a Cross-Reference

A **cross-reference** is a note that refers the reader to another location for more information about a topic. You can create cross-references to headings, bookmarks, footnotes, endnotes, and tables. A typical cross-reference looks like this: **See page 4 for more information about pizza toppings.**

For files you make available via email or on an intranet, you create an electronic cross-reference, such as the hyperlink you created in the last lesson. However, if you are distributing printed copies of your document, you need printed references so the readers can find the location themselves.

In this lesson, you create a cross-reference to another section in the document.

To Create a Cross-Reference

❶ In the open `Personal Interview` document, find the section titled Nonverbal Communications at the bottom of page 6.

❷ Position the insertion point to the *left* of the sentence that begins with `In addition to this`.
The previous sentence refers to a point made earlier in the document.

❸ Type `For more information, see page` and press `Spacebar`.
You are now ready to insert the field that generates the page number for the cross-reference.

❹ Choose Insert, Cross-reference.
The Cross-reference dialog box appears.

❺ Click the Reference type drop-down arrow and choose Heading.
When you choose Heading, the For which heading list box lists all headings in the report that are formatted with Heading styles. You can choose the heading to tie the reference to (see Figure 17.9).

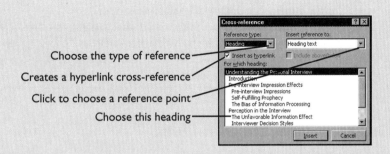

Choose the type of reference

Creates a hyperlink cross-reference

Click to choose a reference point

Choose this heading

Figure 17.9
The Cross-reference
dialog box helps you
create a cross-
reference notation.

 Inside Stuff: **Heading Cross-Reference**
You must use the Heading styles in order to use headings as cross-
references. Although you shouldn't manually format headings, you can edit
the Heading styles to format the headings as you desire.

---

6 **Choose The Unfavorable Information Effect in the For which heading
list box.**

Choosing a heading cross-reference refers to the reader to that location.
Providing a page number is helpful, so the reader can quickly go to that page and
review that information.

7 **Click the Insert reference to drop-down arrow and choose Page number.**

Choosing Page number instructs Word to display the page number that the
cross-reference heading is on.

8 **If the Insert as hyperlink check box is selected, deselect it.**

When this check box is selected, it creates a hyperlink cross-reference that is
similar to the hyperlink you created in the last lesson. If you are providing a
printed copy of the document, a hyperlink cross-reference is irrelevant for your
reader.

9 **Click Insert and then click Close.**

The cross-reference displays page 4—the page that contains the heading you
cross-referenced. When the insertion point is on the cross-reference, it appears
in gray, which indicates it is a field.

10 **Type a period and press** Spacebar.

Figure 17.10 shows your cross-reference when the insertion point is on it.

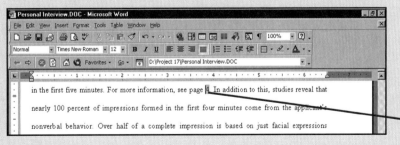

Figure 17.10
The cross-reference
displays a page
number.

Cross-reference field

11 **Save the document and keep it onscreen to continue with the next
lesson.**

Inside Stuff: Updating Cross-References

If you add or delete text, the cross-reference might still display the original page number. You can click the cross-reference field and press F9 to update the cross-reference. If you have several cross-references and don't know where they are located, you can select the entire document and press F9.

 # Lesson 4: Creating an Index

An *index* is a listing of topics covered in a book or long document and the page numbers on which the topics are discussed. An index typically appears at the end of the document or book.

You create an index by first marking words or phrases you want to include in the index. Then, you choose an index design and generate the finished index. Word generates the index by collecting entries that you mark in your document, sorting them alphabetically, referencing their page numbers, and removing duplicate entries from the same page.

In this lesson, you create a simple index for the Personal Interview document. You mark the index entries in the first exercise and then compile the index in the second exercise.

To Mark Index Entries

1 **In the open `Personal Interview` document, double-click the word `validity` in the first paragraph on page 1 in section 2.**
You must select the text you want to include in the index.

2 **Press Alt+↑Shift+X.**
The Mark Index Entry dialog box appears (see Figure 17.11). The process of designating text to include in an index or table of contents is called *marking*. You can edit or change the text in the Mark entry text box.

Figure 17.11
Specify settings for marking an index entry.

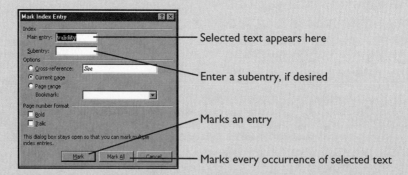
Selected text appears here
Enter a subentry, if desired
Marks an entry
Marks every occurrence of selected text

3 **Click Mark All to mark the selected text as an index entry.**
Word marks text throughout the document that matches the casing of the entry you entered. If your index entry is in uppercase and lowercase letters, only those occurrences are marked. Word marks each index entry by inserting a field immediately after the entry text in your document. Click the Show/Hide ¶ button to see the index fields (see Figure 17.12). EX represents an index field.

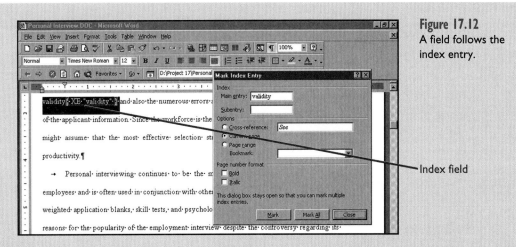

Figure 17.12
A field follows the
index entry.

Index field

The Mark Index Entry dialog box remains onscreen so you can mark additional text in the document.

4 **Select each of the following words and phrases; use the same process you used in steps 2 and 3 to mark the text as index entries.**
Keep the dialog box open as you mark entries. Move the dialog box to a different location onscreen to view text as you scroll through the document. Then click the dialog box again to activate it.

- **Pre-interview Impressions**, located in the bulleted list at the bottom of the first page in section two
- **Stereotypes**, located in the bulleted list at the bottom of the first page in section two
- **credentials**, located in the first paragraph in the **Pre-interview Impressions** section
- **nonverbal**, located in the first paragraph of the **Nonverbal Communications** section

---

(i) Inside Stuff: Deleting an Index Field
If you accidentally mark the wrong text or decide not to use an index entry, select and delete the XE field to the right of the text you marked.

You can also mark text to be a subentry of another index entry. For example, you might want to list **perception in the interview** as a main heading with **unfavorable information effect**, **interview decision styles**, and **physical characteristics** as subentries.

5 **Select Unfavorable Information Effect, part of the Heading 3 below Perception in the Interview on page 4; then press** (Alt)+(⬆Shift)+(X).
The selected text appears in the Main entry text box, but you need to insert it in the S̲ubentry text box.

6 **Delete the existing text in the Main e̲ntry text box and then type perception in the interview.**
Now, you need to enter the text to generate the subentry.

7 **Type unfavorable information effect in the S̲ubentry text box.**

8 **Click M̲ark.**
You want to mark additional subentries.

continues ▶

To Mark Index Entries (continued)

9 Using the process discussed in steps 5–8, mark the following Heading 3 levels as subentries of `perception in the interview.` Use title case when you type the entries.

`Interviewer Decision Styles`

`Physical Characteristics`

10 Click Close.

11 Save the document and keep it onscreen to continue with the next exercise.

 Inside Stuff: **Creating a Concordance File**

A *concordance file* is a two-column table that contains the words and phrases that you want to include in an index. Type the word or phrase *exactly* the way you want Word to search for it, including capitalization, in the first column. Type it the way you want the index entry to appear.

Although the second column often contains the same word or phrase that you used in the first column, it doesn't have to. For example, you might type **inserting bookmarks** in the first column and **bookmarks: inserting** in the second column. Word searches for **inserting bookmarks**. The main index entry is **bookmarks** and **inserting** is a subentry. Figure 17.13 shows an example of a concordance file and the resulting index entries it produces.

Figure 17.13
A concordance file contains entries to compile an index.

Exact words and phrases to find in document

Entry

Subentry

Entry with subentry in index

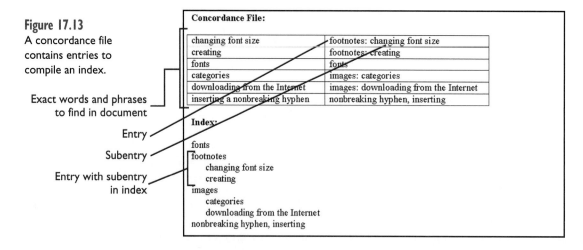

After marking entries, you are ready to compile the index page. You typically compile the index on a separate page.

To Compile the Index

1 With `Personal Interview` onscreen, press Ctrl+End to position the insertion point at the end of the document.

You need to insert a page break to generate the index on a separate page.

② **Press** Ctrl+↵Enter.

The index page needs a title that identifies the page as an index.

③ **Click the Styles drop-down arrow, choose Heading 1, type Index, and press** ↵Enter.

Make sure the style displays Normal after you press ↵Enter.

④ **Choose Insert, Index and Tables, and make sure the Index tab is active.**

Figure 17.14 shows the index options. By default, the index is formatted into two newspaper columns. You can change the number of columns, if desired. You can choose the index format, such as Fancy.

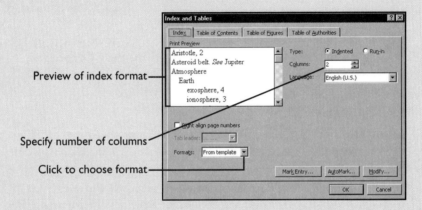

Preview of index format—

Specify number of columns—

Click to choose format—

Figure 17.14
Choose the formats for the index.

⑤ **Click the Formats drop-down arrow and choose Fancy.**

The Print Preview window shows how the index will be formatted.

⑥ **Click OK and click the Print Layout View button.**

Word generates the index at the insertion point's location (see Figure 17.15).

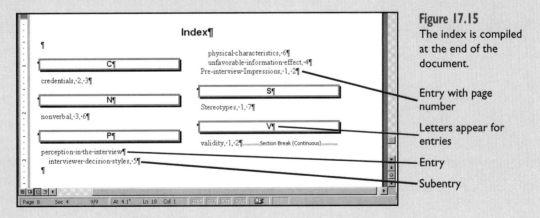

Figure 17.15
The index is compiled at the end of the document.

Entry with page number

Letters appear for entries

Entry

Subentry

⑦ **Save the document and keep it onscreen to continue with the next lesson.**

 Exam Note: **Updating a Field**

If you edit the document, the pagination might change. You need to update the index when pagination changes or when you insert additional index entries. To do this, click inside the index field and press F9, or right-click inside the index field and choose Update Field from the shortcut menu.

Lesson 5: Creating a Table of Contents

A **table of contents** provides readers with a guide to topics covered in a long document or book. Unlike the index that is placed at the end of the document, a table of contents is placed at the beginning of the document. The table of contents lists topics in the order in which they are presented rather than in alphabetical order.

You can create a table of contents quickly if you've applied Heading styles throughout your document or you can mark text to include in a TOC.

In this lesson, you create a table of contents. Because your document is formatted with Heading styles, you'll use those to create the table of contents.

To Create a Table of Contents

1 In the open Personal Interview **document, position the insertion point at the bottom of the title page—after the text Corporate DoubleSpeak, Inc.—and press** Ctrl+↵Enter.
You want to insert a new page for the table of contents. Make sure that the new page is in section 1, not section 2.

2 **Click the Center button, click the Bold button, type** Table of Contents, **turn off Bold, press** ↵Enter **twice, and then click the Align Left button.**

 Inside Stuff: **Formatting the Table of Contents Title**
Do *not* apply a Heading style to the table of contents title. If you do, Word will include it when it compiles the table of contents. Typically, a table of contents does not include an entry for itself.

3 **Select Table of Contents and choose 14-point Arial; then press** ↓ **to scroll back down to the left-aligned text in 12-point Times New Roman.**
You are ready to specify the format for the table of contents.

4 **Choose** I**nsert,** Inde**x and Tables; then click the Table of** C**ontents tab.**
Figure 17.16 shows the Table of Contents options. You can choose how many heading levels you want to include. In this document, you need to show three levels.

Figure 17.16
Set the table of contents formats.

Choose a tab leader option

Click to set a format

Specify the number of heading levels to include

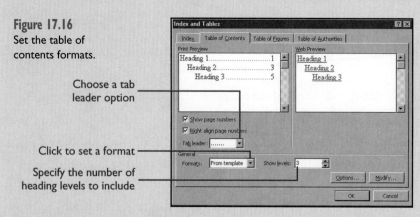

5 **Make sure that 3 appears in the Show** l**evels box.**

6 **Click the Formats drop-down arrow and choose Formal.**

The Print Preview window shows a sample of the Formal format with three levels.

7 **Click OK.**

Word compiles the table of contents from the first three heading levels in your document (see Figure 17.17).

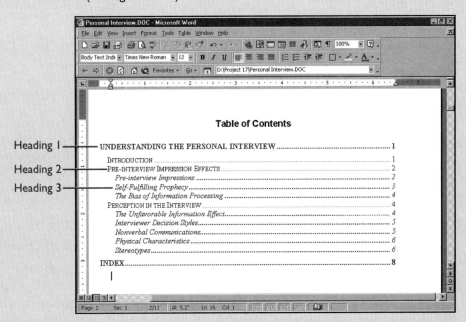

Figure 17.17
Word compiles the table of contents from the headings.

The table of contents entries are formatted as hyperlinks. When you position the mouse pointer over the table of contents, it looks like a hand. Click the mouse button to move the insertion point to a particular heading in the document.

8 **Click Nonverbal Communications.**

Word moves to that heading within the document. You can click the Back button on the Web toolbar to go back to the table of contents.

9 **Save the document and close it; then choose View, Toolbars, Web to hide the Web toolbar.**

 Inside Stuff: **Updating a Table of Contents**

If you make changes to your document, the table of contents might not accurately reflect the headings and their respective page numbers. To update the table of contents, scroll within the table of contents. When the entire table of contents appears in gray, press F9. The Update Table of Contents dialog box appears (see Figure 17.18). Choose the first option if only the pagination changed. Choose the second option if you added, deleted, or changed headings. Then click OK.

Figure 17.18
Update the table of
contents after making
changes in the
document.

Selected table of
contents field

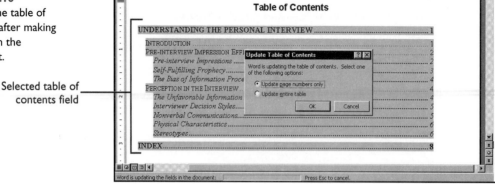

 Inside Stuff: Marking Table of Contents Entries
If you used your own formatting or created your own heading styles, you might
need to mark these headings to include in the table of contents. Select the headings
and press [Alt]+[Shift]+[O] to display the Mark Table of Contents Entry dialog box.
Specify the level number, such as 1 for a first-level entry and 2 for a second-level
entry, and then click OK.

 # Lesson 6: Creating a Master Document and Subdocuments

Working with long documents can be cumbersome. When a document is over 30 pages,
you definitely notice your computer slows down. Scrolling, finding and replacing, editing, and
formatting take longer. To solve this problem, you should create a **master document**, a
document that acts like a binder for managing smaller documents known as **subdocuments**.

You can create a master document from scratch, including the subdocuments, or you can
create a master document by adding existing files as subdocuments.

In this lesson, you create a master document from scratch. The master document contains
short subdocuments in which you can compose text.

To Create a Master Document

 **❶ In a new document window, click the Outline View button, which is to
the right of the horizontal scroll bar.**
You create an outline for the master document to serve as its skeleton. Use
Word's built-in heading styles or use the Promote and Demote buttons on the
Outlining toolbar to set the outline levels (see Figure 17.19). The Master
Document toolbar is on the right side of the Outlining toolbar.

Figure 17.19
The Outlining and
Master Document
toolbars help you
create a master
document.

Master Document toolbar

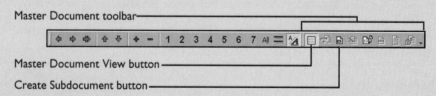

Master Document View button

Create Subdocument button

**❷ Type the outline shown in Figure 17.20. Press [Enter] between outline
entries, press [Tab] to create lower-level entries, and press [Shift]+[Tab]
to create higher-level entries.**

> ◇ **Word Processing Applications**
>   ◇ *Working with Styles and Templates*
>   ▫ Using a Word Template to Create a Document
>   ▫ Creating a New Template
>   ▫ Creating and Applying Styles
>   ◇ *Automating Your Work*
>   ▫ Using AutoComplete
>   ▫ Creating and Inserting AutoText Entries
>   ▫ Recording and Running Macros
>   ◇ *Using Mail Merge*
>   ▫ Creating a Data Source
>   ▫ Creating a Main Document
>   ▫ Merging the Documents

Figure 17.20
Create the outline that will become subdocuments.

You are ready to separate the outline into subdocuments. You need to select the headings and text that you want to place in subdocuments.

❸ Click and drag on the left side of the headings, starting with Working with Styles and Templates.

❹ Click the Create Subdocument button on the Master Document toolbar.

This button creates individual subdocuments for the selected headings and text. Because you start selecting at Heading 2, Word creates a new subdocument at each Heading 2 in the selected area. If you start selecting with Heading 1, Word creates subdocuments starting with each Heading 1. A box surrounds each subdocument (see Figure 17.21). You see a subdocument icon in the top left corner of each subdocument box.

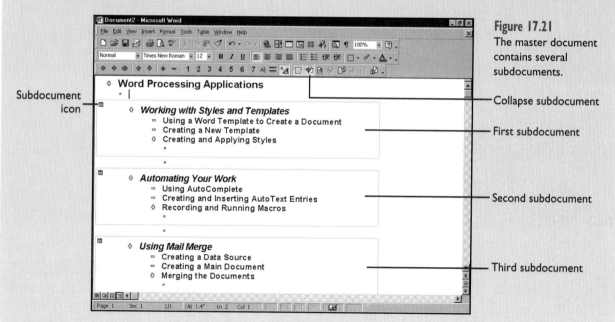

Figure 17.21
The master document contains several subdocuments.

Subdocument icon
Collapse subdocument
First subdocument
Second subdocument
Third subdocument

❺ Save the document as Word Processing Master Document.

Word saves the master document and creates a document for each subdocument. Each subdocument is saved under a name that matches the first line in the subdocument. Your three subdocument names are `Working with Styles and Templates.doc`, `Automating Your Work.doc`, and `Using Mail Merge.doc`.

continues ▶

To Create a Master Document   (continued)

6 **Click the Collapse Subdocuments button.**
Figure 17.22 shows how the master document appears when you collapse it in the subdocuments. Instead of displaying the subdocument headings and text, Word displays the subdocument filenames.

Figure 17.22
The master document displays the subdocument filenames.

Expand Subdocuments button

Subdocument 1's filename

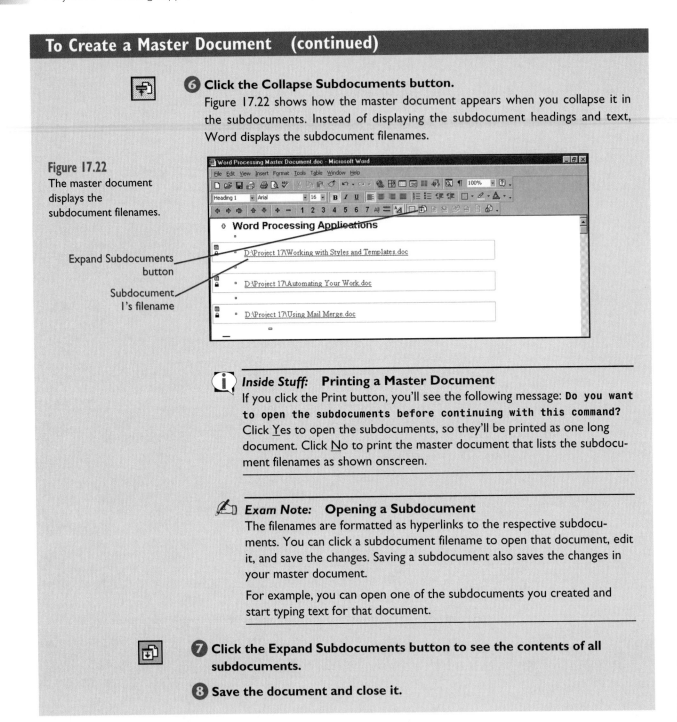

ⓘ *Inside Stuff:*   **Printing a Master Document**
If you click the Print button, you'll see the following message: `Do you want to open the subdocuments before continuing with this command?` Click Yes to open the subdocuments, so they'll be printed as one long document. Click No to print the master document that lists the subdocument filenames as shown onscreen.

✍ *Exam Note:*   **Opening a Subdocument**
The filenames are formatted as hyperlinks to the respective subdocuments. You can click a subdocument filename to open that document, edit it, and save the changes. Saving a subdocument also saves the changes in your master document.

For example, you can open one of the subdocuments you created and start typing text for that document.

---

7 **Click the Expand Subdocuments button to see the contents of all subdocuments.**

8 **Save the document and close it.**

ⓘ *Inside Stuff:*   **Formatting a Master Document**
After completing all subdocument text, display the master document and expand the subdocuments. You can create headers and footers, mark index entries and compile an index, and create a table of contents. Then, you can print the master document with the subdocuments to produce one long, continuous document complete with continuous page numbering!

Exam Note: **Using Existing Documents as Subdocuments**

By the time you decide to create a master document, some documents you need for subdocuments may already be in progress or you may have a set of existing documents that you want to add to the master document.

To insert an existing document into the master document, follow these steps:

1. Open the master document and click the Outline View button, if needed.

2. Expand the subdocuments by clicking the Expand Subdocuments button on the master Document toolbar.

3. Place the insertion point where you want to insert an existing document. This should be in a blank line *between* existing subdocuments.

4. Click the Insert Subdocument button on the Master Document toolbar.

5. In the Insert Subdocument dialog box, enter the filename of the document you want to use as a subdocument; click <u>O</u>pen.

If you have created a document that you want to convert to a master document, follow these steps:

1. Open the document you want to convert to a master document.

2. Click the Outline View button.

3. Apply Word's built-in heading styles or specify outline levels to set up the outline of the master document.

4. Select the headings and text you want to divide into subdocuments. Remember to format the first heading you select with the heading style or the outline level that you want to use to designate the beginning of each subdocument.

5. Click the Create Subdocument button on the Master Document toolbar.

6. Save the master document. Enter a filename and location for the master document; then click <u>S</u>ave. Word assigns a filename for each subdocument based on the first heading within each subdocument.

The Master Document toolbar also contains buttons to remove a subdocument, merge selected subdocuments, or split a subdocument into multiple subdocuments. Furthermore, you can lock a subdocument from being edited by anyone else on your organization's intranet.

Summary

You now know how to make documents more accessible, whether you provide your readers with a printed copy or an electronic file. You can use bookmarks and hyperlinks to quickly jump to locations within the file, and you can create cross-references for printed documents to direct readers to a particular section. In addition, you can mark entries for an index and compile the index, generate a table of contents, and create master documents with subdocuments.

You are definitely an intermediate user now! To enhance your skills in using the features presented in this project, explore the topics in Help, complete the following exercises, and work through the appropriate PinPoint activities.

Checking Concepts and Terms

True/False

For each of the following, check *T* or *F* to indicate whether the statement is true or false.

__T __F   **1.** A bookmark refers to a location with another document, whereas a hyperlink must refer to a location within the same document. [L1, 2]

__T __F   **2.** A traditional cross-reference is designed to refer a reader to another location within the document for additional information. [L3]

__T __F   **3.** When you mark selected text for an index entry, you can enter different text as the main index entry. [L4]

__T __F   **4.** A table of contents is typically found at the end of a document. [L5]

__T __F   **5.** When you save a master document, Word prompts you to save the subdocuments. [L6]

Multiple Choice

Circle the letter of the correct answer for each of the following.

1. You can use the Go To command to go to what element? [L1]

a. hyperlink

b. cross-reference notation

c. bookmark

d. table of contents

2. You can create a hyperlink that jumps to what? [L2]

a. a bookmark

b. another document

c. a Web page

d. all of the above

3. What is the keyboard shortcut for updating a cross-reference field, an index field, or a table of contents field? [L3-5]

a. ⏎Enter

b. F9

c. Ctrl + ⏎Enter

d. F1

4. Which of the following is *not* a characteristic of an index? [L4]

a. It has an alphabetical order of topics.

b. It is compiled from marked entries.

c. Index entries do not have to match selected text to mark.

d. It is typically created at the beginning of the document.

5. What is a master document composed of? [L6]

a. subdocuments

b. concordance files

c. overall document

d. all of the above

Screen ID

Label each element of the Word screen shown in Figure 17.23.

Figure 17.23

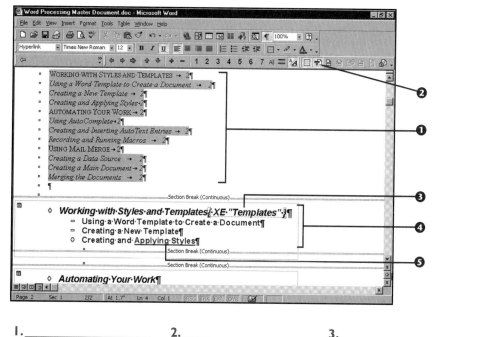

A. Collapse Subdocuments

B. hyperlink

C. index entry

D. subdocument

E. table of contents field

1._____   2._____   3._____

4._____   5._____

Skill Drill

Skill Drill exercises reinforce project skills. Each skill reinforced is the same, or nearly the same, as a skill presented in the project. Detailed instructions are provided in a step-by-step format.

I. Inserting a Bookmark and a Hyperlink

You want to create a bookmark to jump to a table of dates. In addition, you want to create a hyperlink from a line on the title page to the benefits section in the newsletter.

1. Open **W-1702** and save it as **Electronic Newsletter**.

2. Position the insertion point in the first cell of the table. It is on page 1 of section 2.

3. Choose Insert, Bookmark.

4. Type **Conference_Dates** and click Add.

5. Position the insertion point at the beginning of the document.

6. Press Ctrl+G, choose Bookmark, click Go To, and then click Close.

7. Select Dental Benefits at the bottom of the first page.

8. Click the Insert Hyperlink button and then click Bookmark in the dialog box.

9. Click Headings, if needed, to display the headings in the document.

10. Click Dental Benefits, click OK, and then click OK to close the dialog boxes.

11. Click the Dental Benefits link to jump to the Dental Benefits heading on page 3.

12. Save the document and keep it onscreen to continue with the next exercise.

2. Compiling an Index and Table of Contents

You want to create a short index for the newsletter and then generate a table of contents.

1. In the open **Electronic Newsletter** document, go to the first page in section 2.

2. Select Technology Training Conference, press Alt+⬆Shift+X, and click Mark.

3. Select Riverfront Resort Center, press Alt+⬆Shift+X, and click Mark in the Mark Index Entry dialog box.

4. Select **customer service branch** in the paragraph below the New Customer Service Branch heading, press Alt+⬆Shift+X, click Mark in the Mark Index Entry dialog box.

5. Select **Myrtle Beach** in the paragraph below the New Customer Service Branch heading, press Alt+⬆Shift+X, click Mark All in the Mark Index Entry dialog box.

6. Select **key card system** in the paragraph below the New Key Card System heading, press Alt+⬆Shift+X, click Mark in the Mark Index Entry dialog box.

7. Select **dental benefits** in the paragraph below the Dental Benefits heading, press Alt+⬆Shift+X, click Mark All in the Mark Index Entry dialog box.

8. Click Close, position the insertion point at the end of the document, and press Ctrl+⏎Enter.

9. Click the Style drop-down arrow and choose Heading 1.

10. Type **Index** and press ⏎Enter twice.

11. Choose Insert, Index and Tables, and click the Index tab.

12. Click the Formats drop-down arrow, choose Modern, and click OK.

13. Position the insertion point to the right of the Dental Benefits hyperlink on the title page, and then press Ctrl+⏎Enter to insert a page break.

14. Type **Table of Contents** and press ⏎Enter twice.

15. Select the heading, choose 14-point Arial, click the Bold button, and click the Center button.

16. Press ⬇ twice, and choose Insert, Index and Tables.

17. Click the Table of Contents tab, click the Formats drop-down arrow, choose Distinctive, and click OK.

18. Save, print, and close the document.

3. Creating a Master Document and Subdocuments

You plan to create a reference manual for employees. Because it will be a long document, you want to start by creating a master document with subdocuments for the headings, so you can later add the information into the subdocuments.

1. In a new document window, click the Outline View button.

2. Type **Office Reference Manual** as a first-level heading.

3. Press ⏎Enter, press Tab, and type **Punctuation** as a second-level heading.

4. Press ⏎Enter, press Tab, and type **Commas** as a third-level heading.

5. Press ⏎Enter, and type **Semicolons** as a third-level heading.

6. Press ⏎Enter and type **Colons** as a third-level heading.

7. Press ⏎Enter, press ⬆Shift+Tab, and type **Document Formats** as a second-level heading.

8. Enter the following text as third-level headings: **Letters**, **Memos**, and **Reports**.

9. Select the second- and third-level entries, and then click the Create Subdocument button.

10. Save the document as **Office Reference Manual Master Document**.

11. Print the document.

12. Click the Collapse Documents button.

13. Click the Print button and then click No when prompted to open the subdocuments.

14. Close the documents.

Challenge

Challenge exercises expand on or are somewhat related to skills presented in the lessons. Each exercise provides a brief narrative introduction followed by instructions in a numbered-step or bulleted-list format that are not as detailed as those in the Skill Drill section.

I. Inserting Bookmarks and Hyperlinks

You want to insert bookmarks in a document, so you can quickly return to these locations as you review the document. In addition, you want to add a hyperlink for your readers who will receive the document via email attachment.

1. Open **W-1703** and save it as **Training Conference**.

2. Insert a bookmark before Word 2000 in the first bulleted item. Name the bookmark **Word_2000**.

3. Insert a bookmark before Internet training in the next bulleted item. Name the bookmark **Internet_Training**.

4. Insert bookmarks for Multimedia training and Presentation Graphics in the last two bulleted items. Use appropriate bookmark names.

5. Use the Go To command to go to each bookmark you created.

6. Select **Internet experience** in the paragraph below the Training Sessions heading. Insert a hyperlink that links to the appropriate bookmark you created.

7. Click the hyperlink to make sure it works and then click the Back button.

8. Save the document and show your bookmarks and hyperlink to your instructor.

2. Creating a Cross-Reference, Compiling an Index, and Generating a Table of Contents

You created a document on the Great Depression. You realize that it needs a cross-reference to another section. Plus, you want to create an index and generate a table of contents.

1. Open **W-1704** and save it as **Great Depression**.

2. Go to the top of page 2 in section 2.

3. Type the following text before the period ending the first sentence, which ends with **people didn't listen**.

   (for more information about how people reacted, see * on page **)

   Make sure you have a space before the beginning parenthesis.

4. Delete * and create a cross-reference to the heading Effects on People. Choose Heading text from the **Insert reference to** list.

5. Delete ** and create a cross-reference to the same heading, but use the Page number reference this time.

6. Mark the following text as index entries:

Text to Mark	Location
Stock Market	first paragraph under Introduction
Great Depression	second paragraph under Introduction
Black Thursday	in heading Chapter 1. Black Thursday
stock values	first paragraph under Chapter 1. Black Thursday heading
New Deal	first paragraph under heading THE NEW DEAL
Congress	first paragraph under heading THE NEW DEAL
Civilian Conservation Corps	first paragraph under heading THE NEW DEAL

7. Mark **Dupont stock** and **share prices crashed** as subentries of **stock values**.

8. Mark **Roosevelt** as a subentry named **Roosevelt, Franklin D.** under the entry **presidents**.

9. Mark **Hoover** as a subentry named **Hoover, Herbert** under the entry **presidents**.

10. Create a page break at the end of the document and type **Index** as a Heading 1 style with one hard return after it.

11. Compile the index using the Fancy format style.

12. Insert a hard page break before the section break after the title page.

13. Type the title **Table of Contents** in the Title style, press 〔↵Enter〕 twice, and choose the Body Text style.

14. Generate a table of contents with the Formal format style.

15. Save, print, and close the document.

3. Creating a Master Document

You are preparing a presentation about your company, Computer Training Concepts, Inc. You have already created several documents that you can use as subdocuments for a master document you're about to create.

1. Open **W-1705** and save it as **CTC Master Document**.

2. Make sure the document is displayed in Print Layout View.

3. At the end of the document, insert **W-1706** as a subdocument.

4. Collapse the master document, saving it when prompted.

5. Print the collapsed master document.

6. Display the nonprinting symbols and create a table of contents at the end of the first section.

7. Display the document in the Print Layout View and print the table of contents only.

8. Display the document in Outline View and collapse the document, saving it when prompted.

9. Close the document.

Discovery Zone

Discovery Zone exercises help you gain advanced knowledge of project topics and/or application of skills. These exercises focus on enhancing your problem-solving skills. Numbered steps are not provided, but you are given hints, reminders, screen shots, and/or references to help you reach your goal for each exercise.

1. Creating Graphics and Text Hyperlinks to Bookmarks

You are sending a proposal via email attachments to a bank to review. Your restaurant is requesting a loan to expand. You want to create a bookmark in two documents, insert a graphical hyperlink to a bookmark within the current document and a text hyperlink to a bookmark in the other document.

Open **W-1709** and save it as **Cafe Loan Proposal**. Open **W-1710** and save it as **New Food Cafe**. In the **New Food Cafe** document, insert an appropriately named bookmark in front of **lunch menu** in the second paragraph. Save and close this document, but keep **Cafe Loan Proposal** open. Insert an appropriately named bookmark in the first row of the **Quarterly Net Profits** table on page 3.

At the beginning of the first paragraph, insert an appropriate image from the Food & Dining clip art category. If you want, check out the Microsoft Clip Gallery Live to select an appropriate image. Apply a 2.5 inch width with a square wrap option. Format the image as a hyperlink that links to the bookmark you created for the profits table. Create a hyperlink ScreenTip that says **Smell the Profits!** when the mouse pointer is on top of the hyperlink graphic.

Select **menu** in the first paragraph below the **Anticipated Expenses** table. Create a hyperlink to the bookmark you created in the **New Food Cafe** document.

Make sure your hyperlinks work. Close **New Food Cafe** without saving it again. Save the **Cafe Loan Proposal** document. Demonstrate how your links work to your instructor.

2. Creating a Master Document, Index, and Table of Contents

You want to use several documents as subdocuments for a master document. This way, you can work on isolated documents without using a long document that slows down your computer speed.

Open **W-1711**, save it as **DP Title Page**, and close it. Open **W-1712** and save it as **DP Design**. Open **W-1713** and save it as **DP Spacing**. Open **W-1714** and save it as **DP Bibliography**. Open **W-1715** and save it as **DP Index**.

Create the following concordance file named **DP Concordance**:

typography	typography
font face	font characteristics: font face
weight	font characteristics: weight
font size	font characteristics: font size
sans serif	sans serif font
serif font	serif font
Times New Roman	serif font: Times New Roman
Bookman	serif font: Bookman
Garamond	serif font: Garamond
Arial	sans serif font: Arial
Helvetica	sans serif font: Helvetica
font style	style of font
font size	font size
text-intensive	font size: text-intensive documents
headings	font size: headings
spacing	spacing
margin	margin
leading	spacing: leading
descenders	descenders
line spacing	line spacing

Display the **DP Title Page** document in the Outline View mode. Insert the following files as subdocuments in this order: **DP Design**, **DP Spacing**, **DP Bibliography**, and **DP Index**. Save the master document as **DP Master Document**. Remove the **DP Index** by clicking the appropriate button to make it part of the master document. Make sure you have a new page section break, not a continuous section break, between the last subdocument and the index.

Click the AutoMark button in the Index section of the Index and Tables dialog box to select your concordance file. Then, compile the index.

Save the master document, switch to Print Layout View, and print the index only. Switch back to Outline View, collapse the subdocuments and save the master document. Print the collapsed document.

PinPoint Assessment

You have completed this project and its associated lessons, and have had an opportunity to assess your skills through the end-of-project questions and exercises. Now use the PinPoint software Evaluation Mode to further assess your comprehension of the specific exam activities you have just learned. You can also use the PinPoint Trainer Mode and the Show Me tutorials to practice these exam activities.

Project 18

Managing Files and Customizing Word

Key terms introduced in this project include

- details
- docked toolbar
- Favorites
- file size

- file type
- file maintenance
- floating toolbar

- modified
- root directory
- subfolder

Objectives	Required Activity for MOUS	Exam Level
➤ View File Details		
➤ Create, Rename, and Delete Folders	Create a folder	Core
➤ Copy, Move, Rename, and Delete Files		
➤ Create Favorites		
➤ Create a Toolbar	Customize toolbars	Expert
➤ Add and Remove Toolbar Buttons	Customize toolbars	Expert
➤ Customize Word Settings		

Why Would I Do This?

As you become more experienced in using Word, you need to start managing your files. For example, you need to organize them into categories, make backup copies, and delete files you no longer need. Although you can use the Windows My Computer or Windows Explorer to perform file-management tasks, you can also perform these tasks within Word.

In addition to file management, you might want to customize Word by creating a brand-new toolbar with the buttons you use most often. In this project, you create a new toolbar, and add, remove, and rearrange buttons.

Lesson 1: Viewing File Details

As you know, the Open and Save As dialog boxes display files you have saved. You also know how to select a drive by clicking the Look in or Save in drop-down arrows. You clicked the Files of type drop-down arrow to specify types of files to display, as well. For example, you chose Document Template (*.dot) when you saved templates; you chose MS Access Databases (*.mdb;*.mde) when opening a data source for mail merge.

In addition to selecting a drive, folder, and filename to open or save, these dialog boxes contain other valuable tools to work with your files.

In this lesson, you use the View options to change the view of the list of files you see in the Open and Save As dialog boxes.

To View File Details

1 **Click the Open button on the Standard toolbar.**
You can display either the Open or Save As dialog box. When you change View options in one dialog box, Word changes the View options in the other dialog box.

2 **Display the contents of the** `Project 18` **folder on your CD-ROM.**
You probably see a one-column list of the files in that folder. If the folder contains more files than you can see in the list box, you'll see scrollbars to scroll through the list of files.

3 **Click the Views drop-down arrow and choose** <u>D</u>**etails.**
Figure 18.1 shows the list of files in the Details view. The *Details* option displays the filename, file size, file type, and modified. *File size* refers to the amount of space in kilobytes. The larger the number, the bigger the file is. *File type* refers to the kind of file it is, such as a Microsoft Word or Microsoft Excel file. This information helps you know what program to use to open a particular file. *Modified* indicates the last date and time the file was saved.

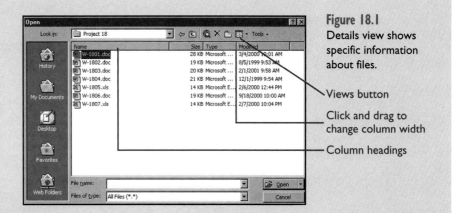

Figure 18.1
Details view shows specific information about files.

Views button

Click and drag to change column width

Column headings

 Inside Stuff: **Changing Column Width**

If you can't see the full data in a column, you can click and drag the vertical line between the column headings to increase or decrease the column width.

---

4 **Click the Modified column heading to arrange files in chronological order by date.**

The oldest file is listed first. In this case, W-1802 is the oldest file. The newest file, at the bottom of the list, is W-1803.

5 **Click the Modified column heading again.**

Clicking the heading a second time arranges the list in the opposite direction. Now, the newest file is listed first. The rest of the files are listed in reverse chronological order (see Figure 18.2).

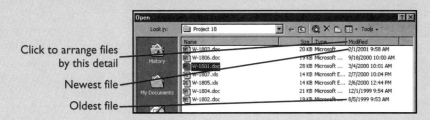

Click to arrange files by this detail

Newest file

Oldest file

Figure 18.2
Click the column heading to arrange the list of files.

6 **Click the Name column heading.**

The files are now listed in alphabetical order by the filename.

7 **Click W-1802 to select it, but don't open it!**

8 **Click the Views drop-down arrow and choose Pre_view._**

A Preview window appears on the right side of the dialog box (see Figure 18.3). It displays the contents of the file you selected.

continues ▶

To View File Details (continued)

Figure 18.3
Use Preview to see a document's contents before opening it.

Selected file

Preview of selected file's contents

Scrollbar to scroll through Preview window

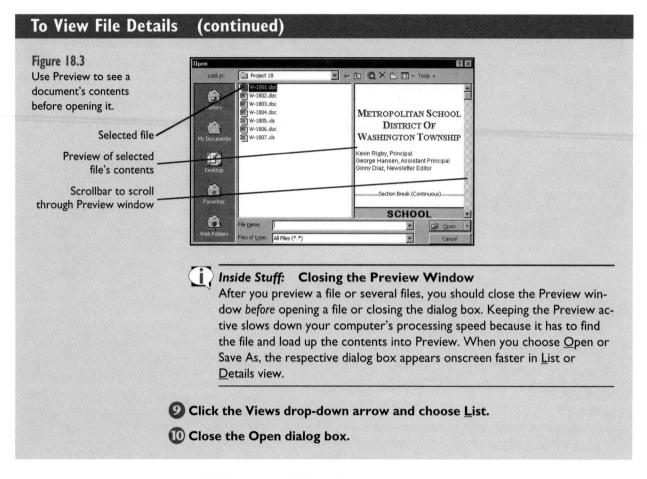

> **Inside Stuff:** **Closing the Preview Window**
> After you preview a file or several files, you should close the Preview window *before* opening a file or closing the dialog box. Keeping the Preview active slows down your computer's processing speed because it has to find the file and load up the contents into Preview. When you choose <u>O</u>pen or Save As, the respective dialog box appears onscreen faster in <u>L</u>ist or <u>D</u>etails view.

9 **Click the Views drop-down arrow and choose <u>L</u>ist.**

10 **Close the Open dialog box.**

> **Inside Stuff:** **Displaying Extensions**
> Depending on the Windows settings, you might not see the three-letter filename extension, such as .doc or .xls. To display these extensions in the Open and Save As dialog boxes, display the My Computer or Windows Explorer window. Choose <u>V</u>iew, Folder <u>O</u>ptions; click the View tab; deselect the `Hide file extensions for known file types` check box; and then click OK.

Lesson 2: Creating, Renaming, and Deleting Folders

You have worked with folders throughout this textbook. In Project 2, "Working with a Document," you learned that a folder is a category for storing and organizing similar files. The folder that holds all other folders on a storage device is called the **root directory**, or root folder. For example, the 3 1/2 inch Floppy (A:) is a root directory.

As you continue working with files, you'll start noticing that several files relate to the same thing, such as a conference or a client's portfolio. You can create folders on most storage devices to organize your files. To create folders, you can use My Computer, Windows Explorer, Word, or other applications.

In this lesson, you create and rename folders.

> **Inside Stuff:** **Folders Created in Word**
> The folders you create in Word are available for storing other files besides Word files. You can store Excel, PowerPoint, and Access files in the same folders.

To Create a Folder

1 **Click the Open button to display the Open dialog box.**

2 **Make sure you are in the root directory for a floppy disk, Zip disk, or personal network drive.**
You can't create a folder on the CD-ROM that accompanies this textbook.

3 **Click the Create New Folder button.**
The New Folder dialog box appears (see Figure 18.4). It displays the drive and folder, if any, that you're creating a folder in. A folder within a folder is known as a *subfolder*.

Figure 18.4
Assign a name to the new folder.

4 **Type** Essentials **in the Name box, and click OK.**
When you create a folder, Word makes that the active folder.

 If You Have Problems...
If you get an error message, stating that folder cannot be created, make sure you are creating a folder on a storage device that allows this. If you are trying to save to a floppy disk and receive this message, make sure the write-protection tab is not in place on the disk.

5 **Click the Up One Level button.**
This button takes you out of the current folder and up one level in the folder hierarchy.

6 **Leave the dialog box open to continue with the next exercise.**

 Inside Stuff: **Renaming a Folder**
After you create a folder name, you might realize that the name has a typographical error in it, or you might want additional words in the filename. To rename a folder, select the folder name and then press F2 or right-click the folder name and choose Rename. You can type a new name or you can scroll within the folder name and make slight changes. Press ↵Enter to accept the new name.

 Inside Stuff: **Deleting a Folder**
If you no longer need a folder, you can delete it. Select the folder and click the Delete button, or right-click the folder and choose Delete from the menu. Click Yes to confirm the deletion.

If the folder contains files, Word deletes those files as well as the folder name. If you want to keep those files, you should move them to another location before deleting the folder name. The next lesson discusses moving files.

Lesson 3: Copying, Moving, Renaming, and Deleting Files

You should periodically review your files and perform file maintenance. **File maintenance** involves copying files to create backup copies, deleting files you no longer need, moving files into folders to organize them, and renaming files.

In the first part of this lesson, you copy files from one storage device to another; in the latter part of the lesson, you move files from one location to another.

To Perform File Maintenance

1 **In the Open dialog box, change the Look in option to the drive containing the CD-ROM that accompanies this book.**

2 **Display the contents of the Project 18 folder.**
You want to copy W-1803.doc, W-1805.xls, and W-1807.xls to the folder you created in the last lesson. Make sure the Files of type option is All Files (*.*).

3 **Click W-1803.doc and press and hold down Ctrl while you click W-1805.xls and W-1807.xls.**
Only the first file and the files you clicked while holding down Ctrl are selected.

 Inside Stuff: **Selecting Consecutively Listed Files**
If the files are all listed together, you can click the first one and press and hold down ◆Shift while you click the last file. All files in between are selected.

4 **Right-click one of the selected files to display the shortcut menu (see Figure 18.5).**

Figure 18.5
Use the shortcut menu to perform file maintenance.

Selected files

Cuts (removes) selected files

Copies selected files

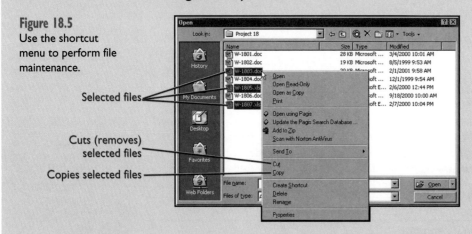

5 **Choose Copy from the shortcut menu.**
You want to place the duplicate files in the root directory on your floppy disk, so you need to display that drive.

6 **Change the Look in option to the 3 1/2 inch Floppy (A:) or whichever drive you created your folder in during Lesson 2.**

7 **Right-click in the empty space in the list box area and choose Paste to paste a copy of the files there.**

If You Have Problems...
If a folder name is highlighted when you choose Paste, Word pastes the files inside that folder. This is why you must ensure that no folder or filename is highlighted when you use the Paste command.

8 **Leave the dialog box open to continue with the next exercise.**

The files are located in two places: on the original CD-ROM and in the root directory of the floppy disk. Having two copies in different locations is beneficial in case one file becomes corrupt, or if that storage device is damaged. You can use your backup file instead of re-creating the document.

 Inside Stuff: **Copying Folders**
You can copy a folder with the files inside it. Simply select the folder without going into it, and then use the Copy and Paste commands to make a duplicate of the folder and its contents in another location.

 Inside Stuff: **Send To**
The Send To option creates a copy of the selected files to the root directory of the 3 1/2 inch Floppy (A:), Zip drive, or other device.

As you review files, you'll probably decide that some files should be moved into different folders. To move files, you use the Cut and Paste commands. In the next exercise, you move the three files you just pasted from the root directory to the Essentials folder you created.

To Move Files

1 **Select the three files—W-1803.doc, W-1805.xls, and W-1807.xls—if they are not already selected.**

2 **Right-click any selected file and choose Cut from the shortcut menu.**

3 **Double-click the Essentials folder.**
Now, you're ready to paste the files there.

4 **Right-click an empty space within the folder and choose Paste.**
The three files are now moved out of the root directory and are placed in the Essentials folder (see Figure 18.6).

Current folder ———
Files moved here ———

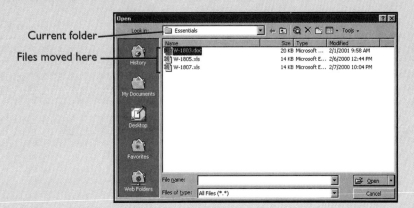

Figure 18.6
Files are moved into the Essentials folder.

continues ▶

To Move Files (continued)

 Inside Stuff: **Refreshing the File List View**
If the files do not appear after using the Paste command, you might need to refresh the view. Press F5 to refresh the view, and you should see any files you've pasted in the current location.

5 **Keep the dialog box open to continue with the next lesson.**

 Inside Stuff: **Renaming Files**
You can rename a file by pressing F2 or by right-clicking it and choosing Rename. You can rename all or part of the filename. However, make sure you keep the period and filename extension—.doc, for example. Otherwise, the system won't recognize which program created that file.

  Inside Stuff: **Deleting Files**
You should delete files when you no longer need them. Select the file or files you want to delete, click the Delete button in the dialog box, and click Yes to confirm the deletion.

You can't undo a deleted file from the floppy disk, Zip disk, or network drive. However, if you delete a file from the hard drive, you can use the Windows Recycle Bin to restore it. Refer to Windows Help to learn more about the Recycle Bin.

Lesson 4: Creating Favorites

You probably notice that you use some folders quite frequently and how much time it takes to click your way to a subfolder. For example, your organization might have clip art files buried deep in the organization's intranet. For example, these files might be at G:\Network\Shared\Graphics\Clipart. You can save time getting to these files—even from the Insert Picture dialog box. You can use the **Favorites** feature to create a shortcut to your favorite folders. When you need to quickly get to those folders, you choose the Favorite instead of working your way through the folder hierarchy to find them.

In this lesson, you create a Favorites location to the **Essentials** folder.

To Add a Folder to Favorites

1 **Make sure you see the Essentials folder within the Open dialog box.**

 2 **Click the Up One Level button.**

3 **Click the Essentials folder to select it, but do not double-click it.**

 4 **Click the Tools button, and then choose Add to Favorites.**

5 **Click the Favorites button to see a list of Favorite locations.**
Figure 18.7 shows items in the Favorites location. Your items will vary.

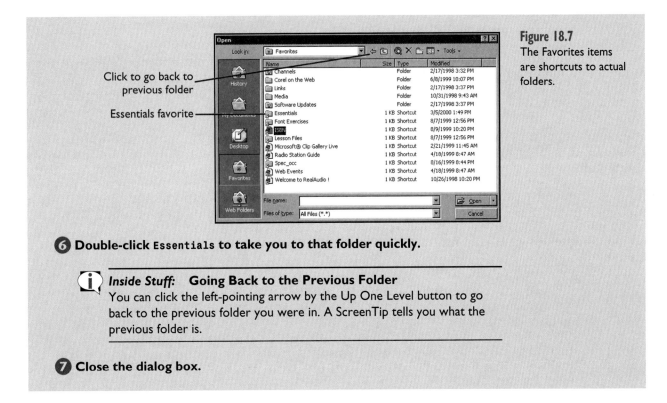

Click to go back to previous folder

Essentials favorite

Figure 18.7
The Favorites items are shortcuts to actual folders.

6 Double-click Essentials **to take you to that folder quickly.**

 Inside Stuff: **Going Back to the Previous Folder**
You can click the left-pointing arrow by the Up One Level button to go back to the previous folder you were in. A ScreenTip tells you what the previous folder is.

7 **Close the dialog box.**

 Inside Stuff:—Removing a Favorites Item
If you no longer need a Favorites shortcut, you can remove it. Click the Favorites button to see a list of Favorites shortcuts. Click the item you want to remove, click the Delete button, and click Yes to confirm the deletion. Deleting a Favorite deletes the *shortcut* to the folder, not the actual folder itself.

Lesson 5: Creating a Toolbar

By now, you're familiar with many Word toolbars: Standard, Formatting, Header and Footer, Picture, AutoText, Clipboard, Drawing, and WordArt. Although you typically keep the Standard and Formatting toolbars visible at all times, the other toolbars appear when you work on a specific task, such as headers and footers. Figure 18.8 shows several toolbars you should already be familiar with.

Figure 18.8
Toolbars you have used.

AutoText toolbar docked below Formatting toolbar

Floating toolbars

Drawing toolbar appears above status bar

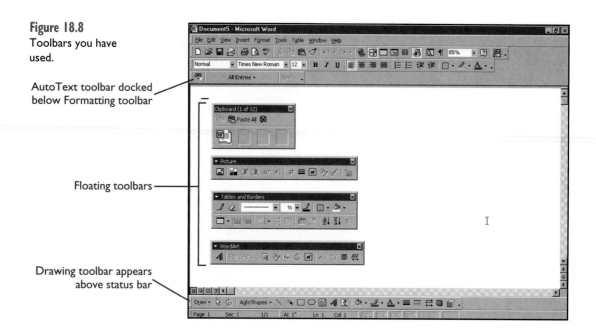

Toolbars that appear at the top or bottom of the screen are **docked**, which means they are "anchored" at that location. Toolbars with title bars that appear in the middle of the screen are **floating toolbars** because they "float" around on the screen by changing their locations as you work. You can click and drag floating toolbars around on the screen or dock them at a side of the screen.

You can also create your own toolbars with buttons that you use frequently. In this lesson, you create a toolbar.

To Create a Toolbar

1 In a new document window, choose View, Toolbars, Customize.
The Customize dialog box appears, so you can customize the toolbar settings.

2 Click the Toolbars tab.
The Toolbars tab displays the available toolbars (see Figure 18.9). The active toolbars are indicated by check marks.

Figure 18.9
Customize the toolbar settings.

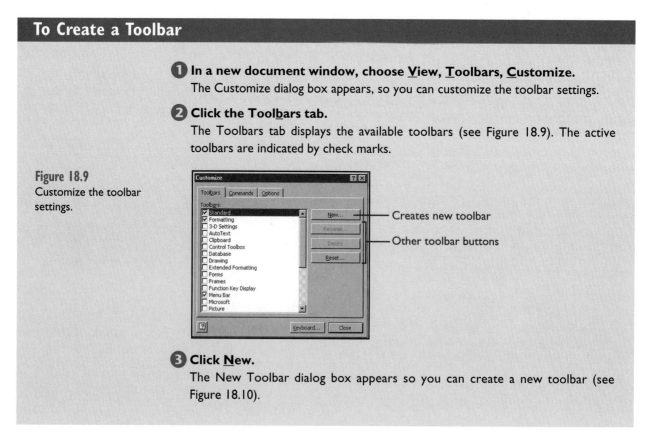

Creates new toolbar

Other toolbar buttons

3 Click New.
The New Toolbar dialog box appears so you can create a new toolbar (see Figure 18.10).

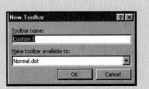

Figure 18.10
Name the new toolbar.

4 Type Essentials: Keith, substituting your name after the colon, and then click **OK**.

Figure 18.11 shows a tiny toolbar to the side of the dialog box. It is mainly gray until you add buttons to it.

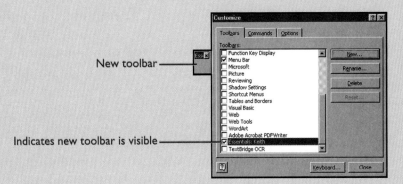

New toolbar ——

Indicates new toolbar is visible ——

Figure 18.11
Your new toolbar appears onscreen.

5 Leave the dialog box onscreen to continue with the next lesson.

 Inside Stuff: **Moving a Toolbar**
You can move a toolbar by dragging it to the top of the screen. When it is docked, you can click the raised gray vertical line to move the toolbar elsewhere.

Lesson 6: Adding and Removing Toolbar Buttons

You can customize a new or existing toolbar by adding and removing buttons. For example, some people like to click a button that displays the Print dialog box instead of immediately sending the document to the printer.

In this lesson, you add buttons to the toolbar you created in the last lesson.

To Add Toolbar Buttons

1 Make sure your toolbar is displayed and the Customize dialog box is still onscreen.

2 Click the Commands tab in the Customize dialog box.
The Commands tab shows commands and buttons you can add to your toolbar (see Figure 18.12).

continues ▶

To Add Toolbar Buttons   (continued)

Figure 18.12
Choose command
buttons for your
toolbar.

Categories —

— Commands for selected category

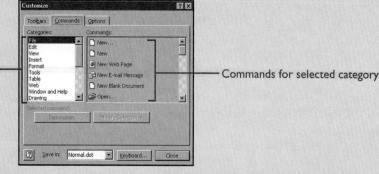

③ **Scroll through the Commands list and click Close All.**

④ **Click and drag Close All to the gray space on your toolbar, which should be onscreen.**
Figure 18.13 shows the command being added to the toolbar.

Figure 18.13
Add commands by
clicking and dragging
them to the toolbar.

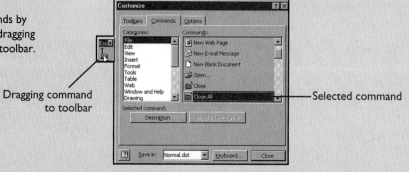

Dragging command
to toolbar

— Selected command

⑤ **Scroll through the Commands list and then click and drag Page Setup to the toolbar.**

⑥ **Scroll through the list and find Print... and Print.**
Print is like the default button—it prints the document. Print... displays the Print dialog box. If you need to know more about a button, click Description.

⑦ **Drag Print... to the right side of your toolbar.**
Figure 18.14 shows your toolbar after adding three buttons to it.

Figure 18.14
Your toolbar has three
buttons.

Now you want to move the Print button to the left of the Page Setup button.

⑧ **Click the Print button on your new toolbar and drag it between the Close All and Page Setup buttons.**
As you drag a button on the toolbar, you see a vertical insertion point letting you know where the toolbar button will be located when you release the mouse button. Figure 18.15 shows the new location of the Print button.

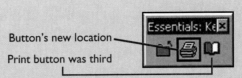

Button's new location

Print button was third

Figure 18.15
The Print button is
second now.

9 **Click the Toolbars tab and click the Essentials: Keith check box to hide the toolbar; leave the Customize dialog box onscreen to continue with the next lesson.**

 Exam Note: **Removing Toolbar Buttons**
You can remove a button from a toolbar if you want. Make sure the toolbar is visible and display the Customize dialog box. Drag the button straight down from the toolbar and release the mouse button.

Lesson 7: Customizing Word Settings

You can customize other Word settings, such as Menu options and View options. Throughout this book, you've seen Inside Stuff notes referring you to the Customize or Options dialog box.

In this lesson, you customize a few settings.

To Customize Word Settings

1 **Make sure the Customize dialog box is open. If it isn't, choose Tools, Customize.**

2 **Click the Options tab.**
Figure 18.16 shows the Options tab selections. In Project 1, "Getting Started with Word 2000," you deselected the first option to show the Standard and Formatting toolbars on separate rows.

Make sure this is deselected

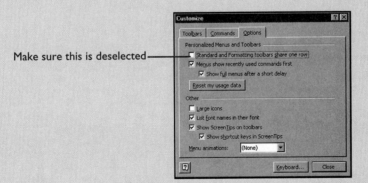

Figure 18.16
Specify options for
customizing Word.

3 **Click Menus show recently used commands first to deselect it.**
Recall that the menu-bar menus show short menus followed by full menus. Deselecting this option displays the full menus each time you choose a category from the menu bar.

4 **Click Close.**

continues ▶

To Customize Word Settings   (continued)

⑤ **Choose Format.**

Notice that you see the full menu immediately. You don't see down-pointing arrows at the bottom of a short menu.

⑥ **Close the menu without selecting an option.**

You can further customize Word by choosing Tools, Options to display the Options dialog box (see Figure 18.17).

Figure 18.17
Customize the Word environment in the Options dialog box.

Summary

After completing this project, you are ready to adjust the view of files in the Open and Save As dialog boxes. You can also create, rename, and delete folders; and copy, move, rename, and delete files. In addition, you know how to create and add a folder to the Favorites list to get there quickly, and you can create your own toolbar. Finally, you can add and remove buttons from a toolbar.

You should practice performing file-maintenance tasks and explore the other options in the Open and Save As dialog boxes. In addition, explore the Customize and Options dialog boxes to see how you can adapt the Word environment. To enhance your skills, complete the following activities.

Checking Concepts and Terms

True/False

For each of the following, check T or F to indicate whether the statement is true or false.

__T __F **1.** The List view shows file size and date modified. [L1]

__T __F **2.** The base level of a storage device on which folders are created is called the root directory. [L2]

__T __F **3.** You use the Cut and Paste commands to move a file from one location to another. [L3]

__T __F **4.** When you delete an item from Favorites, you also are deleting it from its original location. [L4]

__T __F   **5.** With the Customize dialog box on-screen, you can add command buttons to any visible toolbar. [L6]

Multiple Choice

Circle the letter of the correct answer for each of the following.

1. In the Save As dialog box, which details column displays the last date and time you saved files? [L1]

    a. Name

    b. Size

    c. Type

    d. Modified

2. What keyboard shortcut lets you rename a folder or a file? [L2–3]

    a. F1

    b. ⬆Shift+F3

    c. F2

    d. F5

3. You can restore files that you've deleted from what storage device? [L3]

    a. floppy drive

    b. Zip drive

    c. network drive

    d. hard drive

4. What dialog box is required to create a new toolbar? [L5]

    a. Customize

    b. Options

    c. Open

    d. Commands

5. How do you remove a button from a toolbar? [L6]

    a. Right-click the button and choose <u>D</u>elete.

    b. Click and drag the button down while the Customize dialog box is onscreen.

    c. With the Customize dialog box onscreen, click the button and then press Del.

    d. Without having the Customize dialog box open, click and drag the button into the document window.

Screen ID

Label each element of the Word screen shown in Figure 18.18.

Figure 18.18

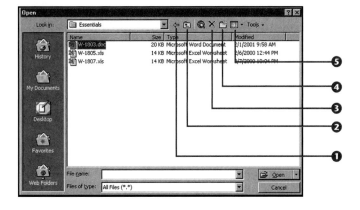

A. Create New Folder

B. Delete

C. Displays previous list of files

D. Up One Level

E. Views

1._____   2._____   3._____

4._____   5._____

Skill Drill

Skill Drill exercises reinforce project skills. Each skill reinforced is the same, or nearly the same, as a skill presented in the project. Each exercise includes a brief narrative introduction, followed by detailed instructions in a step-by-step format.

1. Creating and Renaming a Folder

One of your coworkers is inexperienced in Word and has asked your help in showing file details and creating a folder.

1. With a new document onscreen, click the Save button.

2. Click the Views button and choose Details.

3. Insert a formatted floppy disk into the computer.

4. Click the Save in drop-down arrow and choose 3 1/2 inch Floppy (A:).

5. Click the Create New Folder button, type **Orders**, and click OK.

   Your coworker changed his mind and wants the folder to be called Back Orders.

6. Click the Up One Level button.

7. Click the **Orders** folder name one time to select it.

8. Press (F2) to rename the folder.

9. Press (Home), type **Back**, press (Spacebar), and press (↵Enter).

10. Keep the dialog box open to continue with the next exercise.

2. Managing Files

You need to copy files from the CD-ROM to the floppy disk, so you'll have a backup of important files. You later decide to rename a file and then delete another one.

1. With the Save As dialog box onscreen, display the drive containing the CD-ROM that accompanies this book.

2. Double-click your way to find the Project 18 folder.

3. Click the Project 18 folder name without going into it.

4. Right-click the selected folder, choose Send To, and choose 3 1/2 inch Floppy (A:).

5. Click the Save in drop-down arrow and choose 3 1/2 inch Floppy (A:).

6. Double-click **Project 18**.

7. Click **W-1801.doc**, and press and hold down (↑Shift) while you click **W-1804.doc**.

8. Right-click a selected filename and choose Copy.

9. Click the Up One Level button, and then double-click the **Back Orders** folder you created.

10. Right-click in an empty part of the list box and choose Paste. If the filenames don't appear, press (F5) to refresh the view.

11. Click **W-1801.doc**, press (F2), type **Newsletter.doc**, and then press (↵Enter).

12. Close the dialog box.

3. Customizing the Formatting Toolbar

You want to add two buttons to the Formatting toolbar. The More Buttons drop-down arrow lets you display or remove various buttons on the toolbar. After adding the buttons, you reset the toolbar to its default buttons.

1. Click the More Buttons drop-down arrow on the far right side of the Formatting toolbar. It is the last drop-down arrow you see.

2. Choose Add or Remove Buttons.

3. Choose Single Spacing and choose Double Spacing. *Note:* You see two more buttons on the right side of the toolbar.

4. Click outside the drop-down menu to close it.

5. Click the More Buttons drop-down arrow on the right side of the Formatting toolbar.

6. Choose Add or Remove Buttons.

7. Choose Reset Toolbar.

8. Click OK.

9. Click Yes if you see the following message: **Do you also want to save changes to the document template?**

Challenge

Challenge exercises expand on or are somewhat related to skills presented in the lessons. Each exercise provides a brief narrative introduction, followed by instructions in a numbered-step or bulleted-list format that are not as detailed as those in the Skill Drill section.

1. Managing Files

You want to organize files on your disk. You need to create some folders and move files into these folders.

1. Create the following folders on a data disk: **Letters**, **Reports**, **Newsletters**, **Miscellaneous**.

2. Preview files in the Project 13 folder on your CD-ROM. Select and copy newsletter files into the Newsletter folder on your data disk.

3. Rename the files you just copied into the Newsletter folder. Preview the files to provide meaningful filenames. Remember to keep the filename extensions.

4. Find the files you created when you completed Projects 1–4. Don't use the CD-ROM files. Locate files containing letters and copy them to the Letters folder on your data disk.

5. Search through the files you created for Projects 5 and 6. Move any long document to the Reports folder on your disk.

6. Delete the Miscellaneous folder from your data disk.

7. Submit your data disk to your instructor to verify your file-maintenance tasks.

2. Creating a Toolbar

You want to create a toolbar containing frequently used buttons. Then, you'll hide the Standard toolbar and display the new toolbar.

1. Create a new toolbar called **Word Toolbar:** and type your name after the colon.

2. Add these commands from the File category: New Blank Document, Open..., Close All, Save As..., Save, Page Setup..., and Print....

3. Add these commands from the Edit category: Undo, Cut, Copy, and Paste.

4. Add these commands from the Insert category: Date, AutoText..., Symbol..., File..., and Clip Art....

5. Add this command from the Tools category: Spelling....

6. Hide the Standard toolbar and dock your toolbar above the Formatting toolbar.

7. Edit your toolbar by doing the following tasks:

   a. Move Page Setup... to the right of Print....

   b. Add the Zoom command to the right side of the toolbar.

   c. Add the Insert Table... command to the left of the Zoom button.

   d. Move the Spelling... button to the right of Print....

   e. Move File... to the right of Open....

   f. Remove AutoText... and Date.

8. Show the toolbar to your instructor.

9. Hide your toolbar and display the Standard toolbar in its typical location.

3. Customizing Word Options

You want to see the effects of changing some options in the Customize dialog box.

1. Display the Customize dialog box.

2. Click the Options tab.

3. Click the option to show recently used commands first.

4. Reset your usage data.

5. Choose a menu animation.

6. Close the dialog box.

7. Choose menu options. See whether the short menus appear first and that the option list is fairly short. Also notice the animation effect.

8. Select another menu animation and study its results.

9. Change the menu animation back to None and close the dialog box.

Discovery Zone

Discovery Zone exercises help you gain advanced knowledge of project topics and/or application of skills. These exercises focus on enhancing your problem-solving skills. Numbered steps are not provided, but you are given hints, reminders, screen shots, and/or references to help you reach your goal for each exercise.

1. Exploring Options for Opening Files

You noticed several options for opening files on the shortcut menu that appears when you right-click a filename. You want to explore these options.

Open **W-1802**, save it as **Open Exploration**, and close it. In the Open dialog box, open the file by choosing the different options on the shortcut menu. Make changes and try to save the file under the same filename. Type a brief description of each method, save the information as **Open Options**, and print it.

2. Finding Files

After working with an enormous number of files, you often forget where something is stored. Or, you might want to quickly find files saved during a certain time period. In the Open dialog box, you can use the Find command from the Tools button to help locate files.

Find files in all subfolders that are Microsoft Excel file types on the CD-ROM that accompanies this book. Delete the default find condition. After Word finds files of this type, press Alt+PrtSc to make a copy of the dialog box as a picture. Then, in a new Word document, use Paste to paste the image there. You can then use the Picture toolbar to adjust its size to a 4 inch width, Top and Bottom text wrap, and Center horizontal position. Type a description of what you found as a caption.

Find files that were last modified between 12/1/99 and 3/1/00 in the Project 18 folder. Remove the file type restriction. Use the Print Screen option to save the image to the Clipboard; then paste it below the previous image. Use the same Picture formats. Create a caption that describes the files found.

Save your document as **Files Found** and print it.

PinPoint Assessment

You have completed this project and its associated lessons, and have had an opportunity to assess your skills through the end-of-project questions and exercises. Now use the PinPoint software Evaluation Mode to further assess your comprehension of the specific exam activities you have just learned. You can also use the PinPoint Trainer Mode and the Show Me tutorials to practice these exam activities.

Collaborating on Documents

Key terms introduced in this project include

- accept change
- comment
- comment mark
- Comment pane

- password
- protection
- read-only
- reject change

- revision mark
- track changes
- version

Objectives	Required Activity for MOUS	Exam Level
➤ Insert and View Comments	Insert comments	Expert
➤ Edit and Delete Comments		
➤ Track Changes	Track changes to a document	Expert
➤ Accept and Reject Changes	Track changes to a document	Expert
➤ Save Different Versions of a Document	Create multiple versions of a document	Expert
➤ Protect Documents	Protect documents	Expert

Why Would I Do This?

Today's business environment requires that many people work together to plan, develop, write, and edit important documents. Various individuals submit ideas, provide comments and feedback, review progress, and rewrite material. This process can be confusing and time consuming when it is necessary to incorporate other people's changes on printed copies.

Word includes collaboration tools to help people work together to create documents. Word helps control the organizational tasks in collaboration, such as tracking changes made by different people, dating different versions of the same document, and identifying the source of comments inserted in a document. You and your coworkers can then focus on more important things, such as writing and preparing the document.

In this project, you work with Word's collaboration tools.

Lesson 1: Inserting and Viewing Comments

You can make suggestions to another author or team member by inserting comments into a document. A **comment** is a note or other text that appears onscreen as a ScreenTip, but it does not affect regular document text. A Word comment is similar to writing on a 3M Post-it® self-stick note.

In this lesson, you insert two comments in a cost-containment report.

To Insert and View Comments

1 **Open W-1901 and save it as Cost Containment Report.**
You are a member of the panel that is preparing this report.

2 **Choose View, Toolbars, Reviewing.**
The Reviewing toolbar contains buttons you need for inserting comments and tracking changes.

3 **Position the insertion point at the end of the first paragraph.**
You want to insert a comment about this sentence.

 4 **Click the Insert Comment button on the Reviewing toolbar.**

 Inside Stuff: **Inserting a Comment**
You can also insert comments by choosing Insert, Comment.

Word highlights the previous word, inserts a comment mark, and opens the Comment pane (see Figure 19.1). A **comment mark**, which appears in yellow highlight, is a designation where a comment is inserted. The **Comment pane** is the window that contains the comment text, reviewer's initials, and the sequential comment number.

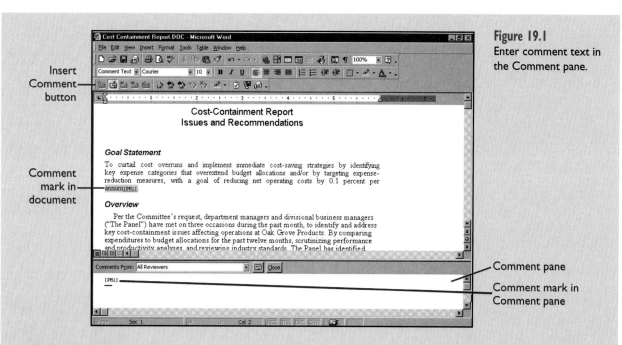

Figure 19.1
Enter comment text in
the Comment pane.

⑤ Type Verify target goal with upper management.

The comment text appears in the Comment pane. You can continue working in the document with the Comment pane open, or you can close the pane until you are ready to insert, review, or edit comments.

⑥ Position the insertion point in the word three in the first sentence in the Overview section.

⑦ Click the Insert Comment button on the Reviewing toolbar.

Word inserts another comment mark and moves the insertion point into the Comment pane.

⑧ Type I thought we met four times.

Your document has two comments (see Figure 19.2).

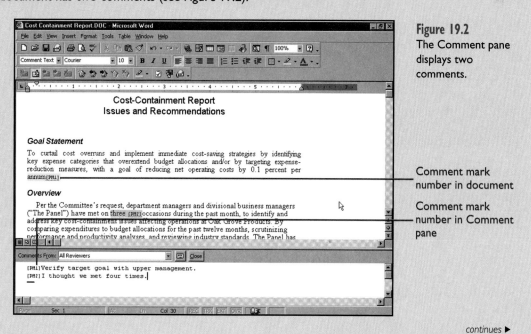

Figure 19.2
The Comment pane
displays two
comments.

continues ▶

To Insert and View Comments   (continued)

9 **Click the Close button at the top of the Comment pane.**
The Comment pane closes, and Word hides the comment marks. The comment locations are highlighted in the document in light yellow.

 If You Have Problems...
If you still see comment marks even after closing the Comment pane, Word is set up to display hidden text. You can keep it displayed or hide it. To hide hidden text (including comment marks), choose Tools, Options, click the View tab, deselect the Hidden text check box, and then click OK.

If the Hidden text check box is marked, you see the comment marks when you click the Show/Hide ¶ button to display the nonprinting symbols.

You want to make sure the comment displays onscreen.

10 **Position the mouse pointer over the highlighted word annum.**
You briefly see a Comment icon, and then a ScreenTip appears that displays the reviewer's name and the comment text (see Figure 19.3).

Figure 19.3
The comment
ScreenTip appears.

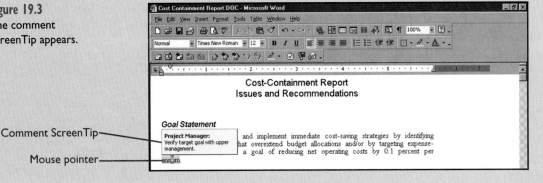

Comment ScreenTip
Mouse pointer

 If You Have Problems...
If a ScreenTip does not appear when you point at the comment highlight, check two things. First, make sure that you are not moving the mouse pointer at all. Second, make sure the ScreenTips are turned on in the Options dialog box.

11 **Save the document and keep it onscreen to continue with the next lesson.**

  Inside Stuff: **Inserting Audio Comments**
You can record audio comments if your computer contains a sound card and a microphone. After clicking the Insert Comment button as usual, click the Insert Sound Object button at the top of the Comment pane and record your verbal comments. To play back the comment, double-click the sound button at the top of the Comment pane.

Inside Stuff: **Changing the Reviewer's Name and Initials**
You can change the reviewer's name and initials that appear for comments. Choose Tools, Options. Click the User Information tab, type the reviewer's name in the Name text box, type reviewer's initials in the Initials text box, and then click OK.

New comments inserted after making this change appear with the new name and initials; comments created before changing the name and initials maintain the original name and initials.

Lesson 2: Editing and Deleting Comments

After creating comments, you might want to edit them. You can also delete comments after others have read them and taken action, or print comments for reference.

In this lesson, you edit and delete comments.

To Edit and Delete Comments

1 **In the open Cost Containment Report document, click the Edit Comment button on the Reviewing toolbar.**
The Comment pane opens, displaying the list of comments in the document.

 Inside Stuff: **Opening the Comment Pane**
If the nonprinting symbols are displayed, you can double-click a comment mark to open the Comment pane.

2 **Double-click four in the second comment and type five to change the text.**

3 **Position the mouse pointer on the second comment, which is the word three in the document.**
The ScreenTip displays the edited comment text (see Figure 19.4).

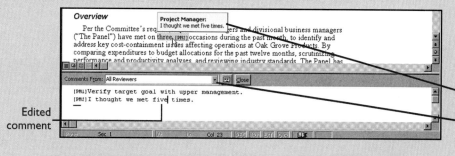

Figure 19.4
Comment changes are immediately shown in the ScreenTip.

Updated ScreenTip

Click to see list of reviewers

 Inside Stuff: **Showing Comments for a Particular Reviewer**
By default, you see comments for all reviewers. You can display comments for a particular reviewer by clicking the Comments From drop-down arrow and choosing a person from the list.

One of your team members verified the accuracy of the data in the first paragraph, so you can now delete that comment.

continues ▶

To Edit and Delete Comments (continued)

4 **Select the word annum and click the Delete Comment button on the Reviewing toolbar.**
Word deletes the comment, removes the highlight from the document text, and renumbers the remaining comments in the document.

5 **Click the Close button at the top of the Comment pane.**

6 **Save the document and keep it onscreen to continue with the next lesson.**

Inside Stuff: **Printing Comments**
You can print the document with its comments. Display the Print dialog box, click Options, click the Comments check box, and click OK.

You can print the comments only by clicking the Print what drop-down arrow and choosing Comments. This prints the comments without printing the document text.

Lesson 3: Tracking Changes

To help you monitor document revisions, you can **track changes** while you edit. Word indicates all changes made to a document by applying noticeable formatting called **revision marks**. Word marks deleted text with strikethrough and insertions with underline. The inserted and deleted text also appears in color, such as blue, red, or green. Word uses different colors for different reviewers who edit the document. You can position the mouse pointer over revision marks to see who made the change and on what date.

In this lesson, you use track changes.

To Track Changes

1 **In the open Cost Containment Report document, click the Track Changes button on the Reviewing toolbar.**
The Track Changes feature is on. The TRK indicator on the status bar is bold. By default, Word tracks changes onscreen and in printed documents.

Inside Stuff: **TRK Indicator**
You can double-click the TRK indicator on the status bar to turn on or off the Track Changes feature.

2 **Select the heading Goal and type Mission to replace it.**
Word applies the default revision mark formatting, as shown in Figure 19.5. Instead of removing deleted text, Word changes the font color and applies strikethrough formatting. Inserted text appears in a different color and underlined. A vertical black line appears in the left margin, indicating the lines where changes have been made.

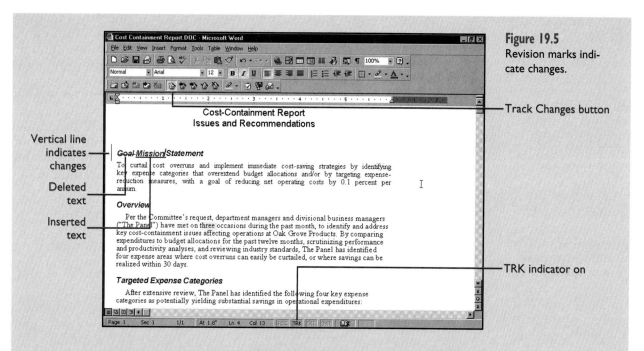

Figure 19.5
Revision marks indicate changes.

Track Changes button

Vertical line indicates changes

Deleted text

Inserted text

TRK indicator on

---

i *Inside Stuff:*   **Revision Mark Formatting**
The color and format of the revision marks might vary on your computer.

---

3 **Type the word** actual **and press** Spacebar **before** expenditures **in the paragraph below the Overview heading. Be sure to press** Spacebar **after typing the new word.**
The inserted word is underlined and in a different color.

4 **Select** twelve **in the same paragraph and type** 12 **to change it.**

5 **In the paragraph below the Targeted Expense Categories heading, change** key **to** primary, **and change** substantial **to** significant.
Word applies revision marks to all changes. The document should look similar to the one in Figure 19.6.

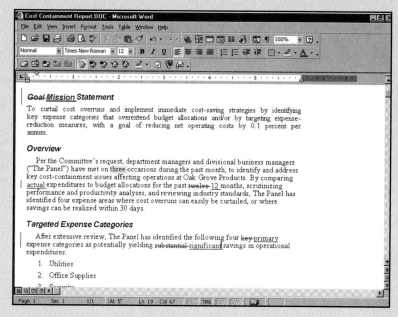

Figure 19.6
Revision marks appear throughout the document.

continues ▶

To Track Changes (continued)

6 Save the document and keep it onscreen to continue with the next lesson.

 Exam Note: **Changing Revision Mark Formatting**
Choose Tools, Options, and click the Track Changes tab (see Figure 19.7). You can select a color and formatting scheme for inserted text, deleted text, changed formatting, and changed lines. To make sure Word uses different colors for each author, set all the Color options to By author.

Figure 19.7
Choose options for tracking changes.

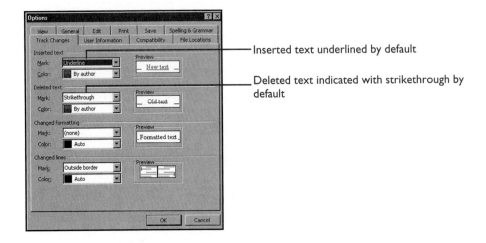

— Inserted text underlined by default

— Deleted text indicated with strikethrough by default

 Exam Note: **Routing a Document to Revise**
Instead of sending a document as an email attachment to multiple people, you can route a copy of the document. This way, a team member works on the document and then sends it to the next person on the list, thus having one document with all edits instead of multiple documents with individual edits. Eventually, the routed document is sent back to its originator.

To route a document, you must first prepare a routing slip. Choose File, Send To, Routing Recipient to open the Routing Slip dialog box. Refer to Help for more information on routing documents. Enter **route a document** when the Office Assistant appears.

 ## Lesson 4: Accepting and Rejecting Changes

After you and your team members finish tracking changes, you need to review the changes and either accept or reject them to prepare the final document. If you like a suggested change, use the ***accept change*** option to remove the revision mark and incorporate it into the regular document text. If you don't want to use a suggested change, use the ***reject change*** option to remove the revision mark and the tracked change, thus restoring that part of the document to its original state.

In this lesson, you accept and reject changes.

To Accept and Reject Changes

1 In the open `Cost Containment Report` document, press ⌃Ctrl+⌘Home to position the insertion point at the beginning of the document.

2 Click the Next Change button on the Reviewing toolbar to highlight the next change.

When you position the mouse pointer on the revision mark, you see a ScreenTip that tells you who made the change and the date and time the change was made (see Figure 19.8).

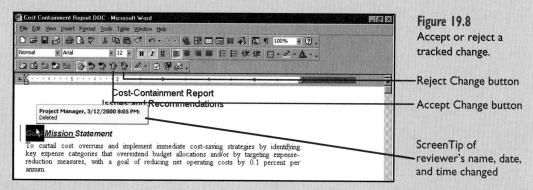

Figure 19.8
Accept or reject a tracked change.

— Reject Change button

— Accept Change button

ScreenTip of reviewer's name, date, and time changed

3 Click the Accept Change button.

Word accepts the change by actually deleting it as suggested. The vertical line in the left margin disappears when you accept or reject a change.

4 Click the Next Change button.

The underlined text `Mission` is highlighted. Because you accepted the revision of deleting `Goal`, you want to also accept the revision to insert `Mission`.

5 Click the Accept Change button.

 Inside Stuff: Accepting and Rejecting Changes
You can right-click the mouse on the revision mark and then choose Accept Change or Reject Change from the menu.

---

6 Click the Next Change button and then click the Accept Change button to accept the revision to insert `actual`.

7 Click the Next Change button and accept the revision to delete `twelve` and accept the revision to insert `12`.

8 Click the Next Change button.

You don't want to delete `key`, which is the next revision mark. Therefore, you'll reject it.

9 Click the Reject Change button.

Word removes the suggested inserted text.

10 Use the Next Change and Reject Change button to reject these changes: inserting `primary`, deleting `substantial`, and inserting `significant`.

Figure 19.9 shows the document after accepting and rejecting changes.

continues ▶

To Accept and Reject Changes   (continued)

Figure 19.9
The document is complete after reviewing changes.

Inserted text accepted

No vertical lines

Deleted text rejected

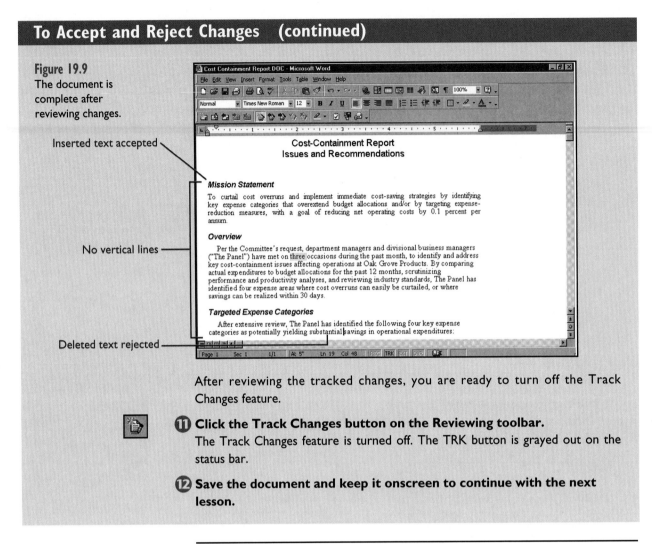

After reviewing the tracked changes, you are ready to turn off the Track Changes feature.

11 Click the Track Changes button on the Reviewing toolbar.
The Track Changes feature is turned off. The TRK button is grayed out on the status bar.

12 Save the document and keep it onscreen to continue with the next lesson.

Exam Note: **Highlighting Tracked Changes**
You can control whether tracked changes appear onscreen and on printed documents. Choose Tools, Track Changes, Highlight Changes. Select or deselect options in the Highlight Changes dialog box and then click OK (see Figure 19.10).

Figure 19.10
Choose onscreen and print options.

Exam Note: **Accept or Reject Changes Dialog Box**
Choose Tools, Track Changes, Accept or Reject Changes to display the Accept or Reject Changes dialog box (see Figure 19.11). You can accept or reject *all* changes at one time, if desired. However, you should preview a document before accepting or rejecting all changes.

Figure 19.11
Select options in the Accept or Reject changes dialog box.

Lesson 5: Saving Different Versions of a Document

Saving versions of a file is useful for keeping track of documents that are routed for review. Each **version** is a "snapshot" of the document and is marked with the name of the person who saves it, as well as the date and time that the version was saved. Using versions helps you keep copies of your original version, the version edited by reviewers, and the version that incorporates the reviewers' changes.

Saving versions is different from using the Save As command. With the Save As command, you create two or more totally separate documents. With the Versions feature, you save each version with the original document. The Versions feature actually saves disk space; only the differences are saved with the document, not a totally separate copy of the version.

In this lesson, you save a version of a file and then view a file version.

To Save Different Versions of a Document

1 **In the open Cost Containment Report document, click the Save Version button on the Reviewing toolbar.**
The Save Version dialog box appears, as shown in Figure 19.12. The dialog box displays the name of the person who saved the version, along with the date and time when the version was saved.

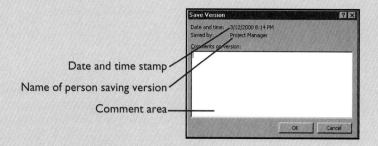

Date and time stamp

Name of person saving version

Comment area

Figure 19.12
Include comments to differentiate the versions.

2 **In the Comments on version section, type Changes have been incorporated, and then click OK.**
Word saves the version of the file and keeps the original file open. You can continue editing it or you can close the document. Changes that you make now are not included in the version that you just saved. A Versions icon appears on the status bar.

3 **Select Issues and Recommendations in the title and type Targeted Expense Categories to replace it.**
This version of the document has a different title from the version you just saved.

4 **Save the document under the same filename.**

5 **Choose File, Versions.**
The Versions in Cost Containment Report dialog box appears (see Figure 19.13). All versions of this document that have been saved are listed. You can open or delete a version, or you can display the full comment text.

continues ▶

To Save Different Versions of a Document (continued)

Figure 19.13
Select the version you want to open or delete.

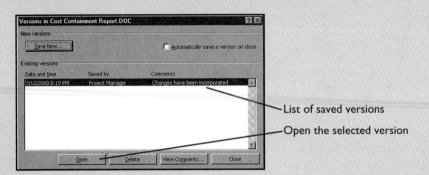

List of saved versions

Open the selected version

6 Click Open.
Word opens the version and displays it in split-screen view along with the regular document (see Figure 19.14). The saved version is active. Notice the date stamp in the title bar, as well as the difference between the two versions—the original has the new report title that you typed in step 3.

Figure 19.14
Compare the original and saved versions.

Current document

Saved version

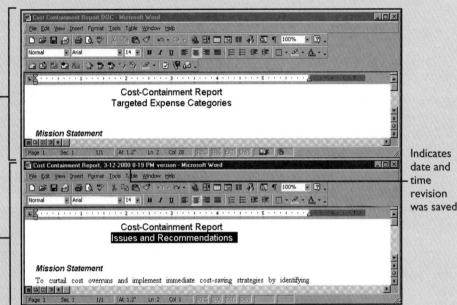

Indicates date and time revision was saved

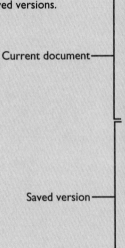

(i) *Inside Stuff:* **Saving a Version as a Document**
You can open a version and then save it as a separate document by using the Save As command.

---

7 Choose File, Close to close the saved version.

 8 Click the Maximize button to maximize the remaining document window.

9 Save the document and keep it onscreen to continue with the next lesson.

Inside Stuff: **Deleting a Version**

To delete a version, choose <u>F</u>ile, V<u>e</u>rsions, select the version to delete, and then click <u>D</u>elete. Word asks if you are sure you want to delete the version because it cannot be recovered after it is deleted. Click <u>Y</u>es to delete the version or click <u>N</u>o to keep it.

Lesson 6: Protecting Documents

At times, you need to control when and how people make changes to a document. For example, if you are the primary author or the project manager responsible for keeping track of all contributions, you need a way to be sure that no unauthorized changes are made. You can use Word's **protection** features to make sure no authorized changes are made. You can control access to a document in the following ways:

- Require a password for users to open, edit, and save the document.

- Require users to open the document as *read-only*, which means they can edit the document, but they must save it with a different filename.

- Recommend that users open the document as read-only. Users see a dialog box reminding them that they should open the document as read-only; however, users can still open, edit, and save the document if they choose to do so.

- Prevent changes to a routed document but allow users to use the track changes feature or to insert comments.

In this lesson, you protect your document against unauthorized use.

To Protect a Document

1 **In the open** Cost Containment Report **document, choose <u>T</u>ools, <u>P</u>rotect Document.**

The Protect Document dialog box appears (see Figure 19.15), so you can select the type of protection for the document.

Figure 19.15
Protect your document from unauthorized changes.

 Exam Note: **Using a Password**

You can also set a **password**—a secret word you choose that requires a user to enter it before accessing the document. After typing a password and clicking OK in the dialog box, you see the Confirm Password dialog box. You must retype the password *exactly* as you originally typed it to set the password.

To remove the password, choose <u>T</u>ools, Un<u>p</u>rotect Document. You must enter the correct password in the Unprotect Document dialog box to actually remove it.

---

continues ▶

To Protect a Document (continued)

② **Click the <u>C</u>omments option and then click OK.**
Word protects the document from changes. You and others can insert comments, but you can't change the document. Let's try deleting text.

③ **Select the title and press** Del.
The title is not deleted because you can't edit the document.

④ **Click inside the first line of the title and then click the Insert Comment button on the Reviewing toolbar.**
Word inserts a comment and opens the Comment pane. The comment is inserted with revision marks.

⑤ **Type Developed by panel members.**
Figure 19.16 shows the underlined comment text, which indicates a tracked change.

Figure 19.16
Comments are inserted with revision marks in a protected document.

Tracked change

Comment mark

Comment revision underlined

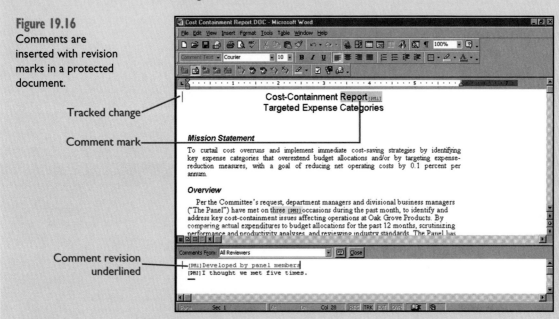

⑥ **Click the <u>C</u>lose button at the top of the Comment pane.**

⑦ **Choose <u>T</u>ools, Un<u>p</u>rotect Document.**
Word removes the document protection. Changes made while the protection was enabled remain highlighted with revision marks. The unprotected document can now be edited.

⑧ **Save and close the document.**

Exam Note: **Password-Protecting a Document**

You can protect a document by assigning a password to open it. To do this, open the document, choose <u>F</u>ile, Save <u>A</u>s. In the Save As dialog box, click **Tools** and choose <u>G</u>eneral Options from the menu. Figure 19.17 shows the Save dialog box. Type a password in the <u>P</u>assword to open text box to prevent unauthorized individuals from opening the document or type a password in the Password to modif<u>y</u> text box to allow users to open a document (they must enter a password in order to edit the document, however).

Passwords can be up to 15 characters long and can include letters, numbers, symbols, and spaces. As you enter a password, only asterisks appear in the box, which keeps people from reading the password over your shoulder.

Type password to
modify document

Type password to
open document

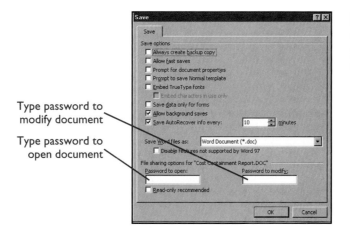

Figure 19.17
Create a password to
protect your
document.

Summary

You now know several methods for collaborating with others. You can insert comments, track changes, and accept or reject changes. In addition, you can save a version of a document for reference and protect a document from unauthorized use.

To enhance your collaboration skills, complete the following exercises, explore these topics in Help, and use the PinPoint program to practice related tasks.

Checking Concepts and Terms

True/False

For each of the following, check *T* or *F* to indicate whether the statement is true or false.

__T __F   **1.** To see a comment, position the mouse on top of the comment mark. [L1]

__T __F   **2.** Word inserts a vertical line in the *right* margin when you track changes. [L3]

__T __F   **3.** Double-clicking a tracked change accepts it. [L4]

__T __F   **4.** When you save a version of a document, Word saves it as a totally separate file. [L5]

__T __F   **5.** You can protect your document from being edited but allow comments by using the Protect Document dialog box. [L6]

Multiple Choice

Circle the letter of the correct answer for each of the following.

1. Which toolbar contains buttons for collaborating on documents? [L1]

   a. Standard

   b. Formatting

   c. AutoText

   d. Reviewing

2. What is the default format for inserting text when the Track Changes feature is active? [L3]

   a. strikethrough

   b. redline

   c. all caps

   d. underline

3. What does Word insert into the left margin to identify a tracked change? [L3]

   a. vertical line

   b. underline

   c. asterisk

   d. plus sign

4. What steps do you take to see a list of saved versions for a document? [L5]

   a. Click the Save Version button.

   b. Choose File, Versions.

   c. Click the Tools button and choose General Options in the Save As dialog box.

   d. Click the Show/Hide ¶ button.

5. Which option is *not* included in the Protect Document dialog box? [L6]

   a. Versions

   b. Password

   c. Comment

   d. Track Changes

Screen ID

Label each element of the Word screen shown in Figure 19.18.

Figure 19.18

   A. Accept Change

   B. comment mark

   C. comment text

   D. indicates tracked change

   E. Reject Change

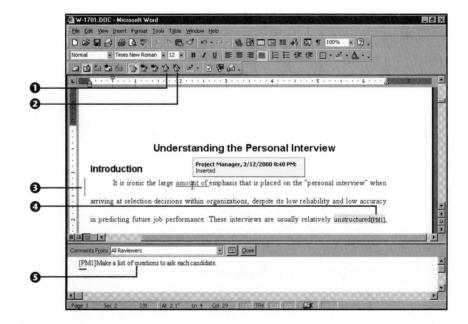

1._____	2._____	3._____
4._____	5._____	

Skill Drill

Skill Drill exercises reinforce project skills. Each skill reinforced is the same, or nearly the same, as a skill presented in the project. Each exercise includes a brief narrative introduction, followed by detailed instructions in a step-by-step format.

1. Inserting and Printing Comments for a New Café Announcement

You've been asked to review an information sheet about a new café called New Food Café. Because you plan to email the document back to the café owners, you will insert comments.

1. Open **W-1902** and save it as **Cafe Information**.

2. Choose <u>V</u>iew, <u>T</u>oolbars, Reviewing to display the Reviewing toolbar, if it is not displayed.

3. At the end of the Fish and Chips line, click the Insert Comment button on the Reviewing toolbar.

4. Type **I thought fish and chips were available on Friday only.**

5. Click in the document window, scroll down, and click after **Dumais**.

6. Click the Insert Comment button, and type **Is this the correct spelling of your name?**

7. Click after **25 people** at the end of the second-to-the-last paragraph.

8. Click the Insert Comment button, and type **The fire marshal states that the room can only hold 20 people.**

9. Click the <u>C</u>lose button to close the Comment pane.

10. Save the document.

11. Display the Print dialog box, click <u>O</u>ptions, click the <u>C</u>omments check box, click OK, and then click OK.

12. Click the second comment mark and then click the Delete Comment button.

13. Click the Edit Comment button, delete **20** and type **22**.

14. Click the <u>C</u>lose button at the top of the Comment pane.

15. Save the document and keep it onscreen to continue with the next exercise.

2. Tracking, Accepting, and Rejecting Changes in the Cafe Announcement

You need to turn on the Track Changes feature, make changes, and then accept and reject changes.

1. In the open **Cafe Information** document, click the Track Changes button.

2. Select **diverse and eclectic** on the third line of the first paragraph and then press (Del).

3. Type **wide** and press (Spacebar) where you left off from deleting text.

4. Click before the word **lunch**, type **daily**, and then press (Spacebar).

5. Delete **on a daily basis**, including the space before **on**, but do not delete the colon at the end of that line.

6. Delete **displayed** in the paragraph below the bulleted list.

7. Insert **daily** and press (Spacebar) before **specials** in the paragraph about the chef.

8. Select the space and **daily** at the end of that sentence and press (Del).

9. Delete **11:30** and type **11:00**.

10. Save the document and click the Track Changes to turn off this feature.

11. Display the Print dialog box, click <u>O</u>ptions, click the <u>C</u>omments check box to deselect it, click OK, and then click OK.

12. Click in the deleted **diverse and eclectic** phrase and then click the Accept Change button.

13. Click the Accept Change button to accept inserting **wide**.

14. Click the Next Change button to highlight the inserted **daily**; then click the Accept Change button.

15. Click the Next Change button to highlight the deleted **on a daily basis** and then click the Accept Change button.

16. Click the Next Change button to highlight the deleted **displayed** and then click the Reject Change button.

17. Continue clicking the Next Change button and then accept or reject changes as follows:

   a. Accept the inserted **daily**.

   b. Accept the deleted **daily**.

   c. Reject the deleted **11:30**.

   d. Reject the inserted **11:00**.

18. Save the document, print it, and keep it onscreen to continue with the next exercise.

3. Saving Versions and Protecting the Document

You want to save a version of the document, change the subtitle, and then protect the document.

1. In the open **Cafe Information** document, click the Save Version button on the Reviewing toolbar.

2. Type **This one contains the original slogan.** as a comment and click OK.

3. Save the document.

4. Select **those in the know** and type **eclectic connoisseurs**.

5. Click the Save button.

6. Choose File, Versions.

7. Click Open to open the selected version to see the version with the current version.

8. Scroll up in each document window to compare the subtitles.

9. Close the **those in the know** version and then click the Maximize button to maximize the current document window.

10. Choose Tools, Protect Document.

11. Click the Comments option and then click OK.

12. Select the subtitle and try to delete it (you can't).

13. Click after **connoisseurs**, click the Insert Comment button, type **this is a better slogan**, and then click the **Close** button at the top of the Comment pane.

14. Save the document, print it with comments, and then close it.

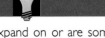
Challenge

Challenge exercises expand on or are somewhat related to skills presented in the lessons. Each exercise provides a brief narrative introduction followed by instructions in a numbered-step or bulleted-list format that are not as detailed as those in the Skill Drill section.

1. Using Comments in a Prospectus

A coworker asked you to review a prospectus and provide electronic comments. You use Word's Comments feature to do this.

1. Open **W-1903** and save it as **Prospectus**.

2. Insert a comment after **August 1, 1983** that states that you thought the date was 1984.

3. Select **$15.7** and insert a comment that you're not sure about this amount.

4. Insert a comment after **$1,000** that questions whether the amount was raised to $1,500 recently.

5. Select **$1.00** and insert a comment that the amount was raised to $5.00 last month.

6. Delete the second comment.

7. Edit the Comment Text style to display comments in 12-point Arial.

8. Save the document and print it with the comments.

2. Tracking Changes in a Desktop Publishing Guidelines Document

You were asked to review a document about desktop publishing guidelines. Use the Track Changes feature to insert, delete, and format text.

1. Open **W-1904** and save it as **Edited Desktop Publishing**.
2. Turn on the Track Changes feature.
3. Delete **are preparing** and insert **prepare** in the first paragraph.
4. Select and italicize **typography** in the first paragraph.
5. Select **as many different** in the paragraph below the **Font Faces** heading; type **oodles of** to replace the selected text.
6. Bold and italicize **serif font** in the second sentence of the second paragraph in the **Font Faces** section.
7. Bold and italicize **sans serif font** in the third sentence of the second paragraph in the **Font Faces** section.
8. Insert **Old Style** to the right of **Bookman** in the bulleted list.
9. Select **AvantGarde** and type **Century Gothic** in the paragraph below the bulleted list.
10. Bold and italicize **font style** in the second paragraph below the bulleted list.
11. Change the heading **Weight** to **Density**.
12. Change the heading **Font Size** to **Point Size**.
13. Change **chapter title** to **document title** in the second paragraph in the **Font Size** section.
14. Bold and italicize **leading** in the paragraph below the **Leading** heading.
15. Turn off the Track Changes feature.
16. Save and print the document.
17. Review the tracked changes and do the following:
    a. Accept all bold, italicized changes.
    b. Accept all changes in the first paragraph.
    c. Reject the changes to delete **as many different** and to insert **oodles of**.
    d. Accept the change in the bulleted list.
    e. Accept changing **AvantGarde** to **Century Gothic**.
    f. Reject the change of **Weight** to **Density**.
    g. Reject the change of **Font Size** to **Point Size**.
    h. Accept the change of **chapter title** to **document title**.
18. Save the document and print it.

3. Saving Versions and Protecting a Job Responsibilities Document

You are editing a list of job responsibilities for lab assistants. Before obtaining final approval to copy the document, you want to save a couple of versions to present to your supervisor. In addition, you want to protect the document by allowing tracking changes only.

1. Open **W-1905** and save it as **Lab Assistant Duties**.
2. Create a header with your name on the left side and **First Draft** on the right side.
3. Save the document, and then save a version of the document with the comment **Original document**.
4. Delete **your supervisor** in the first bulleted item and type **supervising instructor**.

5. Change **Be on time** to **Arrive on time**.

6. Add **Find another lab assistant to cover for you if you must be absent.** in italics at the end of the third bulleted item.

7. Save a version of the changes with the comment **More specific guidelines** and then save the document itself.

8. Edit the header by changing **First Draft** to **Second Draft**; save a version with a comment called **More specific guidelines 2**. Save the document itself.

9. Display the Versions in dialog box and delete **More specific guidelines**, the second version.

10. Open the original version to compare the differences in it and the newest version.

11. Print both versions and then close the original version.

12. Maximize the new version.

13. Protect the document by allowing tracking changes only.

14. Select **difficultly** and type **difficulty** (notice the slight variation of the word).

15. At the end of the **Pass back graded homework to students** bulleted item, insert **Do not discuss grades with students.**

16. Insert a new bullet after the current one with this sentence: **Remain objective. Do not agree or disagree if a student believes the instructor is wrong. Advise the student to visit with the instructor.**

17. Italicize **not** in the bulleted item that begins with **Do not use a computer**.

18. Insert **Proofread carefully!** at the end of the second-to-the-last bulleted item.

19. Save and print the document. Don't save the versions if prompted.

Discovery Zone

Discovery Zone exercises help you gain advanced knowledge of project topics and/or application of skills. These exercises focus on enhancing your problem-solving skills. Numbered steps are not provided, but you are given hints, reminders, screen shots, and/or references to help you reach your goal for each exercise.

1. Tracking Changes in an Apartment Complex Newsletter

As assistant manager of Mountain View Apartment Complex, you need to edit the monthly newsletter prepared by the manager. Because she wants final approval, use the Track Changes feature to record your edits. Open **W-1906** and save it as **Edited Apartment Newsletter**.

Use Help and refer to the lessons to learn how to change tracking changes settings. Set Blue color and Italic mark option to track inserted text. Set Red color and Strikethrough mark to track deleted text. Set Green color and Double Underline to mark format changes.

Track these changes:

- Delete the tab to indent the first paragraph.

- Delete **typical** and insert **routine** in the first paragraph.

- Delete the space and the word **and** after **safe**. Insert a comma.

- Change **December 15** to **November 1**.

- Insert **not** between **do** and **turn off** in **the Thermostat Settings** section.

- Bold the word **not** in the first sentence of the **Sidewalk Salt** paragraph.

- Tab in the last two lines in the document.
- Italicize the last two lines in the document.
- Change **8** to **7:30**, and change **10** to **8:00**.

Turn off the Track Changes feature. Save the document and print it (preferably on a color printer). Refer to the lesson on accepting and tracking changes to learn how to accept all revisions. Then perform this action. Save the document as **Edited Apartment Newsletter 2** and print it.

2. Password-Protecting a Document and Inserting Audio Comments

You want to insert a couple of audio comments and then create a password so users must be authorized in order to access the file. Open **Edited Apartment Newsletter 2** and save it as **Edited Apartment Newsletter 3**.

If you have audio capabilities, record the following comments. If not, insert traditional comments.

- after November 1: **Should we recommend disconnecting hoses by the middle of October?**
- after November 20: **Let's start winter laundry hours on November 1.**

Save the document under the same filename, but assign the password **snow** to open the file again. Close the file and try to reopen it with the password **SNOW**. It shouldn't open. Now try reopening it with the password **snow**. Edit the comments and double-click the speaker icon to hear your audio comments. Save the document and close it. Be ready to demonstrate these tasks for your instructor: opening with the password and listening to the audio comments.

PinPoint Assessment

You have completed this project and its associated lessons, and have had an opportunity to assess your skills through the end-of-project questions and exercises. Now use the PinPoint software Evaluation Mode to further assess your comprehension of the specific exam activities you have just learned. You can also use the PinPoint Trainer Mode and the Show Me tutorials to practice these exam activities.

Creating Forms

Key terms introduced in this project include

- calculating form field
- check box form field
- drop-down form field
- form
- form field
- text form field

Objectives	Required Activity for MOUS	Exam Level
➤ Create a Form Template	Create and modify a form	Expert
	Set default file location for workgroup templates	Expert
➤ Insert Text Form Fields	Insert a field	Expert
➤ Insert Form Fields in a Table	Insert a field	Expert
➤ Set Text Form Field Options for Dates	Create and modify a form control (e.g., add an item to a drop-down list)	Expert
➤ Set Options for Drop-Down and Check Box Form Fields	Create and modify a form control (e.g., add an item to a drop-down list)	Expert
➤ Perform Calculations in a Form		
➤ Use an Onscreen Form		

Why Would I Do This?

A *form* is a document designed for collecting data. Forms are used in a variety of applications, such as software registration, job applications, bank account applications, purchase orders, and invoices. You can create a Word form that people can complete by typing or writing on printed paper or by completing online.

In this project, you design, create, and use a simple form that can be printed or filed out online. You learn how to create and customize the three basic types of form fields: text, check box, and drop-down list. A *form field* is an area in an onscreen form where users can enter information by typing, selecting from a drop-down list, or marking a check box.

Lesson 1: Creating a Form Template

Word forms are stored as templates so the form itself is protected from being changed; the user can only insert data into text fields and use other form fields.

Word forms contain standard text and graphics. The standard text consists of labels that instruct the user what to enter, such as Last Name. Form fields appear where the user enters information. When you create a form, you should spend time planning the layout before you begin. Reviewing the pros and cons of other forms helps you plan your form.

In this lesson, you edit an existing document and save it as a form template.

To Create a Form Template

1 Open `W-2001` **and save it as** `Oak Grove Invoice`.
The invoice is a regular document. To ensure that it retains its settings, you want to edit it and then save it as a form template to be used again and again.
It contains variable data, such as a person's name and address, which you need to delete before saving it as a form.

2 Delete the following information, but do *not* delete the label text or paragraph marks:

```
4/10/02
Ms. Monique Parsia
Forsythe Enterprises
340 North Main Street
Prescott, AZ 86301
```

This information changes on each invoice that is filled out; therefore, you need to delete it.

 If You Have Problems...
Display the nonprinting symbols by clicking the Show/Hide ¶ button. Also choose Table, Show Gridlines if you want to see the table gridlines.

3 Delete the data on the second row of the table.
Delete 4/5/00, Tulip bulbs, 10, $5.95, and $59.50, but not the row itself.

4 Delete the total price, which is $59.50 in the total row.
This is the last variable data you need to delete; everything else is standard text that should remain in the form. Your document should look like the one in Figure 20.1.

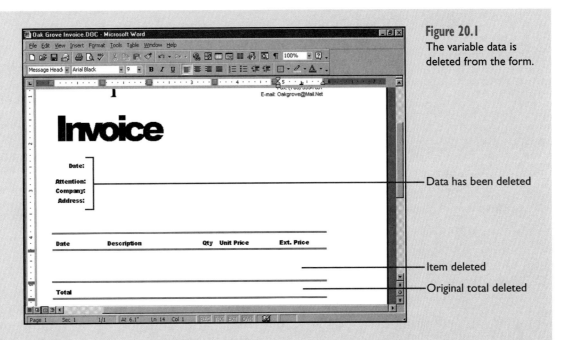

Figure 20.1
The variable data is
deleted from the form.

Data has been deleted

Item deleted

Original total deleted

You need to protect the document so that an unauthorized user cannot change the basic layout, graphics, and text.

⑤ Choose Tools, Protect Document.
The Protect Document dialog box appears (see Figure 20.2).

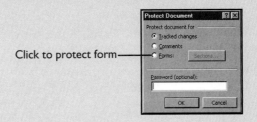

Click to protect form

Figure 20.2
Protect the document
from unauthorized
changes.

⑥ Click the Forms option and then click OK.
Word protects the invoice so that the standard text, graphics, and layout cannot be modified. Because the document contains no form fields, you cannot edit the document.

⑦ Choose File, Save As to display the Save As dialog box.

⑧ Click the Save as type drop-down arrow and choose Document Template (*.dot).
Word displays the Templates folder and a list of all current template documents.

⑨ Type Invoice Form in the File name box and then click Save.

⑩ Keep the document onscreen to continue with the next lesson.

ⓘ **Inside Stuff: Printing Forms**
When you need printed forms, create a document from the template and print as many copies as you need. A printed form needs standard text and lines or table lines for people to write on.

Exam Note: **Changing Workgroup Templates**
If you want to store the template on an intranet drive so others in your organization can access it, choose <u>T</u>ools, <u>O</u>ptions. Click the File Locations tab, click Workgroup templates, click <u>M</u>odify, type the new path, click OK, and then click Close.

For more information about creating and saving templates, refer to Project 14, "Working with Styles and Templates."

 ## Lesson 2: Inserting Text Form Fields

If you want users to fill out a form online, you must add form fields to the form template. You can insert the following three types of form fields:

- **Text form fields** allow users to enter text or numbers.

- **Check box form fields** let users select or deselect to mark an item, similar to the Effects check boxes in the Font dialog box.

- **Drop-down form fields** display a list from which users can select an option, similar to the Style drop-down arrow on the Formatting toolbar.

In this lesson, you insert text form fields to the Invoice Form template. To modify a form template, you must unprotect it first.

To Insert Text Form Fields

 1 **In the open Invoice Form template, click the Protect Form button on the Forms toolbar.**

> *Inside Stuff:*   **Protecting and Unprotecting Documents**
> The Protect Form button is a toggle: Click it once to protect the form; click it again to unprotect the form.
>
> You can also choose <u>T</u>ools, Un<u>p</u>rotect Document.

Word removes the protection, so you can edit the document.

2 **Display the nonprinting symbols and choose <u>V</u>iew, <u>T</u>oolbars, Forms.**
The Forms toolbar contains buttons for you to use to insert items into a form (see Figure 20.3).

Figure 20.3
Customize the form with the Forms toolbar buttons.

```
┌──────────────────────────────── Text Form Field button
▼ Forms                        ☒
abl ☑ 圖 圄 ╱ ▦ 圊 圝 🔒 ── Protect Form button
```

 3 **Position the insertion point to the left of the paragraph mark at the end of the Date line. Then, click the Text Form Field button on the Forms toolbar.**
Word inserts a text field at the insertion point location (see Figure 20.4). The field is created with the default settings so that it accepts any number of characters of typed data. The field is lightly shaded in gray onscreen.

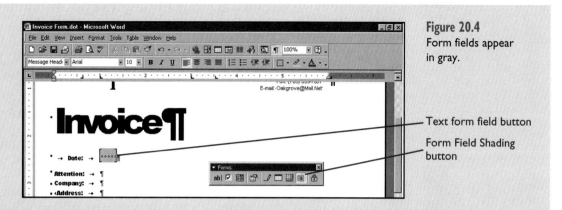

Figure 20.4
Form fields appear in gray.

Text form field button

Form Field Shading button

X   *If You Have Problems...*
If the form fields do not appear shaded, click the Form Field Shading button on the Forms toolbar.

4 **Press ⬇ to move the insertion point to the left of the paragraph mark on the Attention line; then click the Text Form Field button on the Forms toolbar.**

5 **Repeat step 4 four times to insert text form fields for the company and address lines.**
The top of the template contains text form fields to enter data for individual invoices (see Figure 20.5).

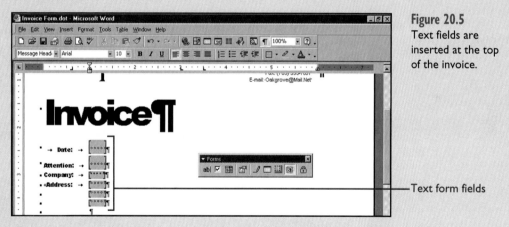

Figure 20.5
Text fields are inserted at the top of the invoice.

Text form fields

6 **Save the Invoice Form template and keep it onscreen to continue with the next lesson.**

  Inside Stuff: **Order of Form Fields**
When a user completes an online form, Word moves through fields in the order in which you insert them. You should plan how you want users to fill out the form before inserting form fields. If you want users to move from left to right across the page, insert form fields from left to right. If you want users to move down the page, insert form fields down the page.

Lesson 3: Inserting Form Fields in a Table

Using a table in a form template helps you align fields so that they look good, and makes the form easier for users to fill out. In addition, you can use Word's Table features to format and manipulate the fields and data in the table to improve the form. For example, in Lesson 6 you learn how to create calculating form fields in the table.

In this lesson, you insert text, drop-down, and check boxes form fields in the **Invoice Form** template document.

  Inside Stuff: **Inserting a Table**
In the Invoice Form template you're working on, the original document contained a table. However, you can create a table from scratch by clicking the Draw Table button or Insert Table button on the Forms toolbar.

To Insert Form Fields in a Table

1 **In the open Invoice Form template document, move the insertion point into the first cell of the second row in the table—the cell under the label Date.**

Inside Stuff: **Displaying Gridlines**
Choose Table, Show Gridlines if the gridlines are not visible.

 2 **Click the Text Form Field button on the Forms toolbar.**
Word inserts a text form field in the cell.

3 **Press Tab.**
The insertion point is in the cell below Description. This is where you insert a drop-down form field so that users can select from a list of available products.

 4 **Click the Drop-Down Form Field button.**
Word inserts a drop-down form field in the cell. In Lesson 4, you learn how to set form field options.

5 **Press Tab and insert a text form field in the cell below Qty.**
This is the field where users can enter the number of items purchased.

6 **Repeat step 5 twice to insert text form fields in the cells below Unit Price and Ext. Price.**
These two form fields are used to display the cost information. Now, add a text form field for the total invoice amount.

7 **Press ↓ to position the insertion point on the row labeled Total, in the cell below Ext. Price, and insert a text form field.**
Now, you insert check box form fields next to the three payment method options.

 8 **Click at the left side of the cell containing Money Order; then click the Check Box Form Field button.**
Word inserts a check box form field in the cell to the left of the text. Users can mark the check box form field next to the payment method they want to use for an invoice.

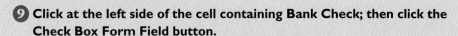

9 **Click at the left side of the cell containing Bank Check; then click the Check Box Form Field button.**
Word inserts a check box form field to the left of the text. Now, insert the last form field into the template document.

10 **Click in the cell containing Visa/MC; then click the Check Box Form Field button.**
These are all the form fields you need in the Invoice Form template. The bottom half of the document should look similar to the document shown in Figure 20.6.

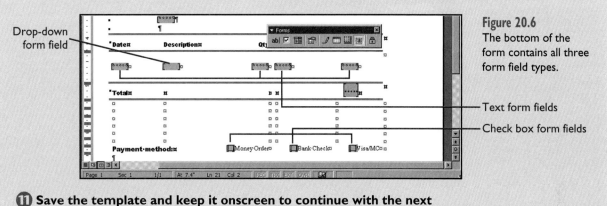

Drop-down
form field

Figure 20.6
The bottom of the form contains all three form field types.

Text form fields

Check box form fields

11 **Save the template and keep it onscreen to continue with the next lesson.**

Lesson 4: Setting Text Form Field Options for Dates

Expert

When you insert form fields, Word creates them with the default settings. For example, text form fields accept any type of regular text and an unlimited number of characters. You can customize the form fields for your form by setting form field options.

In this lesson, you set form field options for date fields to accept only valid dates.

To Set Form Field Options for Dates

1 **In the open `Invoice Form` template, click the first field of the document (the text form filed on the Date line).**
The form field is highlighted.

2 **Click the Form Field Options button.**
The Text Form Field Options dialog box appears (see Figure 20.7), so you can specify the type of text accepted, how many characters are accepted, and the text format.

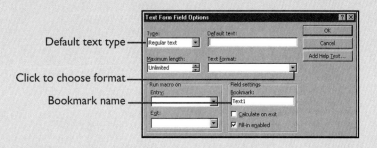

Default text type

Click to choose format

Bookmark name

Figure 20.7
Customize your form fields.

continues ▶

To Set Form Field Options for Dates (continued)

 Inside Stuff: **Displaying Text In Form Fields**
You can insert default text that appears in a text form field. For example, you can display instructions such as `Type phone number here`. To do this, type the desired text in the D**e**fault text box. This text appears onscreen in the text form field every time the form is opened.

You need to set the type of data to be accepted. You can choose from Regular Text, Number, Date, Current Date, Current Time, and Calculation.

3 **Click the Ty**p**e drop-down arrow and choose Date.**
The text form field accepts only dates now.

4 **Click the Date** f**ormat drop-down arrow and choose MMMM d, yyyy.**
This format displays the date in a month, date, year format, such as September 15, 2002.

5 **Select the default name in the** B**ookmark box, type** `InvoiceDate`**, and click OK.**

 Inside Stuff: **Bookmark Names**
Bookmark names can be up to 30 characters long, but they *cannot* include spaces.

 6 **Click in the text form field in the cell below Date in the table; then click the Form Field Options button.**
The Text Form Field Options dialog box appears. You need to set this field to accept only date entries, but you use a different format.

7 **Click the Ty**p**e drop-down arrow and choose Date; then click the Date** f**ormat drop-down arrow and choose M/d/yy.**
Dates in this field appear in numerical format, such as 9/16/02.

8 **Change the default bookmark name in the** B**ookmark text box to TransactionDate and click OK.**

9 **Save the template and keep it onscreen to continue with the next lesson.**

 ## Lesson 5: Setting Options for Drop-Down and Check Box Form Fields

You can also customize drop-down and check box form fields. The Form Field Options dialog box options change, based on the current form field. When you set form field options for drop-down fields, you enter the items to display in the drop-down list. When you set form field options for check box fields, you specify how large you want the check box to appear and whether it should start out blank or marked with an X.

In this lesson, you customize drop-down and check box form fields.

To Set Options for Drop-Down and Check Box Form Fields

1 **In the open Invoice Form template, click in the drop-down form field below Description and then click the Form Field Options button.**
Figure 20.8 shows the Drop-Down Form Field dialog box. This is where you enter the items you want to appear in the drop-down list.

Type item name here —

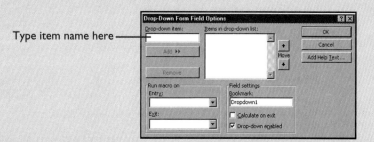

Figure 20.8
Use the Drop-Down Form Field Options dialog box to customize drop-down form fields.

2 **Type `Tulip bulbs` in the Drop-down item box and then click Add.**
Word adds the item `Tulip bulbs` to the Items in drop-down list box.

3 **Repeat step 2 to add the following items: `Hyacinth bulbs`, `Crocus bulbs`, and `Day Lily bulbs`.**
The drop-down list contains four items (see Figure 20.9).

Items listed —

Click to delete selected item —
Click to move selected item up or down in list. —

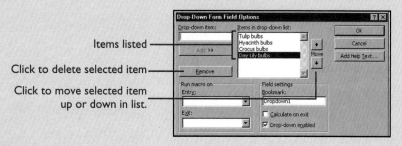

Figure 20.9
You can view the items added to the drop-down list field.

4 **Click OK.**
The first item, Tulip bulbs, appears in the field in the table (the drop-down arrow appears only when the field is selected for data entry).

5 **Click the text form field in the cell below Qty, click the Form Field Options button, and enter the following information in the dialog box:**
- Type: Number
- Default number: 10
- Number format: #,##0
- Bookmark: Quantity1
- Calculate on exit: selected

 Inside Stuff: **Naming Bookmarks**
Naming bookmarks such as `Quantity1` instead of just `Quantity` is helpful when you want to add product items. The next row can contain a bookmark named `Quantity2`.

6 **Click OK to close the dialog box.**
The text form field accepts only numbers and uses 10 as the default number. The bookmark name is used to set up a calculating field in the next lesson. Checking Calculate on exit tells Word to update calculations after users enter numbers.

continues ▶

To Set Options for Drop-Down and Check Box Form Fields (continued)

7 **Click in the form field in the cell below Unit Price, click the Form Field Options button, and enter the following information in the dialog box:**

- Type: `Number`
- Default number: `0`
- Number format: `$#,##0.00;($#,##0.00)`
- Bookmark: `UnitPrice1`
- Calculate on exit: selected

8 **Click OK to close the dialog box.**
The text form field displays numbers as dollar values. After you complete Lesson 6, the field is calculated when you enter numbers.

9 **Click the Money Order check box form field and then click the Form Field Options button.**
The Check Box Form Field Options dialog box appears (see Figure 20.10).

Figure 20.10
Customize check box form fields.

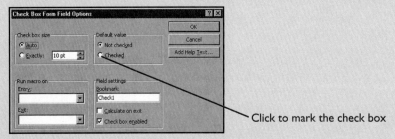

Click to mark the check box

10 **Click the Checked option and then click OK.**
The Money Order check box field is selected automatically when you open the template form.

11 **Save the template and keep it onscreen to continue with the next lesson.**

 Exam Note: **Including Macros with Templates**
Macros are powerful tools when combined with templates. They can automate the task of completing documents created with a template and are particularly useful when working with online forms.

When you create a template for an online form, you insert fields on that form. Any macro in the form template can run automatically when the insertion point enters or exits a form field.

To automate a template by adding macros, you must first create the macros you want to run in the template. Then, do the following:

1. Create or open the form template that you want to automate.
2. Unprotect the form, if needed.
3. Create the macros to use in the template, and store them in the template.
4. Add the form fields you need in the template.
5. For each form field to which you want to attach a macro, double-click the form field to see the Field Options dialog box.

6. In the Run macro on section, select the macro you want to use with that field from the Entry drop-down arrow if you want the macro to run when the insertion point enters the field. If you want the macro to run when the insertion point exits the field, select the macro from the Exit drop-down arrow.

7. Click OK, and test the template to see that the macros work correctly.

Lesson 6: Performing Calculations in a Form

When you use a table within a form, you can take advantage of Word's Table feature to perform calculations automatically in form fields by using values entered in other fields. For example, you can calculate sales tax or outstanding balances. A **calculating form field** is a field that contains a formula to perform a mathematical calculation.

In the invoice form you have been creating, two fields could benefit from automatic calculations: the Ext. Price, which displays the result of multiplying the Quantity field value by the Unit Price value, and the Total field, which displays the result of adding all Ext. Price fields in the table.

When calculating in a table or in a form field, use the standard mathematical operators listed in Table 20.1.

Table 20.1   Mathematical Operators

Operation	Operator
Add	+
Subtract	–
Multiply	*
Divide	/
Exponentiation (raise to power)	^
Less than	<
Less than or equal to	<=
Greater than	>
Greater than or equal to	>=

In this lesson, you set options for calculating fields.

To Perform Calculations in a Form

1 **In the open `Invoice Form` template, click the text form field in the cell below Ext. Price; then click the Form Field Options button.**

2 **Click the Type drop-down arrow and choose Calculation.**
Word displays an Expression text box and enters an equal sign (=) in it. The equal sign is the symbol Word uses to specify that you are creating a mathematical formula.

3 **Type `Quantity1*UnitPrice1` after the equal sign in the Expression text box.**
This formula multiplies the value in the Quantity form field by the value of the UnitPrice form field.

continues ▶

To Perform Calculations in a Form

④ Click the Number format drop-down arrow, select the setting $#,##0.00($#,##0.00), and then click OK.

The Ext. Price field immediately displays $0.00, which is the result of multiplying the default value of 10 in the Quantity field by the default entry 0 in the Unit Price field.

⑤ Click the text form field in the Total row below Ext. Price field and then click the Form Field Options button.

You want Word to add all values in as many fields as appear in the Ext. Price column. You use the SUM function to add values in all fields in this column.

⑥ Click the Type drop-down arrow, choose Calculation, click in the Expression text box, and type SUM(ABOVE) after the equal sign.

This expression adds all values that appear above the current cell in that column.

⑦ Click the Number format drop-down arrow, select $#,##0.00($#,##0.00), and then click OK.

The results display as a dollar value. The form should look similar to the one shown in Figure 20.11.

Figure 20.11
The form contains two fields that perform calculations.

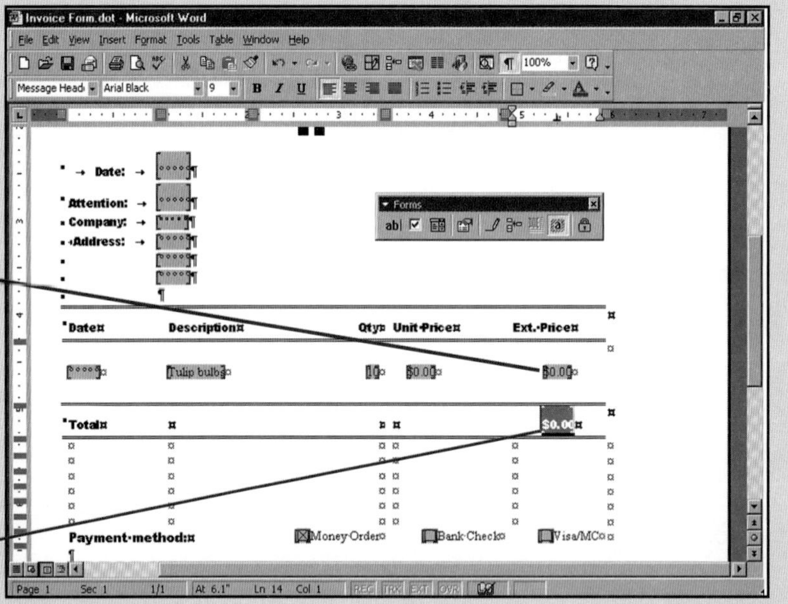

Multiplies quantity by the unit price

Adds all values in the column

Now that you completed the Invoice Form template, you must save the changes and protect the document.

⑧ Click the Protect Form button and then click the Save button.

⑨ Close the Forms toolbar and the Invoice Form template document.

Lesson 7: Using an Online Form

After saving the form template, you can use the template to create forms that can be filled out and saved online with Word. When you use a form template, Word does not let you edit any of the template text or the form structure. You can insert text within the form fields.

In this lesson, you use the Invoice Form template to create and fill out an invoice.

To Use an Online Form

1 **Choose File, New.**

2 **Click the General tab, select the Invoice Form template, and then click OK.**
Word creates a new document based on the Invoice Form template. By default, the first form field is selected.

3 **Save the document as Garden Club Invoice.**
The Formatting toolbar and some other buttons are grayed-out when you open a protected form. This prevents you from changing the form text and formatting; you can only enter data into the fields.

4 **Type 4/30/02 and press Tab⇄.**
Word enters the date in the field in the format you specified when setting form field options and moves to the next form field. Pressing Tab⇄ in a form moves to the next field; pressing ⇧Shift+Tab⇄ moves to the previous field.
The selected field appears in darker gray. A selected text form field has a bold black underline, a selected drop-down form field displays the drop-down arrow, and a selected check box form field has a bold black border.

5 **Type Mr. Alfred Taylor and press Tab⇄.**
Word enters the name in the field and moves to the next form field. The field expands to let you enter as much text as you want.

6 **Type Garden Club Designs, press Tab⇄, type 5050 Lantern Road, press Tab⇄, type Hanover, NH 03755, and press Tab⇄.**

7 **Press Tab⇄, type 4/22/02, and press Tab⇄.**
Word enters and formats the date and moves to the Description field. The drop-down arrow appears to the right of the field.

8 **Click the drop-down arrow.**
Figure 20.12 shows the drop-down list.

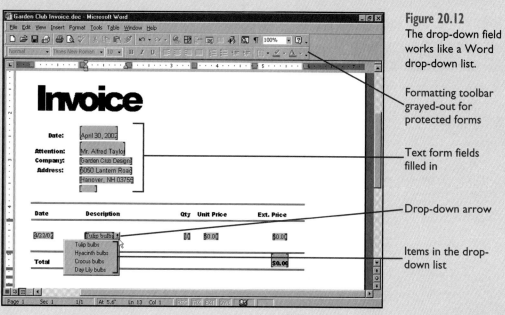

Figure 20.12
The drop-down field works like a Word drop-down list.

Formatting toolbar grayed-out for protected forms

Text form fields filled in

Drop-down arrow

Items in the drop-down list

continues ▶

To Use an Online Form (continued)

9 Select Day Lily bulbs and press `Tab`.
Day Lily bulbs appears in the Description field and then moves to the Qty field.

10 Type 50, press `Tab`**, type 1.50, and press** `Tab`**.**
As soon as you press `Tab` to move out of the Unit Price field, Word calculates the Ext. Price and the Total. It fills in the two calculating fields, and moves forward in the form to the Money Order check box field (see Figure 20.13).

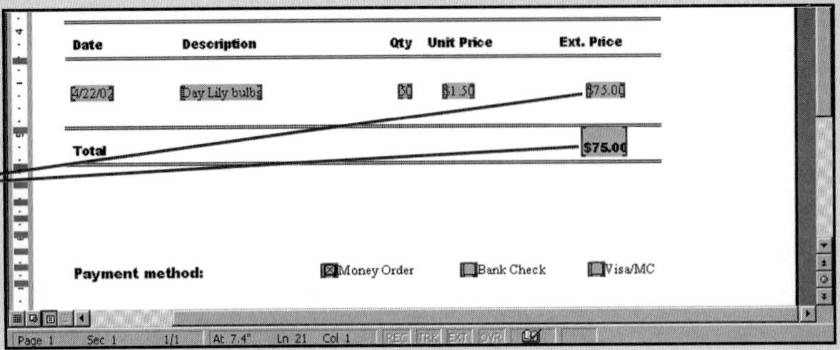

Figure 20.13
Word updates values in calculating fields.

Calculating fields

The Money Order check box is checked by default, but this customer is paying by bank check.

11 Press `Spacebar`**.**
Word unmarks the Money Order check box. You can mark or unmark check box fields by pressing `Spacebar` or by clicking the field with the mouse.

12 Press `Tab` **and then press** `Spacebar`**.**
This moves to the Bank Check check box and marks it with an X. You have completed filling out the form.

13 Save, print, and close the document.

Summary

You have created a basic form template. You can insert text, drop-down lists, and check box fields. In addition, you know how to perform calculations within fields. Finally, you used your invoice template to fill it out onscreen.

To enhance your knowledge and skill in creating forms, use Help, complete the following exercises, and work through the applicable PinPoint activities. After completing these types of exercises, you will be able to create a variety of forms.

Checking Concepts and Terms ✔

True/False

For each of the following, check *T* or *F* to indicate whether the statement is true or false.

__T __F   **1.** You can create a form from a regular document. [L1]

__T __F   **2.** You can set up a text form field to accept a particular date format. [L4]

__T __F   **3.** The default check box form field contains an X. [L5]

__T __F   **4.** Calculating form fields can use bookmark names in the formulas, such as =rate*time. [L6]

__T __F   **5.** Protecting a form keeps users from entering data into the fields. [L7]

Multiple Choice

Circle the letter of the correct answer for each of the following.

1. You should do all of the following to create a form template, *except:* [L1]

   a. Save the template document with a .dot extension.

   b. Save it to your hard drive if you want others throughout your organization to have access to it.

   c. Protect the template with the Form option.

   d. Insert form fields where needed.

2. By default, how do form fields appear onscreen? [L2]

   a. shaded gray

   b. outlined in red

   c. shaded blue

   d. double-underlined

3. Which of the following is the Form Field Options button? [L4–5]

   a.   `abl`

   b.   `☑`

   c.   `▦`

   d.   `▧`

4. What type of form field lets users choose from a list of options? [L3, 5]

   a. Text

   b. Check Box

   c. Drop-down

   d. Date

5. When you are filling out an online format, what key do you press to move to the next field? [L7]

   a. Enter

   b. Tab

   c. Shift + Tab

   d. Ctrl + Enter

Screen ID

Label each element of the Word screen shown in Figure 20.14.

Figure 20.14

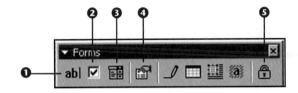

A Check Box Form Field

B Drop-Down Form Field

C Form Field Options

D Protect Form

E Text Form Field

1._____ 2._____ 3._____

4._____ 5._____

Skill Drill

Skill Drill exercises reinforce project skills. Each skill reinforced is the same, or nearly the same, as a skill presented in the project. Each exercise includes a brief narrative introduction, followed by detailed instructions in a step-by-step format.

1. Creating a Fax Form from an Existing Document

You want to create an online fax form that users can complete. After users complete the fax, they can use the Send To, Fax Recipient option to fax the document directly from their computers.

1. Open **W-2002**.

2. Choose File, Save As; click the Save as type drop-down arrow and choose Document Template (*.dot); type **Fax Form** in the File name text box; and then click Save.

3. Choose View, Toolbars, Forms.

4. Create a field by completing the following steps:

   a. Delete the first *.

   b. Click the Text Form Field button on the Forms toolbar.

5. Repeat step 4 to create text form fields to replace all asterisks *except* the one for the From line.

6. Save the form template and keep it onscreen to continue with the next exercise.

2. Inserting and Formatting Drop-Down and Check Box Form Fields

Four people in your office will have access to the fax form template. You want to create a drop-down list of their names in the From category to save them time typing their names.

1. In the Fax Form document template, delete the * to the right of From.

2. Click the Drop-Down Form Field button.

3. Double-click the drop-down form field you just inserted and do the following:

   a. Type **Jeremy Long** in the Drop-down item box and click Add.

   b. Type **Belinda Mathers** in the Drop-down item box and click Add.

   c. Type **Alisha Vaughn** in the Drop-down item box and click Add.

   d. Type your name in the Drop-down item box and click Add.

   e. Click OK.

4. Click to the left of Urgent and click the Check Box Form Field button.

5. Repeat step 4 to insert check box form fields to the left of the remaining four items on that row.

6. Double-click the For Review check box, click the Check**ed** option, and click OK.

7. Click on the line below Comments and then click the Text Form Field button.

8. Click the Protect Form button.

9. Click the Save button and then close the template.

3. Using an Online Form

You want to make sure the fax form works before making it available for other users.

1. Choose File, New.

2. Choose Fax Form and click OK.

3. Type **Ethel Frantz** in the first text field.

4. Press Tab↹, click the From drop-down arrow, and choose your name.

5. Press Tab↹ and type **219-555-8122** in the Fax field.

6. Continue pressing Tab↹ and typing in the following information in the respective fields:

Pages	**1**
Phone	**219-555-8702**
Date	**7/3/02**
Re	**Confirmation of Workshops**

7. Press Tab↹ until the For Review check box is selected; then press Spacebar to remove the X.

8. Press Tab↹ twice and press Spacebar to select the Please Reply check box.

9. Press Tab↹ twice and type the following in the Comments text field:

Ethel, this fax is to confirm that I will be at your office next Friday to conduct Word 2000 workshops. Please let me know how many people will attend the workshops. Thanks.

10. Save the document as **Fax to Ethel**, print, and close it.

Challenge

Challenge exercises expand on or are somewhat related to skills presented in the lessons. Each exercise provides a brief narrative introduction followed by instructions in a numbered-step or bulleted-list format that are not as detailed as those in the *Skill Drill* section.

1. Creating and Using an Evaluation Form

You want to create an evaluation form that managers can use online.

1. Open **W-2003** and save it as **Evaluation Form**.

2. Delete the asterisks and insert text form fields.

3. Edit the text form field to the right of Number and select Number type with 10 as the maximum length.

4. Edit the text form field to the right of Years and select Number type with 2 as the maximum length.

5. Insert check box form fields for **Excellent**, **Very Good**, **Good**, and **Fair** in the Attendance row.

6. Select and copy these check boxes for the rest of these rows.

7. Insert text form fields in each cell in the Comments column.

8. Center the fields vertically and horizontally in their respective cells.

9. Apply Pale Blue shading to all cells in the first row *except* the empty cell.

10. Protect the form.

11. Save the document as a template named **Evaluation Form.dot** and print it.

12. Choose the Evaluation Form template from the New dialog box.

13. Enter the following information in the evaluation form:

Brandon Yeates

33438710

Programmer

3

14. Check the Excellent fields for the first two items; check the Very Good fields for the last three items.

15. Type **Should continue to improve with experience** in the last Comment text form field.

16. Save the document as **Evaluation of Brandon** and print it.

2. Adding Calculations to a Form

After reviewing the Invoice Form template you created in the project lessons, you decide you need more rows for customers who order more than one item. Therefore, you want to modify the template.

1. Open **Invoice Form** as a new *template* and display the Forms toolbar, if needed.

2. Unprotect the form.

3. Select Invoice and choose Expanded as the Spacing option in the Font dialog box.

4. Click in the row that contains fields for entering an item purchased; insert two rows below this one.

5. Edit the Description drop-down form field and add **Perennials**; also use the Move buttons to arrange the items in alphabetical order.

6. Copy the fields to the two new rows you inserted.

7. Edit fields on the second row by doing the following:

   a. Assign the bookmark name **Quantity2** to the second quantity form field.

   b. Assign the bookmark name **UnitPrice2** to the second unit price form field.

   c. Using the formula to multiply the correctly named quantity and unit price bookmarks for the second row.

8. Use the same process in step 7 to edit form fields on the third row of items to purchase.

9. Protect the form, save it as **Invoice Form New**, print it, and then close it.

10. Use the Invoice Form New form template to create a document. Enter the following information:

5/3/02

Mr. Drew Seeger

City Mortgage Company

210 North Stone Avenue

Tucson, AZ 84701

11. Enter the following data for the items purchased:

4/27/02	**Perennials**	**50**	**2.25**
4/27/02	**Tulip bulbs**	**10**	**1.75**
4/29/02	**Day Lily bulbs**	**18**	**3.15**

12. Use the field that indicates the person is using a Visa credit card; deselect other payment methods.

13. Save the document as **Seeger Invoice** and print it.

3. Creating a Shipping Request Form

Upper management is concerned about escalating shipping costs. A manager created the basic idea for a request form for employees to complete online to email to their supervisors for electronic signature approval. You were asked to insert the actual fields into the form template.

1. Open **W-2004** and save it as a document template named **Shipping Request Form.dot**.

2. Insert text form fields into all empty cells in the table.

3. Insert a check box form field and a space for each item in the Carrier Request section. Make sure the U.S. Postal Service check box is selected by default.

4. Insert a check box form field and a space for each item in the Special Shipping Request section. Make Regular Ground checked by default.

5. Insert a text form field after Other (specify).

6. Insert a text form field one double-space below the Package Contents section.

7. Insert a check box and a space for each item in the Other Request section.

8. Delete * and insert a text box with Number type and currency number format.

9. Insert a text form field after (specify).

10. Protect the form template, save, print, and close it.

11. Display the New dialog box and select Shipping Request Form to create a new template. Unprotect the template.

12. Insert a drop-down form field to the left of the current form field for the recipient's name. Enter the following items for the drop-down field: **Ms.**, **Mrs.**, **Mr.**, and **Dr.**

13. Protect the form template and save it as a template named **Shipping Request Form 2**.

14. Display the New dialog box and select Shipping Request Form 2 to create a new document.

15. Type your name in the first field, **Marketing** in the Dept field, and **3482** in the Reference field.

16. Enter the following information in the respective fields for the recipient:

    Mr. Nicholas Feightner

    Express Printing Services

    109 East Elm Street

    Tipp City, OH 45371

17. Select UPS with Next Day Afternoon delivery.

18. Type **Proofs of brochures for spring sale** in the Package Contents form field.

19. Save the document as **Shipping Request for Marketing Brochures** and print it.

Discovery Zone

Discovery Zone exercises help you gain advanced knowledge of project topics and/or application of skills. These exercises focus on enhancing your problem-solving skills. Numbered steps are not provided, but you are given hints, reminders, screen shots, and/or references to help you reach your goal for each exercise.

1. Creating an Expense Report Form Template

You are in charge of creating a travel authorization form. You have the basic design created but need to insert form fields. Open **W-2005** and save it as a document template named **Travel Expense Form**.

Insert text form fields in the heading area. Use the current date format for the Request Date form field. Use date formats for the other two dates. All dates should be formatted as M/d/yy.

Within the table, insert text form fields with number formats for the second and third columns. For the third column, also apply currency number format and set the fields to calculate upon exiting. Assign bookmark names to the fields in the second and third columns (e.g., **Breakfast** and **PerBreakfast**). Edit fields in the second and third columns to provide a note (Add Help <u>T</u>ext inside the Text Form Field Options dialog box) on the status bar to tell the user what to do (e.g., **Type number of miles driven** and **Type mileage allowance**).

Insert text form fields in the first column in the Other Expenses category.

Insert fields in the last column with number and currency format. For rows that have number fields in the second and third columns, create a calculation field. For example, **=Breakfast*PerBreakfast** to calculate the amount of allowance for breakfasts during a trip.

Insert a calculation field in the last cell with this formula: **=SUM(D1:D16)**.

Protect the form, save it, and print it. From the New dialog box, create a new document from the template. Use appropriate data in the first part. Insert the following data in the table fields:

Shuttle		**25**
Airplane		**375**
Hotel	**4**	**100**
Breakfast	**3**	**10**
Lunch	**4**	**15**
Dinner	**4**	**20**
Convention Fee		**110**

Save the document as **My Travel Form**, print it, and then close it.

2. Automating Template Fields and a Macro

You want to use an existing document that contains some form fields to create a form template with drop-down fields, check box form fields, and a macro that inserts a paragraph if a certain check box is selected when the form created with the template is filled out.

Open **W-2006** and save it as a template named **Registration Form**. Delete each * and create a drop-down list of these courses: **Word Basic**, **Word Intermediate**, **Word Advanced**, **Excel Basic**, **Excel Advanced**, **PowerPoint Basic**, and **Access Basic**. *Hint:* Create one drop-down form field and copy it for the other two choices. Delete each ** and insert a check box.

Record a macro named **Color** that is stored *only* with the Registration Form template, not the Normal.dot template. Record the macro to move the insertion point to the end of the document and type the following text in Dark Blue font color: **We can help you purchase an inkjet printer at a substantial discount! Please call Liz at 555-1234 for more information!**

Delete the text from the template document after recording the macro.

Edit the Color Printer check box form field. Choose Color as the macro to run when you exit from the field during completion. Protect the template, save it, and close it. Use this template to create a new document. Fill out the form with your name and address; select Word Basic, Excel Basic, and Access Basic as the three choices; select the Color Printer check box; and press ⟨Tab⁺⟩. The paragraph should be inserted at the end of the document. Save the document as **My Registration** and print it.

PinPoint Assessment

You have completed this project and its associated lessons, and have had an opportunity to assess your skills through the end-of-project questions and exercises. Now use the PinPoint software Evaluation Mode to further assess your comprehension of the specific exam activities you have just learned. You can also use the PinPoint Trainer Mode and the Show Me tutorials to practice these exam activities.

Project 21

Creating Web Pages

Key terms introduced in this project include

- form control
- frame
- frame page
- home page
- hypertext
- hyperlink

- Internet
- list box
- round-tripping
- scrolling text
- theme

- uniform resource locator (URL)
- Web Layout View
- Web page
- Web site
- World Wide Web (Web)

Objectives	Required Activity for MOUS	Exam Level
➤ Use the Web Page Wizard	Create a new document using a wizard	Core
	Save as Web Page	Core
	Use Web Page preview	Core
➤ Insert Text and Files		
➤ Change a Theme and Background		
➤ Format a Web Page		
➤ Insert Graphical Elements on a Web Page	Insert graphics into a document (WordArt ClipArt, Images)	Core
➤ Insert Scrolling Text and Drop-down Boxes	Create and modify a form control (e.g., add an item to a drop-down list)	Expert
➤ Insert Hyperlinks on a Web Page	Create hyperlinks	Core
➤ Round-Trip a Document from HTML Format	Round trip documents from HTML	Expert

Why Would I Do This?

usiness is booming on the World Wide Web (also known as the Web). Millions of people around the world have access to the Internet, with more people getting on-line every day. Today, the Web might be the most effective way to spread information.

Originally, publishing on the Web was difficult and costly. Documents had to be formatted in HyperText Markup Language (HTML), which most people didn't know how to use. With Word 2000, you can create a document and save it in HTML format without even knowing HTML language! You can then store the pages on a Web server so that others have access to your Web pages.

In this project, you use the Web Page Wizard to create and format a new document specifically for the Web.

 Inside Stuff: Internet Information

The **Internet** is a worldwide conglomerate of computer networks. It isn't owned and operated by any one person or company; it is one network of computers that can talk to another network.

The **World Wide Web (Web)** is a component of the Internet; it is a collection of documents accessible through the Internet. These documents contain special technology called **hypertext** that is read by a Web browser program such as Internet Explorer.

When you click hypertext, you are taken to a new document (called a **Web page**) or to a Web page on a different computer (called a **Web site**). The hypertext that links to other pages or information is called a **hyperlink**.

The Web uses a type of address called a **uniform resource locator (URL)** to identify specific documents and locations.

 ## Lesson I: Using the Web Page Wizard

Before you create a Web page, you should plan how you want the page to look. You can design an exciting page using tables, styles, font formatting, bulleted lists, and graphics. However, the easiest way to start creating a Web page is to use the Web Page Wizard. The Web Page Wizard provides step-by-step instructions to guide you through creating a Web page.

In this lesson, you use the Web Page Wizard to create a Web document for Oak Grove Products.

To Use the Web Page Wizard

❶ Choose File, New; select the Web Pages tab; click the Web Page Wizard; and then click OK.
The Web Page Wizard appears. The left side displays the major steps it will take you through.

❷ Click Next at the bottom of the dialog box.
Word advances to the second screen, so that you can enter a title and select where you want to save the Web page (see Figure 21.1).

Type a title for your Web site ——

Type a location to save the
Web site...

...or click to select drive and
folder in which to save site

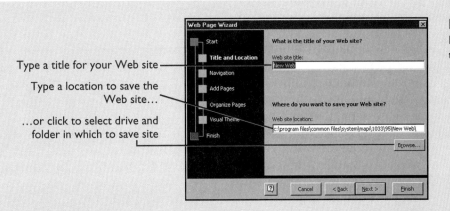

Figure 21.1
Enter the Web page
title and location.

 Inside Stuff: **Viewing a Previous Screen**
Click Back to display a previous screen of options while working with the
Web Page Wizard.

3 **Type Oak Grove Products in the Web site title box; type a location, such
as D:\Project 21\Oak Grove\, in the Web site location box; and then
click Next.**
The Navigation screen appears, so you can select a frame option. The default option is Vertical frame, which creates a frame of links on the left side of the
screen. You see a description for the selected option.

4 **Click Next to advance to the Add Pages screen.**
The Add Pages screen lets you add pages, select a template page, or use an existing document (see Figure 21.2).

Indicates that you're on
the Add Pages screen

Click to add new page ——

Removes selected page ——

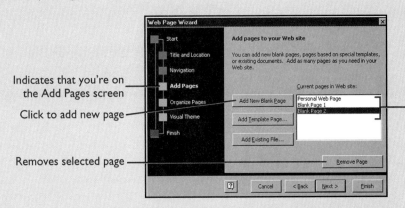

Figure 21.2
The Add Pages screen
helps you add more
Web pages.

— List of pages

 Inside Stuff: **Adding Web Pages**
Click Add Template Page to add template pages such as Frequently Asked
Questions. These pages contain headings and text to use a guide for your
Web page.

5 **Select Personal Web Page in the Current pages in Web site list, and
then click Remove Page.**
Word removes the page from the list.

6 **Click Add New Blank Page to add another blank page to the Current
pages in Web site list; then click Next.**
The Organize Pages screen appears, so you can arrange pages in a different order
or rename pages.

continues ▶

To Use the Web Page Wizard (continued)

7 **Select Blank Page 1 and then click <u>R</u>ename.**
The Rename Hyperlink dialog box appears (see Figure 21.3), so you can rename the current hyperlink.

Figure 21.3
Rename blank pages with relevant names.

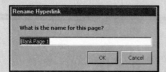

8 **Type Introduction and click OK to rename the page.**

9 **Adapt steps 7 and 8 to rename Blank Page 2 as Garden Tools and Blank Page 3 as Plants & Flowers; then click <u>N</u>ext.**
The Visual Theme screen is next. The default visual theme is Straight Edge, which you'll keep.

 If You Have Problems...
If Straight Edge is not the default visual theme, click Browse <u>T</u>hemes, select Straight Edge from the Choose a <u>T</u>heme list, and then click OK.

10 **Click <u>N</u>ext to advance to the Finish screen; then click <u>F</u>inish.**
Word creates your Web page, which is named default.htm. The document is displayed in ***Web Layout view***, which is the mode for viewing Web pages (see Figure 21.4). The Web Page Wizard creates a table of contents frame, which lists the Web pages you named. Each item in the table of contents frame is a hyperlink to a Web page of that same name. The main Web site page is called a ***home page***.

Figure 21.4
The Wizard creates the table of contents frame and the first Web page.

Default Web page name

Web page title

Table of Contents frame

Web page name

Frames toolbar

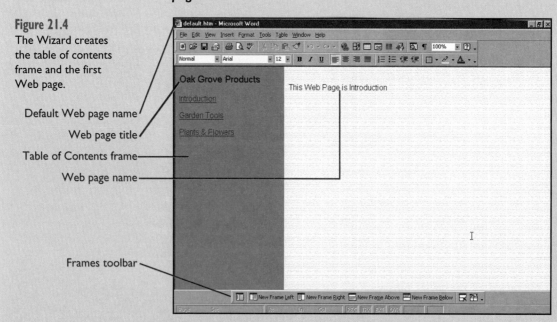

11 **Choose <u>F</u>ile, Save <u>A</u>s.**
As Figure 21.5 shows, Word creates a folder for each Web page contained in your Web site (e.g., Garden Tools_files). Each folder contains a .gif file for each graphic and background item. You also see .htm files for each page you created.

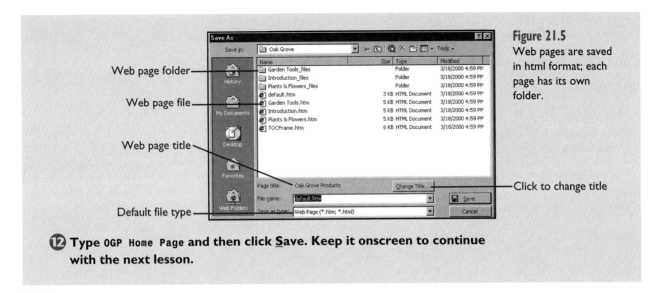

Figure 21.5
Web pages are saved in html format; each page has its own folder.

Web page folder

Web page file

Web page title

Click to change title

Default file type

12 Type OGP Home Page and then click **S**ave. Keep it onscreen to continue with the next lesson.

ⓘ **Inside Stuff: Changing the Web Page Title**
In the Save As dialog box, the page title is listed above the File **n**ame box. To change the title, click **C**hange Title, type a new title, and click OK.

ⓘ **Inside Stuff: Opening and Editing Web Pages**
You can open a Web page like a regular Word document. After opening a Web page, you can edit it and save it again with the html format.

✍ **Exam Note: Saving and Viewing a Regular Document in HTML Format**
You can create a regular Word document and save it in HTML format. Choose **F**ile, Save as Web Page. The default file type is html. You can name the Web page document and also change the title of the Web page.

You can click the Web Layout View button above the status bar to see how a regular document would look on the Web.

Choose **F**ile, We**b** Page Preview or click the Web Page Preview button (if you customized your toolbar) to see the Web page in Microsoft Internet Explorer.

Core

Lesson 2: Inserting Text and Files

The Web Page Wizard divides the Web site into sections called **frames**. Each frame that appears is saved as a separate Web page. The collection of all frames is called the **frame page** and does not appear to the user. The frame is basically ready to go, and you are ready to type text in the Web page. If you already have text saved in a file, you can easily insert a file within a Web page document to save typing time.

In this lesson, you add text and insert a file into the Web document

To Insert Text and a File

1 In the open OGP Home Page Web document, select This Web Page is Introduction and type Oak Grove Products.
The selected text is replaced with the text you just typed.

continues ▶

To Insert Text and a File (continued)

2 **Press** ⏎Enter **twice. Type the text shown in Figure 21.6, making sure to press** ⏎Enter **between sentences.**

Figure 21.6
Create Web page text like a regular document text.

Type this text ————

Oak Grove Products

Welcome to Oak Grove Online, a unique shopping environment offering products and services for your home and garden.

Here is a sampling of products available from Oak Grove Online:

Garden Tools
Bulbs
Flowering Shrubs
Non-flowering Shrubs

Shop Oak Grove Online for the best selection, quality, and customer service!

 Inside Stuff: **Spelling Errors**
Even in Web Layout View, you see red marks below misspelled words. Correct spelling errors the same way you do in a regular document: right-click and choose the correct spelling, click the Spelling and Grammar button on the toolbar, or double-click the Spelling and Grammar Status button on the status bar.

3 **In the Table of Contents frame, click** Garden Tools **so your mouse pointer becomes a hand; click it again to display the Garden Tools page.**
Word displays the Garden Tools Web page. You also see the Web toolbar. The taskbar contains a button indicating that a file named OGP Home Page:2 is open.

 Inside Stuff: **Hyperlink ScreenTip**
When you position the mouse pointer on an item in the Table of Contents frame, you see a ScreenTip that tells you the file that the link jumps to.

4 **Select** This Web Page is Garden Tools **and type** Oak Grove's Garden Tools.

5 **Press** ⏎Enter **twice and type the rest of the text shown in Figure 21.7.**

6 **In the Table of Contents frame, click** Plants & Flowers, **so the mouse pointer becomes a hand; then click again to jump to the Plants & Flowers Web page.**
You see a third open file on the taskbar. The file is named OGP Home Page:3.

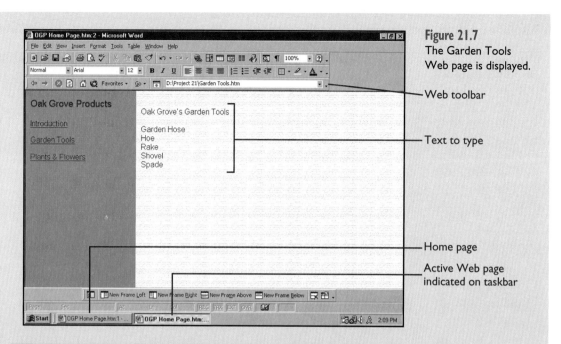

Figure 21.7
The Garden Tools
Web page is displayed.

Web toolbar

Text to type

Home page

Active Web page
indicated on taskbar

ⓘ *Inside Stuff:*   **Open Web Page Files**
Every time you edit a Web page frame and then either use a hyperlink in
the Table of Contents frame or click the Back or Forward button on the
Web toolbar, a new open document appears on the taskbar. Because all
hyperlink pages are now open, you use the taskbar to move between them
to avoid opening additional Web pages.

The numbered open documents do *not* correspond with the order of the
Web pages. They are numbered sequentially based on the order in which
you open them with the hyperlink or Back/Forward buttons.

---

⑦ **Select** `This Web Page is Plants & Flowers` **and press** `Del`.
Instead of typing new text, you insert an existing Word file within the Web page.

⑧ **Choose Insert, File; choose** `W-2101` **and then click Insert.**
Word inserts the file into the current document (see Figure 21.8). A bookmark
is inserted by each heading. You need these bookmarks when you create hyperlinks later in this project.

✖ *If You Have Problems...*
If you do not see the bookmark symbols, choose Tools, Options, click the
View tab, select Bookmarks, and then click OK.

---

continues ▶

To Insert Text and a File (continued)

Figure 21.8
Insert existing files within a Web page.

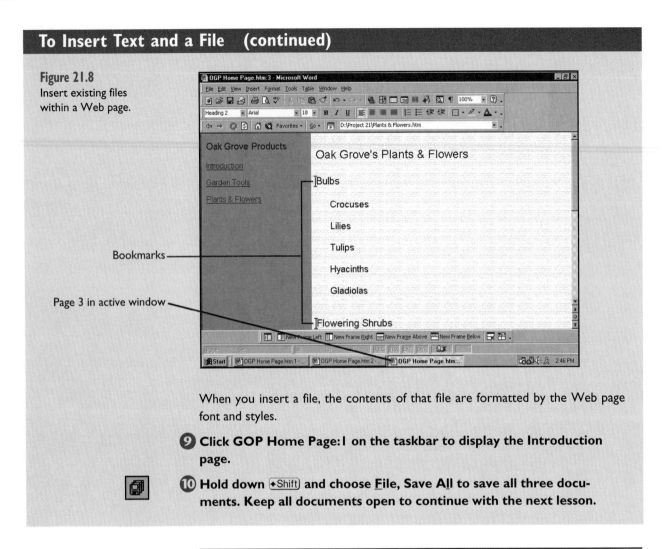

Bookmarks

Page 3 in active window

When you insert a file, the contents of that file are formatted by the Web page font and styles.

⑨ Click GOP Home Page:1 on the taskbar to display the Introduction page.

 ⑩ Hold down ⚫Shift and choose File, Save All to save all three documents. Keep all documents open to continue with the next lesson.

ⓘ *Inside Stuff:* **Save All Button**
You can add the Save All button to your toolbar and click it to save all open documents. Refer to Project 18, "Managing Files and Customizing Word," for information on customizing a toolbar.

ⓘ *Inside Stuff:* **Adding and Deleting Frames**
With the Frames toolbar displayed, select a frame option, such as New Frame Left, that you want to insert into your Web page. Word creates a new html document for the new frame using the first few characters that you type. You can assign a different name by right-clicking the frame, selecting Save Current Frame As, typing the name in the File name box, and clicking Save.

You can delete a frame that contains the insertion point by clicking the Delete Frame button on the Frames toolbar.

Lesson 3: Changing a Theme and Background

Web pages are more interesting when you choose a theme and background. A ***theme*** is a set of design elements that includes background images, bullets, numbering, fonts, lines, and other graphical elements. Word provides an abundance of themes such as Blends, Blueprint,

Construction Zone, and Romanesque. You should choose a theme that relates to the content of your document or Web site pages. You can also adjust the background color to further enhance a theme.

In this lesson, you apply a different theme and color to your Web site.

To Change a Theme and Background

1 **In the open OGP Home Page:1 document, click in the Table of Contents frame.**

 Inside Stuff: Opening the Home Page
If you closed the Web pages after completing a lesson, open **OGP Home Page** only. When specified to click OGP Home Page:1, OGP Home Page:2, or OGP Home Page:3, click the appropriate link in the Table of Contents frame to display the respective Web page in the frame on the right side.

2 **Choose F__o__rmat, T__h__eme.**
The Theme dialog box appears (see Figure 21.9). Straight Edge is the default theme.

Choose this theme ——

Preview of selected theme ——

Default theme ——

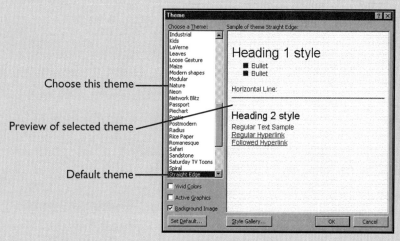

Figure 21.9
Choose a theme for your Web site.

3 **Click Nature in the Choose a T__h__eme list and then click OK.**
Word applies that theme to the Table of Contents frame.

 If You Have Problems...
If Nature is not installed on your computer, choose another theme or use the Microsoft 2000 CD to install all themes.

4 **Click in the Introduction frame and then repeat steps 2 and 3 to apply the Nature theme to that frame.**
Both the Table of Contents and Introduction frames are formatted with the Nature theme (see Figure 21.10). Word applies a variation of the theme to these two frames. You should use the same theme for all pages within a Web site to maintain consistency.

continues ▶

To Change a Theme and Background (continued)

Figure 21.10
The Nature theme is applied to both frames.

Different variation of Nature theme for table of contents frame

Nature theme

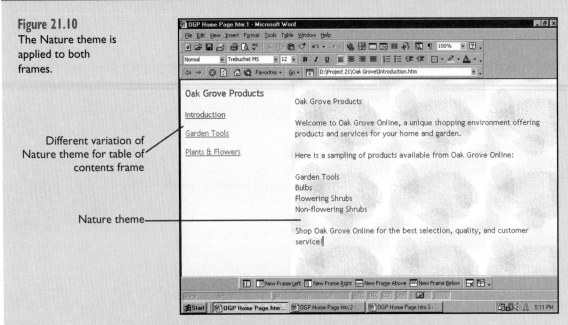

5 Click inside the Table of Contents frame title again.

6 Choose F**o**rmat, B**a**ckground; then click Light Green.

7 Click OGP Home Page:2 on the taskbar, click in the Garden Tools frame heading, choose F**o**rmat, T**h**eme, choose Nature, and then click OK.

8 Use the same process in step 7 to apply the Nature theme to OGP Home Page:3.
Heading 2, which was originally applied to the heading, is adapted to the theme (see Figure 21.11).

Figure 21.11
The Nature theme is applied to the third Web page.

Table of contents frame remains onscreen

Light Green background color for frame

Nature theme for frame

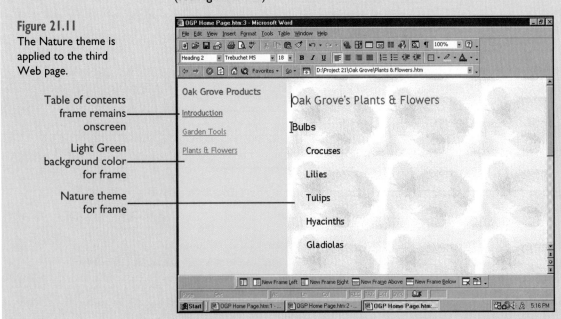

9 Hold down **⬆Shift** and choose F**i**le, Save A**l**l to save all three documents. Click OGP Home Page:1 on the taskbar to make it the active window.

Lesson 4: Formatting a Web Page

You can enhance the readability of your Web pages by applying fonts and font sizes to direct your readers' attention to particular parts of the Web page. You can also format items as bulleted lists or as numbered lists.

In this lesson, you format text on the Web pages by selecting styles and formatting items as a bulleted list.

 Inside Stuff: **Opening the Web Pages Again**
If you closed the Web pages at the end of the last lesson, open **OGP Home Page.htm**. Click the links in the Table of Contents frame to open the other files instead of clicking buttons on the taskbar.

To Format a Web Page

1 **In the open OGP Home Page:1 document, select Oak Grove Products in the Introduction frame.**
You want the heading to stand out more.

2 **Click the Style drop-down arrow and choose Heading 1.**
The four items would look better if you format them as a bulleted list.

3 **Select the four-item list, beginning with Garden Tools; then click the Bullets button.**
Word formats the bulleted list based on the Nature theme.

4 **Select Oak Grove Products in the Table of Contents frame, click the Font Color drop-down arrow, and choose Dark Green; deselect the heading.**
Your frames should look similar to those in Figure 21.12.

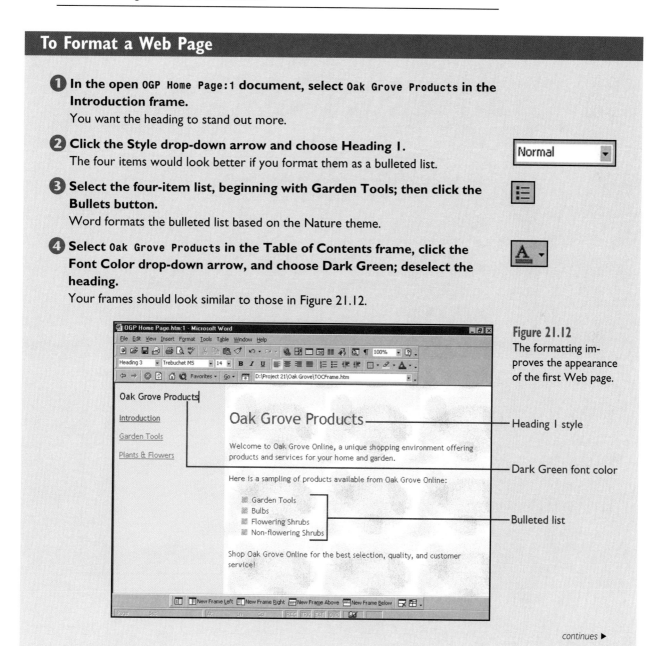

Figure 21.12
The formatting improves the appearance of the first Web page.

Heading 1 style

Dark Green font color

Bulleted list

continues ▶

To Format a Web Page (continued)

5 Click **OGP Home Page:2** on the taskbar, click in the Oak Grove's Garden Tools heading, click the Style drop-down arrow, and choose Heading 2.

You need to format the items as a bulleted list.

6 Select the five-item bulleted list, beginning with Garden Hoses, and click the Bullets button. Then, deselect the bulleted list.

Figure 21.13 shows the formatted Web page.

Figure 21.13
The second Web page is formatted.

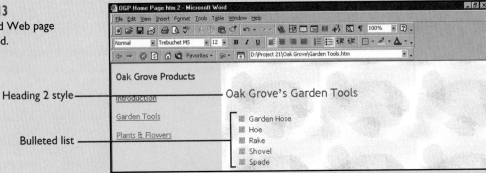

Heading 2 style ——

Bulleted list ——

7 Click **OGP Home Page:3** on the taskbar.

You want the main categories to stand out.

8 Select and italicize the following text: Bulbs, Flowering Shrubs, and Non-flowering Shrubs.

Figure 21.14 shows the italicized category headings.

Figure 21.14
The italicized category names stand out.

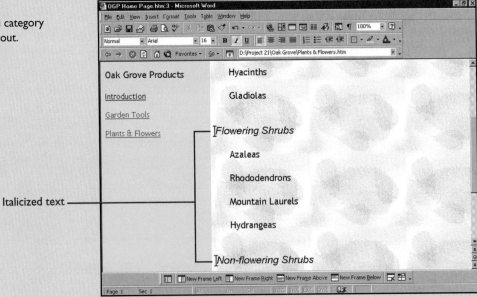

Italicized text ——

 9 Hold down ◆Shift and choose **File, Save All**. Keep OGP Home Page:3 on-screen to continue with the next lesson.

Lesson 5: Inserting Graphical Elements on a Web Page

Many Web page elements are actually graphics files linked to the HTML document. You can enhance a Web page by inserting and formatting JPEG or GIF images.

In this lesson, you insert horizontal lines and a picture into the document.

To Insert Graphical Elements

1 **In the open OGP Home Page:3 page, position the insertion point on the blank line *above* the heading Flowering Shrubs.**
This is where you want to insert a horizontal line.

2 **Click the Outside Border drop-down arrow on the Formatting toolbar and then choose Horizontal Line.**
Word inserts a horizontal line that is formatted by the Nature theme.

 Inside Stuff: **Line Formatting**
The line takes on the formats assigned by the current theme. You can re-size the line, but you can't change its color.

If you want a custom line, click the Line button on the Drawing toolbar and draw a line. You can then customize that line by using the Line Color buttons on the Drawing toolbar.

3 **Place the insertion point on the blank line *above* the heading Non-flowering Shrubs and insert a horizontal line like you did in step 2.**
Your Web page should look like the one shown in Figure 21.15.

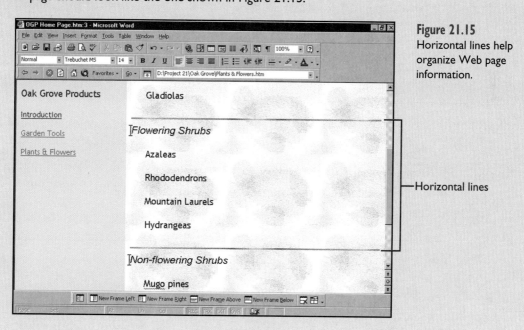

Figure 21.15
Horizontal lines help organize Web page information.

Now, you want to insert a clip art image in the Table of Contents frame.

4 **Click on the blank line below Oak Grove Products in the Table of Contents frame.**

5 **Choose Insert, Picture, Clip Art.**

continues ▶

To Insert Graphical Elements   (continued)

6 **Click the Nature category, right-click the trees picture, choose Insert from the menu, and then close the dialog box.**

Word inserts the image. You can click it and use the sizing handles to adjust its height and width. For a specific measurement, display the Picture toolbar and click the Format Picture button. You can specify a variety of picture formats.

Exam Note: **Inserting Other Image Types**

You can insert other types of images, such as JPEG or BMP, by choosing Insert, Picture, From File.

---

7 **Place the insertion point to the left of Introduction in the Table of Contents frame, and then press ⏎Enter to insert a blank line.**

Your Table of Contents frame looks more inviting with the clipart image (see Figure 21.16).

Figure 21.16
Images enhance Web pages.

Inserted clip art ——

Blank line between image and heading ——

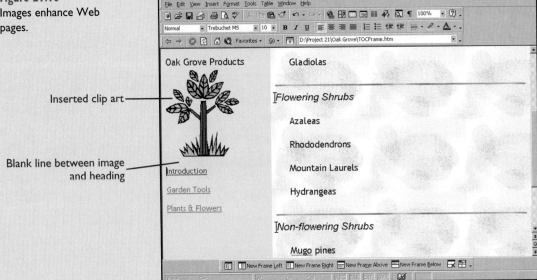

8 **Hold down ⬆Shift and choose File, Save All to save all three documents; click OGP Home Page:1 so it is onscreen to continue with the next lesson.**

Inside Stuff: **Inserting Tables**

You can insert a table in a Web page. A table is a great way to organize information. Refer to Project 7, "Creating and Formatting Tables," and Project 8, "Using Additional Table Options," for information about tables.

Lesson 6: Inserting Scrolling Text and Dropdown Boxes

You can customize Web pages by inserting special items such as scrolling text. *Scrolling text* is text that moves across a Web page, either continuously or for a limited number of times.

You can also insert *form controls*, elements that collect or provide data. These controls require special support files and server support. Therefore, you should work with a Web master or network administrator to plan a form.

In this lesson, you use the Web Tools toolbar to insert scrolling text and a dropdown box.

To Insert Scrolling Text

1 **In the open OGP Home Page:1 page, place the insertion point on the blank line above the title.**

2 **Choose View, Toolbars, Web Tools.**
The Web Tools toolbar contains buttons for inserting special Web page elements, such as scrolling text (see Figure 21.17).

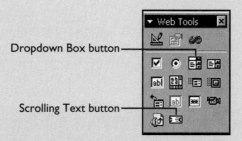

Dropdown Box button

Scrolling Text button

Figure 21.17
Use the Web Tools toolbar to insert Web items.

3 **Click the Scrolling Text button on the Web Tools toolbar.**
The Scrolling Text dialog box appears (see Figure 21.18).

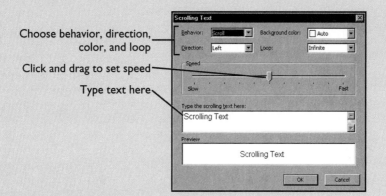

Choose behavior, direction, color, and loop

Click and drag to set speed

Type text here

Figure 21.18
Type and format the scrolling text.

4 **Type Shop Oak Grove Products online for all your home and garden needs! in the Type the scrolling text here box.**

5 **Click and drag the Speed pointer to the left two notches, and then click OK.**
The scrolling text appears in a box at the top of the Web page (see Figure 21.19).

Figure 21.19
The scrolling text appears onscreen.

Text scrolls across in the Scrolling Box area

continues ▶

To Insert Scrolling Text   (continued)

 Inside Stuff: **Editing the Scrolling Text**
Double-click in the scrolling text area to display the Scrolling Text dialog box again, so you can make changes.

 6 Hold down ⬆Shift and choose File, Save All to save all three documents; click OGP Home Page:1 so it is onscreen to continue with the next exercise.

 Inside Stuff: **Formatting Scrolling Text**
Click the scrolling text to select it. You can apply font color, bold, and font size.

In the next exercise, you insert a dropdown box that lists items to choose from.

To Insert a Dropdown Box

1 Click OGP Home Page:2 on the taskbar and then choose View, Toolbars, Web Tools.
You must display the Web Tools toolbar on each Web page.

2 Place the insertion point after Spade, press ⏎Enter twice, type Select your item, and press ⏎Enter.

3 Click the Dropdown Box button on the Web Tools toolbar.

 4 Click the Properties button on the Web Tools toolbar.
The Properties dialog box appears (see Figure 21.20). You need to insert the items you want to appear in the drop-down list.

Figure 21.20
The Dropdown Box is inserted as a form control.

Insert drop-down items

Dropdown Box

Exit Design Mode button

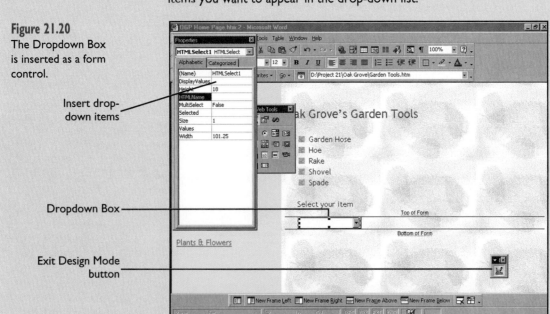

You need to insert the items you want to appear in the drop-down list. You type the item names separated by semicolons.

5 **Click to the right of DisplayValues in the Properties dialog box and then type** `Garden Hose;Hoe;Rake;Shovel;Spade`.

6 **Click the Close button.**

You can't view the drop-down items until you click the Exit Design Mode button.

 Inside Stuff: **Inserting a List Box**

You can insert a *list box* to display available choices in a list format, similar to a list box within a dialog box in Word.

---

7 **Place the mouse pointer on the center-right Dropdown Box object handle to become a double-horizontal arrow; click and drag to the right about one inch to widen it.**

8 **Click the Exit Design Mode button.**

The Design Mode is off, and the drop-down arrow appears to the right of the box.

9 **Click the Dropdown Box arrow to show the list of items.**

Figure 21.21 shows the drop-down list.

Figure 21.21
The Dropdown Box lets Web users select an item to purchase.

List of items

 Exam Note: **Editing and Deleting Form Controls**

To edit a form control such as the Dropdown Box, click the Design Mode button and then click the Properties button. Make desired changes, close the Properties box, and then click the Exit Design Mode button.

To delete a form control, select all items, including the top of form and bottom of form text; then press Del.

---

10 **Hold down** `⬆Shift` **and choose** **F**ile, **Save A**ll **to save all three documents; click OGP Home Page:1 so it is onscreen to continue with the next lesson.**

 Exam Note: **Inserting a Submit Button**

After users have filled out the items they want to order in the drop-down list or list box, they need a way to submit their orders. Click the Submit button on the Web Tools toolbar to insert this button, so that users can submit their selections to you.

Lesson 7: Inserting Hyperlinks on a Web Page

Web sites are designed to provide information in an efficient manner. To do this, individual Web pages should be fairly short. The smaller the Web document and the fewer graphics the document contains, the faster that page loads for Web users. To make a Web site more manageable, you break it into Web pages with hyperlinks to jump users from one page to the next.

You've explored hyperlinks in Project 17 in a regular document. Remember that text hyperlinks appear in a different color and are underlined. After you click a hyperlink, the color changes. When the mouse pointer is positioned over a hyperlink (text or graphics), it resembles a hand.

In this lesson, you insert hyperlinks to jump to pages within the Web site.

To Insert Hyperlinks

1 **In the open OGP Home Page:1 page, select Garden Tools in the Introduction frame.**

2 **Click the Insert Hyperlink button on the Standard toolbar.**
The Insert Hyperlink dialog box appears (see Figure 21.22).

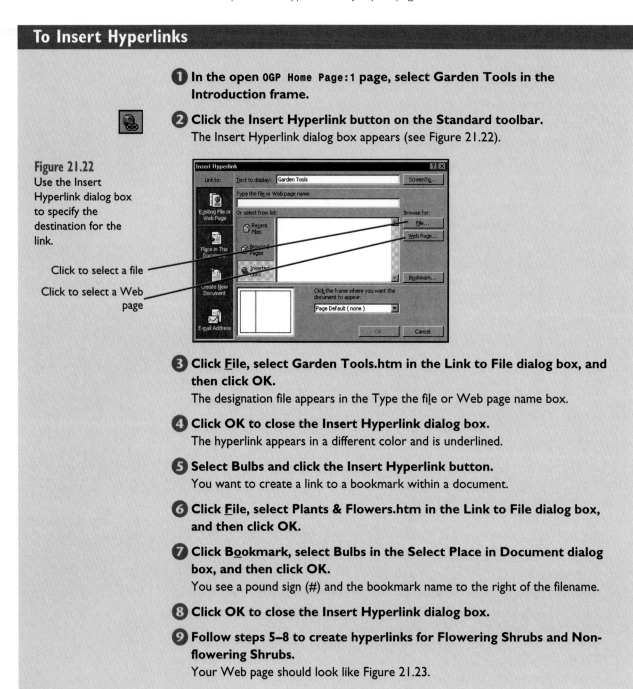

Figure 21.22
Use the Insert Hyperlink dialog box to specify the destination for the link.

Click to select a file

Click to select a Web page

3 **Click File, select Garden Tools.htm in the Link to File dialog box, and then click OK.**
The designation file appears in the Type the file or Web page name box.

4 **Click OK to close the Insert Hyperlink dialog box.**
The hyperlink appears in a different color and is underlined.

5 **Select Bulbs and click the Insert Hyperlink button.**
You want to create a link to a bookmark within a document.

6 **Click File, select Plants & Flowers.htm in the Link to File dialog box, and then click OK.**

7 **Click Bookmark, select Bulbs in the Select Place in Document dialog box, and then click OK.**
You see a pound sign (#) and the bookmark name to the right of the filename.

8 **Click OK to close the Insert Hyperlink dialog box.**

9 **Follow steps 5–8 to create hyperlinks for Flowering Shrubs and Non-flowering Shrubs.**
Your Web page should look like Figure 21.23.

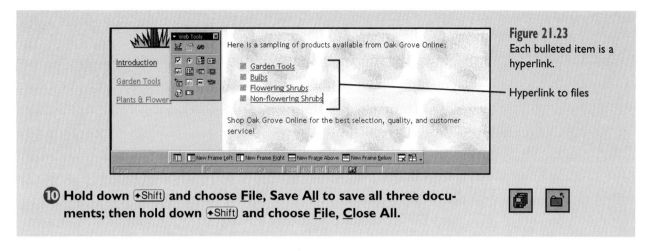

Figure 21.23
Each bulleted item is a hyperlink.

Hyperlink to files

10 **Hold down** ⟨⏵Shift⟩ **and choose** **F**i**le, Save A**l**l to save all three documents; then hold down** ⟨⏵Shift⟩ **and choose** **F**i**le,** **C**l**ose All.**

Inside Stuff: Hyperlink to Home
Well-designed Web sites provide a hyperlink in each page to go back to the home page.

Lesson 8: Round-Tripping a Document from HTML Format   Expert

You learned how to create Web pages and save them in HTML format without even knowing that language! At any time, you can open those files in Word and edit them without having to convert them first. When you display Web pages in the Internet Explorer browser, you can use an edit option to launch Word and open the Web page within Word to edit the document. This process of editing a Web page saved in HTML formatting is called **round-tripping**.

In this lesson, you start Internet Explorer, open the home page, and round-trip the document to make edits.

To Round-Trip an HTML Document

1 **Click the Start button, choose** **P**r**ograms, and then choose Internet Explorer.**
You want to see what the Web page looks like when viewed through a Web browser.

2 **Choose** **F**i**le,** **O**p**en; click** **B**r**owse, browse through your data disk and click OGP Home Page.htm. Then, click** **O**p**en and then click OK in the Open dialog box to open the Web page.**
Figure 21.24 shows the Web page in Internet Explorer.

continues ▶

To Round-Trip an HTML Document   (continued)

Figure 21.24
The Web page is displayed in Internet Explorer.

Back button

Microsoft Internet Explorer browser

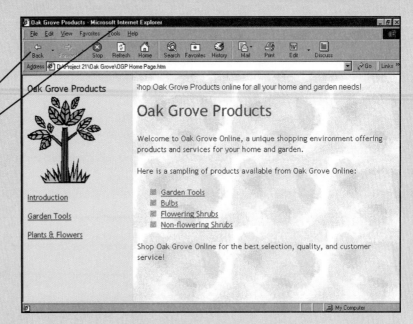

3 **Click the Garden Tools link.**
Clicking the hyperlink jumps to that Web page.

4 **Click the Back button on the toolbar.**
Clicking the Back button takes you back to the previous Web page.

 Inside Stuff: Forward Button
After you click the Back button, the Forward button is available, so you can go forward through the Web pages you've displayed.

5 **Choose File, Edit with Microsoft Word for Windows.**
This option opens the Web page in Word, so you can edit the document without having to use HTML programming language. If Word isn't the active window, click it on the taskbar.

6 **Select Oak Grove Online at the top of the Web page, click the Font Color drop-down arrow and choose Green, and click the Bold button.**

7 **Repeat step 6 to format Oak Grove Online at the bottom of the Web page.**

8 **Save the document.**
Now, you want to see the Web page in Internet Explorer again.

9 **Click the Internet Explorer button on the taskbar to toggle back to that program.**
The browser probably does not show the changes you just made. Therefore, you need to refresh the view.

10 **Click the Refresh button on the toolbar.**
The updated Web page now reflects the change you made to Oak Grove Online—Green font color and boldface (see Figure 21.25).

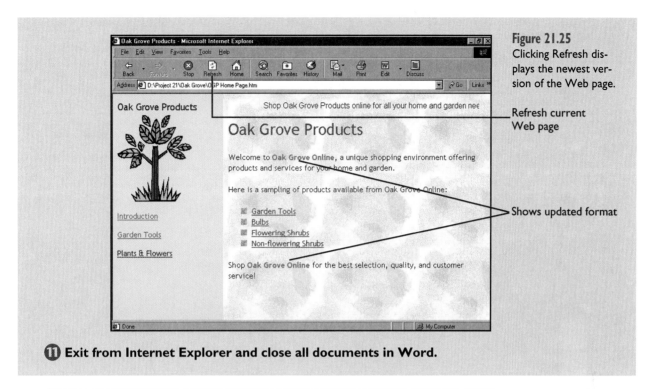

Figure 21.25
Clicking Refresh displays the newest version of the Web page.

Refresh current
Web page

Shows updated format

11 **Exit from Internet Explorer and close all documents in Word.**

 Inside Stuff: **Posting on the Web**
To post your Web pages on the World Wide Web, you must upload them to a Web server. Your organization might have a Web server, or you may have access to a Web server through your Internet Service Provider (ISP), such as America Online. Some colleges and universities allow students to upload personal Web pages to the institution's Web site, provided the material meets certain guidelines. Contact your local ISP for more information.

Summary

After completing this project, you can create Web pages by using the Web Page Wizard or by saving an existing document in html format. You know how to create hyperlinks to jump to other Web pages, format Web pages, and save all open documents. In addition, you can enhance a Web site by applying an appropriate theme and background. Finally, you can view the Web page in Microsoft Internet Explorer and round-trip the html document to edit it back in Word.

The Help feature provides additional information about creating Web pages. Plus, spend some time exploring the buttons on the Web Tools toolbar. Now, complete the following exercises and the relevant PinPoint activities to further your learning.

Checking Concepts and Terms

True/False

For each of the following, check *T* or *F* to indicate whether the statement is true or false.

__T __F   **1.** The Web Page Wizard lets you select a theme for the Web page. [L1]

__T __F   **2.** Word saves each frame as a separate Web page. [L2]

__T __F **3.** You should apply a different theme to each page within your Web site. [L3]

__T __F **4.** Scrolling text is helpful to grab people's attention on your Web page. [L6]

__T __F **5.** A text hyperlink is designated with a different color and underline. [L7]

Multiple Choice

Circle the letter of the correct answer for each of the following.

1. What is the file type for a Web document? [L1]

a. doc

b. txt

c. Web

d. html

2. Which button do you click to see how a Web page will look in Internet Explorer? [L1]

a.

b.

c.

d.

3. What type of form control should you insert to display a list of items which the user clicks a down-pointing arrow? [L6]

a. dropdown box

b. check box

c. list box

d. scrolling text

4. Which of the following hyperlink destinations does *not* make sense? [L7]

a. to another Web page

b. to a bookmark within another document

c. to a bookmark within the same Web page

d. to itself

5. What term refers to editing a Web page that you're viewing in a browser? [L8]

a. road-mapping

b. round-tripping

c. circular reference

d. refresh

Screen ID

Label each element of the Word screen shown in Figure 21.26.

Figure 21.26

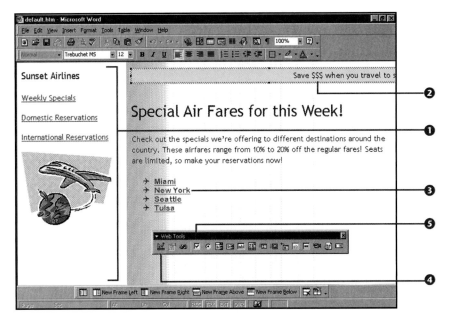

A. Design Mode button

B. Dropdown Box button

C. hyperlink

D. scrolling text

E. Table of Contents frame

1._____   2._____   3._____

4._____   5._____

Skill Drill

Skill Drill exercises reinforce project skills. Each skill reinforced is the same, or nearly the same, as a skill presented in the project. Each exercise includes a brief narrative introduction, followed by detailed instructions in a step-by-step format.

1. Creating a Web Page with the Wizard, New Text, and Existing Text

Heavenly Scents Candle Company hired you to create a Web site. You decide to use the Web Page Wizard to get started.

1. Choose File, New; click the Web Pages tab; click the Web Page Wizard; and then click OK.

2. Click Next and do the following in the Title and Location screen:

    a. Type **Heavenly Scents Candle Company** in the Web site title box.

    b. Type a location, such as **D:\Project 21\Candles**, in the Web site location box.

3. Click Next to display the Navigation screen.

4. Click Next to display the Add Pages Screen and do the following:

    a. Click Personal Web Page and then click Remove Page.

    b. Click Add New Blank Page.

5. Click Next to display the Organize Pages screen and do the following:

    a. Click Blank Page 1, click Rename, type **General Information**, and click OK.

b. Click Blank Page 2, click <u>R</u>ename, type **Fragrances**, and click OK.

c. Click Blank Page 3, click <u>R</u>ename, type **Ordering Information**, and click OK.

6. Click <u>N</u>ext to display the Visual Theme screen and do the following:

   a. Click Browse Themes.

   b. Choose Blends in the Choose a <u>T</u>heme list.

   c. Click OK.

7. Click <u>N</u>ext to display the Finish screen and then click <u>F</u>inish.

8. Select **This Page is General Information** and type **A Warm Welcome to Heavenly Scents Candle Company**.

9. Press ↵Enter twice and type the following paragraphs:

   Fresh, inviting fragrances: That's what Heavenly Scents Candle Company is all about!

   Our candles provide hours of enjoyment by freshening up your home or office. Plus, they make wonderful wedding, birthday, and graduation gifts.

10. Click Fragrances twice in the Table of Contents frame and do the following:

    a. Select **This Page is Fragrances** and press Del.

    b. Choose <u>I</u>nsert, Fi<u>l</u>e; select **W-2102**, and click In<u>s</u>ert.

11. Click Ordering Information twice in the Table of Contents frame and do the following:

    a. Select **This Page is Ordering Information** and press Del.

    b. Choose <u>I</u>nsert, Fi<u>l</u>e; select **W-2103**, and click In<u>s</u>ert.

12. Hold down ⬆Shift and choose <u>F</u>ile, Save All; keep the documents open to continue with the next exercise.

2. Formatting the Web Pages and Inserting an Image from the Web

You want to add some formatting to the Web pages for the candle company.

1. Click the taskbar button to display the Fragrances page.

2. Select Standard Scents and do the following:

   a. Click the Style drop-down arrow and choose Heading 2.

   b. Click the Highlight drop-down arrow and choose Yellow.

3. Select Exotic Scents and apply the same formatting that you applied in the previous step.

4. Select the six items below the Standard Scents heading and click the Bullets button.

5. Select the items below the Exotic Scents heading and click the Bullets button.

6. Double-click below the last item in the Table of Contents frame and do the following:

   a. Choose <u>I</u>nsert, <u>P</u>icture, <u>C</u>lip Art.

   b. Click <u>C</u>lips Online, click OK if prompted, and click Accept if prompted.

   c. Search for candles in the Household category with Photos results.

   d. Click an appropriate image and then click the download icon by it in its preview window.

   e. Close Internet Explorer.

7. Maximize Word, if needed, click the Insert ClipArt button on the taskbar, and then do the following:

   a. Right-click the image you downloaded.

   b. Choose <u>I</u>nsert.

   c. Close the Insert ClipArt dialog box.

8. Click the image and choose <u>V</u>iew, <u>T</u>oolbars, Picture, if the Picture toolbar does not appear; then do the following:

   a. Click the Format Picture button.

   b. Click the Size tab.

   c. Type **2.3"** in the Wi<u>d</u>th box and then click OK.

9. Deselect the image and insert a blank line above it.

10. Hold down ⬆Shift and choose <u>F</u>ile, <u>C</u>lose All.

3. Round-Tripping the Web Page and Inserting Additional Hyperlinks

You are ready to view the Web page in Internet Explorer and round-trip it to insert a scrolling text box.

1. Click the Start button and choose Programs, Internet Explorer.

2. Choose File, Open; click Browse, and browse through your data disk and click Heavenly Scents Candle Company.htm. Click Open and then click OK in the Open dialog box.

3. Click the Fragrances link in the Table of Contents frame.

4. Click the Ordering Information link in the Table of Contents frame.

5. Click the General Information link in the Table of Contents.

6. Choose File, Edit with Microsoft Word for Windows.

7. Select fragrances in the second paragraph and do the following:

   a. Click the Insert Hyperlink button.

   b. Click File, choose Fragrances.htm, and click OK to close the Link to File dialog box.

   c. Click OK to close the Insert Hyperlink dialog box.

8. Hold down ◆Shift and choose File, Save All.

9. Hold down ◆Shift and choose File, Close All.

10. Click the Internet Explorer button on the taskbar.

11. Click the Refresh button to see the updated Web page.

12. Click the fragrance hyperlink to see the Fragrances Web page.

13. Close Internet Explorer.

Challenge

Challenge exercises expand on or are somewhat related to skills presented in the lessons. Each exercise provides a brief narrative introduction followed by instructions in a numbered-step format that are not as detailed as those in the Skill Drill section.

1. Creating a Restaurant Web Page with the Wizard

You want to create a Web page for New Food Café. You use the Wizard to create the basic layout and format and then insert existing files into each Web page.

1. Start the Web Page Wizard.

2. Type **New Food Cafe** as the title and choose an appropriate drive and folder in which to save the Web site.

3. Remove Personal Web Page and insert two additional blank Web pages.

4. Rename the blank Web pages with the following names: **Introduction**, **Daily Lunch Items**, **Personnel**, and **Hours of Operation**.

5. Choose the Citrus Punch theme while still in the Wizard.

6. After completing the Wizard, save the file as **Cafe Home Page** in HTML format.

7. Select the **Introduction** placeholder, delete it, and insert the file **W-2104**.

8. Select and delete the Daily Lunch Specials placeholder on its page, and then insert **W-2105**.

9. Select and delete the Personnel placeholder on its page and then insert **W-2106**.

10. Select and delete the Hours of Operation placeholder on its page and then insert **W-2107**.

11. Save all open documents and keep them onscreen to continue with the next exercise.

2. Formatting the Web Pages

After creating the basic format for the Web pages, you need to format the text and insert some graphical elements.

1. In the open Web pages, click the button on the taskbar to display the Cafe Home Page.htm:1 window. Apply Heading 1 to the first title and Heading 2 to the subtitle.

2. Center the last two lines in the introduction window.

3. Create a customized bulleted list for the daily lunch items. Use the Webdings image of a plate and silverware. (Refer to Lesson 6 in Project 5, "Formatting Documents," for more information about creating customized bulleted lists.)

4. Add a new line at the top of the personnel page that displays Key Personnel in the Heading 1 style.

5. Insert a Horizontal Line (from the Outside Border drop-down arrow) between the two paragraphs in the Key Personnel page.

6. Select and cut the last line in the Operating Hours page. Display the Web Tools toolbar, and create a scrolling text box with this data (by pasting it in the appropriate dialog box option). Slow down the speed by two notches and use a Yellow background.

7. Apply a Light Green color background to the Table of Contents frame.

8. Use the Web Page Preview to see how the Web page looks, and then click close Internet Explorer.

9. Save all open document windows and then close them.

3. Viewing a Web Page and Round-Tripping HTML Documents

You are ready to check out the links by opening the Web pages within Internet Explorer.

1. Start Internet Explorer and open **Project 21\New Food Cafe\Cafe Home Page**.

2. Click each link to make sure it works. Also make sure the scrolling text works.

3. Use the option to edit the html document within Word.

4. Bold New Food Café on the Introduction page.

5. Type **The above items are 10% off during the lunch hours (11 a.m. to 1 p.m.).** one double-space below the last bulleted item in the Daily Lunch Specials frame.

6. Add bold and Green font color to the title in the Table of Contents frame.

7. Type **Special Sunday Brunch!** one double-space below the last paragraph in the Daily Lunch Specials frame. Create a hyperlink of this text that links to the Hours of Operation file.

8. Insert an appropriate clip art image in the Table of Contents frame.

9. Save all open documents and close them.

10. Refresh the view in Internet Explorer and make sure all changes display. Also, check out the new link you added to the Daily Lunch Specials Web page.

11. Print the frames from within Internet Explorer, if requested. Select the **As laid out on screen** option in the Print dialog box.

Discovery Zone

Discovery Zone exercises help you gain advanced knowledge of project topics and/or application of skills. These exercises focus on enhancing your problem-solving skills. Numbered steps are not provided, but you are given hints, reminders, screen shots, and/or references to help you reach your goal for each exercise.

1. Creating a Fitness Club's Web Page

You want to create a Web page for HealthFirst Fitness Club using the Web Page Wizard. Use the title **HealthFirst Fitness Club**, delete the Personal Web Page and make sure you have six blank Web pages that you rename: **Home Page**, **Aerobics**, **Cardiovascular**, **Personal Trainers**, **Weights**, and **Contact Us**. Select an appropriate theme and save the Web page as **HealthFirst**.

Insert **W-2108** into the Introduction page; select the title and apply the Title style to it. Insert **W-2109** into the Contact Us page.

Delete each asterisk (*) and insert a Textbox. Delete each plus sign (+) and insert a Checkbox. Delete the Gender double asterisks (**) and insert a Dropdown Box with these two options: **Male** and **Female**. Delete the Age Group double asterisks and insert a Dropdown Box with these options: **18-25**, **26-35**, **36-45**, **46-56**, **Over 56**.

Use Help to learn about form controls you can use on a Web page and read about the Submit button. Insert a Submit button that performs the action of mailing it to your email address.

Learn about aerobics, cardiovascular, and weights. Develop Web pages for these topics to link from the Table of Contents frame. Create a list of trainers to include on the Trainers Web page.

Insert an appropriate graphic image on each Web page. Use images you have or search through the images on Microsoft's Web page (via the Insert ClipArt dialog box).

Add appropriate formatting, fonts, etc. Apply the workout person symbol to the list of items in the Introduction page. Also explore the Frames toolbar to insert a better frame between the Table of Contents frame and the other frames. Include any hyperlinks you can to other files or suitable Web sites.

Save and print your pages. Explore them in Internet Explorer. If needed, round-trip the Web pages to edit them back in Word. Save all changes. Demonstrate your Web site to the class and your instructor.

2. Creating a Reference Center Web Page

You want to create a Web site that serves as a reference to other Web surfers. Select four or five categories (e.g., Airlines). Use the Web Page Wizard to create your Web site named **Web References**. Rename the blank pages with your category names you selected. Choose an appropriate theme.

Within each Web page, enter a formatted title and a list of Web sites to visit. Create a hyperlink to each Web site. For example, the Airlines category can have data for several major airlines (e.g., American Airlines, Delta Airlines, United Airlines). You can have a short paragraph that mentions some of its major hubs. Then, you can create links to jump to those respective Web sites.

Insert relevant clip art, frames, background color, and so on. You might want to create a separate Web page with form controls, such as having people evaluate your Web site. You can have evaluation questions and then check boxes for them to choose from. Save all documents, open the home page in Internet Explorer, and round-trip it if necessary to edit it on Microsoft Word. Be prepared to demonstrate your Web pages to the class and your instructor. Have fun with it!

PinPoint Assessment

You have completed this project and its associated lessons, and have had an opportunity to assess your skills through the end-of-project questions and exercises. Now use the PinPoint software Evaluation Mode to further assess your comprehension of the specific exam activities you have just learned. You can also use the PinPoint Trainer Mode and the Show Me tutorials to practice these exam activities.

Appendix A

Using the MOUS PinPoint 2000 Training and Testing Software

Objectives

➤ Install and Start the PinPoint Launcher

➤ Start and Run PinPoint Trainers and Evaluation

➤ View Trainer and Evaluation Results

➤ Recover from a Crash

➤ Remove PinPoint from Your Computer

Introduction to PinPoint 2000

P inPoint 2000 is a software product that provides interactive training and testing in Microsoft Office 2000 programs. It is designed to supplement the projects in this book and will aid you in preparing for the MOUS certification exams. PinPoint 2000 is included on the CD-ROM in the back of this text. PinPoint 2000 Trainers and Evaluations currently run under Windows 95, Windows 98 and Windows NT 4.

The MOUS PinPoint software consists of Trainers and Evaluations. Trainers are used to hone your Office user skills. Evaluations are used to evaluate your performance of those skills.

PinPoint 2000 requires a full custom installation of Office 2000 to your computer. A full custom installation is an option you select at the time you install Microsoft Office 2000, and means that all components of the software are installed.

The PinPoint 2000 Launcher

Your PinPoint 2000 CD contains a selection of PinPoint 2000 Trainers and Evaluations that cover many of the skills that you may need for using Word 2000, Excel 2000, PowerPoint 2000, and Access 2000.

Concurrency

PinPoint 2000 Trainers and Evaluations are considered "concurrent." This means that a Trainer (or Evaluation) is run simultaneously with the Office 2000 application you are learning or being tested in. For example, when you run a Pinpoint Word 2000 Trainer, the Microsoft Word 2000 application is automatically started and runs at the same time. By working directly in the Office 2000 application, you master the real application, rather than just practice on a simulation of the application.

Today's more advanced applications (like those in Office 2000) often allow more than one way to perform a given task. Concurrency with the real application gives you the freedom to choose the method that you like or that you already know. This gives you the optimal training and testing environment.

Trainer/Evaluation Pairs

Trainers and Evaluations come in pairs. For example, there is a Trainer/Evaluation pair for Word 2000 called "Expert Creating a Newsletter." This means that there is both a Trainer and an Evaluation for "Expert Creating a Newsletter."

Pinpoint Word 2000, Excel 2000, PowerPoint 2000, and Access 2000 all have such sets of Trainers and Evaluations.

Tasks

Each Trainer/Evaluation pair, or *module*, is a set of tasks grouped according to level (Core or Expert) and skill set.

Trainers

If you need help to complete the task, you can click the Show Me button and activate the Show Me feature. The Show Me will run a demonstration of how to perform a similar task.

After you attempt the task, the program checks your work and tells you if you performed the task correctly or incorrectly. In either case you have three choices:

- Retry the task.
- Have the Trainer demonstrate with the task's Show Me an efficient method of completing the task.
- Move on to the next task.

After you have completed all of the tasks in the module, you can study your performance by looking at the report that appears when you click the Report tab on the Launcher. Reports are covered in Lesson 7.

You may take a Trainer as many times as you like. As you do so, the Launcher keeps track of how you perform, even over different days, so that when you run a Trainer another time, the Trainer is set up to run only those tasks that were performed incorrectly on all of your previous run(s).

Evaluations

Since an Evaluation is really a test, it does not give you immediate feedback. You also cannot go back to a previous task or watch a demonstration of how to do the current task. You simply move from task to task until you have attempted all of the tasks in the Evaluation.

When you have finished, you can look at the report in the Reports section to see how you performed.

You can take an Evaluation as many times as you like. While you do so, the Launcher program keeps a record of how you have performed. As a result, if you take a Trainer after the corresponding Evaluation has been taken, the Trainer will set up to run only those tasks that were performed incorrectly on the Evaluation.

System Requirements

Table A.1 shows the system requirements to run PinPoint 2000 software on your computer.

Table A.1   PinPoint 2000 System Requirements

Component	Requirement
CPU	Minimum: Pentium
	Recommended: 166 MHz Pentium or better
Operating System	Windows 95, Windows 98 or WindowsNT 4.0 sp5
Installed Applications	Full Custom Installation of Office 2000*
	Printer
RAM	Minimum: 16 MB
	Recommended: 32 MB or higher

*Office 2000 must be installed before installing PinPoint 2000. If a Full Custom Installation of Office 2000 has not been performed, some tasks will not be available, because the components required for those tasks will not have been installed. The tasks will not be counted as right or wrong but recorded as N/A.

Table A.1   PinPoint 2000 System Requirements   (continued)

Component	Requirement
Hard Drive Space	Minimum: Installing PinPoint 2000 software requires about 4 MB of hard drive space.
	Recommended: For efficient operation, however, you should make sure you have at least 100 MB of unused drive space after installing PinPoint 2000.
CD-ROM Drive	4X speed or faster
Video	Minimum: Color VGA video display running at 640x480 resolution with 16 colors.
	Recommended: Color VGA video display running at 800x600 (or higher) resolution with 16 colors.
	Note for Gateway computer users: If running a P5 90 (or less) Gateway computer, obtain the latest ATI "Mach 64" video driver from Gateway. This can be downloaded from Gateway's web site.

Running PinPoint 2000

Now that you know what PinPoint 2000 is and what is required to use it, you now see how to install and use the Launcher, and start and run Trainers and Evaluations. You also see how to view Trainer and Evaluation reports. Lastly, you find out how to recover from a crash of PinPoint 2000, should one occur.

Lesson 1: Installing the Launcher on Your Computer

To run the PinPoint 2000 Trainers or Evaluations, you must first install the Launcher program.

To Install the Launcher

1 **Start Windows on your computer.**

2 **Be sure that Office 2000 has already been installed to your computer with a Full Custom Install. If this is not the case, perform this installation before you continue with step 3.**

3 **Insert the PinPoint 2000 CD into your CD-ROM drive.**

4 **From the Start menu, select Run.**

5 **In the Run dialog box, enter the path to the SETUP.EXE file found in the root directory of the CD. For example, if your CD-ROM drive has been assigned the letter D, you would enter D:\setup.exe as shown in Figure A.1.**
Note: If your CD-ROM drive has been assigned a letter different from D, use that letter to begin the path in this dialog box. For example, if your CD-ROM drive has been assigned the drive letter E, enter E:\setup.exe in this dialog box.

6 **Click OK.**

7 **When the Setup Type screen appears, select Normal Single-User Installation.**

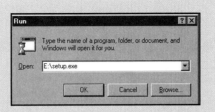

Figure A.1

8 **Click Next to continue.**

You are given a choice concerning the location of the PinPoint 2000 folder

The recommended location of the PinPoint 2000 folder is shown as the default. (*Note:* Two files that initially take up only 109 KB will be placed in this folder.)

If you prefer to use a different path or name for the `PinPoint 2000` folder click the B<u>r</u>owse button and navigate to the location you prefer, or rename the folder.

9 **Click <u>N</u>ext to continue.**

After the installation is complete, the PinPoint 2000 program group window appears.

10 **Close the PinPoint 2000 program group window.**

If the installation has occurred correctly, the following changes have been made to your computer:

- A PinPoint 2000 shortcut icon has been installed that will enable you to run the Launcher program via the Start menu.

- A new folder called PinPoint 2000 has been created on the hard drive of your computer (see Figure A.2).

PinPoint 2000 folder

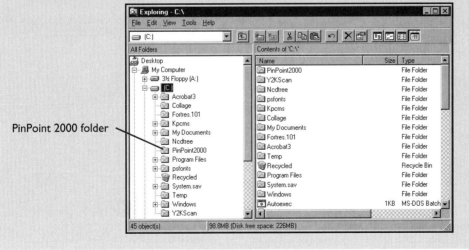

Figure A.2

The PinPoint 2000 folder contains:

- An empty database file, CC_Admin.mdb. As you run Trainers and Evaluations, this file records your performance.

- A small file, Uninst.isu, that is used for removing PinPoint 2000 from your computer.

Note: If your computer is configured so that file extensions are turned off, the CC_Admin.mdb file will appear without the .mdb extension.

Some files necessary for database access have been added to the Windows\System folder.

Lesson 2: Preparing to Run the PinPoint 2000 Launcher

Before running the PinPoint 2000 Launcher, it is necessary to initialize each of the Microsoft applications (Word 2000, Excel 2000, PowerPoint 2000, and Access 2000) at least one time. If you have already used each of these applications, you can ignore this section.

Initializing these applications enables PinPoint training and testing to run in a more stable environment. You will need to provide user information in the first application that you run.

Preparing to Run PinPoint 2000

1 **Start Microsoft Word 2000.**

2 **When the User Name dialog box appears type your Name and Initials.**

3 **Click OK to confirm.**

4 **When the Word window is completely set up and ready for use, you can close the application.**

5 **Start Microsoft Excel 2000.**

6 **When the Excel window is completely set up and ready for use, you can close the application.**

7 **Start Microsoft PowerPoint 2000.**

8 **When the PowerPoint window is completely set up and ready for use, you may close the application.**

9 **Start Microsoft Access 2000.**

10 **When the Access window is completely set up and ready for use, you can close the application.**

You are ready to run the Launcher program and begin Trainers and Evaluations.

Lesson 3: Starting the PinPoint 2000 Launcher

The Launcher program enables you to run Trainers and Evaluations. It also gives you a performance report after you have taken a Trainer or Evaluation.

To Start the PinPoint 2000 Launcher

1 **Select Start, Programs, PinPoint 2000, PinPoint 2000 (see Figure A.3).**

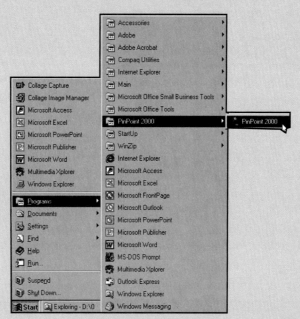

Figure A.3

2 **Enter a user name and password (see Figure A.4).**

Figure A.4

The user name and password can consist of any characters, as long as neither of them exceeds 50 characters. They are NOT case sensitive: It doesn't matter if you use upper- or lowercase letters.

If more than one person will be running PinPoint 2000 from your computer, each person must enter a different user name. However, passwords can be the same.

3 **Click OK in the Logon dialog box.**
If you are logging on for the first time, you need to enter some information in the User Information dialog box.

4 **Enter the requested information and click OK.**
The PinPoint 2000 Launcher screen appears (see Figure A.5).

continues ▶

To Start the PinPoint 2000 Launcher   (continued)

Figure A.5

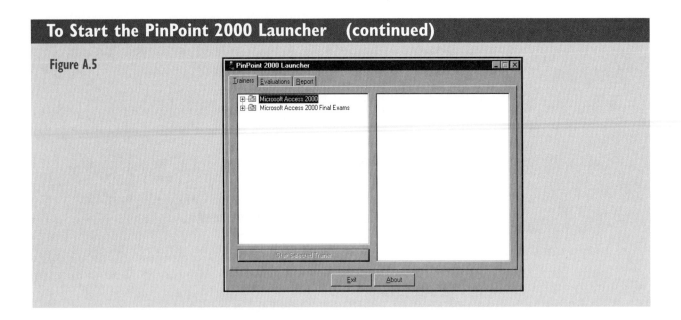

You are now ready to run PinPoint Trainers and Evaluations.

Lesson 4: Starting PinPoint 2000 Trainers and Evaluations

To Start Trainers and Evaluations

① **From the PinPoint Launcher, click the Trainers tab if you want to start a Trainer, or the Evaluations tab if you want to start an Evaluation (see Figure A.6).**

Figure A.6

Trainer tab

Evaluation tab

Report tab

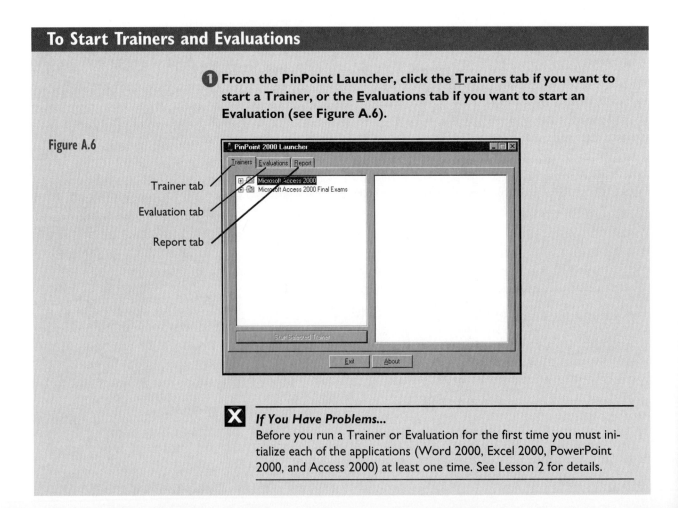

X ***If You Have Problems...***
Before you run a Trainer or Evaluation for the first time you must initialize each of the applications (Word 2000, Excel 2000, PowerPoint 2000, and Access 2000) at least one time. See Lesson 2 for details.

2 **Click the plus sign (+) to open an application's modules and exams. The plus sign becomes a minus sign (–), as shown in Figure A.7.**

Click here to open and close the modules and exams

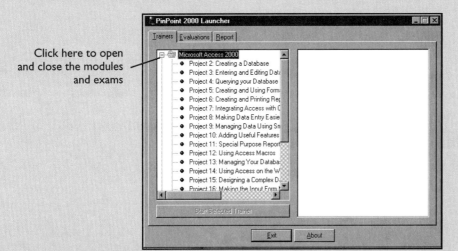

Figure A.7

3 **Select the module or exam that you want to run.**

The individual tasks that are part of the Trainer or Evaluation appear in the pane on the right.

4 **If you are running a Trainer without an Evaluation, you can select or deselect individual training tasks by clicking on the box beside the task name (see Figure A.8).**

The tasks that are deselected will not run during the Trainer. This enables you to adjust your training to include only those tasks that you do not already know how to do.

When running an Evaluation, however, you cannot deselect individual tasks. All tasks will run.

Select or deselect tasks here

Start Selected Trainer button

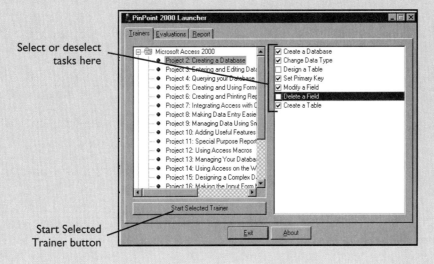

Figure A.8

continues ▶

To Start Trainers and Evaluations   (continued)

⑤ Click Start Selected Trainer button if you are starting a Trainer. Click the Start Selected Evaluation button if you are starting an Evaluation.

⑥ When you start the Trainer, you might encounter a warning message instructing you to change your computer's Taskbar settings (see Figure A.9).

If this message appears, follow its instructions before proceeding. Changing your taskbar settings in this way is necessary for proper functioning of a PinPoint Trainer. You can carry out the instructions given without canceling the box.

Figure A.9

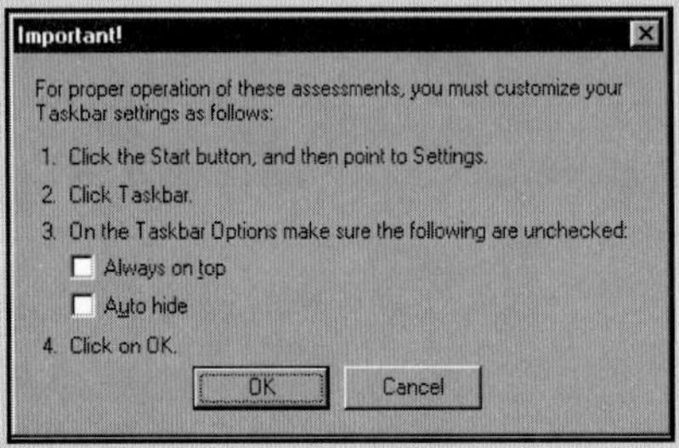

The PinPoint 2000 Launcher dialog box with your name and module selection appears (see Figure A.10).

Figure A.10

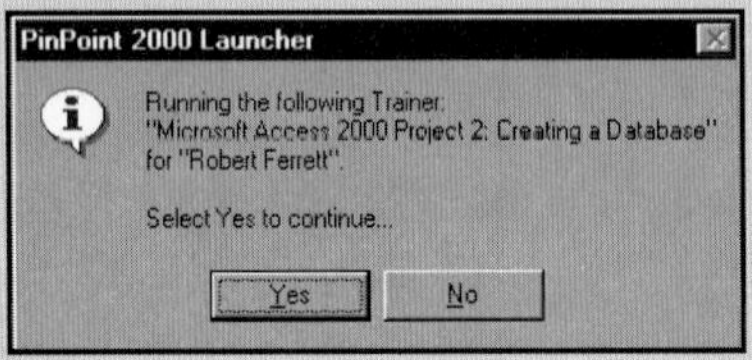

⑦ Click Yes to continue.
The Trainer or Evaluation starts.

Proceed to the next two sections to see how to run Trainers and Evaluations.

Lesson 5: Running a Trainer

This lesson shows you how to run a Trainer. It also details how to handle some of the situations you might encounter during a Trainer.

To Run a Trainer

❶ Once your name and the selected module are displayed, click OK to begin the Trainer.
The PinPoint 2000 launcher dialog box appears before a Trainer runs (see Figure A.11).

2 **Click Yes to continue.**

The first thing you see is an introduction to how all PinPoint 2000 Trainers work. If you want to see the demonstration of how a PinPoint Trainer works and how to use the PinPoint 2000 controls, press any key or click the mouse to continue.

3 **Skip through the introduction for now and go directly to a task.**

After initializing, the Trainer opens the first selected task.

 Inside Stuff: Exiting the Introduction

You can exit the introduction at any time by pressing Esc and moving straight to the training.

The task instructions display in a moveable instruction box that hovers over the application (see Figure A.12).

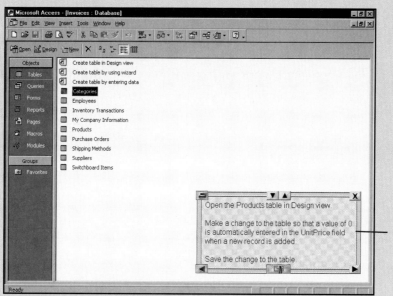

Figure A.12

The instruction box can be moved to different parts of the screen

---

 If You Have Problems...

If the instruction box is blocking your view of something, you can drag it to another part of the screen. To instantly move the box to the other side of the screen, right-click the instruction box.

Notice the PinPoint control buttons that appear on the perimeter of the instruction box. Use these buttons to interact with the Trainer according to your needs (see Figure A.13).

continues ▶

To Run a Trainer   (continued)

Figure A.13

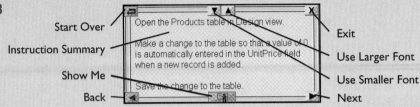

Start Over
Instruction Summary
Show Me
Back

Open the Products table in Design view.

Make a change to the table so that a value of 0 is automatically entered in the UnitPrice field when a new record is added.

Save the change to the table.

Exit
Use Larger Font
Use Smaller Font
Next

The features of the instruction box in Figure A.13 and their descriptions are listed here:

■ The Instruction Summary displays the task to be completed. Instructions remain visible during the task.

■ The Start Over button starts the current task again.

■ The Back button returns you to the previous task.

■ The Show Me button gives you a step-by-step demonstration using a similar example.

■ The Use Larger Font and Use Smaller Font buttons enlarge or reduce the size of the box and text.

■ The Quit button ends the current training session and returns you to the Launcher.

■ The Next button checks a finished task for correct performance and moves you to the next task.

4 **Try to do the task exactly as instructed in the PinPoint instruction box.**

5 **Click the Next button (refer to Figure A.13).**
PinPoint 2000 gives you feedback in the Results dialog box.

Whether you performed the task correctly or not, you now have three choices:

■ Click the Show Me button to display a step-by-step demonstration using a similar example.

■ Click the Try Task Again button to set up the task so you can attempt it again.

■ Click the Next Task button to move on and attempt the next task.

If you click the Show Me button, a demonstration of how to perform a similar task is given. This demonstration, called a Show Me, begins with a summary of the steps required to perform the task.

6 **Press any key or click the mouse to advance the next Show Me box.**
Usually the key concept behind the particular skill is explained during the Show Me.

After the instruction summary (and possibly a key concept), each of the instructions in the summary is explained and demonstrated in detail.

 Inside Stuff: **Exiting Show Me Demonstrations**
If you want to exit from the Show Me demonstration at any point, press Esc to return to the PinPoint task.

During the Show Me demonstration, the mouse pointer moves and text is entered automatically when appropriate to the demonstration, but whenever the description or action is completed the demonstration halts until the user prompts it to continue with either a mouse click or a key stroke.

After the demonstration is complete, you can perform the task yourself.

7 Continue through the PinPoint Trainer at your own pace, attempting each task and watching Show Me demonstrations when you need help.

When you have finished with the training session, the Trainers screen of the Launcher is visible again. You can see a report of your performance by clicking the Report tab in the Launcher (viewing reports is covered in Lesson 7).

 Inside Stuff: **Exiting Trainers**
You are free to exit from the training at any time by clicking the Exit button (refer to Figure A.13). When you attempt to exit a Trainer before it is finished, you are asked to confirm this decision (see Figure A.14).

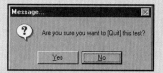

Figure A.14

If you want to exit from the trainer at this point, click Yes.

Lesson 6: Running an Evaluation

This lesson shows you how to run an Evaluation. It also details how to handle some of the situations you might encounter during an Evaluation.

To Run an Evaluation

1 When you start the Evaluation, you might encounter a warning message instructing you to change your computer's Taskbar settings (refer to Figure A.9).
If this message appears, follow its instructions before proceeding. Changing your taskbar settings in this way is necessary for proper functioning of a PinPoint Trainer. You can carry out the instructions given without canceling the box.

2 After you have carried out the steps listed, click OK to continue.
The Pinpoint 2000 Launcher dialog box appears before an Evaluation runs (refer to Figure A.11).

3 Click Yes to continue.
The first thing you see is an introduction to how all PinPoint 2000 Evaluations work. If you want to see the demonstration of how an Evaluation works and how to use the PinPoint 2000 controls, press any key or click the mouse to continue past each screen. If you do not need to see the demonstration, press Esc to go straight to the testing.

continues ▶

To Run an Evaluation (continued)

Like a Trainer, an Evaluation presents you with a task to perform. In an Evaluation, however, the Start Over, Back, and Show Me buttons are all disabled. Therefore, you cannot restart a task, return to a previous task, or run a Show Me demonstration of how to perform the task.

4 After attempting a task, click the Next button to continue to the next task.

Normally, you would attempt all of the tasks in the Evaluation. But if you need to finish early and click the Exit button before you have attempted all of the tasks, the message box in Figure A.14 will display. Click the Yes button if you want to exit the Evaluation and go back to the Launcher program.

5 You can view a report of your performance by clicking the Report tab in the Launcher.

See the next section for details about viewing reports.

Inside Stuff: **What to Avoid While Running Trainers and Evaluations**
Keep the following in mind for PinPoint 2000 Trainers and Evaluations to run properly:

- Only perform actions that the PinPoint task instructions ask you to perform.

- Do not exit from the Microsoft Office 2000 application in which you are training or testing unless you are told to do so.

- Do not close the example document (the document that PinPoint opens for you when you begin a task) unless you are told to do so.

- Do not run other programs (such as email, Internet browsers, virus shields, system monitors, and so on) at the same time as running PinPoint, unless you are asked to do so.

- Do not change views in one of the Office 2000 applications unless you are asked to do so.

- Do not change the way your Windows operating system or Office 2000 applications are configured by default.

- Do not turn off your computer in the middle of a PinPoint Trainer or Evaluation. Instead, first exit from the Trainer or Evaluation, and then turn off your computer.

Lesson 7: Viewing Reports in the Launcher

After you have taken at least one PinPoint 2000 Trainer or Evaluation, you can view detailed reports at any time concerning your performance on any of the modules that you have taken.

To View Reports in the Launcher

1 **If the Launcher is not running, click Start, Programs, PinPoint 2000, PinPoint 2000 to run it. Then log on.**

2 **Click the Report tab.**

The Report screen appears (see Figure A.15).

Click the Report tab to view a detailed report of your performance

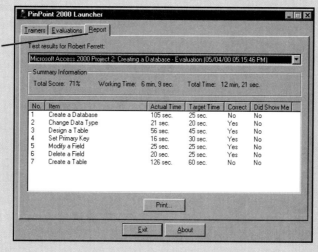

Figure A.15

The very last Trainer or Evaluation that you ran displays onscreen. The information displayed in the Report screen is as follows:

- *Total Score*—The percentage of the correctly performed tasks out of the total number of tasks set to run.

- *Working Time*—The total time you actually spent working on all of the tasks in the Trainer or Evaluation.

- *Total Time*—The total time you spent running the entire Trainer or Evaluation.

- *Item*—The name of the task.

- *Actual Time*—The time you took to perform the task.

- *Target Time*—A reasonable amount of time required to perform the task by an efficient method.

- *Correct*—Displays Yes if you performed the task correctly; No if you did not.

- *Did Show-Me*—Displays Yes if you ran a Show Me demonstration for that task; No if you did not.

Note: A blank or dotted line running through the task line, or N/A, indicate that the task was not taken.

3 **If you want to print a report, click the Print button.**

4 **If you want to see a report for a Trainer or Evaluation that you took previously, select it from the Test results for <your name> drop-down list.**

The reports are listed in the order in which they were taken.

Note: You will see only your own reports on the Reports screen and not the reports for anyone else using PinPoint on your computer.

> **Inside Stuff: User History**
>
> An important feature of the PinPoint 2000 Launcher is its capability to keep track of your history of running Trainers and Evaluations. The Launcher uses your history to reconfigure a Trainer each successive time you run it. To "re-configure" means to change the tasks that will run.
>
> The Launcher does not reconfigure an Evaluation the same way it does a Trainer. No matter which tasks you have performed correctly in the past (on either a Trainer or Evaluation), all tasks are automatically selected to be run when you attempt to take an Evaluation.

Lesson 8: Recovering from a Crash During a Trainer or Evaluation

If your computer crashes while you are running a Trainer or Evaluation, all the work you have already done is not wasted. You do not need to start the Trainer or Evaluation over again from the beginning. To recover from a crash during a Trainer or Evaluation, follow these simple instructions.

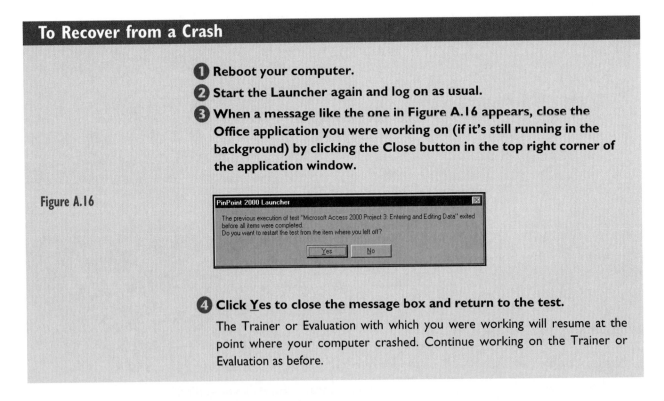

To Recover from a Crash

1 **Reboot your computer.**

2 **Start the Launcher again and log on as usual.**

3 **When a message like the one in Figure A.16 appears, close the Office application you were working on (if it's still running in the background) by clicking the Close button in the top right corner of the application window.**

Figure A.16

> **PinPoint 2000 Launcher**
>
> The previous execution of test "Microsoft Access 2000 Project 3: Entering and Editing Data" exited before all items were completed.
> Do you want to restart the test from the item where you left off?
>
> [Yes]   [No]

4 **Click Yes to close the message box and return to the test.**

The Trainer or Evaluation with which you were working will resume at the point where your computer crashed. Continue working on the Trainer or Evaluation as before.

Removing PinPoint 2000

When you have finished training and testing with PinPoint 2000, you may want to remove the Launcher program from your computer. PinPoint 2000 can be removed using the procedure for removing most other applications from your computer.

Lesson 9: Removing PinPoint 2000

To Remove PinPoint 2000

1 **From the Start menu, select Settings, Control Panel.**

2 **Double-click the Add/Remove Programs icon.**
The Add/Remove Programs Properties dialog box displays.

3 **Select PinPoint 2000.**

4 **Click the Add/Remove button.**

5 **Confirm the removal of PinPoint 2000 by clicking Yes in the dialog box.**

6 **If the Remove Shared File? dialog box appears, click the Yes To All button (see Figure A.17).**

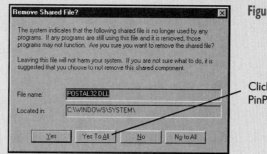

Figure A.17

Click here to uninstall PinPoint 2000

7 **When the Remove Programs From Your Computer dialog box reports** Uninstall successfully completed, **click OK.**

8 **Click OK in the Add/Remove Programs Properties dialog box.**

9 **Close the Control Panel window.**
PinPoint 2000 has now been completely removed from your computer.

Summary

PinPoint 2000 is a very valuable tool for preparing yourself for a MOUS Exam. You've learned how to install and start the PinPoint Launcher. You can now run Trainers and Evaluations, and view a report of their results. You also know what to avoid while running Trainers and Evaluations. You've seen how to recover if PinPoint crashes. And finally, you've learned how to uninstall PinPoint when you no longer need it. You are now equipped to take full advantage of the PinPoint 2000 training and testing software.

Preparing for MOUS Certification

This appendix gives you information that you need regarding the certification exams—how to register, what is covered in the tests, how the tests are administered, and so on. Because this information may change, be sure to visit www.mous.net for the latest updates.

What This Book Offers

This text is certified for both levels of certification:

- Core—You are able to manage a wide range of real world tasks efficiently.
- Expert—In addition to the everyday tasks at the Core level, you are able to handle complex assignments and have a thorough understanding of a program's advanced features.

In addition to the Core and Expert levels, Microsoft now offers a Master certification, which indicates that you have a comprehensive understanding of Microsoft Office 2000 and many of its advanced features. A Master certification requires students to successfully pass all five of the required exams: Word, Excel, PowerPoint, Access and Outlook.

Each exam includes a list of tasks you may be asked to perform. The lessons in this book identify these required tasks with an icon in the margin. You can also review the MOUS Skill Guide in the front of this book to become familiar with these required tasks.

In addition to these icons, this book contains various study aids that not only help you pass the test, but also teach you how the software functions. You can use this book in a classroom or lab setting, or you can work through each project on your own using the PinPoint CD-ROM. You don't have to move through the book from front to back as each project stands on its own. Each project is broken down into lessons, which are then broken down into step-by-step instructions.

The PinPoint CD-ROM includes Project Review Tests for each MOUS Exam skill set. The coverage has two parts: a Task and a Show Me. The Task requires you to do something, (for example, format a document) and the Show Me demonstrates how to perform that task. In addition, each PinPoint has a practice test that mirrors the actual MOUS exams.

Follow the steps within each of the lessons, and use the PinPoint software as an evaluation of your comprehension. If you get stuck, be sure to use the Show Me demonstration.

Registering for and Taking and the Exam

All MOUS exams are administered by a MOUS Authorized Testing Center (ATC). Most MOUS ATCs require pre-registration. To pre-register contact a local ATC directly. You can find a center near you by visiting the MOUS Web site at www.mous.net. Some ATCs accept walk-in examination candidates, allowing on-the-spot registration and examination. Be sure to check with a specific ACT to make certain of their registration policy.

The exam is not written and there are no multiple choice or true-false questions. You perform the required tasks on a computer running the live Microsoft application. A typical exam takes 45 to 60 minutes to complete. You must work through each task in the exam as quickly as you can.

All examination data is encrypted, and the examination process is closely monitored so your test scores are completely confidential. Examination results are provided only to the candidate and to Microsoft.

The Day of the Exam

Bring the following items with you to the testing center on exam day:

- Picture ID—driver's license or passport
- Your MOUS identification number (if you have take a previous MOUS certification exam)
- ATC Student ID, if applicable

At the exam center, you can expect to first complete the candidate information section, which provides the information necessary to complete your MOUS certificate.

After confirming your ID, the administrator will seat you at the test computer, log you onto the test system, and open your test module. You are now ready to begin.

To start the test, click the "Start Test" button and you're ready to begin your certification exam.

The Exam Itself

Instructions are displayed in a separate window on the screen. You can close the instruction window by clicking on it. You can restore it by clicking "Instructions" on the test information bar at the bottom of the screen. Read the test instructions carefully. Once you have started, a box in the bottom right corner of the screen indicates the question on which you are currently working. (For example, "question 3 of 50".)

If anything abnormal happens during the exam, or if the application "crashes," stop immediately and contact the administrator. The administrator will restart the test from where you left off. You will not be penalized any time for this.

When you have completed your exam, the computer will calculate your score. The scoring process takes a short time, and you will be notified onscreen whether you passed or failed. You may then ask the administrator to give you a printed report.

If you complete the exam successfully, your MOUS certificate will be delivered within 2-3 weeks.

General Tips

Unlike earlier MOUS exams, the results of the Office 2000 MOUS exams are expressed as a value on a 1000-point scale, rather than a percentage.

Each activity or question on the Office 2000 MOUS exams is comprised of several individually scored subtasks. A candidates's score is derived from the number of subtasks successfully completed and the "weight" or difficulty assigned to each.

Pay close attention to how each question is worded. Answers must be precise, resolving the question exactly as asked.

You can use any combination of menus, toolbars and shortcut keys to complete each assigned task. Answers are scored based on the result, not the method you use or the time taken to complete each required task. Extra keystrokes or mouse clicks will not count against your score as long as you achieve the correct result within the time limit given.

Remember that the overall test is timed. While spending a lot of time on an individual answer will not adversely affect the scoring of that particular question, taking too long may not leave you with enough time to complete the entire test.

Answers are either right or wrong. You do not get credit for partial answers.

Important! Check to make sure you have entirely completed each question before clicking the NEXT TASK button. Once you press the NEXT TASK button, you will not be able to return to that question. A question will be scored as wrong if it is not completed properly before moving to the next question.

Save your Results Page that prints at the end of the exam. It is your confirmation that you passed the exam.

Take note of these cautions:

- DON'T leave dialog boxes, Help menus, toolbars, or menus open.
- DON'T leave tables, boxes, or cells "active or highlighted" unless instructed to do so.
- DON'T click the NEXT TASK button until you have "completely" answered the current question.

Lastly, be sure to visit the mous.net Web site for specific information on the Office 2000 exams, more testing tips, and to download a free demo of the exams.

All key terms appearing in this book (in bold italic) are listed alphabetically in this glossary for easy reference. If you want to learn more about the feature or concept, turn to the page reference shown after the definition for the first use of the term. You can also check the index for its other significant occurrences.

accept change   The process of removing the revision mark and incorporating it into the regular document text. [pg. 460]

action   Any task or change you make in a document. [pg. 81]

adaptive menu   A menu that adapts the list of commands first shown when you display the menu. After you choose an option from the full menu, it appears on the adaptive menu. [pg. 5]

alignment   The placement of text between the left and right margins. The default alignment is left, which perfectly aligns text at the left margin. [pg. 100]

anchor   The location that an object is attached to. [pg. 223]

arrow   The drawing tool of a line with an arrowhead, circle, or diamond at the end. [pg. 224]

associated keywords   Words associated with a clip on Microsoft's Web page. The keywords help you locate other clips that have some of the same characteristics. [pg. 204]

attachment   A separate file or document sent along with an email message. [pg. 268]

AutoComplete   A feature that helps you complete text that's saved in the AutoText feature. For example, if you start typing today's date, you'll see a ScreenTip that displays the entire date. Press ⏎Enter to complete the date automatically. [pg. 35, 362]

AutoCorrect   A feature that automatically corrects typos and some capitalization errors "on the fly." [pg. 82]

AutoFormat   A feature that applies predefined styles, such as borders and shading, to tables. [pg. 188]

AutoSum   A function that automatically calculates the values in table cells directly above or to the left of the current cell. [pg. 180]

AutoText   A feature lets you store many different pieces of text or graphics and retrieve them instantly into a document. [pg. 362]

bar tab   A tab marker that produces a vertical bar or line between columns when you press Tab⇄. [pg. 287]

blind courtesy copy   A copy of an email message sent to another person, but the primary recipient does not know that someone else is receiving the email. [pg. 271]

boilerplate text   Standard text that appears in a template. [pg. 335]

bookmark   An electronic bookmark that marks your location within a document. [pg. 410]

border   A line style that surrounds text, table cells, or an object. [pg. 107, 163, 208]

bullet   A special symbol to attract attention to text on a page. [pg. 104]

bulleted list   An itemized list or enumeration that contains bullet symbols at the left side of each item. [pg. 104]

buttons   Little pictures that represent tasks. When you click a button, Word performs a task or provides menus for making specific selections. [pg. 7]

calculating form field   A field that contains a formula to perform a mathematical calculation. [pg. 485]

casing   Capitalization style of text. [pg. 74]

catalog main document   A merge main document that creates a list during the merge instead of separately merged pages. [pg. 400]

cell   The intersection of a column and row in a table or Excel worksheet. [pg. 152, 256]

cell margins   The amount of space from the cell borders to the text within a table. [pg. 178]

cell reference   A designation of a cell within a table, typically used to refer to a particular cell while calculating. For example, B1 refers to the second column (B) in the first row (1). [pg. 179]

character effects   Special formats, such as strikethrough and emboss, that you apply to characters. [pg. 56]

character spacing   The amount of space between printed characters. [pg. 58]

character style   A style that formats a portion of the text *within* a paragraph. Unlike a paragraph style that can format font, border, language, line spacing, alignment, and indents, a character style can format only fonts, borders, and languages. [pg. 344]

chart   A visual representation of numerical data that enhances the reader's understanding and comprehension of values. [pg. 236]

chart area   The white area that contains all chart elements. [pg. 242]

check box form field   A field that allows users to select or deselect to mark an item, similar to the Effects check boxes in the Font dialog box. [pg. 478]

Click and Type feature   Lets you double-click and type new text virtually anywhere in a document—even in a new area. Depending on where you double-click, Word inserts left tabs, centers the text, or aligns the text at the right margin. [pg. 10]

clip art   Graphic images, pictures, or drawings. [pg. 196]

Clip Gallery   A collection of clip art images, photographs, sound clips, and movie clips that you can insert in your document. [pg. 196]

close   The process of removing a document from the screen. [pg. 19]

close button   A button that closes the window or dialog box. [pg. 4]

column   A group of table cells arranged vertically. [pg. 152]

column headings   Text that appears at the top of table columns to identify the contents of each column. [pg. 155]

column width   The horizontal measurement of a column. [pg. 158]

comment   A note or other text that appears onscreen as a ScreenTip, but does not affect regular document text. [pg. 454]

comment mark   A designation appearing in yellow highlight that indicates where a comment is inserted. [pg. 454]

Comment pane   The window that contains the comment text, reviewer's initials, and sequential comment number. [pg. 454]

concordance file   A two-column table that contains the words and phrases that you want to include in an index. [pg. 418]

continuous section break   A break that divides the document into sections but continues the next section on the same page instead of starting a new page. [pg. 314]

Control menu box   Displays a menu that controls the application program. Double-click the box to exit (close) the application. [pg. 4]

copy   Makes a copy of the selected text or object and places the copy temporarily in the Office Clipboard. [pg. 75]

cross-reference   A note that refers to the reader to another location for more information about a topic. [pg. 414]

cut   Removes text or an object from its location and places it temporarily in the Office Clipboard. [pg. 75]

data labels   Values that appear above each data series in a chart. [pg. 242]

data series   A set of values arranged in columns or rows to create a chart. [pg. 237]

data source   A document that contains a record of information for each recipient. [pg. 284]

datasheet   A table containing values and labels to be used for creating a chart. [pg. 237]

decimal tab   A type of tab that aligns values at the decimal point. [pg. 182]

default   Refers to a standard setting determined by Microsoft and used unless you change it. For example, the default top margin is one inch. [pg. 3]

demote   Changing an outline entry to a lower-level entry. [pg. 295]

designer font A special font used in creative documents, such as wedding announcements, fliers, brochures, and other special-occasion documents. Examples of designer fonts include Broadway BT, Comic Sans MS, and Keystroke. [pg. 54]

destination program The program that you bring external data into. [pg. 254]

details An option in the Open or Save As dialog box that displays the filename, file size, file type, and modified. [pg. 434]

docked toolbar A toolbar that appears at the top or bottom of the screen. [pg. 442]

Document Map Displays a window that lists the structure of headings in your document. [pg. 139]

document window A screen area that displays text and formats for documents you create. [pg. 9]

double indent Indenting text from both the left and the right margins. [pg. 102]

double-space Text that leaves one blank line between text lines. [pg. 99]

drop cap A big character that drops below the current line. It is often used in published documents. [pg. 318]

drop-down form field A field that displays a list from which users can select an option, similar to the Style drop-down arrow on the Formatting toolbar. [pg. 478]

drop-down list A list of options that drops down when you click a drop-down arrow (a down-pointing arrow). For example, clicking the Save in drop-down arrow displays a drop-down list of options. [pg. 12]

em dash A dash the width of a lowercase m, to indicate a pause or change in thought. [pg. 65]

embedding The process of importing data that can be edited within the destination program. [pg. 259]

en dash A dash the width of a lowercase n, to indicate a series, such as pages 9–15. [pg. 65]

endnote Reference for information you obtain elsewhere or annotations to text. This reference appears at the end of the document. [pg. 131]

end-of-document marker Small horizontal line that shows the end of the document in Normal view mode. [pg. 4]

exit The process of closing the Word application program. [pg. 19]

Favorites A feature to create a shortcut to your favorite folders. [pg. 440]

fields Individual components of data in a merge data source document. Common fields in a data source include first name, last name, address, city, state, and ZIP Code. [pg. 384]

file maintenance Routine procedures that involve copying files to create backup copies, deleting files you no longer need, moving files into folders to organize them, and renaming files. [pg. 438]

file size Refers to the amount of space in KB. The larger the number, the bigger the file is. [pg. 434]

file type The kind of file it is, such as a Microsoft Word or Microsoft Excel file. [pg. 434]

fill The shading color used within a graphics object, drawing object, or text box. [pg. 208]

filter A set of criteria that each record must meet to be included in the merge process. [pg. 398]

first line indent Indents the first line of a paragraph. [pg. 104]

floating toolbar A toolbar with a title bar that appears in the middle of the screen. [pg. 442]

font Style, weight, and typeface of a set of characters. The default font is Times New Roman. [pg. 54]

font size The height of the characters, typically measured in points, where 72 points equal one vertical inch. [pg. 54]

footer Document information, such as a filename or date, that appears at the bottom of every page. [pg. 135]

footnote A reference for information you obtain elsewhere or annotations to text. This information appears at the bottom of the page that contains the footnote reference mark. [pg. 131]

footnote reference mark The number, letter, or symbol that appears in text to refer the reader to a footnote or endnote of the same number, letter, or symbol containing citations or additional information. [pg. 132]

footnote text the actual citation or supplemental text for a footnote. [pg. 132]

form A document designed for collecting data on printed paper or in a Word document. [pg. 476]

form control An element that collects or provides data from a Web page. [pg. 510]

form field   An area in an onscreen form where users can enter information by typing, selecting from a drop-down list, or marking a check box. [pg. 476]

form file   Also known as a main document, this file contains the information that stays the same for all recipients. [pg. 384]

Format Painter   A feature that helps you copy existing text formats to other text. [pg. 59]

formatting marks   Nonprinting symbols and characters that indicate spaces, tabs, and hard returns. You display these symbols by clicking the Show/Hide ¶ button on the Standard toolbar. These symbols are useful when selecting text. [pg. 62]

Formatting toolbar   The toolbar that contains a row of buttons that help you format text. For example, this toolbar helps you select a font, boldface text, and select text alignment. [pg. 4]

frame   A section of a Web site saved as an individual document. [pg. 501]

frame page   A collection of all frames for a Web site. [pg. 501]

full menu   Refers to an entire pull-down menu from the menu. You display the full menu by pointing to the arrows at the bottom of the short menu. [pg. 5]

Full Screen view   This view displays the document for the entire screen. You do not see the title bar, toolbars, and other screen elements. [pg. 39]

functions   Predefined mathematical formulas that perform tasks. For example, the SUM function adds the values in a group of table cells. [pg. 197]

gradient   A fill appearance that blends two or more colors. [pg. 209]

grayed-out option   A button or option that appears in gray, indicating that it is not currently available. [pg. 6]

gridlines   Horizontal and vertical lines that separate cells within a table. [pg. 153]

grouped objects   Selected objects that act as a single object. You can move and format grouped objects at one time. [pg. 228]

gutter   A desktop publishing term that refers to the space between columns. [pg. 311]

hanging indent   Paragraph format that keeps the first line of a paragraph at the left margin and indents the remaining lines from the left margin. [pg. 105]

hard page break   A break you insert to immediately start text at the top of the next page. [pg. 121]

hard return   Defines the end of a line where you press ⏎Enter. [pg. 62]

header   Document information, such as a filename or date, that appears at the top of every page. [pg. 135]

heading   Text between paragraphs or sections that help identify the content of that section. [pg. 53]

Help   Onscreen assistance or reference manual. It provides information about features, step-by-step instructions, and other assistance. [pg. 16]

Help Topic Pane   The right side of the Help window. It contains information about the topic you select from the Navigation Pane. This window provides information, links to other topics, and step-by-step instructions for performing tasks. [pg. 17]

highlight   Places a color behind text, like a highlighter pen, to draw attention to text. [pg. 61]

home page   The main Web page for a Web site. [pg. 500]

horizontal scrollbar   The scrollbar that adjusts the horizontal view of text going left to right. [pg. 4]

hyperlink   An electronic code that jumps the insertion point to a different location or document when clicked. [pg. 412, 198]

hypertext links   Underlined words or phrases that appear in a different color. In Help, clicking a hypertext link displays another topic. On the Web, clicking a hypertext link displays a different Web page. [pg. 17, 204, 498]

hyphenation zone   Area at the end of a line that determines whether a word can potentially be hyphenated. [pg. 322]

import   The process of bringing in data into the current or destination program that was created with another software program known as the source program. For example, bringing Excel data into Word is a form of import. [pg. 243, 256]

index   A listing of topics covered in a book or long document, with the page numbers on which the topics are discussed. An index typically appears at the end of the document or book. [pg. 416]

Insert mode   When you type within existing text, Word inserts the new text and keeps the other text; it does not replace text to the right of the insertion point. [pg. 35]

insertion point   A blinking vertical line that shows the current location in the document or in a dialog box text box. [pg. 4]

inside address   The address of the person who will receive your letter. [pg. 35]

Internet   A worldwide conglomerate of computer networks. [pg. 498]

kerning   Automatically adjusts spacing between characters to achieve a more evenly spaced appearance. [pg. 58]

landscape   The page orientation that positions text parallel with the long side up. [pg. 309]

layering   The process of stacking objects on top of each other, creating layers like a collage. [pg. 226]

leader   A tab option that produces a series of dots, a dashed line, or a solid line between tabulated columns. [pg. 290]

left indent   An indent format that indents a paragraph from the left margin. [pg. 102]

legend   A color-coded key that indicates what color represents what region or data series. [pg. 238]

line spacing   The amount of vertical space from the bottom of one text line to the top of the next text line. The default line spacing is single. [pg. 98]

linking   The process of inserting an object from another program in which the object is dynamically linked to the original data; if you change the original data, the linked data also changes. [pg. 265]

list box   A Web page box that displays available choices in a list format, similar to a list box within a dialog box in Word. [pg. 513]

macro   A small computer program you create to speed up repetitive tasks. [pg. 368]

mail merge   The process of bring the main document and data source together. [pg. 384]

main document   Also known as a form file, this file contains the information that stays the same for all recipients. [pg. 384]

margins   Amount of white space around the top, left, right, and bottom of text on a page. [pg. 96]

marking   The process of designating text to include in an index or table of contents. [pg. 416]

master document   A document that acts like a binder for managing subdocuments. [pg. 422]

masthead   Also known as a nameplate, this is the area on the first page of a newsletter that contains the title and date of the newsletter. [pg. 314]

mathematical operators   Types of calculation symbols that instruct the user or program to perform a calculation such as add, subtract, multiple, and divide. [pg. 179]

maximize button   Clicking this button, located in the top-right corner, displays the window in its full size. You will see either the maximize button or the restore button, depending on the current view of the application or document. [pg. 4]

menu   A list of commands. [pg. 5]

menu bar   A row of menu names displayed below the title bar. Tasks are categorized by nine different menus. [pg. 5]

merge cells   The process of combining cells into one cell within a table. [pg. 176]

merge field   A field contained in a main document that refers to a field within a data source. [pg. 385]

Microsoft Visual Basic   The program that records macro commands and text. [pg. 372]

minimize button   Clicking this button, located in the top-right corner of the Word window, reduces the current document to an icon on the taskbar. [pg. 4]

modified   Indicates the last date and time the file was saved. [pg. 434]

nameplate   Also known as a masthead, this is the area on the first page of a newsletter that contains the title and date of the newsletter. [pg. 314]

Navigation Pane   The left side of the Help window. It contains Contents, Answer Wizard, and Index tabs. These tabs provide different methods for accessing onscreen Help. [pg. 17]

nonbreaking hyphen   A special type of hyphen that prevents hyphenated words from separating by the word-wrap feature. For example, you can insert hard hyphens to keep 555-1234 from word-wrapping. [pg. 65]

nonbreaking space   A special type of space that prevents words from separating by the word-wrap feature. For example, pressing Ctrl+Shift+Spacebar keeps October 16 from word-wrapping. [pg. 64]

Normal view   This view shows text without displaying space for margins, page numbers, headers, or other supplement text. [pg. 38]

object   A non-text item, such as a clip art image. [pg. 75]

Object Linking and Embedding (OLE)
Technology that lets you use objects between programs. [pg. 259]

Office Assistant   An animated image that provides onscreen assistance and help. You can click it and ask it a question to learn how to do something in Word. [pg. 16]

Office Clipboard   An area of memory designed to store items that you cut or copy from a document. The Office Clipboard holds up to 12 different pieces of data, which you can paste within the same application or other applications. [pg. 75]

opening   The process of retrieving a document from storage, such as from a data disk, and displaying it onscreen. [pg. 28]

organization chart   A chart showing the hierarchy of positions within an organization. [pg. 232]

Organizer   A tool that enables you to copy styles, AutoText entries, and other shareable items between two documents or between a document and a template. [pg. 246]

orphan   The first line of a paragraph that appears by itself at the bottom of a page. [pg. 128]

outline numbered list   A list that contains several levels of numbering in an outline format. [pg. 293]

Overtype mode   When you type in this mode, the text you type replaces existing text at the insertion point. [pg. 34]

page orientation   The way printed text appears on a sheet of paper. [pg. 309]

paragraph spacing   Controls the amount of space before or after the paragraph. [pg. 100]

paragraph style   A style that applies formats to an entire paragraph or text separated by hard returns. Paragraph styles can include font formats and paragraph formats such as line spacing, indents, alignment, and spacing before and after the paragraph. [pg. 341]

password   A secret word you choose that requires a user to enter it before accessing the document. [pg. 465]

paste   Inserting the contents of the Office Clipboard in the insertion point's location. [pg. 75]

placeholders   A temporary text or fields where you type your own text, such as in an organization chart. [pg. 232]

plot area   The area that displays the charted data series. [pg. 242]

portrait   The default page orientation that positions text parallel with the short side up. [pg. 309]

position   A font option that raises or lowers text from the baseline without creating superscript or subscript size. [pg. 58]

Print Layout view   This view shows you what the document will look like when it's printed. You see margins, page numbers, headers, and so on. [pg. 38]

promote   To change an outline entry to a higher-level entry. [pg. 295]

protection   Features that ensure no authorized changes are made. [pg. 465]

query   A database term that refers to a filtering tool to select records that meet particular criteria. [pg. 398]

range   A rectangular block of cells in a worksheet. [pg. 257]

read-only   An attribute that allows users to edit a document, but they must save it with a different filename. [pg. 465]

record   A group of fields for a particular person or thing. [pg. 384]

record macro   The process of creating a macro. [pg. 368]

Redo feature   Reverses an undo action. [pg. 84]

regrouping   Process of grouping objects back together again after ungrouping them. [pg. 229]

reject change   The process of removing the revision mark and the tracked change, thus restoring that part of the document to its original state. [pg. 460]

Repeat command   Duplicates or repeats the last action or command you executed. [pg. 82]

restore button   Clicking this button, located in the top-right corner of the Word window, restores the window to its previous size. [pg. 4]

reverse text effect   An appearance that uses a darker background with a lighter text color. For example, a yellow text font on a blue background creates a reverse text effect. [pg. 108]

revision mark Indicates changes made to a document by applying noticeable formatting. [pg. 458]

root directory The folder that holds all other folders on a storage device. [pg. 436]

round-tripping The process of editing a Web page saved in HTML formatting within Word. [pg. 515]

row A group of table cells arranged horizontally. [pg. 152]

row height The vertical space from the top to the bottom of a row. [pg. 158]

ruler Shows the location of tabs, indents, and left and right margins. [pg. 4]

run macro The process of playing back or using a macro. [pg. 370]

salutation A greeting in a letter. It usually appears as Dear Ms. Sullivan. [pg. 35]

sans serif font A font that does not have serifs. This type of font is useful for headings, so they stand out from body text. [pg. 54]

save The process of storing a document for future use. [pg. 11]

scale Increases or decreases the text horizontally as a percentage of its size. [pg. 58]

ScreenTip A little yellow box that displays the name of a button when you position the mouse on the button. ScreenTips also appear for AutoComplete and other tasks. [pg. 7]

scribble line A drawing tool line that lets you "scribble" to create the line. [pg. 224]

scroll buttons Clicking and dragging these square or rectangular buttons moves you quickly through a document. You can scroll up or down a page at a time or scroll to a particular object within the document. [pg. 4]

scrolling The process of moving the insertion point through your document. [pg. 30]

scrolling text Text that moves across a Web page, either continuously or for a limited number of times. [pg. 510]

section break A marker that divides a document into sections; section breaks allow you to have different formats, such as page numbering. [pg. 120]

selecting The process of defining a section of text. After you select text, you can delete, format, or cut it. [pg. 32]

selection bar The space in the left margin area where you see a right-pointing arrow. [p. 32]

separator line A horizontal line that separates the body of the document from the footnotes. [pg. 132]

serif font A font that displays tiny little lines or extensions at the tops and bottoms of most characters in the font. The serifs guide the reader's eyes across the text. [pg. 54]

shading A colored background, similar to highlight, except that space within the area is also colored; it is also the background color within a table cell or group of cells. [pg. 107, 163]

shape A graphics object, such as a circle or lightning bolt. [pg. 222]

short menu Also known as an adaptive menu, it is a pull-down menu from the menu bar. When you first select from the menu bar, you see a short menu of the most commonly used tasks you use. The short menu adapts, based on your usage of the features. [pg. 5]

shortcut A fast keyboard method for performing a task. For example, the keyboard shortcut for bolding text is Ctrl+B. [pg. 7]

single-space Text lines that are close together, one immediately above the other. [pg. 98]

sizing handles Little black boxes that appear around a selected object, so you can change the size or move the object. [pg. 198]

soft page break Page breaks inserted by Word when you fill an entire page. These breaks adjust automatically when you add and delete text. [pg. 121]

Sort Ascending Arranges text in alphabetical order or values in sequential order. [pg. 183]

Sort Descending Arranges text in reverse alphabetical order or from the highest to lowest numerical value. [pg. 183]

sorting The process of rearranging text, paragraphs, or table rows in a particular order, such as arranging names in ascending order. [pg. 183]

source program The program used to create the original data. [pg. 254]

spacing A font option that controls the amount of space between two or more characters. [pg. 58]

spinners Up and down arrows that increase or decrease a numeric setting in a dialog box. [pg. 97]

splitting cells The process of separating a cell into multiple table cells. [pg. 178]

Standard toolbar The toolbar that contains a row of buttons that perform common tasks, such as save and print. [pg. 4]

status bar Appearing above the taskbar, this bar displays the current page number and location of the insertion point. [pg. 4]

style A group of formatting settings that you can apply to characters or paragraphs. [pg. 339]

subdocument A smaller document that is part of a master document. [pg. 422]

subfolder A folder within a folder. [pg. 437]

submenu A menu that appears to the side of a main pull-down menu. It provides more specific options and features. For example, choosing View, Toolbars displays the Toolbars submenu that lists specific toolbars. [pg. 6]

suppress Hides or removes something onscreen. For example, suppressing the page number prevents the number from displaying and printing on a page. [pg. 125]

synonym A word that means the same as another word. Word contains a feature that helps you select appropriate synonyms for words. [pg. 86]

table A series of rows and columns that organize data effectively. [pg. 152]

table alignment The horizontal position of a table between the left and right margins. [pg. 166]

table of contents A list that provides readers with a guide to topics covered in a long document or book. [pg. 420]

tabs Markers that specify the position for aligning text when you press Tab↹. [pg. 287]

template A framework of specifications for creating a document; it specifies a document's formats and might include some text and graphics. [pg. 334]

text box A graphic box that contains text. It's treated as an object so you can size and place it on a page. [pg. 206]

text enhancements Formats such as bold and font color that enhance the appearance of text. [pg. 52]

text form field A field that allows users to enter text or numbers. [pg. 478]

theme A set of design elements that includes back-ground images, bullets, numbering, fonts, lines, and other graphical elements. [pg. 504]

tight wrap A wrapping style that lets text contour or wrap tightly around the outer edges of the image itself instead of the square border area that surrounds an image. [pg. 201]

Tile Windows Vertically option Windows option that lets you display two document windows side-by-side at the same time. [pg. 265]

title bar Shows the name of the file you are currently working on, as well as the name of the application. Dialog boxes also have title bars that show the name of the dialog box. [pg. 4]

track changes A feature that helps you monitor document revisions by displaying changes in a different color and format. [pg. 458]

Undo feature Reverses action that you perform in the document. Actions are undone in reverse sequential order; that is, the last action performed is the first reversed. [pg. 80]

ungrouping The process of separating grouped objects back into individual objects. [pg. 229]

uniform resource locator (URL) A type of address that identifies a specific document and location. [pg. 498]

value (z) axis title A heading that describes the values on the left side of a chart. [pg. 240]

version A "snapshot" of the document; it is marked with the name of the person who saves it, as well as the date and time that the version was saved. [pg. 463]

vertical alignment Positions text between the top and bottom edges on a page. [pg. 121]

vertical scrollbar Moves up and down in a document. [pg. 4]

view buttons Switches between different view modes, such as Normal, Web Layout, Print Layout, and Outline view. [pg. 4]

watermark A washed-out graphic object or text that typically appears behind text. [pg. 229]

Web Layout view The viewing mode for viewing Web pages. [pg. 500]

Web page A document that displays on the Web. [pg. 498]

Web site   A collection of related Web pages for an organization. [pg. 498]

What's This?   Displays character and paragraph formatting when you click within text. [pg. 110]

widow   The last line of a paragraph that appears by itself at the top of a page. [pg. 128]

Wizard   A feature that guides you through creating a document by asking questions and having you select from various options. [pg. 337]

WordArt   A feature that creates interesting shapes and designs for text. Useful for creating banners and titles on fliers and advertisements. [pg. 210]

word-wrap feature   Continues text on the next line if it can't fit at the end of the current line. [pg. 9]

workbook   An Excel document or spreadsheet. [pg. 243, 256]

worksheets   Pages of workbook data arranged in column and rows of numerical data, descriptions, and formulas. [pg. 243, 256]

World Wide Web (Web)   A component of the Internet; it is a collection of documents accessible through the Internet. [pg. 498]

wrapping style   Specifies how text wraps around an object, such as a clip art image. [pg. 201]

WYSIWYG   Stands for "What You See Is What You Get." This means that your printout will look like what you're seeing onscreen. [pg. 62]

x-axis   The horizontal axis of a chart that typically indicates time periods. [pg. 238]

x-axis labels   Descriptions for the items on the x-axis of a chart. [pg. 238]

z-axis   Commonly called the y-axis, the vertical axis typically displays quantities. The taller the bars on the axis, the greater the value. [pg. 238]

z-axis labels   Commonly called the y-axis labels, the consistent values that appear in increments help the reader interpret the value of the bars. [pg. 238]

zoom   Specifies the magnification percentage of how your document appears onscreen. [pg. 39]

Index